THE REFORMATION IN ENGLAND

III
"TRUE RELIGION NOW ESTABLISHED"

BLESSED CUTHBERT MAYNE
PROTOMARTYR OF THE SEMINARY PRIESTS

THE
REFORMATION
IN ENGLAND

III
"TRUE RELIGION NOW ESTABLISHED"

BY

PHILIP HUGHES

NEW YORK
THE MACMILLAN COMPANY
1954

NIHIL OBSTAT : CAROLVS DAVIS, S.T.L.

CENSOR DEPVTATVS

IMPRIMATVR: E. MORROGH BERNARD

VICARIVS GENERALIS

WESTMONASTERII : DIE V NOVEMBRIS MCMLIII

MADE AND PRINTED IN GREAT BRITAIN
AT THE ABERDEEN UNIVERSITY PRESS

First published in the U.S.A. in 1954

History does not bring out clearly upon the canvas the details which were familiar to the ten thousand minds of whose combined movements and fortunes it treats. Such is it from its very nature ; nor can the defect ever fully be remedied. This must be admitted : . . . still no one can mistake its general teaching in this matter, whether he accept it or stumble at it. Bold outlines, which cannot be disregarded, rise out of the records of the past, when we look to see what it will give up to us : they may be dim, they may be incomplete, but they are definite; there is that which they are not, which they cannot be.

NEWMAN,

The Development of
Christian Doctrine

Tanti sunt apud nos exempla principum : quod enim regis exemplo fit, id vulgus, ut scis, non dubitat recte fieri.

JEWEL, TO PETER MARTYR,
APRIL 14, 1559.[1]

When the adversarie made M. Maine this proffer of his life if he would but sweare upon a booke that the Queene was head of the Church of England, and if he did refuse, then to be hanged, drawen and quartered, he tooke the Bible into his hands, made the signe of the crosse upon it, kissed it and said, The queene neither ever was, nor is, nor ever shall be the head of the Church of England.

BLESSED CUTHBERT MAYNE,
TO THE MINISTERS OF RELIGION,
THE EVE OF HIS MARTYRDOM,
LAUNCESTON, NOV. 29, 1577.

For answer I could wish some expert learned man would frame an answer as from a number of Catholics that notwithstanding their evil contentment for religion should profess their obedience and promise both their lives and power against all strange powers offering to land in this realm, and to advertise the Cardinal that he is deceived in his opinion to think that any nobleman in this land, or any gentleman of possessions, will favour the invasion of this realm.

LORD BURGHLEY TO SIR FRANCIS WALSINGHAM,
JUNE 12, 1588.[2]

---

[1] Cf. *infra*, p. 61. [2] Cf. *infra*, p. xxvi.

CONTENTS

PART ONE: THE SECOND CONVERSION OF ENGLAND

CHAPTER I

GRANDDAUGHTER OF HENRY VII

CHAPTER II

THE DECISION OF 1559

vii

CHAPTER III

THE SCHOLARLY APPROACH

CHAPTER IV

THE POPULAR MISSION

I

CONTENTS

CHAPTER V

DIFFICULTIES FROM WITHIN

1. AN INSUFFICIENT MINISTRY

2. HOSTILITY TO THE SETTLEMENT OF 1559

3. CARTWRIGHT

4. THE BISHOPS OF 1583–1593

5. ARCHBISHOP WHITGIFT

6. HOOKER

CONTENTS

PART TWO: DELENDA

CHAPTER I

DRIFT

I

3

CHAPTER II

LEADERSHIP

I

CHAPTER III

CONFLICT

I

CONTENTS

CONTENTS

CONCLUSION

APPENDICES

MAPS

LIST OF ILLUSTRATIONS

From a print in the Hope Collection, at the Ashmolean Museum, Oxford. For the life of Cuthbert Mayne, cf. R. A. McElroy, C.R.L., *Blessed Cuthbert Mayne*, 1929, and J. H. Pollen's (1924) edition of Challoner's *Memoirs of Missionary Priests*. The martyr was born near Barnstaple in 1544, educated (like Harding and Jewel before him, and Hooker after him) at Barnstaple Grammar School and at Oxford, where he received orders according to the new rite and served for some years as chaplain at St. John's College. Among the fellows of St. John's at this time were Edmund Campion and Gregory Martin. To their efforts Cuthbert Mayne's conversion was largely due, and by 1573 he had followed them to Douay. He was ordained priest in 1575 ; sent to England as a missionary in April 1576 ; arrested at Golden, near Probus in Cornwall, June 1577 ; tried September ; put to death at Launceston, November 30, 1577. Cuthbert Mayne was beatified by Leo XIII, December 29, 1886. His skull is preserved as a relic at the Carmelite Convent of Lanherne, the ancient home of the Arundels in Cornwall.

The drawing reproduced is the frontispiece to Christopher Saxton's *Atlas of England and Wales*, 1579.

At this date, 1579, Elizabeth, now 46, is well past the great crisis of her reign, when the bitter opposition of the nobles to her chief adviser, Sir William Cecil, came to a head (cf. *infra.*, pp. 260 ff.). For England the international situation is now easy, the King of Spain facing the revolt of the Low Countries, and France given over to the recurrent civil war ; the imprisoned Queen of Scots is now politically isolated ; the excommunication has proved a dead letter ; since the savage repression of the rising of 1569 England has been perfectly quiet ; the Protestant movement against the queen's settlement of religion has been quietened. It is a moment in the reign when there is seemingly realised the ideal of the Latin verses which the drawing carries, the ideal which an increasing majority of the English—the queen's own contemporaries and the newer generation—will take for granted is realised in Elizabeth.

The two sets of verses may be translated :

i. " In this noble picture there shines forth for men to gaze upon, the mild and kindly governess of the British realm."

Of this celebrated Elizabethan there is no authentic contemporary portrait. No better memorial can be desired than the pages of the original edition of this tiny book, *Rationes Decem*. They are here reproduced, at the actual size of the type, the page somewhat reduced, from the recently discovered fourth copy, now at Campion Hall, Oxford.

For the meaning of the text, I may be allowed to quote the translation of Fr. Joseph Rickaby, S.J., printed in the 1914 edition of the work, which Fr. J. H. Pollen edited for *The Catholic Library*.[1]

The first page of text reproduced is from the fifth of the *Ten Reasons*—the authority of the ancient writers called the Fathers of the Church. The translation (p. 114) is as follows :

> Calvin, in his rage, says he [i.e. St. Gregory the Great] was not brought up in the school of the Holy Ghost, seeing that he had called holy images the books of the illiterate.
>
> Time would fail me were I to try to count up the Epistles, Sermons, Homilies Orations, Opuscula and dissertations of the Fathers, in which they have laboriously earnestly and with much learning supported the doctrines of us Catholics. As long as these works are for sale at the booksellers' shops, it will be vain to prohibit the writings of our controversialists ; vain to search houses, boxes, desks, and book-chests vain to set up so many threatening notices at the gates. No Harding, nor Sanders, nor Allen, nor Stapleton, nor Bristowe, attack these new-fangled fancies with more vigour than do the Fathers whom I have enumerated. As I think over these and the like facts, my courage has grown and my ardour for battle, in which whatever way the adversary stirs, unless he will yield glory to God, he will be in straits. Let him admit the Fathers, he is caught ; let him shut them out, he is undone.

The two pages which follow are from the tenth reason : the argument from witnesses of every kind—here of the Christian princes from the beginning. It has been chosen because of the address to Elizabeth with which it ends. The translation (pp. 141–143) is as follows :

> O Christ, what cause can I allege to Thee why Thou shouldst not banish me from Thine own, if to so many lights of the Church I should have preferred these petty fellows, dwellers in darkness, few, unlearned, split into sects, and of bad moral character !
>
> I call to witness likewise Princes, Kings, Emperors, and their Commonwealths, whose own piety, and the people of their realms, and their established discipline in war and peace, were altogether founded on this our Catholic doctrine. What Theodosiuses here might I summon from the East, what Charleses from the West, what Edwards from England, what Louises from France, what Hermenegilds from Spain, Henries from Saxony, Wenceslauses from Bohemia, Leopolds from Austria, Stephens from Hungary, Josaphats from India, Dukes and Counts from all the world over, who by example, by arms, by laws, by loving care, by outlay of treasure, have nourished our Church ! For so Isaias foretold : *Kings shall be thy fosterfathers, and queens thy nurses* (Isaias xlix. 23).

---

[1] I have ventured, in one or two places, to modify the translation.

Hearken, Elizabeth, most powerful Queen, it is to thee this great prophet utters his prophecy, therein to teach thee thy part. I tell thee : one and the same heaven cannot hold Calvin and the Princes whom I have named. With these Princes then, link thyself and be worthy of thy ancestors, worthy of thy genius, worthy of thy excellence in letters, worthy of thy praises, worthy of thy fortune. To this effect alone do I labour about thy person, and will labour, whatever shall befall me, for whom these adversaries so often augur the gallows, as though I were the enemy of thy life. Hail, good Cross. The day will come, Elizabeth, the day will surely come, that will show thee clearly which of the two have loved thee, the Society of Jesus or the brood of Luther.

I proceed. I call to witness all the coasts and regions of the world, wherever the Gospel trumpet has sounded since the birth of Christ. Was this a little thing, to close the mouth of idols and carry the kingdom of God to the nations ? Of Christ Luther speaks : we Catholics speak of Christ. *Is Christ divided?* (1 Cor. i. 13). By no means. Either we speak of a false Christ or he does. What then ? I will say. Let Him be Christ, and belong to them, at whose coming in Dagon broke his neck.

and all necessaries, no not of pyoneers and vitells in every Countye of the realm without exception, and which as it was most to be marvelled no man compelled to serve, every man voluntarely offered

This memorandum is in the P.R.O. (SP/12, vol. 230, no. 57). It has been printed in *C.R.S.*, V, pp. 178–179. It reads as follows :

> Remembrance for theis Warrants to be mayd forthewith for Mr. Topclyff. Graunted at the Counsell Table.

> A Warrant to the M[aster] and Keeper of Brydewell to receve and kepe as cloase prisoners Crystofer Baylles alias Evers a Seamenary preest, Jhon Baylles his brother a tayller, Henry Goorney haberdasher, Antony Kaye and Jhon Coxed yoman. And no person to resort to any of them but Mr Richard Topclyff and Mr. Richard Younge who is appoynted to examine them, and to procede furder with them according to direction gyven to them by the Lords.

> Directed to the M[aster] and Keeper of Brydewell.

> Another warrant from ther Lordships to Richard Topclyff and Richard Younge Esquiers to examyn the sayd persons Cristofer Baylles alias Evers a Seamenary Priest, John Baylles tayller, Henry Goorney, Antony Kaye, and Jhon Coxed from tyme to tyme, and if they see furder occacyon to commytte them or any of them unto suche torture upon the wawle as is usuall for the better understanding of the trewthe of matters agenst her Majestie and the Stayte etc.
> Directed to Richard Topclyff and Richard Younge Esquiers. *Endorsed.*—Remembrances for Mr. Topclyff.

The question put to Christopher Bayles, when under torture, was where he had said Mass and who had kept him. When, at his trial, Christopher Bayles—indicted and condemned under the 27 Eliz. c. 2—was asked why sentence of death should not be passed on him, he answered, " This only do I want to know, whether St. Augustine sent hither by St. Gregory was a traitor or not ". To which the Court said not. And the priest proceeded, " Why then do you condemn me to death as a traitor. I am sent by the same see : and for the same purpose as he was. Nothing is charged against me that could not be also charged against the saint " (Dr. Richard Barrett's contemporary relation, quoted in *C.R.S.*, V, 179). Christopher Bayles was executed March 4, 1590, at the corner of Fleet St. and Fetter Lane, hard by where the P.R.O. now stands. Over his head was set an inscription *For treason and favouring foreign invasions.* For all this see *C.R.S.*, V, 178–179.

As to " torture upon the wawle ", see, in addition to the next note, the accounts of Fr. John Gerard, *Autobiography* (1951), pp. 108–115, and of Fr. Robert Southwell, *A Humble Supplication* (1953), p. 34.

This is an autograph letter of the professional priest-catcher Richard Topcliffe, asking the queen's pleasure in the torturing of Fr. Robert Southwell, S.J. This priest, who was ultimately put to death, February 21, 1594, had already written to his Roman superiors (January 16, 1590) of the hideous personage who was now to sate himself in such tortures as he described to the queen, *Unum istud purgatorium timemus omnes* [i.e. Bridewell] *in quo duo illi carnifices Topcliffus et Youngus omnem habent cruciandi libertatem*, i.e. That particular purgatory we are all afraid of, where those two butchers Topcliffe and Young have full licence to carry out their tortures. (*C.R.S.*, V, 329–330). It was at Young's door that the Brownists laid the corpse of Roger Rippon (*infra*, p. 215, *n.*). This letter of Topcliffe is in the British Museum, Lansdowne MSS., vol. 72, no. 39. It has already been printed by Strype, *Annals*, IV, 185–186.

Most gracious sovereign Having fr. Robert Sowthwell (of my knowledge) [Jhezuite in my stronge chamber in Westminster churche yard. I have mayde hi assewered for startinge, or hurtinge of himself, By puttynge upon his armes a pair hande gyesves and there and so can keepe hym either from view or conference wi any But Nicholas the underkeeper of the Gaythowse and my Boye. Nicholas bein the man that caused me to tayke hym by settinge of hym into my hands, X em myl from here.

I have presumed (after my lytell [?]) To runne over this exam[ination] inclose faythfully tayken and of him fowlye and suspiciously answered, and somewhat knowi the natture and doinges of the man, may it please yr. ma. to see my simple opynic Constraigned in dowty to utter it.

Upon this present tayking of him It is good foorthwith to inforce him to answ trewlye and dyrectly and so to proove his answers trewe in hast, To the ende th such as bee deeply conserned in his treacheries have not tyme to start or make shyf

To use any meannes in common prisons either to stande upon or against the waw (wherein above all thinges excedes and hurteth not) will gyve warninge But if yo highness pleasour bee to knowe any thinge in his harte, To stande against the waw his feet standinge upon the grownde and his hands Put as hyghe as he can reatc against the wawle, lyke a Tryck at Trenshermean, will inforce him to tell all, and t trewthe prooved by the sequelle, The answer of him to the questyon of the Counte of Arundell, and That of father Parsons descypheareth [?] him. It may please yo majesty to considere that I never did take so weighty a man if he be rightly considere

The letter ends:

Here at Westminster with my charge and ghostly father, this Monday the 22 June, 1592

Your majesty's faithful servant   Ryc. Topclyff.

" F. Southwell was apprehended at one mr. Bellamys 15 miles from London, about the 12 of July. . . . Topclif coming thither to apprehend him. . . . Topclif carried the Father with him to his own house in Westminster, and there he hath exceedingly tormented him at four several tymes . . . hanged by the hands against a wall many hours together, and Topcliffe [*sic !*] left him hanging and so went abroad. Because the often exercise of the rack in the Tower was so odious, and so much spoken of of the people, Topclif hath authority to torment priests in his own house, in such sort as he shall think good, whose inhuman cruelty is so great as he will not spare to extend any torture whatsoever. Our Lord of his infinite mercy strengthen and comfort this good father and all such as shall fall into his merciless hands. . . ." (Richard Verstegan to Fr. Persons—at Madrid—from Antwerp, Aug. 3, 1592; in *C.R.S.*, V, 211–212).

The autograph letter of Allen to Lord Paget dated January 30, 1590, the last page of which is here reproduced, is in the P.R.O. (SP/12, vol. 230, no. 17). The letter is printed in Knox, *Letters and Memorials of William, Cardinal Allen* (1882), pp. 315–316. As this work is not at every reader's disposal, here is the text of the whole, as printed. The asterisk marks the point at which the page reproduced begins :

My good Lord ; Yours of the XIVth came to me X dayes sith, being right sory for that foule fact your L. writeth of, and that irremidiable disunion amongst our banished men, which is a plage of God farre more heavye then our banishment it selfe ; and wo upon them that are thoccasion thereof, who so ever they be. I have ever with much tolleration sought to reconcile all such breaches, and so I will do still, and will as much as in me lyeth, and as authority and jurisdiction shall be given unto me, seeke by force of law to redresse the same and correct all disorders without partialitye, as farre as God shall give me his grace and assistance. I trust it is a thing that concerneth that young mans folly onely, trusting verily that no man of compt or honestye wold ether counsel or encourage him to any such fact. Nether can it sinke into my heade as yet that such men as your L. seemeth somwhat to suspect (whereof doctor Griffeth here over and above your letter gave me insinuation) should be any wise acquainted with such foule matters. God forbid they should ; and me think I might be so bold to warrant your L. there of. All my ciphers at the time of my daungerous sicknes, when I departed from Reims and looked for no other but death,[1] I made awaye, and I had cleane forgotten to tell your L. before that therefore I could not discipher those few words you wrot in your former in Mr. Charles[2] his alphabet. Your L. must pardon that my negligens. We shall cum, I suppose, er it be long nerer together, that we shall not neede to use ether letter or ciphers ; for I think your L. hath * hearde that his M.[3] hath nominated me for Machlins. the revenewes whereof, as the times now be, are so little, that, but in respect of servise, and that his M. will otherwise provide I durst not adventure to coom thether, where I am like to find nothing but misery and discontentment of our coontrymen, and no lesse want and calamity in myne owwne province and bisshopricke, having not welthe nor meanes to healpe as my heart desireth nether thone or thother. But how and when so ever I coom, all parts shall prove so great a good will and desire to serve the common and particular, that I verily suppose all will be glad and contented, though not all satisfyed, or soch men as is desired or required. Fare you well, my good Lord Paget, with my commendations to all others,

Your L. assuredly,

THE CARDNALL.

Jan. 30, 1590.
[Addressed] All Illmo il Sigr. Barone Pagetto come fratello ossmo., Bruselles.

I gratefully acknowledge permission to reproduce photographs as follows : *to the curator of the Ashmolean Museum for the frontispiece ; to the Bodleian Library for No. 12 ; to the master of Campion Hall for No. 21 ; to the president of St. John's College, Oxford, for No. 23; to the Cambridge University Press for No. 15 ; to the president of St. Cuthbert's College, Ushaw, for No. 19 ; to the Victoria and Albert Museum for No. 27 ; to the Public Record Office for Nos. 30 and 32 ; to the National Portrait Gallery for Nos. 2, 14, 16, and 18 ; to the British Museum : (a) the Print Room, for Nos. 1, 3, and 26 ; (b) Department of Manuscripts, for Nos. 29 and 31 ; (c) Department of Printed Books, for Nos. 4, 5, 6, 7, 8, 9, 10, 11, 13, 17, 20, 22, 24, 25, and 28.*

---

[1] August 3, 1585.   [2] Charles Paget, brother of Lord Paget.   [3] King Philip II.

PART I

THE SECOND CONVERSION OF ENGLAND

CHAPTER I

GRANDDAUGHTER OF HENRY VII

THE death of Queen Mary Tudor, on November 17, 1558, brought the country up sharply, for the third time in twelve years, against the grave uncertainty of its fortune as a nation, in the immediate future. Her death may well have been a relief, and the welcome accorded the new queen especially joyous. But there was much to cause serious anxiety, on all sides. What was to happen to the late queen's religious policy ? Would the barely-inaugurated restoration of Catholicism endure ? Would the new government be able, without grave disorder, to re-establish things as Edward VI had left them ? And would the new, political and military, alliance with Spain continue ?—and, if not, how would the country stand, with France militantly hostile ? And would there still continue that general drift of national affairs towards catastrophe which had been continuous since the disappearance from public life of England's last great man of affairs, Thomas Cromwell, now eighteen years ago ? That drift—in itself neither Catholic nor Protestant—the gigantic dishonesty of the men who dominated the reign of the child king, Edward VI, had speeded up until it had run like a mill race. With Mary's accession, dishonesty had indeed lost its best opportunity, but incompetence had remained ; moreover, once Stephen Gardiner had gone, there had come upon the country the colossal misfortune of entanglement in Spain's feud against France, to do England far more damage financially than all that Northumberland and his like had been able to effect. And to the average Englishman, to Queen Mary herself indeed, the war had meant, so far, one thing only—the loss of Calais. Even outside the ranks of the Protestant party there can have been little regret for the régime that came to an end on November 17, 1558, save among those—and how many were they ?—who foresaw with apprehension what the new reign would bring to the ancient faith and its adherents.

What no man could know, at the moment, was that England, at last, was to be in the hands of rulers who were extremely capable, if not great ; that the drift towards catastrophe was, at last, to be arrested ; and that, along with a new firmness and consistency in the administration, a new age of prosperity was to begin for that middle class whose well-being is what has always mattered most, in modern times, to the tranquillity of states ; that while there was indeed to be a new religious policy, this, from the beginning, would be linked with the new prosperity, and be bound up, ultimately, in the second generation, with a fervid rebirth of national feeling. What no man could know, in November 1558, was that the new sovereign was to be one of the most capable of all, in many respects Henry VII come again as in 1485, so in 1558, the main novelty in the resolution of a national crisi. was a new ability in the ruler.   And, as in 1485, the ruler was to be served with unusual competence, as well as with fidelity.   William Cecil, now in his thirty-ninth year, whom Elizabeth chose for her principal minister, was an administrator of the first class, as competent, as great indeed, as was ever Wolsey or Cromwell, and as honest as they were corrupt.   Truly as great, and from the beginning, Cecil had his plan, a plan which, for the more immediate problems, was remarkably complete.   It was a plan to save the country from the seemingly inevitable financial destruction ; and, rooting out the old religion, once and for all, it proposed to refound the half-ruined nation upon the basis of a new religious unity within a reformed national church, over which the monarchy should preside.

Cecil was one of those statesmen, of whom his great adversary Philip II is perhaps the most notable, who never in a long lifetime took, or desired to take, so much as an hour's holiday from the task of observing and studying, in all possible detail, all that went on in the nation they ruled.   Cecil, working himself hard in the pursuit of his policies, came to such a knowledge of England and of Englishmen that it is a temptation to make the little exaggera-tion of saying that, for a long generation, the whole life of the country lay in his hands.[1]   The mild kindly face of his serene old age, with its complexion of innocent childhood, and the denial which these proclaim of the actuality as we know it, must not distract us from the actuality.   We are gazing on one of the shrewdest and most pitiless of English rulers.   Cecil has not debauchery to his discredit, nor jobbery.   His family life was as careful and good as his own hands were clean of other men's wealth.   But if lies matter, and treachery, plots to encompass innocent men whom it was desirable to remove, and ruthlessness towards such in the hour of mastery ; then, despite his tempera-mental *sophrosyne*, Cecil is a very bad man indeed.   He hated the Catholic religion and he hated it logically, for he was a very sincere, pious and whole-hearted Protestant [2] after the fashion of that generation in which he first came to know the Reformed religion and to embrace it.   His new sovereign was to reign for almost forty-five years—the longest reign in four centuries of English history ; for forty years of the reign—until the day of his death, that is to say—Cecil was to command her entire confidence, and England, after the years of restless change which followed the fall of Wolsey, was thus at last to know once more, and for more than a generation, the tranquillity of a land free from political or administrative crisis.   Given the Englishman's aver-sion from all change that is apparent, this very continuity of rule was not the least powerful of the factors that shaped his new age, and reconciled him to it.

[1] Hallam's saying has already been quoted, that Cecil governed like " the prying steward " administering some great nobleman's estate.   Let Mr. Rowse tell us how this worked out in practice : " no-one felt safe—it was desirable that no one should feel too safe. . . . At the centre of the web the queen was watching.   Distrust expresses itself in every accent of these men's words " ; these men being the queen's ministers. *The England of Elizabeth*, p. 282.

[2] Cf. the opinion of Roger Ascham that Cecil was " next to God and the queen, the most firm support " of sound religion in England ; to Sturmius, April 11, 1562 in *Z.L.*, 133.

Cecil had already shown his quality : in Edward VI's time as the hench-man, first of Somerset and then of Warwick ; in Mary's reign as the pious Catholic of Wimbledon who, secretly, managed to reconcile himself—a henchman of the Dudleys—to the Princess Elizabeth whom they had set aside, as a bastard, in 1553.[1] The lords of the council who, waiting on Elizabeth at Hatfield to announce to her that she was queen, found Cecil already by her side, would have no doubts what was toward.

But what of the queen herself ? After all these centuries, and all the enthusiastic labour of her friends, and of her foes, in all the archives of Europe there still remains about the queen so much that is enigma that he would be rash indeed who professed really to know her. Elizabeth eludes us still as she eluded her own time. None will doubt her remarkably keen intelligence, her tenacious will, her sense of sovereignty as something beyond all human rights of control, her moral indifference about ends (however she might scruple and hesitate about particular means)—but what did she believe, in those matters about which, in all her lifetime, Europe fought and bled and killed ? about God for example, and His plan for man whom He had created ? about the Reformed theology, and its teaching, say, that it is faith alone which justifies the sinner, or that human nature is utterly and incurably corrupt, or that man's will is not really free, or that sinfulness in man justified will not be any barrier to his eternal salvation, or that only those can be justified whom God has predetermined from all eternity that He will call to salvation, and that the rest of mankind God, before He created them, predetermined to everlasting damnation in order to manifest to man how mysterious is His justice ? What did Elizabeth believe about these, and about many other related topics ? And whom did Elizabeth ever love ? or who ever loved her ?

We may think—and pityingly, if only for human nature's sake, where her own hard century might even have thought such pity as ours an irrele-vancy—of her birth, the child of a union which no one, not even her parents, really believed to be a marriage ; of her father's judicial murder of her mother while Elizabeth was still a baby not yet three years old, and of her father's public defaming of her mother—and of her own birth—by an Act of Parlia-ment still, at her accession, the law of the realm ;[2] of the childhood dragged out in various provincial manors of the crown, with obscurities from the lesser nobility for her guardians and governors ; of her emergence, in her adoles-cence, into such high society as the lecherously ambitious brother of Protector Somerset might typify ; of the dangerous years when Mary ruled, the half-sister who did not believe Elizabeth to be Henry's daughter at all, but the offspring of Anne Boleyn and one of those put to death with her by Henry as her adulterous accomplices. Mary had all the family ruthlessness, and once Elizabeth, now heiress-presumptive, began to be the focus of plots, her danger was very real. Her cousin, Jane Grey, had gone to the block, at sixteen, for

---

[1] Cecil, for Black, *op. cit.*, 7, is an " eminently safe, if not heroic figure ", who, in Mary's reign, " had cleverly dissimulated his protestant leanings ". For Ridley, those who so acted were marked with the mark of the beast (cf. Foxe, VII, 576–8).

[2] 28 Henry VIII, c. 7 (1536).

matters in which she had had far less of a part really her own. In Mary's reign Elizabeth had gone through a feigned conversion to Catholicism—a political act to stave off some of her sister's ill-will.[1] It was a conversion whose reality Mary never ceased to doubt; and when, in the last weeks of her life, she finally acknowledged Elizabeth as her father's daughter and her own successor, she demanded of her a declaration and promise to stand by the Catholic faith. " Might the earth open and swallow her ", the queen-to-be is said to have protested, " if she ever believed else." Elizabeth, born of the Royal Supremacy as truly as she was of Anne Boleyn, was bred in whatever it was that her father believed, modulated through the personal inclinations of those who managed her household—inclinations more and more markedly towards the Reformed religion as the years went by. The best of her tutors were of this way; and her foreign tutors, Italians, were finished sceptics, only too typical of the age of Pomponazzi and Machiavelli that had bred them. Italians also, it has been noted, were her favourite divines, Peter Martyr Vermigli, for example, and the one-time general of the Capuchins, Ochino, whose career was now ending in really spectacular scepticism. Never, at any period of her life, was Elizabeth a Catholic; [2] and it is hard to see how, in the circumstances, she can ever have been other than what she was.

What of the queen's personal attitude to the religion in which, for safety's sake, she had recently professed her belief? How far would Elizabeth, left to herself, have proceeded in the reaction of 1559? Would she have penalised so severely the practice of Catholicism? Would she, in 1563, have so sharpened the laws? We know—in some detail now[3]—what her opposition to the united front of ministers, bishops and parliament achieved in later years. Here we touch the long debated problem of Cecil's hold upon the queen. Was he, in fact, the real ruler—the brains of the business and the will also? manoeuvring the queen, to whom he

[1] There is evidence that the " conversion " (whether real or feigned) shocked some conscientious Protestants. William Fuller, writing to the queen, many years later, reminds her that " Our gracious God in great mercy towards Your Majesty and his Church, preserved your life, that were unworthy by reason of your yielding to that Idolatry . . .' July 1585. Peel, II, 51. Hooker took another view. Elizabeth, he wrote (Works, I, 487), was " a most glorious star . . . whom [God] himself had kept as a lamb from the slaughter of those bloody times; that the experience of his goodness in her deliverance might cause her merciful disposition to take so much the more delight in saving others whom like necessity should press."

[2] " More than one Catholic who spoke with her in later days was struck by her ignorance of Catholic verity." Maitland, in C.M.H., II, 563. For her early knowledge of the new, cf. Hooper's account. After telling Bullinger of the informed enthusiasm of the twelve year old Edward VI, he continues, " The daughter of the late king by Queen Anne is inflamed with the same zeal for the religion of Christ. She not only knows what the true religion is, but has acquired such proficiency in Greek and Latin that she is able to defend it by the most just arguments . . . so that she encounters few adversaries whom she does not overcome." The date of this letter is Feb. 5, 1550, when Hooper was preacher at the court. O.L., I, 76. Elizabeth was in her seventeenth year. J. G. Nicholls has preserved another interesting item (Narratives of the Reformation, Camden Soc., 1859, p. 52, note e): " Mr. Offor [editor of the 1836 reprint of Tyndale's New Testament] has a copy of the first edition, in small 4to, published in May, 1528, once the property of the princess afterwards queen Elizabeth. It has her autograph beautifully written, but with all the pomp worthy of a Tudor, Elizabeth daughter of England and France."

[3] Cf. Neale, Elizabeth I and her Parliaments (1953).

was indispensable, by endless manipulation of the truth, and by panic induced in her highly strung soul,[1] to consent to policies she loathed ? It is of course easy to exaggerate, and to read into recorded incidents more than the facts. But the problem, which puzzled contemporaries too,[2] is by no means yet solved.

Now, in the closing weeks of the year 1558, Elizabeth appeared before her people as the queen—twenty-five years of age, tall, attractive, vivacious, skilled to please, *la plus fine femme du monde*,[3] and completely English ; but betraying nothing of her mind, determined to be obeyed, and already inspiring more fear than her sister had ever done.[4] Observers who knew the country, who had seen from close quarters all that had happened since Henry VIII went, and what it had all cost, were, however, doubtful of the outcome ; and when it began to be evident that the new régime would choose the side of the Reform, their doubts increased. In the circumstances, this policy must indeed have seemed to many plain madness.[5]

England—it is useful again to recall the basic facts—was a poor country of perhaps 3,000,000 people only,[6] that lay on the fringe of European life, not able to influence that very much greater thing, nor ever wholly influenced by its strong tides. The standard of living here was low ; the industrial technique was still backward ; and the prosperity that came of the revolutionary changes in the organisation of industry, in commerce and in agriculture, which had once promised so well for those who directed them, had steadily declined during that economic and social crisis which, after twenty years, seemed likely to become the country's permanent condition. Expenditure had, of late, increased fantastically. Taxation did not produce anything like enough to meet the expenditure—and taxation could not be increased. The country was heavily in debt. The coinage was in a

---

[1] The queen's habitual, super-human indifference to danger is part of the legend. Sir John Perrott's famous outburst at the council table in Dublin about her panic at the prospect of a Spanish attack, would have been impossible had such a marvel been a generally accepted truth ; Naunton, *Fragmenta Regalia*, 43. It was in the reaction from such moments that Elizabeth showed herself cruel ; *after* the crisis of 1569 in the north, for example ; *after* the " discovery " of the Babington plot. And did she not suffer from Philip II's " fear to be final " ?

[2] The queen's attitude to Mary Stewart is part of the mystery. " Cecil was [Mary's] sworn enemy ", Leicester could say to the French ambassador in 1571, " and he continually diverted the queen [i.e. Elizabeth] from doing anything in her favour." Leicester is, of course, not an impartial witness where Cecil is concerned, nor was he a man habitually truthful. Fénélon, III, 100, quoted Lingard, VI, 240.   [3] So Henry III of France.

[4] " She seems to me ", Philip II's ambassador reported from London, barely a fortnight after her accession, " incomparably more feared than her sister was, and she gives her orders and has her way as absolutely as her father did " : Dec. 14, 1558, *Span. Cal.*, p. 7.

[5] Cf. Maitland, *op. cit.*, 559. " William Cecil was to be her secretary, and England was to be Protestant. [Elizabeth's] choice may surprise us. When, a few months later, she is told by the Bishop of Aquila that she has been imprudent, he seems for once to be telling the truth " ; and also (*ibid.*, 562) " . . . when, after some years of fortunate and dexterous government, we see how strong is the old creed, how dangerous is Mary Stuart and its champion, we cannot feel sure that Elizabeth chose the path which was, or which seemed to be, the safest ".

[6] Two and a half to three millions is Black's estimate, *op. cit.*, 195.

deplorable condition. And it was only with the greatest difficulty that Mary had been able to raise, abroad, the money she needed ; and this at the ruinous interest of 14 per cent.

Moreover, this nation, so enfeebled and dispirited, did not then enjoy its modern security of a territory wholly insular. Beyond the Cheviots there lay, in 1558, the bitterly hostile independent kingdom of Scotland ; and with the Scots the English had been at war, intermittently, during all those years of drift.[1] The ruler of Scotland, at this time, was also a woman, and the country's first queen-regnant : Mary, the daughter of Elizabeth's first cousin James V, and now a girl just turned sixteen.[2] The Queen of Scots, however had for many years lived beyond the seas, in her mother's country France ever since the English had attempted to capture her at the age of five and thus to solve, in their own interest, one of the problems of the centuries The queen of this hostile people had, moreover, a place in the English succession that might prove important : her father's mother was Henry VII's eldest daughter. If Henry VIII's famous will continued to hold, Elizabeth's next heirs were the sisters of Lady Jane Grey and their issue. But if that will were disregarded—and this was to be its ultimate fate—then Mary of Scotland had a better claim than the Greys ; perhaps, even, a better claim than Elizabeth herself, whom an Act of Parliament, still standing, declared " preclosed, excluded and barred " from all claim to the throne.[3] In this very year,[4] Mary of Scotland had married the heir to the throne of France and so, at Elizabeth's accession England was, already, more exposed than ever before to the chances of a simultaneous attack from France and from Scotland [5]—when the Queen of Scots' claim would be anything but a piece of archaeology. Indeed the news of Mary Tudor's death no sooner reached Paris than the King of France had his daughter-in-law proclaimed as her successor, and had the arms of England quartered on her shield.

With France itself England, at Elizabeth's accession, November 17, 1558 was still, technically, in a state of war as the ally of Spain ; but the peace talks had already begun a few weeks before, in October, that were to produce the treaty of Cateau-Cambrésis, signed on April 3, 1559. Spain, it seemed was England's sole hope against the new menace from France and Scotland— but Spain was so Catholic that a Spanish alliance with a country in the process of actively rooting out Catholicism would be a contradiction in terms Whence the general feeling in Europe, in 1559, that the new régime in England would not last. Many things conspired to save it—the genius of Cecil was one of them, and the King of Spain's fear of France was another

For although England was badly placed, geographically, for a contest where France and Scotland would be, practically, a single opponent, there

[1] " It was plain that in the age of great monarchies England would be feeble so long a she had a hostile Scotland behind her." Maitland, op. cit., 555.   [2] Born Dec. 8, 1542.
[3] This was the act of 28 Henry VIII. But, also, " She had an unrepealed statute in he favour " (Maitland, op. cit., 559), namely 35 Henry VIII, c. 1.   [4] April 24, 1558
[5] " After the fall of Calais in Jan. (1558) England was panic-stricken. The French wer coming ; the Scots were coming ; Danes and Hanseats were coming." Maitland, op. cit. 561.

as one possible advantage that offered itself—were England a country where he ruler had taken the side of the Reformation. This advantage came from he presence, in both France and Scotland, of a minority of determined, and recently persecuted Protestants,[1] conscientious adherents (in part) of that wing of the Reform whose inspiration was Calvin, but also, in part, powerful nobles, political opponents of the governments of France and Scotland,[2] or whom religious differences were a convenient opportunity and no more. In the event of a war of England against France combined with Scotland, were he English government as Catholic as that of the French or the Scots, here would be nothing to move any good Frenchman or Scot to assist his country's enemy. But if England were on the Protestant side, then, in both countries, it was at least possible that these Protestant minorities would work against the national cause in the hope of shaking off the Catholic rulers and establishing the Reformed beliefs and system. It was Cecil's first great achievement as Elizabeth's minister that he was to understand this truth well, to organise his relations with the rebels in Scotland in masterly fashion, and then, despite the queen's reluctance, carry the policy to action, and with great success. With remarkable boldness,[3] considering the insecurity of his whole position, in the very year when he had found it so difficult to force through parliament the government's laws fundamental to the new religious arrangement for England, Cecil also did all that was necessary to secure the triumph of the Protestant party in Scotland too. It was a first victory—the crucial victory it may be thought—for " the queen's policy of establishing relations with the elements of disorder in the dominions of [other] monarchies " ;[4] a policy to be pursued constantly, henceforth, against the Kings of France and of Spain, and without any declaration of war, at times when these princes were at peace with the English queen.[5]

The danger from France through Scotland was practically ended, by the time the Treaty of Edinburgh was signed (July 6, 1560), for all that the Queen of Scots was, by now, Queen of France also. For the effect of the treaty was the return to France of the small army lent to the Queen-regent of Scotland— the only force upon which she could rely in her contest with the rebel lords. The regent had died three weeks before the surrender the treaty implied (June 10). The lords were now the real rulers of Scotland. Only five months later, in the last weeks of 1560, the King of France, who was Queen Mary's husband, also died ; and when Mary returned to Scotland (August 19, 1561) to take up her inheritance, what Cecil's aid had accomplished was already too firm to be shaken by anything she could do against it.

[1] But, cf. Maitland (*C.M.H.*, II, 558) " . . . the Protestant martyrs had not been numerous [in Scotland] even when judged by the modest English standard ".

[2] For Scotland, cf. Maitland's phrase " . . . there was combustible material lying about in large quantities, and sparks were flying ", *ibid.*, 555.

[3] " True that for Protestant eyes there was light on the horizon. Anyone could see that there would be religious troubles in France and Scotland. Geneva was active, and Rome seemed to be doting." Maitland, *op. cit.*, 561.   [4] Black, 87.

[5] " Intrigue succeeds intrigue ; with France, with Spain, with Scotland ; all cunning, hardened, and faithless ; some of them merely dishonest, some criminal ; in that age every country produces the same kind of worthless, cruel, and valiant leader." Dixon, V, 275.

In all these months, while Cecil was thus skilfully undermining the powe
best placed to harass the government's plans [1] (and with what a world (
difficulties he had had to contend, the hesitations and fears and vacillations (
Elizabeth) the King of Spain had looked on.   Whatever weakened Franc
must make in Spain's favour, so it seemed.   And Philip II now first shows t
the full how far caution and procrastination, and expectation of the onl
really appropriate moment, can carry him, as before his eyes Elizabeth an
Cecil establish themselves, in a short twelve months, in an insular securit
such as no English king before them had ever known.   Never again, for a
that Scotland remains an independent state, need England fear a war on tw
fronts and perilous days such as those from which only the miracle of doubl
victories had delivered her, Neville's Cross and Crécy in the fourteent
century, Flodden with Guingates in the sixteenth.   The English success i
Scotland in 1559–60 [2] stands out in marked contrast to the blundering o
Henry VIII in 1544 and of Somerset in 1547.   What had made all th
difference in 1559 was the organised strength of the Scottish Reform party
and Cecil's skill in using them while he assisted them.   It was a first sign—
had there been, to note it, any contemporary with sufficient knowledge o
what had been done—of the coming Elizabethan restoration, to which indee
it was a vitally necessary preliminary.

In these first twenty months of the reign that had thus seen the most urger
danger from abroad warded off, the new government had also solved the mos
pressing of its domestic difficulties, and had laid the foundations of the res
toration of commercial prosperity.   Its agent here was Sir Thomas Greshan
an experienced adventurer in trade, and in the fields of high finance ;
man whose fame and prestige were international, indeed, and who was, alsc
one of the pioneers of the new, scientific understanding of the laws of wealth
The queen's natural thriftiness was also a great asset.   The French ambassadoɪ
writing in 1559, describes this true descendant of the first Tudor king as
" from her accession . . . scraping money together from all sides, payin
nothing and giving nothing to her people, and spending very little ".   A
Elizabeth could scrape went to paying off the heavy debts contracted a
Antwerp ;   and so effectively was English credit restored thereby, that Greshan
was able to borrow new money—short term loans—at a much lower rate
The Saturnian age was over.   Though public morality might remain low
very low, for generations yet, and few men not die very much the richer—
at the public expense—after a life spent in the service of the state,[3] the happ
days were over when the plundering could be done openly and on the grea
scale.   The liberality of the crown, too, was exhausted ;   and the queen showeᵈ
herself just as sparing in her distribution of honours.   Very few, even of he
most distinguished and influential servants, achieved anything higher than
simple knighthood.   Cecil himself was given no more than the lowest ste

[1] " But Scotland was the key-stone of the arch of England's safety."   Pollard, in *H.E.*, VI
222.   [2] " Perhaps [Cecil's] greatest triumph ", *ibid.*, 237.
[3] Cf. Black, 218–219, reviewing the whole reign :   " Money was power—it was more tha
this, it was the national divinity. . . . The plain fact is that public morality was low, and th
great officials who died poor . . . were the exception rather than the rule."

1 the peerage. Retrenchment was the policy universally—a policy as
ongenial to the sovereign as to the minister.

And while the queen thus cut expenses to the bone in order to regain the
onfidence of the world of finance, the bold decision was taken to solve the
urrency problem by calling in all the debased money and recoining it.   This
vas daring, if only because unprecedented ; and the government began by
ducating public opinion in a series of explanatory proclamations.   The
ffect of the financial manipulations of Henry VIII and Edward VI—lessening
he weight of the silver coin, and in the coin thus lightened diminishing the
roportion of silver to alloy—had been that the money at Elizabeth's accession
ontained but one seventh the silver it had contained at the fall of Wolsey,
hirty years earlier.   What had been coined as a silver penny, for example,
ince 1551 was an ingot weighing one-sixth of an ounce, three quarters of it
lloy ; in 1529 the same coin had been twice as heavy, and less than one twelfth
f it was alloy.   The coining of this debased money was now brought to an
nd.   Coins of later date than 1543 were called in, and new money was given
1 exchange for them—not a new coin of like face value for every old one
urrendered, but new coins to the actual value of the silver in what was
urrendered.   The great experiment was successful ; the old money was all
urrendered, and the new accepted at the government's rate—and nowhere was
here any disturbance. And the government made a profit on the operation.

This remarkable achievement did not, of course, check that steady rise
1 prices which was the effect, in all the markets of Europe, of Spain's ex-
·loitation of the newly discovered silver mines of the Americas.   By the
ear 1600, so it has been calculated, the amount of coin in circulation in
·urope—an amount that had been almost stable for centuries—had, in less
han a hundred years, increased fourfold.   The first effect of the upheaval
vhich followed—and the most permanent—was such a rise in prices as to
nake the lot of the labourer, who had but his wage to look to, so hard, that,
ften enough, it was only by leaving his work and taking to begging that he
ould keep himself alive.   The problem of these " beggars ", whose plight
s already one of the things that most move More's pity in the *Utopia*, pursued
very government through the whole of the sixteenth century ; and it is
gain a merit of the new government under Elizabeth that it found the solution
—not an idealistic solution by any means, but a workable solution [1]—which
.eld English life together until the Industrial Revolution called into existence
he very different England that we know—the England of the last 150 years.

The problem of the poor and propertyless man was not, of course, at that
ime, peculiar to England : every country in western Europe then knew it.
And in the treatment of the problem, it goes without saying, the rights of man
the rights, that is to say, of the common man—of the patient) as part of his
·ery humanity, were a consideration that never entered in to complicate a
·overnment's task.   That task, in England, was so to provide that the land-
ord should be certain of labour for his farms, and the budding capitalist be

---

[1] Which worked at the expense of the poorer man most of all, of course.

assured of a constant supply of trained workmen for his industries ; the drif
of landless peasants from the countryside had to be stopped, and the drif
of workmen from the corporate towns, where the industrialist, more and more
was ruler as well as employer.   The lower orders, once they were controlle
in the general interest, and assured of employment and a living, would b
happier and more peaceable ; and the violent oscillation of chronic disconter
would cease, that had for so long endangered the stability of the nation.

The problem of organising labour in the general interest of the landlore
the employer and the lower orders, was given its solution in the Act passe
in the fifth year of the queen's reign—the Statute of Apprentices or Statute c
Artificers.[1]   This was a real code of industrial regulation, and one of the mos
influential of all Acts of Parliament ; for it endured, in whole or in part, as
main reality shaping English life, for the next 250 years, to within a couple c
years of the battle of Waterloo.   All workmen, it enacted, were to be hired
henceforward, by yearly contract ; and a minimum wage for work was to b
assessed locally, from year to year, for every trade, by the justices of the peace
subject to an appeal to the council.   The plan of a maximum wage, fixed off
cially for the whole nation, such as the earlier Statute of Labourers of 1351 ha
attempted, was now abandoned ; all apprentices were to follow the custor
of London, and serve seven years; and in order to discourage the flight from th
corporate towns, the amount of property that a man must possess who wishe
to apprentice his sons was, for dwellers in such towns, reduced by a third
The whole business of enrolling apprentices, and the policing of the systen
once it began to operate, was laid upon the craft guilds, i.e. the new, rising
industrial companies.   The statute also provided for the needs of the farme
by enacting that, at harvest time, all workmen could be called upon to wor
in the fields, and that no exemptions should then be granted.

The parliament which enacted the Statute of Apprentices, dealt als
with the problem of the " sturdy beggars "—and of others too—the un
employed; and the Act which it passed established a new principle that i
operative to this very day.   Already, twenty-seven years before this time
a statute of Henry VIII [2] had laid the foundations of a new social policy when
distinguishing between the " sturdy and valiant " beggar (whom this Ac
proposed to treat as a criminal) and the weak and ailing, it enacted that sucl
impotent poor were to be sought out and succoured by the authorities o
their own parish.   The expense of this was to be met from what was placee
in the alms box now ordered to be set in every parish church ; and the clergy
were bidden, in the royal injunctions for this year (1536), ceaselessly to exhor
the parishioners to give alms for this purpose.   Now, in 1563, Elizabeth'
government revived the severities which the older Act had provided for th
" sturdy " beggar ; and it introduced the new principle that each parish shoule
tax itself for the relief of the " impotent, aged, and needy " ; those whe
refused to pay the tax were to be punished by the justices.   Nine years late

---

[1] 5 Elizabeth, c. 4.   With reference to the remark in the preceding note, Clapham'
comment (p. 213) is of interest, " . . . the Act shows that legislators still thought of a
people who had no property as semi-servile ".   [2] 27 Henry VIII, c. 25.

a second Act orders that the justices and, in corporate towns, the mayors, shall fix this local poor rate, and collect the needy and impotent in " homes ", while their children are to be put to service as apprentices. In 1576 a third Elizabethan Act sets up centres in each town where the poor who are in receipt of parish aid shall be compelled to work for their keep : the wool, hemp, flax or other raw material being bought by the corporation, and the wage fixed according to the work done—the workhouse has arrived. Finally, in 1598, a maximum poor rate is fixed by law ; the justices are to name " overseers " of the poor for each parish, who shall manage the parish workhouse ; and the age at which the apprenticeship of pauper children shall finish is fixed at twenty-one for girls and twenty-four for boys. Begging remains the crime it has been since Henry VIII's Act of sixty-two years before, but now a distinction is made : there are the ordinary vagabonds, who are merely to be whipped " until his or her back be bloody ", and then imprisoned until a master is found to take them ; and there are the dangerous, for whom the penalty is banishment from the realm and, if ever they return, the galleys and the gallows.

This last Act was passed in the year that Cecil died, an ancient close on eighty. It had provided a last means to keep the lower orders in their proper station—above the starvation line indeed, and employed—under the control, as officers of state, of the landlord and the capitalist : an England organised in the interest of England no doubt (and strengthened because organised), but, inevitably, the age being what most ages have been, organised also—and very much so—in the interest of those who really ruled. It was a further concession—and not the least important—to the same class, that in 1571 it was made lawful to take interest on all money loans, the one restriction being that the interest must not exceed 10 per cent.[1]

The long reign of Elizabeth is in more than one respect a real turning point in the history of the English, but in nothing was the action of the queen and her ministers more important than in this policy of economic and social reconstruction. From that day to this there has never been any serious chance of England foundering. And whatever the miseries of all too many of the English people, during the queen's own reign, and in the ensuing two centuries and a half, their condition never sank to that of their fellows in the France and Spain and Germany of, say, the hundred years before the Napoleonic wars. For the moneyed classes, for the landowners and the new capitalists [2]

---

[1] Cf. " There is a strong suggestion that Elizabeth's trade policy was dominated by rich merchants and by the powerful men who farmed the customs, two groups inimical to home industry, and careless of the interests of the consumer." Professor E. G. R. Taylor, *Camden's England*, in Darby, 384, note.

[2] " Our merchants also are to be installed as amongst the citizens (although they often change estate with gentlemen, as gentlemen do with them, by a mutual conversion of the one into the other) whose number is so increased in these our days that their only maintenance is the cause of the exceeding prices of foreign wares, which otherwise, when every nation was permitted to bring in her own commodities, were far better, cheaper and more plentyfully to be had. . . . Certes, among the Lacedaemonians it was found out that great numbers of merchants were nothing to the furtherance of the state of the commonwealth : therefore

and the new merchant seamen (the classes from which came the administrators, the politicians, the members of the House of Commons) this competent and successful, practical, social policy was all that was needed to rivet to the cause of the queen and of her policies what had, so far, been but attached ; and to attach whatever was wavering. The national prestige of a government that had successfully drawn the nation from the brink of a bottomless slough was perhaps, of all things, its greatest asset in the business of persuading " the nation " not to reject the settlement which it proposed in matters of religion. From such a government the appeal to accept the settlement as patriotic duty would not sound hollow—to those classes, at least, who understood how they had been saved, and what they owed to the government for present prosperity and for the prospect of its continuance.

If the age was what the social historians declare it to have been, it will have been precisely by such considerations that those classes will, for the most part, have been guided, upon whose support and active co-operation the stability of public affairs depended, and the "implementing" of the royal policies, when they reflected on what the new government had devised in 1559 as the religion of the nation. It is but sober fact, as one of the greatest of our historians has noted, that " The Elizabethan religion . . . was satisfying many people . . . for (to say nothing of intrinsic merits or defects) it appeared as part and parcel of a general amelioration ".[1]

What the social historians declare, or the general historians who are specialists in the history of the reign—I have in mind such pregnant sayings as : " The prevailing tone of society was intensely secular " ; [2] the same writer's already quoted remark that money was now " the national divinity " [3] and again, " Behind the imposing façade of the law, society was at war with itself ; and the root of the turbulence and factiousness was covetousness " ;[4] again Professor Taylor, writing that " Beggary, vagrancy, and crime at home, piracy on the high seas abroad, had alike swollen to high proportions in England in the 1570's "—which increase of crime " the more thoughtful (such as the Hakluyts) ascribed . . . not to human wickedness but to unemployment and lack of opportunity for legitimate advancement " ; [5] the statement, " Political jobbery and corruption were another sign of morbidity. They were inherent in the Elizabethan system " ; [6] or, Professor Black once more, " We must be careful, however, not to credit the reign of Elizabeth with more than its due. . . . The most striking feature of rural history between 1558 and 1603 [i.e. the history of the great mass of ordinary Englishmen during this reign] was the prevalence of unrest—an unrest provoked, in large measure, by the continued activity of the inclosers for pasture [7] . . . Of the sufferings of the poorer classes there can, unfortunately, be no doubt . . . private charity had grown cold since the dissolution

---

it is to be wished that the huge heap of them were somewhat restrained, as also of our lawyers so should the rest live more easily upon their own, and few honest chapmen be brought to decay by breaking of the bankrupt." Harrison, 9–10.   [1] Maitland, *op. cit.*, 598

    [2] Black, 237.   [3] *Ibid.*, 218.   [4] *Ibid.*, 220.   [5] *Op. cit.*, 382.
    [6] J. E. Neale, *The Elizabethan House of Commons*, 244.   [7] *Op. cit.*, 212.

f the monasteries ".[1] The complaint is indeed frequent, with Elizabethan riters, about the general indifference to the vast amount of human misery ; nd one common point with these social writers is that this indifference a new thing.

We may profitably weigh well every detail of this author's summary,[2] ho sees the reign as a transitional period in social life, characterised by a eneral appreciation, that is new, of the possibilities of a more civilised, and deed luxurious, way of living—" A hundred different ways of spending e discovered and practiced, old fashions give way to new and the whole utlook of society is transformed." Clothes, food, housing, furniture : all these it was in England a time of transformation, with the generality of nen consumed by the passion to have their share in every aspect of it ; a me whose spirit was one " of egoism, paganism, and epicureanism " ; when nto fashionable life there had come, along with the new poetry and the new nusic, the new manners also, and other new, Italianate accomplishments, the ew scepticism and the new " bawdy books " of which Ascham complains, nd the new cult of unnatural vices.

This cultural revolution, however, was a force which, for many years et to come, hardly affected life save in the very few towns recognisably nch. It was all, in a sense, chiefly a matter of London life, and of the fe of the country houses of the great men. What could it mean to Hodge nd his fellows [3] that the apparatus of " life " was yearly more Persian ? ne fantastic dress of his masters, for example, a single suit of which cost nore than Hodge would earn in a long lifetime's labour ; the new in-ecencies in the costume of the great ladies and the wives of merchant rinces ; the new silks and taffetas and velvets, the enormous ruffs and ne farthingales ; the new houses of brick and stone, with their timbered oors and plastered ceilings and panelled walls and the novelty of a multi-ide of private sleeping chambers ; the novelties, too, of carpets and feather eds, of stoves and chimneys, and the new luxury of the great glass windows. Vhat did the great writers mean to Hodge, when these at last appeared, ne Spensers and the Marlows, Camden and Holinshed and Hakluyt, hakespeare himself ? There were indeed writings of another sort which ame to him, as we shall see ; and which, ultimately, made a profound ifference. But the great life, the " Elizabethanism " of the age, was an rban product : its gradual transformation of England was yet another ictory for the cultivated urban minority over the rural mass—a mass that not actively hostile to the transformation, nor indeed hostile at all, unless s natural inert conservatism, its suspicion of novelty, be hostility.

---

[1] J. E. Neale, *The Elizabethan House of Commons*, 215.   [2] Black, 225–235.
[3] " Bullcalf o' the green and Mouldy ", for Clapham (p. 210) ; who considers their class— ne day labourers—makes up almost two-thirds of the agriculturally employed population ; nce the same authority estimates this agriculturally employed population as four-fifths the whole (p. 125), Bullcalf and Mouldy—Hodge—would mean one Englishman in vo, in Elizabethan times. " . . . for members of this class . . . Shakespeare's England as a poor place." *Ibid.*, 210. Their " situation looks so bad that historians have been the look-out for extenuating circumstances. . . . But when all has been allowed for, remains certain that the material position of the mere wage-earner deteriorated under e Tudors—unless every figure lies." *Ibid.*, 212.

Chapter II

THE DECISION OF 1559

PARLIAMENT was actually in session when Mary died on Novembe 17, 1558 ; and the Archbishop of York, the lord chancellor, immed ately proclaimed Elizabeth as queen. There was not, from ar quarter, any suggestion of dissent.

By the queen's death parliament was automatically dissolved, and th council also that Mary had chosen to serve her. To choose new councillo was Elizabeth's first important action as sovereign. Little by little, durin the next ten days, their names were announced, eleven of the late queen council and seven new members. The next consideration was the ne parliament, and on December 5 the writs went out ; parliament was to me on January 23.

The intervening weeks were packed with rumour and surmise ; eve incident of court life was studied for what it might reveal of the queen intentions in the matter of religion ; while, from Germany and from Switze land, the Protestants who had gone into exile now began to return. A Paul's Cross, on the Sunday following Mary's death, the sermon was preache by one of the new queen's chaplains, Dr. Bill : he was a married priest and well-known Reformer.[1] On the following Sunday the Bishop of Chichester replied to him—and for his pains was reprimanded by the council and bidde to keep his house. On December 14 Mary's funeral took place in Wes minster Abbey, and again a bishop was in trouble. This time it was White Winchester, whose sermon praising the dead queen for her repudiation of the Royal Supremacy gave offence.[3] He too was haled before the counc and also put under house arrest.

Elizabeth, maintaining all the religious usages of her sister's reign, cor tinued, however, to go to Mass in state ; and her proclamation, made th day following her accession, was strictly enforced that forbade any " breacl alteration, or changes " in religious services. Then, on Christmas Day, th queen herself attempted a very great change when she sent orders to th Bishop of Carlisle,[4] preparing to sing Mass in her presence, that he was not t elevate the Blessed Sacrament after the consecration. He answered tha this was a command he must disregard ; and so the queen, after the gospe

---

[1] One of the six royal chaplains of Edward VI, appointed (Oct. 1552) to consid Cranmer's draft of forty-five articles. The five associated with him were John Harle Robert Horne, Edmund Grindal, John Knox, and Andrew Perne. Cf. Hardwick, 73, 28
[2] John Christopherson.
[3] The sermon is printed in Strype, *Memorials*, III, pt. ii, 536–550. The legend that White offence was a comparison of Mary to Elizabeth as a dead lion to a living dog, has long ag been dealt with, notably by Dixon (vol. V).   [4] Owen Oglethorpe.

eft the chapel. Two days later a second proclamation [1] ordered that the epistle nd gospel of the Mass, and the litany before the Mass, should be in English. But this same proclamation also forbade, in explicit terms, the Reformed lergy who had been deprived under Mary to resume " their former office in preaching and ministering ", noting how their sermons had provoked breaches f the peace ; and it likewise forbade the clergy in possession to preach. The queen, in this same proclamation, threatens pains and penalties, demands complete obedience from all, and announces that parliament will presently take measures "for the better conciliation and accord of such causes, s at this present are moved in matters of ceremonies of religion ".

The next day, December 28, the general election began. Before it was over Elizabeth had been crowned, and the ceremony, on Sunday, January 15, 559, was the occasion for the most striking demonstration so far that the Marian restoration was doomed. The bishops, sure by now of the queen's intentions, and unwilling to co-operate in a coronation oath that must be a mockery, and indeed perjury, had resolved to refuse to crown her. At the last moment, however, the Bishop of Carlisle, characteristically, gave way. But the Mass of the coronation—with which the rite was interwoven—was sung by one of the Reformed clergy, a married man, Dr. George Carewe; here was no elevation ; and again, the preacher was one of the Reformers. [2]

The last doubts of the Catholics must, by now, have been fully resolved. The better informed doubtless knew that, since the first days of December, a group of heretical divines and politicians had been at work devising the new service that was to replace the Mass. And Cecil and Bacon and the other lawyers were at work drafting the new statutes that would restore the Royal Supremacy, and the Prayer Book of 1552.

Parliament was opened on January 25. The records of the election are defective ; we do not even know the names of very many of the members. [3] Was this a parliament " packed " beyond the wont of sixteenth-century parliaments ? Had the government done its best to secure the election of members known to favour the Reformed religion ? It would have been a very unusual government for its century if it had shown itself indifferent to use, for that purpose, whatever means it might possess. But what the question, so often asked, really means is whether, if the election had been conducted as freely as are modern elections, the result would have been the same.

[1] Text in G. & H., no. LXXVII, pp. 416–417 : date Dec. 27, 1558, not Dec. 30 as Pollard, *H.E.*, VI, 194.

[2] There were Reformers, however, who, none the less, were gravely displeased—to these Protestants the coronation was Elizabeth's second surrender ; " the most hurtful step ", Fuller wrote to her, in later years, " that Satan could then invent to make shipwreck of all godly zeal and conscience in Your Majesty, your councillors, nobility, clergy and people. Which most horrible thing was Your Majesty's yielding to be crowned and anointed at a most monstrous and idolatrous Mass, and by Antichristian Bishops, instead of God's holy ministers." Peel, II, 53.

[3] I.e. of 60 boroughs (120 members) and 14 counties (28 members) ; so Dixon, V, 54 n., who speaks of " sweeping changes ", while Pollard, *H.E.*, VI, 199, says that about one-third of the members of Mary's last parliament were re-elected (Dixon says 53) and that " the change in personnel was less than it had been in 1558 " ; Black, however, says that " the bulk " of the late parliament was re-elected.

The government bloc in the House, that amounted to one-fifth of tl whole [1]—the councillors, courtiers and officers of state—would nc perhaps, have been so certainly elected. Given the constituency of 1559 the north and the midlands must still have been under-represented, ar the countrysides under-represented as compared with the always " ove represented " towns, if the misleading phrase be allowed to pass.[3]

But when we speak of the towns as " electing ", there are other cor siderations to be borne in mind beyond the fact that " in a substanti majority of Elizabethan boroughs the electorate was the corporation ".[4] V can now profitably study [5] the fact that while for fifty years before the electic of the Reformation parliament (1529) the local gentry had been " infiltra ing " into the House of Commons as members for the boroughs, since th date, or thereabouts, the movement had become an " invasion ". In tl borough seats of Queen Elizabeth's parliaments there were four gentlem to every townsman. And the gentlemen had not invariably secured the election through their own personal influence with the magnates of tl little towns. To understand their parliamentary careers we need to stu the interaction, upon the boroughs, of the influential peers, and of su departments of state as the Duchy of Cornwall and the Duchy of Lancast well-centralised administrations that were influential, politically ar socially, over crown estates in two-thirds of the counties of England— weigh well such a fact, for example, as that " the Chancellor [of the Ducl of Lancaster] was tantamount to a viceroy in Lancashire," and that " the six parliamentary boroughs of Lancashire . . . were within tl Duchy ".[6] And once we begin to grasp the reality that, by 1559, and f reasons that had nothing at all to do with religious belief, there was electoral system in possession, we may then proceed to ask ourselves, hc much pressure was needed from the new sovereign, in 1559, to induce tl election of members whom her government favoured ? After all, for tl ordinary man with a stake in the national fortunes there were other probler to settle besides that of the Church. Was not the very nation in jeopardy

These anti-Catholic legislators of the Elizabethan parliaments, the Protestant critics of the Elizabethan settlement of religion, are not, in tl

---

[1] The estimate of Bayne in *E.H.R.*, XXIII (p. 908) quoted and discussed in Magee, and foll., whose conclusion (p. 13) is " The House of Commons was certainly ' packed ' the extent of the ' official element ' of 21 per cent. It may have been more heavily packe but the evidence is not absolutely conclusive." I should prefer to say that what eviden there is, is not conclusive at all.

[2] Ninety-six new seats had been created since 1529, bringing the total membership the House of Commons to 406 : 27 seats given to Wales and Monmouth, by the Statute 1536 that incorporated Wales with England, and 4 to the county and the city of Ches by the same Act ; the other 65 were borough seats, 22 north of the Trent (making a to of 42 seats there), 20 in the midlands ; J. E. Neale, *The Elizabethan House of Comm* (1949), 140, 141 ; who usefully warns us (p. 145) against misinterpreting the geographi distribution of the new boroughs.

[3] In Edward I's reign 75 towns sent 150 members ; in Richard II's reign, a centu later, 83 towns sent 166 ; in 1529, 117 sent 236 ; and now, in 1559, 165 towns sent 31 out of the total 406 members.   [4] Neale, 247.

[5] See Neale, *op. cit.*, especially chapters VII and X.   [6] Neale, 224.

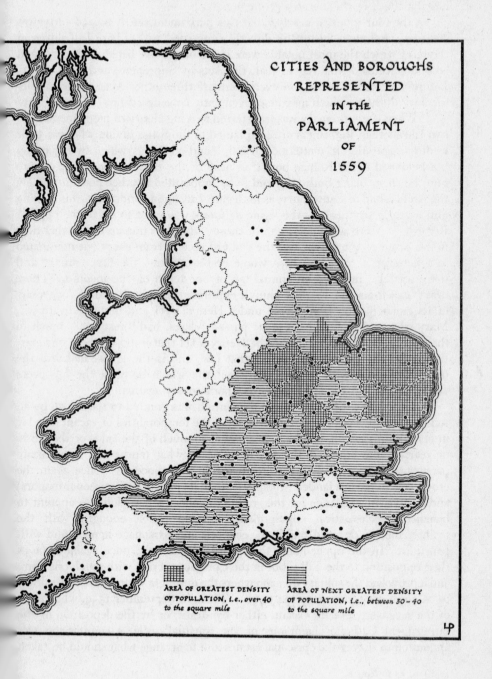

CITIES AND BOROUGHS
REPRESENTED
IN THE
PARLIAMENT
OF
1559

AREA OF GREATEST DENSITY
OF POPULATION, i.e., over 40
to the square mile

AREA OF NEXT GREATEST DENSITY
OF POPULATION, i.e., between 30 - 40
to the square mile

mass, the middle class traders of the town oligarchies, but, very much more largely, they are the country gentlemen.

In the four months, nearly,[1] that this parliament sat, it passed forty-two statutes. Religious history is directly concerned with a bare half dozen of them, of which the most notable were those ultimately listed as the first and second statutes of this regnal year, the Acts of Supremacy and Uniformity. Before we come to these, however, there are three other Acts, really supplementary to them, which may be conveniently considered first.

" When the supremacy was transferred to King Henry of pious memory ", two Elizabethan Reformers once explained to the Swiss divine who was their leading inspiration in matters doctrinal, " and all things which by the canon law belonged to the Roman pontiff as head of the church were made over to him, he then, being both king and pope, appointed another person, namely the Archbishop of Canterbury, as his legate, but upon condition of his making him a yearly payment, as the legate *de latere* was wont to do to the pope of Rome ".[2] More accurately, one of those " things " transferred at that time to the profit of the crown, was the right to receive from every one nominated to a benefice a fee equal to a whole year's income—the first fruits ; and there was also imposed an annual tax of one-tenth of the income. These heavy exactions the English church endured through all the twenty years of its emancipation from Rome under Henry VIII and under Edward VI. Mary who, as the Act about to be passed relates, had " restored " much to the church, had repealed the law of Henry VIII that imposed these burdens. Elizabeth now proposed to revive that law, and in the House of Lords the new bill passed with heavy majorities,[3] the whole body of the lay peers voting for it, but the spiritual lords unanimously against.

A second new title to plunder the church was granted to the crown by an Act that empowered the queen, whenever the temporalities of vacant sees lay in her administration, to take in possession so much of the lands of the see as in yearly value equalled the yearly value of what tenths and impropriate parsonages were owned by the crown within that diocese.[4] Once again the crown was to receive landed property (it took its pick of the episcopal manors) and to give, in exchange for this, rights to collect tithes, rights to appoint to benefices—ecclesiastical appointments saddled (often enough) with the maintenance of decayed buildings, chancels and parsonage houses, and with pensions. In the upper house the spiritual lords were, once again, alone in their opposition to the Bill ; but in the Commons it met with much criticism, and it provoked the solitary division where the numbers voting have come down to us, for it only passed by 134 to 90. Then, in September 1559, when most of the sees were already vacant, either by death, or by the deposition of the intransigent Catholic champions of the spiritual order, a commission was appointed to survey the episcopal estates and to arrange what should be taken

[1] Jan. 25 to May 8.
[2] George Withers and John Barthelot to Bullinger and Gualter, Aug. 1567 ; *Z. L.*, 282.
[3] 1 Elizabeth, c. 4 ; cf. Dixon, V, 54–55 ; Birt, 59–60.
[4] 1 Elizabeth, c. 19 ; Dixon, V, 55.

and what given in exchange. On this commission there sat those birds of ill omen, Sir Walter Mildmay and Richard Keilway, who had, ten years before, presided, to the profit of the crown, over the destruction of the schools. This measure moved to action the Protestant divines now designated to fill the vacant sees but, as yet, waiting in the wings until their predecessors were disposed of, and a means devised to give themselves lawful entry. They spoke of the Act violently as sacrilege : Parker, Barlow, Scory, Grindal and Cox—who was especially strong about it all—even offering, in order to be quit of the Act, an annual thousand marks each to the crown.[1]

Thirdly, there came an Act dissolving the half dozen monasteries which Mary had managed to restore : the Benedictines at Westminster Abbey, the Carthusians of Sheen, the Franciscan Observants at Greenwich, the Dominican Friars at Smithfield, the Bridgettine nuns and brethren of Syon, and the Dominican nuns at Dartford. All this property was annexed to the crown ; and to all the religious who would renounce their vows and acknowledge the supremacy, a pension was offered. As for the religious life itself, the Act now said openly what the previous dissolutions had conveyed in sign, that it was a thing " repugnant to the usage of the Holy Catholic and Apostolic Church of Christ ".[2]

It was in the Commons that the government's scheme for " the alteration of religion " made its first appearance, on February 9, 1559. What exactly the Bill then introduced proposed to do, we do not know. It was committed to Sir Francis Knollys [3] and Sir Antony Cook,[4] for revision, on the 13th or 15th ; and then it disappeared. On February 21 a new Bill was introduced—

[1] Parker's *Correspondence* (Parker Society), p. 97 ; 5000 marks a year would be (using the multiple of 30) £100,000 a year of our (1939) purchasing value. Elizabeth, however, preferred the better part—and, this time, the crown kept what it took for 150 years.

[2] 1 Elizabeth, c. 24, repealed 1926.

[3] Now a man of about forty-five. He came of London merchant stock. His father had been in the personal service of Henry VII at the beginning of the century, and Francis Knollys had been similarly employed all his life so far. He owed his knighthood to Protector Somerset (1547). By that time he was, apparently, a convinced and enthusiastic reformer. He had married Catherine Carey, the daughter of Anne Boleyn's elder sister Mary, whose liaison with Henry VIII had complicated the first stages of the great marriage suit and then (perhaps) provided Cranmer with his good reason for pronouncing that Anne had never been Henry's wife at all. Francis Knollys' wife—and this is the all-important thing—was Elizabeth's first cousin, and her nearest woman relative not of royal blood, a woman about three years Elizabeth's senior, to whom the queen was closely attached ; and from Edward VI's reign Knollys was on familiar terms with the future queen. The marriage brought him seven sons and six daughters—the most famous of these last being Lettice who, by her first marriage, was the mother of that young Earl of Essex for whom Elizabeth, in her old age, conceived such a " romantic " attachment. The second husband of Lettice Knollys was the queen's older favourite, the Earl of Leicester. Sir Francis Knollys was a leader in the " exile " during Mary's reign ; and throughout Elizabeth's reign he remained staunch to the religion of those days, a supporter of Cartwright and of the " prophesyings " ; and also an openly contemptuous critic of the parasites whom at court the queen delighted to see fawning upon her—" King Richard II's men " he called them. Knollys lived on until 1596.

[4] A man ten years older than his fellow zealot and exile, Knollys. Cook was a man of vast learning and great culture and the wonder of his time for the success with which he

whose terms, again, are not known to us. From the Venetian envoy's corre
spondence we learn that, on February 15, a Bill was introduced, " For the orde
of service and ministers in the church ", that it was discussed on the 16th a
" the book for Common Prayer and ministration of the Sacraments "
and that it then disappeared.

What was introduced on February 21 was, it seems certain, a composit
Bill—i.e. one that dealt, not only with the liturgical matter of abolishing th
Mass and providing a Communion Service in its place, but also with th
repudiation of the doctrine of the pope's authority and the restoration of th
Royal Supremacy. This Bill went through all its stages in the Common
in four days, and it appeared in the Lords to be read there a first time o
February 28—a day upon which something else happened ; which some
thing else was, possibly, the cause of the delay of a fortnight that no
occurred. For on February 28 the Lower House of Convocation voted
strong, reasoned, detailed protest against all that Elizabeth and her govern
ment had in mind, and denied utterly that any government could posses
any " authority to treat of or to define whatever concerns the faith, th
sacraments and ecclesiastical discipline ", for this, they say, " has hithert
belonged, and ought to belong, to the pastors of the church alone, whon
the Holy Ghost has placed in the Church of God for this purpose, and no
to laymen ".[1]

Here, at last, is the note we might have expected to hear continuousl
from Convocation, from the moment when Henry VIII first raised thes
questions in 1532, the note that had sounded indeed in 1515, the instinctiv
utterance of Catholic clerics facing Caesar's invasion of the things that are no
Caesar's. The protest speaks of " the public and universal agreement o
Christian peoples ", and of how the beliefs now endangered have bee
" handed down without discord from the Apostles even to ourselves "
it is Catholicism in the traditional manner, conscious as always of its ow
consistent continuity, and seeing in this the final argument that proves th
doctrinal innovator, *ipso facto*, heterodox. And so, " moved by the exampl
of our forefathers, whose lot fell often in times like these our own ", Con
vocation makes its public profession " of the faith which we believe "
on the five points which follow.

" We affirm ", they say, " and, so God help us in the day of judgment
we assert :

" 1. That in the sacrament of the altar, by force of the word o
Christ duly pronounced by the priest, there is present really, under th

had educated his own large family. This fame brought him the all-important appointmer
to be tutor to the future Edward VI. When the little boy came to the throne Cook wa
knighted and he soon figured on all the commissions which began to revolutionise Englis
religion. One of his daughters married Nicholas Bacon, now, in 1558, Elizabeth's sub
stitute for Lord Chancellor ; she is the Lady Bacon who, as we shall presently see, did th
Elizabethan establishment the great service of translating Bishop Jewel's *Apologia* into a mos
readable English. Francis Bacon, Lord Chancellor and philosopher-essayist, was their sor
A second daughter of Sir Antony Cook was married to William Cecil. Cook died in 1576.

[1] Latin text in T.-D., II, p. cclxi, from Wilkins, *Concilia*, IV, 179 ; translated in Phili
Hughes, *Rome and the Counter-Reformation in England* (1942), 138-139.

appearances of bread and wine, the natural body of Christ, conceived of the Virgin Mary; and in the same way His natural blood.

"2. That, after the consecration, the substance of bread and wine does not remain, nor any other substance, except the substance of God and man.

"3. That in the Mass the true body of Christ and His true blood is offered, a propitiatory sacrifice for the living and the dead.

"4. That, to the apostle Peter, and to his lawful successors in the apostolic see, there has been given, as the vicars of Christ, the supreme power of pasturing the church militant of Christ, and of strengthening their brethren.

"5. That the authority to treat of or to define whatever concerns the faith, the sacraments and ecclesiastical discipline has hitherto belonged, and ought to belong, to the pastors of the church alone, whom the Holy Ghost has placed in the Church of God for this purpose, and not to laymen.

"We, the aforesaid lower clergy, for the reasons we have mentioned, by the tenor of these presents, set forth to Your Paternities this our assertion and our affirmation and our faith."

In the Lords, when the Bill was again produced, on March 14, the bishops fought it manfully, and, it would seem, with some success. They brought it about that a committee was named to revise it, and as revised it appeared (and passed the Lords on March 18) as a Bill which, if it restored the Supremacy, did not affect the Mass, or impose a Communion Service in its place.[1] It was during these debates that the Archbishop of York and the Bishop of Chester made the great speeches which have come down to us.[2]

To forsake and flee the see of Rome, as the Bill proposed, said the archbishop, would be "to forsake and fly from the unity of Christ's church". As to the proposal to acknowledge the queen's supremacy in church affairs, and the argument that this is already hers by right, because she is the sovereign —was Herod, by right, Supreme Head of the church at Jerusalem? was Nero the Supreme Head at Rome?[3] or was there no Supreme Head anywhere for the 300 years before the first emperor appeared who was a Christian?

---

[1] So the Mantuan, Schifanoya, Birt, 77, quoting *Ven. Cal.*, March 21, 1559.

[2] Printed in Strype, *Annals*, I, ii, 399–407 (Heath) and 408–423 (Scot). The speeches were reprinted, some years ago now, in a handy form, by the Catholic Truth Society of London, under the title, *The New Religion*, with a preface by The Lord Seaton.

[3] This point had been put explicitly to Cranmer, three years before, at his trial before the Bishop of Gloucester acting as delegate of the pope. "Every king in his own realm and dominion", said the archbishop, "is supreme head, and so was [Henry VIII] supreme head of the church of Christ in England". Upon which, "Is this always true?" asked Dr. Martin, one of the three commissioners sitting in judgment, "and was it ever so in Christ's church?" "It was so", Cranmer answered. "Then what say you by Nero?" said Martin; "He was the mightiest prince of the earth after Christ was ascended: was he the head of Christ's church?" "Nero was Peter's head", Cranmer replied. Dr. Martin would not be put off. "I ask", he pursued, "whether Nero was head of the church or no? If he were not, it is false that you said before, that all princes be, and ever were, heads of the church within their realms." "Nay, it is true", Cranmer answered, "for Nero was head of the church; that is, in worldly respect of the temporal bodies of men, of whom the Church consisteth; for so he beheaded Peter and the apostles. And the Turk too is head of the church in Turkey." To which Dr. Martin said, "Then he that beheaded the heads of the church, and crucified the apostles, was head of Christ's church; and he that was never member of the church, is head of the church, by your new-found understanding of God's word"; Foxe, VIII, 57.

And where else, except from the Bishop of Rome, did England receive its Christian faith ? Heath then analysed closely the authority over the church which the bill proposed to acknowledge in the queen. Spiritual authority meant, first of all, that power of binding and loosing of which Our Lord spoke when he said, " ordaining Peter to be the chief governor of his church : To thee I will give the keys of the kingdom of heaven : whatsoever thou shalt bind shall be bound also in heaven, and whatsoever thou shalt loose shall be loosed also in heaven." Was parliament about to say to the queen " We will give you the keys of the kingdom of heaven " ? and if so by what authority ? Government in spirituals meant, again, what Our Lord had in view when, again speaking to Peter, he said " Feed my lambs, feed my sheep ". Was this what parliament was now saying, to Elizabeth ? It was Peter's office, by divine command, to confirm his brethren, and this " by wholesome doctrine and administration of the blessed sacraments "—how could a woman in any way fulfil such a rôle in that church where, from the beginning, it had been the rule that women were silent ?

The speech is a closely reasoned analysis, as dispassionate and impersonal as a theological lecture, and so too is the much longer speech of Cuthbert Scot, the Bishop of Chester.

Scot began by noting, as one of the difficulties of the situation, that this was a matter in which the queen was an interested party : to oppose the Bill was to oppose the queen. Then he acknowledged the concessions made by the revising committee which had struck out the proposed liturgical changes, and had also lightened the penalties to which clergy would be liable who disobeyed the law. Nevertheless, he had, he declared, no choice but to speak against the bill. Our faith and religion " is maintained and continued by no one thing so much as by unity", and the unity of the church ultimately depends on the union of all its parts with the " one High Bishop, called the pope, whose authority being taken away, the sheep, as the Scripture saith, be scattered abroad ". To avoid such a disaster Our Lord had prayed " that we might all be one, as His Father and He be one ", and He had said " There shall be one pastor and one sheepfold " ; as " He set one Holy Ghost to rule and govern His people inwardly, so He appointed one Governor to rule and lead them outwardly ". Who is this one governor, divinely appointed ? Not temporal princes ; or there would be many heads to the church, and the church a monstrous thing. And Scot now repeats the point made by Heath, that Our Lord spoke to an apostle, and " not to Herod, Pilate nor yet to Tiberius the emperor " when He said " Feed my lambs ", and when He gave the keys. " In these keys, and in exercising of the same, consisteth all authority ecclesiastical given by God unto any man ; unto whom He hath not by Scripture given these Keys, they have no right to it."

The bishop is aware that to this traditional interpretation of the texts, objections can be raised ; and, in anticipation, he deals with the objections. Peter, that is to say in our time the pope, is the rock of which Our Lord spoke when He said " Upon this rock I will build my Church ", as the facts of the situation alone must show. For from what other apostle has there come down any church still firm and stable in faith, or indeed any church at all ? " At this present there be abroad in Christendom thirty-four sundry sects of opinions, whereof never one agreeth with another and all differ from the Catholic Church. And every one of these sects do say and affirm constantly that their profession and doctrine is builded upon Christ, alleging Scripture for the same." What possibility is there of a way out of this chaos if we cease to acknowledge that Peter is the rock Our Lord spoke of ? " Peter and his successors, whereunto men might safely cleave and lean, as unto a sure and unmoveable rock, in matters of Faith."

Scot knows all the stories of contemporary papal wickedness and, allowing them all to pass as true, he sets them aside as beside the point at issue. Had Our Lord said to Peter, " I have prayed for thee that thou sin not ", then the evil life of the popes might indeed have been a proof that they were not Peter's successors. But the prayer was " that thy faith fail not " ; and so " the lives of the popes of Rome, were they ever so violent, cannot be prejudicial to the authority given to Peter and his successors by the mouth of our Saviour Christ ". Again, what has been the fate of the Greek Church since it separated itself from the pope ?—" extreme miseries, captivity and bondage ". And has Germany been any happier since the separation ?

The bishop came back to the main point with his declaration that " a particular or provincial council can make no determination against the universal church of Christ ".[1] As for the innovators, St. Paul, centuries ago, described their like, " Always learning, and never coming to the knowledge of Truth ",[2] men who " vary among themselves, one from another, so no one of them doth agree with himself in matters of religion two years together. And as they be gone from the sure rock and stay of Christ's church, so do they reel and waver in their doctrine, wherein no certainty nor stay can be found." Again if, with St. Paul, we consider the teacher from whom the doctrine comes, whence has all the novelty come if not " of the Germans ", who got it from Luther, who, self confessedly, in his book *De Missa Angulari*, declares he had it from the devil. Let us stand by the doctrine we had from " our forefathers within the same church " against these adversaries whose doctrine " is not yet fifty years old ", and who, as St. Irenaeus said, 1200 years before, since they "depart from the principal succession " are by the fact to be held suspect of heresy or of hypocrisy.[3]

The bishops, however, failed to secure the whole of what they fought for, and on the third reading, March 18, with the Earl of Shrewsbury and Lord Montague, they voted *contra*.[4] The Bill as now amended went back to the

[1] The very argument of More at his trial in 1535.

[2] 2 Tim. iii. 7.

[3] The bishop makes an interesting reference to the bishops and other prelates who, twenty years before, acknowledged Henry VIII as Supreme Head. " Of the learned men that were the doers there [i.e. in the convocation that ' abolished and disannulled ' the pope's supremacy] so many as be dead, before they died were penitent, and cried God mercy for that act ; and those that do live, as all your Lordships do know, have openly revoked the same, acknowledging their error."

[4] The ten Lords Spiritual present and voting were : Heath of York ; Bonner of London ; White of Winchester ; Pate of Worcester ; Kitchin of Llandaff ; Bayne of Coventry and

Commons ; and what the Commons did to it [1] the Lords accepted, on March 22—the bishops once more voting solidly against it. It was now the Wednesday in Holy Week. All that was lacking was the royal assent. The plan was that Elizabeth should give this in state on the Friday—Good Friday —and dissolve the parliament. But the plan was changed. On the Friday the House of Commons met, indeed, but only to be adjourned.

Why the Bill did not, at this stage, receive the little it now needed in order to become law, is one of the many mysteries that hang over this fateful campaign. Easter was approaching. Was the Englishman to receive his Easter communion as a Catholic, or as one of the Reformed ? A proclamation was prepared announcing the new law ; and then, on the very day, Elizabeth changed her mind. The queen, it seems, boggled at the style " Supreme Head on earth of the Church of Christ in England ". Catholics were by no means the only ones to disapprove, and to deny that such a thing could be. That the " scruple " which one of the most famous of the returned exiles, Thomas Lever, " wisely " put into Elizabeth's head [2] was, to her, a religious scruple is highly unlikely. But his protest may have revealed a possibility of future domestic trouble ; and if an ambiguity in the style might avert this ? The bishops, moreover, had hung together so decidedly against all change, that England was, very evidently, about to see the novelty of a law that altered the religion of the country " by and with the advice of the lords spiritual and temporal ", but a law against which every lord spiritual had voted on every possible occasion—a difficulty too novel for any man to say how it would be solved.[3] The Easter recess fell conveniently. Other plans might be devised—the new difficulty be well considered. Parliament was not dissolved on March 24, but adjourned until Monday in Low Week, April 3.[4]

Lichfield ; Turberville of Exeter ; Scot of Chester ; Oglethorpe of Carlisle ; Feckenham, Abbot of Westminster.

[1] Seemingly they restored all that the Lords had cut out—i.e. they abolished the Mass and set the Communion Service of 1552 in its place.

[2] Edwin Sandys to Matthew Parker, April 30, 1559, in *Parker Correspondence*, 66 ; " wisely " is Sandys' word. Allen, twenty-five years later, has a reference to this, in his *Defence of English Catholics*, I, 17 : " . . . when they abolished the Pope's authority, and would have yielded the same authority with the title of Supreme Head to the Queen, as it was given before to her father and brother : divers, specially moved by Minister Calvin's writing (who had condemned in the same Princes that calling), liked not the term, and therefore procured that some other equivalent but less offensive, might be used ".

Thomas Lever was born near Bolton, Lancs., 1521 ; educated, St. John's, Cambridge of which master, in 1551 ; a supporter of Lady Jane Grey in 1553, he entertained Northumberland at Cambridge in the fatal " campaign " of that year against Mary. During the next five years he was busy among the exiles in Germany and Switzerland. On his return he was named archdeacon of Coventry : he remained faithful to his primitive principles ; died 1577.

[3] Cf., " . . . the English Church by its constitutional organs refused to reform itself the Reformation would be an unprecedented state-stroke ". F. W. Maitland, of these events, *C.M.H.*, II, 550.

[4] Professor Neale (*E.H.R.*, July, 1951, pp. 304-32) has lately re-examined the parliamentary history of the Elizabethan Acts of Supremacy and Uniformity, with very interesting results. The main suggestion of his extremely careful study is that the queen's government none too confident of overthrowing the work done by Mary without some tumult, intended originally, to re-impose the royal supremacy only, in this first session of Parliament, and t

The government's solution was to organise the alteration of religion through two separate Acts—one treating of the Supremacy only, and the other of the Mass—and to ignore whatever risk there might be in the novelty of a lay majority forcing these changes on the Church in the teeth of the unanimous opposition of the spiritual lords and of the whole clergy assembled in convocation. On April 10 the Supremacy Bill was introduced in the House of Commons. It went through all its stages, without a division, in four days ; on the 15th it went to the Lords, and it passed finally on April 29. Four days after this Bill first left the Commons for the Lords, the government, on April 18, presented the Lower House with the Bill to abolish the Mass. Again no division was challenged, and in two days this also had gone through all its stages and was ready for the Lords. It was six days, however, before they were ready to debate it. It was read there a first time on April 26.

Once more the Bishop of Chester made a vigorous critical attack.[1] The Bill, he said, called into doubt and denied articles of the Christian faith. How could our Faith depend upon an Act of Parliament ? what one King established by statute, his successor could repeal.[2] And the Abbot of

have the restoration of the Book of Common Prayer until a later session. The hypothesis is presented as no more than a hypothesis, but one (it is claimed) which fits all the facts known and explains them all. The " vital clue " (op. cit., 309) is the clause in the Act of Supremacy which, reviving 1 Edward VI, c. 1 (G. & H., p. 322–328), makes communion under both kinds obligatory, independently of what an Act of Uniformity may provide about Prayer Book. This, it is suggested, was done in order to secure a key change, even should other, " more radical ", policies founder in the event of conflict between Elizabeth and the Protestant divines about the character of the future Prayer Book. The pattern of events of Edward VI's reign was now to be repeated : Mass plus the Order of Communion of 1548, Prayer Book of 1549, Prayer Book of 1552. A subsidiary, but important hypothesis is that the leading Protestant divines " played a great part behind the scenes ; that " they kept in touch with the left wing leaders in the House of Commons, some of whom had actually been fellow-exiles " (p. 311) ; cf. also (p. 313), " the divines in London—Cox, Sandys, Grindal and others—who were probably behind this move in the Commons " (which " move " is itself only a hypothesis). By p. 320 the hypothesis begins to be treated as a fact, e.g. " the divines interested in guiding the work of parliament " ; (and a later writer, Mr. Trevor Roper, can now—by virtue of this study ?—note " How much . . . we owe to that low-church group, ' the Marian Exiles ', who, thanks to their internal organization, parliamentary tactics and qualified royal support, provided the Elizabethan Church with its basis, its bishops, and its famous Via Media ! " History To-Day, Aug. 1952, p. 539. Rarely have we had such a chance to see how swiftly learned hypothesis can become a " fact " of popular knowledge !) The new government's dependence on the lately exiled clergy (shown by its choice of so many of them for bishops, and as speakers for the Reformed party in the Westminster disputation) proves (for Professor Neale) " the pressure which potentially they could exercise " (p. 325) ; " the skilful use of their power by the protestant exiles " was a factor that " must have undermined the policy of gradualness " (ibid.). However, what, in the end—even in this new hypothesis—settled the matter, was not any pressure from the Protestant divines, but the will of Elizabeth ; and the queen made up her mind once she knew the Peace of Chateau-Cambrésis was safe. No summary can do justice to this highly elaborate, carefully thought out reconstruction (and I have not mentioned the texts in the Zurich Letters, quoted in support). But, with all respect, how happily Jewel could have retorted on Harding— When were any of you consulted ? "—this story of himself and his colleagues as the pressure group of 1559 : had this hypothesis of 1951 been a fact within the bishop's own experience ! cf. next note but one.

[1] Strype, op. cit., 448.
[2] This point, that the new religion was the creation of parliament (and, indeed, of the laymen there) raised in the very debates on the creative Acts, was too important not to be urged in later years by the dispossessed Catholics. And the Reformers were very sensitive

Westminster, Dr. John Feckenham, followed in the same strain.[1] No ma
could think, " that this new religion, here now to be set forth in this book, ha
been observed in Christ's Church of all christian men at all times and in a
places," and universality of this kind is one of the criteria of the true religio
What had the book behind it ? a few short years of the reign of Edward V
Feckenham recalled how rapidly the Reformation was itself splitting in
hostile factions ; and how, once a man slipped away from the Catholic fait
he soon ceased to be consistent with himself, and lost all stability of belie
as witness, said he, Dr. Cranmer and Dr. Ridley. Would the new beli
bring about a change for the better in those who went over to it ? The abb
spoke of what London had seen, week by week, since the news sprea
of what the government intended : " . . . spoiling of churches, pullir
down of altars, . . . most blasphemous treading under foot of Sacrament
and hanging up the knave of clubs in the place thereof . . . scratching ar
cutting of the face and legs of the crucifix and the image of Christ . . . ope
flesh-eating and shambles-keeping in Lent. . . . Obedience is gon
humility and meekness clear abolished, virtuous chastity and strait livir
denied, as though they had never been heard of in this realm. . . ." [2] A thir

to its implications. " Yet truly we do not despise councils, assemblies, and conferences
bishops and learned men " ; says Jewel in the *Apology*, " neither have we done that we ha
done altogether without bishops, or without a council. The matter hath been treated
open parliament, with long consultation, and before a national synod and convocation
(*Apology*, in *Works*, III, 93), upon which his Catholic critic, Harding, comments as follow
" If ye mean (as by reason ye must) the parliaments of these latter days, the first of all [i.
the parliament of 1559] did make the most of you [i.e. made most of you what you no
are] ; and yet how open was it for you ? Had ye any place at all in it ? Consider the
with what consultation your purposes were concluded. Did they tarry many months abo
it ? Had they bishops ? Had they divines and the most learned to reason to and fro wi
all liberty ? Was the authority of the universal church of Christ and the doctrine of th
ancient fathers considered ? Ye say, in Latin, *Plenis comitiis*, that is, ' in the full and who
assembly ', as though none at all had there resisted, but every man had yielded to yo
matters. What say ye then of the spiritual lords, a great part of the parliament, and witho
all doubt the part which must be chiefly and only regarded, when the question is
religion ? How many of them gave you their voice to your gospel ? Yea, which of the
all did not resist it ? . . . As, of the spiritual lords ye had none at all . . . so of th
temporal ye had not all ; and so had ye also in the lower house very many, and well learne
that spake against you. . . ." Text in Jewel, *Works*, IV, 902–903.
   Here is interesting, contemporary comment on the debates of 1559. And, if Hardi
seems to insist that the arrangements finally agreed were the arrangements of laymen, ar
laymen only, had not his very adversary, Jewel himself, then *in minoribus*, said as much at th
time when he confided to Peter Martyr his uneasy feeling that all was not going so well a
he had hoped ? " The scenic apparatus of divine worship is now under agitation ", b
had written from London to Switzerland, " and those things which you and I have so ofte
laughed at, are now seriously and solemnly entertained by certain persons (for *we* are n
consulted) . . ." The italics are Jewel's ; *Z.L.*, p. 33, an undated letter, but written a
1559 after the writer had been commissioned for the visitation of the western sees. " ∙
Zurich ! Zurich ", he is moved to exclaim, " how much oftener do I now think of thee tha
ever I thought of England when I was at Zurich . . . we are yet strangers in our own country.
But could anything have been more characteristic of the Elizabethan age, " the age of th
layman uncontrolled either by priest or presbyter " ? (The quotation is from R. Bayn
writing on *Religion* in *Shakespeare's England*, 1926, I, 49.)
   [1] Strype, App. 9, and in the Catholic Truth Society's publication already noticed, p
26–32.
   [2] Were these outrages, indeed, the fruits of a spirit which, if misdirected, was pure

spiritual lord, active in these last stages, was Thirlby of Ely, just returned from his great diplomatic effort at Cateau-Cambrésis. He spoke "very well and like a Catholic" the Spanish ambassador wrote home to King Philip, "saying he would sooner die than change his religion".[1]

But the Bill to abolish the Mass went through its final reading on April 29 —by the very narrow majority of 3. The minority included, besides nine bishops,[2] the following nine lords, the Marquis of Winchester, the Earl of Shrewsbury, Viscount Montague, Lords Morley, Sheffield, Dudley, Wharton, Rich, and North. Winchester was the Lord High Treasurer, Shrewsbury was President of the Council of the North, Wharton the warden of the marches.

The Elizabethan Act of Supremacy began by reviving, wholly, ten Acts which Mary's parliaments had repealed : nine Acts of Henry VIII and one of Edward VI ; and with these it revived also a tenth Act of Henry VIII as this was modified by a statute of Edward VI. All that these fundamental Acts gave to Henry VIII belonged as fully to the queen, so the Act that now revived them declared.[3] The new statute explicitly enacted that no foreign

---

religious, " an ebullition of public feeling against the church ", or were they merely the act of " the looting mob led by Calvinist preachers ", of the same kind as that which in " the five memorable August days, the 14th to the 19th, of 1566, destroyed all over the Netherlands hundreds of churches and monasteries and thousands of priceless treasures of art " ? Chudoba, 134. For an account of this English destruction, cf. the non-Catholic contemporary, quoted Birt, 511, from *Harleian*, 6021, no. 3, saying that the " common people " show great " fervency ", " especially in beating down, breaking and burning images . . . declaring themselves no less disordered in defacing of them, than they had been immoderate and excessive in adoring them before, . . . as if it had been the sacking of some hostile city ". Also, the queen's proclamation of Sept. 19, 1560, " against breaking or defacing monuments of antiquity being set up in churches or other public places, for memory and not for superstition ".

[1] Dixon, V, 72, quoting Strype, *Annals*, I, 448.

[2] Heath of York, Pate of Worcester, Bonner of London, Thirlby of Ely, Kitchin of Llandaff, Bayne of Coventry and Lichfield, Turberville of Exeter, Scot of Chester, Oglethorpe of Carlisle. As to the other seven spiritual lords then alive Watson of Lincoln and White of Winchester were prisoners in the Tower ; Goldwell of St. Asaph and named for Oxford, was " in process of translation " and not summoned to the parliament ; Morgan of St. David's was seriously ill (he died on Dec. 23, 1559) ; so too was Poole of Peterborough ; Tunstall, also, was not summoned to the parliament but left in charge of the north ; Bourne of Bath and Wells is mentioned as present on January 31 but he then returned to his see. Heath held the proxies of Tunstall, Bourne, Poole and Morgan.

[3] The text of the Supremacy Act of 1559 is in G. & H., 442–458. The ten Acts which : revived were :

* 23 Henry VIII, c. 9 (1532) Forbidding church courts to cite a man for trial outside the diocese in which he lives.

* 23 Henry VIII, c. 20 (1532) Annates Act ; G. & H., 178–186 ; cf. Vol. I, 236–7.

* 24 Henry VIII, c. 12 (1533) Statute of Appeals ; *ibid*, 187–195 ; cf. Vol. I, 245–6.

* 25 Henry VIII, c. 19 (1534) Submission of Clergy Act ; *ibid.*, 195–200 : cf. Vol. I, 57.

* 25 Henry VIII, c. 20 (1534) Ecclesiastical Appointments Act ; *ibid.*, 201–209 ; cf. Vol. I, 256.

* 25 Henry VIII, c. 21 (1534) Papal Dispensations Act ; *ibid.*, 209–232 ; cf. Vol. I, 256.

* 26 Henry VIII, c. 14 (1534) Suffragan Bishops Act ; *ibid.*, 253–256.

* 28 Henry VIII, c. 16 (1536) Dispensations Act.

37 Henry VIII, c. 17 (1546) Married men may be ecclesiastical judges.

prelate should for the future exercise any spiritual or ecclesiastical jurisdiction within any of the queen's dominions ; and, furthermore, it enacted that all such jurisdiction used hitherto lawfully, by any spiritual authority, for the visitation, reformation and correction " of the ecclesiastical state and persons " and " of all manner of errors, heresies, schisms ", and other offences, should for ever " by authority of this present Parliament " be " united and annexed to the imperial crown of this realm " ; this ecclesiastical jurisdiction the queen was empowered to exercise, when and as she thought fit, through commissioners whom she would name.

It was not, however, left to the commissioners, or to the queen, to decide what was and what was not heresy. Nothing is more persistent, in all the history of the Reformation in this country, than the complaint that since the layman is, by definition, invincibly ignorant of the legal meaning of heresy— this is a " mystery " proper to churchmen—he is, in this respect, at the mercy of the cleric—which is by no means always the same thing as being subject to the *magisterium* of the Church. The layman complains throughout that it is the cleric who decides what heresy is, and whether the layman is guilty of heresy ; that it is clerical law that makes the mere suspicion of heresy cause for arrest, whereupon, at the cleric's bidding, the layman must clear himself of the suspicion and prove his innocence ; [1] and should he fail to do this, to the satisfaction of the cleric, it is the cleric who thereupon hands the layman over to the secular arm to experience the famous *animadversio debita* ; and the layman complains, also, that the affair is judged in a system of jurisprudence un-English in character. From the very opening of the complicated story of the change of religion in England this topic has recurred continually. And now, when the layman is, once more, given full scope to trim the clergyman's authority after his own heart, and is busy reviving all those restrictive anti-clerical statutes of Elizabeth's father, he does not, in 1559, accept the guidance of the clerics who are good orthodox Reformers, and enact the laws *de Haeresibus* proposed by Cranmer ; [2] instead he proposes and enacts, what none would have ventured to propose twenty-five years earlier,[3] his own layman's statutory definition of heresy ; transferring the whole business, thereby, from the exclusive hearing of theologians and

---

[1] Edward VI, c. 1 (1547) Against revilers of the Sacrament ; G. & H., 322–328 cf. Vol. II, 101, 102 n.

The Act revived in part is 32 Henry VIII, c. 38 (1540)—an Act concerning precontract of marriage and touching degrees of consanguinity, which was repealed in part by 2 & Edward VI, c. 23. The Acts marked with an asterisk are those now declared to apply to Elizabeth " as fully and largely as ever [they] did . . . to the said late King Henry VII your highness's father." G. & H., 445.

[1] " Qui autem inventi fuerint sola suspicione notabiles, nisi iuxta considerationes suspicionis, qualitatemque personae, propriam innocentiam congrua purgatione monstraverint anathematis gladio feriantur . . . ita quod si per annum in excommunicatione perstiterint ex tunc velut heretici condemnentur " ; such is the law since 1215 (Lateran Council IV canon 3 ; cf. Schroeder, 562, translation *ibid.*, 242).   [2] Cf. Vol. II, 129–132.

[3] Cf. K.P., II, 230–231, noting how the statute of 1534 (25 Henry VIII, c. 14), repealing the *De Haeretico Comburendo* Act of 1401 (for procedural reasons), " regretted the absence of any definition of heresy (so that on captious interrogatories the wisest might be caught out) ".

anonists—for the interpretation of statutes is matter for the king's courts ; nd giving the layman an assurance for all time that, in this field, too, nothing hall be done against him without his own consent.[1]

Nothing, henceforth, is to be charged against a man as heresy unless it is udged to be heresy in Holy Scripture ; or by the councils of Nicaea (325), Constantinople (381), Ephesus (431), or Chalcedon (451) ; or " by the High Court of Parliament of this realm, with the assent of the clergy in their convocation " ; and nothing enacted in religious matters by the present parliament is ever to be adjudged heresy, whatever stands to the contrary. " Popery " then is no heresy, although not to conform may be, on a second or third refusal, treason ; and almost all varieties of Protestantism are safe from the bishops and the stake. These laymen are more tolerant than Cranmer, here silently set aside. And the move of the extremists, twelve years later, to revive Cranmer's grim proposals will also be ignored. Arians and the Anabaptists, however, the verdicts of these ancient councils of eleven and twelve hundred years ago doubtless rule out :[2] these are still beyond the pale, and the new bishops will, on occasion, burn them,[3] the repeal of *De Haeretico Comburendo* being no obstacle even to a Protestant bishop burning, once he has lawful matter before him and is willing to proceed.

The Act of 1559 also imposed an oath. By this it was acknowledged that the queen alone was the " supreme governor of this realm, and of all other her highness' dominions and countries, as well in all spiritual or ecclesiastical things or causes, as temporal " ; and the oath also denied, explicitly, that any " foreign . . . prelate . . . has, or ought to have, any . . . juris-diction, power, superiority, pre-eminence or authority, ecclesiastical or spiritual within this realm ", and it explicitly renounced all foreign juris-dictions. This oath was to be taken by all ecclesiastics, of whatever degree, and by their officers ; by all who enjoyed fee or wages from the crown ;

[1] As to this last matter, cf. Coke, arguing in 1609–1610 against Archbishop Bancroft, " Acts of Parliament made by King, the Lords and Commons, are part of the laws of England, nd are to be interpreted by the judges of the laws of England, and not by any Canonist or ecclesiastical judge. . . . If any Act of Parliament do authorise the ecclesiastical judge that which before he could not do, the judges of the Common Law shall judge and deter-mine whether the ecclesiastical judge have pursued his authority given by the statute, or by colour of that statute hath done wrong to any of the king's subjects or no." (In his answer to Archbishop Bancroft's argument against Prohibitions, cited Usher, *Reconstruction*, I, 242.) And cf. also Lord Chancellor Audley, teaching Stephen Gardiner that the Royal Supremacy marks the layman's triumph over the cleric. " Look at the Act of Supremacy . . and there the king's doings be restrained to spiritual jurisdiction ; and in another act it is provided, that no spiritual law shall have place contrary to a common law or act of parliament. And if this were not, you bishops would enter in with the king, and, by means of the supremacy, order the laity as ye listed. But we will provide that the prae-munire shall ever hang over your heads ; and so we laymen shall be sure to enjoy our in-heritance by the common laws, and acts of parliament." Gardiner to Somerset, 14 Oct. 1547, in Foxe, VI, 43.

[2] " We have good reason to fear that in their eyes a law for the burning of Arians and Anabaptists was in full harmony with the word of God, and no one could say that it was condemned by any English statute " ; Maitland's remark (*Canon Law in the Church of England*, 178) is as true of 1559 as of 1547. Cf. *infra*, Appendix III.

[3] Not, it is true, very often : the record is, 1575, 2 ; 1579, 1 ; 1589, 1 ; 1610, 2.

by all persons sueing livery of lands, or doing homage, or entering the queen service ; by all receiving Holy Orders ; by all who took a degree in a un versity ; by " all and every temporal judge, justice, mayor, and other lay (temporal officer and minister ".[1]

The second fundamental law, the Elizabethan Act of Uniformity explicitly revived the second Act of Uniformity of Edward VI.[3] Th Prayer Book of 1552 was once more, as from June 24, 1559, to be " in fu force and effect " ; all " ministers in any cathedral or parish church or oth place ", being, from that date, " bounden to say and use the Matins, Even song, celebration of the Lord's Supper and administration of each of th sacraments, and all their common and open prayer " as these are set out in th book, " and none other or otherwise ".[4]

There were, however, certain " alterations and additions added ar appointed by this statute " to the Book of 1552, and specified, in the Ac as " one alteration or addition of certain lessons to be used on every Sund; in the year, and the form of the Litany altered and corrected, and tv sentences only added in the delivery of the sacrament to the communicar . . .". From the petitions in the Litany there was, in fact, struck o the phrase " From the tyranny of the Bishop of Rome and all his detestab enormities [Good Lord, deliver us] ". In the rite of the Holy Communio the words, retained from the Book of 1552, " Take and eat [drink] this remembrance that Christ died for thee, and feed on him in thy heart wi thanksgiving ", were now preceded by a phrase taken from the Book 1549, " The Body [Blood] of our Lord Jesus Christ, which was given f thee, preserve thy body and soul unto everlasting life ". There is o other change from the Book of 1552 as this was printed—an omission— which the statute makes no mention, and, indeed, need make no mentio since what is now omitted was never a statute-authorised part of the boc

---

[1] Cf. *infra*, pp. 72-76 for a discussion of meaning of the Elizabethan Supremacy, and t origin of this particular oath.　　　　[2] 1 Elizabeth, c. 2, text in G. &. H., 458-467.

[3] 5 and 6 Edward VI, c. 1 ; *ibid.*, 369-372.

[4] ". . . it may be questioned ", writes Black, 15, " whether . . . the average Englishm was conscious of any marked change in the ministration of religion beyond, perhaps, the u of English in the service in place of Latin ". This might have been, with regard to the services which were prayer services only—the change from Vespers according to the use Sarum to Evensong according to the Book of Common Prayer, for example. But who there who would not have been immediately conscious of very " marked change " inde when the Communion Service displaced the Mass—even were the Communion Servi carried out with the ritual reverence (on the part of the congregation and the clergy) that nc obtains universally ? who is there—if accustomed to either, believing in what he is accustom to and loving it—who would not immediately be aware that much more than the langua had been changed ? Against a view which is by no means peculiar to this eminent Elizabeth specialist, we might put that of a contemporary Archbishop of Canterbury, " Not the simpl and most ignorant papist ", says Whitgift to the Puritans, " could mistake the Communi for the Mass " ; Maitland, in *C.M.H.*, II, 592. And the Devonshire peasants, ten years befc the Settlement of 1559, could detect the change from the Mass to the First Prayer Book 1549, and mock the change as " a Christmas game ". And, since the Communion Servi speedily became a rite celebrated only once a quarter, the replacing of the Sunday M; by the new Morning Prayer—the surpliced clergyman reading from the desk instead of t priest vested at the altar—" the marked change " would have been evident in all the fulln of its authors' intentions ; see *infra*, p. 103, n. 9, for a contemporary on the new rite.

hat is now restored. This was the so-called Black Rubric, which explains hat although " it is ordained in this office . . . that the Communicants hould receive [the sacrament] kneeling. . . . It is here declared, that hereby no Adoration is intended, or ought to be done, either unto the Sacramental Bread and Wine there bodily received, or unto any Corporal Presence of Christ's natural Flesh and Blood " ; and that to adore " the Sacramental Bread and Wine [that] remain still in their very natural sub- tances . . . were Idolatry, to be abhorred of all faithful Christians "; nd that " the natural Body and Blood of our Saviour Christ are in Heaven, nd not here ; it being against the truth of Christ's natural Body to be at one time in more places than one ". This rubric was a concession to the cruples of the boy king, Edward VI, stirred up by a sermon from John Knox preached while the authorised text was actually in the presses of he royal printers. It was as late as October 27, 1552, five days only before he date at which the Prayer Book was to come into force, that the Black Rubric was ordered to be put into the book, by this time already printed. " The inset sheet was duly printed and duly bound in, though neither in ill, nor in the same places, of the copies." [1]

Both Acts bristled with sanctions for the disobedient. The Supremacy Act envisaged two classes of offenders : those who refused the oath ; and hose who, " by writing, printing, teaching, preaching, express words, deed or act " maintained and defended the spiritual or ecclesiastical jurisdiction, hitherto claimed or exercised in the queen's dominions by any foreign prince or prelate. To refuse the oath entailed as a punishment the loss of all offices held, and lifelong disablement from holding any office. Any defence or maintenance of the repudiated papal authority was punishable, on a first offence, by the loss of all goods and chattels " as well real as personal " ; [2] on a second offence the punishment was as in cases of *Praemunire*, namely, he loss of all property and imprisonment for life ; a third offence was high reason. As for the Act of Uniformity, clergy who break this law by refusing o use the new Prayer Book, or who use " any other rite, ceremony, order, orm, or manner of celebration of the Lord's Supper, openly or privily, or Matins, Evensong, administration of the sacraments, or other open prayers, han is set forth " in this book, or who speak in derogation of the book, orfeit a whole year's income and go to prison for six months. If they

---

[1] Morison, 84. Why did not the promoters of the Act of 1559 cause this extraneous ubric to be made part of the text of the book they were reviving ? Fear lest so patent a ontradiction of the traditional faith might cause a storm, in the House of Lords, at least ? There can be no doubt about the Eucharistic beliefs of those responsible for the changes of 559. Twenty-four years later an observer of these events who had, by then, risen to be Archbishop of Canterbury, John Whitgift, was answering, in his characteristic, blunt way, he Puritan demand for a rubric forbidding the Communicants to kneel. " . . . the rubric of kneeling ", he found it sufficient to reply, " is now not necessary, for all the world knoweth hat the church of England kneeleth not to adore the Sacrament, but for comeliness. The esture in receiving is indifferent, standing, sitting, or kneeling, but this is thought most neet for us." *Reply to the Ministers of Sussex*, Peel, I, 212.

[2] If the value of these did not amount to £20 then, besides the loss of them, the offender was to go to prison for a year. Also, if the offender held any ecclesiastical benefice he forfeited : upon conviction.

offend a second time they go to prison for a year and, *ipso facto*, lose all their benefices.   For a third offence the punishment is imprisonment for life Clergy who are not beneficed will go to prison for a year on the first conviction, and for life if they offend a second time.   Next there come penalties to discourage the lay critics of the liturgical change.   All who, in any way speak or write in derogation of anything the book contains, or do anything to cause any clergyman to use any other form of service than what it contains or who interrupt or hinder the performance of those services, are liable, for a first offence, to a fine of 100 marks ; [1] for a second offence there is a fine four times as great ; [2] and for a third offence the penalty is loss of all goods and chattels and life imprisonment.   Furthermore, it was made an offence for anyone to absent himself from the Sunday service in his parish church the experience of 1549-52 had shown that, the " service " being changed people ceased to attend.[3]   All Englishmen were now commanded by law to attend the parish church every Sunday and holy day, under penalty of fine of twelve pence for each time they were absent—the fines to be levied by the church-wardens, and to go to the use of the poor of the parish.[4]

One novel feature of the penal clauses of this Act of Uniformity is that the bishops are given explicit assurance that they can, with impunity, use all their spiritual powers to correct with excommunication those who offend against it : the spiritual authority of the bishops now derives from that of the queen—there is no longer any reason to fear it as for its own sake.   And the queen is given power, advice taken of her high commissioners or of " the metropolitan ", to " ordain and publish " further ceremonies, should any contempt or irreverence arise from " misusing of the orders " here appointed Otherwise no other service is to be tolerated but what is contained within the covers of the new Prayer Book.

These laws were much more severe than those made, for the same objects by Edward VI ; but they were milder than the corresponding Acts passed under Henry VIII.   The Edwardine Acts of Uniformity had enacted for lay offenders fines of only £10 and £20 ; where, under the new law, the fines were £66 13s. 4d. and £266 13s. 4d. respectively.   These earlier Acts had

---

[1] £66 13s. 4d.

[2] £266 13s. 4d. ; all these sums need to be many times multiplied to give an idea how heavy the new fines were.

[3] " Where there has been a very godly order set forth by the authority of Parliament for common prayer and administration of the sacraments ", says the Act of 1552, imposing the Second Prayer Book of King Edward VI (G. & H., 369), ". . . yet this notwithstanding a great number of people in divers parts of the realm . . . do wilfully and damnably before Almighty God abstain and refuse to come to their parish churches where common prayer is used . . . upon the Sundays and other [holy days] . . .".

[4] Under penalty, also, of excommunication.   It is interesting that Jewel, in the letter to Peter Martyr where he makes so merry about the punishments now enacted for saying Mass or being present when Mass is celebrated (cf. *infra*, 258, n. 4), says nothing of this particular method of ensuring a national acceptance of the new services.   And most historians seem to notice the smallness of the fine, or the scanty evidence whether it ever needed to be levied rather than the unique (?) character of this particular penal obligation.   Cecil, it is true was later to say that " the pain being no greater than twelve pence, no officer did seek to charge any offender therewith . . .". (Conyers Read, *Walsingham*, II, 273, n.).   But 52 shillings yearly was the half of many a parson's benefice.

left to the bishop's censure only, the parishioner who now began to absent himself from church ; where the new law also fined him. The new law also revived the heavy penalties provided for the congregation who assisted at Mass.[1] As to the Act of Supremacy, the penalty for refusing the oath, under Henry VIII's Act of 1534 that inaugurated the Supremacy, had been life imprisonment ; and the penalty for denying the Supremacy, death ; and the oath was to be sworn by the whole adult population ; the words of the oath of 1534, moreover, were a more explicit acknowledgment of the king as " Supreme Head on earth of the Church of Christ in England " ; the king's claim to be, for England, all that the pope claimed to be, and had hitherto been acknowledged to be, was unmistakable. The later statutes of Henry VIII (1536, 1544) changed the text of the oath, and punished refusal to swear as high treason.[2] The long oath of 1544 was the most explicit of all, and its clear enunciation of the claim survived in Edward VI's reign too, although Somerset then abolished the penalty of death for refusing the oath and for denying the supremacy.

This comparative clemency of Elizabeth's Act of Supremacy was far indeed, it has been suggested, from what her government originally had in mind : the Lords, at a critical moment in the Bill's fortunes, had mitigated the penalties and the government had had to yield. But four years later, in the new parliament of 1563, the penalties were sharply increased.[3] To refuse the oath meant, after the Act then passed, much more than loss of office—loss of all property, indeed, and life imprisonment, for a first offence ; death as a traitor for the second. And the same more terrible penalties were also now enacted for the crime of defending the old belief that the pope's spiritual jurisdiction is co-extensive with the Church of Christ ; and it is also expressly said, in this statute of 1563, that the crime so punished is the maintenance of " the authority, jurisdiction and power of the bishop of Rome, or of his see, heretofore claimed, used or usurped within this realm ". Moreover the scope of the Supremacy legislation is, in 1563, very notably enlarged : henceforward, all those elected to the House of Commons are to take the oath ; all barristers and attorneys ; the sheriffs ; all officers of all courts ; all schoolmasters, " and public and private teachers of children ". But—a highly significant reservation—" this act shall not extend to compel any temporal person of or above the degree of a baron of this realm to take the oath aforesaid ".

Was the Church of England, as by law established in 1559, a compromise between the doctrines of the country's ancient faith and what was new in the Reformed religion ? In no way ; nor, if compromise means agreement

---

[1] Six months imprisonment for a first offence, twelve months for a second, life imprisonment for a third.

[2] 28 Henry VIII, c. 10 ; 35 Henry VIII, c. 1. These two oaths are in T.-D., I, 417.

[3] By the statute 5 Elizabeth, c. 1, which came into force April 1, 1563. For which Act, cf. G. & H., 202–209 (the full text) or Prothero, 39–41 (the important clauses). In this second parliament of the reign almost all were new members : " not more than 50 were returned who had sat in " that of 1559, Dixon, V, 368.

made between contending parties, was it any more a compromise between the various schools of thought among the English Reformers. The settlement suited no one wholly, it is true ; and in the sense that all were now meant to put up with what no one of them wholly liked, it has about it something of the appearance of what compromises do produce. But it was a thing devised by laymen—the queen and her ministers—behind closed doors ; put through parliament in the face of much opposition ; sanctioned finally by parliament—the whole body of bishops, and convocation too, voting *contra* to the end—and then introduced to the country through the agency of a very small handful of clerics, who saw that the thing was as much as they were likely to get of what they had dreamed.

The Act of 1559 left it to the queen to determine when and by whom the new oath should be administered to those actually in office. On May 23, just fifteen days after the Bill became law, a commission was issued under the great seal to eighteen individuals, laymen, all of them, and privy councillors,[1] empowering them (or any five of them, so long as one of the five were Bacon, Winchester, Arundel, Parry, Rogers, Knollys or Cecil) to administer the oath to all these office-holders whom the act obliged to swear it—the bishops, the whole body of the clergy, the judges, and those hundreds of justices of the peace who were then the chief agents of the Crown for the administration of the law and the actual local government of the country.[2] The commissioners first turned their attention to the bishops—the consistently strenuous leaders of all the opposition so far made to what was now beginning to work.   There were sixteen of them in all, ten sees being vacant by this time. It was everywhere expected that they would all refuse the oath, and, in striking contrast to the bishops of twenty-five years before, this is what they did. Between May 29 and the first week in November all were summoned before the commissioners, were offered the oath, refused to take it and were deprived of their sees.[3]

---

[1] Sir Nicholas Bacon, Lord Keeper of the Great Seal ; the Marquises of Winchester (Lord Treasurer), and Northampton ; the Earls of Arundel, Shrewsbury (President of the Council of the North), Derby, Bedford, and Pembroke ; the Lords Clinton (Lord High Admiral), and Howard of Effingham (Lord Chamberlain) ; Sir Thomas Parry, Treasurer of the Household ; Sir Edward Rogers ; Sir Francis Knollys, Vice-Treasurer of the Household ; Sir William Cecil, Secretary ; Sir Ambrose Cave, Chancellor of the duchy of Lancaster, Sir William Petre ; Sir Richard Sackville ; Sir John Mason.

[2] The (Latin) text of the Commission is in Gee, 39–40.

[3] Here are the dates of the deprivations, so far as they are known : May 29, Edmund Bonner of London ; June 21, Owen Oglethorpe of Carlisle, Cuthbert Scot of Chester, Ralph Bayne of Coventry and Lichfield, Richard Pate of Worcester, Thomas Goldwell of St. Asaph ; June 26, John White of Winchester, Thomas Watson of Lincoln ; July 5, Nicholas Heath, Archbishop of York, and Thomas Thirlby of Ely ; Aug. 10, Henry Morgan of St. David's and James Turberville of Exeter ; Sept. 28, Cuthbert Tunstall of Durham ; Oct. 18 (about) Gilbert Bourne of Bath and Wells ; November (first week) David Poole of Peterborough.   We do not know the date on which Antony Kitchin of Llandaff took the oath, nor indeed that he ever took it : but on July 18 he signed a curious paper in which he promised, in consideration of the queen's goodness in deferring his obligation to take the oath, that he would carry out " the whole course of religion now approved in the state of her Grace's realm ", and " would require the said oath of others receiving office ecclesiastical and temporal, as in the statute thereof provided ", cf. Dixon, V, 122, note §, who reprints the complete text.

The first six of the bishops had already been swept out of public life in this way when, beginning on June 24,[1] the Letters Patent began to be issued which provided for the application of the Acts to the general body of the clergy. The means proposed was a general ecclesiastical visitation of the whole country, after the pattern of those carried out by royal commissioners in 1536 and 1547. The queen, said the Letters Patent, would not be able to give a perfect account to God for His English people committed to her care unless she had propagated the true religion and a sincere worship of God in all parts of her dominions ; and so the peers, gentry and clergy named, to whom the queen granted " in our place full faculties in the Lord ", were to make a visitation of all the churches of the country—cathedrals, collegiate churches, parish churches—of the whole ecclesiastical fabric, material and spiritual, examining the clergy's way of living, punishing where punishment was called for, granting probates of wills, publishing the royal injunctions now committed to their charge, declaring vacancies, settling disputes about livings, recording presentations to them and inducting those presented, summoning synods, collecting the sums due on account of such, commissioning preachers, deciding appeals. The commissioners for the Northern Province were the Earls of Shrewsbury, Derby, and Northumberland ; William, Lord Evers ; Sir Henry Percy, Sir Thomas Gargrave, Sir James Crofts, Sir Henry Gates ; Richard Bowes, Christopher Estofte, George Brown and Richard Kingsmill, gentlemen ; Henry Harvey, doctor of laws and Edwin Sandys, D.D. It was not required that the whole fourteen should always be present ; two commissioners would suffice, and, in fact, the work was almost entirely done by Sandys and Harvey. Their duties and powers to enforce the new laws recently passed are set out in the Letters Patent as incidental to their task of enquiring into the conduct of the clergy—" to punish with appropriate penalties those who are guilty of crime and those who obstinately and peremptorily refuse to subscribe to the religion received ".[2]

The action of the commissioners was regulated by the official Articles of Inquiry supplied to them ; and the directions which the commissioners gave are the Royal Injunctions of 1559. With the evidence which these offer about the beliefs and practices of the new religion we shall be concerned in a later chapter ; the commission interests us here for one part alone of the task it undertook—how far the commissioners actually put into operation that requirement of the Act of Uniformity that all the clergy should, by oath,

---

[1] Date of the commission for the four sees of the Northern Province, which is here described. The dates of the other commissions—the text of which is lost—were as follows : July 18, Wales and the dioceses of Worcester, and Hereford ; July 19, dioceses of Salisbury, Gloucester, Bath and Wells, Bristol, and Exeter ; July 22, dioceses of Lincoln, Peterborough, Oxford, Coventry and Lichfield ; August 21, dioceses of London, Norwich and Ely ; a sixth commission (date unknown) visited the sees of Canterbury, Rochester, Chichester, and Winchester.

[2] " Criminosos ac susceptae religioni subscribere obstinate et peremptorie recusantes " ; Gee, p. 90 (3), who prints (pp. 89–93) the full text of the Letters Patent. For the text of the Royal Injunctions, ibid., 46–65 (also G. & H., 417–442) ; for the text of the Articles of Inquiry, Gee, 65–70 (not in G. & H.).

recognise the queen's supremacy and repudiate that of the pope. " Gentle and judicious management ", so Bishop Frere considered,[1] was the characteristic of this royal visitation of 1559. About certain of its effects there has been considerable difference of opinion—which does not affect one main point, namely, that the parochial clergy, on the whole, made no open resistance to the change. Even were one to take the most optimistic view of the affair (the hypothesis of Dom Birt's learned study, for example) no less than three-fourths of these priests now abandoned both the Mass and the pope as easily as the priests of twenty-five years earlier had abandoned the Roman Supremacy alone.

And here the interesting point arises about the terms in which the new oath was proposed to the clergy—and whether, indeed, it was as an oath that anything at all was proposed to them.[2] It was in June and July that the various commissions were made out. " Representative visitors must have met together after their nomination in order to settle some *modus operandi*. One of the chief matters discussed would be the manner of tendering the oath to the clergy, and here an important piece of information is given us in a paper written somewhat later by Dr. Parker.[3] He there speaks of ' the form of a subscription which we devised to be used in the order of visitation '. This form we possess in records of the visitation for North and South, in which it appears in substantially the same words, so that it is clear that the phrasing was settled by common conference before the visitation began . . . it was determined not to administer the Supremacy Oath pure and simple. . . " [4] The declaration to which, in place of "the Supremacy Oath pure and simple ", some thousands of clergy now, in 1559, set their signatures, was, it seems, that subscribed by those of the chapter of York Minster who conformed ; this runs, " We, the clergy of the Cathedral and Metropolitical Church of York, whose names are subscribed, do humbly confess and acknowledge the restoring again of the ancient jurisdiction over the state ecclesiastical and spiritual to the crown of the realm, and the abolishing of all foreign power repugnant to the same, according to an oath thereof made in the late Parliament begun at Westminster the 23rd day of January, in the first year of the reign of our sovereign lady Queen Elizabeth, and there continued and kept until the 8th day of May next after ensuing. We confess also and acknowledge the administration of the Sacraments, the use and order of divine service and manner and form as it is set forth in the book commonly called the Book of Common Prayer, &c., established also by the same Act, and the orders and rules contained in the Injunctions given by the Queen's Majesty, and exhibited unto us in the present visitation, to be according to the true word of God, and agreeable to the doctrine of the primitive Church. In

---

[1] *The English Church in the reigns of Elizabeth and James I*, 40.

[2] Historians have usually written as though the statutory oath was now actually offered to all the clergy. For example, " It is, however, fairly certain that many of the Marian clergy took the oath ", Conyers Read, *op. cit.*, II, 276, n.

[3] I.e. the future Archbishop of Canterbury.

[4] Gee, 45 ; the quotation of Parker's words is given by Gee as from Strype's *Parker*, I, 95.

witness whereof, and that the premises be true, we have unfeignedly hereunto subscribed our names."[1]

It may also be noted that, while the earlier commission of May 23, 1559, to the Privy Councillors, gives them authority in the most explicit terms to administer the new oath,[2] and while the later commission of May 5, 1562, to the prelates and notabilities of the north, for the visitation of the northern province, uses the same explicit phrases,[3] there is not, in the commission for the visitation of 1559, a single word about the oath, nor so much as a hint that any authority is given the commissioners to demand it.[4] With this before us, and the text of what was put before the general body of the clergy in 1559, is it too much to hazard that no oath was then anywhere demanded of them ?[5]

The only part of the official report of the great visitation of 1559 that has survived is that of the commissioners for the four sees of the northern province—York, Durham, Carlisle and Chester. For the rest of England, eighteen sees of the province of Canterbury, we have no more evidence of what happened than the signatures to the declaration of some 1804 clergy, and a few references in the private correspondence of the visitors.[6]

The northern report[7] tells us that, in a total of something like 968[8] parishes, 314 priests absented themselves from the visitation. Were the

[1] Text in Gee, 77–78 ; also in Birt, 148, and in Usher, *Reconstruction*, II, 298.

[2] " Sciatis quod dedimus vobis . . . plenam potestatem et auctoritatem recipiendi de omnibus et singulis Archiepiscopis etc. quoddam sacramentum corporale super sacrosancta Evangelia coram vobis . . . corporaliter per ipsos et eorum quemlibet praestandum, declaratum, et specificatum, in quodam Actu in Parliamento nostro apud Westmonasterium 25⁰ die Januarii anno regni nostri primo tento, edito, iuxta vim formam et effectum eiusdem actus ; Gee, 39–40.

[3] " . . . per praesentes damus et concedimus vobis . . . plenam potestatem et auctoritatem capiendi et recipiendi de omnibus et singulis archiepiscopis etc, etc., quoddam sacramentum corporale (rest as in previous note) ; *ibid.*, 172–173.

[4] Jewel and his colleagues, in their visitation of the diocese of Bath and Wells did not tender the oath to the bishop, Gilbert Bourne. This was done by four Somersetshire justices, in virtue of a commission dated Oct. 18, 1559 ; for the text of which cf. Rymer's *Foedera*, XV, p. 545.

[5] Cf. the letter of Horne, Bishop of Winchester, to Cecil (June 8, 1561) describing his visitation of Surrey, where all the " ministers . . . conforming themselves as it was required of them . . . in testification thereof have subscribed to the declaration for Uniformity of doctrine ". Birt, 41 (P.R.O., *Dom. Eliz.* XVI, n. 23).

[6] For what now follows, see the map, p. 43.

[7] The itinerary of the commission in the northern province was as follows, sessions of the visitation being held at all the places named :—

Aug.	22,	Nottingham	Sept.	21,	Bishop Auckland
„	24, 25,	Southwell	„	22, 23,	Durham
„	26,	Blyth (Notts.)	„	27,	Newcastle-upon-Tyne
„	28,	Doncaster	Oct.	3, 4,	Carlisle
„	31,	Halifax	„	6,	Penrith
Sept.	4,	Otley	„	9,	Kendal
„	6–9,	York	„	12,	Lancaster
„	11,	Hull	„	16,	Wigan
„	12,	Beverley	„	18, 19,	Manchester
„	14,	Malton	„	20,	Northwich
„	15,	Northallerton	„	24,	Tarvin
„	18,	Richmond	„	26,	Chester

[8] Figures according to the *Valor Ecclesiasticus*, 1536.

majority of these absent because resolved not to submit to the new arrange
ments, albeit too " prudent " to make a public announcement to this effect
One might like to think so, and it may very well be so.[1] But all we know i
that they were absent. Reading the innumerable laments of the new
Reformed bishops while, in the next ten years, they are labouring to " es
tablish religion " in the north, and noting the frequent suggestions in thei
complaints, not only about priests " lurking " in every countryside, but abou
the body of clergy still in possession as almost wholly sulky if not sullen
hostile to the new régime and suspected of being, at heart, still attached t
the old, we may think that one in three of the clergy is not an impossibl
proportion for wilful absentees who have successfully evaded subscription
The number of priests who appeared before the visitors, boldly avowe
their non-acceptance, and were thereupon deprived, is not large—90 onl
for the whole northern province.[2]

What the number was of those who refused to subscribe in the provinc
of Canterbury no one knows. Nor do we know the number of absentee
there : all that we possess are the signatures of 1,804 priests who accepted th
settlement in six of the 18 English sees of the province. For the twelv
sees of Canterbury, Rochester, Chichester, Winchester, Salisbury, Worcester
Hereford, Gloucester, Bristol, Bath & Wells, Exeter, and Peterborough
we have just no information at all—and in these sees were nearly one hal
of the total number of parishes in England. The six sees which supply
the names of the 1,804 subscribing clergy are : London, where 413 subscribed out of 800 ;[4] Norwich, 495 out of 600 ;[5] Ely, 98 subscriptions
(number of clergy not known, but 152 benefices) ; Oxford, 104 signatures,
where there were 171 parishes ; Coventry and Lichfield, 351 signatures
where " about 500 parishes " ;[6] and Lincoln, where the record of 343
signatures in a diocese of 1,246 parishes is noted as " imperfect ".[7] Nc
more than in the northern province are there, in the figures for these six

[1] Two years later than this, Horne had the same experience of absentees when he mad
his first visitation of Winchester. Despite a general conformity, " I have found many absent "
he wrote to Cecil, " partly through the wilfulness of some who have purposely withdrawr
themselves . . . partly under pretence that they serve noblemen . . ." June 8, 1561. Birt
pp. 413–414.

[2] We meet some of these priests a few years later, when the queen writes to the Bisho
of Chester, William Downham (Feb. 21, 1568), about the priests " who having been late
ministers in the Church, were justly deprived of the offices of ministry for their contemp
and obstinacy, be yet (or lately have been) secretly maintained in private places in that ou
county of Lancaster " ; Birt, p. 533, n. 2, from P.R.O. *Eliz.* XLVI, no. 32.

[3] The following counties, that is to say : Kent, Sussex, Surrey, Hampshire, Berkshire
Wiltshire, Dorset, Somerset, Cornwall, Devon, Gloucester, Worcester, Hereford, part o
Shropshire, part of Warwickshire, Northampton, Rutland. See the map, p. 43.

[4] 800 is the estimate of Rev. G. Hennessy in Gee, 96, n. 1. A complete list, in alpha-
betical order, of all these subscriptions, is printed in Gee, 102-129.

[5] This is Dr. Jessopp's estimate of the total number of clergy, quoted by Gee, 96, n. 2 ;
there were at this time 1148 parishes in the diocese of Norwich, *Valor.*

[6] So Gee, 98, quoting a " diocesan return " of 1593 in Harl. MS. 595 ; the *Valor* gives
451, and as Lichfield lost 92 parishes in 1541 to the new see of Chester, it would have 359
in 1559.

[7] By Gee, 98 ; the return in the *Valor* gives the number of parishes in Lincoln as 1,736.
It lost 171 to Oxford and 319 to Peterborough in 1541.

es,[1] any signs that the new " settlement " of religion was hailed by the
enerality of contemporaries as an emancipation after years of servitude ;
this is not the evidence which proves a general enthusiasm for the Reformed
ligion on the part of the parish clergy, free to express itself at last, after
ears of oppressive persecution.[2]

The work of these commissioners was brought to an end in October
id November.[3]   A second royal commission, set up under another of the
ew statutes, had also, by this time, sorted out the manors which the crown
roposed to take from the sees in exchange for tithes and advowsons.

" By the beginning of November [1559] England had not a single bishop
ft : the spiritual jurisdiction, originated by St. Augustine nearly a thousand
ears before, had come to an abrupt termination." [4]   To make a reality of
ie royal ecclesiastical jurisdiction set up in its place, the government must
ow instal its own men as bishops of the various sees.   The most of these
ere, of course, already chosen : they were men thought likely to be suitable
ents for the government's policy of reconciling to the new arrangements
oth the conservative mass of the nation, and the mass of the party of the
eform.   Here are the elements on which the Elizabethan via media pro-
oses to work.   The new bishops must, also, be installed according to law
-it must not be open to troublesome fellows, from either of the parties
itical of the new thing, to object that the new incumbents of the sees are,
law, no bishops at all.   And here, as Cecil's own papers make known to
s, the government faced a double difficulty.   First, the newly revived
ct of Henry VIII,[5] which now once again regulated episcopal appoint-
ents, required that the elections of bishops be confirmed by the arch-
shop, and the elections of archbishops be confirmed by an archbishop
id two bishops or else by four bishops [6]—and, as Cecil noted, " There is
o archbishop nor four bishops now to be had. Wherefore *querendum*
c." [7]   The second difficulty was that the new Act of Uniformity, which
id abolished the Catholic rite and made it a crime to use that rite, had not
ithorised the new rite for the consecration of bishops drawn up under

---

[1] The territory covered by these sees is that of the following counties ; Middlesex, Hert-
rd, Bedford, Essex, Suffolk, Norfolk, Cambridge, Huntingdon, Lincoln, Leicester, Derby,
afford, part of Shropshire, part of Warwickshire, Oxford, Buckingham.

[2] That notable contemporary Reformer, Thomas Lever, was presently to complain that
iong these parochial clergy who had conformed there were not, in the whole country,
ove 70 or 80 able and willing to preach the new doctrines. Cf. *infra*, p. 134 ; and for other
stimony too, that this conformity of 1559 meant no more than external acquiescence,
d that it is by no means evidence of any change of heart.   For the further, highly im-
rtant, fact that the enacted Supremacy was proposed to the clergy in this visitation veiled
the dishonest " *Admonition* " of the queen " *to simple men deceived by malicious* ", which
duced " almost to nothing the change against which all the bishops, supported by a
animous convocation, had fought for three months in parliament " (Pollard, *H.E.*, VI,
7) cf. *infra*, pp. 73-74.   [3] Dixon, V, 191, note ; Gee, 141.

[4] A. Gordon Smith, *William Cecil*, 66.

[5] 25 Henry VIII, c. 20 ; G. & H., 201–209.   [6] *Ibid.*, pp. 207.

[7] Public Record Office, *Dom. Eliz.*, V, no. 25, facsimile in Estcourt, *Anglican Ordina-
ns*, 86 ; cf. also Birt, 242.

Edward VI. " This book ", wrote Cecil, " is not established by Parli
ment." [1] If it were used would not the government be violating
own new, fundamental principle ? Therefore, no doubt, *querendum* on
more.

These difficulties had been present to Cecil's mind throughout t'
summer of 1559, and he had made at least one effort to bring some of t'
Catholic bishops, as yet not deposed, to confirm the election of Parker
Archbishop of Canterbury and to consecrate him.[2] Finally a commissi
was made out, three months later, to a second very varied group of personage
bishops in various senses, both by consecration, and by diversity of episcop
occupation or employment : Kitchin, Barlow, Scory, Coverdale, Hodgki
Salisbury and Bale. These seven or any four of them were hereby direct
to confirm the election and to consecrate the elect " according to the form
the statutes set forth and provided in that behalf "—and the insinuation
this formula, that what the seven were commissioned to do was a lawful a
and its effect good in law, it was hoped to save from being no more th
so much politician's verbiage by the clause which followed, " a speci
clause, not found in any other instrument of the sort ever issued ".[3]

In this clause the queen declares that, " by our supreme authority roy
we nevertheless supply whatever is or shall be lacking, of those things whic
by the statutes of this realm or by the laws of the church, are required or a
necessary in this business, whether it is a lack in what shall be done by y
in carrying out our command, or whether the lack is in you, or in any one
you, by reason of your condition, status, power for the performance of t
aforesaid " ; and the clause ends by explaining that it is demanded by all t
circumstances of the time and what needs to be done.[4] And so little certa
of the value in law of this clause were the government, that they not on
submitted the question to a number of experts—canonists and civilians-
but took good care to get and preserve their signed opinion that the queen
action was indeed lawful, and that those whom it authorised might " exerci
the act of confirming and consecrating, in the same to them committed "
All this detail illustrates, of course, the characteristic Tudor care to secu
the sanction of legal appearances for every act of the crown in the great a
teration ; and it shows, surely, something of that uncertainty about t
event which ever accompanies attempts to give an appearance of customa
legality to what is in fact novel, unprecedented and revolutionary.

Five years later, nearly, the commission thus carefully drafted, and
novel clause, seemed likely to come under the professional scrutiny of t
Common Lawyers and of a common jury in open court. For the queen

[1] Estcourt, *ut supra*.

[2] Letters Patent of Sept. 9, 1559, to Tunstall, Bourne, Poole, Kitchin, Barlow, and Scor
text in Rymer, XV, 541 ; cf. Birt, 236 & foll., Dixon, V, 199 & foll.   [3] Dixon, V, 203

[4] Dixon, V, 203, prints in full the Latin text of this commission of Dec. 6, 1559 ; t
Supplentes clause is on p. 204 ; the last phrase runs, *Temporis ratione et Rerum necessitate*
postulante.

[5] *Ibid.*, 204, for the text. The signatories are William May, Robert Weston, Edwa
Leeds, Henry Harvey, Thomas Yale and Nicholas Bullingham.

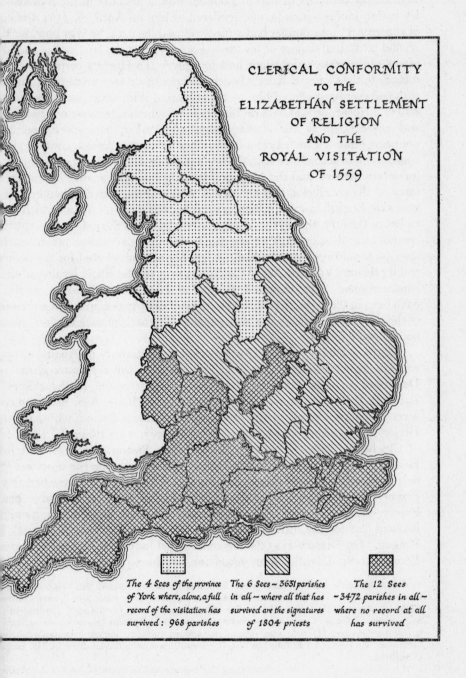

CLERICAL CONFORMITY
TO THE
ELIZABETHAN SETTLEMENT
OF RELIGION
AND THE
ROYAL VISITATION
OF 1559

The 4 Sees of the province
of York where, alone, a full
record of the visitation has
survived: 968 parishes

The 6 Sees ~ 3631 parishes
in all ~ where all that has
survived are the signatures
of 1804 priests

The 12 Sees
~ 3472 parishes in all ~
where no record at all
has survived

Bishop of Winchester, Robert Horne, thirsting for the blood of Edmu
Bonner, the deprived Bishop of London, who, a prisoner in the Marshals
lay within Horne's jurisdiction, tendered to him on April 26, 1564, the oa
of supremacy. As Bonner had already refused the oath, he was now, for tl
second refusal, in danger of his life. Forty years at the law, and in the hi
places of the state, taught him how to reply.[1] To Horne's certificate of t
refusal, to the Court of King's Bench, Bonner made answer denying that t
oath had ever been offered him by the Bishop of Winchester, as the certific
stated. Horne, he said, was no Bishop of Winchester, because not confirm
and consecrated as the statutes required—Parker, Horne's consecrat
not being himself a lawful archbishop, since he was not himself confirmed a
consecrated in accordance with the law's requirements. The case dragged
for several terms ; and the judges, discussing Bonner's answer in chambe
came to the conclusion that the doubt which he suggested, whether Hor
was what English law said a bishop must be, was a matter of fact which mi
be left to the jury, should the case come to trial ; and the judges thought tl
on this plea, Bonner must be acquitted. So the government preferred tl
the case should not come to trial ; it left Bonner unmolested for the futur
and it procured a special Act of Parliament to cover the whole legality of the
consecrations.[2] The deprived Bishop of London would seem, then,
have been in the right, the more so as the Act of 1567 declared that all tend
of the oath so far made by the bishops, and all refusals of such tenders, shou
be of none effect.

Matthew Parker, who had been elected to Canterbury on August 1, 15!
was confirmed as archbishop-elect, by virtue of the *supplentes* clause,
December 9 ; and eight days later he was consecrated in the chapel
Lambeth Palace, where so many bishops of the Middle Ages had been co
secrated, at six o'clock in the morning, by William Barlow who had be
Henry VIII's Bishop of St. David's, John Scory, once Edward VI's Bish
of Chichester, Miles Coverdale, Edward VI's Bishop of Exeter, and Jo
Hodgkin, Henry VIII's suffragan Bishop of Bedford : the rite used was tl
first imposed by a (now repealed) statute of Edward VI and attached to t
Prayer Book of 1552. Four days later, December 21, in the same pla
Parker, using the same rite, consecrated Edmund Grindal for Londo
Richard Cox for Ely, Edwin Sandys for Worcester, and Roland Meyrick 1
Bangor. On January 21, 1560, he consecrated four more bishops : Thom
Young for St. David's, John Jewel for Salisbury, Richard Davies for :

---

[1] The bishop's legal advisers were Edmund Plowden, reputed the greatest comn
lawyer of his generation (" Bonner, with the expert Plowden to guide him ", says Maitla
Collected Papers, III, 126), Christopher Wray (destined, as Lord Chief Justice, to
and sentence Edmund Campion, seventeen years later) and William Lovelace, who, accord
to Strype (*Parker*, II, 168) was refused an appointment by Parker " because he ne
mentioned the matter [of Bonner] to him ". I owe this note to the kindness of Mr. Rich
O'Sullivan.

[2] 8 Elizabeth, c. 1.—" An act declaring the making and consecrating of the Archbish
and Bishops of this realm to be good, lawful and perfect ". For an account of this cri
cf. Dixon, VI, 29–36, who prints the Bishop of Winchester's certificate and extracts, fr
Dyer's reports, of the judges' debate. For the Act of Parliament, *ibid.*, 146–150.

aph, and Nicholas Bullingham for Lincoln ; and on March 24 another
ree, Gilbert Berkeley for Bath and Wells, Thomas Bentham for Coventry
d Lichfield, Edmund Guest for Rochester. Barlow had been given
nichester, and Scory Hereford, on December 20. William Alley was con-
crated to Exeter, July 14, 1560 ; John Parkhurst to Norwich, September 1,
llowing ; Robert Horne to Winchester and Edmund Scambler to Peter-
rough, February 16, 1561. The four northern sees were also filled
at same year.[1] Then, in 1562, Gloucester (with Bristol) was given to
chard Cheney.[2] Oxford was left vacant the whole of the reign, save for
few months in 1567 when Hugh Corwen, once Archbishop of Dublin, oc-
pied it, and for the three years of John Underhill's episcopate (1589–1592).

The government had not seemingly had any large variety of choice, when
came to fill the sees which its policy had emptied. Of the 18 new nominees
the English sees, 12 were taken from the small band of clerics who had
nctioned as chaplains and preachers in the late exodus to the Continent.
gain, as many as 15 of the 18 had been, until dislodged by the Marian
storation, university professionals. Of the 12 bishops lately exiles, 10
d been university figures. Four of these were from Cambridge : Robert
orne had risen,[3] at 34, to be fellow of St. John's ; [4] Edmund Grindal, at 34,
llow of Pembroke Hall ; James Pilkington, at 33, master of St. John's ;
d Edwin Sandys had been, at 37, master of St. Catherine's and vice-
ancellor. The six Oxford men were : Thomas Bentham who, at 40,
d been a fellow of Magdalen ; Nicholas Bullingham, fellow of All Souls at
; John Parkhurst, at 44 fellow of Merton, but resident at his benefice of
eeve in Gloucestershire ; Thomas Young, 46 when he went into exile,
as a one time master of Broadgate Hall, but in 1553 a dignitary of the cathe-
al church of St. David's ; Richard Cox, the senior of the new bench, 52 in
53, Dean of Christ Church and vice-chancellor ; and John Jewel (the only
e, besides Parker, to survive, even as a name, for the general reader of history)
llow of Corpus Christi at the time of the hejira and 31 or 32 years of age.

Of the other exiles now promoted, two, William Barlow and John Scory,
d already functioned as bishops under the Supreme Headship of Henry VIII
d Edward VI ; the third, Gilbert Berkeley, was like them an ex-religious,[5]
d now (in 1559) 51.

Only six of the new bishops had spent the late reign in England.[6]
mehow they had escaped the persecution ; and also, what was later to
important, they came to their new task with a Protestantism untouched
so remarkable an experience as life at the very heart of the Reformed

[1] York : William May, nominated in June 1560, died before consecration ; Thomas
ung translated from St. David's, Feb. 20, 1561 ; Durham : James Pilkington, March 2 ;
rlisle : John Best, March 2 ; Chester, William Downham, May 4.
[2] Consecrated, April 19, 1562.
[3] By the date of Mary's accession—and so for the remainder of the names in the list.
[4] Dean of Durham, also.
[5] He had been a Franciscan Conventual, Barlow an Austin Canon and Scory a Dominican.
[6] But Bentham had returned from the continent to direct the London Congregation of the
formed through the last two years of Mary's reign.

religion in Strasburg, Zurich or Geneva. The new Archbishop of Cant
bury, Matthew Parker, was one of these six, a one-time master of Corp
Christi college, Cambridge [1] and (at 49) Dean of Lincoln at the time
Mary's accession ; he was a learned antiquarian, whose great care, amid t
contemporary ruin of learning, to collect ancient manuscripts has won h
sympathy from all historians. Edmund Guest had been vice-provost
King's, at 35 ; unlike almost all the rest he was, and he remained, unmarrie
something which was to win him a great place in Elizabeth's regard. Anoth
King's man was William Alley, who, at 39, had turned physician in Mar
reign to shield himself. A fourth of these bishops was Edmund Scambl
no older than John Jewel, and one of the bishops who have done most to w
the bench hard words from the historians.[2] Richard Cheney, who
Mary's accession found a man of 42 and Archdeacon of Hereford, has t
distinction of being the solitary Lutheran among these bishops : he was
be one of the storm centres in the long controversial years ahead. The six
bishop of this group, William Downham, the only one of them from Oxfor
where he had been a fellow of Magdalen, had in early life been a religiou
one of the community of Bonhommes at Ashridge in Buckinghamshire, whi
house had later come to be the residence of Elizabeth. Downham had be
one of the queen's private chaplains in the days of her misfortunes, and
was possibly this early link with his sovereign that saved him when, in t
years to come, his slackness about Catholics in Lancashire drew him in
frequent trouble with the council.

What part theology was to play in the lives of the new apostles ; how
was to complicate their relations with one another, with their fellows now al
returned from exile, but not promoted to sees, with their one-time maste
at Zurich and elsewhere ; all this is a great part of the history of the ne
formative twenty years. Leaving aside, for the moment, all consideratio
of the theological views which they shared, and of the points where they we
divided, we can note that of the whole bench only three were canonists
legists, Young of York, and Meyrick of Bangor, and Bullingham of Lincol
And we can also note that not a single one of these new bishops of the Refor
has come to his see after a career in the service of the state. If the now great

[1] All of this group but William Downham were Cambridge men.

[2] The worst that has ever been said of them, in a single paragraph, is I suppose wh
Herbert Hall has written in his *Society in the Elizabethan Age*, pp. 105, 170 : " The State
society was the worst that had ever before been in the land. . . . And where, all this tim
was the influence of the Church at work ? There was no pretence even of such an influenc
The Bishops were mostly starveling pedants, creatures of a court faction, whose finge
itched after filthy lucre ; or else good, plodding, domesticated men, with quiverfuls to provi
for ; graziers or land-jobbers who had mistaken their vocation. Narrow, harsh, graspin
servile, unjust, they were despised as much by their masters as they were hated by th
flocks. . . . In fact, there seems to have been a consensus of opinion unfavourable to t
English bishop. Denounced alike by Catholics, Anglicans, and Puritans, they existed on
by good will of the Crown or rather by its contemptuous toleration. Even well-meani
bigots like Parker and Whitgift appear in pleasant relief to theologians of the school of Aylm
and Cox—except for purposes of religious or political partisanship." This is by no mean
generally accepted view nowadays, as will be seen.

poverished episcopate is no longer to be a means for the crown to reward
more eminent servants, those high offices of state are, on the other hand,
be closed henceforth to all but the layman.   The Lord Chancellorship,
d the many courts that depend on this, the high places of the " Foreign
ffice " and the diplomatic service—these are, henceforth, to be filled, as is
ght, by the laymen.[1]   In the considerations which guide their manifold
tivities, questions of right will, it is to be feared, have even less place than
ey had of yore with the clerical legists.   The laymen has not won his final
ctory over the cleric in order to fetter himself, in the government of the
untry, by what, henceforward, will more and more come to be thought of
the scrupulosity of parsons.   But if the bishops have gone for ever who were
tle more than high civil servants in rochets, the bishops who have arrived
their place are none the less—and as bishops—the servants of the crown,
pendent ultimately upon the Supreme Governor, who, behind all trans-
rencies of verbal denial, is still in law the Supreme Head ; and these bishops
e to be more and more rigorously confined to the pastoral work of super-
sing the conduct of the clergy.   The national life is now the layman's
air, and so too is the layman's own life.

[1] No bishop or archbishop is even a member of the council until, nearly 30 years after the
olution of 1559, Elizabeth appoints Whitgift in 1587.

Chapter III

THE SCHOLARLY APPROACH

THE pages in which, all too briefly, an attempt is made to descri[ ]
what the new religious laws of 1559 actually brought about in t[ ]
forty years that followed, ought to be the least dogmatic of all—so litt[ ]
do we know the religious life of Everyman. Scholars of a generation pa[ ]
indeed, could write about it all with a certitude which today amazes : "
England, generally, the religious settlement was welcomed by the peop[ ]
and corresponded to their wishes ".[1] Such scholars saw that one part,
any rate, of the revolution of 1559 had fully succeeded—Catholicism, as
principal force in English life, did indeed disappear within a lifetime ; a[ ]
it seems to have been, with scholars of that generation, a kind of axiom th[ ]
revolutions do not succeed to this extent unless the bulk of the communi[ ]
is actively sympathetic.

Since Creighton wrote, now sixty years ago,[2] there has come a generatic[ ]
that is not only something less than certain about the absolute value of wh[ ]
was inaugurated in 1559—and less embarrassed by the knowledge of [ ]
fundamental weaknesses—but a generation that is considerably more famili[ ]
with the way in which all revolutions seem to work. " Lenin was cle[ ]
from the outset that to make a revolution it was necessary to make a party
a student of contemporary history can tell us, as one reciting a platitud[ ]
and, the very day on which this page is written, another observer—of even[ ]
in Roumania—is explaining in *The Times* how, a very small minority havi[ ]
gained control, " The whole apparatus of the state was turned against t[ ]
historic parties . . .". That a revolution succeeds is not, by any mean[ ]
proof that what it means to accomplish must be a thing generally desired[ ]

[1] Creighton, *Queen Elizabeth* (ed. 1899), 53. The remarks that follow, in the text,
made with respect to the treatment of facts generally known. But beyond this, the warn[ ]
of Ronald Bayne, in *Shakespeare's England*, I, 49 (1926), still holds, that it is difficult
summarise the religious history of the reign because many problems still await investigati[ ]

[2] Fifty years after Mandell Creighton a scholar of our own time can take for gran[ ]
ideas that destroy the bishop's thesis absolutely. " That the Elizabethan settlement [ ]
only proved most favourable to the ' interest of the state ', but was actually devised by [ ]
scrupulous politicians to square with the needs of a ruthless policy of national autono[ ]
can, of course, hardly be denied ", D'Entrèves, *Medieval Political Thought*, 141.
There was another side to the politicians' profit that was not hidden from clerical conte[ ]
poraries. " The Church of England ", wrote William Harrison in 1577, " is no less co[ ]
modious to the prince's coffers than the state of the laity, if it do not far exceed the same, si[ ]
their payments are certain, continued, seldom abated ". Harrison, p. 73. The whole
Harrison's ch. VI, *Of the Ancient and Present Estate of the Church of England*, should
read. One interesting point is its witness how the tradition of untruth about the religion
the Middle Ages is forming : the association of monastic life as such with immorality, p. 2[ ]
the habitual immorality of the clergy, p. 79 ; the failure to foster universities, p. 75 ; a[ ]
p. 261, Henry VIII as the protector of universities against those who would despoil them

y more than the success of the revolution is proof that what has been accom-
ished is something wholly good.[1] If it were declared that the great religious
ange that has come to be called the Elizabethan Settlement, was as much
e work of a minority, and accomplished with as great a disregard of national
shes, as certain political settlements which our own day has seen effected
various parts of eastern Europe, our first reaction to evidence offered in
pport of such a theory would not, today, be that incredulity, that astonish-
ent that reasonable men should be asked even to consider the possibility
such obvious nonsense, which the mention of the theory would have had
face sixty or seventy years since. If a determined minority can, for a
ole generation, command " the whole apparatus of the state ", who will
w set limits to what it may effect upon the minds of the majority ?

When the fundamental Acts had been got on to the statute book, the
atholic bishops displaced, and divines from the Reform party installed in
eir places ; and when the first royal visitation had made it evident to the
ole country that a new religious policy, yet again, demanded its obedience,
o things still remained to be done which could only be done over a
riod of years : the establishment of the Reform party so firmly that it
uld never again lose hold ; and the de-Catholicising of whatever proportion
the nation still regarded the Reform with suspicion, if not with active
slike.[2] It is this double process which is the subject of this part of the
ok.
We cannot begin by making general statements about what " the mass "
the nation desired, or disliked, in 1559. Creighton, sixty years ago now,
id very definitely that the mass was Reform-minded. Pollard, forty years
o, thought it Catholic to this extent that, left to itself, it would never have
oved towards the Reform ; and Usher, about the same time, was saying
at as late as 1583, after twenty-four years of the new régime, " The majority
ill inclined to the old mass ".[3] A writer of our own time considers it
true to say that the vast bulk of the nation were untouched by any marked
sire to revolt from the old faith ".[4] He also adds—and this, of course, is
ry important—" it is equally true to affirm that they were not moved by
y marked desire to defend it ".
Nicholas Sander who in 1559 was a man of 32, and professor of Divinity
of Canon Law at Oxford, has left us an all-too summary judgment,
ow the Common People of England are disposed, with regard to the Catholic
ith, that should be quoted. It was written in 1561, for the information
Giovanni Morone, cardinal-protector of England, the erstwhile friend

---

[1] " It is a common assumption that historical success has depended on moral excellence,
t truth and morality have generally, if not always prevailed, and that there is at least a
ong presumption that the victorious cause has been that of justice and right." A. F.
llard, Factors in Modern History (1948 reprint), p. 9.
[2] " If protestantism was to have a foothold in the country it was necessary to alter the
igious outlook of the nation. This, briefly, was the work the new governors of the church
d taken in hand." Black, 26, of the situation in 1559.
[3] Reconstruction, II, 266. [4] Black, 12.

of Reginald Pole. " While the common people consist of farmers, shep
herds and artisans, the farmers and shepherds are Catholics, nor are an
of the artisans infected by schism except those engaged in sedentary craft
weavers, for example, and cobblers, and some of the idlers about the cour
Again, the most distant parts of the kingdom are most averse to heres
Wales, for example, and Devon, Westmorland, Cumberland and Northum
berland. Since cities are few in England, and small, and since heresy do
not live in country districts, and scarcely at all in the distant cities, it
the firm judgment of those in a position to know, that not so many as on
in a hundred of the English are infected, so that the Lutherans too spea
of their flock as ' small '." [1]

But we are not at the end of our problem when we have determined th
numerical strength of the opponents of the Reform : the quality of the
Catholicism is no less important, how far they understood their faith as we
as how far they attended services.

It is now, in 1559, thirty years since the fatal day when the pope's lega
adjourned his court in order to defeat that petitioner who was Kir
Henry VIII, in what seemed the very hour of royal triumph ; and in a
those thirty years, this one thing at least is certain, the religious life e
England has been in ceaseless turmoil. Never, at any time, can the English
man have been more conscious that his religion mattered—if not to himsel
then to his rulers and to the vast array of their officers and administrati
servants, temporal as well as spiritual. And a whole generation had con
into existence, by 1559, that had never known that normal English Cathol
life which had continued peaceably without a break through all the fi
hundred years and more between the Danish wars and the time of Kir
Henry VIII ; that normal life when, whatever the troubles—between prie
and people, between king and bishops, between king and pope—that can
of conflicting human desires, all men took for granted the one corpus e
beliefs about God and God's plans for man, the one church through whos
teaching these were known, the one system of grace-communicating ritua
the one standard of moral conduct in public life and in private life ; fi
hundred years and more, in which all could take for granted what—in ve
different circumstances—we also can take for granted, namely, that the pro
fession and practice of religion, as one had learnt it from one's elders, as it wa
professed and practised by all around, could never involve peril of posses
sions, of liberty, of life. It was upon a race that took such peace fe
granted that the Reformation had come, ten rapid and violent years,[2] mor

---

[1] *C.R.S.*, I, 22. Translation mine. The statement that no more than 1 per cent.
the population were Protestant when Elizabeth came to the throne is, curiously enoug
in exact agreement with what a leading English Reformer was writing, at this very tim
about the religion of the clergy (i.e. those who had accepted the arrangement of 1559), vi
that not more than 1 per cent. were willing and able to preach the new doctrines. (Thom
Lever to Bullinger, July 10, 1560, *Z.L.*, 109.) And eleven years after Sander's report, a
anonymous observer declares, in 1572, that, outside London, less than one in forty of th
people are " good and devout Gospellers ". Brit. Mus., *Lansdowne*, 21, no. 2.

[2] " These ten grim unlovely years ", H. A. L. Fisher, *Political History of England*,
328, in which " the reformation was unalterably riveted upon the English people ".

anges in a quarter of a lifetime than a thousand previous years had seen.
hen came reaction—or restoration ; and now there was change once more.
/hat, after all this, would the mentality be, in matters of religion, of one
ho, in 1559, was a man of thirty ? and who, if he lived, would be an old
an of sixty in the year of the Armada.

This man had been a boy of seven at the Pilgrimage of Grace, ten when the
st of the abbeys went ; he did not remember a time when the king did not
t as the supreme earthly master of his subjects' religion ; but, if he were
e average man, he had been taught in boyhood to believe that the Mass
as a sacrifice, offered to God by the priest for the living and for the dead,
d that in the Sacrament was Jesus Christ—really, substantially, corporally
resent, body and soul, God and man ; and, until he was eighteen, like all
her orthodox believers, he had prepared himself to receive Holy Communion
y a confession of his sins to his parish priest ; then, as a young fellow of
om eighteen to twenty-three, he saw the official repudiation of these sacra-
ental doctrines, and a new service introduced, with the benediction of the
ng and most of the bishops, which displaced the Mass and which, by ritual
ords and gestures, proclaimed as gospel truth what he had, until now,
een taught was heresy. Pilgrimages he could not remember ; nor the
nturies-old cultus of the local saints, their glorious shrines and the venerated
lics they contained—these, with the statues and pictures relating to them,
ad been destroyed in his childhood, by the time he was ten or eleven. And
ow, as he watched the Mass in process of the transformation that would
estroy it, he saw the chantries disappear, and the schools in jeopardy, saw
e last round-up of church plate and costly furnishings, the very altars
rn down, the churches turned into whitewashed meeting-houses such
the Zwinglians used in Switzerland. Perhaps all this appealed to him
d was welcome. He was, anyhow, a young man of twenty-four, who
ad never known anything religious likely to stay unchanged for long,
hen, in 1553, Mary came to the throne—and the great movement was
augurated that was to restore the world to what it had been before he
as born.

Such was the life story of all Queen Elizabeth's subjects under thirty
ears of age [1] at the beginning of her reign ; the queen herself was then 25,
/alsingham 28, Leicester the same ; the Duke of Norfolk 22 ; of coming
ligious leaders Jewel was 37, and Whittingham 34 ; of future archbishops
Canterbury, Grindal was 39, and Whitgift 29 ; William Allen was 26 ;
homas Cartwright 23 ; Drake was 18, and so was Edmund Campion.
ecil was 38.

[1] We may here recall the opinion of the Venetian ambassador, some eighteen months
fore Elizabeth's accession that practically no one under 35 years of age was truly a Catholic
that Cecil's own generation was, on the whole, lost to the faith. (For the report, cf.
l. II, Appendix, pp. 347–348.) The ambassador does not say, nor mean, that this
neration had been won to the Reformed doctrines : he is most explicit that what held
e younger generation was the new prospect of not needing to believe anything at all which
s a restriction upon their desires. It must also be noted that, speaking generally, all that
e foreign ambassadors knew of England was London and the court.

We shall not expect to find, after thirty years of this sort, any gre
enthusiasm, for religious dogma as such, among the nobility and the peop
of the court, or among the merchant princes—among those classes for whic
the religious changes have been the opportunity to develop, at the gener
expense, social changes which they had already found profitable. And th
mass of the English people are peasantry, farmers and farm labourer
owning and not owning ; half of them, at least, unable to read or writ
poor and oppressed in very large part ; victims, in the most populate
districts of all, of the " progress " that is making the fortunes of their better
living in a continual state of agitation and unrest.   These are the people wh
rose in 1536 and 1549 and 1553, and again in 1554, to remedy social wrongs
to undo the religious revolution.   This is the ordinary Englishman.   Wha
in 1559, is his attitude to the question, Catholic or Reformed ?

Whatever the general knowledge of the Catholic faith which this averag
Englishman possessed who was formed in the far-off time before 152
knowledge *what* and knowledge *why*, and knowledge of the differing in
portance of the various acts and rites and ceremonies of his religion, is it to
much to suggest that the thirty years of dislocation, and of unhindered ant
Catholic propaganda,[1] and of the fluctuations of the far from well-instructe
parish clergy, must have greatly diminished and obscured that knowledge a

---

[1] As a reminder, written by a contemporary, of the kind of thing that had been pou
into the mind of the Catholic Englishman by his own clergy, we might consider the followin
actually written in the very year of Elizabeth's accession, by a writer who is evidently ce
brating the event by an assault on the Catholic prelates late the persecutors of his party, a
now themselves about to be cast down ; there is no charge, it will be observed, that those
attacks had ever taught the new heresies about Justification, or about the Holy Euchar
Here we have some evidence of what the fruits could be, in the popular mind, of the Bisho
Book and the King's Book and the Homilies.

" Who taught us that Thomas Becket was no saint, but a devil, no true subject, but a fa
traitor, that did disobey and contend with his Prince, and took part with the Pope ? . . . W
(I pray ye) put into the prayers of the Primer : From the tyranny of the Bishop of Rome a
all his detestable enormities, O Lord, deliver us ?—and whether the acts of our blessed Bishc
the Pope's executioners, have been such as we have needed (if we mought) so to pray st
I report me to you.   Who made it one chief part of their matter in pulpits, still to shew
of his intolerable arrogancy and abuse of Princes, of his tyranny, war, quarrelling, avari
apostacy, simony, sacrilege, whoredom . . . malice, pride, poysonings, and all kinds
wickedness and abominations beside, so continually exercised by him, and all his whole h
company, his cardinals and court ?   Who taught us that his dispensations, his pardons, a
Bulls, were but false trumpery, wicked for him to give and folly for us to receive, and utte
damnable for any to trust in ?   Who taught us that Scripture never made mention of P
gatory after this life, or if there were any such pains, yet were they not redeemable by
Pope's pardons, by Monks' masses, or Priests' penny-prayers ?   Who taught us, that it w
meetest for us to have the law, that we all professed, and to have divine service, in that langua
that we best knew ?   Who taught us to pluck images out of churches for doubt of idolatr
Who taught us to make our prayers, not to Our Lady, nor any other bisaints, but only
God ?   Who taught us all this, *and ten times more*, than I have leisure to tell, or ye to he
and now can recant it every whit ?   Who, I say, who and who, I pray ye ?   Marry who I
even they and they of their coat ?   Our Bishops, our Suffragans, our Doctors, our Deaco
our Parsons, our Chaplains, our hedge Priests and all, whereof many yet alive both quick a
queathing."

The quotation, in Foxe, VII, 797, is from a tract entitled : " A speciall grace, appoint
to have been said after a banket at Yorke, upon the good nues and Proclamation thear,
the entrawnce in to reign over us, of our Sovereign lady Elizabeth, in November 1558
signatures D.i and iii.

limmed it with doubt ?   And how little had been done in Mary's short time owards undoing the mischief of the preceding twenty years.   The Catholic eaders had never really begun, what was called for immediately and before ll else, that great campaign of popular re-education which should explain vhat had been wrong in the revolution and why.

And along with the effect of those thirty years of change upon these peasants and work folk, we should need to know how it all appeared to the parochial clergy who worked amongst them, and shared so much of their daily life ; and how little we know of these ! In this mass of the ordinary clergy, there have been few signs of positive enthusiasm, in all these thirty years, about what has been going forward ; outside a few centres there have been no noteworthy individuals, except critics and opponents. For nearly twenty years or so now, fewer and fewer have offered themselves for Holy Orders—in some years almost none at all ; [1] and in every part of the country here are very many parishes without priests. Again we need to ask, what proportion of these clergy of 1559 could remember the normal Catholic life, or had been trained—whatever that may ever have meant—to accept with imple faith the traditional teaching and the practices that derived from this nd supported it ? Even the youngest man who was already a priest at the ime when Wolsey fell from power and the Reformation parliament began its vork was, by the time Elizabeth came to the throne, a man approaching ixty ; and at sixty, sixteenth-century man was nearing the end of his life. Again, all but the very youngest of these clergy had, at one time, publicly vorn their repudiation of the pope ; and if they had not been learned nough to preach that his primacy was a fraud, they had regularly read the Iomilies which proclaimed this discovery. They had fed on the doctrine of the Bishops' Book and the King's Book in the sixteen years before Mary's ccession—more subtly dangerous, by far, to faith than open Lutheranism. A great number of them had married in the time of Edward VI—six to twelve ears ago now—and had then put away their wives when Mary came in, had lone penance and been reconciled, and re-appointed.[2] But in all these

---

[1] The statistics of ordinations for the period 1517–1559 have never been studied. Here re some figures from the registers of Stephen Gardiner (Winchester 1531–1541), and of 'uthbert Tunstall (Durham, 1530–1559), the first published in 1930 (Canterbury and York ociety), the second in 1953 (Surtees Society). In the diocese of Winchester there were ordinations in those ten years, in which a total of 8 priests were ordained, one of them a monk of Hyde, and 3 others secular priests for other dioceses—i.e. a total of 4 priests for 1e diocese of Winchester ordained in the diocese. Gardiner was the ordaining prelate n one occasion only. At Durham, in startling contrast, in the five years 1531–1535 inclusive, 33 priests were ordained, of whom 101 were of the secular clergy. But in the next six years iere were no ordinations at all. In 1542, 6 priests were ordained ; in 1543, 6 again, and a 1547, 8. In the eight years 1548–1555 inclusive there were no ordinations. In 1555, 10 riests were ordained ; in 1558, 4 ; in 1559, 14. But of these 28 priests ordained a Queen Mary's reign, 7 only were for the diocese of Durham ; 9 were for Carlisle, and 12 or Chester. The first of Queen Elizabeth's bishops—James Pilkington, 1561–1576— rdained in all 12 priests (ordinatus fuit in ministrum, the register sometimes notes) ; 9 of 1em for Durham.

[2] The total number of priests who took advantage of the statute of Edward VI and married not known. Dixon (IV, 144–160) gives the following, from the register of the various es : Coventry and Lichfield, 550 livings, 43 deprived for marriage ; Canterbury, 380

years, save for the last four of Edward's reign, they had always said Mass and had administered the traditional Catholic sacraments.

One very great difference indeed there was, between the England of 1559 and that of the preceding years, as the event soon showed—the party, or section, ready for " Catholicism without the pope " had disappeared entirely. This was really remarkable ; for from 1534 this had been, to all appearances, the party of the mass of the nation, and its views had been, for the first fifteen years of the change, the country's official religion, more or less. In fact, however, this was never any more, with most, than the official orthodoxy —commanded, enforced, but on all sides only passively accepted. To the great mass of those who accepted this form of Christianity, to the church of the Royal Supremacy in its earliest phase, that is to say, all the doctrines which particularised the church of the Supremacy in its Elizabethan stage were heresy—to the great mass, for some of the leaders already, even in those earliest years, held these doctrines in secret. At Henry's death religious leaders of this type gained control. But when, six years later, the failure of Northumberland's plot ended their triumph, their victorious opponents did not thereupon re-establish the régime of 1534. The official orthodoxy was not, in 1553, to be the " Catholicism without the pope " of Henry VIII and of the *De Vera Obedientia*, but Catholicism itself. " Catholicism without the pope " was now, as a possible solution and system, not only dead, but dead and damned. If, and when, the now defeated party of the Reform ever came back to power, it would be Catholics whom it would everywhere find in possession, and the issue henceforward would be clear between the two. Mary's short reign provided the opportunity whereby this important issue was clarified, so that Catholicism re-appeared after being lost to sight for a generation behind the ambiguities of the régime of Henry VIII ; the reign had also provided the opportunity for the party of Gardiner and Heath and Bonner to hear condemned, with all the fullness of Catholic authority, that Supremacy before which it had bowed, and the opportunity of admitting whatever sin it had committed in so doing.

And the reign had seen the return to Catholicism of many who had accepted, not only the Royal Supremacy but the new Continental doctrines of the Reform also. From three of the newly returned Marian exiles we have statements about this, divines already designated for the vacant sees who are describing, to their friends and mentors abroad, the religious state of England in the first months after their return, and the prospects of their party. Many of the Reformed, they say, have been won back to Catholicism, and are now standing firmly by it : Elizabeth's restoration has not been for them an opportunity to revert to the new beliefs now fashionable once more.[1]

---

livings, 73 deprived ; Bath & Wells, 390 livings, 69 deprived ; London, 700 livings, 143 (?) deprived ; Norwich, 1,120 livings, 335 deprived.

[1] Bullinger's exhortation from Zurich, to be firm and resolute, was much needed, wrote Jewel to Henry Bullinger, May 22, 1559 ; " For we have at this time also not only to contend

The Reformers were indeed, after 1559, the party in power, but it was in a country where all outside the party was Catholic—in some sense ; those who belonged to the party were very conscious how few they were, and what hazards their venture still faced. " A few Calvinists of one little island ", said a Catholic controversialist ; [1] very scornfully it may seem—yet the Reformers' own language, in their private correspondence, suggests that, in their own hearts, they felt much the same. Jewel speaks of there being but one " minister of the word then in London", at the moment of Elizabeth's accession.[2] There was never a time, in the worst days of Elizabeth's persecution of the Catholics when the number of priests in the capital sank so low as this : which is not said with any reference to the comparative courage, in adversity, of one party or the other, but as suggesting that the Reformed were in truth a mere handful, at the time when the change of sovereign put them into power. Foxe, again, gives an account of the " marvellous preservation " during Mary's reign of what he calls " The Congregation of London ". He speaks of " their minister ", and " their deacon " ; and he tells us that " From the first beginning of Mary's reign, they had divers ministers ", whose names he gives : Edmund Scambler (whom in 1560 Elizabeth made Bishop of Peterborough), Thomas Foule, John Rough (an ex-Friar Preacher and a Scot, burned in Smithfield in 1558), Augustine Bernher, and, lastly, that Thomas Bentham mentioned by Jewel (who was made Bishop of Coventry and Lichfield in 1560). Foxe also tells us that, " In this church or congregation there were sometimes 40, sometimes 100, sometimes 200, sometimes more and sometimes less. About the latter time of Queen Mary it greatly increased ".[3] Is this really the sum total, in a city of 80–100,000 people, of the adherents faithful to the religion established under Edward VI and about to be restored by the government of Elizabeth ? [4]

---

with our adversaries, but also with those of our friends who, of late years, have fallen away from us, and gone over to the opposite party ; and who are now opposing us with a bitterness and obstinacy far exceeding that of any common enemy " ; Z.L., 41. " Under the cruel reign of Mary though but for the space of five years, papacy so much increased both in numbers and strength ", Richard Cox wrote to Weidner, May 20, 1559, " that it was hardly to be imagined how much the minds of the papists were hardened ; so it was not without great difficulty that our pious queen, with those about her who stood forth with alacrity on the side of truth, could obtain room for the sincere religion of Christ ". Z.L., 36. And Grindal wrote, May 23, 1559, to Conrad Hubert, " We are labouring under a great dearth of godly ministers : for many who have fallen off in this persecution are now become papists in heart ; and those who had been heretofore, so to speak, moderate papists, are now the most obstinate ". Z.L., 44–45. There is nothing here to suggest any expectation on the part of the Reformers that—the Marian terror over—" godly ministers " will now be revealed in every priest, or most priests, or even in many priests. One very notable friend, of late years fallen away, was Thomas Harding, who will presently be in controversy with Jewel, and who had gone over to the new doctrines in his schooldays at Winchester. Archdeacon Louth was to recall, in 1579, that it was Harding who, when " I was in Wykham's college . . . delivered me John Frith's Purgatory to read . . .". Cf. his reminiscences in Nichols, Narratives, 55. Harding, born 1516, went to Winchester in 1528 ; Louth, who was born in 1519, in 1534.

[1] Thomas Harding, answering in 1564 Jewel's Apology ; Jewel, IV, 903.
[2] To Peter Martyr, Jan. 26, 1559, Z.L., 16–17. The minister was Thomas Bentham.
[3] Foxe, VIII, 558–560.
[4] Is Hooker (born 1553) a witness that the Reformers of 1559 knew themselves to be but

Against this interpretation we may set another piece of information fro
Jewel, written in March 1560, shortly after his consecration as Bishop (
Salisbury : " Religion is now somewhat more established. . . . The peop'
are everywhere exceedingly inclined to the better part. The practice (
joining in church music has very much conduced to this. . . . You ma
sometimes see at Paul's Cross . . . six thousand persons . . . all singin
together." [1]

Two years or so after the passing of the Acts of Supremacy and Uniformit
and the deposition of the bishops, the great cathedral of London was struc
by lightning and its spire, the tallest thing the world then knew, was des
troyed. Whereupon cries that this was the judgment of God on 1559, an
a furious controversy, in which the chief figure was James Pilkington, soo
to be Bishop of Durham. " In the fierceness of Pilkington the anxiety (
the conflict and the issue still uncertain is reflected : he describes his ac
versaries as by no means despondent, but waiting for a change of affairs. . . ."
The Reformers themselves are surely conscious how few they are. " W(
that little flock, who for these last five years, by the blessing of God, hav
been hidden among you in Germany . . . ", wrote Cox, in May 1559.[3] Thre
years later he is still fearful of the temper of the country (whether of h
Cambridgeshire see, or of England), and says " We can hardly dare to expe(
a long continuance of the Gospel in these parts. There is an immens
number of Papists." [4] And Horne, three years later still, writing as Bisho
of Winchester, uses the same language. The new controversy about cleric;
dress and vestments, he says, " has occasioned a great strife among u;
so that our little flock has divided itself into two parties . . . ". In contra
he speaks of his fears : " the papists are forming a secret and powerfu
opposition ".[5]

" The English Reformers ", it has been written of their situation at th
moment of Mary's death, " were without a chief ; beyond Elizabeth the
had no pretender to the throne ; they had no apostle, no prophet ; they wer
scattered over Europe and had been quarrelling, Knoxians against Coxian;
in their foreign abodes. Edward's reign had worn the gloss off the nev
theology." [6] Nor were they at all, in the first moments at any rate, ab
solutely certain of the queen. After reporting the news that Elizabet
" has taken good Christians into her service in the room of papists ", on
writer, a returned exile to whom the queen was soon to give the see o
Worcester, goes on to say, " and there is good hope of her promotin

---

a handful when, thirty-four years later, he writes of " the reformed religion, a thing
her [i.e. Elizabeth's] coming to the throne even raised as it were by miracle from the dea
a thing which we so little hoped to see, that even they which beheld it done, scarcely believe
their own senses at the first beholding " ? Hooker, I, 488.

[1] To Peter Martyr, March 5, 1560 ; Z.L., 90.

[2] Dixon, V, 338.   [3] To W. Weidner, May 20, 1559 ; Z.L., 36.

[4] To Peter Martyr, Aug. 5, 1562 ; ibid., 148.

[5] To Rudolf Gualter, July 17, 1565 ; ibid., 200. Cf. also, Cox to the Privy Counc
in 1564 : " True religion is dangerously declining in the most part of the churches in th
realm." Camden Miscellany, IX, 23–26 for his letter.

[6] Maitland, in C.M.H., II, 562.

he Gospel, and advancing the kingdom of Christ to the utmost of her power. That she may do this, God must be entreated by all religious persons." [1] Fuller's letter to Elizabeth, already quoted, also makes clear how anxious ome of the Protestants were. Recalling to her, in 1585, " the right godly ringing up and good report which Your Majesty had for religion and all virtue and good learning, even when Your Majesty was but a child " he proceeds to tell how, in the early months of Queen Mary's reign, Elizabeth had disappointed all her admirers: " . . . from Hatfield House I was advertised by godly friends, that had woeful hearts . . . that Your Majesty went to the antichristian abomination, and travailed to bring all your amily also thereunto ", and " afterwards that Your Majesty in process of time was so marvellously altered, in mind, manner and many things, hat there was no hope of any such reformation (when Your Majesty should ome to the crown) as was before hoped for . . . the effects of the said advertisements were confirmed by divers that came out of England to Geneva [and] my former hope of great good was turned into fear of great evil . . .".[2] Again, it could seem much, to one of the great laymen among the exiles, that, " if the reports from Antwerp are to be depended upon, the spirits of the papists are entirely cast down, and that they will not offer to attack us, unless our own discord should afford them an opportunity ".[3] And six months after the parliamentary victory, Jewel, on his return from that tour of the west as a royal commissioner during which, so he said, " The ranks of the papists fell of their own accord ", could also write, " Pray to God that we may at length bring our vessel . . . into harbour. For the rage of the papists among us at this time is scarcely credible . . . who most impotently precipitate and throw all things into confusion." [4]

In this correspondence, and in the sermons of the leading Reformers, there is more than one hint that the religious situation is far from simple ; and nothing, seemingly, was less evident to the returned leaders than that they had come back to a country which had long been secretly yearning

---

[1] Edwyn Sandys to Bullinger, Dec. 20, 1558 ; *Z.L.*, 5–6.

[2] Peel, II, 57. Fuller, it must be explained, is writing in 1585, after twenty-six years of disappointment, anxiously warning the queen of the punishment that awaits her disregard of that miracle of God's work, viz. " that little Mount Sion of this age " Geneva, and her " not fetching thence [her] chief advice and pattern as from the most tried and approved ", for this " hath greatly offended God . . . and furthered Antichrist's kingdom ". Peel, II, 61, n. 1.

[3] Sir Antony Cook to Bullinger, Dec. 8, 1558 ; *ibid.*, 1.

[4] Jewel to Gualter, Nov. 2, 1559 ; *ibid.*, 63. The phrase about " the ranks of the papists " is amazingly expanded by Black, 16 (no references given) and made to mean more than it contains : " The government commissions that began their perambulation of the country in August returned to London in October with the comfortable feeling that ' the ranks of the papists have fallen almost of their own accord '." Cf. also the unexplained anxiety of a curious note, in which one Swiss reformer comments to another about English affairs in the first week of the reign : " We are afraid, however, that they [the exiles] have returned too soon ; but as we consider that their presence will be necessary, we cannot blame their resolution." The senate at Berne is sending a letter recommending these exiles of Aarau, under Lever, to Elizabeth : will not Bullinger's people do the same ? J. Haller to Bullinger, Berne, Jan. 11, 1559 ; *Z.L.*, 6–7.

for the liberation they proposed to offer.[1] Sceptics, for example, abounded :
" Many will believe neither side, whatsoever they allege. Bring they
truth, bring they falsehood ; teach they Christ, teach they antichrist ;
they will believe neither, they have so hardened their hearts ; . . . nothing
will move them, nothing will please them. . . . " [2] There were heretics
also : " I have had to contend, both from the pulpit and in mutual conference,
with those horrid monsters of Arianism . . .", so Parkhurst ; [3] and Thomas
Sampson reported to Peter Martyr, " We have papists, anabaptists, and very
many gospellers, who are enemies both to learning and a godly reformation ".[4]
There was not " the same alacrity among our friends, as there lately was
among the papists ", said Jewel.[5]

And once the Reform was legally established, the inevitable happened :
the " little flock " became fashionable, and strange sheep indeed began to
show in the fold. While the situation was doubtful, wrote Thomas
Lever, there were, through the new preaching, many sincere conversions.
" And now popery is at length abolished by authority of parliament, and
the true religion of Christ restored : this unclean world, both in the one
and the other, seeks after nothing but base lucre and filthy pleasure.
Very many persons are so drawn over from that to this, that they are
neither willing to purify the dross of the one, nor to embrace the purity
of the other, but are disposed to frame themselves after the fashion of this
world." [6] Three years later Parkhurst, now Bishop of Norwich, makes
the same complaint : " To be plain with you, I fear many evils are
hanging over our heads. For almost all are covetous, all love gifts. There
is no truth, no liberality, no knowledge of God . . . what Empedocles said
of his Agrigentines, I may also say of my English. The English indulge in
pleasures, as if they were to die tomorrow ; while they build, as if they were
to live forever." [7]

We might set in contrast with this picture of their own early difficulties and
disappointments, what the same well-placed observers have to say about the
attitude of the clergy whom they found in possession.[8] The " propaganda ",
and the parliamentary campaign made no immediate difference, it would
seem : " At length many of the nobility, and vast numbers of the people,
began by degrees to return to their senses ; but of the clergy none at all. . . .

---

[1] It is surely to a preacher thought to have been engaged for years in the missionary work of
converting a whole people, that Bullinger writes to Horne, now Bishop of Winchester
seven years after Elizabeth's accession : " For I doubt not but that you have met with so
much success in your ministry, as that you have many throughout the whole kingdom . .
who are most favourably disposed to religion. . . ." Nov. 3, 1565, *Z.L.*, 203.

[2] Jewel, preaching before Elizabeth ; Jewel, II, 1014.

[3] To Bullinger, May 21, 1559. *Z.L.*, 39.

[4] Dec. 17, 1558 ; *ibid.*, 3.   [5] ? May, 1559 ; *ibid.*, 33.

[6] For an account of this first preaching in the winter of 1558–59 and its effect see the whole
of Lever's letter to Bullinger of Aug. 8, 1559, *Z.L.*, 57–58 : the quotation is from p. 59.

[7] To the same, April 28, 1562 ; *ibid.*, 140.

[8] Clergy, of course, who had made their submission to the new regime, and whose inertia
must be borne in mind when such statements are considered as in Black, 17, " The one
indubitable fact is that the Marian pastorate in overwhelming numbers *passed over into the*
service of the establishment without a murmur ". Italics mine.

'or the whole body remained unmoved . . ."; [1] and the clergy's first reaction
o the new laws was to leave the churches to those who alone had now, in law,
he right to use them.[2] " If inveterate obstinacy was found elsewhere ",
aid Jewel, of his visitation of the western counties in 1559, " it was altogether
mong the priests, those especially who had once been on our side." [3] Lever,
n the summer of 1560, speaks as though the obstinacy was still noticeable :
" Many of our parishes have no clergyman . . .", and the number is very
mall of those " who, throughout this great country, administer the sacraments ".[4] Antony Gilby, ever bitter, is still more vivid, describing what
he found when he came back from Geneva in the first years of the reign :
" Old monks and friars, and old popish priests and notorious idolaters,
penly perjured persons, halting hypocrites and manifest apostates, are allowed
n place of true and faithful pastors ".[5]

It has, indeed, actually been claimed that the England of Edward VI
was a " Protestant " country ! And more often, and more plausibly, that by
559, thanks to the mistakes, the incompetence, and the cruelty of Mary's
dministration, the country was ripe for the change of religion.[6] These zealous
nd energetic pioneers of the Elizabethan Reform do not seem to have been
t all aware of the fortunate circumstance. They were under no illusions
s to what had actually been accomplished—or how ; and they did not doubt
hat they were only at the beginning of a very arduous task, the task of
onverting the mass of their fellow-countrymen to the ideologies which they
hemselves so fiercely believed to be the only saving truth of Christ. " Now
et us behold the present state of our country ", said Bishop Jewel, preaching
one day before Elizabeth ; " the poor people lieth forsaken, and left as it were
heep without a guide . . . *they are commanded to change their religion*, and
or lack of instruction they know not whither to turn them : they know not
neither what they leave nor what they should receive ".[7]

And the lay leaders—those nobles and gentlemen who are, likewise,
most sincere believers in the Reform as a religious doctrine—use the same
anguage. It is surely one of a party which, if victorious, recognises that,

[1] Cox to Weidner, May 20, 1559 ; *ibid.*, 36.
[2] " Now that religion is everywhere changed ", Jewel wrote on Aug. 1, 1559, " the mass-
riests absent themselves altogether from public worship, as if it were the greatest impiety
o have anything in common with the people of God. But the fury of these wretches is so
reat that nothing can exceed it. They are altogether full of hope and anticipation . . . that
nese things cannot last long." To Peter Martyr, *ibid.*, 54.
" The popish priests among us are daily relinquishing their ministry, lest, as they say,
ney should be compelled to give their sanction to heresies." Cox to the same, undated but
ater than Dec. 21, 1559 ; *ibid.*, 81–82. [3] To the same, Nov. 2, 1559 ; *ibid.*, 60.
[4] To Bullinger, from Coventry, July 7, 1560 ; *ibid.*, 109.
[5] From *An hundred points of Poperie yet remaining*, a tract written in 1581, reprinted in
rber, *An Introductory Sketch to the Martin Marprelate Controversy* (1879), p. 31. For
Gilby, see *infra*, p. 228, n.
[6] But cf. Conyers Read, II, 275, " When we consider the work it [i.e. the machinery of
riyy Council, High Commission, etc.] had to perform of changing Catholic England as
Mary had left it to Protestant England as Elizabeth desired it . . .".
[7] Italics mine. Jewel is very clear about the meaning of 1559 ; he does not dispute the
ght of the government to order the change—it is, indeed, their duty to order it : as it is
ne " poor people's " duty to obey the order. The sermon (undated) is in Jewel, II, 1024.

despite its victory, it is nothing more, as yet, than a party and that all it
work still lies before it, who writes, " You cannot be ignorant that the firs
beginning of nascent affairs is attended with the most difficulty . . . ant
that religion, like everything else, has crude and weak beginnings, as well at
its increase, and progress, and maturity . . . this our religion . . . now, by
God's blessing, again beginning in some measure to revive, will strike its
roots yet deeper and deeper ; and what is now creeping on and advancing
little by little, will grow up with greater fruitfulness and verdure ".[1]

The contemporary observer who could so write, was well aware that
the Acts of 1559 had by no means " achieved the glorious work " ; that
the Acts had, indeed, merely secured the pioneers their desired opportunity
The preaching of the new doctrine to the generality of the nation was a task
it remained to begin. *Non lex ecclesiam congregavit sed fides Christi*, Jewel
quoted from St. Ambrose, in that sermon which complained of the sceptics ;[2]
and he went on to urge, from the more familiar words of the Apostle,[3] the need
of more and more preachers, and of an ever greater generosity in the maintenance of those schools where the preacher must be trained. Nothing is
more remarkable, in all Jewel's sermons, than his return, time and again
to this theme—than his constant, declared anxiety that unless preacher
are found, and educated preachers, the new venture cannot thrive.

Protestantism is not mere anti-Catholicism. It is a positive doctrine
In the upheaval of 1529–1553 old certitudes were destroyed, and the
destruction went on for many years yet to come. After the question is
answered, whether the English were " protestantised " by the time
Elizabeth came to the throne—if only in the sense that they were alienated
permanently from the old religion—a second question must be faced,
when and how the new positive certitudes were implanted in their minds i
And how long did this process take ? What of the interval before the work
of evangelisation began to bear fruit ? Nature abhors a vacuum. Into
the void there crept unbidden, unpreached, the great idea that religion
doesn't really matter—religion, that is to say, as dogma, and dogmatic
certitude. To the fact that a kind of " agnosticism " in regard to the truth
about the specifically Christian mysteries was now developing among
ordinary people, we have evidence from contestants on both sides of the
Reformation division. There is, for example, the heretic who, in Mary's
reign, warned his judges about the prevailing " third religion " ;[4] there

---

[1] Francis Russell (2nd Earl of Bedford) to Gualter, Jan. 21, 1560 ; *Z.L.*, 83. This i
nearly eight months after the parliamentary triumph. Cf. also Kennedy's phrase, written
of the first beginnings of the reign : " The new bishops entered upon a task of inconceivable
difficulty " ; *Interpretations*, 14.   [2] Sermon in Jewel, II, 1023.

[3] " How shall they believe him whom they have not heard ? And how shall they hea
without a preacher ? " Romans x, 14.

[4] " My lord, there are in England three religions. . . . The first is that which you hold
the second is clean contrary to the same ; and the third is a neuter, being indifferent—
that is to say observing all things that are commanded outwardly, as though he were o
your part, his heart being wholly set against the same." Ralph Allerton, to Bonner, April 8
1557 ; Foxe, VIII, 407.

are the references to the " atheists ", and " sceptics " in the sermons and correspondence of Hooper and of Jewel. And to the fact that during these generations of constant change the unguided Catholics could simply drift away, we have an interesting piece of testimony in a biographical reminiscence of the Benedictine mystic of these times, Dom Augustine Baker.[1] Thousands who in their youth, he tells us, had sincerely and contentedly professed the Catholic faith, " in tract of time and *sensim*, and indeed as it were unawares to themselves, became neutrals in religion, viz. neither true Catholics . . . not yet mere Protestants ".

" If the queen herself would but banish [the Mass] from her private chapel, the whole thing might easily be got rid of. Of such importance among us are the examples of princes. For whatever is done after the example of the sovereign, the people, as you well know, suppose to be done rightly " ; so Jewel wrote to Peter Martyr,[2] in the last weeks before the Act of Uniformity made it legally obligatory for Elizabeth to banish the Mass. The letter may serve to introduce yet another consideration in this survey of the forces and the parties, of the hopes and fears and antici- pations, that agitated English religious life in 1559—what were the anticipations of Elizabeth and her ministers? What, when Cecil had finished the drafts of the two Bills, did he expect would be the " nation's " reaction? In what spirit did he propose to administer these laws whose purpose was to establish the identity of the two *res*—the nation and religion : to bring it about that all England belonged, *ipso facto*, to this church of which the English sovereign was the chief ruler? and to secure that this church was not to be a religion in which the chief act of worship is the Mass.

Did Cecil really expect that all priests would become Hornes and Jewels— or Parkers—overnight? and their people with them? Did Cecil think the mass of priests were already such? and only waiting for it to be legally safe in order openly to proclaim the fact? and their people with them? Or did Cecil anticipate a lively resistance?[3] demonstrations—riots, for example— everywhere?

---

[1] Born in 1575 of parents who had lapsed from Catholicism—Catholics of Cecil's own generation—bred in the religion of the Settlement of 1559, educated at Christ's Hospital, London, at Oxford (Broadgates Hall) and at Grays Inn. He became a Catholic and then a monk (1607). He died in 1641. *C.R.S.*, 33, pp. 18-20.   [2] April 14, 1559 ; *Z.L.*, 28-29.

[3] " The Visitation [of 1559] ", thinks Kennedy, " must have exceeded their wildest hopes " (i.e. of Elizabeth and Cecil), *E.E.A.*, I, p. clii. There had been no popular rising (as in 1549) ; the number of deprivations was small ; there had been no signs that the laymen were disposed to organise in opposition to the " settlement " ; *ibid*. A contemporary witness, the Douay Missionary, Edward Rishton (1550–1585), wrote, later, to the same effect, " Meanwhile the queen and her ministers considered themselves most fortunate in that those who clung to the ancient faith, though so numerous, publicly accepted, or by their presence outwardly sanctioned, in some way, the new rites which they had prescribed. . . . They were not a little pleased that even priests were found who did not shrink from the new service ; for they were at first afraid that they would not be able to persuade them to accept it, contrary to the example and commandment of their bishops and the voice of their own conscience ". Lewis 268.

Or did he expect no more than, and would he (whatever the *mens* of the clergy and people) be satisfied with, a mere non-refusal of the Act of Supremacy and a peaceful carrying out (in whatever spirit) of the new Prayer Book—provided the Mass was really discontinued in the parish churches ? Would so little as this suit his plans in 1559 ? and would his acceptance of this suit the kind of Catholic which so many of the priests of 1559 were ?

Certainly Cecil had a double policy. As against the only real leaders the Catholics possessed—their bishops—Cecil demanded a conformity to the settlement that was real : they must publicly apostatise or be driven from public life. To them, and with great publicity, the oath contained in the Act of Supremacy was truly and formally tendered. From the rest of the nation very much less needed to be asked, in 1559, and very much less was asked.[1] If the Mass ceased to be said, or was only said in such secrecy that the number of those who could assist was negligible ; if the bulk of the nation assisted at no other services than those provided in the new Prayer Book ; and if some kind of an engagement to be loyal to the new arrangements were subscribed by the mass of the clergy, then (whether they observed the engagement faithfully, or less faithfully—the government do not wish to be too exactly informed of this) then, with the " whole apparatus of the state " in their hands, and all the twenty-six sees, what more would the government, at this moment, desire ? The whole nation is now " in " the new church ; the Mass will, with the years, disappear entirely ; there is no need to enforce, in every part of the country, on individuals here and there, to any notable number, penalties whose severity may affront local feeling—no occasion or ground will be given to " agitators " to organise such feeling ; all connection with Rome is broken ; ambiguity in the policy will tolerate (because at the moment, ambiguity is the most useful ally of all) ambiguity in the subjects ; nothing will do more to end Catholicism than ambiguity persevered in—ambiguity, that is to say, and time.

And, what was that to which, in 1559, England was to be converted ? Here, it perhaps needs to be said at the outset, we are concerned with one thing alone : the religious beliefs and views of those leading personages in whose hands, from the end of this crucial year 1559, the future of

---

[1] " Why should compulsion be used on us and lenity to the Papists ? " William Whittingham, once Knox's ally at Frankfort, and now Dean of Durham, wrote to Leicester : " How many Papists enjoy liberty and livings *who have neither sworn obedience to the Queen,* nor yet do any part of their duty towards their miserable flocks. They triumph over us : they brag that they trust the rest of their things will follow " (quoted Dixon, VI, 109. No date is given, but seemingly the letter was written in 1566 or 1567). For Whittingham, cf. *infra,* pp. 207 n., 228–230. Italics mine.

" If popish priests ", Sandys, then Bishop of Worcester, wrote to the Council in 1564, " which misliking religion, have forsaken the ministry and yet live in corners, are kept in gentlemen's houses and had in great estimation with the people, where they marvellously pervert the simple and blaspheme the truth, were restrained of their liberty and put to the oath of the Queen's Majesty's Supremacy . . . ." And we know how, in these same years, Edmund Campion was able so to arrange matters that Robert Parsons took his degree without the prescribed oath being tendered to him ; cf. Simpson's *Campion,* 6, and Birt, 507.

English religion lay ; what follows is not, in any way, meant as a description of the religion of any individuals—or of any of the parties—in any religious body in later centuries. One thing alone is intended—to describe the alternative actually presented in 1559 and the years immediately following, for the sake of which the Englishman was bidden and constrained to give up what he and his had believed for a thousand years : a re-organised church, over which the sovereign now functioned as supreme governor ; a new conception of worship ; a new set of beliefs on all the fundamental points of man's relations to God ; a new morality ; a whole set of new religious motives and habits.[1]

It would be a great mistake to assume that this new entity was of the same nature as the old ; on that assumption, to demand from it the kind of activity to be expected in the old ; and, then, to appraise the new according to the correspondence of its way of acting with the way the old always acted. It would be, implicitly, a confession of ignorance of the problem awaiting solution for a writer to look for and to discover in the new society, for example, such an official view of its doctrine as would make logical consistency, or unity, the new society's own criterion of the truth of the doctrine or of its apostolicity. It would be unjust to posit (or oneself to construct from sources) a common belief, among those who accepted the new, on all the points where issue was joined with the old, and then to think of this synthesis as a thing held to be necessarily, authoritatively, binding on all in the same sense—and it would be unjust to use such a synthesis as a means to judge either individuals or the whole. There are many views, and all will develop. And it is from sources very varied in kind that we come to learn what was in the mind and intentions of the leaders : from their private correspondence, from their apologetic and controversial writings, from their published sermons, from joint manifestoes,[2] from the injunctions they issued (if they were bishops), and from such corporate and official declarations as the Thirty-nine Articles of Religion [3]—sources which must each be used according to its own kind, and none made to mean more than a source of its kind can mean. None of these sources, for example, even professes to be of such a kind as those other, well-known, contemporary, ecclesiastical productions the decrees and canons of the Council of Trent ; [4] and Jewel's classic

[1] " Where present controversies are bound up so closely with questions of history, it is difficult in the extreme to be sure that one has seen the facts oneself without prejudice, and almost impossible to convey them to the reader in the exact proportion that one understands them without their being interpreted by his prejudices without his knowledge," Dix, *Shape of the Liturgy*, 614.

[2] For example, *A Declaration of doctrine offered and exhibited by the protestants to the Queen at the first coming over of them* ; for the text of which cf. Dixon, V, 107–116.

[3] Which, it needs to be noticed, do not profess to be a complete official statement of beliefs. They are " Articles . . . agreed by the Archbishops and Bishops of both provinces and the whole clergy . . . for the avoiding of the diversities of opinions, and for the stablishing of consent touching true Religion " (Articuli . . . ad tollendam opinionum dissensionem, et firmandum in vera Religione consensum). The texts of the Articles (Latin) of 1563 and (English) of 1571 are printed in parallel columns with those of the Articles of 1553 in Hardwick (ed. 1884), pp. 289–353.

[4] Which are conveniently consulted in Denzinger.

Apologia Ecclesiae Anglicanae, is not, in intention or in fact, another *Institutio Christianae religionis*.

The famous *Apologia Ecclesiae Anglicanae* appeared in 1562 ; and was translated (by Lady Bacon) as *An Apologie or answere in defence of the Church of England with a brief and plaine declaration of the true Religion professed and used in the same* in 1564.[1]   The *Apology* " was regarded as the official statement of the position of the Church of England under Elizabeth " says one modern Anglican historian ; [2] and, for Professor Black, it " is indispensable for an understanding of the principles of the settlement ". " Of Jewel, what shall be said " ; so Canon Dixon [4] opens his panegyric " he wrote an *Apology* . . . of admirable elegance and strength ".   Grindal proposed to Convocation, in 1563, to draft a series of articles embodying its main points, and to impose these upon all the clergy.[5]   Parker favoured a plan to print the whole *Apology* along with the Thirty-nine Articles and that it should be taught in all the universities and all grammar schools, with the same penalties for those who attacked it or belittled it as were provided in the Act of Uniformity for the protection of the Prayer Book ; and in 1573, he wrote reprovingly to Jewel's old tutor, Parkhurst, now Bishop of Norwich, that the Bishop of Salisbury's " last book ", i.e. the *Defence* of the Apology against Harding, should " be had in the rest of the parish churches within your diocese wherein they be not ".   Parkhurst demurred : Jewel had printed *verbatim* the criticisms of Harding which in this work he was answering, and the Bishop of Norwich seemed to think more harm would be done by people reading Harding on Jewel than the good hoped from Jewel's reply to Harding.[7]   A generation later Jewel still counts, and one of the things put to Bancroft's credit by contemporaries was his great effort to place in every parish, along with the Prayer-Book, the Bible, and the Canons, the works of Bishop Jewel.[8]

The differences between the new version of the Christian religion and the old were well nigh infinite, said this leading apologist of the new.[9]   Allowing for the pardonable exaggeration, how shall we not lose ourselves in the endeavour to set out the contrast ?   Perhaps by recalling as a leading principle that, despite all seeming evidence to the contrary, the quarrel between the old and the new was really about a practical, everyday matter, the most practical matter of all : how man shall save his soul, and how, in the first place, man shall come to any certainty as to the way of salvation appointed him by God.

---

[1] For which see the Parker Society edition of Jewel's works (1848), Vol. III, 5–47, for the Latin text, and 52–108 for the English version which runs to about 50,000 words, e.g. about eighty pages of such a book as this.

[2] Ronald Bayne, in *Shakespeare's England*, I, 71.   [3] *Elizabeth*, 416.

[4] V, 301.   [5] Dixon, V, 387.   [6] Dixon, V, 397.

[7] *Parker Corr.*, p. 417.   [8] Usher, *Reconstruction*, I, 265.

[9] " But, not to tarry about rehearsing all points, wherein we and they differ (for they have well nigh no end) . . . sunt enim prope infinita ", *Apologia*, in Jewel, III, 35 (Latin text) 92 (English).

Clemens et Regni moderatryx iusta Britōm
Hac forma insigni conspicienda nitet.

Tristia dum gentes circum omnes bella fatigant;
Cæciq; errores toto grassantur in orbe:
pace beas longa, vera et pietate Britannos:
An Dñi Iustitia moderans miti sapienter habenas. 1579
Chara domi, celebrisq; foris, longenaq; regnū
Hic teneas, regno tandem fruitura perenni.

THE ENGLISH QUEEN

JOHN JEWEL, BISHOP OF SALISBURY, 1559-1571

Cujus in hac humili confusus imagine pendes,
Et maciem hanc spectas pallidaq; ora senis:
Edidit hunc Bostona parens: Oxonia nutrix
Erudijt: scripsit Martyres: occubuit.

G: Glouer scul.

JOHN FOXE, 1516-1587

a Which was
til witſiſti-
de, when the
holie Goſt was
ſent from hea-
uen.

Mar.16.19.
act.1.9.

of Ieruſalem, a vntil ye be endued with
power from an hie.
30 Afterwarde he led them out into Betha-
nia, and lift vp his hands, & bleſſed them.
31 And it came to paſſe, that as he bleſſed
them, * he departed from them, and was

caryed vp into heauen.
51 And they worſhipped him, and returned
to Ieruſalem with great ioye,
53 And were continually in the Temple,
praiſing, and lauding God, Amen.

THE HOLY GOSPEL
of Ieſus Chriſt, according to Iohn.

CHAP. I.
8.14.17.The diuinitie, humanitie, & office of Ieſus Chriſt.
15 The teſtimonie of Iohn. 39 The calling of An-
drewe, Peter, &c.

*Or, before the
beginning
a Chriſt is
God before
all time.

b The Sōne is
of the ſame
ſubſtance with
the Father.
c No creature
was made with
out Chriſt.
d Whereby all
thigs are quic-
kened and pre-
ſerued.
e The life of
man is more
excellent then
of any other
creature, be-
cauſe it is ioy
ned with light
and vnderſtan-
ding.
Mat.3.1.
mar.1.4.
luk.3.3.
f Mans minde
is ful of darke-
nes becauſe of
the corruption
thereof.
*Or, are borne.
Ebr.11.4.
g Becauſe they
did not wor-
ſhip him as
their God, Ro.
1,21. act.14,15.
h To the Iſrae
lites who we-
re his peculiar
people.
i Meaning
priuiledge, or
dignitie.
Mat.1.16.
luk.2.7.
Mat.17.2.
2 pet.1.17.
Coloſ.1.19.
& 2.9.
k He was for-
med and made
man by the
operation of
the holie Goſt
without the o-
peration of mā
*Or, proceding
frō the Father.
*Or, more excel-
lent thē I.
l More abun-
dant grace thē
by Moſes.

I N the beginning was
the Worde, and the
Worde was with a God
and that Worde was
God.
2 The ſame was b in
the beginning w̄ God.
3 All things were made by it, & c without it
was made nothing that was made.
4 In it was d life, and the life was the e light
of men.
5 And the light ſhineth in f ȳ darkenes, &
the darkenes comprehended it not.
6 ¶ There was a man ſent frō God, whoſe
name was Iohn.
7 The ſame came for a witnes, to beare witnes of the light, that all mē through him
might beleue.
8 He was not that light, but was ſent to beare witnes of the light.
9 That was the true light, which lighteth
euerie man that cometh into the worlde.
10 He was in the worlde, and the worlde
was * made by him: & the worlde g knewe
him not.
11 He came vnto h his owne, and his owne
receiued him not.
12 But as many as receiued him, to them
he gaue i power to be the ſonnes of God,
euen to them that beleue in his Name,
13 Which are borne not of blood, nor of
the wil of the fleſh, nor of the wil of man,
but of God.
14 *And the Worde was k fleſh, and
dwelt among vs, (and we * ſawe the glorie
thereof, as the glorie of the onely begotten Sonne of the Father) *ful of grace and
trueth.
15 ¶ Iohn bare witnes of him, & cryed, ſaying, This was he of whome I ſaid, He
that cōmeth after me, is preferred before
me: for he was before me.
16 And of his fulnes haue all we receiued,
and l grace for grace.
17 For the Lawe was giuen by Moſes, but
grace and trueth came by Ieſus Chriſt.

18 *No man hathe ſene God at any time:
the onely begotten Sonne, which is in the
m boſome of the Father, he hathe n declared him.
19 ¶ Then this is the recorde of Iohn, whē
the Iewes ſent Prieſts and Leuites from
Ieruſalem, to aſke him, Who art thou?
20 And he confeſſed and denyed not, and
ſaid plainely, I * am not the Chriſt.
21 And they aſked him, What thē? Art thou
Elias? And he ſaid, I am not. Art thou the
o Prophet? And he anſwered, No.
22 Then ſaid they vnto him, Who art thou
that we may giue an anſwer to them that
ſent vs? what ſaiſt thou of thy ſelf?
23 He ſaid, I * am the voyce of him that
cryeth in the wildernes, Make ſtraight the
way of ȳ Lord, as ſaid the Prophet Eſaias.
24 Now they which were ſent, were of the
Phariſes.
25 And they aſked him, and ſaid vnto him,
Why baptizeſt thou then, if thou be not
the Chriſt, nether Elias, nor the Prophet?
26 Iohn anſwered them, ſaying, I baptize
with water: but there is one among you,
whome ye knowe not.
27 *He it is that commeth after me, which
is preferred before me, whoſe ſhoe latchet
I am not worthie to vnloſe.
28 Theſe things were done in Bethabara
beyonde Iordan, where Iohn did baptize.
29 ¶ The next day Iohn ſeeth Ieſus cōming
vnto him, and ſaith, Beholde the lambe
of God, which taketh away the p ſinne of
the worlde.
30 This is he of whome I ſaid, After me cometh a mā, which is preferred before me:
for he was before me.
31 And I knewe q him not: but becauſe he
ſhulde be declared to Iſrael, therefore am
I come, baptizing with water.
32 So Iohn bare recorde, ſaying, I ſawe *the
Spirit come downe from heauen, like a do-
ue, and it abode vpon him.
33 And I knewe him not: but he that ſent me
to baptize with water, he ſaid vnto me,
Vpō whome thou ſhalt ſe the Spirit come
downe, & tary ſtil on him, that is he which
baptizeth with the r holie Goſt.
34 And

il
1.14
m
is
re.
ly
one
bar
tur

tha
wa
it
the
A
o
lo
be
as
D

If
m
la

I
m
la
at

è
è

p
or
wi
ſin
re

?
la
ly
la

M
a
m
la

e
m
rel
tei

The Catholic, learned or illiterate, found out what God had made known about all this by listening to the Church.[1] Taking as revealed what the Church told him God had revealed, he believed—because God had revealed it—the revelation thus communicated to him ; and then, to the best of his good will, he put it into practice. The "man of the Reformation ", if he could read, found out what God had made known by studying his Bible—in theory : for in practice he generally found it out by listening to the preachers, and by accepting what seemed to him the facts of the matter, as the preachers made their criticism of the religion so far in possession, which both they and he had so far professed, and as they put before him their view of the meaning of the Scripture's message.

What the Church said that God had said, and what the preachers affirmed to be God's message, were in many respects very different. All, indeed, agreed that there is a God ; and that man is God's creation ; all agreed that man, by the sin of the first man and by his own sin, was alienated from God and that this alienation had only been terminated by (and could only have been terminated by) an initiative on God's part—in the first place by God's willingness to terminate the alienation and then by the redeeming death of God Himself, incarnate, as the means. But the Church and the new preachers differed in what each had to say about the effect upon human nature of the first, alienating sin of Adam ; and they also differed in their account of the way in which the reconciliation effected by the redeeming death becomes operative for each individual human being.

These were differences that went to the very foundations ; and it was inevitable that from the Reformers (restoring, as they contended, the basic Christianity of the Church in its earliest days) there should come a vast, practical criticism of every aspect of the religion in which they had themselves been bred—criticism in the light of what they now held on these two fundamental points. It is to their belief on these points that all the details of their charges, and their two main general charges also—that Catholicism was, of its nature, superstitious, and that it was idolatrous—are related in their own minds ; and the details must be seen as so related, if we are to understand the violence of the contest which everywhere ensued. For the English Reformers, now in the saddle in 1559, have to detach all those who cling to the old way, and to detach also whatever of the old way still clings, in any measure, to themselves or to their disciples. It is to these details that their propaganda is first of all directed—to the things all men can see immediately, matters where the point of criticism is immediately grasped, and immediately taken up ; matters that are " practical " issues. The Elizabethan propaganda does not begin with the abstract doctrines which are fundamental to the new religion—and from this there will

[1] As the popular Catechism of today expresses it, " I am to know what God has revealed, by the testimony, teaching and authority of the Catholic Church ".

ensue, it may be thought, the weakness in the religious life of the English as a whole, that they will now never grasp the fundamentals of their own religion.

This criticism now made of the old religion is, in the main, negative, destructive ; and it is disingenuous.   The leading theme that gives unity to an undertaking that is necessarily complex is that of liberation—liberation from specified ritual " superstitions ", and from the false doctrines whence they derive.   The criticism says, for example, that the Presence in the sacrament of the Holy Eucharist is not an objective reality—and therefore the sacrament is not received unless received under both kinds.   The criticism denies any reality to the Holy Eucharist as a sacrifice—there is therefore no power in the Holy Eucharist to profit the souls in purgatory ; moreover, there are no souls in purgatory to stand in need of what Catholics believe the Mass can do for them.

Acts of piety—prayer, all such acts of public worship as receiving sacraments, assistance at divine service, processions, and pilgrimages, fasting, almsdeeds—whatever their part in the life of a true believer, these do not, for they cannot, in any way work towards the believer's salvation.   In the practice of such acts the believer is always exposed to the danger of thinking that they possess some saving value in God's sight, and so of transforming his act of piety into a superstition.   Hence the new teaching that the monastic life—not the monastic life as encrusted with abuses, but the monastic life in its ideal state, lived in fidelity to the vows of performing such acts of piety —is one of the greatest of all snares.

Where the criticism is disingenuous is in its sham attack upon " superstitions " of its own devising, and upon abuses constantly condemned by the Church, but now denounced as though these superstitions and abuses were what the Church had, on the contrary, fostered and blessed : so, for example, the Catholic Church is denounced for the idol worship alleged to be given to images, for a cult of the saints as intercessors in the sense in which Christ Our Lord is our sole mediator, for a doctrine about the efficacy of the sacraments that makes these rites a kind of magic ; for teaching that sins of impurity in the clergy do not matter, and for licensing the faithful to commit sin ; for asserting that the pope is omniscient, and the ultimate source of right and wrong, morality for Catholics being no more than what the pope makes it to be ; for preferring a laity that is ignorant about God's revelation, and, for this reason, forbidding the Scriptures to be translated out of the old dead tongues, and using Latin exclusively in the liturgy and administration of the sacraments.

It was, of course, upon a generation bewildered, baffled and, it may be, bored to a sceptical indifference in very great part, by thirty years of religious change, that the evangel of 1559 was released.   The novelty of change had, by now, long ago disappeared—and, it may be, any general enthusiasm for religion as a doctrine had disappeared with it.   The English of this time were not an ideal congregation for the exposition of speculative theology—ever had that theology been a simple thing, which held together with a logic that was self-evident ; even had those pressed for the service of setting it out been, all of them, competent for the task.

The Elizabethan propaganda for the Reformed religion consists, next, in a critical offensive against those " corruptions " in which the fundamental error of Catholicism has issued. Some of these " corruptions " are merely disciplinary arrangements ; but they are not any the less a most useful target for the Reformers' purpose. For it is not possible to defend all developments on the ground that they are expressly commanded or allowed in Holy Writ, or even that the Scripture makes mention of them. And it is by this one test, whether Scripture commands a thing or forbids it, that all religious practices are now to be judged. The authority of the teaching church, the fact that the teaching church has so decided, is no longer to be a valid argument—that authority, that very conception of the Church as something instituted by God in order to teach with authority, is itself one of the things now most vehemently denied.

The Reformers are in control of all. To them has passed the initiative and it is their action which settles the lines of the first discussions. The real issues of the revolution are clouded—for the man who is not by training a theologian—by the immense array of detailed objections against Catholic practices and the doctrines immediately related to them, by the impressive tale of Catholic ill-doing and carelessness and mismanagement. Now it is that there are laid the foundations of all that tradition that Catholicism is an active superstition, a something that breeds scandals—and is bound to breed them—by its very nature. Three hundred years after Jewel, it is still Jewel whom Newman will be answering [1] in his enquiry why the Englishman of 1851, if he does not hate and fear, at least mistrusts, not perhaps any longer his Catholic fellow-countrymen, but, very certainly, the Catholic Church.

The fundamental differences, about the effects of original sin and about the nature of justification—it is often held—do not make the show in the popular Reformation in England which they made in the churches of the Continent, or of Scotland. England, apparently, has always been England.[2] But whatever of these fundamentals did, or did not, get across to the average

---

[1] And Newman is, seemingly, conscious of this : " Since attack is much easier and pleasanter than defence ", he wrote, " it has been the way with certain disputants, especially with the Anglican school, instead of accounting for their own serious departure in so many respects from the primitive doctrine and ritual, to call upon us to show why we differ at all from our first Fathers, though partially, and intelligibly, in matters of discipline and in the tone of our opinions. Thus it is that Jewel tries to throw dust in the eyes of the world and does his best to make an attack upon the Papacy and its claims pass for an Apology for the Church of England ; and more writers have followed his example than it is worth while, or indeed possible, to enumerate." This, in a lecture, delivered in 1850, on *Difficulties* [felt by Anglicans] *in accepting the Communion of Rome as One, Holy, Catholic and Apostolic*, published in *Difficulties of Anglicans*, Vol. I. The quotation is from p. 365. As to the " charges of ambition, cruelty, craft, superstition and false doctrine against a great Church ", Newman says elsewhere (*Via Media*, I, 126, note 9), " Such a serious indictment against Rome was the only defence of the Reformation, a movement which was a heinous sin, if it was not an imperative duty ".

[2] " It is not at all easy (humanly speaking) to wind up an Englishman to a dogmatic level ", so Newman in the *Apologia*, standard edition (Longmans), 206.

Englishman of 1559–1600 from the average pulpit, no one of them ever ceased to be present to the divines, and to be present to them all as fundamental : they appear in all the formularies ; they are common to all sections of the Reform ; and even when, after 1566, and still more after 1572, the sections are beginning their exceedingly bitter fight on other points, here all remain agreed, throughout this generation and well on into the next.

The Reform leaders of 1559 are all, again, very conscious that they form a different thing from the body to which those bishops belong whose places they have taken ; and they are anxious to make this plain to all. The Reformers have returned to the church of Christ ; and to do so they have left the synagogue of Satan. " We have forsaken the church as it is now ", says Jewel, " not as it was in old time. . . . Let [our opponents] compare our churches and theirs together, and they shall see that themselves have most shamefully gone from the apostles, and we most justly have gone from them.[1] . . . True it is we were brought up with these men in darkness, and in the lack of knowledge of God, as Moses was taught up in the learning and the bosom of the Egyptians. . . . This was a rueful state : this was a lamentable form of God's church. It was a misery to live therein, without the gospel, without light, without all comfort . . . how just cause we had of our departure." [2] When it is urged against them that they have then left, as it were, the ark of Noe, Jewel does not deny the leaving, but justifies it, " What if some thief or pirate invade and possess Noe's ark ? " [3] What if the " desolation " foretold in the gospel stand openly " in the holy place " ? [4] The time came when, by the work of Catholics, " nothing remaining in the church of God that hath any likeness of this church ",[5] Christianity had disappeared from it entirely. " The doctrine of Christ this day, Master Harding, succeedeth your doctrine, as the day succeedeth the night ; as the light succeedeth darkness ; and as the truth succeedeth error." [6] Consciousness of opposition in fundamentals could hardly be stated more clearly ; and in this work, which is the time's classic statement of the Elizabethan Reformers' position, such passages abound.

And as the Reformer is clear about what he now enjoys, so is he explicit in describing the road by which he came to attain it. " We, *in altering religion* . . . have gone from that church which had power to err . . . and we are come, *as near as we possibly could*,[7] to the church of the apostles and of the old Catholic bishops and fathers . . . and have directed according to their customs and ordinances not only our doctrine, but also the sacraments, and the form of our common prayer." Like Abraham they have left " Chaldee ", or " even as Lot in times past gat him out of Sodom " ; [8] and " *We have searched out of the holy bible,*[9] which we are sure cannot deceive, our sure form of religion, and have returned again unto the primitive church of the ancient fathers and apostles . . .".[10]

---

[1] *Apology, ut cit.*, 92.   [2] *Ibid.*, 91.   [3] *Ibid.*, 77.   [4] *Ibid.*

[5] " Nam isti quidem, cum in ecclesia Dei, nihil ecclesiae simile reliquerint . . ." : the Latin text is *ibid.*, 24.

[6] In the *Defence* of the *Apology* against Harding, Jewel, III, 339.

[7] Italics mine.   [8] *Apology*, 106.   [9] Italics mine.   [10] *Apology*, 106.

It is all a private enterprise of biblical and patristic learning, reconstructing, from literary remains, doctrine and ritual too. Nowhere is the claim made, by any of these Reformers, that this new knowledge of the truth comes from some new divine revelation, nor that any of the pioneers is inspired as were the prophets of the Old Testament or the evangelists of the New. It is really in the name of honest scholarship that the missionaries stand forth, with no other credentials than the books they have read and their *apparatus criticus*.[1] Nor are these pioneers dismayed, either by the newness of it all or by the latent implication that they are condemning, as unworthy of attention, the spiritual history of a thousand years that can also claim to be Christian.[2] They are, in a sense, proud of the newness of it all: it is the newness of truth re-discovered; and they use the fact to exhort to newness of life: " It is not enough to change our religion, it is not sufficient to alter our faith; but we must also change our old life . . . we must walk as becometh the professors of a new religion, as becometh them that are of a right faith. . . ." [3]

These Elizabethan Reformers are also—for the most part—very conscious that they are one in faith with those Continental theologians who, in Cranmer's time, had filled the chairs of divinity at Oxford and Cambridge and who, in these last five years, were hosts to the exiles at Strasburg and Zurich and Geneva. " We have exhibited to the queen ", Jewel assured Peter Martyr in the first months of the return, " all our articles of religion and doctrine, and have not departed in the slightest degree from the

---

[1] " As near as we possibly could ", said Jewel. Here we may consider some remarks of a modern historian that relate to the competence of the Reformers for this work, rather than to the question " By what authority ? "

" Obviously the thing to do, in Calvin's mind (and his influence became strong over all Europe outside of Germany), was to restore the church of primitive Christianity. But what was the primitive church ? *No one knew*, and so all started to read with avidity the Scriptures and the Fathers to discover what form of church and what manner of doctrine Christ had really instituted." But " neither the leaders nor their adherents were equipped with sufficient classical learning to read with more than approximate accuracy what the old texts said . . . and every man who possessed the most superficial acquaintance with the classical tongues felt himself fully able to approach the most abstruse theological matters couched in the most difficult Greek . . .". So Usher, *Reconstruction*, I, 85–86 ; who speaks of failure " to understand what was really in the documents before them . . . no critical use of the sources . . . inability to detect forgeries and interpolations, and to distinguish between text and glosses . . . complete readiness to believe whatever was proved to be old. . . Even by the end of the [16th] century, the leaven of scholarship, begun by Erasmus, had produced little effect in deepening the general spirit of critical research." It had, however, " enormously increased the number of those who boasted some knowledge of the humanities . . . a rank and file on the whole . . . unfitted to use the results of the labours of the literary giants . . . [and] unwilling to accept the authority of the experts . . .". Also, which is to the point and very much so, " If this was the condition of affairs on the Continent, how much more was it true in England, where the level of classical scholarship and of the critical spirit was by no means so high as it was along the Rhine and the Seine." *Ibid.*, 86–87.

[2] " Forty years agone and upward . . . when, in the midst of the darkness of that age, first began to spring and to give shine some glimmering beam of truth . . . when also Martin Luther and Hulderic Zwinglius, being most excellent men, even sent of God to give light to the whole world, first came unto the knowledge and preaching of the gospel ; whereas yet the thing was but new, and the success thereof uncertain. . . ." Jewel, *Apology*, 74.

[3] Jewel, in Sermon XIII ; Jewel, II, 1091.

Confession of Zurich ; " [1] and three years later, nearly, he repeated this : " As to matters of doctrine, we have pared everything away to the very quick, and do not differ from your doctrine by a nail-breadth. . . ." [2]

Jewel was, by now, Bishop of Salisbury and busy with the composition of his *Apologia*. From Winchester his brother bishop, Robert Horne, wrote in a similar strain, nearly two years later still, to Henry Bullinger, " We have throughout England the same ecclesiastical doctrines as yourselves ; as to rites and ceremonies . . . [3] nor, as the people are led to believe, do we at all differ in our estimation of them ". [4]

And as the years went by, and university life began to revive, it was the minds of Bullinger and Peter Martyr and Calvin, " so revered a father, and so worthy an ornament of the church of God ", [5] that more and more formed the thought of the rising generation of the educated clergy ; while the works of these first founders, translated now into English, were imposed, along with the Bible, for the daily study of the unlearned parochial clergy. [6] And the Bible meant, in practice, the annotated translation produced at Geneva by English exiles who were actually members and ministers of Calvin's own *ecclesia*. [7]

Between these churches of Switzerland—all, since the Pact of Zurich, in close doctrinal alliance with Geneva and Calvin—and the disciples of Luther, there yawned, however, a very abyss ; and in 1559 the anxiety of the Reformed [8] was great indeed that to popery there should not succeed, in England, a revival of the scarcely less reprehensible errors of Lutheranism, even as Melanchthon had rationalised this. There must be no going back to the days of Henry VIII, when, to the English, Wittenberg was the only known alternative to the Middle Ages. When Richard Hilles, who had now returned to London, wrote to Bullinger at Zurich (February 28, 1559) that the godly were expecting either the religion of Edward VI or that set forth in the Confession of Augsburg, Bullinger, passing on the news to Utenhove, prophesied that there would be trouble in England if this were done. " This gives vexation ", he went on to say, " to all the purer churches, and would infect them with all its leaven " ; and, " I pray God restrain men otherwise pious ", he added, " but sufficiently troublesome to godly men and the purer religion . . . King Edward's reformation satisfieth the godly ". [9] The Lutherans, in fact, so Bullinger's second-in-command at Zurich explained to the English, were but half-hearted reformers, whose counsels " appeared

---

[1] The *Consensus Tigurinus* of May, 1549, between Calvin and Bullinger, i.e. *Consensio mutua in re sacramentaria ministrorum Tigurinae Ecclesiae et D. Ioannis Calvini ministr Genevensis Ecclesiae.* For the text of this, cf. Kidd, *Documents of the Continental Reformation* 652–656 ; and for the history of the entente, André Bouvier, *Henri Bullinger, le successeu de Zwingli*, pp. 110–149, *Un accord oecuménique : le Consensus Tigurinus.* Jewel's letter i dated April 28, 1559 ; *Z.L.*, 31–32.

[2] Feb. 7, 1562 ; *Z.L.*, 124.   [3] The manuscript is here illegible.

[4] Dec. 13, 1563 ; *ibid.*, 189 ; and cf. Maitland, " Dr. Horne, Elizabeth's Bishop of Winchester, had been the pastor of a Presbyterian flock of English refugees at Frankfort " *C.M.H.*, II, 593. For Horne at Frankfort cf. Vol. II of the present work, 316–320.

[5] Jewel, replying to Harding ; *Works*, III, 370.

[6] Cf. *infra*, p. 141.   [7] Cf. *infra*, pp. 228–230.

[8] The name given on the Continent to the non-Lutheran bodies.   [9] *Z.L.*, 21 and note

to the carnal judgment to be full of moderation, and especially adapted to the promotion of concord ", but in reality they retain " the seed of popery ", inventing a form of religion of a mixed, uncertain, and doubtful character.[1]   Once again, in fact, as in the days of a former Supreme Head, the way of foreign politics was uneasy, and Elizabeth, like her father, had it in mind, so Jewel feared, to join with the Lutheran princes and states.[2]

There is one argument, however, to prove the truth of doctrine, an argument familiar enough to many of those who listened to these sermons or who studied the tracts or books, which no Elizabethan Reformer ever uses : namely, the argument from what the Church of Christ—wherever on earth this may be—is actually teaching at this present moment.   For, in the eyes of these evangelists of 1559 there is no ultimate surety or finality about the Church of Christ considered as a teacher.   It is the Bible which, first and last, is the source of man's knowledge of God ; this is the measure of the church's orthodoxy ; here, indeed, is " the very sure and infallible rule whereby may be tried whether the church doth stagger, or err . . .".[3]   " For thereby [i.e. by ' the truth that God hath revealed to us in his holy word '] shall ye be able to reform her, if she happen to do amiss.   For it is not possible the scriptures may err. . . .   To conclude, like as the errors of a clock be revealed by the constant course of the sun, even so the errors of the church are revealed by the everlasting and infallible word of God." [4]

The Reformers realise how very important is this difference between their idea of what the Church of Christ is, and that which is held by the Catholics ; and they declare that the Catholics must be got away from their theory of the Church, or they will not be able to yield to the word of God—they must be wrenched away from it as Antaeus, in the match with Hercules, had to

---

[1] Gualter to Richard Masters (Elizabeth's physician), Jan. 16, 1559 ; Z.L., 14.

[2] April 28, 1559 ; ibid., 31.   It was, of course, barely four years since, by the Peace of Augsburg, Catholic and Lutheran princes had come to an agreement not to interfere in one another's religious policies ; Elizabeth announcing herself a Lutheran would be able to take her people away from Rome without danger from any Catholic state—so the uneasy non-Lutheran protestants may have read the queen's temptation.   Certainly the Lutheran princes of Germany were watching the English situation very closely in those weeks of 1559 while the Acts of Supremacy and Uniformity were under discussion.   Cf. the letter of Vergerio (Stuttgart, Feb. 1, 1559) to Sir Henry Killigrew, Elizabeth's envoy to the Duke of Würtemberg, shuddering at the rumour that the queen has sent for Peter Martyr, explaining what injury her interests would suffer if the Protestant princes of Germany had reason to think she had gone over to Calvinism, and what advantages would come (in her relations with Philip II also, and with France) if the queen accepted the Confession of Augsburg.   Foreign Calendar, Eliz., 1558–1567 (1863), no. 297.

Grindal and Horne write to Zurich in the most bitter anti-Lutheran strain, that, for the bishops of their way of thinking to resign their sees, would be to open the way for " a papistical, or at least a Lutherano-papistical ministry " : to Bullinger and Gualter, Feb. 6, 1567, ibid., 277.   George Withers, one of those then opposing the bishops in the controversy about the use of the surplice was here in agreement.   " Satan ", he explained to the Elector Palatine, " is making secret attacks upon the church of England ; and as he is unable to restore popery altogether, he is endeavouring imperceptibly . . . to bring us back to Lutheranism " ; ibid., 299.   [3] Jewel, Apology, in Works, III, 62.

[4] Jewel, against Henry Cole, late Dean of St. Paul's, deprived for refusing to acknowledge the Royal Supremacy, and now imprisoned, in Works, I, 79.

be lifted from the earth before he could be overcome.[1] Again, unity and concord do, indeed, "best become religion; yet is not unity the sure and certain mark whereby to know the church of God".[2]

The Church of Christ, then, has not any divinely protected commission to teach—it is not endowed with that infallible *magisterium* which Catholic tradition has always claimed for it.[3] And of that Church, in these dominions of Queen Elizabeth, the queen is—what? "The highest governor, next under God", so Bishop Jewel will explain in a sermon.[4] "Supreme Head" she was to have been openly voted, as her father and brother before her, in the first Bills presented to parliament. There was opposition, and this style disappeared from the Bill. The Act as ultimately passed revived, however, other Acts which contained the very title, and still more; and the Bishop-to-be of Norwich, John Parkhurst, was but stating the fact when, just a fortnight after the Act of Supremacy received the royal assent, he wrote to Zurich, "The queen is not willing to be called the Head of the church of England although this title has been offered to her; but she willingly accepts the title of *governor*, which amounts to the same thing."[5] It does, indeed! So much so that Henry VIII has already used it to describe his ecclesiastical office, and has compelled his loyal subjects to use it also. His daughter's choice of the term has the best of precedents, and she has no need that subtle legists (or theologians) shall rack their brains to devise an appropriate oath: the Act of 1559 simply takes over the oath imposed by Henry VIII's Act of 1536.[6] And, for the kind of power it implied, Jewel said from the pulpit to Elizabeth,[7] "Your grace hath already redressed the doctrine, now cast your eyes towards the ministry". The royal authority is, in fact, a necessary element in the vocation of every preacher of the gospel, "For, as God calleth him inwardly in the heart whom he will have to be a minister of his word, so must he be authorised of his prince by outward and civil calling: . . . It pertaineth therefore also to kings and princes to send out labourers into the harvest."[8]

---

[1] Jewel, *Apology*, 78: the Latin text is on p. 25, "ita adversarii nostri ab ista matre sua, hoc est, ab ista inani specie atque umbra ecclesiae quam prae se gerunt, levandi sunt; alioqui non possunt cedere verbo Dei".

[2] *Non tamen est [unitas] certa et propria nota ecclesiae Dei*: the quotation is from Jewel's *Apology*, 18; p. 69 for the English version.

[3] Jewel is well in accord with the teaching imposed on the *Anglicana* in 1553 by authority of Edward VI: "As the Church of Jerusalem, of Alexandria, and of Antioch hath erred, so also the Church of Rome hath erred, not only in their living, but also in matters of their faith". Article XX, Hardwick, 316.

General Councils too, ". . . when they be gathered (forasmuch as they be an assembly of men whereof all be not governed with the spirit, and the word of God) they may err and sometimes have erred, not only in worldly matters, but also in things pertaining unto God". Article XXII, *ibid.*, 318.

And this teaching the articles adopted by Convocation in 1563 and imposed under Elizabeth in 1571, repeat, of course, substantially, Articles XIX, *Of the Church*, and XX *Of the Authority of General Councils*, *ibid.*, 317, 319.

[4] Sermon V, in Jewel, IV, 1025.   [5] To Bullinger, May 21, 1559; *Z.L.*, 38.

[6] 28 Henry VIII, c. 10: *An Act for extinguishing papal authority*. For the text of th oath, cf. T.-D., I, 417.

[7] Sermon III in *Works*, IV, 1015.   [8] Sermon IV, *ibid.*, 1022.

But in 1559, with the Statutes barely enacted, the government was well aware of the various sources from which the newly established supremacy might expect opposition—conscientious opposition—and clerical refusals of the new oath. And within a few weeks of the royal assent to the Act, it had ready a characteristically ambiguous declaration about the meaning of what had been done, *An Admonition to simple men, deceived by malicious*.[1] The simple whom the queen's explanation professed to have in view were clergy, " sundry of her native subjects, being called to the ecclesiastical ministry of the Church". Their simplicity, " sinister persuasion and perverse construction " of the statute had " induced to find some scruple " in the oath now imposed—some novelty unknown to the Supremacy as " the most noble kings of famous memory, King Henry VIII and King Edward VI ", had been acknowledged to possess it. The new Supremacy, the simple are now explicitly told, involves no more than did the old. And then comes explicit reference to the sinister and perverse and malicious report —that what the oath acknowledges in the sovereign is " authority and power of ministry of divine offices in the Church ". To drive home her denial of such a slander the queen repeats, with suppressions that make the *Admonition* an immense *suggestio falsi*, what exactly the Act has acknowledged as her authority, the limits beyond which (no more than her two predecessors mentioned) she will never go, " that is, under God to have the sovereignty and rule over all manner persons born within these realms, dominions, and countries, of what estate, either ecclesiastical or temporal, soever they be, so as no other foreign power shall or ought to have any superiority over them ". It is as meaning this, and no more than this, that the oath has been imposed, says the *Admonition*, and with an acceptance of the oath, in this sense, the queen will be satisfied, " and shall acquit [all those who so take it] of all manner penalties contained in the said Act against such as shall peremptorily or obstinately refuse to take the same oath ".

This *Admonition* was attached, as a kind of appendix, to the Royal Injunctions taken round the country and proposed for the subscription of the clergy by the commissioners of 1559. This was the explanation—the official explanation—of the government's mind given to the thousands of parish clergy who, in the summer of that year, were bidden to accept the new régime or be deprived, of which thousands how many had seen, could possibly have seen, the all-important text of the new Statute ?

The suggestion of the *Admonition*, that the Supremacy enacted in 1559 actually meant, to those who had devised it—and the law which imposed a sworn acceptance of it under such heavy penalties—nothing more than the abolition of clerical privilege before the English law, will not bear examination. The Act of Supremacy of 1559 is clear ; and it is the plain fact that the Royal Supremacy meant, in law, under Elizabeth and under her successors for three hundred years nearly,[2] all that it had meant under King Henry VIII.

---

[1] Text in G. & H., 438–439.
[2] Until Parliament took away from Victoria, in 1863, something of what, in 1559, it had conferred on Elizabeth. Maitland, *Collected Papers*, III, 204.

The Act of 1559 is explicit that the jurisdiction acknowledged in the queen is the fullness of all that ecclesiastical authority has hitherto enjoyed over the " ecclesiastical state " no less than over " ecclesiastical persons ", of all the old power to correct, for example, " heresies and schisms " ; and the very words of the oath speak of the queen as sole, supreme governor " in all spiritual . . . causes ", and explicitly pledge those who take it to defend the queen's right to " all [these] jurisdictions . . . privileges and authorities ".[1] Moreover, the Act recalls to life, and makes once more English law, an Act of Henry VIII that not only explicitly gives the sovereign the title of " supreme head of the Church of England and also of Ireland ", but states that this place and these powers are given divinely to the English sovereign, and are vouched for in Holy Scripture.[2] The Supremacy of 1559 is, in essence, and in the intention of those who devised it, the Supremacy of Stephen Gardiner's *De Vera Obedientia*.[3]

It is in the light of these facts that we may meditate on Elizabeth herself meditating on the religious scruples of Thomas Lever, and consider the shocked tones of Jewel rebutting the Papist slander that in the Church of England the queen is, as it were, pope.[4] And we might meditate on the

[1] The Royal Supremacy in ecclesiastical affairs acknowledged by the Act of 1559 is a sovereign power. The Act does not only say that kings may do this or that in practice, but declares with whom, in the matter of religion, the last word lies, the place of the ultimate authority. Nor did that ultimate authority ever show any shyness in exercising its ecclesiastical jurisdiction, whether the controversy was about ritual or belief.

[2] The Act is the 37 Henry VIII, c. 17, which declares that the king's " most royal majesty is and hath always been, by the word of God, supreme head in earth of the church of England, and hath full power and authority to correct, punish, and repress all manner of heresies . . . and to exercise all other manner of jurisdiction commonly called ecclesiastical jurisdiction ". The same act also declares that the king " is the only undoubted supreme head of the Church of England, and also of Ireland, to whom by Holy Scripture all authority and power is wholly given to hear and determine all manner of causes ecclesiastical ". This statute Maitland calls " the *Unam Sanctam* of the royal supremacy, since it bases that supremacy upon the very Word of God ". It was repealed in 1863, by 26 & 27 Vic. c. 125. But the repeal is not to affect " any principle or rule of law ". Maitland, *Collected Papers*, III, 204.

[3] " A judicious proclamation ", says Pollard of the *Admonition* (H.E., VI, 217), " which whittled down almost to nothing the change against which all the bishops, supported by a unanimous convocation, had fought for three months in parliament. It was not a statesman's part to advertise the revolutionary character of a religious settlement imposed upon the clergy by the secular arm ". And, " There is then a marked discrepancy between the gloss put by the queen on the statute and the powers it actually conferred or was believed to confer ". Black, 15. " Why was this so ? There seems to be only one reason, namely, a desire on the part of the government to quieten public opinion on the Catholic side, which strongly resented anything in the nature of a regal supremacy by a lay person over the church. A jurisdictional authority, merely temporal in character, would not carry the same obnoxious implications." This was the reason also for altering " the only supreme head in earth of the church of England ", of Henry VIII and Edward VI, to " the only supreme governor of this realm, as well in all spiritual and ecclesiastical things or causes as temporal " ; which " qualitative difference in the wording, be it noted, sacrificed nothing of the substance of power, but it was intended to soften the impact of the measure on the catholic conscience, and to make the transference of ecclesiastical power to the Crown as little obtrusive as possible " ; Black, 15.

[4] Elizabeth, says Maitland, " had managed to get a little credit from Philip's envoy and a little from zealous Calvinists by saying that she would not be Head of the Church, and she could then tell appropriate persons that she scorned a style which the Pope had polluted . . . sensible men saw that having the substance she could afford to waive the irritating name." C.M.H., II, 568, 569.

possible effects upon the general morale of those who submitted to a spiritual régime inaugurated by such ambiguity. The queen's subjects may continue to be Catholics so long as they pretend to be Protestants, and to live as Protestants and to use the new rites as though they are Protestants. They do not need to believe anything of what they profess to believe. And not only may the Catholic satisfy the government by taking the oath as though this meant what, in his heart, he knows it cannot mean, but the government makes the perjury easier by publicly declaring that it understands that this is what he will do, and that it demands no more from him than this. Such is the moral, the ethical level of the statesmen whose re-arrangement of the Christian religion, so the English are invited to believe, is the divinely guided return to the primitive truth : such are the men doing anew the work for which God once became Man, men converted long ago, to the new *Heilslehre*, and accomplishing now the new *Kirchenbegriff*. " Unprecedented state-stroke ",[1a] indeed.

This carefully devised ambiguity of the *Admonition* which, for the ordinary man, might well mask the intent of the foundation statute of the Elizabethan settlement of religion, was not left to the chance that it would perish with the passing of the critical hour it was meant to weather. Six years earlier Mary, at her accession, had found the new doctrine about the relation of Christian prince and the Church of Christ set out with blunt simplicity indeed, in the Thirty-sixth Article of 1553 : " The king of England is supreme head in earth, next under Christ, of the Church of England, and Ireland " [1] But when, in the Convocation of 1563, these Forty-two Articles of Edward VI were revised, before being imposed anew, this blunt statement disappeared, and what was now written into the article, *De civilibus Magistratibus*, was the wilful ambiguity of the *Admonition to simple men* of 1559.[2]

The defence made by Jewel of the Elizabethan Supremacy as a point of faith—a truth revealed by God—is no more profound than was Gardiner's upon its invention by the queen's father. Jewel repudiates the style " Supreme Head " : " We use it not ", he says with dignity ; but the substance he admits. For the prince, he says, " had both the tables of the law of God evermore committed to his charge ; as well the first that pertaineth to religion, as also the second, that pertaineth to civil government ".[3]

---

[1] Hardwick, 342.   [1a] Maitland, *C.M.H.*, II, 550.

[2] This is Article 36 of the Latin articles of 1563, and Article 37 of the English text of 1571, then imposed for subscription by parliament ; it runs, " The Queen's Majesty hath the chief power in the Realm of England, and other her dominions, unto whom the chief government of all estates of this Realm, whether they be Ecclesiastical or Civil, in all causes doth appertain, and is not, nor ought to be, subject to any foreign jurisdiction.

" Where we attribute to the Queen's Majesty the chief government, by which titles we understand the minds of some slanderous folks to be offended : we give not to our princes the ministering either of God's word, or of Sacraments, the which thing the Injunctions also lately set forth by Elizabeth our Queen doth most plainly testify : but that only prerogative which we see to have been given always to all godly Princes in holy Scriptures by God himself, that is, that they should rule all estates and degrees committed to their charge by God, whether they be Ecclesiastical or Temporal, and restrain with the civil sword the stubborn and evil doers." *Ibid.*, 343, 345.   [3] *Defence* [of the Apology] in Jewel, IV, 974.

And like the royal apologists of Henry VIII's time, it is to the Old Testament that Jewel goes for his scriptural argument. Elizabeth—and presumably all Christian princes everywhere—has these powers in 1559 over the church of Christ because, centuries before the coming of Christ, Moses, Josue, David, Solomon, Ezechias, Jehosophat and Josias, exercised certain rights over the priests and the Levites of Israel. From the New Testament the bishop does not attempt to draw a single argument. The only support for his doctrine which Christian times afford him is the caesaro-papistical part played, in the fourth and fifth centuries, by such emperors as Theodosius and Marcian.[1] Nowhere, perhaps, is the " donnish ", not to say pedantic, quality of the thought which built up so much of the Reformers' *corpus* of religion more evident, than in these attempts to endow this novelty of novelties with a pedigree of ancient lineage.

And the kings of Israel being cited, and this handful of early Christian invaders of ecclesiastical jurisdiction—whose acts, if sometime borne with, were never acknowledged as rightful—Jewel is then in a position to ask his opponent, " What offences have our princes of this day committed, that they, being in the like degree, may not have leave to the like ? " Harding's reply is simple, " We answer, It was never lawful in any temporal prince to judge in causes of religion. Neither did any prince before this time ever use it. . . ." [2] In which Harding had with him, not only all the Catholicism both of his own century and of all antiquity, but all the varied theological production of his own century too—except Jewel and those who, in this new church, agreed with Jewel. Lutherans, Zwinglians, Calvinists, no less than Anabaptists, Brownists, Separatists—and many even of Jewel's own following, sealed with the Elizabethan election in its fullness—rejected and abhorred the novelty quite as openly, and as vehemently, as did the Catholic writers of Louvain.

" Kings and emperors ", said Harding, " have their first authority by the positive law of nations, not by supernatural grace from God, as priests have " ; and hence, they " can have no more power than the people hath, of whom they take their temporal jurisdiction ". This is a consideration of a deeper kind than anything Jewel has to offer, anywhere, on the matter. He can only retort, " Untruths, three together, open and manifest " ; and, " This is your Lovanian divinity, master Harding ".[3]

From the very idea, however, of a " headship " of the Church of Christ, Elizabeth, so her apologists explained, shrank with horror. It was an idea too defiled by the long papal usurpation for any christian mind to tolerate it : [4]

---

[1] *Apology*, Jewel, III, 98.

[2] *Defence*, in *ibid.*, IV, 1038 ; for the discussion on the text in the *Apology*, 98, cf. *Defence*, pp. 973–990 in Jewel, IV.

[3] For all this cf. the *Defence* (1567) in Jewel, IV, 1035, 1036.

[4] " She seriously maintains that this honour is due to Christ alone, and cannot belong to any human being soever ; besides which these titles have been so foully contaminated by Antichrist that they can no longer be adopted by any one without impiety." Jewel to Bullinger, *Z.L.*, 33. Jewel offered a most interesting explanation of Henry VIII's lamentable fall into this blasphemy : the king's assumption of the Supremacy had been the fruit of a Catholic plot : " Your fathers, master Harding, first intituled that most noble and most

he truth being that, of the Church of Christ as a universal thing, " there
either is nor can be any one man who may have the whole superiority " ; [1]
here can no more be a head of the whole church or universal bishop, from
mong mortal men, than there can be from among them a spouse or light or
ife of the church.[2] Hence the Bishop of Rome, who today claims such a
rimacy, is " Lucifer and a forerunner of antichrist ".[3]

This is putting it mildly ; from the very beginning of the reign, even
efore the law was passed that repudiated the pope, this aspect of the matter
ad been declared much more bluntly. Cox, for example, soon to be Bishop
f Ely, described to the pastor of Worms how, " We are thundering in pulpits,
specially before our Queen Elizabeth, that the Roman Pontiff is truly
Antichrist,[4] and that traditions are for the most part mere blasphemies ".[5]
And " Lucifer's " supporters were wasting their time when they sought to
stablish, as against the Reform propaganda, that he was St. Peter's successor,
nd to use this fact to prove that, as teacher of the Christian church, the
ope cannot err. For, " God's grace is promised to a good mind, and to one
hat feareth God, not unto sees and successions.[6] . . . We have departed
rom him . . . who had nothing to say for himself, but only I know not
vhat virtue or power of the place where he dwelleth and a continuance of
uccession." [7]

But although the pope is thus most justly departed from, the church—
hat is to say, ecclesiastical authority—is, in this " religion of Christ . . .
ately restored and as it were coming up again anew ",[8] a force with which
he Christian must still reckon. The early dream of a brotherhood of men
piritually equal, founded on their common zeal, and their love for the printed
vord of God which each could interpret as he considered the Spirit instructed

---

vorthy prince, King Henry the Eighth, with that unused and strange style, as it may well
e thought, the rather to bring him into the talk and slander of the world." The *Defence*,
bid., 974.

[1] Jewel in the *Apology, ut cit.*, 59.   [2] *Ibid.*, 60.   [3] *Ibid.*

[4] For a very much later view of the part which the thesis, *The Pope is Antichrist*, was
hought to have played in the propaganda to convert the English from whatever they had
een to an acceptance of that wherein the *novatores* presided, cf. Newman explaining how to
e anti-Romanist was part of the essence of his being as a member of the Church of England :
" Such a protest was necessary as an integral part of [the Church of England's] controversial
asis : for I adopted the argument of Bernard Gilpin, that Protestants ' were not able to give
ny firm and solid reason of the separation besides this, to wit, that the Pope is Antichrist',"
Apologia, 55. This is Newman's view in 1834 or so as he describes it thirty years later.
Again, in 1840, on the practical usefulness of the belief : " . . . when the simple principle
s once mastered that the Pope is Antichrist, nothing more is necessary in the Controversy.
t answers to the dogma of the Pope's infallibility in the Roman system. A bold, forcible,
lecisive argument is taken, intelligible to the meanest capacity. . . ." *The Protestant Idea
f Antichrist*, reprinted in *Essays, Critical and Historical*, q.v., II, 132. It is not peculiar to
Newman. " The palmary, the most effective argument of the Reformers against us ", he
vrites, as a Catholic, in 1871, " was that Rome is Antichrist. It was Mr. Keble's idea,
hat without this tenet the Reformers would have found it impossible to make head against
he prestige, the imposing greatness, the establishment, the momentum of Catholicism."
Newman goes on to note that " wherever Protestantism has been earnest and (what is called)
piritual, there this odious imagination has been vigorous . . . the received teaching of
Anglican bishops and divines from Latimer down to Dr. Wordsworth ". *Essays, Critical
nd Historical*, I, 218–219.   [5] To Weidner, May 20, 1559 ; *Z.L.*, 36.

[6] Jewel, *Apology, ut cit.*, 103.   [7] *Ibid.*, 105.   [8] *Ibid.*, 106.

him was, by 1559, at an end everywhere. The famous twelve months o
1530 that had seen the appearance of the two first "confessions", th
Augustana and the Tetropolitana, had been the beginning of the end of th
dream. These explanatory expositions had, almost overnight, becom
obligatory creeds—to all intents and purposes. For the future, the pro
fessional theologians might debate the details, and pursue with as muc
diplomacy as learning the will o' the wisp of a new religious unity ; for th
ordinary man life was no more than a choice between two, and more, officia
orthodoxies equally insistent. The moral chaos that spread wherever th
old was repudiated, the licentiousness that took hold so firmly before th
virtues of the new had been explained, had already impressed the leaders.
Then came Calvin ; and by 1559 his powerful new synthesis of the Reforme
belief had raised up as an ideal the union of believers in an organisation eve
more rigid, even more dogmatic, just as infallible for all practical purposes as
and much more effectively equipped with sanctions than, the religion so latel
abandoned. And even though Calvin's theories were not accepted *en bloc*
the prestige of his powerful example strengthened everywhere, outside th
Lutheran camp, the natural tendency to reorganise the mass of mankind fo
religious purposes in definite, law-bound, societies.[2] And within all these, th
ruling power was no less hostile to the exercise of private judgment agains
what itself ruled as orthodox, than had ever been any ancient pope. "It falletl
not within the compass of every man's understanding ", Richard Bancroft
the future Archbishop of Canterbury, was to announce in the course of hi
epoch-making sermon of 1589,[3] " to determine and judge in matters of religior
but of those experienced and well exercised in them ".[4] Hooker, almos
contemporaneously with Bancroft, will use against the position of the lates
disciples of Tyndale—and against the principle which is basic to the whol

---

[1] " The history of the early years of the Reformation has already proved to him [i.
Melanchthon] how easily the newly won liberty is ' used for an occasion to the flesh '.
And so he is brought to the conclusion, " quod doctrina libertatis non sit tradenda iis, q
non sunt recte instituti ". Hildebrandt, 34. " The whole law is abrogated ", the sam
Reformer wrote in the first edition of the *Loci Theologici* (1521), " not only the law of leg
forms and ceremonial, but the ten commandments also." In 1532, however, he is sayin
that these last " are retained, both because they prove the fact of sin and teach a spiritu
message ". *Ibid.*, 39. And an English Reformer of Edward VI's time is quoted as speakin
of the " licentious life which some would be apt to take from it [i.e. the doctrine tha
Justification is by only faith] if it should be taught to the common people ". Stryp
Memorials, II, i, 527–530.

[2] Cf. " Au libre examen, à l'Individualisme primitif de la Réforme se substituait ur
orthodoxie ", Imbart de la Tour, IV, 52.

[3] Quoting St. Gregory Nazianzen. Cf. *infra*, p. 211.

[4] Hickes' edition, p. 272 ; Usher, who quotes this phrase, *op. cit.*, I, 86, summarises muc
when he writes, " While all the reformers had eagerly encouraged the reading of the Scripture
as long as the study seemed to hasten the downfall of Rome in the public eye, they soon bega
to discountenance ' undue curiosity ' and ' unholy prying ' into the mysteries when their ow
conclusions seemed threatened." There was a tendency in them, he continues, " to beliex
that the first thing found, and the first notion of it conceived, were unalterably correct "-
a very natural and very common tendency with all of us, but one which, of course, " tende
to perpetuate any errors made ". And so, " In fact, theological controversy both on th
Continent and in England soon lost its early character of a search for truth at any cost, an
became a defence of what had already been set forth " ; *ibid.*, 88.

xteenth-century revolt against the Catholic Church—the very argumentation
hich, sixty years before him, Catholics had used against Tyndale himself.
When they and their Bibles were alone together ", he writes, " what strange
intastical opinion soever at any time entered into their heads, their use was
o think the Spirit taught it them." [1] A criticism not far removed in substance
om More's condemnation of the state of things in which the word of God is
ecome something for " every lewd lad to keep a pot-parliament on ".

In England the Catholic, after 1559, might accept the queen's untruthful
xplanation that the Supremacy meant no more than that the priest, hence-
orth, was answerable to her for his conduct as fully as was the layman ;
e might, on Sundays, sit in the parish church beside his neighbour who
as of the Reform, and join with him in the Morning and Evening Prayer of
ie new Liturgy, and find little or nothing therein that contradicted any
elief he had ever held ; but all the time, and before the Catholic came to any
ich test as the new Communion Service, there was nevertheless, whether
e knew it or not, a deep abyss between himself and the man at his side—
ie abyss that must forever separate two religions that differ in their accounts
f what reconciliation with God means, the one building upon a belief that
race is a reality *in* the soul, the other upon the belief that grace is no more
ian an acceptability in God's sight.[2] This second belief is at the heart of
ll the religious revolution of the time ; it is a belief that affects all Europe
iore powerfully than anything else ; it is this which transforms whatever is
ransformed. England is no exception to this. The more evident and more
pectacular controversies about the liturgy, and even the debate about the
Ioly Eucharist from which these derive, are, in England also, all secondary
o the main controversy on the nature of Justification.

The Reformers' first solution to the agelong problem, how shall man
urvive the chronic anxiety that comes of his consciousness that he is end-
essly in rebellion against God ? was to suggest that Christianity is a divine
eligion given to man in order to reassure him that it is possible for him to be,
nd to remain, truly reconciled with God, although at the same time in chronic
—and, as it were, inevitable—rebellion against Him. This idea is, in some
orm or another, at the basis of all the Reformed religion ; this is, indeed,
he consolation which the Reformed religion offers the sinner driven crazy
y the torments of his conscience ; and the endeavour to keep the advantages
f such a situation while getting away from the embarrassment of the
bviously untenable theory, to say nothing of the embarrassment of the mis-
hievous conclusions that could be drawn from the theory, is a leading problem

---

[1] *Laws*, Preface, viii, 7 ; *Works*, I, p. 185 (1888 ed. Church and Paget).
[2] Cf. St. Thomas, *Summa Theol.*, 1–2, q. 110, a. 1, *Utrum gratia ponat aliquid in anima*,
here the first difficulty is an argument that apparently proves, from Scripture, that " when
is said that a man has God's grace, nothing is placed in his soul, but there is signified only
divine acceptation " (Ergo per hoc quod homo dicitur gratiam Dei habere, nihil ponitur
i anima, sed solum significatur acceptatio divina). That the theory here refuted took
o hold, seems to follow from this, that Cajetan, whose commentary is published on the
ve of Luther's great denial of what St. Thomas is teaching, does not feel it necessary to
id a word of comment to this article.

for all the new theologians. Again, it is a practical problem : not so much
" Is what I want to do, or what I have done, a bad thing ? " but rather
"What will be the consequences to me in eternity of my doing this bad thing ?
Is theft, or adultery, in fact, a grave sin which, if deliberate, alienates me from
God eternally unless I repent ? or is it a very regrettable, all but inevitable
incident even in the life of the justified, deriving from the inherited and
corruption of his human nature, which even God's grace does not heal, a
incident which now, because of the sinner's "faith ", is no longer " imputed
to him by God as sin ?

The first drastic statements of the doctrine summarised in the word
" Justification by Faith alone " had, of course, been greatly challenged in the
course of the forty years between Luther's announcement of it and the
official imposition of it in England in 1563–71 as part of the restoration of the
true religion of Christ our Lord—and not merely the statement or wording
of the doctrine had been challenged. But whatever the qualifications, after
a lifetime's controversy, the theory was always linked with the belief that the
effect of Adam's sin was that all men were born wholly bad in their very
nature—needing restraint and punishment and threats of punishment to
govern them. It is now, in 1559, held and taught by all the new lights in
England, and it will be taught for generations, that part of God's revelation
to man about man is that he is born utterly corrupted in his very nature—
not merely " prone to evil from his very childhood ", but actually evil.
Infidels, said Jewel, and by this he explicitly says that he means Jews, Turks
and all heathen people, " are not able to think any good, to conceive one
good thought, because they fight under [Satan's] banner . . .".[2]

How much of all this new teaching about grace passed into England and
was currently accepted by the new chiefs as the religion of Christ our Lord
The doctrine, certainly, that grace does not really heal the corrupted human
nature ;[3] that the ensuing inclination to sin—which is now part of human
nature—is itself a sin, in all men but the justified, and that this inclination

---

[1] Once again, there is no question here of what is now believed or held by any party or
individual—only of what the beliefs were for the sake of which, in the sixteenth century
Englishmen left the Catholic Church, the beliefs which they then strove to bring about should
be the beliefs of the whole nation.   [2] Sermon IX ; Jewel, II, 1061.

[3] Original Sin, say the Articles (no. VIII of 1553 ; no. IX of 1563), " is the fault and
corruption of the nature of every man " (vitium et depravatio naturae cuiuslibet hominis
It brings it about that man " is of his own nature inclined to evil " (ad malum sua natura
propendeat) " and therefore in every person born into this world [original sin] deserves God
wrath and damnation " (unde . . . iram Dei atque damnationem meretur). This " infection of human nature " (haec naturae depravatio) is not even healed by regeneration ;
remains in the justified and, as a result, what is called the " desire of the flesh " is not controlled
by God's law (manet etiam in renatis . . . qua fit, ut affectus carnalis . . . legi Dei non
subjiciatur). In itself this " concupiscence and lust " has the nature of sin ; but " for them
that believe and are baptised " there is, for Christ's sake, no condemnation on account of this
This, as a doctrine of Justification, is Melanchthon summarily expounding Luther in the
Confession of Augsburg (part i, c. ii) ; for this last cf. Kidd, Documents of the Continental
Reformation, 262 ; for the Articles cf. Hardwick, 99 and 300–303. For the Augsburg
Confession on this point, and for Melanchthon's own further elucidation of what his statements
meant, cf. Möhler's Symbolism, Bk. I, sec. vi. (pp. 54 and foll. in the English translation
edit. of 1905).

ᴀerits the damnation that will be its punishment ; [1] that the way out for man ᴇs in his actual confidence [2] that God, for Christ's sake, imputes to him the ghteousness of Christ, has freely accepted him and is reconciled to him ; ᴀe doctrine that the corruption of original sin continues even in the just, ɔr even in them " fleshly inclinations " have not, by grace, been made subject ɔ God's law ; [3] that this law, a most perfect thing, it is not possible for man, ᴀ any circumstances, perfectly to fulfil ; [4] that good works are a necessary ffect of justification, flowing from the faith which is the condition of attaining ᴀis ; [5] that even the *good* acts, of those who have not, through this faith, ᴇen justified are, in God's sight, terrible sins ; [6] that the Christian must, ᴇven when justified, give himself none the less to the constant exercise of all ɔod works. [7]

And what, in practice, is all this to mean in the daily life of the ordinary ᴀhristian ? who would like to know peace of mind, and to have a conscience

---

[1] See note 3, p. 80.

[2] The Articles nowhere say what they mean by " faith ", but in the Declaration of 1559 ᴇ read that by Justification is understood " Pardon of sins, as free acceptation into God's ᴠour and a full and perfect reconciliation to God for Christ's sake, wherein Christ's righteous-ᴇss is imputed " ; and also that the faith by which a man is justified is " a certainty and full ᴇrsuasion wrought in the heart of man through the Holy Ghost, whereby he is assured of ᴀe mercy of God promised in Christ, that his sins are forgiven him . . . freely of God's ᴀodwill and mercy, without all respect of works and deserving of our parts " ; also, " After ᴀis reconciliation to God thus wrought through the Spirit of God, necessarily follow all nd of good works " ; cf. Dixon, V, p. 110 (the note), for the Declaration of 1559.

[3] See note 3, p. 80.

[4] Cf. Jewel in *Apologia*, ii, ch. 19. " We say also, that every person is born in sin, and ᴀadeth his life in sin ; that nobody is able truly to say his heart is clean ; that the most ghteous person is but an unprofitable servant ; that the law of God is perfect, and requireth f us perfect and full obedience : that we are able by no means to fulfil that law in this worldly ᴀfe ; that there is no mortal creature which can be justified by his own deserts in God's ght " (*Works*, III, 65–66). The Latin text is " Dicimus hominem natum esse in peccato, ᴀ peccato vitam agere : neminem posse vere dicere, mundum esse cor suum : justissimum ᴀuemque servum esse inutilem : legem Dei perfectam esse, et a nobis requirere perfectam ᴇ plenam obedientiam : illi a nobis in hac vita satisfieri non posse ullo modo : neque esse ᴀortalium quemquam qui possit in conspectu Dei propriis viribus justificari ".
Much of this is, by itself, patent of a Catholic interpretation. But Harding comments *ibid.*, p. 579) : " We know what mark ye shoot at, by your doctrine uttered in other places. ᴀour meaning is that no man in this life is able by the grace of God to fulfil the command-ᴀents. . . . We believe God commandeth us nothing impossible to us." This, says Jewel ᴀ reply, is " a horrible heresy ", and he quotes St. Augustine in support.
" Otherwise ", Harding goes on, " how could God justly punish for not doing that ᴀommandment which by no means we are able to fulfil ? We are sure that God punisheth ɔ man unjustly. . . ."
Jewel's comment is : " A fond question. For God punisheth infants for their original ᴀin ; yet they are by no means able to avoid it."

[5] Cf. Article XII of 1563 : The good works which are the fruit of faith and follow after ᴀstification " do spring out necessarily of a true and lively faith " (ex vera et viva fide necess-ᴀio profluunt) so that they are a sign that faith is indeed " true and lively ". Hardwick, 305.

[6] Cf. Article XIII of 1563 (XII of 1552). Works done before Justification " are not ᴀleasant to God (minime Deo grata sunt) . . . yea rather . . . we doubt not but that they ᴀave the nature of sin " (Immo . . . peccati rationem habere non dubitamus) *ibid.*, 304–307.

[7] Cf. the Declaration of 1559, for example, stating that the Christian " thus freely saved " ᴀay not, however, henceforward " live according to his fleshly liking " ; he " must . . . ᴀall upon God diligently " in prayer ; " he must fast . . . to subdue the body and make it ɔbedient to the spirit " ; he must liberally give alms . . .". Dixon, V, p. 111 (in the note).

6

free from the chronic fear that in the next world an eternity of torment awai‹
him in just punishment for his sins in this, and whose natural interest i‹
speculative theology as such is no greater than his interest in metaphysic‹
What is such a one to be given as the practical conclusion to which all th‹
exegesis tends, and by which he may guide his life ?   That it is still necessar‹
for man to make efforts, although he is justified, forgiven, accepted an‹
reconciled ? still necessary for his better self to struggle with his lower sel‹
if he is to save his soul from hell ? just as necessary as it was according to th‹
old way of looking at these matters ?   And, if so it be, how, in practice, is th‹
new way a gain ?

Moreover, to that plain man for the sake of whose peace of mind th‹
university professors and the preachers have stood the theological univers‹
on its head, there might reasonably seem to be radical ambiguities and in‹
coherencies—as well as practical insufficiencies—in the answer now offere‹
to that most practical of all questions, " What must I do to be saved ? ".

For example, these good works which are the sign that a man is reconcile‹
with God " do spring out necessarily ", in those who are justified—so thes‹
English Reformers hold—from the faith which is theirs and which has mad‹
them acceptable to God.[1]   Does this mean that the will of the justified cease‹
to be free ?   It is nowhere stated, nor (I think) implied.   Wherein, then, lie‹
the necessity ? Apparently in the nature of the faith that justifies, the fait‹
from which the works " do spring out " : i.e. that kind of faith being what i‹
is, good works necessarily result in the life of one who has that faith.   And s‹
it is that, in order to resolve the anxious practical question, Do my presen‹
misdeeds affect my prospects of eternal happiness ? the plain man mus‹
interest himself in what, seemingly, is a purely speculative question, namel‹
what is meant by faith, when it is said that " Justification by faith only‹
is " a most wholesome doctrine and very full of comfort ". [2]

It can certainly be said of charity that good works " do spring out neces‹
sarily " from it.   If a man is charitable—loves God with all his heart and min‹
and strength, and loves his neighbour as he loves himself—he necessaril‹
does charitable acts ; to say that he is charitable, and to say that he does goo‹
acts, are but two ways of saying the same thing.   Similarly it is true of the ma‹
who has faith that he believes ; or, if by faith is understood what Luthe‹
meant, that he trusts.   But unless it is true that wherever there is knowledg‹
of the right thing to be done the right thing is necessarily done ; unless it b‹
true that a man cannot ever believe a certain course of action to be the righ‹
and proper thing, and yet choose to do otherwise ; then good acts (i.e. othe‹
than the acts of believing and trusting) do *not* necessarily flow from th‹
possession of faith.

Or again, what is it that this confidence which is " faith " [3] does to th‹
personality of the one who possesses it ?   We know what, according to th‹

[1] Article XII of 1563 ; a new article then added to those of 1553. The Latin versio‹
runs : *Ex vera et viva fide necessario profluunt.*
[2] Article XI of 1563 and 1553 : *Doctrina . . . saluberrima ac consolationis plenissima.*
[3] This " certainty and full persuasion wrought in the heart of man through the Hol‹
Ghost, whereby he is assured, etc. . . . " ; cf. note 2 on p. 81.

eory, God thereupon does with regard to the person who possesses this
ith ; what is it that the person's " faith " does to him ? It gives him, in-
ed, a certain assurance about his own state, and destiny ; it relieves him
om a pressing, present anxiety ; and from that relief there should come
ratitude. But, again, is it impossible for beneficiaries to neglect and to
isregard and even to injure their benefactors ? is affection for the
enefactor a necessary consequence of being conscious that one is a
eneficiary ? Does charity necessarily follow upon knowledge ?

If, along with faith, charity, too, were needed to bring about justification,
nd were a part of that process, then good actions would follow and, in so far
s a man cannot continue for a moment to be a man of charity and yet refuse
 do actions that are charitable, these acts might be said necessarily to flow
om the charity that is in him, to be part and parcel of that charity. But if
he faith were merely *accompanied* by charity, could these good works be said
 flow, in any sense, from the faith ? There is a faith which is not merely
ccompanied by charity, but is so associated with charity that it is actually
nformed by it ; and this is a really different thing from faith isolated, from
aith alone, from faith which is purely an intellectual assent, or a trusting
dherence based on a belief in a promise. Faith so *informed* is a really virtuous
hing, i.e. it is not only a good thing itself but it is a thing which makes *good*
and not merely believing or trustful) the man who possesses it. For without
harity—i.e. unless it is thus given the " form " of charity—no virtue
o-called is really a virtue at all : a man may have any of them, or the whole
f them, but if informing charity be lacking he remains the horror he
lways was, the more monstrous indeed as he has about him more and
nore of these dead regularities. This traditional, Catholic explanation
f the need of charity to quicken faith and to make it virtuous by lending
o it charity's own form, and the teaching of the Catholic theologians that
aith can only avail to save man if it is thus informed by charity, that with
aith not so informed man cannot be a doer of the word but only a hearer
—this was one of the points of the old belief which Luther held most in
bhorrence ; never was his language more violent, his abuse of Catholicism
more scurrilous, than when the ghost of this realism re-appeared in his
till troubled, if emancipated, life.

According to the Reformer it is faith and " faith alone ", in the simple
literal meaning of the phrase, that justifies—Luther was constant here, from
first to last, whatever the theological or scriptural difficulties presented by his
teaching, whatever the criticisms, the storm of criticisms, which it provoked.
One never-ceasing criticism, to which the Reformers were extremely sensitive,
was that the doctrine made for loose-living. This was a charge made from
very early on in the movement, and by critics who had not, as support for their
argument, any knowledge of such a document as the famous " Pecca Fortiter "
letter of Luther to Melanchthon.

" Amongst other things ", wrote Stephen Gardiner, " [I] noted the devil's
craft, what shift he useth to deceive man whose felicity he envieth, and therefore coveteth to have man idle and void of good works, and to be led in that

idleness, with a wan hope to live merely and at his pleasure here, and yet have heaven at the last. And for that purpose procured out pardons from Rome wherein heaven was sold for a little money, and for to retail that merchandise the devil used friars for his ministers : now they be gone with all their trumpery, but the devil is not yet gone, for now the cry is that ' heaven needs no works at all, but only belief, only, only, and nothing else '." [1]

And earlier still St. Thomas More had said similar things about " the liberty that Luther so highly commended unto the people, bringing them in belief that having faith they needed nothing else. For as for fasting, prayer and such other things, he taught them to neglect and set at naught as vain and unfruitful ceremonies, teaching them also that being faithful Christians, they were so near cousins to Christ, that they be in a full freedom and liberty discharged of all governors, and all manner laws spiritual or temporal, except the Gospel only . . . [As to obedience to princes, Luther] says that the people be so free by faith that they be no more bounden thereto, than they be bounden to suffer wrong. And this doctrine teacheth Tyndale also in the special matter of his holy book of disobedience." [2] " Who can place less value on His commandments ", said the saint elsewhere, " than they who upon the boldness of faith only, set all good works at naught, and little consider the danger of their evil deeds upon the boldness that a bare faith and slight repentance, without shrift or penance, suffices. . . ." [3]

" Because we say that justification standeth only upon the free grace and mercy of God, the adversaries report that we forbid good works ", said Jewel and his complaint, made many years later than these particular criticisms, may, not unfairly, I think, stand for the Reformers' general answer : that the Catholic critics have not really understood.[5] But the difficulty persists

---

[1] *A declaration of such true articles as George Ioye goeth about to confute*, fol. ix.
[2] *A Dialogue etc.* (1528), bk. IV, ch. 7, in *English Works* (1557), p. 257 ; reprinted 1932.
[3] *The Confutation of Tyndale's Answer, ibid.*, p. 341.
[4] Sermon V ; Jewel, II, 1026.
[5] A writer of our own time protests much more warmly : " All the Reformers from Luther onwards admitted the need of good works, and the statement to the contrary is the sillies superstition of the modern Catholic caricature of Protestantism." Rupp, 183. That good works were not forbidden, but on the contrary strenuously urged upon the congregation in these years, the various *Homilies* are witness (cf. *infra*, 111–112). But although the thing urged to be done was the same thing which the priests of old had insisted on, the intention now recommended and insisted on as the soul of the thing done was quite other. In reality, fasting new-style and fasting old-style were different actions—in inspiration purpose and presumed effect. And, in practice, good works very soon disappeared from religious life based on the theory of *Justification by faith alone.* The Bishop of London, Grindal, writes to Secretary Cecil, in 1563, of " the matter of fast, which we utterly neglect ' and of how this is a point where the Catholic critics score easily. Seventeen years later, his successor, Aylmer, reminds Cecil that Catholics " commonly upbraid us that we never fast and seldom pray ". In 1571 the Fishmongers' Company, petitioning parliament to help their necessities by imposing abstinence from meat, declares that the butchers do more business in Lent than the fishmongers, despite the queen's proclamations and the ordinance of religion. Birt, 524, quoting Grindal's *Remains*, Aug. 21, 1563 ; Aylmer–Cecil, April 22 1580, Lansdowne MSS. 30, no. 49, and P.R.O. *Eliz.* LXXVII, no. 69. As to " the superstition " being quite so silly, when Hooker, explaining " the outward profession of those things which . . . are necessarily required in every particular Christian man " declares that " the want of these virtues [i.e. ' those virtues that belong unto moral righteousness and honesty of life '] excludeth from salvation ", his fellow-Protestants immediately asked

at, at the heart of the new teaching, there is apparently a real inconsistency ; or while a man's good conduct, before or after justification, is without consequence as regards that divine acceptance which justifies him in this world and saves him in eternity, and while such good conduct flows " necessarily " from that " faith " through which he was justified, this justified man is nevertheless exhorted, by the very exponents of the teaching, to the practice of good works and to a high standard of conduct just as though such works would not and did not now flow *necessarily* in him, as though it were still possible for him to choose to produce bad acts—i.e. to sin ; and as though his sins would lose him all that justification had brought him.   Luther, at the beginning, had said in all baldness, that once one was accepted of God through " faith " sins subsequently committed made no difference—provided they were not the sin of withdrawing this " faith ".   And there is still, in 1559, a strong echo of this primitive teaching in the earliest exposition of doctrine put out by the new bishops : " Man can sin after receiving the Holy Spirit, and can again recover also ", they declare, " And there is no man who lives without sinning although to those reborn in Christ the sin is not imputed ".[1]

Other, no less striking, difficulties arose, from the very beginning, about the exposition of the new version of another doctrine closely associated with the theory of Justification and Works—the mystery of Predestination.   For, according to many of the Reformers, it is only those whom God has from eternity predestined to salvation who can be justified.   It is these, and these alone, who are " called ", who " obey the calling ", and who are " justified freely ", who " walk religiously in good works ".   Is it, then, impossible for the predestined to do actions that are bad ? or is it that, for the doer who is predestined, bad actions have no ill consequences in eternity ?   All we are told, in this " official " statement, is that, because of their predestination, those who are thus " called ", " walk religiously in good works ".[2]   As to the possibility—which Catholic critics constantly urged—that men would reasonably draw from this doctrine " encouragement to carnal and ungodly life ", or that it would beget a " dulness of slothfulness to piety and godly exercises ", this is only answered by the vehement, if vague, rebuke that

---

be shown " what Scripture approved such a saying ? " Hooker, *Works*, I, 341.   The doctrine of these critics, Hooker notes (*ibid.*, n. 4), " would well have pleased Caligula, Nero, and such other monsters to hear ".   Cf. also, *supra*, p. 78, n. 1.

[1] This " exposition " is a clause in a document headed " Resolutions concerning the Injunctions ", i.e. the Queen's Injunctions of 1559, imposed on all the clergy by the Royal Visitation of that year.   Of this document, " a set of modifications produced for working purposes " (p. xli of the edition to be quoted), its editor says also, " There can be no doubt that it shaped the policy of Parker and his brethren in more respects than one, and represents a sort of mutual basis for the episcopal policy " (Prefatory Note—see also p. 16 of Dr. Kennedy's essay, which is a study of the document in its relation to the Elizabethan Prayer Book).   The clause quoted in the text is from a section of the document prescribing a declaration of belief which the ministers of religion are to sign, drawn up in twenty-three clauses: see Kennedy, W. M., *The " Interpretations " of the Bishops and their influence on Elizabethan Episcopal Policy* (Alcuin Club Tracts, VIII), London, 1908.   The original of the clause is Latin : Post acceptum Spiritum Sanctum potest homo peccare, ac denuo etiam resipiscere. Nemoque sine peccato vivit, quamvis regeneratis in Christo non imputetur ; *op. cit.*, 35.

[2] The quotations are from Article XVII (of 1563, repeating here the same article of 1553), *of Predestination and Election*.

whoever so interprets the teaching can be certain " that he hath no rigl
consideration neither of himself nor of God's merciful sure goodness promise
us in Christ. For those agitations, which proceed from God's spirit, ten
always to the overthrow of the Devil's work and sin, and not contrariwise t
minister provocation unto sin." [1] The divine decree of predestination i
indeed, " full of sweet, pleasant and unspeakable comfort "—but only to tl
truly godly ; those who are " curious and carnal . . . lacking the spirit t
Christ " [2] had best leave it alone : since, for such as these to have it befoi
their eyes, " is a most dangerous downfall whereby the devil doth thru
them either into desperation, or into recklessness of most unclean living
no less perilous than desperation " [3]—the very thing which the Catholi
critics had always averred to be the natural consequence of brooding over th
new presentation of the great mystery. [4]

What, now, of the meaning and function of religious ritual in the net
religion ? and especially of those rites technically called " sacraments "
Of these, it was said in the Forty-two Articles of 1553, " Our Lord Jesu
Christ hath knit together a company of new people with Sacraments " ;
but no definition of the term was then attempted. Jewel will explain nin
years later that sacraments are " certain holy signs and ceremonies, whic
Christ would we should use, that by them he might set before our eyes th
mysteries of our salvation, and might more strongly confirm our faith whic
we have in his blood, and might seal his grace in our hearts ". [6] This i

[1] The signatories of the *Declaration of 1559*, from which the three quotations in th
sentence come.

[2] Article XVII of 1553 and 1563.

[3] Article XVII : the Latin text is : " Ita hominibus curiosis, carnalibus, et spiritu Chris
destitutis, ob oculos perpetuo versari Praedestinationis Dei sententiam, perniciosissimum e
precipitium, unde illos Diabolus protrudit, vel in desperationem, vel in aeque perniciosai
impurissimae vitae securitatem ". Hardwick, p. 313.

[4] Cranmer, publishing these articles in 1553, and Parker and his hierarchy re-adoptin
them in the Convocation of 1563, the first Convocation after 1553 where the Reformers wei
masters, are as close to Geneva as disciples need to be. Only a year before that re-adoptio
the Bishop of London, Grindal, is found defending the Calvinian theology about Predestinatio
and about the freedom of the will, against Lutheran critics in Germany, and endeavouring t
convict these of inconsistency, " For what else do Bucer, Calvin, and Martyr teach that Luthe
has not maintained in that treatise " (i.e. *de Servo Arbitrio*) ; letter to Conrad Hubert c
June 6, 1562, *Z.L.*, 142. And in the year following the re-adoption Grindal's brother c
Ely, Richard Cox, was begging the Council to punish " free-will men " (linked with " in
corrigible Arians ", and " Pelagians "), by sending them " unto some castle in North Wale
or Wallingford, and there to live of their own labour and exercise, and none others be sufferee
to resort unto them but their keepers until they be found to repent their errors ". Nov. 1564
Cox is here quoting a joint resolution of the bishops ; cf. Kennedy, *Interpretations*, p. 3c
Are these " free-will men " Protestants who refuse assent to such a doctrine as Grind:
is here, by implication, upholding ? Or are they only of the same mind as those whc
thirty years later, attacked Hooker when, to the question " Must the will cease to be itsel
because the grace of God helpeth it ? ", he replied in the negative ? (*Works*, II, 537) thereby
it would seem, going contrary to the teaching by now universal in the reformed *Anglicana*
it is noteworthy that Hooker calls not a single reformer—English or foreign—to suppoi
his answer ; his chief guides are St. Augustine and St. Thomas Aquinas.

[5] Article XXV, *Of the Sacraments* ; these are the opening words. The Latin is "Dominu
noster Jesus Christus Sacramentis numero paucissimis . . . societatem novi populi colligavit '
Hardwick, 322.   [6] *Apology, ut cit.*, p. 62.

pretty much the orthodoxy received at Zurich since 1549.[1] The sacraments are not indeed " bare signs : it were blasphemy so to say " ; [2] but they do not *confer* grace, as Catholic sophists contend. To all this Jewel is still faithful when, in 1567, he comes to defend his *Apology* against Harding's criticism.

Meanwhile, in 1563, Convocation has produced, after much discussion between various types of Reformer, the Elizabethan revision of Cranmer's Forty-two Articles of 1553. From that which speaks *De Sacramentis* there has now been struck out the condemnation which it contained—as a thing in no way godly but very superstitious—of the doctrine that the sacraments confer grace *ex opere operato*. The sacraments, the revised text declares, following Cranmer in 1553, are " effectual signs of grace ".[3] What they are said to effect is a quickening of the all-important faith, a strengthening and confirming of it. There are only two such rites instituted by Christ our Lord—Baptism and the Lord's Supper. The five rites called sacraments in common parlance are, it is repeated, either states of life (marriage, for example) or practices only regarded as sacraments through a misunderstanding of what the Apostles had done.

The purposes of Baptism are described with something of that vagueness which ever tends to shroud the language of the Reformers when they are explaining the new and not attacking the old. The person baptised is thereby " grafted into the church " ; and, through the sacrament as an instrument, God's promises to forgive sins and adopt us as sons are " visibly signed and sealed " ; the faith of the one baptised is " confirmed " and, " by virtue of prayer unto God ", grace is increased.[4]

Nowhere—it is proverbial—has the Christianity of the Reformers more evidently appeared a different thing from that of the Catholic Church, than in what they professed about the sacrament of the Holy Eucharist ; and in no other point, as is generally known, did Reformers differ so acutely, so bitterly even, one from another. Some of the English Reformers of 1559, in the first months after the Mass had been put to the ban and their own rite established by law, were still anxious about this matter of their second sacrament—anxious perhaps that the theories of Zurich should not be displaced by Lutheranism ? " The doctrine of the Eucharist, as yet by God's blessing unimpugned, remains to us ", wrote Jewel to Peter Martyr, " and we hope will continue to remain, pure and inviolate. For both myself and my episcopal brethren will maintain it, by God's help, to the utmost of our power,

---

[1] " Of the various ends for which the sacraments were instituted. . . . This is the leading end among them, that God may through the sacraments represent and seal to us his grace. For although they signify nothing else than what is announced by the Word himself, it is nevertheless a great thing that living images as it were should be thrown before our eyes, which make us better, as though by leading us to the thing itself ; while they recall to our memory the death of Christ and all his benefits so that faith may be more exercised. . . ." So the *Consensus Tigurinus* of 1549 ; cf. Latin text in Kidd, p. 653, VII. The translation is mine.

[2] Jewel, *Treatise on the Sacraments*, in *Works*, II, p. 1101.

[3] *Efficacia signa gratiae*, Article XXV of 1563 and 1571 ; XXVI of 1553. Hardwick, 323.

[4] Article XXVII, " . . . fides confirmatur, et vi divinae invocationis, gratia augetur " ; ibid., 329.

as long as we live ".[1] It is Zurich which Jewel, explaining this sacrament, again recalls in the *Apology*—in language at any rate—and again he is vague : " In the Lord's Supper there is truly given unto the believing, the body and blood of the Lord. . . ." [2] The sacrament is " an evident token [3] of the body and blood of Christ, wherein is set, as it were, before our eyes, the death of Christ and his resurrection, and what act soever he did whilst he was in his mortal body " ; [4] and by frequently receiving this sacrament " we may daily renew the remembrance of that matter . . . Christ himself . . . is so presently given unto us, as that by faith we verily receive his body and his blood." [5]

The Holy Eucharist, in classical Catholic teaching, is, primarily, the Christian sacrifice, commonly called the Mass ; it is, secondarily, Holy Communion received.[6] In the new religion, however, and in every form of it, the very idea that there could be a Eucharistic sacrifice was cried down as a blasphemous abomination.

None were more conscious than all these Reformers that their Communion Service was a different kind of thing from what Catholics declared the Mass to be.[7] The Communion Service was far indeed, in their eyes, from being no more than an English form of the Mass. " Christ saith by way of a parable unto his disciples ", Jewel wrote, in answer to Harding, " ' The kingdom of heaven is likened unto a man that sowed good seed in his ground ; but when the folks were asleep, that man's enemy came and sowed tares and cockle among the corn.' Christ is the husbandman : he planted the holy communion in his church ; and so it continued many hundred years. Afterward, when the priests and bishops became careless, and fell

[1] April 1, 1560 ; *Z.L.*, 98.

[2] *Apology, ut. cit.*, p. 62. The Latin Text (*ibid.*, p. 12) is : " Diserteque pronunciamus in coena credentibus vere exhiberi corpus et sanguinem Domini . . .".

[3] Symbolum conspicuum. [4] *Ibid.*, 63 ; Latin text, 13.

[5] " Et illis Christum ipsum, verum panem aeternae vitae, sic nobis presentem exhiberi, ut eius corpus et sanguinem fide vere sumamus " ; *ibid.*, 13 for Latin text, 63 for English.

[6] Cf. St. Thomas Aquinas, in the *Summa Theologica* : (*a*) sacramentum eucharistiae perficitur in ipsa consecratione materiae, alia vero sacramenta perficiuntur in applicatione materiae ad hominem sanctificandum. 3, q. 73, a. 2 ad 3.

(*b*) . . . hoc sacramentum perficitur in consecratione materiae. Usus autem fidelium non est de necessitate sacramenti, sed est aliquid consequens sacramentum. 3, q. 74, a. 7.

(*c*) . . . Perfectio huius sacramenti non est in usu fidelium, sed in consecratione materiae. 3, q. 80, a. 12 ad 2.

(*d*) . . . in hoc sacramento sacerdos consecrat . . . panem et vinum ; in qua consecratione perficitur sacramentum. Usus autem sacramenti est consequenter se habens ad hoc sacramentum. 3, q. 82, a 4, ad 2.

(*e*) . . . Opportunitas autem sacrificium offerendi non solum attenditur per comparationem ad fideles Christi, quibus oportet sacramenta ministrari, sed principaliter per comparationem ad Deum, cui consecratione huius sacramenti sacrificium offeretur. 3, q. 82, a. 10.

(*f*) . . . hoc sacramentum perficitur in consecratione eucharistiae, in qua sacrificium Deo offertur. *Ibid.*, ad 1.

[7] For Edmund Grindal, the first of the new line of bishops of London, the Mass was " an accursed abomination and a diabolical profanation of the Lord's Supper ' (to Bullinger Aug. 29, 1567, Z.L., 311). Edwin Sandys, his successor, describes to Cecil a raid on a congregation assembled for Mass, " to apprehend such as [the sheriff] should find there committing idolatry. There was found the altar prepared, the chalice, and their bread-god " March 2, 1573, in Birt, 461. Both Grindal and Sandys had said Mass in their time.

ist asleep, the devil came with negligence and ill disposition and want of evotion of the people, and planted your mass. The servants said to their master : ' Sir, did not you sow good corn in your field ? From whence then be these tares ? ' Even so may we say : Did not Christ deliver us the oly communion, that the people should feast and communicate together, and ublish the benefits of his passion ? From whence then is this private anquet, that one man receiveth all alone ? The servants knew not who sowed he tares ; neither do you know who founded your mass. Notwithstanding here is no less difference in the church of God between your mass and the oly communion, than is in the field between wild tares and wholesome orn. The one was planted by day, the other by night. But Christ saith : Every plant that my heavenly Father hath not planted shall be taken up y the root '." [1]

The very idea of an actual sacrifice disappeared as utterly, wherever he new Christianity triumphed, as did that other idea that the Church of Christ is founded to be mankind's infallible teacher. What was left, as he sacrament of the Lord's Supper, was a devotional exercise preparatory o the faithful man's receiving the holy tokens which commemorated Our Lord's sacrificial offering of himself for us upon the cross—and in the moment when the faithful man so received this consecrated bread and wine, Christ was mysteriously received by him in his heart, " only after an heavenly and spiritual manner ".[2]

It is still hard for a Catholic to grasp the fact that these theories and rites were, in very great measure at least, the accomplishment of men who were priests, who had not only received the Catholic sacraments, but had said Mass ; and who had now come to be satisfied with this, and without any ign of regret that the old could not be.

One thing was immediately evident—that in the new religion the collective piety of the church was not to be dominated by the Lord's Supper as the collective life of Catholicism has, from the beginning, been dominated by the Mass. The Reformers had had much to say about the Catholic discipline as it regulated the reception of Holy Communion : for example, that it was administered under one kind alone, and that at most of the many Masses said daily, none communicated but the priest who said the Mass. In such a discipline, they protested continually, the layman was defrauded. The layman did, indeed, in the Middle Ages, receive Holy Communion all too rarely ; and the obvious policy of apostolic reformers in this matter, it might be thought, was to work for a great renewal of devotion to the sacrament, and to strive that the average layman should receive it more frequently, that reception of the sacrament should more and more become the centre of every layman's life—and this the saints of the time, all of them, did : St. Thomas of Villanueva in Spain, St. Philip Neri in Italy, St. Ignatius Loyola, and others too.

[1] *The Defence of the Apology*, in Jewel, III, 338–339.
[2] Article XXVIII, *Of the Lord's Supper* ; these words are part of the addition of 1563 to Cranmer's article of 1553 ; *tantum cœlesti et spirituali ratione*, is the Latin text.

But the Reformers did nothing of the kind. Their theories destroye
all belief in the objective reality of the Presence in the sacrament. If the
were right, then Holy Communion was a great deal less than it had alway
been held to be. There had indeed been too few communicants at th
numerous daily Masses, even though all present held the Catholic teaching—
but the Reformers' policy not only worked against all " private " Masses
it worked out of existence the daily parish Mass itself. Not even once
week, on Sunday, was the new Communion Service of 1559 to be used.
Within a year or two that new service was only being said once a month i
the very cathedrals ; and in the parish churches it had become universall
that once-a-quarter celebration that it remained until a day which is only jus
going out of memory. In the eyes of the Reformers their new rite never ha
the importance which the Mass has always held for the Catholic. It coul
never have been said, " It's the Lord's Supper that matters "—and ha
it been said, in the sense of the classic saying about the Mass so familiar t
us all, the Reformers would have been the first to deny the saying. An
as they knew so well the nature of what they had devised, they knew als
the power of what they had rejected. In one sense they still paid mor
attention to the Mass than to their own Eucharistic rite, for agains
the Mass itself they never ceased to wage war ; and all through thes
first generations of the Reform the flood of bitter, lying—and even indecen
—propaganda against it, and against the doctrine of the Real Presence
never ceased. None were more zealous in opposing the changes of 1559
said Jewel, than those won back to Catholicism in Mary's reign : *Tan*
est semel gustasse de missa ; and to attack the Mass immediately was, there
fore, the best strategy of all : *Vident erepto illo palladio omnia ventura i.*
periculum.[2]

The Catholics were idolaters, it now began to be declared by the bes
wits among the Reformers, and to be repeated by all the party until, as th
party grew to be the nation, this became an article of the national credo
Jewel, for example, in the *Apology*, makes it a boast that the new religion i
free from " the carrying about and worshipping of bread and such othe
idolatrous blasphemies ", and he declares that, " We justly blame the bishop
of Rome who . . . set before the people the sacramental bread to be wor
shipped as God ".[3] Cranmer, ten years before, had likewise ridicule
the popular piety at the elevation in the Mass, " tooting and gazing at tha
thing which the priest held up in his hands, . . . and saying ' This day hav
I seen my Maker '."[4] And, of course, things truly vile could be mentioned

[1] Cranmer, in the *Reformatio Legum Ecclesiasticarum*, had forbidden the receiving c
Holy Communion except on Sundays and feasts of Our Lord : " [Coena Domini] solur
in Dominicis diebus et ad aliquam Domini propriam memoriam spectantibus sumetur "
de Divinis Officiis, cap. 7.

[2] To Peter Martyr, not dated but probably in May 1559. For the Latin cf. Jewel, IV
p. 1209 ; English version in *Z.L.*, 34 : " This it is to have once tasted of the mass " ; " The
perceive that when that palladium is removed, everything else will be endangered."

[3] As quoted, 64.

[4] Cranmer, P.S., I, 229. What was it that Cranmer thought he himself " held up i
his hands " when he sang the Mass at the coronation of Edward VI ?

one by Reformers, that proved beyond proof what their beliefs in this matter
were. Transubstantiation—not the name, merely, but the Catholic belief
that what, after the consecration in the Mass, is really present, under the appearances of bread and wine, is the Body and Blood of Christ, and nothing else
but this—was now stated officially [1] to be a belief that conflicted with " the
plain words of scripture ", and that had " given occasion to many superstitions " ; and it was also declared that it was no part of the wisdom of Our
Lord in instituting this sacrament that it should be " gazed upon or be carried
about ", " lifted up or worshipped ".[2]

Between the Catholic belief about the real presence in the Blessed
Sacrament and about the real sacrifice in the Mass, and the Catholic belief
about Justification there is a close organic connection. Wherever this last
doctrine is abandoned " the Mass must be rejected with a sort of instinct
and the doctrine of the real presence also ". " In the Lord's Supper Luther
could not find Christ alone—bread and wine ever recurred to his mind, because, in the will of those regenerated in Christ, he saw a permanent dualism,
a perpetual co-existence of a spiritual and a carnal inclination, so that the
latter—the evil principle in man—could never be truly converted into the
former." [3] No mind that believed mankind to be so ruined morally by the
first man's sin that God Himself was not able to repair the damage, could
possibly tolerate the notion of the intimate union between man and God that
is part of the function of the sacrament of the Holy Eucharist as Catholics
believe this. One who accepted this new theory of Original Sin was a happier
man in that he was able to say, with Calvin and Bullinger, that Christ is as far
away from the Eucharist as heaven is from earth.[4] The religion that did
not believe that a bad man could really be turned into a good man, did not,
because it could not, believe in transubstantiation. And the presence in the
sacrament is a reality by virtue of the power of Him who is present—He is
not " there or not there ", when the sacrament is received, according to
the internal disposition of my mind in His regard. " The differences are
almost without end ", Jewel had said.

This summary account may close with a reference to the new teaching
about Holy Order, and about the Sacrament of Penance, commonly called,
in England, Confession. It is not any part of the religion of 1559 that whoever feels himself suited for or called to the task may thereupon and forthwith
" minister in the congregation " ; [5] may preach, that is to say, or administer
the sacraments. For this to be lawful, he who officiates must be " lawfully
called and sent to execute the same " ; [6] by which is meant that he must " be
chosen and called to his work by men who have public authority given unto
them in the congregation, to call and send ministers into the Lord's vine-

---

[1] Article XXVIII.   [2] Article XXV.
[3] Möhler, *Symbolism*, Eng. trans., 5th edition (1906), 244–245.
[4] *Consensus Tigurinus*, XXV, in Kidd, p. 656.
[5] Article XXIII.
[6] *Ibid.* : " legitime vocatus et missus " is the Latin text, of 1553 and 1563.

yard ".[1]   But the rite or ceremony by which the man " called " and " sent "
becomes a minister—deacon, priest, or bishop—is not a sacrament " ordaine
of God ".[2]   Whether Holy Order is " a state of life allowed in the scriptures
or is a rite mistaken for sacramental through " a misunderstanding of th
Apostles ", does not appear ; " the book of ordering Ministers of the Church "
which is to be used henceforth—that " set forth in the time of Edward VI an
confirmed by . . . the authority of Parliament "—is merely presented a
containing nothing " that of itself is superstitious or ungodly ".[3]   From tha
rite attached to the Prayer Book of 1552, and now to be used once more, car
has been taken to eliminate every word and gesture that could support th
old notion of the priest as one whose specific function is the offering of
sacrifice ; and such a well-accredited contemporary as Jewel will say plainly
" . . . this ministry of the church was not ordained to offer sacrifice fo
forgiveness of sins.   Whosoever taketh that office upon him, he doth wron
and injury to the death and passion of Christ. . . . He alone is our Hig
Priest. . . . All others whatsoever, apostles, prophets, teachers, and pastors
are not in office to offer any propitiatory sacrifice, but are called to the ministr
of the saints, to the edification of the body of Christ, and to the repairing c
the church of God." [4]   He will tell the audience to whom he is explainin
the true doctrine of the sacraments, that " The preaching of the word o
God and . . . the due and reverent administration of the sacraments "
are the means by which " the mystery of our salvation " is set forth—in whic
setting forth " the holy ministry of the church standeth " ; and also tha
" The principalest part of this office is to preach repentance . . .".[5]

Repentance : " some, of late years ", says the bishop, " have change
this into penance, and thereby have also made a sacrament " [6]—here is ye
another mistaken " following of the Apostles ".   The traditional Catholi
doctrine about the sacrament of Penance had always been related, in ex
planations and defences of it (and was related by the Catholic writers of th
Reformation century), to the words of Our Lord to the Apostles, " Whos
sins you shall forgive they are forgiven them ", and also His words to St
Peter, " To thee I will give the keys of the kingdom of heaven ; whatsoeve
thou shalt bind on earth shall be bound also in heaven, and whatsoeve
thou shalt loose on earth shall be loosed also in heaven ".   This " loosing "
so Jewel will now say,[7] means that " the minister should either offer by th
preaching of the gospel the merits of Christ and free pardon " to those wh
with contrite hearts sincerely repent,[8] or else the reconciliation with th
Christian community of those banished therefrom by great offences
" Binding ", once more, means preaching—the denouncing of God's ven
geance and everlasting punishment against unbelieving and stubborn persons

---

[1] " . . . per homines, quibus potestas vocandi ministros atque mittendi in vineam Domir
publice concessa est in Ecclesia, cooptati fuerint et asciti in hoc opus "—Latin text of 155
and 1563.   [2] Article XXV.
[3] Article XXXVI of 1571.   [4] *Treatise on the Sacraments*, in *Works*, II, 1131.
[5] *Ibid.*, for all citations.   [6] *Ibid.*   [7] *Apology*, as quoted, p. 60.
[8] Words which suggest that " Faith alone " is not really sufficient for the sinner
justification ?

s for " the keys of the kingdom " : " Our doctrine is plain, that there be
vo keys in the church of God ; the one of instruction, the other of correc-
on ".[1] As for the Catholic practice of confessing to a priest : " Private
onfession to be made unto the minister is neither commanded by Christ
or necessary to salvation." [2] And however it may be allowed for in the new
ligion, such private confession is hardly regarded favourably—if the
nguage of Jewel is any guide : " Christ's disciples ", the bishop says, " did
ceive this authority [i.e. of binding and loosing, of opening and closing]
ot that they should hear the private confessions of the people, and listen to
teir whisperings, as the common massing priests do everywhere nowadays ";[3]
nd again, replying to Harding's use of a passage from St. Paul against him,
e says, " But did the Apostles or John Baptist hear private confessions ?
•id they sit upon a stool in a corner, and hearken what each man should
everally say unto them ? " [4] That " the priests should hear the private
onfessions of the people, and listen to their whisperings ; that every man
tould be bound to their auricular confession, it is no commandment or
rdinance of God ".[5]

Sacred Scripture, says Jewel,[6] speaks of three kinds of confession :
o God alone, to the whole congregation, and " the third privately unto our
rother " ; and it is this third which the bishop has in mind when he says
we . . . think it not unlawful . . . to make the like confession in
rivate . . .". For, to continue the quotation, " Touching the third, if it
e discreetly used, to the greater comfort and better satisfaction of the
enitent, without superstition or other ill, it is not in any wise by us re-
roved. The abuses and errors set apart we do no more mislike a private
onfession than a private sermon." Nowhere is there any hint of a
elief that the penitent's " greater comfort " lies in the knowledge that
te one to whom he has confessed his sins has forgiven them by his priestly
uthority and power. As to this power, " . . . remission of sins may be
t the priest as in the messenger, in the word of God as in the instrument,
t the penitent party as in the receiver. . . . The offering hereof is in the
tinister ; but the effect and force is in the sinner." [7] It is, seemingly,
tly " as a judge, together with the elders of the congregation " [8] that,
cording to Jewel, the priest " hath authority both to condemn and to
osolve ", i.e. in a system of penitential discipline obsolete now for centuries,
s he remarks.[9]

Was the kind of private confession which Jewel is prepared to allow,
onfession preparatory to a priest's absolution considered as forgiving the
ns confessed ? Or was it the kind of thing which Calvin also had in mind ?

[1] *Defence of the Apology*, in Jewel, III, 369.
[2] *Ibid.*, 351.   [3] *Apology*, p. 61.   [4] *Defence* . . . 352.
[5] *Treatise on the Sacraments*, Jewel, II, 1133.
[6] *Defence* . . . 351.   [7] *Ibid.*, 358.   [8] *Ibid.*, 360.
[9] *Ibid.*, 361 ; cf. also (*ibid.*, 375) " We mislike no manner confession, whether it be private
public. For as we think it not unlawful to make open confession before many, so we think
not unlawful, abuses always excepted, to make the like confession in private, either before
ew or before one alone."

Calvin, of course, did not believe that there was such a thing as the sacrament
of Penance ; he attacked as an intolerable yoke, and as contrary to Holy
Scripture, the doctrine that private confession of sins was a thing prescribed
by God.[1] But he made a place, none the less, for a voluntary private confession of sins, as his own words show, the letter written to his one-time colleague
Farel, in 1540 : " I have often testified that it does not seem to be a service
to religion to abolish confession without putting something in its place, and
I have just started something like this myself. When the day for the Lord's
Supper is drawing near, *I order* [2] that all who wish to communicate shall first
present themselves to me, and I explain to them why I have summoned
them : that those who, as yet, are ignorant of their religion may receive some
instruction ; that those who stand in need of some special correction may
receive it ; and finally, that those tortured by some anxiety of conscience
may be given some consolation." What is done for these last ? " If the
believer goes to his pastor and privately informs him of the bad thing, and the
pastor speaking to him assures him that the words of Christ ' Thy sins are
forgiven thee ' apply to him in particular, the man will be delivered from all
his anxiety." [3]

Cranmer, in the *Reformatio Legum Ecclesiasticarum*, had made provision
for a pre-Communion exercise very similar to this : " Those who are going
to receive communion must, the day before, come together in the minister's
presence that he may take time to examine their consciences, and to deal
with them should there be going to be done, on their part, anything unseemly
or superstitious by which there might be some common offence to the Church.
Then the minister should sound their faith, in order to correct their ignorance,
or to frighten them out of their insolence, or to strengthen them against
doubts. For no man ought to be received to the Lord's table whose faith
is not perfect in every part. And so, if any of those who are preparing
themselves for the Lord's table is shaky in any part of religion, or wounded
in his conscience, he should have free access to the minister, and should
take from him consolation and a lightening of his sickness, and if he shall
have proved himself fully to the minister, should there be need of it let him
be absolved (si opus fuerit, solvatur)." [4] Is this the Catholic sacrament of
Penance—confession of sins with a view to absolution, and then the priest
forgiving the sins so confessed through the words of absolution ?

Or did those " abuses and errors " in the matter, of which Jewel speaks,
and which, he says, must be removed if private confessions are to be allowed,
include the belief professed by all Catholics that the priest had the power of
forgiving sins ?

There is, of course, in the very Prayer Book to which Jewel, with the
whole nation, was now bound,[5] a formal absolution of sins to be pronounced
by the minister after private confession—it is to be found in the Visitation of

---

[1] Inst. III, iv, 4.   [2] Calvin, *aetat*, 31.
[3] Op. Calv., XI, col. 41 ; quoted in Imbart de la Tour, IV, 101–102 : italics mine.
[4] *De Divinis Officiis*, cap. 7. Translation mine, as also in last passage noted.
[5] The Prayer Book as Cranmer finally revised it.

he Sick.   Surely it is singular that when, in the great controversy, Harding
rges the point that, there being no absolving priests in Jewel's church, the
aithful are deprived of a great and necessary benefit, Jewel does not refer
ɔ the priest's power of absolution which seems, at least, to be implied in this
articular office—and which, if it means what it seems to mean, so effectually
ettles the matter against Harding.[1]

[1] Jewel, *Works*, III, 362.   That these words in the Visitation of the Sick could be taken
y an authoritative contemporary to mean something very far removed from their *prima*
cie meaning, some words of Whitgift are evidence.   The future archbishop is answering
Protestant criticism of the ordination service.   For the bishop to say to the candidate
ɔr orders " Receive the Holy Ghost " is blasphemous, it is urged—for the Holy Ghost
ɪe bishop cannot give.   Whitgift replies, " The bishop by speaking these words doth not
ɪke upon him to give the Holy Ghost, no more than he doth to remit sins, when he pro-
ɔunceth the remission of sins . . .".   Hooker, *Works*, II, 459, n. 1.

CHAPTER IV

THE POPULAR MISSION

I

THE religious re-education of England that now began, in 155
was not, however, just such an academic business as the argumentati
conversion of one set of theologians by another. Nor was it destine
to proceed in a long-drawn-out campaign of prayer and evangelical preachir
where the new bishops and the other chiefs would play the part whic
centuries later, was Wesley's. It had indeed its academic side—directe
mainly, and in the first instance, to the edification of the brethren abroad
Jewel's *Apologia*, the classic production of the movement so considere
was written in Latin. But the main work of turning the English away fro
what Catholic beliefs still held their affections must be done through popul
sermons : through sermons, in the first place, of the clergy licensed to preac
—a select band, indeed, and far too few in number for the task before ther
as the new bishops are unanimous in lamenting all through the next twen
years ; [1] but, most of all, it had to be accomplished through official sermor
drafted for the use of the mass of the clergy, too ignorant—as it is declare
on all sides—to be able to think out sermons of their own. These offici
sermons were those contained in the Book of Homilies published in 154
by authority of King Edward VI and in a second, still longer,[2] book no
prepared. They were ordered to be read Sunday by Sunday, feast d
by feast day, throughout the year.[3] Alongside these, there were, too, oth
official texts of popular religious instruction, which also were of obligatio
and which were indeed the basis of all the popular education which tl
age knew—the Catechism, namely, and the Primer.

The pages of these once well-thumbed volumes contain the half
least of what we need if we are to reconstruct the process of conversion as
fills the forty-four years of Elizabeth's reign. In these books we may becon
as familiar as were ever those long dead generations, not only with the doctri
which the Reformers strove to instil as the revelation of God to man throug
Christ our Lord, but with the kind of religious spirit in which that doctri
was conceived, and in which it was conveyed ; with the purpose of the
criticism of that religion hitherto believed and practised but now forbidde
the English by law ; and with the kind of thing which that criticism itse

[1] Cf. *infra.*, pp. 137-140—where some statistics for the diocese of Lincoln are given.
[2] Three hundred and ninety pages in the Oxford edition of 1832 ; about 290 pages su
as this.
[3] " And when the foresaid book of homilies is read over, her majesty's pleasure is, that t
same be repeated and read again "—Preface to the edition of 1562 reprinted in that of 18
p. 6.

as. And we can note—as in the learned *Apology*, so in the more popular ndling of the same themes, in the *Homilies* for example—what topics the eformers preferred for their exposition, and the tactics which dictated their oice. Thus can we revive again, at least in part, the spirit of the religious ovement which, in all these years while England was slowly finding itself ain socially and economically, was constantly at work upon that mass Englishmen neither enthusiastically Catholic in 1559 nor fervently pro-eform, that mass which at last ceased to be Catholic at all—whether it came Protestant in any real, that is to say positively doctrinal, sense or not.

Jewel's *Apology*, hailed by contemporaries as a masterpiece, and con-dered such down to our own day, is not merely a statement of certain official liefs considered vital in the new establishment—a rôle as to which some-ing has already been said—but it is a powerful piece of anti-Catholic opaganda. As such, it was to serve as the pattern in all the party warfare r generations ; and to be a main source whence men less learned drew hat argumentation or evidence they offered in disproof of the Catholic aims. In this book the whole business of the propaganda is as well studied the book is well written. Moreover, in Francis Bacon's mother the Bishop ' Salisbury found a contemporary translator of genius, an early stylist whose ame would be in all the text books had her subject been more congenial the age that discovered " Eng. Lit.".[1]

The *Apology* offers itself, by its name, as an answer or defence. And an nswer it is ; but not a real answer to any actual treatise directed against the stitution which Jewel is defending : it is a propagandist's answer, directed what he chooses to consider is charged against him ; it is an answer meant begin the attack ; and Jewel is, in fact, using the rhetorician's classic vice to bring his enemy to battle on ground of his own choosing. The ethod had the great advantage that, if the Catholics were once caught up the controversy thus begun, they would hardly be able—except at the price never-ending digression—to expose the new order at other points. The pology is not, then, a systematic explanation of the whole being of the newly -organised religion, but is rather an attack on chosen positions in the old ; d what was selected for attack has, not unfairly, been described as " a edley of doctrine and practice, of revelation and observance, of human— d therefore changeable—law and custom . . . [an attack] wholly confusing any but a trained mind ".[2] Brilliantly written, in the style of the classic atory, this learned work is an attack on the church of the popes in the name the Reformation generally.[3]

---

[1] The translation appeared in 1564, just two years after the original Latin work. It was troduced by a grateful and admiring preface from Matthew Parker, in which it is said that th Jewel and himself have reviewed and passed the translation.

[2] Birt, 408—and the description applies pretty well to the whole of Jewel's controversial rk.

[3] We can note in it explicit declarations that show how conscious the writer is of the lidarity of the English movement and the Continental. The martyrs of the one, for ample, are the martyrs of the other—" so many thousands of our brethren in these last enty years " who " have borne witness unto truth in the midst of most painful torments ", wel, III, 55.

7

The topics on which Jewel chooses to make his stand, the points as
which, in the famous " Challenge " sermon wherein the *Apology* is fir
adumbrated, he defies his adversaries to bring against him any declarati
in Holy Scripture, or any witness from the primitive church—these topi
are the points where, to the ordinary observer of current events, the chang
in religion are most evident ; and the debate is so initiated as to turn on t
wisdom and the fairness of these very striking changes, on the profitable thi
they are to the ordinary man—and to show, consequently, in immedia
and eloquent contrast, the foolishness, the tyranny, the worldly selfishne
of the religion now displaced.   What the *Challenge*, or the *Apology*—for t
method is the same in both—does not mention is, *ex hypothesi*, somethir
that no one has questioned, or it is a thing of only secondary importanc
" Here is the worst *they* have to say of us ", the book suggests ; " this is t
sum of what they have against us.   This is why they hate us.   And wh
does it amount to ? "   The mentality is that of a party which understan
well enough that it has more before it than merely to inscribe the new messa
on minds virginal in their ignorance of all religion : there is evidently
great deal of Catholicism, and of attachment to Catholicism, that nee
yet to be erased.   In all this there is, as well as great learning, psychologic
and political genius of a high order.   And while the layman is thus to I
brought to realise how numerous are those rights of which Catholicism h
deprived him—and which the new order now restores—he is also present
with the reasoned catalogue of the sins and abuses and corruptions of t
old system : so many, it is suggested, so deep-seated, so hoary, so much
part of the system and so bound up with its very nature, that the thing
which he was enslaved cannot possibly have been the Church of Chris
Popery has been a tyranny ; it has been a fraud ; it has been a blasphem

There are, then, certain points which continually recur in all this pr
paganda ; and in a great sermon preached by Jewel before the queen they a
concisely brought together and set out : namely, that the bread and wir
do not, by virtue of Our Lord's institution, undergo any change in themselv
in the rite of the Eucharist ; that the Eucharist is meant and " must be used
as a communion only—and never used at all unless " frequented with mo
than one " ; that the communion " ought of necessity " to be used und
both kinds ; that public prayers " ought to be in the common tongue "
that the Bishop of Rome ought not to take upon him to be the head of t
universal church ; that the prince is, " of right, and by the authority th
God has given him, the highest ruler of his church and realm, as well of t
ecclesiastical officers as of the temporal ".[1]

The more fundamental matter of the real nature of the Church of Chris
and whether it is the new, or the traditional, conception which better accor
with this, is not raised ; nor such other matters, where the difference
again fundamental, as the meaning of the fall of man, the mysteries of grac
of justification and the way of the forgiveness of sin, of redemption, and t

---

[1] Sermon V, on the text " And some of them said He casteth out devils by Beelzebub
Luke xi. 15 ; in Jewel, II, 1030.

e. These are matters where the effect of the difference of belief is not immediately evident to the eye : this is " theory " ; these topics lend themselves less easily to immediately successful, popular polemic—also, the debate here must ultimately turn on the interpretation of Scriptural texts, of which the other side, too, has its store. In preferring to attack Catholics on such points as their custom of administering Holy Communion under one kind, for example, Jewel selected a matter where, from Scripture, the other side had a direct answer—and, in what his very attack made to seem to matter most, he could win an easy, immediate, debating victory.

The Catholics were, however, by no means blind to their adversary's tactics; and immediately, in their first replies, they sought, by exposing them, to deprive him of his great initial advantage. Harding, for example, in his *Answer to Master Jewel's Challenge* [1] refers to the first reply to the bishop, made by the lately deprived Dean of St. Paul's, Henry Cole, now a prisoner in the Tower. When Dr. Cole asked you, he says, " Why you treat not other matters of more importance than these articles be of . . . [e.g.] of the presence of Christ's body and blood in the sacrament, of justification, of the value of good works, of the sacrifice of the mass . . . you answered that you thought it better to begin with smaller matters ". And why these ? Because you assure yourself we have nothing for confirmation of them. Thus craftily you shift your hands of those greater points wherein you know Scriptures, councils, doctors, and examples of the primitive church to be of our side. . . .

" Verily, Master Jewel, if you had not been more desirous to deface the Catholic Church than to set forth the truth, you would never have rehearsed such a long roll of articles, which for the more part be of less importance ; . . As touching the other weighty points, whereupon almost only your school-masters of Germany, Switzerland, and Geneva, both in their preachings and also in their writings treat, you will not yet adventure the trial of them, with making your match with learned men, and in the meantime set them forth by sermons busily among the unlearned and simple people, until such time as you had won your purpose in these smaller matters." [2]

" You, Master Jewel, persuading yourself to have singular skill in divinity, among the simple people you utter the weighty and high points of Christian religion that be now in question, in such wise as the protestants have written of them, and with vehement affirmations [i.e. you utter them where you have no fear of contradiction or argument to meet] with misconstrued and falsified allegations, and with pitiful exclamations you lead the seely souls into dangerous errors. But in your writings, which you knew should pass the judgment of learned men, the points of greater importance you cover with silence. . . . Wherein you show yourself not to fear controlment of the ignorant, but to mistrust the trial of the learned. . . ." [3]

---

[1] Published at Louvain, 1564 ; the work was completed June 14, 1563, according to the *To the Reader*. This, and the *Preface to Master Jewel*, from which the quotations are taken are reprinted in the Parker Society edition of Jewel, Vol. I, 86–92.
[2] *Ibid.*, 89.   [3] *Ibid.*, 90.

"Wherein the mark you shoot at every man perceiveth what it is ; ev
that, when you have brought the Catholic Church into contempt, and borr
the people in hand we are not able to prove a number of things, by y
denied, for lack of such proofs as you yourself shall allow, in certain particu
points of small force (which falsely you report to be the greatest keys ar
highest mysteries of our religion), then triumphing against us, and despisir
the ancient and catholic religion in general, you may set up a new religi
of your own forging, a new church of your own framing, a new gospel of yo
own device. . . ." [1] You must admit, says the one-time fellow of Ne
College to the one-time fellow of Corpus Christi his contemporary, that y
were a humanist and a Latinist rather than a theologian, " and concernir
divinity your most labour hath been to find matter against the Church, rath
than about serious and exact discussing of the truth." [2]

The duel which now began between these two opponents must thenc
forward have been the main occupation of each for the rest of his life, and
not improbably shortened the lives of both. Whoever needs to form
judgment where the victory lay must study the controversy in their works
it is not in anticipation of any such judgment that the *Apology* is quote
here : it is merely used for the evidence it offers of the kind of statemer
now set forth, as part of the official propaganda, about Catholic belief ar
practice.

Of the Mass, for example, this : " They say . . . that they are able t
their masses to distribute and apply unto man's commodity all the merits (
Christ's death ; this is a mockery, a heathenish fancy. . . . For it is ot
faith that applieth the death and cross of Christ to our benefit, and not th
act of the massing priest ".[3] Because, as Catholics were now to hear fc
centuries, as though Catholicism had been a denial of this truth, we have r
" other mediator and intercessor, by whom we may have access to God th
Father, than Jesus Christ ".[4] More generally : " They have plucked awa
from the people the holy communion, the word of God, from whence a
comfort should be taken, the true worshipping of God also, and the righ
use of the sacraments and prayer ; and have given us of their own to pla
withal . . . salt, water, oil-boxes, spittle, palms, bells, jubilees, pardon
crosses, censings, and an endless rabble of ceremonies. . . . In these thing
have they set all their religion, teaching the people that by these God may b
duly pacified, spirits driven away, and men's consciences well quieted."
Catholicism is just a "racket": "these men and we" might easily be brough
to one " touching all these matters, were it not that ambition, gluttony
and excess did let it. Hence cometh their whining : their heart is o
their half-penny." [6] The real trouble is that the pope's " profits deca
more and more. And for this cause doth he hale us into hatred, all th
ever he may . . ." [7]

---

[1] Jewel V, 90 ; Jewel, it is interesting to note, did not reprint this preface of four an
a half pages though he took ten pages to reply to it.   [2] *Ibid.*, 91–92.
    [3] *Apologia*, Jewel, III, 64.   [4] *Ibid.*, 65.
    [5] *Ibid.*, 89.   [6] *Ibid.*, 107.   [7] *Ibid.*

The pope—here we touch on a topic about which, for now thirty years most continuously, the Englishman has been well indoctrinated in the sense the Reformers; and that, as we have seen, by divines, too, who held as firmly the popes themselves to the traditional belief in the sacraments.   It is the pope, Jewel declares,[1] who is the chronic cause of sedition wherever sedition as plagued the peace of a nation : the pope's claim to be " King of Kings ", is political use of the spiritual weapon of excommunication, his incitations subjects to murder their rulers, his theory that he is the source of all earthly risdiction, the general *libido dominandi* of the papacy (Jewel uses St. ernard's actual phrase) ; here are the root causes of the disorders chronic mong Christian peoples, and he sets them out—with an abundance of ogus history—from a strange medley of medieval writers, very dim figures us perhaps, but to Jewel and his generation not much further removed an are Burke and Chatham from our own time ; and some of them are but contemporaries.[2]

The attack on the papal government of the church is general, and the opes are flayed for declaring in their various decretals (and for allowing lossators and commentators to declare) what Jewel asserts these texts really ean.   Which of the Fathers can be cited, he asks, to support such doctrines (according to his interpretation) are here set forth ?   For example,[3] " that rnication between single folk is not sin " ; " that a priest should not be ut out of his cure for fornication " ; " that the priest which keepeth a oncubine doth live more holily and chastely than he that hath a wife in atrimony ".   And what about " the thousand common harlots in Rome " ? nd the pope's 30,000 ducats annual revenue from the licensed brothels in ome ? and what about Pope Joan ?   The report on the state of the Church ade to Paul III, a bare twenty-five years before this, by a commission of ardinals and prelates,[4] is adduced in support of this thesis ; and the scanalous lives of particular individuals in high places within recent memory. nd which of these has ever been punished ? had they been " heretics ", hat a different story, quite another story !   For a contrast let the reader rn to regard the chaste life of England, where with Parker and his other olleagues, " We diligently put into execution the ecclesiastical discipline ".

Great is propaganda, in the work of destruction.   Here is a masterpiece f the art, and who shall say the minds and souls it damaged, for not to all hom it robbed of the remnants of their Catholic faith—and of faith, indeed, 1 all but the present moment and the opportunity which must not be let o by—did it give the new strange peace which the propagandist professed enjoy.

---

[1] *Apologia*, Jewel, III, 75 and foll.

[2] For example, in the list are Joachim of Flora, Marsiglio of Padua, Petrarch, Platina, alla, Savonarola, Baptista Spagnuolo, and " before all these " (most disingenuously, surely) t. Bernard—an array used to prove that the anti-papalism of the Reformers was not the invention of Luther and Zwingli ; *ibid.*, 81.

[3] *Ibid.*, 71–72, for the remainder of this paragraph.

[4] The *Consilium delectorum cardinalium* for the text of which see Kidd, *Documents of* e *Continental Reformation*.

Let us turn from the *Apology* to what is offered the ordinary man in th
official sermons, read week by week in all the parish churches. Th
Homilies are, indeed, popular discourses where it would be foolish to look f
the rigorous precision of the theologian lecturing to his audience of pr
fessionals. But in the tale they tell and the spirit of the telling they do n
differ from Jewel—since he was himself the author of so many of them th
is hardly strange![1] Like the *Apology*, but with greater urgency, what th
homilies first make known to the congregation is the great deliverance whic
the Reform has wrought.[2] Their old religion, the people are told, is " th
idolatrous church . . . being indeed not only a harlot (as the Scripture calle
her) but also a foul, filthy, old, withered, harlot (for she is indeed of ancie
years) . . . the foulest and filthiest harlot that ever was seen . . . th
great strumpet of all strumpets, *the mother of whoredom* set forth by St. Joh
in his Revelation . . .".[3] And as the parishioner sits in his lately despoile
parish church and gazes on the whitened walls, the plain windows, the mad
up niches, the board with the ten commandments where once the Blesse
Sacrament had been,[4] the royal arms set on the screen in place of the imag
of Christ crucified, the plain, moveable table that has displaced the onc
consecrated altar, he is bidden to rejoice at yet another deliverance. Fo
" Contrary to the . . . most manifest doctrine of the Scriptures . . . th
corruption of these later days hath brought into the church infinite mu
titudes of images ; and the same, with other parts of the temple also, hav

[1] The statement, in Black, 27, that " the *Book of Homilies* published by Parker in 156
for the use of the pulpit, carefully refrained from mentioning points of doctrine a
confined itself to moral precepts concerning . . . matters of a socio-political character
is far from exact : and it overlooks the fact that, by Articles 33 and 34 of 1563, the First Bo
of Homilies (i.e. the book of 1547) was equally imposed for public reading by the clerg
to judge from the numerous editions, both were extensively used ; cf., also, the frequen
with which Elizabethan bishops, down to the end of the reign, ask in the visitations wheth
the minister possesses the two Books of Homilies. " Which homilies ", says Harrison, "
comprehend the principal parts of Christian doctrine, as of original sin, of justification
faith, of charity and such like ". Harrison, 76.

[2] The new liberty is the sole positive attraction of the new faith which the propagan
really exploits and makes much of. And it is brought home, always, by these vivid, u
scrupulous contrasts between what now is and what, most mendaciously, all past ages for
thousand years are declared to have been. " Who is there now, what man so old, or child
young, but may well remember the blindness that hath been in our time, and our father
times before us ? Who is so blind, who so far past knowledge, but may both well see a
remember the dark ignorance that hath been in times past, and the great grace that G
hath now poured down upon us in these our days ? " So Jewel in one of his sermo
(*Works*, IV, 1088). And in another, " The errors that have been taught and preached
the Church of Christ, have been, good brethren, so gross, that such as could not see them wi
their eyes might have felt them even with their fingers . . . , as Christ himself . . . sai
' They have made my church a den of thieves ' " ; (*ibid.*, 1082), with a good propagandi
mistranslation of the Scripture quoted.

[3] *Homilies*, Oxford edition, 1832 ; references are to the Book (I or II), homily (arab
numeral), part, and page ; in this case, II, 2, pt. 3, 239.

[4] " and see that you set up the table of the Commandments on the place where th
Sacrament was hung ". Instructions of Bishop Thomas Bentham, for his diocese of Lich
field and Coventry, 1565, in Dixon, VI, p. 77 note. Also, the same, " that you do take dow
your roodlofts unto the lower beams, and to set a comely crest or vault upon it ". *Ibia*
p. 80. Bentham is here repeating the queen's general order of Oct. 10, 1561—for the te
of which cf. F. & K., III, no. xix ; resumé in Kennedy, *E.E.A.*, I, p. liii.

cked with gold and silver, painted with colours, set them with stone and
arl, clothed them with silks and precious vestures " ; which resulted in
most horrible idolatry " and even, with " the covetous ", in worship of the
ry gold and silver ! [1]

All images, indeed, are idols, the man in the pew is told ; [2] and in 2 Corin-
ians vi. 16 the word εἰδώλων is now (following Tyndale) translated *images*.
And all those names of abomination, which God's word in the holy scrip-
res giveth to the idols of the Gentiles, appertain to our images, being idols
ke to them, and having like idolatry committed unto them." [3] It is therefore
religious duty to destroy all such. Could not a *right* use of images be
aintained, by sermons and instructions ? [4] No ! " Preaching cannot
ossibly stay idolatry, if images be set up publicly in temples and churches " ; [5]
deed, they " can no more be suffered to stand " in God's house " than light
n agree with darkness or Christ with Belial ".[6]

And then these same homilies, which have justified in the sacred name
' God the destruction and plunder that has desolated hundreds and
ousands of churches throughout the whole kingdom, and which have
essed and lauded, by implication, the fanatics and thieves who were the
incipal agents in the work,[7] turn to lecture the congregation on the terrible
ondition in which too many churches actually stand ; and they do this as
ough, between the spirit they have praised and what they now ban, there
ere not a most evident connection. These are printed sermons, written
y the government's commission, ordered by the government to be read
egularly in all churches—it can hardly be thought that what they denounce
not, to the generality of Englishmen, a very familiar sight. " It is sin and
ame to see so many churches so ruinous, and so foully decayed, almost
a every corner . . . defiled with rain and weather, with dung of doves and
wls, stares and choughs, and other filthiness, as it is foul and lamentable
o behold in many places of this country. It is the house of prayer, not the
ouse of talking, of walking, of brawling, of minstrelsy, of hawks, of dogs." [8]
uinous churches are perhaps no new thing, but the next rebuke certainly
oeaks of a decline : " Where there appeareth at these days great slackness
nd negligence of a great sort of people in resorting to the church, there to
erve God . . . as also much uncomely and unreverent behaviour of many
ersons in the same, when they be there assembled." [9]

[1] *Homilies*, II, 2, pt. 1, 166.   [2] *Ibid.*, II, 2, pt. 1, 167.
[3] *Ibid.*,II, 2, pt. 3, 247.   [4] *Ibid.*, II, 2, pt. 3, 221–223.
[5] *Ibid.*, II, 2, pt. 3, 225 ; and cf. this (on p. 223) : " It appeareth not by any story of credit
aat true and sincere preaching hath endured in any one place above one hundred years."
[6] *Ibid.*, II, 1, pt. 2, 159.
[7] *Ibid.*, II, 2, pt. 1, 173–174 and pt. 3, 247. Work often officially ordered, of course ;
ad seemingly never actively discouraged. " This much, however, is clear, the royal visi-
tion of 1559 did not encourage moderation ; and the royal visitors do not appear to have
aade efforts to impress on the church-wardens the difference between ornaments ordered
or destruction and those to be ' retained and in use '." Kennedy, *E.E.A.*, lxiii.
[8] *Homilies*, II, 3, 252 and 253–254.
[9] *Ibid.*, II, 1, pt. 1, 151. Harrison describes the new mode of service : " The minister
aith his service commonly in the body of the church, with his face toward the people, in a
ctle tabernacle of wainscot provided for the purpose, by which means the ignorant do not only

Was the new religion generally welcomed ?   The *Homilies* seem to off
evidence to the contrary that is still more direct : " . . . much wicked people
the congregation is told, " pass nothing to resort to the church . . . f
that they see the church altogether scoured of such gay gazing sights as the
gross fantasy was greatly delighted with, because they see the false religic
abandoned and the true restored, which seemeth an unsavoury thing to the
unsavoury taste " ;   and to illustrate this, the homily tells the story how "
woman said to her neighbour, ' Alas, gossip, what shall we do now at Churcl
since all the goodly sights we were wont to have are gone, since we cann
hear the like piping, singing, chanting, and playing upon the organs, th
we could before ' " ? [1]

The homily, of course, insists that " we ought greatly to rejoice and giv
God thanks, that our churches are delivered of all those things which di
pleased God so sore, and filthily defiled his holy house . . . that such supe
stitious and idolatrous manners . . . are utterly abolished . . .".[2]   The
comes some history.   Images once introduced, all gradually began to u
them, the learned even and the wise, clergy and bishops ;   and so they " fe
into the pit of damnable idolatry.   In the which all the world, as it we
drowned, continued until our age, by the space of about 800 years, unspoke
against in a manner. . . .   So that the laity and clergy, learned and unlearne
all ages, sects and degrees of men, women, and children of whole Christendo
(an horrible and dreadful thing to think) have been at once drowned in abomir
able idolatry, of all other vices most detested of God and most damnable t
man, and that by the space of 800 years and more." [3]   Hence the zeal of tl
Reformer against " the abuse of churches . . . by too costly and sumptuot
decking and adorning of them, as also the lewd painting, gilding and clothin
of idols and images, . . ." [4] and against " . . . the outrageous furnitu
of temples and churches with plate, vessels of gold, and precious vestures "

---

learn divers of the psalms and usual prayers by heart *but also such as can read do pray togeth
with him.*"   Italics mine.
    And here we might ask what became of the religious life of the illiterate, once the on
technique they were used to was destroyed—the crucifix and statues and frescoes, the syr
bolic ceremonial, their beads—and the new rites and new doctrines and new prayers were
lavishly poured over them ?   For some account of what the Elizabethan zeal to rava
the parish churches accomplished, cf. Appendix II, *infra*, pp. 408-410.
    [1] *Homilies*, II, 8, pt. 2, 319.
    [2] As last reference.   Harrison provides a vivid contemporary description of the buildin
as evangelised, and explains how it is that some of the medieval glass survives : " All image
shrines, tabernacles, rood-lofts and monuments of idolatry are removed, taken down and d
faced, only the stories in glass windows excepted, which for want of new stuff, and by reas
of extreme charge that should grow by the alteration of the same into white panes througho
the realm, are not altogether abolished in most places at once, but by little and little suffere
to decay, that white glass may be provided and set up in their room " ;   *op. cit.*, 77.
    [3] *Homilies*, II, 2, pt. 3, 224.
    [4] *Ibid.*, 235.
    [5] *Ibid.*, 238.   A later passage in the same homily may be set beside the well-known tribu
of Erasmus to the glories of the English parish churches.   " Our churches stand full of su
great puppets, wondrously decked and adorned ;   garlands and coronets be set on their head
precious pearls hanging about their necks, their fingers shine with rings set with precio
stones ;   their dead and stiff bodies are clothed with garments stiff with gold.   You wou
believe that the images of our men saints were some princes of Persey land " ;   *ibid.*, 242-24

" The Pope's intolerable pride " [1] is another important and inevitable theme of the *Homilies*; and " the Church of Rome . . . as it is presently and hath been for the space of 900 years and odd . . . the style thereof so far wide from the nature of the true church, that nothing can be more." [2] And how ? Because they " have so intermingled their own traditions and inventions ". For example : " Christ commended to his church a Sacrament of his Body and Blood : they have changed it into a sacrifice for the quick and the dead. Christ did minister to his Apostles, and the Apostles to other men, indifferently, under both kinds : they have robbed the lay people of the cup, saying that for them one kind is sufficient. . . . What our Saviour Christ pronounced of the Scribes and the Pharisees in the Gospel, the same may we boldly and with safe conscience pronounce of the Bishops of Rome, namely that they have forsaken, and daily do forsake, the commandments of God, to erect and set up their own constitutions. . . . If it be possible to be where the true church is not, then is it at Rome " ; [3] and next there is a long litany of papal misdeeds and of bad popes, among whom there figure Boniface VIII, Alexander III (for his victory over Frederick Barbarossa) and St. Gregory VII for his inhumanity to the emperor Henry IV, kept shivering in the snow at Canossa. [4]

In your learned treatises, Harding had complained, you say nothing of the master matter of Justification and the acts of the religious man that relate to this. You reserve your perversion of this capital doctrine for the untrained congregations in the churches. The Reformed doctrine about Justification—one particular version of it—is certainly set out at large in the Homilies ; and, popular expositions though these be, it is to the Homilies, as has been noted, that the very Articles of Religion direct whoever would understand that " most wholesome doctrine, and very full of comfort " namely, " that we are justified by Faith only ". [5]

In their criticism of the personages and practices of the old religion the homilies speak with a clearness and decision that leaves nothing in doubt. Here the Reformers are all agreed, and all know exactly what they have in mind. There is not the same lucidity when they come to set out what they themselves now believe about the fundamental mysteries ; clearness and decision now disappear from the language of the homily—to re-appear at intervals, whenever it is necessary to stigmatise what the Reformers declare to have been the teaching of the pope and his church.

Whoever has tried to set out accurately, in a popular way, what by comparison is a simple matter, the definitions of the Council of Trent on Original Sin, on Justification and Good Works, will readily sympathise with those who

---

[1] *Homilies*, II, 16, pt. 2, 424.   [2] *Ibid.*, 422.   [3] *Ibid.*, 422–423.   [4] *Ibid.*, 424–425.
[5] Article XI of 1563 (XI of 1553 ; the reference to the *Homilies* is an addition to the article of 1553). The homily to which this Article XI refers is the third in Book I, *Of the Salvation of Man by only Christ our Saviour from Sin and Death everlasting* (pp. 25–36 of the reprint of 1832 which is used here). The next homily (pp. 37–48) is *A short Declaration of the true, lively, and Christian Faith* ; and then follows (pp. 49–62) *A Sermon of Good Works annexed unto Faith*. These three homilies are attributed to Cranmer himself.

had the task of putting the English version of the Reformation discoveries [1]
before congregations largely illiterate, bewildered by the years of continual
change, sceptical and indifferent, it may be, because of them, and present at
the sermon because bound to be there under pain not only of excommunication but of fines ; and all of them with many other matters, besides
religion—whether the new or the old—calling most urgently for their
daily attention : a generation upon which many crises had arrived, as it
were, simultaneously.

The fervid perorations of these homilies are clear enough, and often very
moving. How real, to the men who wrote them, the doctrines were that
they yet expounded—be the word allowed to pass—so mistily, is beyond all
doubt. The real meaning of the doctrine, as a whole consistent with itself,
and as the source, or ground, of the practical exhortation and of the fervent
religious relief, is something much less evident. But if this was the day of
liberation, and if the Reformer was conscious that the wisdom of God had
chosen him to be one of the liberators, in nothing was the liberation, for him,
more evident than in this new doctrine about man's justification. The whole
spirituality of the *Homilies* is penetrated by this theory, or rather by the
conviction that the theory is true ; and over the theory itself there broods,
ceaselessly, the thought of God's avenging wrath—just wrath, indeed, and
justly vengeful—and of how this may be averted, averted always by God's
free mercy, and by that alone ; mercy offered, granted, for the sake of the
merits of Our Lord dying as a sacrifice on the cross of Calvary, mercy taken

---

[1] The understanding of which version is by no means always a simple matter even for
leisured minds—and this must, in part, be my excuse for here stepping outside the rôle
of chronicler, and noting my own uncertainty whether I have rightly understood it. After
all, it has been possible for one of the most acute minds which the church of Cranmer and
Matthew Parker ever knew, to maintain that the difference between this English version of the
doctrine of " Justification by only faith ", and the teaching of the Catholic Church is largely
a matter of words—this was Newman's conclusion as an Anglican, and it remained his conclusion after years of familiarity with the Catholic teaching " from within " (see *Lectures on
Justification*, p. ix). Not that Newman's view was generally accepted in the Church of Eng-
land when he put it forth, or (so far as I know) has been generally accepted there since
The Protestant controversy about the teaching of the reformed *Anglicana* on this subject still
continues, indeed, with all its old liveliness, to judge from the comments of the Rev. E. G
Rupp on *The Doctrine of Justification in the Anglican Reformers*, by the Rev. A. H. Rees
(S.P.C.K., 1939), for which see Rupp, *The English Protestant Tradition* (1947), pp. 171–185
A second reason for these notes in comment (whose unexplained presence may seem, otherwise, a mere controversial impertinence) is that summaries, however objective in intention
may be greatly misleading ; and notes, which to the initiated will indicate how far I have
really understood what I am endeavouring to summarise, may thus perhaps redress any actual
unfairness in the summary.

As for the difficulty of understanding what the Reformers meant by their famous theory,
" Melanchthon ", says the Vicar of St. Mary's, Oxford (in 1837), " the most judicious defender
of the chief doctrine of Protestantism, justification by the apprehensive power of faith
whom our Church follows, makes that doctrine intelligible and true by admitting that it is
not to be taken literally, but as a mode of symbolising a protest against the doctrine of human
merit "—which statement Newman supports from the Confession of Augsburg, and a
comment on this by Bishop Bull, viz. " From their own teaching it is as plain as plain can
be that it is by a figure of speech indeed (though not an unsuitable figure of speech) that it
can be said we are justified by faith alone ". Newman, *Lectures on Justification*, p. 181, n.
I have translated the sentence quoted from Bull, *Harm. Apostolica*, II, 18, § 6.

hold of through that act called faith by which comes justification. Sin, and punishment, and remission of sin through the saving death, this is the whole business as it is put to the congregation : with man's concern in it— his confident faith—and man's profit from it, and man's comfort and satisfaction from his faith, as the high lights of the story ; and if sin is denounced unsparingly, and described with fearful realism, it is sin considered in a very material way, the loathsomeness intrinsic to the thing done, the frightfulness intrinsic to the penalty sin must bring. And in the relation of all this to the sinner in the pew the influence of that fear called by theologians " servile fear " is all-important, with an exaggeration of its importance that goes far beyond anything that is peculiar to the psychology of preachers as such.[1]

The homilies begin by describing " the misery of all mankind ", [2] and in doing so they make no distinction between what is good naturally and what is good supernaturally. " Of ourselves we be crabtrees that can bring forth no apples . . . [We be] of such earth as can bring forth but weeds, nettles, brambles, briars, cockle and darnel [3] . . . of ourselves, by ourselves, we have no goodness, help, nor salvation, but contrariwise sin, damnation, and death everlasting " : [4] all this being the " miserable captivity into which we were cast, through the envy of the devil, by transgressing God's commandment in our first parent Adam ".[5] " . . . Of ourselves and by ourselves, we are not able either to think a good thought, or work a good deed : so that we can find in ourselves no hope of salvation, but rather whatsoever maketh unto our destruction." [6]

It is God alone who can deliver us from this state ; and that " righteousness or justification to be received at God's own hands, . . . [and] which we so receive of God's mercy and Christ's merits, embraced by Faith, is taken, accepted, and allowed of God for our perfect and full justification ".[7] In this work,[8] " our justification ", there must be " upon our part, true and lively faith in the merits of Jesus Christ ; . . . [which true and lively faith] nevertheless is the gift of God, and not man's only work without God. [This faith, however,] doth not exclude repentance, hope, love, dread and the fear of God to be joined with faith in every man that is justified ; but it excludeth them from the office of justifying. . . . Nor [does this faith] exclude the justice of our good works, necessarily to be done afterward of duty towards God . . . but it excludeth them so that we may not do them to this intent, to be made good by doing of them."

Lest " the carnal man " misinterpret this,[9] the congregation are warned not to think that it is " this our own act, to believe in Christ, or this our faith in Christ, which is within us [that] doth justify us and merit our justification

---

[1] " Servile fear " is the slave's fear of the whip—the fear of punishment pure and simple, for the pain's sake. In the Catholic belief the rôle of " servile fear ", as preparing the soul of the sinner for the grace of justification, is subordinate : " Servile fear, indeed, is not a requisite, although, often enough, it is extremely useful ", says an authoritative exponent, Christian Pesch, S.J., *Praelectiones Theologicae* (1916), V, 224, Sect. 359 (translation mine).

[2] The title of the second homily in Book I ; *op. cit.*, 17–24.

[3] *Homilies*, I, 2, pt. 2, 21.   [4] *Ibid.*, 22.   [5] *Ibid.*, 22.   [6] *Ibid.*, 24.

[7] *Ibid.*, I, 3, pt. 1, 25.   [8] *Ibid.*, p. 727 for rest of this paragraph.   [9] *Ibid.*, I, 3, pt. 2, 31.

unto us ". No indeed! For " although we have faith, hope, charity
repentance, dread, and fear of God within us, and do never so many works
thereunto ; yet we must renounce the merit of all our . . . good deeds
. . ., as things far too weak . . . to deserve . . . justification ; [1] and
must trust only in God's mercy and in that sacrifice [offered by Christ our
Lord] to obtain thereby God's grace and remission, as well of our original
sin in baptism, as of all actual sin committed by us after our baptism, if
we truly repent,[2] and turn unfeignedly to him again." [3]

The Articles of Religion do not tell us what they mean by Faith, when they
approve as a wholesome doctrine what they call " Justification by Faith
only ". They refer us for an explanation to the homilies, and here is what
the homilies have to say. First of all : that the Faith through which sinful
man is justified is not only the believing that the Old and the New Testaments are true " and all the articles of our faith " ; it is " also to have a
sure trust and confidence in God's merciful promises, to be saved from
everlasting damnation by Christ ; whereof doth follow a loving heart to
obey his commandments ".[4]

And how does this faith actually operate towards our justification
" Faith doth directly send us to Christ for remission of our sins, and . .
by faith given us of God we embrace the promise of God's mercy and of the
remission of our sins ".[5]

What all this meant to the congregation—not as a doctrine broken up
and explained piece by piece by one trained in theology and with some power

---

[1] The Catholic Church teaches that faith (in the Catholic sense of this word), hope and
repentance are necessary elements in the preparation of the soul for justification : other
virtues may or may not be there. Charity is also necessary if justification is not sought
through a sacrament. It should be noted, also, that the faith, hope, repentance and the rest
which prepare the soul for justification are not, so the Catholic Church teaches, activities
merely human and natural : they are acts done under the stimulus of, and as a response to
and accompanied by, God's grace—it is only in so far as they are the product of that grace
that these acts derive whatever power they have to prepare the soul for justification. Another
important point : the Catholic insistence on faith in the Catholic sense (i.e. acceptance of
revealed doctrines as true) was often combated by the Reformers as though the act of
faith were no more than an intellectual operation ; the fact is that, from long before the Reformers came into existence, it was understood that the act of the Catholic believing, say, the
mystery of the Trinity, is primarily an act believing God revealing the mystery. The act of
faith is a substantially supernatural act, whose immediate term is *Deus revelans*—God
believed because God is Truth itself, and so the mystery believed which God reveals. The
assent of faith then, according to Catholic teaching, by itself relates man to God immediately
It is not just the apprehension of a theological proposition, a business void of supernatural
effect, but an act which relates the human mind to God in action upon it.

[2] If there were no repentance, would the faith of the sinner, then, not procure his justification ? Is the presence, or absence, of repentance an evidence of the presence or absence
of " the faith which justifies " ? i.e. of whether the faith which is present is " justifying faith "
or some other kind ? The homily (p. 31) asks, " For how can a man have this true faith
this sure trust and confidence in God, that by the merits of Christ his sins be forgiven, and
he reconciled to the favour of God, and to be partaker of the kingdom of heaven by Christ,
when he liveth ungodly and denieth Christ by his deeds ? " ; it answers " Surely no such
ungodly man can have this faith and trust in God ". And why not ? Because, the ungodly
man knows, " that wicked men shall not enjoy the kingdom of God ".

[3] *Ibid.*, 31.   [4] *Homilies*, I, 3, pt. 3, 34.   [5] *Ibid.*, 33.

of popular exposition, but read out from the book by Sir Oliver Martext,[1] the thirteen pages (as directed) spread over three successive Sundays— we may ponder long, and perhaps instructively, as we study the origins of what was the popular religion of this country in modern times, that which took the place of the popular religion of the Middle Ages. But whatever it meant, this was no more than " Justification by only Faith " as a religious theory, Justification in the abstract. What of Justification as the practical concern of any of the sinners now listening to Sir Oliver ? Time had been when, now and again at any rate, they had all examined their consciences, made their acts of contrition, and firm purposes of amendment, confessed their sins, received the priest's absolution, and done the penances imposed—and so found peace with God and a quiet mind. And now ?

The homilies speak much of Sin, and of its forgiveness : " Sin is come, and so come that it cannot be avoided. . . . And our Saviour Jesus Christ, although he hath delivered us from sin, yet not so that we shall be free from committing sin ; but so that it shall not be imputed to our condemnation ",[2] it is said, in the second homily of the Passion, somewhat ambiguously. And, more practically, " Now resteth to show unto you how to apply Christ's death and passion to our comfort, as a medicine to our wounds, so that it may work the same effect in us wherefore it was given. . . . For . . . the death of Christ shall stand us in no force, unless we apply it to ourselves in such sort as God hath appointed. . . . He hath ordained a certain mean, whereby we may take fruit and profit to our soul's health. What mean is that ? Forsooth it is faith ; . . . the only mean and instrument of salvation required of our parts is faith, that is to say, a sure trust and confidence in the mercies of God, whereby we persuade ourselves, that God both hath and will forgive our sins, that he hath accepted us again into his favour . . . not for our merits . . . but only and solely for the merits of Christ's death and passion. . . . This faith is required at our hands ; and this if we keep steadfastly in our hearts, there is no doubt but we shall obtain salvation at God's hands. . . ."[3]

" Thus have ye heard in a few words the mean whereby we must apply the fruits and merits of Christ's death unto us, so that it may work the salvation of our souls : namely a sure, steadfast, perfect, and grounded faith. For, as well they which beheld steadfastly the brazen serpent were healed and delivered, at the very sight thereof . . . even so all they which behold Christ crucified with a true and lively faith shall undoubtedly be delivered from the grievous wounds of the soul, be they never so deadly or many in numbers. Therefore, dearly beloved, if we chance at any time, through frailty of the flesh, to fall into sin, *as it cannot be chosen but we must needs fall often* ;[4] and if we feel the heavy burden thereof to press our souls, tormenting us with the fear of death, hell and damnation ; let us then use that mean which God hath appointed in his word, to wit, the mean of faith,

---

[1] For some evidence of the ubiquity of Sir Oliver, through these forty years, 1559–1604, cf. *infra*, pp. 133–142.
[2] *Homilies*, II, 13, pt. 2, 388.   [3] *Ibid.*, 390–392.   [4] Italics mine.

which is the only instrument of salvation now left unto us. Let us stead
fastly behold Christ crucified with the eyes of our heart. . . ." [1]

But, despite this insistence on the sole importance of faith, other thing
too are spoken of : " No doctrine is so necessary in the Church of God
as is the doctrine of repentance and amendment of life." [2] " We must b
earnestly sorry for our sins. . . ." [3] Why ? Because they are offence
against God who is " most bounteous and merciful " towards us, and becaus
of the heinousness of sin.[3] And to get this sorrow we must be " diligent t
hear and read the Scriptures " where they speak of the enormity of sin.
Then we must make confession to God ; confession also to one another i
" needful and necessary ", as St. James teaches.[5] This is, however, n
argument for " auricular confession ", i.e. to the priest as a priest, " whic'
hath not his warrant in God's word ".[6] The homily explains, " I do not sa
but that, if any do find themselves troubled in conscience, they may repai
to their learned curate or pastor, or to some other godly learned man, an
shew the trouble or doubt of the conscience to them, that they may receiv
at their hand the comfortable salve of God's word ; but it is against the tru
Christian liberty, that any man should be bound to the numbering of hi
sins, as it hath been used heretofore in the time of blindness and ignorance ".
What the curate, pastor, or " other godly learned man " will do is certainl
not thought of, here, as pronouncing an absolution that forgives the sins witl
which the conscience is burdened—unless, says the homily, " to pray is t
absolve ", and " then the laity by this place [i.e. the text in St. James] hath a
great authority to absolve the priests, as the priests have to absolve the laity ".
Moreover, " What need we then to tell forth our sins into the ear of the priest
sith that they be already taken away ? " [9]

So much, then, is enjoined on the sinner who desires forgiveness—
though nowhere is it said in what sense he must do as he ought to do. On
thing alone is clearly spoken of as absolutely necessary for him—he must hav
" faith, whereby we do apprehend and take hold upon the promises of God
touching the free pardon and forgiveness of our sins ; [10] . . .". And we ma
note that, along with the repudiation of what Catholics had understood as th
Sacrament of Penance, there is set out a travesty of the Catholic doctrin
of contrition that enables the Homilist to stigmatise it as the repentance o
Judas.[11]

Finally, the homilies again move away from Catholicism when they teach
that " under the name of sin not only those gross words and deeds whicl
by the common judgment of men are counted to be filthy and unlawful
and so consequently abominable sins, but also the filthy lusts and inwar
concupiscences of the flesh . . .".[12] And for the comfort of such secre

---

[1] *Homilies* II, 391–392.   [2] *Ibid.*, II, 20, pt. 1, 475.   [3] *Ibid.*, II, 20, pt. 2, 485–486.
[4] *Ibid.*, 486.   [5] *Ibid.*, 486–487 ; the reference is James V 16.   [6] *Ibid.*, 488
[7] *Ibid.*, 489.   [8] *Ibid.*, 488.   [9] *Ibid.*, 488.   [10] *Ibid.*, 489.   [11] *Ibid.*, 489–490
[12] *Ibid.*, II, 20, pt. 1, 477 ; understanding by this last phrase not desires of sin wilfull
fostered, entertained, indulged, developed, but the " instinctive " movement towards the act
as things attractive, that is prior to (and independent of) any judgment whether they are righ
or wrong—the φρόνημα σαρκὸς of Article IX of 1571 (VIII of 1553).

adherents of the ancient faith who nowadays come to church in order, perhaps to please the queen, perhaps to dodge the fines, it is said that by sin is also to be understood " the false and erroneous opinions we have had of God, and the wicked superstition that doth breed of the same, the unlawful worshipping and service of God, and other like. . . . They be here condemned which will seem to be repentant sinners, and yet will not forsake their idolatry and superstition." [1]

The homilies are, very largely indeed, moral instructions : exhortations to better living, and to " good works ", to prayer especially, to almsdeeds and to fasting. And it is always carefully explained in what sense these are commanded, and in what spirit they should be done, lest the Englishman should do them, as his forefathers had done them for centuries—towards the remission of his sins, or in a spirit of penance for sins mercifully forgiven, or as an act beseeching God's favour. " Almsdeeds ", it is now said, " do wash away our sins, because God doth vouchsafe then *to repute* [2] us as clean and pure, when we do them for his sake, and not because they deserve or merit our purging, or for that they have any such strength and virtue in themselves." [3] This is followed by the explanation, " The godly do learn that, when the Scriptures say that by good and merciful works we are reconciled to God's favour, we are taught then to know what Christ by his intercession and mediation obtaineth for us of his Father when we be obedient to his will ; yea, they learn in such manners of speaking a comfortable argument of God's singular favour and love, that attributeth that unto us and to our doings, that he by his Spirit worketh in us and through his grace procureth for us ".[4]

Fasting must be done in the same spirit—that it is of itself utterly ineffective spiritually : " To fast . . . with this persuasion of mind, that our fasting and other good works can make us good, perfect, and just men, and finally bring us to heaven, this is a devilish persuasion, and that fast, so far off from pleasing God, that it . . . is altogether derogatory of the merits of Christ's death. . . ." [5]

But, six pages later, in the second part of this homily, tucked away as an *obiter dictum* indeed, but said none the less, is the statement that there are " works by which, as by secondary means, God's wrath may be pacified and his mercy purchased ".[6] And, which seems to point away from the cardinal doctrine, the congregation is warned, in the opening sentences of the *Homily against Gluttony and Drunkenness*, that it is " necessary . . . for every Christian that will not be found unready at the coming of our Saviour Christ, to live sober minded in this present world : forasmuch as otherwise being unready he can not enter with Christ into glory. . . ."[7]

The best employment of all, however, for the Christian man, is the pious study of Holy Scripture. Here, and here alone, will be found " God's true word setting forth his glory, and also man's duty ".[8] And so to Sacred

---

[1] *Homilies* II.
[2] Italics mine.
[3] *Ibid.*, II, 11, pt. 2, 356–357.
[4] *Ibid.*, 357.
[5] *Ibid.*, II, 4, pt. 1, 260.
[6] *Ibid.*, II, 4, pt. 2, 264.
[7] *Ibid.*, II, 5, 272.
[8] *Ibid.*, I, 1, pt. 1, 9.

Scripture, the homilies declare, men " must apply their minds . . . without the which they can neither sufficiently know God and his will, neither their office and duty ".[1]   Here is " the well of life " to which, and not " to the stinking puddles of men's traditions, devised by man's imagination ", we must go " for our justification and salvation ".[2]   And to those who read the Holy Word with humility and prayer and patience its meaning will ultimately be made clear.[3]   How much richer are not such souls than the " old philosophers ", or even the Scholastics, seeing " what vanity the school doctrine is mixed with, for that in this word they sought not the will of God but rather the will of reason, the trade of custom, the path of the fathers, *the practice of the Church* ".[4]

The homilies speak at length of the need for prayer in a Christian's life ; and, insisting that it is to God alone that we must pray, they caricature the Catholic doctrine about the invocation of saints, and stigmatise the doctrine caricatured as blasphemous.[5]   And an easy transition brings in the question of prayer for the faithful departed : " Let us [not] dream any more that the souls of the dead are anything at all holpen by our prayers : but as the Scripture teacheth us, let us think that the soul of man, passing out of the body goeth straightways either to heaven or to hell, whereof the one needeth no prayer, and the other is without redemption . . .";[6] heaven for " the elect and blessed ", hell for " the reprobate and damned ".[7]   " The only purgatory wherein we must trust to be saved is the death and blood of Christ : which if we apprehend with a true and steadfast faith, it purgeth and cleanseth us from all our sins, even as well as if he were now hanging upon the cross ".[8] Nevertheless, the condition is added, " if they truly repent them of their sins ".[9]

" Justification by faith only " must not then be taken to mean that in a Christian man's life justifying faith alone matters ?   Despite much passionate language that seems, at times, to say the contrary ?   In the homily on the Passion the warning is plainly given, " It shall little avail us to have in meditation the fruits and price of his passion, to magnify them, and to delight *or trust in them*,[10] except we have in mind his examples in passion to follow them." [11]

What of the sacraments ?   There are but two of these, of course, " according to the exact signification ", and a sacrament is, so it is now explained, a " visible sign, expressly commanded in the New Testament, whereunto is annexed the promise of free forgiveness of our sin and of our holiness and joining in Christ . . .".[12]   Or, again, it is a " public and common rite or action, pertaining to the profit and edifying of the poor congregation ";[13] and " to administer a Sacrament is by the outward word and element to preach to the receiver the inward and invisible grace of God " [14]—very Zurich, and very Calvin !   Where the words spoken " in the administration

---

[1] *Homilies* I.   [2] *Ibid.*, 10.   [3] *Ibid.*, I, 1, pt. 2, 14–15.
[4] *Ibid.*, II, 17, pt. 3, 443, italics mine.   [5] *Ibid.*, II, 7, pt. 2, 296–301.
[6] *Ibid.*, II, 7, pt. 3, 307–308.   [7] *Ibid.*, 306.   [8] *Ibid.*, 308.   [9] *Ibid.*
[10] Italics mine.   [11] *Ibid.*, II, 13, pt. 1, 382.   [12] *Ibid.*, II, 9, 324.
[13] *Ibid.*, 325.   [14] *Ibid.*

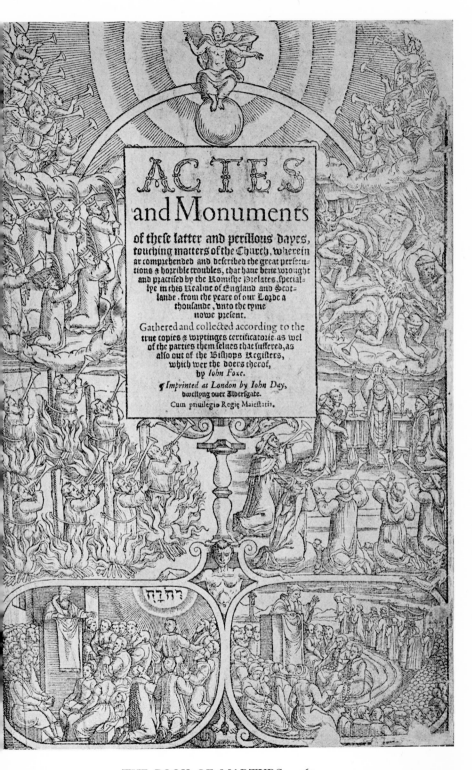

ACTES
and Monuments
of these latter and perillous dayes,
touching matters of the Church, wherein
ar comprehended and described the great persecu-
tions & horrible troubles, that haue bene wrought
and practised by the Romishe Prelates, special-
lye in this Realme of England and Scot-
lande, from the yeare of our Lorde a
thousande, vnto the tyme
nowe present.

Gathered and collected according to the
true copies & wrytinges certificatorie, as wel
of the parties them selues that suffered, as
also out of the Bishops Registers,
which wer the doers therof,
by Iohn Foxe.

¶ Imprinted at London by Iohn Day,
dwellyng ouer Aldersgate.

Cum priuilegio Regiæ Maiestatis.

THE BOOK OF MARTYRS, 1563

Henricus the emperor, with his wife and child, barefoot and barelegd

waiting on pope Hildebrand, three daies and three nights, at the gates of Canusium, before he could be suffered to come in.

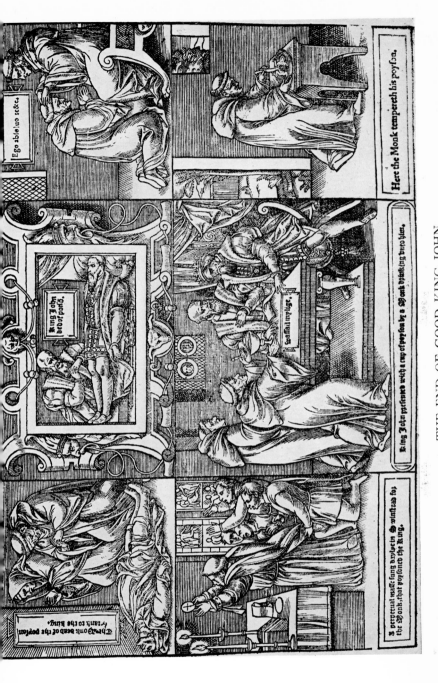

THE END OF GOOD KING JOHN

✠ The ryght Picture and true counterfeyt of Boner, and his crueltye, in scourgynge of Goddes Saynctes in his Orcharde.

of the Sacraments be not understanded of them that be present, they cannot thereby be edified ".[1] Hence " it is required of necessity, that the common prayer be had in a tongue that the hearers do understand ".[2]

The Mass has been forbidden by law, and stigmatised in these homilies as an idolatrous pretence, a horrible blasphemy and worse. What has taken its place, what is presented through the ritual, now revived, of Edward VI's second Book of Common Prayer, is described as : " the public celebration of the memory of [Christ's] precious death at the Lord's table [3] . . . where everyone of us must be guests and not gazers, eaters and not lookers. . . .[4] We must then take heed, lest, of the memory, it be made a sacrifice ; lest, of a communion, it be made a private eating ; [5] . . . Here they [i.e. the faithful] may feel wrought the tranquillity of conscience, the increase of faith, the strengthening of hope, the large spreading abroad of brotherly kindness. . . ." [6] Along with this knowledge of what the sacrament is, there must also be in those who receive it " a sure and constant faith, not only that the death of Christ is available for the redemption of all the world . . . and reconciliation with God the Father, but also that [Christ] hath made upon his cross a full and sufficient sacrifice for thee. . . . This is . . . to applicate his merits unto thyself. Herein thou needest no other man's help, no other sacrifice or oblation, no sacrificing priest, no mass, no means established by man's invention ".[7] As for what has been, " We now see and understand ", the rising generation is calumniously instructed, " what dens of thieves the churches of England have been made by the blasphemous buying and selling the most precious body and blood of Christ in the mass, as the world was made to believe, at diriges, at month's minds, at trentalls, in abbeys and chantries . . .".[8]

Christ our Lord is not actually present in what has been consecrated ; " We have no special regard to the bread, wine or water ", Jewel wrote in 1567, " for they are creatures corruptible, as well after consecration as they were before. But we direct our faith only unto the very body and blood of Christ ; not as being there really and fleshly present, as ye have imagined, but as sitting in heaven at the right hand of God the Father. . . . Christ's body is one thing, and the sacrament is another. The sacrament is in earth : Christ's body is in heaven, at the right hand of God the Father." [9] Jewel's explanation reduces the idea of presence in the sacrament to metaphor. " The sacrament bread is bread, it is not the body of Christ : the body of Christ is flesh, it is no bread . . . . The bread is on the table : the body is in heaven. The bread is in the mouth : the body in the heart. . . ." [10]

And against all this flood of propaganda the other side had, of course, comparatively little immediate remedy. The pulpits were entirely in the control of the Reform party, and in this matter the pulpits were all but

---

[1] *Homilies* II, 326.   [2] *Ibid.*   [3] *Ibid.*, II, 15, pt. 1, 403.
[4] *Ibid.*, 403–404.   [5] *Ibid.*, 404.   [6] *Ibid.*, 407.   [7] *Ibid.*
[8] *Ibid.*, II, 3, 253.   [9] *Defence of the Apology,* in *Works*, III, 527.
[10] *Treatise on the Sacraments, ibid.*, II, 1121.

8

everything : it was an age when half the population could neither read no
write. The press was censored ; printers were few, well-known, an
well-supervised ; not a book could be printed without the leave of the bishops
What little could be done, the Catholics did. The Catholic scholars wh
had crossed the seas, after their dispossession from chairs and headships an
fellowships at Oxford and Cambridge, and who were now established, somewhat precariously, at Louvain began to publish replies to Jewel and exposi
tions of Catholic doctrine on particular points, and gradually these wer
smuggled into England and slowly circulated. Within ten years or so of th
appearance of Jewel's first book (in 1562) there were, Nicholas Sande
thought, some 20,000 copies of the various new Catholic works circulating
in England.[1]

2

To deepen and consolidate the effect of this routine anti-Catholic
preaching and homily reading, there were the active administrative
measures [2] of the new bishops, who, in close contact always with the
Secretary of State, did whatever was possible to put into operation in thei
dioceses that new code of clerical and Christian behaviour, the Royal Injunctions of 1559.[3]

These Injunctions, which " implemented " the new fundamental laws, the
Acts of Supremacy [4] and Uniformity,[5] are presented to the queen's " loving
subjects " as her will and command ; they are the act of " the queen's most
royal majesty ", intending " the suppression of superstition . . . and to
plant true religion " ; and " her highness's displeasure, and pains of the

---

[1] Quoted Pollen, *English Catholics in the Reign of Queen Elizabeth*, p. 111, from the
MS. of the *De Schismate* (English College, Rome), fo. 136b.

[2] Cf. Kennedy, *E.E.A.*, I., p. xxxiv and following, for the regulations which, as a quasi
permanent code, shaped Elizabethan ecclesiastical life, regulations " constantly reflected "
in the visitation documents, and which, in the main, were devised in the early years of the
reign. The items of this " code " are :

1. The Acts of Supremacy and Uniformity, 1 *Eliz.*, cc. 1, 2.
2. The Royal Injunctions of 1559 and the Interpretations (1560).
3. The Admonition of 1560.
4. The Kalendar.
5. The Declaration of Principal Articles of Religion, 1561.
6. The Thirty-nine Articles.
7. Whitgift's Articles of 1583.
8. The Canons of 1576, 1585, 1597—never enforced universally as a whole.
9. The Recusancy Acts.
10. The Royal Order of 1561. F. &. K., III, n. XIX.
11. The Advertisements of 1566.

[3] For the text of the Injunctions cf. G. & H., 417–442. " These Injunctions, with the Acts
of Supremacy and Uniformity, overshadow all other documents of the reign in ecclesiastical
administration. No extant visitation records overlook them." Kennedy, *E.E.A.*, I, p. xlvi.

[4] This Act " runs through the documents as a unifying principle [of administration]
throughout the reign " ; Kennedy, *E.E.A.*, I, p. xxxvii.

[5] This Act is a " fruitful source of inquiry and regulation in all the visitations of the
reign " ; e.g. not only for the liturgical change, but for the matter of church furnishings
and the matter of fines for non-attendance at the new services ; *ibid.*, p. xxxviii.

ame " are the stated sanction accompanying the code. It is addressed, primarily, to the clergy.

The Injunctions open with the declaration that all ecclesiastics charged with a cure of the souls must, four times a year, declare in their sermons that " all usurped and foreign power " [1] has no warrant in God's word and that its abolition is therefore just ; and that between the Englishman and Almighty God there is but one authority, the queen.   The cult of the saints, reverence for their relics, belief in miracles wrought through their intercession, is " superstition and hypocrisy " ; all shrines and images are to be destroyed—even those in private possession—and once a month all ecclesiastics as aforesaid, in exhorting their parishioners to works of faith (i.e. to mercy and to charity), are to instruct them that pilgrimages, setting candles before images and praying upon beads, tend to idolatry and merit the malediction threatened for this sin, " which of all other offences God Almighty doth most detest and abhor ".   The regulation is renewed that in every church a bible is to be set up for the public to read, and with it the Paraphrases of Erasmus. On the other hand, all Catholic vestments and service books are to be sought out and destroyed.   None is to preach even in his own parish unless specially licensed by the Queen, or the bishop, or by " the Queen's majesty's visitors ".

All this is but the repetition of what Edward VI's Injunctions had demanded twelve years before.   To supplement it there are now twenty-five new items and three appendices.   The new religious freedom, we learn, is far from absolute.   No one is to defend heresy, for example ; nor to reason " rashly " about what he reads in Holy Writ, using this to support false doctrines ; nor to dispute about religious matters and dub his opponents, " heretic " or " papist " ; [2] nor is anyone to use charms, witchcraft or sorcery.   A severe censorship of books is established—no book is to be printed without express licence in writing from the queen or her council or the bishops.   The layman is to attend service every Sunday in his own parish church and in no other ; and once there he is not to interrupt the service, " or let or discourage ", whether it be the preacher, or the " minister " saying the new divine service. Special overseers are to be appointed in each parish to see that their fellows come to church—and do not leave before the service is over.   Ale-houses shall be closed during service-time.

No one is to teach without a licence from the bishop.   The Grammar of Henry VIII, " and none other ", is imposed as the universal class book ; and " all teachers of children shall stir and move them to the love and reverence of God's true religion now truly set forth by public authority ".   This education the clergy will supplement by half an hour's catechetical instruction every other Sunday.   In addition to the Sunday services, so it is now laid

[1] Edward VI in 1547, and Henry VIII in 1536 had said, more openly, " the Bishop of Rome's usurped power and jurisdiction " : cf. G. & H., 419, note, and 270.   " The four quarterly sermons appear in most of the [bishops'] orders, and sometimes they were increased to six " ; Kennedy, E.E.A., I, p. xxxvii.

[2] " Papist ", of course, may mean no more, in an argument, than a less perfect kind of Reformer than the one who is using the term.

down, there is to be a service every Wednesday and every Friday—and thi
is to be, not the Communion Service, but " the Litany and prayers "
During the Litany and prayers, at all times of common prayer, the peopl
are " to kneel upon their knees ", and always to bow their heads at the hol
name of Jesus ; and wherever there are foundations for choral services
the present arrangements shall remain—" for the sake of the living of th
singers and the preservation of the laudable science of music " ; and it i
allowed, " for the comfort of such that delight in music ", that a hymn b
sung, at the beginning or end of common prayer " in the best sort of melody
and music that may be conveniently devised ".[1]

The Injunctions add to the vast body of existing regulations for clerical
life a new warning, about care in choosing a wife. The experiment of clerica
marriage under Edward VI was not, it would seem, universally successful
And so, since there has " grown offence and some slander to the Church by
lack of discreet and sober behaviour in many ministers of the Church, both
in choosing of their wives and indiscreet living with them ", deacons and
priests who propose to marry are, in future, to present the lady for " good
examination by the bishop . . . and two justices . . ." of the neighbourhood ; and as well as their permission, the consent of the lady's kinsmen is
required. Those who marry without these formalities will be deprived.
Bishops who propose to marry are similarly subjected to the authority of
their metropolitan or the queen's commissioners; and heads of colleges to the
visitor of the college. All the clergy are to be dressed in the garments and

---

[1] This particular *Injunction*, or rather permission, was soon to be revealed as a stone of
offence throughout the party of Reform. When, in July 1566, Humphrey and Sampson
are listing for Bullinger, " Some blemishes which still attach to the church of England "
no. 2 in the catalogue reads, " To say nothing of the effeminate and over-refined strains of
the music itself, the use of the organ in church is growing more common " (*Z.L.*, 239)
Perceval Wiburn, a canon of Westminster, also speaks of " singing in parts in the churches
and with organs ", as a grievance which the truly reformed must resent (*ibid.*, 271). And
the Bishops of London and Winchester, answering these critics who still remain faithful to
the pre-1559 faith in all its purity, earnestly dissociate themselves from any responsibility
for such music : " We do not assert that the chanting in churches, together with the organ
is to be retained ; but we disapprove of it, as we ought to do " (Grindal and Horne, to Bullinger
and Gualter, Feb. 6, 1567 ; *ibid.*, 275).

" . . . The Reformation ", says a writer of our own time, " ordering the destruction of
all Latin service books (by Royal Letter of Edward VI), abruptly closed down the performance
of Latin music in churches except for such motets and sections of the service, like the *Magni-
ficat*, the *Te Deum*, the *Nunc Dimittis*, as were retained in the Anglican Rite and could still be
sung in Latin at the Universities, foundations of learning where Latin was the customary
ceremonial tongue. The Mass, which was the core of the Latin Rite, and which had formerly
been the inspirational centre of English Church Music was doomed.

" The impact of this on contemporary music was almost as bitter as it was on the spiritual
life of those who clung to the old religion. It was the putting out of a great light. . . .

" . . . You cannot go on for long writing silent music in defiance of the law, half-afraid
always of the sharp, foxy eye of the informer ; in the end it becomes the silence of death.
The inspiration of Latin music was finished. . . ." (Andrews, *Westminster Retrospect*,
1948, pp. 76, 77, 78).

And this comment does not touch another great loss—the hymns of the breviary, and the
wealth of melody in the Missal, Gradual, Vesperal and Processional. For this heritage that
had slowly accumulated through a thousand years of a continuous and ever developing
culture, the desk work of Cranmer through barely as many days (allowing his gifts, and the
unique quality of what he produced) could not possibly be adequate compensation.

quare caps such as were in use in the last years of Edward VI—as matter of
eemliness. Finally, there is a command that in officiating at divine service,
he clergy shall read " leisurely, plainly, and distinctly " ; and there is added
he significant direction, " also such as are but mean readers shall peruse over
before, once or twice, the chapters and homilies . . .".

Of the three " appendices " to the Injunctions, the first is that *Admonition* about the meaning of the Royal Supremacy which has already
been noticed,[1] and the third sets out the new form of the " bidding prayer ".
The second is headed *For tables in the church*. It begins by saying that, for
he future, altars are not to be taken down in the " riotous and disordered
manner " that has been seen in some places, but only with the " oversight of
he curate . . . and the church-wardens ". Then it lays down " that the
holy table in every church be decently made, and set in the place where the
altar stood . . . and so to stand, saving when the communion of the Sacrament is to be distributed ; at which time the same shall be so placed in good
ort within the chancel as whereby the minister may be more conveniently
heard of the communicants in his prayer and ministration, and the communicants also more conveniently and in more number communicate with
he said minister. And after the communion done, from time to time,
he same holy table to be placed where it stood before. " These directions
are binding on the whole nation.

How far indeed the Injunctions of 1559 were from ever becoming a dead
letter, so long as Elizabeth reigned, is apparent from the numerous visitation
documents of the reign now published.[2] In these we can not only study
the principles of action, but see something of the detailed working of that
executive machinery by means of which the old beliefs and practices were
rooted out, and the tender beginnings of the new carefully fostered.[3] And we
can begin to familiarise ourselves with the never-ceasing supervision of the
ordinary man by church officials, lay and clerical, that was now a main
feature of English life.[4] For never, in any department of life, at any time,
even in this much-regimented century when, as Hallam has said, Cecil
governed all England in the way the prying steward of some great noble
administered his estate, were Englishmen so meticulously shepherded, so
systematically spied upon, and their activities and omissions so carefully
reported to the central authority, as in their dealings with God, through what

[1] Cf. *supra*, 73–74.
[2] By the Alcuin Club ; for the period 1558–75, *Visitation Articles and Injunctions of the
Period of the Reformation*, Vol. III, ed. W. H. Frere, listed in these notes as F. & K. ; for the
period 1575–1603, *Elizabethan Episcopal Administration*, Vols. II and III, ed. W. M. P.
Kennedy, here referred to as *E.E.A.*
[3] Their " application to parish life was constant, either *in extenso* or in extracts " ; so
Kennedy, *E.E.A.*, p. xli, noting how they were read in every church once a quarter, and,
hung up prominently in the church, were one of the new permanent furnishings of the very
building. References to orders " according to the Injunctions " or " prescribed by the
Injunctions " are legion. *Ibid.*
[4] A feature more and more predominant, and a supervision that grew in aggressiveness
according as the local authority was more faithful to the example of Zurich and Geneva.

is called religion, in the reign of Queen Elizabeth—all Englishmen, that is save the very greatest.

The most important local agent of this administrative system by which in fact, the slow transformation was wrought which we have called the Second Conversion of England was the churchwarden, " the non-commissioned officer in the army of the new Divine Right of Kings ".[1] Here was the unpaid constable and detective for parochial morality in its widest and in its narrowest sense, and the means whereby the bishop's officials—the vigilant archdeacons and their courts—kept themselves informed about the conduct of the incumbent ; whether he preached and how he preached, and whom besides himself he allowed to preach ; what kind of life he led ; whether, for example, he was one of those who, a papist at heart, " looked for the day " or else, a Reformer of the primitive type, thought sermons so much more important than sacraments that though he preached he never celebrated the Supper. The churchwardens were thus " . . . the earliest points of contact [for the subject] with the national régime. They touched parish life at every point [and were] extraordinarily busy [so visitation records reveal]. The parson himself walked warily before them. The congregation worshipped under their eyes. The weaker brethren . . . found in them no mutilated authority, but the very image and transcript of that wielded at Westminster itself." [2]

The place of the wardens in the system can be understood by examining the questions regarding them, put in all these episcopal visitations. Chaderton, for example, Bishop of Chester (1579–95), asks pertinently in every parish, in 1581, " Whether have your churchwardens assisted your minister in his office and function from time to time ; and whether they have done their diligence to bring such into the Church as stand gazing and talking in the churchyard, or frequent and lurk in alehouses or tippling houses in the time of Divine Service ; and whether they have been careful and diligent to see good order and silence kept in the Church during the time of sermons and service ; and whether they have diligently noted the names of all such parties every Sunday and Holy Day as have been absent from Divine Service at any time, and levied the forfeiture of twelve pence for every absence from Common Prayer, according to the statute, and put the same to the use of the poor of the parish ; or, if they have offended in any of the premises, then how often have they so offended and what be their names ; and what particular sums of money have they forfeited that way and by whom since the last visitation ; and how much of such forfeitures have been levied by the chuchwardens and by them delivered to the use of the poor of the parish, and to whom hath the same been delivered ?

" Whether your churchwardens have yearly given an account of your church-goods committed to their charge, and of other their receipts and expenses ; and whether they have sold any bells or other church-goods without the consent of the Ordinary first had in writing : and whether they have

---

[1] Kennedy, in *E.E.A.*, I, p. cxxxi.   [2] *Ibid.*

mployed such goods, receipts, and sums of money to the use of the Church
r no ; and what be the names of the offenders ?

" Whether the churchwardens and swornmen in former years have,
f any private corrupt affection, concealed any crime or other disorder done
n their times, and have not presented the same ; and if so, then what faults
ave they concealed, and what were the names of such churchwardens and
wornmen so concealing the same ? " [1]

And after the churchwardens the next most important figure, among the
aity, is the schoolmaster. His occupation, too, is carefully regulated, as a
eally vital element in the ecclesiastical system. Before a man can teach he
eeds a licence under the bishop's seal, and this law is rigidly enforced.
3efore the licence is granted he is carefully examined, and about nothing so
arefully as about his loyalty to " the Queen's most godly proceedings ".
'rom the year 1563 the schoolmaster is one of those liable to be called upon
o swear the oath of Supremacy, with penalties in prospect of life imprison-
nent and death should he refuse it. The matter of his teaching is also very
arefully controlled, and official text books are imposed. The ideal school-
naster of the Elizabethan settlement is portrayed in Whitgift's visitation of
he diocese of Bath and Wells in 1583, in a question which other prelates
ake over verbatim, so perfectly does it express the mind of the *Anglicana*
t this moment : "Whether the schoolmasters which teach within your parish,
ither openly or privately in any noble or gentleman's house, or in any other
lace there, be of good and sincere religion and conversation, and be diligent
n teaching and bringing up of youth ; whether they be examined, allowed,
nd licenced by the ordinary or his officers in that behalf ; whether they teach
he grammar set forth by King Henry the Eighth of noble memory and none
ther ; whether they teach anything contrary to the order of religion now
established by public authority ; and whether they teach not their scholars
the Catechism in Latin lately set forth, and such sentences of Scripture as
shall be most expedient and meet to move them to the love and due obedience
and reverence of God's true religion now truly set forth by the Queen's
majesty's authority, and to move them to all godliness, and other honest
conversation ; and what be the names and surnames of all such schoolmasters
and teachers of youth within your parish, as well as of such as teach publicly
as those that teach in the houses of noblemen, gentlemen, or other private
men ? " [2]

These episcopal Injunctions are also a faithful record of the local cam-
paigns against the old beliefs and rites—the destruction of the altars, for
example — and of the effort to provide that the very memory of them, and of
what they stood for, shall be erased. The intention behind such a demand
as this, of Archbishop Sandys, is unmistakable—and it is a demand often
repeated elsewhere, and verbatim, in these documents : " Whether in your
churches and chapels all altars be utterly taken down and clean removed even
unto the foundation, and the place where they stood paved, and the wall
whereunto they joined whited over and made uniform with the rest, so as no

---

[1] *E.E.A.*, II, p. 17, nos. 26–28.   [2] *Ibid.*, III, 156–157.

breach or rupture appear ; and whether your rood-lofts be taken down and altered so that the upper parts thereof, with soller or loft, be quite taken down to the cross-beam, and that the same beam have some convenient crest put upon the same ? " [1] And Archbishop Grindal adds the command that when an altar is thus taken down, the consecrated altar stone upon which the Mass has been offered is to " be broken, defaced and put to some common use "— Grindal, who said, apologetically, to the Puritans he was trying, " I have said Mass : I am sorry for it ". In place of altars there are to be placed in the churches wooden tables, which, the bishops specify, are to be " erected upon a frame "—for there were places where, at the Communion Service, the holy table was no more than a board upon trestles. This was carrying things too far. And while the table was to be covered with a linen cloth on days when the sacrament was administered from it, on all days it was to be covered with a cloth of buckram or silk. But it was not to be " decked " as though it were an altar.

Another matter which everlastingly occupies the vigilant bishops is the conduct of the parishioners during the divine service. The Bishop of Coventry and Lichfield, in 1564, in order to secure attendance at church on Sundays, and due order there, prescribes that in every parish, " eight, six or four " of the best and wealthiest parishioners are to be chosen, who, " having white rods in their hands ", shall police the church during the service, and " shall lead . . . up unto the chancel door " disturbers who disregard their monitions, " and set them with their faces looking down towards the people for the space of one quarter of an hour ". These same worthies shall also, during service time, make the round of the alehouses, and all whom they find tippling, they shall bring to church and set at the chancel door " as is aforesaid ".[2]

And while all this care needs to be taken in order to secure that the parishioners pay the new rite at least the elementary courtesy of allowing it to proceed without interruption, the hunt for the remnants of the old liturgy is ceaselessly pursued. As late as 1590 the Archbishop of York is still asking throughout his province, " Whether all and every antiphoner, massbook, grail, portess (i.e. breviary), processional, manual, legendary, with all other books belonging heretofore to your church or chapel and which served for the superstitious popish service be defaced, abolished, and utterly gone ; and if not, then where and with whom are they? Whether all crosses, vestments, albs, tunicles, stoles, fanons (i.e. amices), pixes, handbells, sacring bells, censers, chrismatories, crosses, candlesticks, holy water stocks, images, beads, and such like relics of popish superstition and idolatry be utterly defaced, broken and destroyed ; and if not, where and in whose custody they remain ? " [3] And

---

[1] Metropolitan Visitation of the Province of York, 1578 ; *E.E.A.*, II, pp. 98–99, no. 31 ; the regulation here brought to the churchwardens' notice goes back to Grindal's visitation of the province in 1571 (F. & K., III, 253 ff.). Sandys' question is repeated at Chester (1581), Coventry and Lichfield (1584), Chichester (1586), and Hereford (1586) ; *E.E.A.*, II, iii ; III, 162, 210, 227.

[2] Dixon, VI, 77–81, gives the full text of these Injunctions.

[3] *E.E.A.*, III, p. 261, nos. 22, 23.

even years later than this, Bancroft, in London, is enquiring " Whether ere be any in your parish who are noted, known, or suspected to conceal keep hidden in their houses any mass-books, portesses, breviaries, or her books of popery or superstition, or any chalices, copes, vestments, albs, any other ornaments of superstition, uncancelled or defaced, which it is be conjectured they do keep for a day, as they call it ".[1]

There are other books, too, which the bishops seek out and destroy—the ntroversial writings from the exiles beyond the seas, whom, in these visita- ons, the bishops are careful to name, as Archbishop Sandys, for the province York, in 1578, asking " Whether there be any person or persons ecclesias- cal or temporal within your parish or elsewhere within this diocese that of te hath retained, or kept in their custody, or that read, sell, utter, dispose, rry or deliver to others any English books set forth of late years at Louvain in any other place beyond the seas by Harding, Dorman, Allen, Sanders, tapleton, Marshal, Bristow or any of them, or by any other English papist, ther against the Queen's Majesty's supremacy in matters ecclesiastical, or ainst true religion and catholic doctrine, now received and established y common authority within this realm ; and what their names and surnames e ? "[2]

Were these episcopal visitations, which took place every three years, alities ? or mere formalities where prelates or their officials asked routine uestions, careless how they were answered so long as the visitation dues ere paid ? Dr. Kennedy, an authority certainly, does not ignore the ossibility that with certain bishops the visitations may easily have een no more than a means of collecting money ; but, while a general nswer is not yet possible, what evidence is available leads him to believe hat on the whole the visitations were carried out " with something like fficiency ".[3]

When the churchwardens " presented " their prey to the bishop's official t a visitation, they set in motion all the ancient ecclesiastical procedure hat came down from the days of the great papal canonists of the early Middle Ages, the procedure of interrogation by the oath *ex officio*, for example, nd the accused clearing himself by the sworn oath of half a dozen neighbours hat they believed in his innocence (compurgation, it was called) ; and for hose who failed to prove their innocence there awaited the penalty of ex- ommunication, a penalty that might entail imprisonment and which, n its more serious forms, deprived a man of the right to sue (though he could till be sued—and could be fined for not going to the services which the ery excommunication forbade him to attend). " The arm was long, the ield wide, the machinery complicated and the toils hard to escape. . . . And nce it had been put in motion, he was a foolish layman who did not seek o extricate himself with all the speed available "[4]—especially in the last years f the reign, when the Court of High Commission had made all this a dread eality indeed.

---

[1] *E.E.A.*, III, p. 346, no. 7.   [2] *Ibid.*, II, 99, no. 34.
[3] *Ibid.*, I, p. cxxxi.   [4] *Ibid.*, I, p. cxxvi.

Whatever we may think of the zeal of the new bishops,[1] and whatever our judgment of the spiritual value of their version of the religion of the New Testament, it seems beyond all doubt that almost nowhere were their efforts received with any general enthusiasm ; that everywhere they had, rather, to contend with opposition, active and passive ;[2] and that, after a quarter of a century, with all the force of the Elizabethan state behind their effort, with the prestige of court fashion in support of it, and the general acquiescence of the moneyed class, the Reformers were still very far from their goal, the conversion of the English into " good and devout gospellers ". Such, at any rate, is the impression left by a consideration of the correspondence between the central government and the various bishops who were in part its agents, in part its professional expert advisers in the enterprise. Here, with as little comment as may be, are some of their experiences.[3]

" I am grown into such displeasure with them ", says Elizabeth's first Bishop of Durham of his subjects, " part for religion and part for ministering the oath of the Queen's Superiority, that I know not whether they like me worse or I them. . . ."[4] His successor, seventeen years later, speaks of " these stubborn, churlish people of the county of Durham and their neighbours of Richmondshire . . . as hard, stubborn and rebellious as ever they were." And of Northumberland this bishop is highly suspicious, " so humble obedience and conformity . . . as (truly and before God) I think better and more plausible cannot be found (saltem ad oculum) . . . I have an external show of some dutiful obedience ".[5]

In the diocese of Carlisle the clergy—the clergy who have conformed, that is to say—" . . . are wicked imps of antichrist ", says the queen's new bishop, " and for the most part very ignorant and stubborn, past measure false and subtle ; only fear maketh them obedient ".[6] Six months later he writes that, " Every day men look for a change and prepare for the same. The people desirous of the same do in manner openly say and do what they will concerning religion and other matters right perilous, without check or punishment. The rulers and the Justices of the Peace wink at all things and look through the fingers." The bishop has had " privy displeasure " for his efforts against those who would not take the Oath of Supremacy.[7] Ten

---

[1] " There has been a tendency to believe that the Elizabethan bishops were slack in administration, and this tradition has passed somewhat into the history of the period. On a review of all the evidence here presented the impression is left that they were very busy. Kennedy, E.E.A., p. xxv.

[2] How does the enthusiasm for (or opposition to) the restoration of the Prayer Book of 1552 in the years following 1559 compare with the opposition to (or enthusiasm for) the restoration of the Mass in 1553 ? How does the proportion of those who, after subscribing to the settlement of 1559, did their best to evade the use of the Prayer Book, compare with the proportion of those who, reconciled under Mary, secretly clung to the Prayer Book ?

[3] For all this see Birt, op. cit., pp. 297–474, The Task of the Elizabethan Bishops, illustrated with a wealth of citation from papers still unprinted, from which much has here been borrowed. Since Birt's work is not easily come by, his references are copied here.

[4] Nov. 14, 1561, James Pilkington to Cecil ; Birt, 309 ; from P.R.O., Eliz., XX, no. 5.

[5] Feb. 11, 1578, Barnes to Cecil ; ibid., 301–310 ; Brit. Mus., Lansdowne, 25, no. 78.

[6] July 19, 1561, Best to Cecil ; ibid., 311 ; from P.R.O., Eliz., XVIII, no. 21.

[7] Jan. 14, 1562, to the same ; ibid., from P.R.O., Eliz., XXI, no. 13.

ars after the great change the story is still the same, " many hollow hearts
our people here touching their obedience unto the Queen's Highness and
t a small number (in mine opinion) of just and true servitors in these
rts ".[1]

When Grindal, himself a north countryman, arrived in York as the second
chbishop of the new line, in 1570, he had to report that, after ten un-
terrupted years of the new régime, and on the morrow of the ferocious
nishment of the Rising of the North, the official opinion was that " the
eatest part of our gentlemen are not well affected to godly religion, and
at amongst the people there are many remanents (sic!) of the old super-
tions . . . so as this seemeth to be, as it were, another Church, rather than
member of the rest ".[2] And when, after another six years, Grindal had
t York for Canterbury the Earl of Huntingdon who, in the queen's name,
led as Lord President of the Council for the North, considered that the
obstinacy of many doth shrewdly increase . . . their number is great ".[3]

Grindal was followed at York by Edwin Sandys who had already succeeded
m at London ; and Sandys, about to begin a personal visitation of the arch-
ocese was very well aware of what he was likely to meet. Offenders—
fending Catholics—he wrote to the queen's council (October 28, 1577),
are too many, whose intolerable insolency, perverse and contemptuous
sobedience is with speed to be repressed, or else hardly the State can stand
quiet safety . . . a more stiff-necked, wilful or obstinate people did I
ever know or hear of. Doubtless they are reconciled to Rome and sworn
the Pope. They will abide no conference, neither give ear to any doctrine
persuasion. . . . To some I have offered lodging and diet in my house,
at I might have conference with them for their conformity, but they choose
ther to go to prison." [4]

Bishop Bentham, of Coventry and Lichfield, asking in 1564 for the
moval from Staffordshire of David Poole, the deprived Catholic Bishop of
eterborough, wrote to the council that " the country is too much hinderly
all good things pertaining to religion ".[5] Fourteen years later, keen to
unt down recusants of wealth for the council, Bentham found it hard to get
e information he needed, " for that I can find few trusty to deal with and
wer willing to utter what they know " [6]—these midland counties being, in
ct, what the bishop's successor, William Overton, described them just
ree years after this, " the stubbornest diocese in all this land " : [7] and
verton had come from Chichester ! [8]

Oxford was a town as notoriously Catholic as any part of Lancashire,
nd when the mayor, in 1561, told the council that there were " not three

---

[1] Jan. 20, 1570, Best to Cecil ; Birt, 313 ; from P.R.O., Eliz., XVII, no. 36.
[2] Aug. 29, 1570, to Cecil ; ibid., 326 ; from P.R.O., Eliz., LXXIII, no. 35.
[3] Sept. 12, 1576, to the same ; ibid., 334 ; from Brit. Mus., Harleian, 6992, n. 26.
[4] Birt, 334-335, from P.R.O., Eliz., CXVII, no. 23.
[5] Birt, 395, from Camden Soc., Miscellany, IX, 39-47.
[6] Feb. 1, 1578, Birt, 400-401, from P.R.O., Eliz., CXXII, no. 28.
[7] June 11, 1581, to Walsingham ; ibid., 401, from P.R.O., Eliz., CXLIX no. 37.
[8] For Chichester, cf. infra, pp. 128-130.

houses in it wherein there were not papists ", he was ordered not to spread th
information further.[1]   Things were not greatly changed when, sixteen yea
later than this, the Dean, excusing gaps in his report to Grindal, spoke
" the lothness of many to utter their knowledge ", and reported there we
many more Recusants (i.e. exclusive of those in the university) than he cou
bring people to inform on.[2]

No less of a Catholic stronghold, in the opening years of the reign, w:
the cathedral city of Hereford and all the hinterland which it influence
Of the whole city council, so the new bishop, John Scory, wrote to tl
council in 1564, there is " not one favourable to this religion ".[3]   At Ludlo
all the town was hostile except six " favourers ".   Priests were receive
favourably in the cathedral city by the great, and especially by William Luso:
a canon residentiary and by the vicars of the choir, all but one of whom a
Catholics, " And of these there be certain who have mass in their houses . . .'
Eleven years later, Scory was still complaining of his " purgatory " ; [4] an
when, in 1577, he ventured to denounce some local Catholics as recusants, l
begged the council to conceal his own share in the proceedings, so muc
reason had he to expect reprisals, the Catholics being still so powerful
The account of Hereford in the first years of Scory's episcopate, as this e:
Dominican gives it, is very striking.   These canons, all but one of whom a
Catholics, and some of whom have Mass in their houses, " come seldom c
not at all to church, which never received the Communion since the Queen
Majesty's reign openly in the church. . . . The Communion was n(
ministered in the Cathedral Church since Easter [it is now October].   Th
canons will neither preach, read homilies, nor minister the hol
Communion, nor do any other thing to commend, beautify or set forwar(
this religion, but mutter against it, receive and maintain the enemies c
religion ",[6] " looking upon such," the bishop writes to Parker, " as if the
are God's angels".[7]

That the " backward " north, and the distant Welsh borders should be thu
" conservative " has never astonished progressive minds.   It is, however, inter
esting to find the same spirit in the south also, in the dioceses of Wincheste
and Chichester.   The first of these did not receive its new bishop, Rober
Horne, for three years yet ; and when, after another year, the late pasto
of Frankfort writes to Cecil, he has to say that he has not so far been abl
" by any means " to " reduce the inhabitants of the city of Winchester t
good uniformity in religion ", to bring them, for example, to attend th
Common Prayer " (which, so far, has been quite neglected) ; . . . and als
that good and sound doctrine might be taught amongst them, which the
as yet do not so well like and allow ".   The people of Winchester are, in fact

[1] Nov. 15, 1561, Birt, 508, from *Chronicon Belg.*, no. DCCCXXIV, ii, p. 643.
[2] Dec. 3, 1577, *ibid.*, 405, from P.R.O., *Eliz.*, CXIX, no. 5.
[3] See *Camden Misc.*, IX, pp. 11–23, for this report.
[4] June 13, 1575, to Cecil ; Birt, 363, from Brit. Mus., Lansdowne, 20, no. 63.
[5] Nov. 2, 1577, Birt, 369, from P.R.O., *Eliz.*, CXVIII, no. 7.
[6] The report of 1564 in *Camden Misc.*, IX, pp. 11–23.
[7] Feb. 17, 1565, quoted Birt, 368.

THE
SEES OF ENGLAND
AND WALES
AS RE~ARRANGED
IN 1541
AND
1555

THE HEAVY LINE SHOWS THE BOUNDARIES OF THE NEW SEES FOUNDED
BY HENRY VIII IN 1541 AND RECOGNISED BY POPE PAUL IV IN 1555

THE STIPPLE MARKS THE AREA OF THE SEE OF WESTMINSTER, i.e., MIDDLESEX, FOUNDED
BY HENRY VIII IN 1541 AND SUPPRESSED BY EDWARD VI IN 1550

" nursled in superstition and Popery " and some of the " priests in th
Cathedral Church . . . inculcate the same daily into their heads ".   Th
citizens of the ancient capital are, indeed, " very stubborn," and a forc
that is keeping the county Catholic.   Behind them, apparently, is th
influence of local grandees, who " hinder as much as they can " the " prc
ceedings in religion "—magnates who have never once received the Com
munion since Mass was forbidden, nearly three years ago now.[1]

Chichester meant, then as now, the county of Sussex ; and its bishoj
the hoary William Barlow, wrote to the council that it is only " fear c
Your Lordships' vigilant authority " that preserves Sussex from the " ope
violence " of the Catholic opposition.   He had not dared to take into hi
confidence any but the Dean of Salisbury and his own chancellor, so doubtfi
is he of the " secretness " of others, " that retinue and alliance being s
great in these parts ".[2]

All this is direct testimony, from the new bishops, about the apathy, an
the hostility, to the " settlement " of religion in more than one part of th
country.   And this apathy and hostility persists, seemingly, in many place
for a good twenty years and more.   The evidence quoted can be supplemente
by what the bishops write, reminiscently, after years of work done in th
various sees.

Sandys, for example, when Bishop of London, and after fourteen year
as a bishop, takes a very low view of the prestige of the new bench in th
country, when he writes to Cecil and Leicester, " Yea, if all of my callin
were joined together we are too weak, our estimation is little, our authorit
is less, so that we are become contemptible in the eyes of the basest sort o
people ".[3]

Lancashire was within the jurisdiction of the indolent Bishop of Chestei
William Downham.   His more active episcopal neighbours kept the govern
ment informed however—and at times stirred up the government to forc
Downham into action.   " It is too lamentable ", Pilkington of Durhar
wrote to Parker, in 1564, of the Lancashire clergy who had conformed
" to see and hear how negligently they say any service there, and how seldom."
Six years later than this, the newly appointed Bishop of Carlisle wrote tha
in Lancashire " . . . on all hands the people fall from religion, revolt t
Popery, refuse to come at Church ; the wicked popish priests reconcile then
to the Church of Rome, and cause them to abjure this (Christ's religion)
and that openly and unchecked ".[5]   And twenty years later than this, th

[1] Horne to Cecil, Jan. 12, 1562, quoted Birt, 416, from P.R.O., *Eliz.*, XIX, 36.
[2] In 1564 ; the letter is in *Camden Misc.* IX, 8–11.   A tenth diocese where, in 155
there is some evidence of strong Catholic feeling was Canterbury where, in the last Corpu
Christi procession held in the Cathedral city, on Sunday, May 28—three weeks after the fat
day of the Royal Assent to the Act that abolished the Mass, and four weeks from the day whe
the Act would come into force—" 3000 people and many persons of worth of the countr
side took part ".   May 30, 1559, the Spanish Ambassador (Quadra) to Philip II, in Bir
505, from *Collection de Chroniques Belges inédites*, no. CCCLIII, i, p. 530.
[3] Aug. 5, 1573, in Birt, 460, from Brit. Mus., Lansdowne, 17, no. 43.
[4] Parker Corres., p. 221.
[5] Oct. 27, 1570, Barnes to Cecil, in Birt, 314, from P.R.O., *Eliz.*, LXXIV, 22.   Barne

tuation had not greatly changed. " The county is mightily infected with
opery : the number of Justices of the Peace which in that country are but
w that take any care in the reformation thereof ; the wives, children and
rvants of some Justices of the Peace . . . are notable recusants ; . . .
oo persons at the last assize . . . stand indicted upon the statute of re-
usants. . . ." [1]

Of the 150 cures in the archdeaconry of Stafford, barely five are, after
venty-five years of the régime, " furnished with a tolerable preacher :
ie country otherwise being so dangerous and superstitious " ; so the
shop of this diocese, Coventry and Lichfield, writes to Walsingham,[2]
id in the general visitation held this year he is still enquiring whether the
ministers be known or suspected as favourers of the Romish Church,
uperiority or religion ", and whether there are " any sometime in Orders,
iat now do live as laymen ? " [3]   This was in 1584 ; and so little seemed to
ive been achieved, only seven years before, in these regions, that the Bishop
London, John Aylmer, was then suggesting to Burghley that the four most
otorious leaders of the section now beginning to be known as Puritans,
amely, William Charke, Edmund Chapman, John Field, and Thomas
Vilcox, might be sent as missionaries into Lancashire, Staffordshire and
hropshire " and such like other barbarous counties to draw the people from
apism and gross ignorance ". If their zeal produced a Protestantism
iore radical than what the government liked, " it would be less labour ",
the bishop thought, " to draw [the converts] back than it is now to hale
iem forward ".[4]

The story is much the same, for these early years, in the counties to the
uth of Shropshire. From Worcester, for example, Sandys, its first
lizabethan bishop, when about to be translated to London after an episcopate
f ten years in the west, writes to Cecil, " I have here long laboured to gain
ood will, the fruits of my travail are counterfeited countenances and hollow
earts . . . hard it is to find one faithful . . . Religion is liked as it may
rve their own turn :" and of the ruling class, ". . . not one that is earnest
id constant. . . . More give their hands than their hearts ".[5]   And in the
isitation which he made in this same year, 1569, Sandys still found it necessary
ask the parishioners whether " your minister " is privately " an hinderer "
f " true religion ".[6]

In Oxford too—not only in the city, or the university, but throughout
ie diocese—Catholics hostile to the régime continued to be numerous,
ven among the well-to-do ; and, as late as 1577, Archbishop Grindal wrote

---

id been Bishop of Nottingham, suffragan (i.e. auxiliary) to the Archbishop of York, from
;67. In 1570 he was a man thirty-eight years old.
[1] 1590 (Feb.) : " An Information touching the Recusants of Lancashire ", Brit. Mus.,
otton, Titus, B III, no. 20, quoted Birt, 319.
[2] July 19, 1584, Brit. Mus. Egerton MS., 1693, fo. 118, quoted Birt, 401.
[3] Birt ; from Second Report of the Ritual Commission of 1868, p. 428.
[4] June 27, 1577, Birt, 466, from Brit. Mus., Lansdowne, 25, no. 30.
[5] Dec. 12, 1569, Birt, 358–359, from Lansdowne, 11, no. 70.
[6] Lansdowne, 11, no. 94 and no. 95, quoted—at length—Birt, 359–361.

to the dean and chapter of the ever vacant see, " I am informed, that the di
cese of Oxford is more replenished with such recusants, for the quanti
thereof, than any other diocese of this realm ".[1]

Hampshire, after twenty-five years, also continued to be actively hostile
and Thomas Cooper, translated to Winchester in 1584 from Lincoln, no
thoroughly evangelised,[2] complains about the boldness of the Recusants a
that, at Easter last, they managed to bring it about that 500 more refused
communicate.[3]   There were, indeed, more convicted recusants in th
county than anywhere in England outside of Yorkshire and Lancashire ; a
the Justices, in 1583, had denounced to the council, Catholics who " bold
affirmed that it is necessary to have Mass and they hope to hear it, and th
had rather hear bear-baiting than divine service ".[4]

As to the neighbouring county of Sussex—a centre of devotion to t
new doctrines, if the comparative statistics of executions for heresy a
proof of this [5]—an interesting picture survives of the almost nothing th
was the fruit of William Barlow's nine years' episcopate, 1559–1568.[6]   T
county and the diocese of Chichester were all but conterminous, and
the diocese there were some 278 parishes, in 1536.   The report says th
in " many " of these churches there has been no sermon for seven yea
in " some " not for twelve years—i.e. since the introduction of the ne
services in 1559 ; this on the evidence of preachers lately sent to the
places.   " Few " churches again, have the quarterly sermons imposed
the queen's *Injunctions*.   Preachers are " very few ", and a list of sevente
is given, three only of whom are beneficed.   Another six are named wh
" preached in Queen Mary's days but do not now, nor will not, and y
retain their livings."   In the twenty parishes that belong to the jurisdicti
of the see of Canterbury there are, however, six preachers.   " In t
Cathedral Church of Chichester there be very few preachers resident,
31 prebendaries scarcely 4 or 5 ", who are named ; " The other some
laymen, some no preachers, and some few absent."

In Chichester itself, to turn to the laity, " few of the aldermen be of
good religion, but are vehemently suspected to favour the Pope's doctrin
and yet they be justices of [the] peace ".   The names are given of half
dozen leading families who " come not at their parish churches nor recei
the holy communion at Easter ".   These well-circumstanced personage

---

[1] Grindal, *Remains* (Parker Society), p. 362, quoted Birt, 403.

[2] So Birt, 394 : " Evidence, then, so far as it exists, would prove that Lincolnshi
had practically ceased to be Catholic ".   For what such " evangelisation " amounted
see *infra*, pp. 137–140.   [3] Birt, 423.

[4] *Ibid.*, from Brit. Mus., Cotton, Titus, B III, no. 29, fo. 73.

[5] At Lewes, Mayfield, East Grinstead and Steyning, a total of 27 convicted heretics we
burned in Mary's reign, 1555–1558.

[6] *Disorders in the Diocese of Chichester contrary to the Queen's Majesty's Injunctio*
P.R.O., S.P. 12, vol. 60, no. 71 (1568).

[7] This last is evidence that, however opposed the queen might show herself to attemp
to compel the English to receive Communion in the new rite, by Act of Parliament, s
was not thereby hindering the inquisition into men's consciences from which, as is sai
this opposition proves she consistently shrank.   From the beginning of her reign un
the end the queen's ecclesiastical law laid the layman open to this particular inquisitio

Easter approaches, " get them out of the country until the Feast be past
and return not again until then ". Again, " Many gentlemen receive the
communion at home in their chapels at Easter times, and then they choose
into them a priest for the purpose to minister unto them there, fetched a
good way off, and do not take their own minister of their parish church,
or receive not three times in the year in their own parish churches, as by
the law they should do . . .".

The report is concerned with " disorders " only. It gives no material
by which we can set off, against these, the spiritual gains of the new regime.
One " disorder ", unmistakably, that causes annoyance is the strong affection for the old that still survives. " In some places the roodlofts do yet
stand, though they were commanded to be taken down, and the timber of
them that be taken down lieth still in many churches ready to be set up
again." Likewise, " In many places ", there are " images hidden and
other popish ornaments ready to set up the mass again within twenty-four
hours warning." And " because the rood was taken away " the parishioners
in some places . . . painted there in that place a cross with chalk, and
because that was washed away with painting, and the number of crosses
standing at graves in the churchyard taken also away, since they have made
crosses upon the church walls within and without, and upon the pulpit
and communion table, in despite of the preachers, and this was done of
very late in Patching since I preached last there, as these can witness ",
and the names follow. And " In many places they keep yet still their chalices
looking for to have mass again ", preferring, so the report avers, to burden
the parish with the cost of buying the new communion cups now commanded, rather than have the old chalices melted down for this purpose
hoping for a day for the use of the same, and some parishes feign that
their chalices were stolen away and therefore they ministered in glasses and
profane Goblets ".

The Communion is a more serious test than the mere presence during
Morning Prayer. The Catholic-at-heart conformist will seek all means
to disqualify himself from so definitive an apostasy : " In many places the
people cannot say the commandments, and some not the articles of their
belief, when they be examined before they come to the Communion and
yet they be of the age of 40 and 50 years some of them as the last Easter
was tried. The ministers there for the most part are very simple." And
these ministers who almost never preach in years and years, " in most places
of the diocese do not use to read the Declaration of certain principal articles
of religion set forth for testimony of unity in doctrine, and appointed to
be read twice in the year . . .".

One single phrase of the report resumes the whole, " Except it be about
Lewes, and a little in Chichester, the whole diocese of Chichester is very
blind and superstitious . . .". And as one of the dignitaries commended
in the report for his zeal as a preacher, Dr. William Overton, the bishop's

---

and to penalties for his failure to receive. The parliamentarians were not introducing a
new liability but merely improving the machinery of the persecution.

9

chancellor, wrote to Cecil about this very time, *Undique enim apud nos Papistarum et Papismatis plena fere sunt omnia*.[1] It is not in the attachmen of these Papists to Spain, nor in their political activities ; not in their plots actual or imagined, against the " state "—to wit, the party in power—or against the life of the queen, that the anxiety of the government lies : but in the fact of their attachment to the ancient beliefs about grace and the sacraments and the way appointed by God for the salvation of a Christian man's soul.

John Aylmer, Elizabeth's third Bishop of London, found north-east Essex—of all places—still troublesome, where there were " divers bold and riotous assemblies of divers Papists at Colchester and there near about . . . by 20 and 30 at a time . . . Mass said commonly ".[2]

In the difficult task of estimating the effect of a revolution of this kind on the ordinary man, such chance remarks and generalisations of the all-important officials in their correspondence with the queen's first minister, the head of all her administration, are perhaps more useful, in the present state of our knowledge of Elizabethan administration, than the mere presentation of the statistics of recusants convicted during these years or than conclusions drawn from hypothetical calculations based on these—as yet —scarcely studied puzzles !

And over it all there still hangs the query, what exactly was the conformity worth of the generality of those who, under pressure of one kind or another, gradually ceased in these twenty years [3] to resist ? As these twenty years draw to their conclusion, the new, missionary priests are beginning to arrive from Douay and from Rome. We shall, presently, be listening to what they have to tell about religion in England. Meanwhile when Edmund Scambler, Bishop of Peterborough, sent into the council in 1577 his list—a very short list indeed—of those known as refusing to attend church, he warned the council not to misinterpret it as a proof of general real conformity, " But if you had charged me *or any other bishop in this realm* . . .[4] to certify you of those that refuse to receive the communion, you should have had a larger certificate of persons dangerous in mine opinion to be unknown to your honours ".[5] This was in 1577, and from Northamptonshire.

Five years before this an anonymous report estimated the " good and devout Gospellers " as less than one in forty of the population, outside London.[6] " Good and devout Gospellers "—to turn the average English-man into such was surely the whole purpose of the Reform. For what other reason was Catholicism banned, except that it was the fatal hindrance to true

---

[1] Aug. 14, 1568. " Almost all places in our part of the world are full of Papists and Popishness ", Birt, 427, from P.R.O., *Eliz.*, XLVII, no. 40.

[2] June, 27, 1577, Birt, 466, from P.R.O., *Eliz.*, CXX, nos. 26, 27.   [3] 1559–80.

[4] Italics mine.   [5] Oct. 26, 1577, Birt, 386, from P.R.O., *Eliz.*, CXVII, no. 16.

[6] " It is terrible to consider that not every fortieth person in England is a good and devout Gospeller (unless it be in London) ". Birt, 435, from Brit. Mus., Lansdowne, 109, no. 31. This is not very far from Sander's estimate of 1561, that the heretics were only 1 per cent. of the population—and the reverse of a judgment now fashionable that not more than 3 per cent. were Catholics. For Sander, cf. *supra*, pp. 49-50.

evangelical godliness ? And until the Reform had made the mass of the English " good and devout Gospellers " it had hardly succeeded. Bishops and council alike were troubled that progress was so slow ; and opinion in these circles was divided about policy. Scambler supported the original plan to be content with non-resistance : " If a man may be won, great haste is not to be required ; if a man in recanting . . . profess at the first no more than he is fully persuaded in . . . he is liker to prove a good member of Christ's Church than some other that speak otherwise and better to please in haste." [1]

Horne, of Winchester, however, ruling a diocese more Catholic than was Scambler's, was for severity : " What troubles and charges overmuch forbearing of the Papists hath wrought, is manifest . . . and will bring forth hereafter a more grievous effect." [2] And Grindal, from York, where the Catholic prisoners are begging to be released, was of the same mind : " If such a general *jubilee* should be put in use in these parts, a great relapse would follow soon after." [3]

The Bishop of Winchester went on to suggest that the local justices should be more carefully chosen and supervised, and to say that that there was " little hope . . . unless the courts were reformed, which I look not for ". This was in 1570. In 1564 Sandys, from Worcester, had discerned the same weakness ; and his suggestions reveal, yet once again, how reluctant the government had been in these early years to administer the new Oath of Supremacy to those indispensable agents the Justices. For the bishop would now have " the oath for the Queen's Majesty's Supremacy . . . tendered to all such as bear rule or be of authority in their country yet known to be adversaries to true religion ". And he would have " gentlemen and such as be in authority . . . enjoined every quarter to receive the Communion and to hear a sermon ".[4] Scambler, too, in that same year, 1564, gave it as his advice that the Act of Supremacy should really be enforced—

[1] Mar. 27, 1575, to Cecil ; Birt, 299, from Brit. Mus., Lansdowne, 21, no. 2.
[2] Jan. 2, 1570, to the same ; *ibid.*, 419, from Lansdowne, 12, no. 27.
[3] Nov. 13, 1574, to the same ; *ibid.*, 330. Grindal's *Remains*, p. 350.
[4] *Camden Miscellany*, IX, 1–8. The oath was never tendered to the justices in Durham and Northumberland until the summer of 1561 (Bishop Pilkington to Cecil in Birt, 305 from P.R.O., *Eliz.*, XXI, no. 27). In York the justices then objected that " no such thing was] required or given before " ; and Archbishop Young's comment to Cecil was " there hath been some sinister practices touching that oath heretofore, and some men think that . . . the fault was in the Justices of the circuit ". From Durham the bishop also notified Cecil that Catholics were the bolder since they saw no punishment inflicted on those in authority who " refuse to acknowledge their due allegiance " (Nov. 11, 1561, Birt, 307). Sandys is evidence for a like state of things in Worcester in 1564. In Sussex, in November 1570, " very many, under one pretext or another had managed not to take it " ; and a letter of March 24, 1577, from Barlow's successor at Chichester, Richard Curteis, reveals also how far from absolute reliability the official returns can be, when, asking Walsingham to arrange that justices who are " backward in religion " should be dismissed or the oath tendered to them, the bishop goes on to say, " for it is commonly and credibly thought that some of them never took the oath although it be otherwise returned ". (*Ibid.*, 430 ; P.R.O., *Eliz.*, CXI, no. 45.) Then, in 1578, we have a complaint from the queen herself. During a progress, the council writes to the Bishop of London, Elizabeth was annoyed to discover that, in various counties, there are justices who " have of late years forborne to come to the church to any Common Prayer and divine service " which the queen notes as contrary to law and a bad example " to the common sort of people ". (*Ibid.*, 522, P.R.O., *Eliz.*, XLV, no. 16.)

that it should be offered to " the straggling doctors and priests who have liberty to stray at their pleasures within this realm [and] do much hurt secretly ", and that all cathedral clergy should be compelled to a manifest declaration of their faith. Also he proposed that, in the first place, " the learned adversaries, being ecclesiastical persons . . . be either banished or sequestered from conference with such as be fautors of their religion, or else the oath to be tendered unto them ".[1] Aylmer of London, in 1577, took up Sandys' idea of compulsory communion as a test. The bishops were agreed on this, and in their name he proposed that " round fines be imposed ", at the bishop's discretion, on non-communicants—something vastly more remunerative to the queen, he suggested, and more painful to the victims, than the beggarly shilling a time for absence from church.[2]

[1] *Camden Miscellany*, IX, 34–37.
[2] June 21, 1577, to Walsingham ; Birt, 464, from P.R.O., *Eliz.*, CXLV, no. 22.

Chapter V

DIFFICULTIES FROM WITHIN

I. AN INSUFFICIENT MINISTRY

THE new bishops were seriously hampered in their task by conditions within the very ranks of the reformed.[1] They had far too few auxiliaries of any real worth in their task of winning over to Protestantism this people that was so indifferent where it was not actually hostile. Next, some of the keenest of these auxiliaries greatly disliked the new official setting in which " true religion " had been established ; and from the very first meeting of Convocation under the new dispensation, in 1563, there was open war between them and those of the brethren whom Cecil had recently persuaded to accept appointment as bishops.

But, from the very beginning, the most acute anxiety of all was where to find clergy willing and able to expound the new message of liberation.[2] In the 9,000[3] or so livings of the *ecclesia anglicana* there were, apparently, something like 7,000 ordained clergy in 1559. From the language which the Reformers used about these, alike in their sermons and in their private correspondence, it is evident that almost the whole body of the clergy who had conformed were, in their eyes, matter rather for conversion themselves, than apostles long restrained, now released, at last, to pursue their true vocation.[4] " We are labouring under a great dearth of godly ministers ",

---

[1] " The new bishops entered upon a task of inconceivable difficulty " ; Kennedy, *Interpretations*, 14. He is writing of the year 1560—and if the Creighton view is right (*supra*, p. 48), and if " Puritanism " is a reaction that the bishops themselves provoke, in that lay the " inconceivable difficulty " of their task in 1560 ?

[2] " The Bishops however soon [i.e. soon after 1562] radically changed their minds, for they found that most of their assumptions were without basis. . . . It became almost immediately evident that they had miscalculated the number of clergy sufficiently learned to weigh the Scriptures as the ordination vow required. Then was borne upon them, with crushing weight, the fact that the great mass of the people . . . clung to the past . . . [The Bishops] began ardently to desire the firm settlement of the new church. . . . They came face to face with the facts, that the learned differed widely upon the form of the new Church, that the people cared little . . . so long as they paid neither fines nor tithes . . . that the Queen was determined, from political reasons, that no such definition of the Church position as the Bishops desiderated] should be promulgated." Usher, *Reconstruction*, I, 202.

[3] A list, in Cecil's own handwriting, which he states to be " extracted out of the Queen's Majesty's records of the First Fruits and Tenths ", gives the number of parishes as 8731 ; so Birt, 414, referring to Brit. Mus., Old Royal MS., 18, D 111, fo. 3.

[4] " . . . most of them are popish priests, consecrated to perform mass ; and the far greater part of the remainder are most ignorant persons, appointed . . . not to the ministry of the word, but to repeat the office of the day or festivals, which almost any child might do without difficulty " ; George Withers to the Elector Palatine, *Z.L.*, 304.

" . . . not only [are] the papists left in possession of the revenues of their benefices, but even of their ecclesiastical offices, upon merely taking an oath to maintain the reformation ;

Grindal wrote in May 1559 to his erstwhile host of Strasburg
Conrad Hubert.[1] Lever thought that no more than one in a hundred—
seventy or so in all England—of the clergy who had conformed to the
Supremacy were both able and willing to preach.[2] Jewel describes the scarcity
as " great and alarming ". " The schools also are *entirely deserted*",
he said, " so that, unless God look favourably upon us, we cannot hope
for any supply in future. The existing preachers, who are few in number
those especially who have any ability, are listened to by the people with
favour and attention." [4] In sermon after sermon, preached before the
queen, Jewel, driving home the truth that without preachers the new faith
must disappear, hints at an extraordinary spiritual dereliction amid the
steadily reviving commercial prosperity. " O lift up your eyes, and consider
how the hearts of your poor brethren lie waste without instruction, without
knowledge, without the food of life, without the comfort of God's word
such a misery as never was seen among heathens. The Turks have teachers
sufficient for their people : the Jews . . . ; the Christians which this day
live in India, Aethiopia, Barbary . . . ; the Christians in old time, when they
lived under tyrants, and were daily put to most shameful death. . . . It
is therefore most lamentable, that Christians, living under a Christian prince
in the peace and liberty of the gospel, should lack learned ministers to teach
them and instruct them in the word of God. . . ." [5]

What preachers there were would soon, the bishop thought, disappear,
" . . . unless we show forth greater zeal than hitherto ; if the years to come
eat up and take away from the ministry as the late years have done, there will
not be left within a while any to speak the word of God out of this place. The
pulpits shall have none to use them. . . . For, of the preachers which now
are, within a few years none will remain alive. . . ." [6]

The new clergy, those ordained since the changeover of 1559, were an
ignorant lot ? Jewel did not deny it : " I know that there are grievous
complaints made that the bishops appoint priests and ministers that are
ignorant, and have no understanding in the Latin tongue. Would God it
were not true . . . But alas are we able to make learned men upon the
sudden ? Or can we make others than come unto us, or will come to live
in misery ? " This, evidently, is not a time of any universal enthusiasm for
the re-discovered primitive gospel of Christ. Even in what must have been
the first fervour of the movement, Jewel, a good witness, makes it clear how
unreasonable it was thought, to expect that men with brains should give their
lives to this gospel for the gospel's sake alone. After all, he said, the better

---

so that godly brethren are for the most part placed under the authority, and compelled to
submit to the jurisdiction of those who are, in general, unlearned and in their hearts most
bitter enemies of true religion " ; Beza to Bullinger, Sept. 3, 1566 ; *ibid.*, 247.

[1] May 23, *Z.L.*, p, 45.   [2] July 10, 1560, to Bullinger ; Birt, 109.
[3] Italics mine. Parliament, about this very time, was making the like complaint.
Addressing the queen, on Jan. 19, 1563, the Speaker said, " I dare say a hundred schools
want in England, which afore this time hath been . . . . The Universities are decayed
. . ." quoted in Neale, *Elizabeth I and her Parliaments*, 99.
[4] Nov. 11, 1560, to Peter Martyr, *Z.L.*, 115–116.   [5] Jewel, II, 1021.
[6] Sermon III (before the queen), *ibid.*, 1014.

rains " are weary and discouraged [at the poor prospect], they change their
tudies : some become prentices, some turn to physic, some to law " :
ould any man wonder at this ? [1]   Benefices have been so pillaged that " all
hun and flee the ministry " ; and even " in the properest market towns
enefices are so simple that no man can live upon them, and therefore no
nan will take them. . . . Many here present know I speak the truth.   And
nyself know the places which have continued still these many years without
 minister resident among them, and have provided themselves, as they
night, with their own money." [2]

And if clerical learning is decayed, it should be remembered that, " the
ivings and provisions which heretofore were given to this use are taken
way ".[3]   The chronic medieval abuse that the patronage of livings tended
o fall out of the church's control was now increased far beyond the worst
hat had ever been seen before,[4] and church revenues were openly and un-
shamedly appropriated by the lay patrons for their own use.[5]   When the
governing classes and the king conspired to rob the monasteries and the
chantries and the other pious funds, Jewel might have added, they sowed a
habit of indifference to theft at religion's expense which was to spread, and
o endure.   " The livings of such as are in the ministry are not in their
hands to whom they are due. . . . [Parsonages and vicarages] seldom pass
nowadays from the patron, if he be no better than a gentleman, but either

[1] " The general contempt of the ministry ", Parson Harrison explains in 1577, is one great
hindrance to any schemes to raise the tone of clerical life.   " . . . the greatest part of the
more excellent wits choose rather to employ their studies unto physic and the laws, utterly
giving over the study of the Scriptures, for fear lest they should in time not get their bread
by the same."   Nor has Harrison any hope that there will be any amendment in his
lifetime ; Harrison, 82.   [2] Jewel, II, 1012.   [3] Ibid., 1011
[4] In 1605 the bishops complained that five-sixths of the ecclesiastical patronage was in the
hands of lay patrons (Usher, Reconstruction, I, 95).   Canon Foster has worked out an interesting analysis for the diocese of Lincoln which shows that, at this date, out of 1255
livings whose patrons are known, the right of presentation in all but 212 was in lay hands.
The bishop himself had but 48 livings in his gift, and the dean and chapter 59.   (L.R.S.,
23, p. lvi.)
[5] It is notorious that the lay patrons robbed the livings by simoniacal pacts with the men
they presented ; that they procured the ordination of the most unlikely candidates, to make
this easier ; and that the first fathers in God of the Elizabethan Anglicana ordained such men
by the hundred.   To quote Harrison, once again, religion had to contend with " the covetousness of the patrons, of whom some do bestow advowsons of benefices upon their bakers,
butchers, cooks, good archers, falconers, and housekeepers, instead of other recompense for
their long and faithful service " ; op. cit., 74.   And also, p. 80, defending clerical wives
against the charge that it is they who are responsible for clerical poverty, he makes the same
point :   " Such a threadbare minister is either an ill man or hath an ill patron, or both ; and
when such cooks and cobbling shifters shall be removed and weeded out of the ministry ",
better men will be found.   What brings about the ordination of such clergy is the poverty of
the living, robbed by the lay patron.   It is only worth the while of a workman to take Orders,
as a supplement to what he gains by his craft, " The very cause why weavers, pedlars and
glovers have been made ministers, for the learned refuse such matches, so that if the Bishops
in times past had not made such by oversight friendship I wot not how such men [i.e. patrons]
should have done with their advowsons, as for a glover or a tailor will be glad of an augmenta-
tion of 8 or 10 pound by the year, and well contented that his patron shall have all the rest,
so he may be sure of this pension ".   (Note in the edition of 1577, quoted by Furnivall in
Harrison, 80.)   For Harrison the church, too, is evidently a world where graft reigns supreme,
and where bribes are needed at every step ; ibid., 81.

for the lease or for present money. . . . And this is done, not in one place
or in one country, but throughout England. A gentleman cannot keep his
house unless he have a parsonage or two in farm for his proviso." [1]

The desolation that had been the lot of the universities in the time of
Somerset and Northumberland, ten and fifteen years before, was come again.
" This noble realm, which ever was famous for the name of learning, is like
thereby to come to such ignorance and barbary as hath not been heard of in
any memory before our time ".[2] Jewel could not understand how it had
happened : " . . . if learning decay, it is likely that religion cannot abide.
Bear with me, if I speak that which may seem more fit for some other place
than this audience. . . . In other countries the receiving of the gospel hath
always been cause that learning was more set by ; and learning hath ever been
the furtherance of the gospel. In England, I know not how, it cometh otherwise
to pass. For since the gospel hath been received, the maintenance for
learning hath been decayed." [3] And as though this thought, that the new
religion would never gain the country unless it could make an appeal to
its intelligence, might fail to move the queen and his courtly congregation,
the bishop evoked the judgment of the future : " Chronicles shall report
this contempt of learning among the punishments and murrains and other
plagues of God. They shall leave it written, in what time and under whose
reign this was done. Or if we grow so barbarous that we consider not this,
or be not able to draw it into chronicle ; yet foreign nations will not spare
to write this, and publish it to our everlasting reproach and shame." [4]

This sermon was preached before the Supreme Governor and her court—
that court at whose immoralities the modern historian so often affects
amusement and shrugs his sophisticated shoulders. But for the courtiers,
the most distinguished of the new religion's converts, the preacher has harsh
words indeed, " . . . You still live in your sins ", he says to them, " in
adultery, in covetousness, and in pride, without any feeling of conscience,
without any fear of God. Your daughters, your heirs, to whom you shall
leave your lands, are stolen away from you : robberies and thefts are so
common as if it were not only lawful, but also commendable ; as if sin were
no sin, and hell fire but a fable." [5]

It was, of course, an England wholly secular, so we are often reminded—
an England whose real God was money ; when, beyond what had ever been
known before, there was opportunity for all ; and when the tale was told
everywhere of fabulous wealth to be had for the taking by whoever was bold
enough when the moment came. And in the thirty years between Wolsey
and Elizabeth's accession, what opportunities ! [6] For that society which was
now in process of " conversion " from may be nominal Catholicism to a

---

[1] Sermon III, Jewel, II, 1011–1012.   [2] Ibid., 1012.
[3] Ibid., 1011.   [4] Ibid., 1013.   [5] Ibid.
[6] One such opportunity, now, was piracy. Dasent, in his Introduction to the volume
of the Registers of the Privy Council (vol. VII) that covers the first twelve years of Elizabeth's
reign, says, " It is scarcely an exaggeration to say that, putting out of consideration the
relations between England and Scotland, the keynote to the present volume is piracy ";
note p. xviii,

ess than wholehearted Protestantism—or in process of adapting itself, yet again, to the policies of the state—the fact of that opportunity and of each family's varying luck before the fact, was the great fact of life : the main fact and the chief memory of many and many a lifetime. What religion has ever survived in a milieu where surrender to such temptation has been general ? "More Christians, less Christianity", the caustic St. Jerome had said, twelve hundred years before, observing the effects, upon the fashionable world, of the new imperial patronage of religion. There was an abundance of conversions of the same kind, in the century of the Reformation, wherever this triumphed. And they scandalised mightily the prelates who were at once the fathers in God of the distinguished converts, and their creatures.

"O almighty God, how fares it now with them that would be called Christians, and be reckoned among professors of the gospel ? . . . how many are there that may be known by changing of their manners ?—unless it be for that they make a mockery of God's holy gospel, and so become more dissolute, more fleshly, more wanton than ever they were afore. . . . If our life should give testimony and report of our religion, sorry I am to speak it, but, alas ! it is too true in too many, it crieth out, *Non est Deus :* . . . I would to God it were no more than I make it." [1] ". . . Preach we never so oft, teach we never so much ", says Jewel in a later sermon, " few, yea, very few, are found that receive the same, and continue therein, and so bring forth fruits of salvation." [2]

It is time to descend from such generalities—the generalities, however, of a well-placed contemporary witness—and to set beside them some concrete facts and particular instances. By no means all the extant diocesan records have yet been studied, and little more is possible, at the moment, than to note some specimens of what has been found in some localities, and what—it *may* be—will be found in all. We can study, for example, the state of the clergy in the diocese of Lincoln during the first fifty years after 1559. [3]

Our first statistic is the number of parishes in that diocese at the time of the religious revolution—that is to say, in the counties of Lincoln, Leicester, Huntingdon, Bedford, and Buckingham and in the northern and western part of Hertfordshire. In a return made between 1562 and 1564, [4] these are given as Lincolnshire 512, [5] Leicestershire 205, Huntingdonshire 167, Bedfordshire 123, [6] Buckinghamshire 185. From a return made in these same years to Parker, as metropolitan, in reply to a question about clerical

---

[1] Jewel preaching before the queen : *Works*, IV, 1033.   [2] *Ibid.*, 1086.

[3] Thanks to the devotion of the Lincoln Record Society, and to the energetic scholarship of Canon Foster, the editor of the papers published in Vol. 23 of its publications, as *The State of the Church in the reigns of Elizabeth and James I* (1926), quoted in these notes as L.R.S., 23.

[4] Statistics from this return (Brit. Mus. Harleian, 618) are printed in L.R.S., 23, pp. 442, 444.

[5] Not including the archdeaconry of Stow, for which the records are missing. Forty years later than this, there were 91 parishes in this archdeaconry, and 517 in that of Lincoln,   [6] This archdeaconry includes the parishes in Hertfordshire.

marriage,[1] we can gather how many clergy then served these parishes—in Lincolnshire (archdeaconry of Lincoln) 317 ; Leicestershire 129 ; Buckinghamshire 194 ; the returns for Bedfordshire and Huntingdonshire are missing ; for the archdeaconry of Stow in Lincolnshire (with perhaps 91 parishes) the number of clergy is 45. There are thus 685 parochial clergy returned for an area where there were, seemingly, 993 parishes.[2]

Sixteen years after Matthew Parker's visitation, the diocese was visited by its own bishop, Thomas Cooper ; and of this visitation of 1576 there survives the record of the clergy in the counties of Lincoln and Leicester.[3] In Lincolnshire, where in 1562–64 there were 362 clergy there are now 396 ; in Leicestershire, the 129 have only increased to 149. In 14 years the number of clergy has but increased by 11 per cent. : there are still only 545 for these two counties which count between them 808 parishes.

We are also given particulars, in 1576, about the ordinations of 337 of the Lincolnshire clergy and of 122 of those of Leicestershire. Of the first, 122 date back to the years before 1559 and 215 have been ordained since ; in Leicestershire 79 (of the 122) have been ordained since 1559, 43 go back to the older régime. The first missionary priests from the seminary at Douay would, if their work took them to Lincolnshire, or Leicestershire, find that after seventeen years of the new régime just about one in three of the parochial clergy were one-time Catholic priests.

This visitation of 1576 also gives us unusual details about the learning of these clergy. Of those 215 now at work in Lincolnshire, whom the new bishops have accepted to ordain, the visitation of 1576 records only 36 as possessing a university degree ; on the other hand, as many as 63 of the 215 were found to be possessed of " insufficient knowledge " in the matter of sacred learning (i.e. nearly one in three of the 215) ; another 45 have no more than a knowledge described as " moderate " ; 87 are credited with " sufficient knowledge " for their position. Of the whole 396 clergy of the shire only 51 are licensed to preach ; [4] seven-eighths of the population still, after seventeen years, is nourished on the Homilies almost exclusively.

The Leicestershire returns of 1576 are so much less creditable even than these, that a higher standard, their editor suggests, must have been demanded by the visitors in this county. Of the 79 clergy here who have been ordained since the changes of 1559, 6 are non-resident and we are given no information about another 4. Sixty-nine, then, remain for consideration : 11 of these

---

[1] In the metropolitical visitation of 1560. The returns (so L.R.S., 23, p. 455) are in Parker MS., xcvii, at Corpus Christi College, Cambridge : the figures quoted here are from L.R.S., 23, p. 455. Of 727 clergy here reported on, 128 are returned as married.

[2] The proportion of clergy who have married, by 1560, is 1 in 5 for Lincoln archdeaconry 1 in 4 for Stow ; 1 in 6 for Buckingham ; 1 in 14 for Leicester ; and 1 in 4 for the Cathedral clergy : out of the 685, 7 are set down as " unspecified ", and there are 12 " unspecified " out of the 61 Cathedral clergy.

[3] For the record of the Lincolnshire archdeaconries cf. L.R.S., 23, pp. 157–213 ; for Leicester, ibid., pp. 33–46. Both are summarised in ibid., pp. 446, 453, 455, 456–460.

[4] L.R.S., 23, pp. 457, 458 for all these figures. There are another 20 of these clergy described as " Preacher (presumably not licensed), preacher in his own cure, preacher sometime, preacher not licensed, able to preach " ; ibid., 458.

have a university degree ; 8 are credited with " moderate " knowledge, and 3 with " sufficient " knowledge of sacred learning ; but no fewer than 48 out of the 69 are considered by the bishop as " insufficient ". In Leicestershire only one in twelve of the clergy is licensed to preach—10 out of the 122 ; there are 4 who preach in their own cure, and 16 described as " Teacher in his cure ".

Eight years later than the date of this record, Cooper was translated to Winchester. William Wickham who succeeded him proceeded immediately to visit the diocese, and of this visitation of 1585 the list of clergy survives, not only for the two counties of Lincoln and Leicester but for the whole diocese. The Elizabethan establishment is now twenty-six years in being. In both the shires just mentioned the nine years between the two visitations have seen very great developments. In Lincoln, the number of clergy has grown from 396 to 573 ; and in Leicester from 149 to 228. Of the 195 Lincolnshire clergy ordained in these nine years, 80—nearly a half—have a university degree, as have 38 of the 63 Leicester clergy ordained in the same period. No details are given, in 1585, of the clergy's professional learning ; but while there are now 573 clergy in Lincolnshire, no more than 88 of them are licensed to preach ;[1] and in Leicestershire no more than 18 out of the total 228.[2]

In the southern half of the diocese, now open to our observation for the first time since 1562–64, Huntingdonshire in 1585 has 180 clergy in all for its 167 parishes. We know the dates (approximately) when 148 of these clergy were ordained, and we can note that, after twenty-six years, there are still 11 survivors from pre-Elizabethan times. Of the 137 clergy whom the new episcopate has ordained, 53 have a university degree. But only 14 out of the 180 are licensed to preach.[3] In the archdeaconry of Bedford, which includes also the Hertfordshire parishes, there are 115 clergy in all, for 123 parishes. The ordaining bishop is known for 106 of these clergy—only 12 are survivors of the old régime. Of the 94 ordained since 1559, 37 have a university degree ; and 16 of the 115 are licensed to preach.[4]

Finally, in the county of Buckingham there are 189 clergy altogether—there were 194 in 1560 [5]—and we know when 149 of these 189 were ordained, i.e. 28 before 1559, and 121 since then. Of these 121 new clergy, 40 have a university degree ; there are only 17 licensed to preach out of the total 189, and there are another 10, with degrees in theology, " presumably " preachers.[6]

As the diocese of Lincoln was in 1585, so it remained for the rest of Elizabeth's reign. In 1603 the bishop was the vigorous William Chaderton, a tough man from the neighbourhood of Manchester, promoted to Lincoln

---

[1] There are also the 10 with degrees in divinity, " presumably preachers " (says the editor of these records, p. 458) ; and another 11 classed as in the last note.

[2] Add (?) the two incumbents with degrees in divinity.

[3] The editor (p. 458) reminds us that there are 13 doctors and bachelors of divinity " presumably " preachers.

[4] Four more are classed as in note 4, *supra*, p. 138.   [5] *Ibid.*, 455.

[6] For the Visitation of 1585, cf. *ibid.*, pp. 63–144 and, for the summaries, pp. 446, 447, 448–452, 454, 458, 459.

after sixteen years zealous service, as Bishop of Chester, against the Catholics of Lancashire. From the *Liber Cleri* prepared for this bishop's visitation of 1604 [1] we learn that nowhere in the diocese have these last eighteen years brought any increase in the number of parochial clergy—in Bedford the number is actually the same as in 1585, in Buckinghamshire and in Lincoln-shire approximately the same ; in Leicestershire it is down by a sixth, and in Huntingdonshire down by a fifth. Where there were 1283 clergy in 1585, there are now 1184 in 1603. But the proportion of educated men among these clergy is, in 1603, very much higher than in 1585. In Lincolnshire one third as many have now a university degree ; in Leicestershire two and a quarter times as many ; in Huntingdonshire twice as many almost ; in Bedfordshire the same ; and in Buckinghamshire nearly three times as many. These degrees are, for the most part, degrees in arts,[2] and by no means every minister with a degree is a licensed preacher ; in more than two-thirds of the parishes the people, who have had the *Homilies* alone for forty-five years, are still condemned to this dreary and sterile repetition.

The problem how to prepare the needed " fit ministers of the word " was one of the first which the new bishops attacked.[3] Within a few months of the first consecrations, and before all the sees had been filled, the pro-duction of " some longer catechism devised . . . for the erudition of simple curates ",[4] was announced as a desideratum ; and the bishops decreed " that young priests or ministers made or to be made be so instructed that they are able to make apt answers concerning the form of some Catechism to be pre-scribed ".[5] This is language which, of itself, seems to show what little hope the bishops had, even in the first flush of their victory, of recruiting the Reformed clergy from men of any education at all.

The queen's *Injunctions* of 1559 had already ordered that every priest with a cure of souls should provide himself with the New Testament in Latin and in English and with the *Paraphrases* (of Erasmus) upon the same ; and they had laid upon the bishops the obligation to examine the clergy " how they have profited in the study of Holy Scripture ". These regulations Arch-bishop Parker's *Advertisements* of 1566 translated practically, in an instruction

---

[1] For which cf. *ibid.*, pp. 253–328. Chaderton had been at Lincoln now eight years.

[2] The particulars for 1603 (from L.R.S., 23, pp. 454, 458) are as follows :

County	Clergy	Degrees in Theology	Degrees in Arts	Licensed Preachers
Lincoln . . .	560	23	187	145
Leicester . . .	188	21	88	50
Huntingdon . . .	143	25	80	56
Bedford . . .	115	9	78	33
Buckingham . .	178	23	111	42
Diocesan Total . .	1184	101	544	326

[3] Cf. Kennedy, *Elizabethan Episcopal Administration*, I, pp. lxxi–cxvii (The Parish Clergy) ; the same writer's *Parish Life in the Reign of Queen Elizabeth* (1914), 29–43.

[4] Kennedy, *Interpretations*, p. 30 ; the Catechism was that written by Alexander Nowell (Dixon, V, 349).   [5] Kennedy, *Interpretations*, pp. 30–31.

:o the archdeacons to set for learning by heart certain passages of Sacred Scripture. In 1571 the archbishop's orders re-appeared in the canons voted by the Convocation of that year, and in 1586 Archbishop Whitgift moved Convocation to impose something much more serious—the systematic study of Bullinger's *Decades*,[1] now translated into English.

But for the first twenty-seven years nothing more than the simple " learning by heart " of prescribed texts seems to have been demanded— and we can now better gauge the intelligence (or the interest in religion— to say nothing of interest in the Bible) of those Lincoln clergy of these first years of Protestantism triumphant (clergy who were the most part of the whole) who for so long fell down so miserably before so simple a task.[2] Everywhere the bishops, as their Injunctions show, provide an abundance of rules and regulations and inspections and tests—but no new colleges, no local centres of teaching ; and the " prophesyings ", which might have done much, were suppressed by the queen, as we shall see, once it was evident that they tended to breed a really religious spirit in the clergy—a spirit, that is to say, which put conscience before the demands of state policy.

The England of Wolsey and Fisher and Thomas More, of William Smyth and Richard Fox and Hugh Oldham and the Lady Margaret, had hardly been indifferent to the practical problem of clerical learning. Nor indeed was England a land where, even before their day, all was to begin, in things of the spirit. But in these first Elizabethan prelates we seem to behold men legislating with no higher hope than to produce a clerical proletariat ; the age of " ignorance and barbary " that Jewel spoke of has, seemingly, arrived already, and the sacred ministry is recruited from an aboriginal level indeed. Yet even with cultural standards as primitive as these, it was hard to find candidates ;[3] and to supply the want of ordained ministers the office

---

[1] Already ordered for Lincoln in 1577 by Thomas Cooper ; *E.E.A.*, II, 16–17. At Norwich, in 1589, Scambler " sets " Calvin's *Institutes* and Peter Martyr's *Commonplaces* (in English) ; *E.E.A.*, III, 255–256. The canon of 1586 ordered that the cleric should read one chapter of Scripture daily, and one sermon of Bullinger's weekly ; that he should summarise these " in his paper book ", which Convocation now ordered him to buy ; and that he should, once a fortnight, show his summaries to the preacher who lived nearest to him ; *E.E.A.*, I, p. viii. The earlier, diocesan rules, given in these visitation records, are Norwich, 1561 ; Winchester, 1562 and 1571 ; Rochester, 1565 ; Lincoln, 1577. On p. cii of *E.E.A.*, I, there is an interesting account of a clergy examination at Durham under Bishop Barnes, in 1578, at which 144 clergy appeared, 62 of whom are marked as having completed their task. The questions are not forthcoming, but the subject for the year was St. Matthew's Gospel. Kennedy considers that these various regulations " throw a rather painful light on the qualifications of the parish clergy ", *ibid.*, p. xcvii.

[2] The same simple requirements and no more may be seen demanded all over the country ; e.g. Sandys at Worcester, 1569, F. & K., III, 223 ; Grindal at York, 1571, *ibid.*, 260 ; Cox at Ely, 1571, *ibid.*, 302 ; Parker at Winchester, 1574, *ibid.*, 384 ; Grindal, for the province of Canterbury, 1576, in Kennedy, *E.E.A.*, II. Cf. for all this, and with many other references, the last mentioned work, Vol. I, pp. xcvii–ciii. And how the Protestant critics jeered at these poor attempts to remedy clerical illiteracy ! " In this court . . . a man shall be excommunicated . . . if he learn not his Catechism like a good boy without book, when it should be more meet he should be able to teach others "; the *Admonition to the Parliament* (1572), in *Puritan Manifestoes*, 33–34. Also, *ibid.*, 10, " . . . first they consecrate them and make them ministers and then they set them to school ".

[3] " When a living is void ", Harrison tells us (1577) " there are so many suitors for it that a man would think the report to be true [i.e. that there are more good preachers than livings

of " reader " was devised. These were laymen, removable whenever the
bishop chose, whose business it was to read the service and the homily—
but never to preach, or to interpret, or to administer sacraments ; they were,
however, allowed to bury the dead and to " purify women after childbirth ".[1]

The new plague also began to show of unordained ministers—not merely
of laymen who held benefices, an abuse which, often enough, the bishops
had to wink at when the layman was a personage, but of such lay incumbents
ministering. So it is that in 1569 Sandys of Worcester is enquiring at visitations whether the parson has been ordained ; Grindal in 1571 is doing the
same at York, Cox also at Ely in that same year, and Parker at Winchester,
three years later.[2]

And so the scandal continued, little abated until the very end of the
queen's long reign, with England fifty years away from the interested
obscurantism of the Bishop of Rome, and seventy years old, very nearly,
in its freedom to be familiar with the written word of God. The testimony
of the critics of the settlement of 1559, popularly called the Puritans, it is
customary to dismiss as less than truthful exaggeration ; such statements,
for example, as that " scarce every tenth congregation can be so provided
for as were to be wished ".[3] This was in 1586. But in this very year
the Secretary of State, Sir Francis Walsingham, analysing the evident
" decay and falling away in religion ", set down as the first necessary
remedies the provision of learned and godly preachers, and the removal
of ministers whose scandalous lives bred offence. He proposed to begin
the reform by " a general examination " whether " ministers presented
since [1571] be qualified according to the statute ".[4] As to the bad men,
" chancellors and archdeacons, for the most part, do rather seek to cover
faults than to remove or reform the corrupted ".[5] Hooker, in 1598, seems
to think the problem is insoluble. He speaks of " numbers of men but
slenderly and meanly qualified ", and complains that " the Church . . .
hath obtruded upon her their service that know not otherwise how to live
and sustain themselves. . . . These . . . are often received into that
vocation whereunto their unworthiness is no small disgrace. Did anything more aggravate the crime of Jeroboam's profane apostasy than that
he chose to have his clergy the scum and refuse of his whole land ? " [6] No
Puritan spoke more strongly than this. Yet the risk was unavoidable. " Is

---

to maintain them] but when it cometh to the trial (who are sufficient and who are not, who are
staid men in conversation, judgment, and learning) of that great number you shall hardly
find one or two such as they ought to be. . . ." Harrison, 70.

[1] See *Injunctions to be confessed and subscribed by them that shall be admitted readers,*
in Kennedy, *Interpretations,* 36–37.

[2] Also Grindal in 1576, for the province of Canterbury, and Aylmer in 1577 for the
diocese of London.   For all this cf. *E.E.A.,* I, p. xxxiii, where the full references are given.
Aylmer already has to ask if any have been ordained " by new presbytery or eldership without
orders taking of the bishop " ; *ibid.*

[3] *Certain points concerning the policy and government of the Ecclesiastical State,* in Peel,
II, 19.

[4] This, apparently, to arrest the abuse that the benefices reserved to the learned clergy
by the statute (for which G. & H., 480) were conferred indiscriminately.

[5] *C.R.,* II, 304–308.   [6] Hooker, *Works,* II, 521.

t not plain that unless the greatest part of the people should be left utterly vithout the public use and exercise of religion there is no remedy but to ake into the ecclesiastical order a number of men meanly qualified in respect of learning ? " And, " to do that we cannot we are not bound ", i.e. keep to what St. Paul requires in a presbyter, who " requireth more in presbyters than there is found in many whom the Church of England alloweth " : St. Paul requiring " such learning as doth enable them to exhort in doctrine which is sound, and to disprove them that gainsay it ".[1]

Were these clergy, as a body, keenly spiritual men ? There is no doubt at all that they were not. Were at least the new clergy, recruited since 1559, keenly spiritual men, in happy contrast to the fruits of less enlightened times ? The answer must be the same.

As to the bishops, the strong—too strong—language of one writer has already been quoted.[2] Certainly no one has yet undertaken to propose these pioneers and founders as types of their own version of Christianity at its best. Even the measured language of Dr. Kennedy is severe,[3] and he seems to suggest that the good and decent were exceptional through all the first thirty years of the Reform.[4] But once the pope had " shot his bolt " in 1570, and the Armada had failed, the Reformed religion could afford to be something more than an anti-Catholic polemic and from now on, so he thinks, " it is possible to trace growing signs of revival ".[5] This reads more like a presumption or speculation than a reasoned judgment based on facts ;[6] the writer appears closer to reality when he states that, " It is evident that there was much moral failure among the Elizabethan clergy—a casual acquaintance with court proceedings easily shows that . . .".[7]

Certainly the new bishops seem to anticipate that, despite reform, the liberation of zeal and the destruction of superstition, to say nothing of the new institution of clerical marriage, they will meet all the old clerical vices as they make the visitation of their dioceses. Wickham's question to the

---

[1] Hooker, *Works*, II, 516, 517.   [2] H. Hall, cf. *supra*, p. 46, n. 2.

[3] " The Elizabethan episcopate contained many unworthy men, and their shortcomings need no further historical elaboration " ; *E.E.A.*, I, p. xxv, is one remark. Cf. also, " There were grave scandals among the Elizabethan episcopate ", *ibid.*, p. xxxix ; but the author notes the " gradual emergence of a higher type ", and pleads that Elizabeth's " reign began with an inherited spiritual and moral exhaustion, and morality was at a low ebb, all the lower owing to the unreality of the Marian experiment " ; *ibid.*

[4] In his earlier work, *Parish Life under Queen Elizabeth*, 158–159, this author commits himself very definitely to this, e.g. " Parish life under Queen Elizabeth was in no healthy state. . . Moral standards did not exist. The entire local government was honeycombed with abuses. There was no such thing as privacy. Spying was not only common but was encouraged. Education was, in the widest sense, neglected. *Genuine religion was so uncommon as to be almost negligible.* . . . It is almost impossible to find anything to praise . . ." (italics mine), and in conclusion Kennedy here quotes Frere : " . . . piety was decayed, and a gloom of spiritual apathy had settled over the land ". Frere, *History of the English Church under Elizabeth and James I*, 208.

[5] *E.E.A.*, I, p. xc ; pages xc–xcvii of this long introductory essay summarise the problem of clerical conduct as the visitation articles envisage it.

[6] But cf. the still more drastic statement of Dr. Frere, " The practice of religion had sunk to a very low ebb . . . there had been a moment when hatred of Spain and Rome seemed to be the only bit of religion left in the English Church " ; *op. cit.*, 284.

[7] *E.E.A.*, I, p. xc.

churchwardens of the diocese of Lincoln in 1585 is a classic formula often repeated in these documents : " Whether your own parson, vicar, or curate be any common resorter to open games, plays, or assemblies whatsoever (in evil causes) ; or do keep, or suffer to be kept, in his parsonage, vicarage or other his dwelling house any alehouse, tippling-house or tavern ; or that he do or have kept any suspicious women [1] in his house ; or that he being unmarried doth keep any woman in his house under the age of sixty years except his daughter, mother, aunt, sister, or niece and those of good and honest name ; or whether he himself be any haunter of alehouses, taverns, or suspected places ; an hunter, hawker, dicer, carder, a swearer, or otherwise do give evil example of life, whereby the word of God and the *form of religion now used by the laws of England* is or may be evil spoken of; and generally whether he behave not himself soberly, godly, and honestly as becometh a minister of God's most holy word ? " [2]

One evil that was at least as serious as moral lapses in the usual meaning of the phrase—and far more widespread than ever before, since so many presentations to livings had come into lay hands—was simony.   This plague began in the very fount of grace, in the practice of the Supreme Governor herself, who " seems to have preferred [for bishops] the weak kneed whom she could easily persuade to corruption".[3]   The law against simony was however, continually brought before the notice of every congregation in every parish church ; the wardens were ceaselessly admonished about their duty to make known simoniacal pacts of any kind between incumbent and patron and an oath was devised and imposed on all new incumbents that there had been no simony of any kind in their acceptance of the living.   And yet " . . . parishes suffered in no small degree from a system of simoniacal robbery . . . covenants and pacts of direct alienation, and fraudulent leases made to obtain promotion witnessed to a deterioration not merely in moral and good fame but in the property of the church ".[4]

The prevalent spirit of jobbery invaded, in these years, the ecclesiastical courts also, and the visitation documents show the bishops as needing to wage war on this wickedness from the beginning of the reign to the very end Whitgift himself testifies how hopeless at times the task appeared, and what a menace to the future of the new establishment was this all too prevalent wickedness of corrupt episcopal officials.   " Unfortunately, as we know too well, the evils continued to flourish.   They remained to hurt both just and unjust, to lower the whole conception of ecclesiastical jurisdiction, to corrupt

---

[1] Here, in English dress, are the *mulieres suspectae* of the canonists, for whom cf. Vol. p. 55, n. 2.

[2] Italics mine.   *E.E.A.*, III, pp. 191–192, no. 21.   In part, what such questionings a these are enforcing is the legislation of the various Convocations since 1559.   Of the rule regulating clerical familiarity with the other sex Kennedy thinks ". . . it is remarkable that in the first canons of the church since the Reformation [this canon about women] should have been included, and that among a body of regulations otherwise singularly pertinent to cor ditions ".   *E.E.A.*, I, p. lxxxviii.

[3] *Ibid.*, p. cl ;   the authority goes on to say, " The history of episcopal promotions an translations during the reign is an unsavoury answer to the challenges of the best puritanism For one such, attempted at Ely, 1595, cf. Strype, *Aurals*, IV, 343-6.   [4] *E.E.A.*, I, p. cl.

ꝙ THE INSTITVTION OF

Chriſtian Religion, vvrytten in Laꝫ
tine by maiſter Ihon Caluin, and tranſlaꝫ
ted into Englyſh according to the auꝫ
thors laſt edition.

ꝙ *Seen and allowed according to the order appointed in the*
Quenes maieſties iniunctions.

ꝙ Imprinted at London by
Reinolde Vvolfe & Richarde Harison.
Anno. 1 5 6 1.

Cum priuilegio ad imprimendum ſolum.

Quamuis autem dicamus nihil nobis esse præsidij in operibus & factis nostris, & omnem salutis nostræ rationem constituamus in solo Christo, non tamen ea causa dicimus luxè & soluè uiuendum esse, quasi initus satis sit homini Christiano, & nihil ab eo aliud expectetur. Vera fides, uiua est, nec potest esse otiosa.

Sic ergò docemus populum, Deum uocasse nos, nõ ad luxum & libidinem, sed, ut Paulus ait, ad opera bona, ut in illis ambulemus: Deum eripuisse nos à potestate tenebrarum, ut seruiamus Deo uiuenti: ut re-scindamus omnes reliquias peccati: ut in timore & tremore operemur salutẽ nostram: ut appareat spiritum sanctificationis esse in membris nostris, & Christū ipsum per fidem in cordibus nostris habitare.

Postremò credimus hanc ipsam carnem nostram, in qua uiuimus, quamuis mortua obierit in puluerem, tamen ultimâ die resituram esse ad uitam, propter spiritum Christi qui habitat in nobis. Tunc uerò quic-quid hic interim patimur eius causâ, Christum abster-surum esse omnem Lachrymam ab oculis nostris: & nos propter illum fruituros esse æterna uita, & sem-per futuros cum illo in gloria. Amen.

Istæ sunt horribiles ille Hereses, quarum nomine bona pars orbis terrarum hodie à Pontifice insimula condemnatur. In Christiam potius, in Apostolos, in sanctos Patres ista intendenda fuit: Nam ab illis ista non tantū profecta, sed etiam constituta sunt. Nisi isti forte uelint dicere, quod etiam fortasse dicent, Christū non instituisse sacrum communionem, ut inter fideles distribuetur

Apologia Ec=
clesiæ Angli
canæ.

ROMA. V.

Non enim me pudet Euangelii CHRISTI, Po-tentia siquidem est Dei, ad salutem omni credenti.

LONDINI
Anno Domini
M. D. LXII.

our obeing his commaundementes, becauſe it hath pleaſed him to binde him ſelfe to that couenant. In reſpect whereof S. Iohn doubted not to make him ſaye of certaine chaſt men, *Ambulabunt mecum in albis, quia digni ſunt* . *They ſhall walke with me all in white, becauſe they be worthy* . Thus we then that ſhould haue ben vnprofitable by nature, are by grace made profitable and worthy to walke with God. *Apoca.3.*

Where ye ſay that his lawe is perfite we confeſſe the ſame. whē ye adde that it requireth of vs perfite and ful obedience, we anſwer, it doth ſo: but in ſuch ſort, as perfectiō may be obteined in this life. For as there is a perfection of childrē, a perfection of mē, a perfection of angels, and a perfectiō of God, euery one a perfection in his kinde, and that a greater alſo in reſpect of a leſſer perfectiō, but the perfectiō of God only abſolute and in it ſelfe perfite: ſo is there one perfection of this life, an other of the life to come. Now the lawe of God requireth of vs in this life ſuch ful and perfite obedience, as may be had in this life, which the fathers call the perfection of wayefaringmen. and requireth ſuch full obedience in heauen, as ſhalbe moſt perfite there. Ye therefore make a ſophiſticall argument, when ye teach, becauſe the lawe of God requireth of vs full obedience, that therefor it can not be ſatiſſied in this life by any meanes. For when ye ſay it requireth of vs full obedience, if ye meane ſuch full obedience, as is required only in this life, then conclude ye falſely, that we can by no meanes ſatiſſie it. But if ye meane ſuch full obedience, as is only performed in heauen, then ye conclude well, that we in this life can not fulfill ſuch perfection, as is required in heauen. But then haue ye ſaid nothing to the purpoſe. For we knowe what marke ye ſhoote at, by your doctrine vttered in other places. Your meaning is that no man in this life is able by the grace of God to fulfill the commaunde mentes. *How the lawe requireth of vs perfite obedience.* *Perfectio viatorum.*

for

FIFTIE GODLIE AND LEAR-

ned Sermons, diuided into fiue Decades, con-
teyning the chiefe and principall pointes of Christian
Religion, written in three seuerall Tomes or Sections, by
Henrie Bullinger minister of the Churche of
Tigure in Swicer-
lande.

WHEREVNTO IS ADIOYNED A TRIPLE
or three-folde Table verie fruitefull and
necessarie.

Translated out of Latine into English
by H. I. student in Diuinitie.

MATTHEWE. 17.
This is my beloued Sonne in whome I am well pleased:
Heare him.

¶IMPRINTED AT LONDON BY RALPHE
Newberrie, dwelling in Fleete-streate a little
aboue the Conduite.
Anno. Gratiæ.
1577.

THE IMMORTAL DECADES, 1577

the officials with the lure of filthy lucre, to cause heart-burnings to good and upright men, to form themes for bitter, merciless and brilliant satire, to fill a dark page in church history, until the tragic broom of the Caroline revolution swept courts and all away amid almost universal rejoicing. When the courts were set up again at the Restoration, they possessed little of their old influence and power." [1]

"The want of a sufficient ministry", said Bishop Overton, of Coventry and Lichfield, in 1584, which he linked with "the corruption of patrons", was the cause of "lamentable inconveniences" to the church of God; and the "lamentable inconveniences" continued until the end of the reign. It would be hard to maintain that by the end of Elizabeth's reign, after forty-five years of government-assisted, government-prescribed religion, the state of the clergy as a whole was really any better than in the opening years. All those clerical abuses, indignant revolt against which, so once it was supposed, was the very life of the Reform movement and the first cause of its success, abominations that must be consumed in the purifying fire of enlightenment triumphant, all these continued, we now know; some of them flourished as never before: pluralities, non-residence, lay patronage, simony, clerical ignorance, clerical ill-living. As in Catholic days so now, there were clerics who throve on the abuses, and clerics who did their best in spite of them, and clerics who bravely protested against them. And the main source of the abuses, now, was the court of the Supreme Head.

While the Catholic, and the Reformer of the primitive type now, as the reign went on, coming to be called a Puritan, protest that to claim such headship is a blasphemy, the very primate of the church is confidentially complaining to Cecil that the court is the "fountain" from which "are sprung all the evil bishops and deans now living in England." [2] Even after thirty years, the party of the Reform is not yet so clean that it has none but the clean for its religious chiefs—thanks to the crown's control of the party through the party's acceptance of the Royal Supremacy as a doctrine of religion, an authority grounded on the word of God. The fact was, of course, that while "the Queen and her advisers cared little if the clergy was ignorant so long as it was loyal ",[3] they cared just as little about the general irreligion of the country, so long as it was neither Catholic nor Presbyterian who influenced the national life. As to the professional competence of the clergy at the end of the reign, the great majority—two thirds at least, it is safe to say —are still "without degrees and, in consequence presumably ignorant, unable to preach and incompetent"; and Whitgift is re-echoing Jewel's

---

[1] E.E.A., I, cxxix. Another contemporary form of ecclesiastical corruption has been, no doubt, responsible for some of the statistics over which historians have so long puzzled : Bancroft, in 1601, asking the wardens whether " a just and perfect note " is taken of the names of communicants, asks also whether the parsons " do not rather, regarding their private gain, receive their offerings at Easter, deliver them tokens, enter them into their book, and so certify as communicants those who never receive ? " ibid., 203, n. 29.

[2] Whitgift to Cecil, July 28, 1586 ; in Hatfield Calendar, III, 153. ". . . and yet where is greater zeal pretended ", the letter continues. And Whitgift asks Burghley to burn it !   [3] Usher, Reconstruction, I, 219.

old complaint and explanation : " For what man of reason will think that £8 yearly is able to maintain a learned divine ? When as every scull in a kitchen and groom in a stable is better provided for ? " [1]

Are the Puritans of 1584 overstating their case when they declare, in a petition to the queen, that one reason why the Catholics are still so hopeful [after twenty-five years of repression] is that " scarce in the tenth parish of this realm . . . there is resident a vigilant and watchful shepherd or pastor . . .". [2]

And if such were the shepherds what of their flocks ? We cannot indict a nation of course ; but, " in Elizabethan times, the parochial and diocesan records disclose a consistency of moral decay in all classes of society which can hardly be paralleled in English history ". [3] The fundamental reason for the catastrophe was that, after sixty years of upheaval, religious conviction had well nigh disappeared, outside the minorities called Papist and Puritan.

2. HOSTILITY TO THE SETTLEMENT OF 1559

The clerics whom, in 1559, the government had charged with the actual guidance of the nation in spirituals, those whom it had invited to fill the vacant sees, had a second, chronic trouble to harass and handicap their effort through the next forty years—the fact that, by many of those who should have been their chief assistants, by fellow-sufferers of Mary's reign—by these " co-mates and brothers in exile " especially—they were held to be traitors to the sacred cause, and this almost from the moment when they accepted to be consecrated. The exiles, in fact, had not come back to a country where they were to be free to worship God in their own way, nor to one where they would be free to harry, after their own heart, all who followed a different way from their way—but to a country where all alike were to worship God in the government's way, or pay the consequences. And in framing the new governmental order none of the brethren had had any share, except those whom the government chose to call in as technical, liturgical experts. The *Anglicana* devised by the politicians of 1559 was far from representative of the English Protestantism of 1559 ; and from the beginning, nay even while the thing was in gestation, there were ominous

---

[1] Strype's *Whitgift*, I, 534, given Usher, 221, as Whitgift ; Usher's ch. X, *The Condition of the Clergy*, 1603, pp. 205–243 and ch. XI, *Attitude of the People towards the Church*, pp. 244–281, should be read. Whitgift declared, in 1585, that not 600 out of the 9,000 or so benefices offered a stipend really adequate for a learned man ; that more than 4,500 benefices with a cure of souls were not worth above £10 a year, most of these being even under £8, and as many as 2978 only £5 and under ; Usher, *op. cit.*, 219.

[2] Peel, I, no. 164, p. 254.

[3] Kennedy, *Parish Life*, 149. Sandys, Archbishop of York, links the prevailing wrong-doing with the shortage of religious teachers—this in 1578, after nineteen years of the new régime. " Here is great want of teachers, by reason whereof an ignorant people. . . The meaner people here is idle . . . given to much drinking, whereof followeth great incontinency, as well appeareth by the multitude of fornicators presented in this my last visitation. Truly the cause hereof is the want of good instruction " ; letter of April 21, 1578, Brit. Mus. Lansdowne MSS., 27, no. 12. It is not only erudite theologians who are lacking in the new clergy.

mutterings. Soon there were brethren as bitterly active against the new bishops as ever they had been against the popes ; and bitter, in very great part, because they looked on these bishops as time-servers and apostates. The history of this duel is so involved that an outline account can scarcely hope to do justice to it ; but certain features of it must be set down, or the picture would not be complete of what that was that the Catholic was now expected to become.

And first of all, we need to note how this anti-Settlement activity on the part of the Protestants is as old as the Elizabethan Settlement itself ; and that its ideals can, at the very beginning of the reign, command at least as many avowed champions within the party of Reform, as uphold the new, official, State version of the Reform. " The men . . . now [1559] advanced in honour . . . were the men who in their exile had stood for the Second Prayer Book of Edward against the extreme sort. . . . The ostensible leaders such as Jewel, Grindal, Pilkington, to say nothing of Cox himself, were not likely to oppose the establishment of the said Book which formerly they had defended. . . . It is like enough, however, that in foreign parts some of them may have been free of their tongues in conversing about the Book of England, that they had said things against it which they were not now ready to repeat, so that their present behaviour took a good deal of explaining to their friends the pastors of the churches abroad." [1] Jewel is himself witness that the division began to show among the London Protestants even before the Acts of Supremacy and Uniformity were introduced into parliament : " Having heard only one public discourse of Bentham's the people began to dispute among themselves about ceremonies, some declaring for Geneva, and some for Frankfort." [2]

The new established church did not start from a point at which all the leaders were agreed, whether about the lawfulness of the Royal Supremacy and the obedience a Christian man owed it, or about the way they accepted,

[1] Dixon, V, 125. In what sense they had defended the Prayer Book of 1552, in what sense this had been attacked, may be learnt from Whittingham's *Troubles at Frankfort* (cf. Vol. II of the present work, 307–320). Under the pressure of controversy it presently began to be fashionable to speak of the Book of 1552 as though it were the very palladium of the Reformation as accomplished by Englishmen, and even to speak of Queen Mary Tudor's victims as " martyrs of the Prayer Book ". The other side did not let pass this attempt to identify the religious policy of the Elizabethan government with the religious movement of an earlier time. " What talk they of their being beyond the seas in Queen Mary's days because of the persecution, when they in Queen Elizabeth's days are come home to raise a persecution. They boast they follow the steps of good Master Ridley the martyr : let them follow him in the good, and not in the bad. What man, martyr or other, is to be followed in all things ? why follow they not Mr. Hooper as well as him, who is a martyr also ? or Rogers, or Bradford, who are martyrs also ? They said all these good men in Queen Mary's days died for the Book of Common Prayer, but they slander them, for they took not so slender a quarrel, they died for God his book, and for a true faith grounded upon the same. Divers of those martyrs would not in those days of King Edward, abide all the orders in that book. . . ." The *Second Admonition to the Parliament*, in *Puritan Manifestoes*, 112.

[2] Letter of Jan. 26, 1559, to Peter Martyr ; *Z.L.*, 17. Bentham was the pastor of the congregation of London in the latter part of Mary's reign. In 1560 Elizabeth gave him the see of Coventry and Lichfield. For the Geneva *v.* Frankfort conflict during the Marian exile, cf. Vol. II, 305–320.

as " wholly in accord with God's word ",[1] the Prayer Book imposed by the
Act of Uniformity. The grave divergences that were to be revealed so
strikingly when first the Reformers came together in Convocation, barely
three years after the fundamental Acts of 1559 were passed, were present and
active from the beginning—they antedated the legal " settlement " of the
Reformed religion. What, in later years, came to be called Puritanism—
and by opponents first of all—was not, in the Elizabethan beginnings,
heterodoxy actively striving to displace, within the queen's *Anglicana*,
primitive orthodoxy ; it was a rival alternative view, with an equal claim to
orthodoxy, with equal rights (save for two Acts of Parliament) and with at
least an equal chance of success in the fight—save for the fact that the queen
would have none of it.

There is even something of a case, at the very least, for the suggestion
that it is this section of the party, critical of, if not absolutely hostile to, the
Settlement of 1559, which is really the primitive English Reformation ; that
in 1559, not only was the Catholic majority hostile to the Reform out
manoeuvred by the government's policy, but along with it the majority also
of that Protestant minority that favoured the Reform ; [2] that from May 8
1559, for a number of years which we may cautiously hesitate to determine
it was in fact a minority within a minority that was controlling the religious
fortunes of England ; that the real inspiration of this minority of a minority
its creator and the source of what being it possessed, was political and lay. To
the Protestant critics, the government's arrangement, and the policy which the
queen imposed on the new bishops, were a regression. Lever, the preacher
who, it is said, had inspired the queen with her conscientious antipathy to the
title of Supreme Head, writes to Bullinger as though her directions about
clerical dress and about vestments were an unlooked-for innovation. All the
Reformed clergy, he explains, had given them up, and what Parliament had
restored was the régime of Edward VI ; the queen's Injunctions, " however "
were prescribing " some ornaments such as the mass priests formerly had and
still retain ".[3] Coverdale, too, speaks of Parker's demands in 1566 as a
departure " from the opinion we have taken up and the custom we have
received" ; [4] and the comment of the two most active of this group, Laurence

---

[1] Text of the submission imposed on all clergy by the Royal Visitation of 1559, cf. *supra*
p. 38.

[2] This is, of course, a highly controversial matter—and the divisions upon it among
historians cut across their own religious differences. Dr. Kennedy, who assuredly speaks
with very high authority, and who has studied the matter as an Anglican and as a Catholic
would seem to hold that there is no case for this assertion, when he writes, of the controversy
now about to be described, " The whole religious life of the country was complicated by the
new extreme Protestant party . . . ; " *Interpretations*, p. 14, italics mine. And again, " The
age was an age of compromise and transition . . ." ; upon which one might ask where there
are any signs of compromise except among the statesmen, who present a *fait accompli* to the
clerics of all sections and beliefs. Even about the most significant element of what was to be
criticised in the new organisation, the episcopate, from whom among the Reformers would
there have come protestations, in 1559, had the statesmen then willed to abolish, and been
successful in abolishing, the episcopate ? And on what grounds would the protest have been
made, had it then been proposed that England should follow a Genevan or Zurich model
of church organisation ?

[3] July 10, 1560, *Z.L.*, 108.   [4] To Beza, July 1566, *ibid.*, 229.

Humphrey and Thomas Sampson implies that what is being demanded is a return to something already given up.[1]

This Thomas Sampson, to whom Elizabeth, in 1559, gave the deanery of Christ Church, Oxford, we have already met.[2] It is not surprising that his private correspondence reveals him to us, in the very hour when the news of Mary's death reached him—he was then at Strasburg—scrupulously mediating whether he could in conscience accept to be one of the new bishops whom the new queen would assuredly need to appoint. It is not only the worldly rank, nowadays inseparable from the office, he writes, which makes him, as a Christian, anxious : there are his doubts whether Elizabeth will allow the exercise of that " discipline "—vital to all the Calvinist churches [3]—without which the episcopal office is a vain show ; doubts also about the " unseemliness of their superstitious dresses " ; and doubts, finally, what his attitude should be towards the Royal Supremacy. In this letter to Peter Martyr, written in the very first month of the reign,[4] we meet the main topics around which controversy within the state-established church was to rage during all the rest of the century : clerical dress, vestments, the Calvinistic system of church organisation and government, the place of the sovereign in the church. Now, for the first time, the Reform had come up against a patron really powerful—something very different in kind from the petty German princes and the toy republics of Switzerland. The Reformers, now, were going to serve : even more than they were served.[5]

[1] " After the expiration of seven years in the profession of the gospel, there has now been revived that contest about habits ", Sampson to Bullinger, Feb. 16, 1566, Z.L., 212. Also, Humphrey and the same, to the same, in July of the same year, " This is not to extirpate popery, but to replant it ; not to advance religion but to recede " ; ibid., 234.

[2] Cf. Vol. II, 193.

[3] Sampson had, long before, made plain what he thought should be done, in the farewell letter to his London parishioners already quoted, Vol. II, 193-195. " Again, if the true ecclesiastical discipline were used ", he told them, " a piece of it ought to be, that the man restored should of his fault make an open confession before the congregation, to declare publicly his repentance. Yea, and a minister may upon just grounds examine any of whom he hath cure, of such a fault as he seeth him worthy to be reproved for. But this is so far from their earshrift [i.e. the Catholics' Sacrament of Penance] that a man most blind may easily judge thereof ". The practice of the discipline, Sampson suggests, is as clear a sign to the Christian that he is in the true Church as the practice of Confession is a sign showing where Belial is triumphant. For Sampson's letter, cf. Strype, Memorials, III, pt. ii, 235. For Cranmer's plan to introduce the discipline in 1553, cf. Vol. II, 134.

[4] From Strasburg, Dec. 17, 1558, in Z.L., 2-3. There were Reformers who would have liked to regulate dress in another sense of the word. The Bishop of London, John Aylmer, in 1577 complains of wives and children of the clergy " proudly and vainly decked in apparel not fit for the state and calling of their husbands ", E.E.A., I, lxxxvi ; and the Bishop of Chichester, Thomas Bickley, issues in 1586 an order that the wives and families of the clergy " be apparelled handsomely without vanity and great charges, fit for the calling of their husbands " ; ibid., II, 183.

[5] They will be disappointed, at times very grievously. Here is Zurich consoling, fifteen years later, one of them who is a bishop : " . . . it is the misfortune of our age, that not even those princes who have opened their doors to the gospel of Christ, will allow all things to be altered and corrected . . .", but " so long as purity of doctrine and liberty of conscience remain inviolate . . . if the most serene queen and the nobles of the realm will not have the existing form of the Church altered ", the brethren ought to bear it with patience. R. Gualter to Richard Cox, Aug. 26, 1573, Z.L., 442, 444.

These " superstitious dresses ", of which so much was to be heard, were
the conventional walking-out dress of the clergy, the official costume of the
Catholic clergy at the time the Reformation began, and which the Elizabethan
régime was to retain and enforce ; and the phrase was also meant as a description of vestments worn in the administration of the sacraments and in
the other church services.

To the first scrupulous questions of Sampson, his mentors from Zurich
replied that there could be no question of " superstition " in the matter of the
outdoor costume now ordered ; as to the " vestments " properly so called,
Bullinger thought it wrong to use them, while Peter Martyr thought that
Sampson, rather than lose the chance of abolishing the use of them which the
episcopate offered, could consent to wear them if this were made a condition
of his appointment.[1]   But if altars and images—to wit the crucifix—are
retained, on no account is it lawful to officiate.[2]

The very day after this was written at Zurich, John Jewel—now designated for the see of Salisbury—was writing to Zurich, from London, on the
same subject, and proposing the same line of conduct about what he called
" the theatrical costume ".   All the best endeavours of Jewel and of those
who thought as he did have failed, he tells his friends ; the " relics of the
Amorites " will have to be endured, that " scenic apparatus of divine worship
. . . and those very things which you and I have often laughed at ".[3]   One
of these days it will be abolished, he hopes ; and no one, he says, will work
more eagerly than himself to bring about that day.

Meanwhile Sampson too was back in England, and cut to the soul to
see popery in the very chapel of the queen who was still proposing to make
him one of her bishops.   " What hope is there of any good ", he wrote to
Zurich, " when our party are disposed to look for religion in these dumb
remnants of idolatry . . . ? "[4]   But Zurich's advice was still the same :
not to refuse office, lest sees be offered " to wolves and antichrists ".   So
long as Sampson continues to denounce the vestments, he can wear them with
a safe conscience.[5]

[1] Dixon (Vol. V, p. 127) describes this advice as " perfidious ", and it is perhaps the right
word—but no more perfidious than the whole Elizabethan religious policy, whose basis was
that the Englishman must conform outwardly whatever his inward mind, whose authors
boasted that the government was indifferent whether the inward mind of the nation corresponded to the outward expression, and that they were only exigent about conformity that
would express outwardly an assent to the royal *mens*.   And the counsels from Zurich do not
approach the humbug of telling the Catholic to rejoice in his good fortune that, so long as he
lived like a Protestant, and practised no other religion than the queen's, the government
would allow him to continue to believe in his heart that Catholicism was true and Protestantism
false—the masterpiece that so many of our modern historians have lauded as the most admirable feature of the Elizabethan settlement, a general invitation to hypocrisy, with heavy
penalties for those who refuse it.

[2] Peter Martyr to Sampson, Nov. 4, 1559 ; *Z.L.*, 66.

[3] To Peter Martyr, Nov. 5, 1559, *ibid.*, 67 ; the last quotation is from Jewel's undated
letter, *ibid.*, 33.

[4] To Peter Martyr, Jan. 6, 1560 ; *ibid.*, 79.   The main anxiety was that in the queen's
chapel a crucifix stood on the table, flanked by candles.   It was an anxiety to Jewel also
(*ibid.*, 69) and to Cox, now Bishop of Ely (*ibid.*, 81), though less painful to endure, it would
seem from their letters.   [5] Peter Martyr to Sampson, Feb. 1560 ; *ibid.*, 84-85.

The queen's crucifix was one day, some years later, found in pieces on the floor of the chapel—there were no enquiries, and it was not restored. But the vestments remained—surplices for the Common Prayer and copes for the Lord's Supper—to cause trouble endlessly. " The outward habits and inward feeling of popery ", Thomas Lever wrote to Bullinger, " so fascinate the ears and eyes of the multitude, that they are unable to believe, but that either the popish doctrine is still retained, or at least that it will shortly be restored." [1]

It would have been no answer to the difficulty to say that, after all, the injunction about dress meant no more than that the cleric must not dress like a layman. Was not this precisely the difficulty ? that the cleric being bidden to wear a special kind of dress meant that the cleric as such was a different kind of Christian, one of a class apart ? What else could this clerical costume convey except some survival of the popish notion that the cleric was indeed a different kind of being, made really different by an ordination that was sacramental ? If the difference between cleric and layman was but a difference of function, what need was there of any special dress outside the performance of the function ? The opposition of these clergy to the clerical dress was then in no way a bid for a greater freedom of life, nor a mere empty scruple, but an opposition closely related to the doctrinal opposition between the old religion and the new. The special clerical dress might suggest that the minister continued to be, in the new religion, all that the priest had been in the old. The " Primitive " objected to being made to dress as the popish priest had been ordered to dress, because he feared that the reason for the order to the popish priest might seem to be the reason for the order given to himself. To the ordinary man—so the " Primitive " feared—the dress must symbolise a doctrine of priesthood which should be abhorred as a thing humanly invented, and which, because it was a human invention thrust into the very heart of divine religion, was a thing pernicious, and indeed blasphemous.

With such deeply rooted differences of opinion among the very leaders of the party of the Reform ; [2] with the sudden influx, in the first two years, of hundreds of new, utterly uneducated clergy ; [3] and with the worked-up

---

[1] Two very different expectations, of course. July 10, 1560 ; *Z.L.*, 109.

[2] Already the stage is reached where bishops discuss the chances of the orthodoxy of brother bishops, and hints of the revealing question, " Is he sound " ? begin to appear. Parkhurst of Norwich notes that Parker is asking for the names of those who will not comply with true religion, and thereupon writes to Zurich, " I gather from this that his grace of Canterbury intends firmly to support the true religion. May the Lord grant it " ; Aug. 20, 1562 ; *ibid.*, 161.

[3] More than 300 were ordained in London alone—155 in one ordination—in the four months that followed Parker's consecration. When Calfhill, in 1565, replies to Marshall he does not deny the charge of his Catholic opponent, which he repeats, viz.," that the inferior sort of our ministers . . . came from the shops, from the forge, from the wherry, from the loom ". He does no more than retort a *tu quoque*, " In the time of popery ye should have found in every diocese forty Sir Johns in every respect worse " ; and urges that in these new inferior clergy there is " more sincerity and learning therefore than in all the rabble of their popish chaplains, Mass mongers and their soul priests ". (Quoted Dixon, V, 96.) Cf. *supra*, p. 135, n. 5, for the testimony of another Protestant contemporary, Harrison, about the poor quality of many of the new clergy and the reason for this. The complaints about

iconoclastic fury, it is not surprising that, " in no small degree the parochia
clergy were their own guides, and there were at times divergences of teachin;
and of ritual as striking as anything which modern times can show ".[1]   " Th
Table standeth in the body of the church in some places ", the queen wa
informed, " in others it standeth in the chancel. In some places the Tabl
standeth altar-like distant from the wall a yard, some others in the mids
of the chancel north and south. In some places the Table is joined, i
others it standeth upon trestles. In some the Table hath a carpet, in other
it hath none. Some administer with surplice and cope, some with surplic
alone, others with none, some with chalice, some with communion cup
others without a communion cup, some with unleavened bread, some witl
leavened. Some receive kneeling, some standing, others sitting."[2]   Upor
which, Kennedy goes on to say, " It can hardly be believed that variety coul
go beyond this summary, but that it did so is abundantly evident. Th
minutiae of differences would fill a large volume. Sometimes there wer
communicants, sometimes none. Sometimes there was a celebration once a
month, sometimes every Sunday. Sometimes the minister ' counterfeitec
the Popish Mass ', or ' crossed and breathed over the sacramental bread and
wine, showing the same to the people to be worshipped and adored ', and
' decked the Lord's Table like an altar '. It is unnecessary to broaden
the picture. Infinite variety was the rule, and private opinion the only
authority."[3]

" I hope for an improvement at the approaching convocation ", Bishop
Parkhurst wrote to Bullinger in 1562.[4] He meant, of course, an improvement in the sense of Zurich, and he nearly had his wish. For that Convocation of 1563, the first gathering of the party of the Reform, with any
official character, since the change of religion four years before, saw all but
victorious that section to which Parkhurst and Jewel and Pilkington, with
Grindal and Horne, belonged at heart, and many another dignitary with them.
Then there came vigorous action from the government—and, above all,
from the queen—to dispel all doubt that there was an " official ", statesman's
conception of the Reformed religion, and that this was to be enforced ;
and, with this, there came all the clarity of the divisions that are familiar.

The best known work of this convocation[5] is the transformation of
Cranmer's Forty-two Articles of 1553 into the Thirty-nine Articles that

---

careless ordinations continue to be made in later years. While such officers as churchwardens are chosen for service of a particular parish, there is no such care for the ministers,
says a Puritan manifesto, " so that at some one ordering of one B[ishop] . . . have been
made ministers without any certain charge, 20, 30, 40, 50, yea, 60 at a time, which hath
brought that reverend order of ministers to that vileness [i.e., cheapness], etc. . . ."
Certaine Notes of Corruptions in the State of our Churche. Peel, I, 131.

[1] Kennedy, *Parish Life under Queen Elizabeth* (1914), 53 ; a popular account, all too little
known, carefully documented.

[2] This document " purports to be an answer to the queen's request to Parker for diocesan
certificates of ' what varieties and disorders there be ' " ; Kennedy, *E.E.A.*, I, p. civ.

[3] Kennedy, *Parish Life*, 72.   [4] April 28 ; *Z.L.*, 139.

[5] For its history see the vivid, documented account in Dixon, V, 382–412.

still endure. Seven of Cranmer's forty-two were dropped,[1] seventeen of the remainder were modified and four wholly new articles were added. The articles that now disappeared treated of Grace, Blasphemy against the Holy Ghost, of the obligation of all men " to keep the moral commandments of the law ",[2] and reproved four heresies : that by the term resurrection of the dead there is to be understood the raising of the soul by Grace " from the death of sin " ; that " the souls of such as depart hence do sleep . . . until the day of judgment ", or that they " die with the bodies " ; the heretical fable of Millenarism ; the " dangerous opinion, that all men, be they never so ungodly, shall at length be saved, when they have suffered pains for their sins a certain time appointed by God's justice ".

The best part of the changes in the thirty-five articles retained were introduced to make the meaning clearer, to strengthen the declaration, to give reasons, and to supply a practical corollary to the doctrine set out. But to Cranmer's article 5 [3] there was added a list of the Canonical Books ; to number 26 [4] there were added the present second paragraph, that Christ our Lord instituted two sacraments, and the explanation that the other five rites " commonly called sacraments . . . have not like the nature of sacraments with Baptism and the Lord's Supper ". A paragraph was omitted from article 29,[5] *Of the Lord's Supper*, explaining that " the real and bodily presence (as they term it) of Christ's flesh and blood, in the Sacrament of the Lord's Supper ", is an impossibility because Christ's body is in heaven since his ascension and no man's body can be " at one time in diverse places ". Cranmer's article 35 declared that the Prayer Book of 1552 and the Ordinal set forth with it were " godly and in no point repugnant to the wholesome doctrine of the Gospel ". The reference to the Prayer Book was now omitted, and the article became the present 36, with its declaration that all consecrated or ordained according to the rites of this book are " rightly, orderly and lawfully consecrated and ordered ". The change in the wording of the article about the Royal Supremacy has been noticed already.[6] In the article *Of Predestination and Election* [7] there is an interesting omission, from the first sentence of paragraph 3, indicated here in italics : " Furthermore, *although the Decrees of predestination are unknown to us, yet* we must receive God's promises as they be generally set forth to us in Holy Scripture, etc., etc. . . ." [8]

---

[1] Articles 10, 16, 19, 39, 40, 41, 42.
[2] The first paragraph of this (the nineteenth) article was added to no. 6, and forms the third paragraph of the present seventh article. [3] The present article 6.
[4] The present article 25. [5] The present article 28.
[6] The present article 37 ; no. 36 of Cranmer's 42. Cf. *supra*, 75.
[7] Article 17 of 1553 and of the present series.
[8] The Latin text is Deinde *licet praedestinationis decreta sunt nobis ignota,** promissiones tamen divinas**** sic amplecti oportet, etc. Hardwick notes (p. 312) that the Forty-five articles, which were Cranmer's first draft, the following bracketed phrase is inserted at the point marked * (*quatenus homines de hominibus judicare possunt*), and at the double asterisk the bracketed phrase (*quibus fides innitens certos nos reddit de nostra salute*). These Forty-five articles were submitted to the judgment of six royal chaplains, one of whom was John Knox, and two others the Elizabethan bishops of London and Winchester in 1563, Edmund Grindal and Robert Horne.

Finally there was added to Cranmer's twenty-first article, *Of the* *Authority of the Church*,[1] an introductory clause which controversy was presently to make famous : The Church hath power to decree Rites or Ceremonies, and authority in controversies of faith.

The four new articles added in the convocation of 1563 were those numbered in the present series 5, 12, 29 and 30, entitled respectively, Of the Holy Ghost, Of good works, Of the wicked which do not eat the body of Christ in the use of the Lord's Supper, and Of both kinds.[2]

This successful readjustment of the Articles of Religion is not, however, the sole reason why this convocation matters to the historian. It was the occasion for many hearts to be opened, as the various draft schemes laid before it show, and, above all else, the close voting on the proposals to carry further the changes authorised by the parliament of 1559. What the " Zurich " party had so nearly carried, in the Lower House, was a set of six articles that would have abolished all saints' days, the sign of the cross in baptism, the obligation to kneel when receiving the communion, the use of all vestments but the surplice, and the use of organs ; and that would have had the minister always facing the congregation during the service at which he officiated. The programme was defeated by one vote only.[3]

The anti-Settlement section of the Reform party had in its favour, seemingly, very many indeed of the influential class[4]—but against it was the queen, and also that instinct of the bureaucrat to oppose whatever may lessen his own control over his fellows ; Cecil, for example, whose personal religion, so far as we know it, was sympathetic to these men, and who tempered the administration in their favour as much as possible, yet who never faltered in his opposition to the principle of the independence of religion *vis-à-vis* the state, for which, ultimately, they stood.

And the queen saw, from the first, that the movement really made for the nullifying of that newly voted supremacy which she meant should be a

---

[1] The present article 6.

[2] Dixon's statement about the Articles of 1563 (V, 398), " The whole of the teaching of the Forty-two upon Grace and Justification was altered ", is the harder to understand since the Articles of 1563 continue to impose, without alteration, the First Book of Homilies, and to refer the believer to it for a fuller explanation of the meaning of the article on Justification.

[3] By 59 to 58 : see an analysis of the votes in Dixon, V, 389, note. The date is, seemingly, the end of February, 1563 ; *ibid.*, 384, note. The text of the six articles is in Prothero, 191.

[4] Burghley, Leicester, Bedford, Bacon, Walsingham, Davison, Mildmay, Knollys, Cave and Rogers—there was not one of these members of Elizabeth's council but favoured the radical beliefs. And it is a commonplace with the historians of the business that these religious radicals were wealthy. It was in the house of a London goldsmith (*lege* banker), James Tynne, that most of the leaders of the Plumber's Hall affair were arrested (Pearson, 79) ; who writes of the " pious and wealthy ladies ", correspondents of Dering, who supported the cause generally (*ibid.*, 117) and notes, of the authors of the first *Admonition to the Parliament*, that it was " well known then that [they] had wealthy supporters behind them " (*ibid.*, 62). This was a matter of complaint to the Bishop of London (Sandys) in 1573 (*ibid.*, 106) ; and it gave the still more radical patriarch of the Independents a point in his controversy against the claim of the party to be evangelised, " They are fed of the rich and upheld by great men ", quoted, *ibid.*, 216–217.

practical instrument of government. This, and this alone, was what mattered for the queen in the religious life of her subjects.[1] "No one is admitted to any ecclesiastical function", said one of the "Primitives", "unless he acknowledge the queen to be the supreme head of the Church of England upon earth. There is no great difficulty raised about *any other point of doctrine*, provided the party is willing to obey the laws and statutes of the realm." [2] This is a statement from a leading opponent, but it seems to be no more and no less than the plain fact. It is a bolder statement than any made at the time in England itself—naturally, for to touch the supremacy was to play with treason. The queen made it a virtue that, in her own celebrated phrase, she made no windows into any man's soul. Whether he was honest or hypocrite in acknowledging her ecclesiastical supremacy, moved her not at all. Subjects must obey, conform, give no trouble, breed no trouble. "Of religious feeling", we may opportunely listen to the judgment of a modern scholar, "she probably had little. Her cold, entirely humanist outlook, nourished by classical study, kept her apart from the deeper spiritual currents of her time." [3]

The Zurich letters throw some light on Elizabeth's own personal interest and influence in this controversy, as various leaders saw it. In 1566 Grindal, the Bishop of London, speaks of the queen's own irritation at the controversy as a major factor in the affair of Sampson and Humphrey [4] and says that Elizabeth had been one of the main obstacles, in 1559, to the general demand of the returned exiles for a removal of all the last remnants of the old religion. Geneva (seven days later) is saying to Zurich, "our own church . . . is so hateful to that queen" that she has never even acknowledged Beza's present of his book on the New Testament. "We are accounted too severe and precise", Beza thinks, "which is very displeasing to those who fear reproof." Would Zurich, then, undertake to intercede with Elizabeth for the Primitives, "a godly and charitable legation", which would be "very agreeable to the queen and the godly bishops".[5] But Zurich, too, had already had a dose, and handed back the poisoned chalice.

[1] "Ye would take away the authority of the prince, and therefore ye suffer justly", said Bishop Edmund Grindal (June 20, 1567) to the Protestant prisoners taken at a forbidden religious service. And Grindal was one who, at heart, sympathised with these radical tendencies : cf. Dixon, VI, 167–168.

[2] *The State of the Church of England as described by Percival Wiburn*, a document drawn up in 1566 for the consideration of Beza and Bullinger ; Z.L., 269, no. 6. The italics in the text are my own. Wiburn was a Canon of Westminster.

[3] Black, 3. Cf. also, Conyers Read, II, 271, "She appears to have possessed little or no religious enthusiasm herself. First to last, she seems to have regarded religion as a matter of policy." Also, *ibid.*, "The only point upon which she really insisted . . . was that there should be no recognition of the Papal supremacy in England"—which statement ignores, of course, the whole policy of the Act of Uniformity, the prohibition, under heavy penalties, of the practice of the old religion, e.g. to say Mass or to be present at Mass. Elizabeth was herself aware of the critics who thought her indifferent to religion as such, and she publicly made her protest, in the course of one of her most famous speeches to parliament, Nov. 5, 1566 : "It is said, I am no divine. Indeed, I studied nothing else but divinity till I came to the crown. . . ." Neale, *Elizabeth I and her Parliaments*, I, 149.

[4] Aug. 27, 1566. Z.L., 243. For the "affair" cf. *infra*, pp. 159 foll.

[5] Sept. 3, 1566 ; *ibid.*, 248.

" The queen ", Gualter wrote in reply, " who has in many respects too much abused her authority up to the present time by her arbitrary power, and has refused to be warned by the advice and remonstrances of her councillors . . . ", will hardly listen to Zurich, in this matter. Why, she has never even noticed the letters Zurich has already sent.[1] Grindal and Horne, in the following spring, write feelingly to Zurich of the effect of the demonstrations of the true blues of the party of Reform, that they " are bringing the whole of our religion into danger. For by their outcries of this kind, we have, alas, too severely experienced that the mind of the queen, otherwise inclined to favour religion, has been much irritated " ;[2] Jewel, a fortnight later, says that the controversy " has at this time occasioned much disturbance. For it is quite certain that the queen will not be turned from her opinion."[3] In August, that same year, the new exiles at Zurich are telling Bullinger that if the bishops would intercede with Elizabeth the ejected clergy would be allowed to keep their livings.[4] Horne of Winchester paints the queen as the all-important, and wholly incalculable, factor in the business : " Our excellent queen, as you know, holds the helm, and directs it according to her pleasure. But we are awaiting the guidance of the divine Spirit, which is all we can do ; and we daily implore him with earnestness and importunity to turn at length our sails to another quarter . . . it would be very dangerous to drag her (i.e. Elizabeth) on, against her will, to a point where she does not yet choose to come to, as it were wresting the helm out of her hands."[5] The Bishop of Ely, three years later, describes the queen as the church's one hope in the crisis : the anti-Settlement party " would bring the church into very great danger, were not our most pious queen most faithful to her principles, and did she not dread and restrain the vanity and inconsistency of these frivolous men ".[6]

By the time that Cox was writing so comfortably to Switzerland, the " most pious queen " had proved herself, in act, the staunchest of all believers in the Settlement of 1559 as the final arrangement of national Christianity. It was indeed due to the queen's own personal determination, that never wavered in the teeth of opposition, at times well nigh universal, from the party whose patron she was, that the Settlement survived unharmed in these critical years. And nowhere is her effect more clearly shown than in the parliamentary history of the years 1566–1572.[7]

The new parliament which sat concurrently with the convocation of 1563, and which was as strongly " radical "[8] in religion as the convocation

---

[1] Z.L. 236–241, 265 ; Sept. 11, 1566.
[2] Feb. 8, 1567 ; ibid., 274.
[3] Feb. 19, 1567 ; ibid., 286.
[4] Bullinger and Gualter to Grindal, Horne and Parkhurst, Aug. 26, 1567 ; ibid., 308.
[5] To Bullinger, Aug. 8, 1571 ; ibid., 355.
[6] To Gualter, Feb. 3, 1574 ; ibid., 454.
[7] The detailed story is set out, for the first time, by Professor Neale in the dramatic pages of his Elizabeth I and her Parliaments, Vol. I, 1559–1581 (1953).
[8] Professor Neale's word for the clergy who were so narrowly defeated in the convocation of 1563, op. cit., 89.

itself, was, in the event, too absorbed by its contest with the queen about the need for her to declare her next heir, and to marry, for it to find time to press on with the completion of what had been achieved in 1559. But this same parliament in its second session, three years later, although occupied more than ever with the succession problem, managed to force the religious issue too, and very strongly. On December 5, 1566, a Bill was introduced in the Commons to give force of law to the Articles of 1563, and to exact from all the clergy a public declaration they accepted them as true.

The Bill went through all its stages in the Commons and had been read once in the Lords (December 14), when the queen intervened. First she sent a message to the Lord Keeper that he was to see the Bill went no further ; and then, when the Commons, and the bishops too, not knowing the cause of the delay, began to press the matter, Elizabeth sent for the bishops to tell them that although she did not dislike the " doctrine of the Book of Religion, for that it containeth the religion which she doth openly profess ", she did indeed dislike " the manner of putting it forth ".[1] And there the matter ended, for this parliament ; despite a further petition from the bishops on December 24.

This petition is, incidentally, interesting evidence what these first Elizabethan prelates thought of the practical importance of the testimony of the church compared with that of the Royal Supremacy, in securing the assent of the ordinary man in matters of doctrine. " The approbation of these Articles by your Majesty ", they declared, " shall be a very good means to establish and confirm all your Highness subjects in one consent and unity of true doctrine, to the great quiet and safety of your Majesty and this your realm ; whereas now for want of a plain certainty of Articles of Doctrine by law to be declared, great distraction and dissension of minds is at this present among your subjects and daily is like more and more to increase and that with very great danger in policy, the circumstances considered, if the said Book of Articles be now stayed in your Majesty's hand, or (as God forbid) rejected." [2]

In the parliament of 1566 Elizabeth had been too much for the " godly ". Five years later, in a new parliament, the trouble began all over again, and this time the queen thought it better, in the end, to compromise. The Bill to enact the Articles of 1563 now passed into law, despite the queen's wishes. On the other hand Elizabeth succeeded in halting a much more rigorous inquisition into the private life of the Englishman, a bill strongly backed by both houses of parliament and by the bishops, which proposed to make annual communion obligatory for all under a penalty of 100 marks. The religious temper of the parliament may be gathered from the demand of the Commons that each day's proceedings should begin with a forty-five minutes' sermon from preachers appointed by the Bishop of London.

There were other proposals, introduced and debated, that never got so far as to challenge the queen's veto, bills designed, yet once again, to

---

[1] Parker, *Correspondence*, 291. [2] Dec. 24, 1566 ; *ibid.*, 292 ; Hardwick, 146.

complete the work of 1559, by purging the church of ministers unable to preach, by enacting the Cranmer Code of Canon Law,[1] and by abolishing caps and surplices, the rite called Confirmation, the interrogations at Baptism, the use of the ring in marriage, the practice of receiving communion kneeling. The nobility of the aim was undisguised, the duty, namely, not to permit " for any cause of policy or other pretence, any errors in matters of doctrine to continue amongst us " ; [2] the debates were animated ; and the queen's opposition unmistakable. " For us to meddle with matters of her prerogative ", said Sir Francis Knollys, in warning to the House, is " not expedient ".[3] And from Elizabeth came the direct message that although she liked well of the said Articles, she " mindeth to publish them and have them executed by the bishops, by direction of her majesty's regal authority of supremacy of the Church of England, and not to have the same dealt in by Parliament ".[4] Yet four weeks later the Bill received the Royal Assent ! [5]

This Act of 1571 [6] was directed, in the mind of those who promoted it —as was the abortive Bill of 1566—against the survivors of the conforming clergy of 1559, the one-time Catholic priests who still formed so large a part of the national clergy, and whose sincerity as true believers of the reformed doctrines was more than suspect. For it was only those benefice holders who had been ordained by Catholic rites in days gone by who were now obliged—under penalty of deprivation *ipso facto*—to set their names to the Articles ; although, for the future, a signed acceptance of them was to be exacted as a condition of ordination, and at every institution into a living. But what the cleric was obliged to declare himself as accepting was " all the articles of religion which only concern the confession of the true christian faith and the doctrine of the sacraments ", not all the Thirty-nine but only these.[7]

The bishops, meanwhile, in this same year 1571, had taken a line of their own in convocation. While parliament was fighting the queen's contention that questions of religion concerned her prerogative, and were not matter for parliamentary initiative, convocation made its own regulations about the acceptance of the Articles of 1563. In a canon, *Concerning Preachers*,[8] it was laid down that " whoever shall be sent to teach the people

---

[1] The *Reformatio Legum Ecclesiasticarum*, which, under the practiced editorship of John Foxe, now made its first appearance in print. This code treated as heresy the main points where Catholic belief differed from the Reformed religion, and provided a death penalty for the obdurate heretic. Cf. for further details, Vol. II, pp. 129-134.

[2] Walter Strickland, April 6, inaugurating the debate in the Commons, cf. Neale, *op. cit.*, 194. [3] Sir Francis Knollys' speech, April 14, *ibid.*, 199. [4] D'Ewes, p. 185.

[5] But the queen, that same day, refused the royal assent to the very popular Bill " concerning coming to the church and receiving of the Communion ". It had passed all its stages in both houses. Only the queen was opposed to it. And she now made an end of it. Why ? " Tolerance was undoubtedly her motive. She refused to go back on her liberal declaration of 1570 ; she would open no window into men's souls." So Professor Neale, *op. cit.*, 216.

[6] 13 Elizabeth, c. 12. The text is printed in G. & H., 477-480.

[7] For the controversy over this clause, cf. *infra*, p. 195, n. 3.

[8] G. & H., 476-477 (Eng. trans.) ; Prothero, 201.

shall confirm the authority and faith of those Articles not only in their sermons but also by subscription. Whoever does otherwise, and perplexes the people with contrary doctrine, shall be excommunicated." As, by this same canon, every incumbent needed the bishop's permission before he could preach even in his parish, this was a rule that could affect the whole body of parochial clergy, and it imposed subscription to the whole of the Articles. What is meant by the phrase "those Articles", is made clear by the words which introduce the command about subscription. "And since the Articles of the Christian religion to which assent was given by the bishops in lawful and holy synod convened and celebrated by command and authority of our most serene princess Elizabeth, were without doubt collected from the holy books Old and New Testament, and in all respects agree with the heavenly doctrine which is contained in them. . . ."

For another two years nearly, after the Convocation of 1563, the uneasy truce endured, and then, in December 1564, Archbishop Parker wrote to Sampson, now Dean of Christchurch, and also to Laurence Humphrey, president of Magdalen College and Regius Professor of Divinity at Oxford, the two most distinguished in rank of the section openly opposed to the new uniformity, and a discussion began, reasons for the surplice, reasons against it, which, at first, left matters where they were. Then, on January 25, 1565, the queen sent her celebrated letter to Parker rebuking him for his slackness in securing conformity to the laws, and bidding him "according to the authority which you have *under us* for this Province of Canterbury", to take measures to put an end to all novelties and diversities. For "we will have no dissension or variety . . . for so the sovereign authority which we have under Almighty God would be made frustrate and we might be thought to bear the sword in vain ".[1] Thereupon an inquisition began, that varied no doubt according to the temperament of the various bishops, but about which we know little ; and in March there came from Parker a new set of articles. For some time these passed from Parker to Cecil and Cecil to the queen, and then back to Parker, to be approved by Elizabeth but refused any public sign of her approval, and to be issued finally, in March 1566, on the archbishop's responsibility, as his own *Advertisements*.[2]

In the meantime Sampson and Humphrey had been cited before the archbishop (April 29, 1565) and on Sampson's refusal to wear the appointed dress or the vestments, and " to communicate kneeling in wafer bread ",[3] he was deprived.[4] The next event was the discovery that Cambridge was as full of Protestants like Sampson as Oxford was said to be of Catholics.

---

[1] Strype, *Parker*, III, 67, 68. Italics mine.
[2] Text in G. & H., 467–475 ; Dixon, VI, 49–55.
[3] Parker's words ; *ibid.*, 60.
[4] Laurence Humphrey, however, continued as president of Magdalen College and regius professor of Divinity—the leading personage in the university—for another twenty-four years : a great attraction for " the politically alert gentry. . . . Many Elizabethan members of parliament went to Magdalen college " and Humphrey's " influence was reflected in the strong puritan tone of the Elizabethan House of Commons ". The quotations are from J. E. Neale, *The Elizabethan House of Commons*, 303–304.

If obedience to the laws about the surplice was demanded, so the vice-chancellor wrote to Cecil, the university must lose a host of pious and learned men. St. John's College and Trinity were especially affected.

The struggle now became sharp indeed, once the *Advertisements* were promulgated, in March 1566. For to this list of thirty-eight new articles, which dealt with doctrine and preaching, public prayer, administration of sacraments, "ecclesiastical policy" and outward apparel, there was appended a series of eight "protestations to be made promised and subscribed", as a condition of appointment to any post in the church—among these were promises not "to preach or publicly interpret but only [to] read that which is appointed by public authority", unless specially licensed; and also a promise to wear the prescribed apparel, and to keep to the rites and ceremonies approved.

On March 26, 1566, Parker had the whole of the London clergy before him at Lambeth, Grindal sitting with him, and the rector of Bow Church functioning as a clerical mannequin, clad to show how all must now be clad.[1] There was no discussion; nothing but a peremptory summons to write *Volo* or *Nolo*. Out of 110 present, all but 37 were willing; and the 37 were immediately suspended, to be deprived of their livings *ipso facto* in three months if they had not submitted. What the legality of these deprivations, or of the very *Advertisements*, is still disputed. Among the clergy deprived were some of the most celebrated Reformers of the day, and protests came in to Cecil from the very bishops. From the commotion that now began, the new establishment was not to be free for another sixty years and more. "Sides were being taken for the mighty conflict which was to turn England into a camp, in another generation, under another dynasty."[2]

Meanwhile both parties consulted the Swiss infallibilities.[3] "The opinions of masters Bullinger and Gualter are of no little weight in our church", the Bishop of Ely was later to write to those venerable personages.[4] And indeed it was from Bullinger and Peter Martyr, more than from any others, that many leading English divines of this time had learned almost all they knew of these mysteries. In this Zurich Correspondence by no means the whole of the story is told. But there is, at times, a great revealing of hearts, for all parties write freely, and do not mince their words. Also the aggrieved say plainly what it is that they want—what those points are in which, so they declare, the bishops have gone back on what all once held and practised, and desiderated for England, as the gospel truth.

---

[1] The clergy were told that they must dress ". . . like to this man, as ye see him." For an account of what Dixon calls a "curious and painful" scene, cf. Vol. VI, 95 and foll.

[2] Dixon, VI, 124.

[3] "Infallibilities" is inaccurate, of course, to the point of libel and slander. What is true is that, "A better example of purely spiritual power could hardly be found than the influence that was exercised in England by Zwingli's successor Henry Bullinger. Bishops and Puritans argue their causes before him as if he were the judge." Maitland, in *C.M.H.* II, 597.

[4] Cox to Bullinger and Gualter, Feb. 3, 1574 : *Z.L.*, 453. Cf. also, the same prelate "that pillar of the church of Christ, master Henry Bullinger", *ibid.*, 422.

To Bullinger, a few weeks before the publication of the *Advertisements*, Humphrey, for example, sends a series of nine doubts for his consideration ; and Sampson, about the same time, sends a list of twelve. Bullinger replies with a solution and then the two Englishmen, in a joint letter, set out their grievances under thirteen heads ; and Percival Wiburn takes over to Switzerland a still more detailed list of thirty-one items.[1] These are the principle statements.

The Swiss divines, for their part, are not eager to take part in this fight. They warn their disciples of the danger of concealing " a contentious spirit under the name of conscience " ; they complain that the leaders of the " conscience " party have " entangled [the subject] in complicated knots " ; and they find it " extraordinary " that Humphrey and Sampson are " perpetually contending in this troublesome way ". And they do not forget to remind them how few are the clergy in England capable of guiding the churches there in the direction of evangelical reform,[2] and how real the danger is that if the dissidents walk out, their flock will be handed over to " wolves ". To which the two Englishmen reply that they " are not merely disputing about a cap or a surplice ", that the controversy " is of no light or trifling character ", and that they " are endeavouring to check at the outset what we fear will come to pass in this country ". They write, from the first, as men of principle : not what may or can be done, they say, is what they are asking, but what ought to be done.[3]

Once the heads of the churches at Zurich and Geneva understood the nature of the new English establishment, they tended to judge it as did the dissidents ; and they expressed themselves about it still more violently. " We hear ", say Bullinger and Gualter to the Earl of Bedford, " that many other things [besides clerical dress] are obtruded upon the godly ministers . . . which were fabricated in the school of antichrist . . . new filth and the restored relics of wretched popery." [4] Bullinger candidly does not approve those who first enacted, or who are now zealous maintainers of, those laws by which " the dregs of popery are retained ". He thinks that " dregs and filthiness of this kind . . . stain and defile " the Reformation. To the Bishop

[1] The dates of these four letters are Feb. 9, Feb. 16, May 1, and July, all in 1566 ; *Z.L.*, 210, 211, 214–224, 233–240. Wiburn's paper (*ibid.*, 269–272), undated, also belongs to the summer of 1566, for Beza's comments on it to Zurich (*ibid.*, 246–252) are dated Sept. 3 of that year, and Zurich's letter to Grindal which it inspired, Sept. 6 (*ibid.*, 253–255). Bullinger's reply to the English letter of July 1566 is dated Sept. 10 (*ibid.*, 256–258). For Wiburn (1533?–1606?), a one-time fellow of St. John's, Cambridge, a refugee at Geneva in Mary's reign, ordained in 1560, cf. *D.N.B.*

[2] In 1566—after seven years of the régime of 1559 !

[3] Cf. also, *Admonition to the Parliament* (1572), " Neither is the controversy betwixt them and us as they would bear the world in hand, as for a cap, a tippet, or a surplice, but for great matters concerning a true ministry and regiment of the church, according to the word ". *Puritan Manifestoes*, 36, n. 2.

[4] Nov. 11, 1566 in *Z.L.*, 260. Zanchy, also, from Calvinistic Heidelberg, wrote of " meretricious adornments . . . adopted by the Roman harlot to allure men to spiritual fornication " ; this in a letter meant for Elizabeth, which Grindal was too prudent to allow to pass ; *ibid.*, 373.

of Norwich, Parkhurst, Gualter writes that " it were rather to be desired that their views might prevail ".[1]

The new liturgy, we gather from these letters of Sampson and Humphrey and Wiburn,[2] is too disfigured by " popish superstition " : for example, the questioning of the infant at baptism through the sponsors, the signing with the cross, and the private administration of this sacrament in urgent cases (? as though, thus administered, it could be effective) ; the use of the ring in marriage ; the very retention of the rite called confirmation,[3] and of " the purification of women after childbirth, which they call the thanksgiving"; feast days that bear the names of saints, and their vigils;[4] tolling of bells on feasts and at funerals ; " the effeminate and over-refined strains of the music itself " and " the use of the organ in church " ; bowing the head at the holy name ; kneeling to receive at the Lord's Supper, and the use of unleavened bread ; they denounce the law that no one shall, either in word or in writing, criticise the liturgy as now set forth, and Parker's new regulation that the minister shall, as a condition of his appointment, put his signature to an approval of the liturgy and to a promise that he will use no other.

There are also other objections to the new régime, to details of what it imposes and to the authority by which all is imposed : for example, the retention of the full ecclesiastical hierarchy, archbishops, bishops, deans, archdeacons, rectors, vicars, curates ;[5] the bishops' control over appointments "to serve a church " ; the law that none shall preach without express leave of the bishop ; " the greater part of the canon law is still in force ", or, as Humphrey

---

[1] Sept. 11, 1566 ; Z.L., 261. Cf., also, Beza to Grindal, June 2, 1566, in Puritan Manifestoes, 43–55.

[2] The " straws and chips of popery " set out in the appendix to the letter of Humphrey and Sampson are in fairly general terms. Wiburn gives substantially the same but with more detail.

[3] This rite, " in which the bishops lay their hands upon the children on their repeating the catechism, and pray the Lord that he may vouchsafe to increase in them the knowledge of his word and godliness " (Cox, Bishop of Ely, to R. Gualter, Z.L., 418), was hardly more esteemed by the official party than by their critics. Hooker, for example, can write that there is " surely great cause to make complaint of the deep neglect of this Christian duty almost with all them to whom by right of their place and calling the same belongeth " (Hooker, II, 345). And whether the Puritan, Robert Cawdry, is correct who said to Burghley in 1587, that " The Bishops themselves, for the most part, these 29 years had not observed it [i.e. the Book of Common Prayer] in not confirming of children ", Whitgift, in a circular letter of September 1591, could complain, " I am very sorry to hear that my brethren, the Bishops of the province of Canterbury, do so generally begin to neglect to confirm children at least to call for and exact both the use of it, and of the catechising children in the church by the minister ". Strype, Whitgift, III, 289 ; and Aylmer, p. 89, for Cawdry, who also remarked that none were supposed to receive Communion who had not been confirmed.

[4] Whitgift, as Archbishop of Canterbury, explained later to the critics, Dec. 5, 1583 that saints' days were kept in the calendar not " to nourish " the superstition that there was any holiness in the saints " but to express the usual times of payments, and the times of the courts, and their returns in both laws ". Peel, I, p. 212, no. 135, viz., A Briefe and true reporte of the proceedings againste some of the ministers and preachers of the diocese of Chichester for refusing to subscribe to certaine articles ; ibid., 209–220.

[5] Cf. Beza's comment on this to Bullinger (July, 1566), " What can it be in a countr where, just the same as under the papacy, they have in the place of a lawfully appointed presbytery their deans, chancellors, archdeacons . . ." ; Z.L., 246, and again (July 29, 1567 " Where did such a Babylon ever exist ? " ; ibid., 294.

d Sampson put it, " In the ecclesiastical regimen there are retained many aces of the church of anti-christ ", words which preface a vigorous denunciation of the whole system of dispensations and fees that still continues the courts of the bishops, " in which, as things are at present, there preside r the most part papists or despisers of all religion ". Behind all this is the uthority of the queen. It is one grievance that, with the advice of the Archishop of Canterbury, the queen is authorised to " change anything in the urch at her pleasure " ; and it is another that "No one is admitted to any clesiastical function, unless he acknowledge the queen to be the supreme ead of the church of England upon earth ".[1] Against this last it is urged at nothing ought " to be obtruded [on the church] by the authority of the vereign without its having been lawfully discussed in a Christian synod ".[2]

" What shall we say respecting discipline, the sinews of religion ? " say umphrey and Sampson : " There is none at all, neither has our church its d, or any exercise of superintendence." [3] For example, the clergy are ot " called to the ministry of the word by reason of any talents bestowed pon them ; great numbers offer themselves ; whence it comes to ass that not very many are found qualified for this function ". Lay atronage still flourishes, and all the abuses that went with it : appropriations, r example, and the sale of advowsons. The clergy have not the unfettered ght to excommunicate—this is the business of the bishops' courts, and the ecisions of the lay judges who sit there bind the clergy: and with these lay dges, too, lies the power of absolving from excommunication. It is these ame lay judges who inflict what punishment is ever inflicted for adultery ; nd for this sin, " even clergymen are not very severely punished ". There is o divorce, for " the popish laws are retained as heretofore " ; [4] and the arriages of the clergy suffer in public estimation from the contradiction that,

---

[1] The idea of the Royal Supremacy seems to have moved Beza very profoundly. " The apacy was never abolished in that country, but rather transferred to the sovereign ", he rites to Bullinger (July, 1566), *Z.L.*, 246. And, two months later, to the same correspondent, e thus speaks of the pledge imposed by the *Advertisements* : " the most grievous thing of all, at persons are admitted to this office of teaching solely upon condition of taking an oath at they will neither by writing nor by word of mouth oppose any part of that reformation, at is those intolerable corruptions, and therefore that they will firmly maintain as law hatever it may please the Queen or the Archbishop of Canterbury to change, take away or dd ; who can submit to this with a good conscience ? " *ibid.*, 251. Gualter, writing to arkhurst, Bishop of Norwich, for Bullinger as well as for himself, speaks still more plainly Sept. 11, 1566) : " Christ is the . . . most determined avenger of his church and will not llow any injury done to his most faithful servants to go unpunished. And it is to him that e must some time render an account of our stewardship, not to the queen, or pope, or those ho assume to themselves the pope's tyranny in the church " ; *ibid.*, 262.

[2] So Coverdale, Humphrey and Sampson to Beza, July 1566, in *ibid.*, 229. The two last ad written much the same thing to Zurich five months earlier, asking, " Whether anything f a ceremonial nature may be prescribed to the church by the sovereign without the assent nd free concurrence of church men ? " *ibid.*, 212, Feb. 16, 1566.

[3] Cf. George Withers, to the Elector Palatine, " . . . the ministry is, in fact nothing at all, or is there any discipline " ; *ibid.*, 304.

[4] Including, it seems, the Catholic doctrine that Christian marriage is indissoluble, e.g. he declaration of the bishops in 1560, " Matrimonium inter Christianos legitime iuxta erbum Dei initum et contractum est indissolubile, nec per traditiones hominum unquam onvellendum " ; in Kennedy, *Interpretations*, 36.

although these marriages are allowed " by permission of Queen Elizabeth '
they are " forbidden by a public statute of the realm . . . in force to thi
day " ; so that the " children are by some persons regarded as illegitimate "
Moreover, " The lord bishops are forbidden to have their wives with ther
in their palaces ; as are also the deans, canons, presbyters, and other minister
of the church, within colleges or the precincts of cathedral churches ".[2]

Such were " These dregs and this leaven of popery ", now declared to b
" the source of the whole controversy ".[3] Here was what caused godl
men to ask " Can tyranny please us in a free church ? " This was ba
enough from the popes ; and now, " Have the bishops any *right* to obtrud
upon pastors, on pain of deprivation, certain habits and ceremonies "
asked the Dean of Wells.[4]

It was no small part of the bitterness of this controversy that very man
of the bishops were known to share the views of the men whom they were
nevertheless, at the queen's behest, condemning and, even, expelling fror
their livings. And in their letters to Zurich these bishops make no secret—
—in defending their submission to the crown—either of their own rea
opinions or of the way they came to their present, " practical ", point of view

[1] " . . . how little are they removed from the law of celibacy, who are forbidden t
marry wives without the express permission of the queen, and the assent of the lord bishor
and some two justices of the peace ; and when married are forbidden to keep their wive
either in colleges or within the precincts of the cathedrals, to wit as counting them impur
or for the avoidance of scandal ". Beza to Bullinger, *Z.L.*, 247.

[2] Almost literally true. As the queen moves around Suffolk, in 1561, the sight of th
married clergy draws venomous comments. " Surely here be many slender ministers, an
such nakedness of religion as it overthroweth may credit ", Cecil wrote to Lambeth, Aug. 1
(Strype, *Parker*, I, 214). " Her Majesty continueth very ill-affected to the state of matrimon
in the clergy. If I were not very stiff therein, she would utterly and openly condemn an
forbid it. . . ." And he sends on the Queen's Injunction of Aug. 9 (*ibid.* 212) " Kee
your wives and children and nurses out of colleges, chapels and cathedral precincts. .
If you will not obey, you shall lose your promotions " ; so Dixon, V, 309, summarisin
this order. Cecil would have liked it suppressed, but Parker published it, " to the perplexit
of the bishops " (*ibid.* 310). And cf. (Strype, *Parker*, III, no. XVII) Parker writing to Ceci
" I was in horror to hear such words . . . as she spake concerning God's holy ordinanc
and institution of matrimony. . . . We alone of our time . . . traduced before the malicio
and ignorant people, as beasts without knowledge to Godward, in using this liberty of h
word, as men of effrenate intemperancy without discretion. . . . In so much, that th
Queen's Highness expressed to me a repentance, that we were thus appointed in offic
wishing it had been otherwise. Which inclination being known at large to Queen Mary
clergy, they laugh prettily to see how the clergy of our time us handled."

Sixteen years later clerical marriage is a much criticised novelty still—and not on religiou
grounds. Harrison feels it necessary to reply, for example, to such charges as that wel
beneficed clergy no longer leave their money to found colleges and hospitals but to the
widows and children ; or that the clergy's widows are not the grave religious women the
might be expected to be. " Eve will be Eve ", he says, " though Adam would say nay
(Harrison, 79). And his will, made when the establishment is thirty years old, itself witnesse
how real, all through the reign of Elizabeth, was the ambiguity of the wife's status. Fe
he leaves " . . . one part and a half unto Marion Harrison alias Marion Isebrande and th
daughter of William Isebrande . . . whom by the law of God, I take for my true and lawf
wife . . ." ; and again, when he comes to appoint his executors, he uses the same caref
language, " Marion Isebrande alias Marion Harrison . . . whom by the laws of God I tak
and repute in all respects for my true and lawful wife " ; July 27, 1591, *ibid.*, pp. xx–xx

[3] Humphrey and Sampson to Bullinger, July 10, 1566 ; *Z.L.*, 237.

[4] William Turner, to the same, July 23, 1566 ; *ibid.*, 232–233.

We who are now bishops ", wrote Grindal, " on our first return, and before we entered on our ministry, contended long and earnestly for the removal of those things which have occasioned the present dispute : but as we were unable to prevail, either with the queen or the parliament, we judged it best, *after consultation on the subject*, not to desert our churches for the sake of a few ceremonies . . .".[1]   And Horne, considered by the critics to be one of the " ferocious " bishops, wrote, in much the same strain. " It was enjoined us who had not then any authority either to make laws or repeal them) either to wear the caps and surplices, or to give place to others. We complied . . . lest our enemies should take possession of the places deserted by ourselves." [2]

A third episcopal witness to the same facts is Pilkington of Durham : " We receive, it is true, or rather tolerate until the Lord shall give us better times " [3] such things as the sign of the cross in baptism, and kneeling to receive the Lord's Supper, and the courts of the Archbishop of Canterbury. " We endure many things against our inclinations, and groan under them, which if we wished ever so much, no entreating can remove. We are under authority, and cannot innovate without the sanction of the queen . . . and the only alternative now allowed us is, whether we will bear with these things or disturb the peace of the church." [4]

It is not to be wondered at that the victims doubted the purity of the bishops' zeal.   " On the expulsion of the papist bishops [new ones were appointed]—most of these were of the number of those who had been exiles. These at first began to oppose the ceremonies ; but afterwards, when there was no hope otherwise of obtaining a bishopric, they yielded, and as one of them openly acknowledged, undertook office against their conscience." [5] Nor was it surprising that, at Zurich, they were shocked, having expected the bishops to defend these clergy—never that the bishops would be such cowards as to connive at the persecution, still less that they would consent to be themselves the instruments of it.[6]   After all, as had been said more than once, " We have the same doctrine as you of Zurich ".   It was logical enough to ask " Why should we not have the same rites ? " [7]

The divisions, of course, continued. How could they have been healed ? Grindal[8] said the extent of the controversy had been ". . . scarcely credible ". Some of the reform party, suspicious, from the beginning, of the settlement of 1559, gradually advanced from criticism and protestation to the positive work of describing in detail what that " more scriptural " organisation was which they considered proper for the Church of Christ ; and here and there attempts were made to set it up. " Many of the more learned clergy ",

---

[1] To Bullinger, Aug. 27, 1566 ; *Z.L.*, 243.   Italics are mine.
[2] To Gualter, July 17, 1565 ; *ibid.*, 200.
[3] Much as a certain type of contemporary Catholic was " tolerating " until a better day arrived !   [4] To Gualter, July 20, 1573, *ibid.*, 425–426.
[5] Withers to the Elector Palatine, *ibid.*, 302. Cf. also, the *Admonition to the Parliament* (1572), " they were once of our mind, but since their consecration they be so transubstantiated, that they are become such as you see ". *Puritan Manifestoes*, 6.
[6] So Gualter to Parkhurst, Sept. 11, 1566 ; *ibid.*, 261.
[7] Humphrey and Sampson to Bullinger, July 1566 ; *ibid.*, 238.
[8] To the same, Aug. 27, 1566 ; *ibid.*, 314.

this same letter of the Bishop of London goes on to say, " seemed to be on the point of forsaking their ministry. Many of the people also had it in contemplation to withdraw from us and set up private meetings." About 200 indeed, more women among them than men, " of the lowest order ", with four or five ministers, " have openly separated from us ", and hold services in private houses, in fields, and in ships, preaching and administering sacraments. " Besides this they have ordained ministers, elders, and deacons, after their own way." [1]   In June 1567 a congregation of true believers was discovered meeting for unlawful liturgies in the hall of the Plumbers' Company. They were dispersed and a score of their leaders were imprisoned.[2]

Three years later, at Cambridge, there were more important developments, in which two new personalities appeared around whose activity these ecclesiastical debates were now to turn for the rest of the reign. These were the Lady Margaret professor of divinity, Thomas Cartwright, and the Master of Trinity College, John Whitgift.

3. CARTWRIGHT

John Whitgift was, in 1569, a man of thirty-nine. He hailed from Grimsby in Lincolnshire, where his father was a well-to-do merchant,[3] and he was the nephew of the last abbot of the local abbey of Wellow. At Cambridge, Ridley had been his master, and John Bradford his tutor. But Whitgift managed, none the less, like many another Reformer, to continue his studies there during the whole of Mary's reign.[4] He was ordained in 1560, in one of the first ordinations of the new régime ; and when, in 1563, he was given the Lady Margaret chair of divinity, the future Archbishop of Canterbury chose for his inaugural lecture the popular, and highly important, theme that " The pope is Antichrist ".[5] In 1567 Whitgift received two great promotions from the crown, the mastership of Trinity College, and the Regius professorship of divinity ; and two years later, on the eve of the great controversy, he preached his first sermon before Elizabeth, and was named one of her chaplains. Here was an intellectual who was also a masterful, and a highly successful, personage.

Cartwright, however, younger by five years than his opponent, was quite equal to Whitgift, both in intelligence and in good fighting quality. He too had climbed high, but from very humble beginnings ; unlike Whitgift he had views of his own. Unlike Whitgift in this also, Cartwright had had to interrupt his university life in Mary's reign, the last two years of which he spent in the study of the Common Law, and as clerk to a barrister. In his early years, at St. John's, Cambridge, Cartwright had known, as masters of the College, two very celebrated Edwardian Reformers, William Bill and Thomas Lever. When he returned to St. John's, after Mary's

---

[1] Same to the same, June 11, 1568 ; *Puritan Manifestoes*, 314.   [2] Dixon, VI, 166 and foll.
[3] Whence, to the future archbishop, a good private fortune.
[4] M.A. in 1557, and fellow of Peterhouse.
[5] For an opinion about the importance of this thesis to the success of the Reformation ropaganda, cf. *supra*, p. 77, n. 4.

eath, it was under the rule of James Pilkington, late an exile at Zurich, and onsidered to be one of the major forces in the " puritanising " of the univer-ity.[1] In 1560 Cartwright completed his master's degree, and became a ellow of his college. Then, in 1562, he moved to Trinity as a fellow, five ears before Whitgift crossed its threshold. For two of those years he was way in Ireland, chaplain to Elizabeth's new primate Adam Loftus, who, n 1567, proposed this young deacon for the see of Armagh. The Archbishop f Dublin's endeavour to be useful failed however ; Cartwright came back o Trinity, where Whitgift now presided. He took his bachelor's degree n theology (1567), was twice named a university preacher (1567, 1568) nd, in 1569, succeeded to Whitgift's old place as Lady Margaret professor.

From that chair, and from the pulpit too, Cartwright now began his life's vork of criticising, and denouncing as contrary to Holy Scripture, the con-titution and hierarchy of the Church of England as the Acts of 1559 had stablished it. Cartwright's procedure was the same simple methodology f Jewel defending the recent repudiation of the papacy. Lecturing on the Acts of the Apostles, he compared the Elizabethan establishment with the Church of Christ as he understood it to be there described : by that com-parison the Establishment stood condemned.

Soon a most violent controversy developed, in which a great part of the university sided with Cartwright. The new Regius professor of divinity, however, William Chaderton,[2] denounced him to the chancellor of the univer-sity—who was none other than Cecil himself ; and Grindal, just promoted Archbishop of York, wrote to Cecil in the same sense.[3] On June 29, 1570, the vice-chancellor and the heads of the colleges intervened to prevent Cartwright from taking his doctor's degree. And once more both parties appealed to Cecil. Letters and memorials poured in on the Secretary of State ; there was an explanation from Cartwright, and a denunciation of Cartwright from Whitgift—the real, leading influence in the event of June 29. The master of Trinity was now in the midst of the great business of remodel-ling the statutes of the university. On September 25 these were promulgated, " the great revolution " was accomplished ;[4] and Cartwright now was doomed. For under the new statutes the heads of the colleges were the rulers of the university, and Whitgift, vice-chancellor in November, had now little difficulty in bringing about Cartwright's expulsion from his chair (December 11, 1570). Despite all the power of the highly-placed laymen who shared his views, despite Cecil's own interest in them, Cartwright, at 35, was broken ; his official and academic career in the Church of England

[1] J. B. Mullinger, D.N.B., art. Pilkington, James.
[2] Appointed in 1570, on Whitgift's resignation of the chair. Chaderton (born c. 1540) was a Lancashire man (from Nuthurst, near Moston, Manchester) and educated at Cambridge (Pembroke College, of which a fellow in 1558). In 1567 he was Lady Margaret professor of divinity ; in 1568 President of Queen's College, through Cecil's influence. He was also one of Leicester's chaplains, and it was through Leicester that, in 1579, he was given the see of Chester, with the wardenship (in commendam) of the Collegiate Church of Manchester. As Bishop of Chester (1579–95) he proved himself a bitterly efficient persecutor of the Catholics of Lancashire.
[3] June 11 and 25, 1570.   [4] J. B. Mullinger, in D.N.B., Art. Whitgift, John.

was ended. He had still thirty-three years of active life before him, but no
less than eighteen of these were to be spent abroad.[1] Like others similarly
placed, before him, and after, Cartwright now crossed the seas—to Geneva
and Theodore Beza. He was most hospitably received, and his theological
competence recognised by an invitation to lecture in the famous academy
that was the main fount of Calvinist learning. The sun did not shine upon
a more learned man, said Beza.[2]

In 1572 Cartwright was in England once again ; in time for the next
round of the fight, provoked by the publication, early in June that year, of
the manifesto of his party called *An Admonition to the Parliament*. This was
Elizabeth's fourth parliament, that had opened on May 8, 1572. Just a fortnight later the queen sent her famous message to the House of Commons
that no Bills about religion were to be introduced that had not previously been
approved by the clergy.[3] This effectively checked a Bill to reform the church
which was already before the house, and the *Admonition*, which appeared
within the month, was in effect, therefore, not a mere exposition of doctrines
and a programme of reform but a reply to the queen's action—one of the
boldest adventures, surely, of the whole Elizabethan age. It repeats, " in
fresh, crisp sentences ",[4] the substance of Cartwright's Cambridge teaching,
that the divinely intended form of church government is the " presbytery "
system ; and it violently attacks the Book of Common Prayer as the last
refuge of Popery. The manifesto was anonymous and it was printed on a
secret (and therefore unlawful) press. By August two more editions had
been sold.

While Whitgift, in close consultation with Parker and Cox, set himself
to compose a reply, the government did its best to track down the printers—
unsuccessfully, however. But it soon discovered the authors, two young
clergymen, John Field and Thomas Wilcox.[5] They were arrested some time
in June, and on October 2, 1572, sentenced to a year's imprisonment, under
the Act of Uniformity.

By this time Whitgift's reply was completed, and he had succeeded also
in depriving Cartwright of the Trinity fellowship that was his last hold on
Cambridge life (September 21).[6] But before the master's book was published

---

[1] (i) Dec. 1570–May 1572 ; (ii) Dec. 1573–April 1585 ; (iii) 1595–1601, in Guernsey.
[2] The latest scholar to occupy himself with Cartwright is more exacting. Dr. McGinn
finds him, in the controversy with Whitgift, ambiguous and evasive. He speaks of his
" arguments more emotional than rational ", and says that, like the Puritans in general,
Cartwright " searched the Scriptures not in order to discover the truth but in order to justify
[his] own hypotheses "—a habit not exclusively Puritan, however. This author also notes
Cartwright's " careless scholarship and loose logic . . . [his] writing, both in construction
and in content, is turbid, tiresome and crude ", the last two of his books against Whitgift
being " poorly organised and muddled in thought ". D. J. McGinn, *The Admonition Controversy*, Rutgers University Press, New Brunswick, N.J. (1949), pp. 92, 86, 107.
[3] Prothero, p. 120, for the text of the message.
[4] Pearson, 60. The *Admonition* is reprinted in *Puritan Manifestoes*, 5–39.
[5] For Thomas Wilcox (1549 ?–1608), a man still in the early twenties, cf. *D.N.B.* He
was a pupil of St. John's, Oxford.
[6] Cartwright had failed to comply with the requirement of the statute that a fellow should
be ordained priest within seven years of his M.A. degree. His " defence " was that such a
statute could have no power to bind him—he had taken the oath to observe it with a mental

—*An Answere to a certen Libel intituled An Admonition to the Parliament*—a new manifesto had appeared, *A Second Admonition to the Parliament*, the work " of a practical, but hot-blooded man, who wields a facile pen " ; [1] it greatly magnified the offence of the first declaration. Cartwright's contribution to the campaign was a much weightier affair—*A Replye to An Answere made of M. Doctor Whitgifte Agaynste the Admonition to the Parliament*, which appeared five months after Whitgift's book, in April 1573. And now there began yet another of those duels so curiously characteristic of English history where, at a particular crisis, the great causes in conflict are admirably represented by personal controversy between the leaders—More and Tyndale, Cartwright and Whitgift, Pitt and Fox, Gladstone and Disraeli. For Whitgift produced, in February 1574, *The Defence of the Answere etc.* ; and in 1575 Cartwright came back with *The Second Replie of Thomas Cartwright etc.* completed, in 1577, by *The rest of the second replie of Thomas Cartvuright* (sic). [2]

The curious printing of the author's name is a reminder that his last two works were printed abroad : Cartwright was, indeed, once more an exile. The summer months of 1573 that followed the publication of his first answer to Whitgift had seen the excitement in London rise rapidly, and the beginnings of what no sixteenth-century government, in any country, could see without alarm, public controversy about state policy. The whole force of the state was now put out against the Cartwright party, and successfully. On 11 June, 1573, a royal proclamation banned his book, and gave all who owned copies twenty days to surrender them. On August 28, the secret press was discovered [3] and the printer, John Stroude, arrested. The chiefs— the clerical chiefs—of the movement were rounded up, Fuller, White, Johnson and others : Cartwright went underground. And when, in December, the High Commission issued a warrant for his arrest, he made his way out of the country once again ; not, this time, to Geneva but to the fervours of the recently Calvinised university of Heidelberg. Thanks to the government, thanks to the queen above all, [4] the Settlement of 1559 had come through— and the letters to Zurich of the various bishops testify how well they knew

---

reservation ; McGinn, 38–42, 47–48. " From this contest Cartwright emerges as a non conformist by temperament, Whitgift as a conformist." *Ibid.*, 48.

[1] Pearson, 73, who rejects the usual ascription of the work to Cartwright, and suggests as its author either Antony Gilby or Christopher Goodman. The *Second Admonition* is in *Puritan Manifestoes*, 80–148.

[2] For a summary of this controversy, cf. Pearson, 88–100.

[3] At Hemel Hempstead, seemingly ; Pearson, 109.

[4] It was a legend among the elect that the queen was, at heart, on their side, accepting them as the true servants of Christ, and signing with tears in her eyes the warrants that consigned them to punishment—as it was believed by many Catholics that she was the innocent tool of heretic ministers. And historians have sometimes seemed to suggest that Elizabeth recognised in the so-called Puritans the doughtiest champions of her throne, the iron core of her strength—which recalls, somewhat, the wishful thinking of the Victorian Orangeman about his place in another queen's affections. Cartwright and his school might flatter themselves, saying to Elizabeth that the surest shield " against conspiracy, treason and rebellion to your own person . . ." was the strength ministered by " the plentiful preaching of the word of faith, obedience and of all dutiful subjection " by preachers such as themselves (Petition of 1586, Peel, II, 177). But the Archbishop of York knew better. " I will tell you

whence had come their salvation. The vigour of the government, however, is more a measure of its alarm at the spectacle of non-official views organising themselves within the church and in the country, than of enthusiasm for any religious doctrine for its own truth.

The anti-episcopal movement had, in fact, been popular ; and the leaders were looked on as heroes. " These authors of sedition ", the Bishop of London, Edwin Sandys, told Cecil, " [are] now esteemed as Gods, as Field, Wilcox, Cartwright. . . . The people resort unto them [i.e. to the prisoners] as in popery they were wont to run on pilgrimage." [1]   To Bullinger the same prelate, describing the changes proposed as " the complete overthrow and rooting up of our whole ecclesiastical polity", writes, "You would not imagine with what approbation this . . . is regarded as well by the people as by the nobility ".[2]

So far, in the eleven years, that is to say, since the re-establishment of religion by the Acts of Supremacy and Uniformity, all the controversy, between men otherwise agreed in belief,[3] has centred, in the first place, around the question whether the use of certain externals of worship necessarily implies and fosters certain beliefs which all parties repudiate equally ; and in the second place, around the question whether civil authority—the queen, in this instance—has any right to impose the use of such externals without consultation of the church, if not without its consent. This second matter, the question of authority, has been there all the time, really there, but—very naturally—latent. It is really the question with whom does authority lie, in the Church instituted by Christ our Lord? and with whom, therefore, in the Church of Christ which, actually, is in England?

Cartwright, in 1570, brings this latent question to the forefront of the controversy : this is his specific service in the modern history of the religious life of the English people. With him there arrives on the scene his party's first systematic thinker.[4] He insists that the question is not one of policy merely, but of fundamental belief. He forces the debate to the question what was it that God meant should be done? what, in fact, has God in Holy Scripture commanded shall be done? That which you speak of as polity, he says in effect to his opponents, is as much a tenet of Christian belief as Justification by only Faith.[5]

---

what the queen's majesty said ", are Sandys' words to the insubordinate John Wilson, " that these puritans were greater enemies to her than the papists." At Bishopthorpe, Jan. 15, 1587 ; *ibid.*, II, 224.

[1] Aug. 5, 1573, *Puritan Manifestoes*, xix.

[2] Aug. 15, 1573 ; *Z.L.*, 439 ; cf. *ibid.*, 421 for Cox, of Ely, saying this also.

[3] Cf. the *Admonition*, " We would to God that as they hold the substance together with us, and we with them, so they would not deny the effect and virtue thereof ". *Puritan Manifestoes*, 37.

[4] And a man who, combining high intellectual quality and great courage, gives courage to others and liberates many who, so far, had cherished these ideas secretly. So the Bishop of London to Leicester and Cecil, Aug. 5, 1573, in Pearson, 105.

[5] Cf. also the *Admonition*, " The right government of the church can not be separated from the doctrine ". *Puritan Manifestoes*, 37.

It is no movement merely to "presbyterianise" the discipline and government of the Church of England, but to " presbyterianise " them because Presbyterianism is the scriptural and divinely appointed way. The régime that now obtains at Zurich and at Geneva is, in fact, how God meant things to be : the régime of 1559 is sinful.

The first implications of all this may indeed be alarming, both to the statesmen responsible for the church of 1559, and to the prelates who are only too conscious how thin is the soil in which this is rooted. Is all now to be called in question once more? the Royal Supremacy, for example—whether explicitly, or by implication—in the conscientious refusal to acknowledge the right of any but the church to control religious affairs. Political necessity is bound to set the statesmen in opposition to the spread of Cartwright's ideas. The statesmen will, inevitably, stand by their own creation and the maintenance of it as it was created ; and none will stand by it more constantly than the one amongst them whose judgment no lingering half-affection for this religion of the brotherhood can ever confuse—Elizabeth herself. In the church the statesmen will promote all who are steadfast against Cartwright and the new danger—Richard Bancroft, for example, very notably. And by a curious paradox (for they do this because it is a thing that it is politic to do), they will thereby open the way for that peculiarly Catholic notion, the *ecclesia docens* and *regens, regens quia docens*, to return to England and in some degree be reinstated. But this is to anticipate events by very many years indeed.

In the years with which we are now dealing, these first years of Cartwright's activity, it is the substance of his effect that he provides the existing partisans of this presbytery system, to say nothing of the men still younger than himself, with a body of reasoned, scripture-based theology, as a foundation for their movement to transform the settlement effected by the statesmen in 1559 ; a theology that is, also, English.[1]

The Cartwright-Whitgift controversy is but another example of what was bound to happen once the theory was launched that the good man's fidelity to his own conscientious private judgment as to what is Christian doctrine, is the basis of Christian life as God intended it ; another example of what had been happening continuously everywhere for now fifty years and more. All agree that Holy Scripture is God's word and that Holy Scripture contains everything man needs to know and to do in order to be saved. All agree that men are bound to follow its teaching and its practical directions. Both Cartwright and Whitgift, in this particular dispute, agree that not every detail of religious organisation is there provided for. Where they differ is in what, from out of this mass of Scripture, each singles out as binding now, on Christian man, in 1573. The jaundiced Catholic would say that, heresy being, by definition, this business of choosing doctrines according to one's own preferences, differences of the gravest kind are inevitable once heretics

---

[1] Cf. Pearson, 44 : " The chief result of his conduct [in 1570] was the resuscitation and reformulation of English Puritanism. He made the question of polity the distinctive and foremost note of the movement."

have the field to themselves, and that such differences must, if the heretical principle is true, be insoluble. " Whitgift holds that the Bible contains all that is necessary to Salvation " : so too, of course, does Cartwright ; " And so Whitgift rejects the sacrifice of the mass and such like ", Cartwright's modern biographer continues, "but he cannot see eye to eye with Cartwright when the Puritan affirms that Presbyterian discipline is an essential part of the Gospel ".[1] Nay more, Whitgift, even in the very defence he makes of the authority of bishops, will still argue against Cartwright that it is not the case that Scripture " doth set down any one certain form and kind of government of the church, to be perpetual for all times, persons and places, without alteration." [2]

To differences of this kind there was, in sixteenth-century Protestantism, no possible solution anywhere : no one, as yet, would have thought of a *modus vivendi* founded on the principle " live and let live ", except as a blasphemous attempt to compromise between light and darkness. Cartwright's personal statement, indeed, of the then universally accepted idea that heresy is the greatest of crimes and should be punished accordingly, is so pitilessly thorough, that, compared with him, the grim Whitgift may seem fatherly, mild, and even tender. " The same severity of punishment that was used against false prophets then ", Cartwright declares, with Zacharias iii explicitly before his mind,[3] " ought to be used now, under the gospel, against false teachers ". As Deuteronomy xiii prescribes, they must be put to death.[4] Bloody doctrine? " If this be bloody and extreme ", says Cartwright, " I am content to be so counted with the Holy Ghost. . . . And although in other cases of idolatry, upon repentance life is given . . . yet in this case of willing sliding back, and moving others to the same . . . I deny that upon repentance there ought to follow any pardon of death which the judicial law doth require." [5] For Cartwright held that all Scripture is

[1] Pearson, 90.

[2] One thing alone, for Whitgift, is certainly set down in Scripture about the government of the Church of Christ, namely, the Royal Supremacy. " I am fully persuaded . . . that there is no such distinction betwixt the Church of Christ and a Christian commonwealth as you and the papists dream of ", he declares, Whitgift's Works (Parker Soc. ed.), III, 160 ; " God hath given the chief authority in the government of his church to the Christian magistrate " (*ibid.*, III, 177). " In every particular church where there is a Christian magistrate, he is chief and principal over the rest " (*ibid.*, III, 181) ; " the chief ' pillar ' indeed that upholdeth the church " (*ibid.*, II, 97), and the " Supreme Governor [of the Church] under God " ; *Defence of the Answere etc., ibid.*, III, 275.

Nor is Whitgift troubled by the fact that this highly important truth is not expressly contained in Holy Writ. It is even he who draws attention to the fact ; in order thereby to answer the critic's argument against archbishops, viz. that God, who even thought of " the besoms and snuffers " when legislating for the services of the Old Law, has made no mention of archbishops in his rules about the New. No more has he made express mention, says Whitgift, of [what all accept] " the chief pillar " etc. (*ut supra* ; see, too, McGinn, 300–302). So there can be highly important truths about the religion of Christ that are not expressly contained in Scripture ! *Naturam expellas furca, tamen usque recurret.*

[3] Verse 3 : [They] shall say unto him : Thou shalt not live : because thou hast spoken a lie in the name of the Lord. [4] Verse 10 : With stones shall he be stoned to death.

[5] *The Reste of the second replie*, p. 74, quoted Pearson, 91. The language of this radical —or fanatic, according to the reader's prepossessions—is, *ex hypothesi*, to be expected. It does but re-echo, however, to the words, the sentiments of one of the most orthodox of

equally binding. Had he had his way, all the death penalties announced in the Old Testament would have been enforced, as well for refusals to attend church, for blasphemy and for adultery, as for murder and heresy.[1] He is, indeed, " an example of the godly man in the sixteenth century whose lack of toleration sprang from conviction ", for whom the end in view was " not the slaughter of men, but the furtherance of God's glory ".[2]

And all this is to happen simply because such is Cartwright's private judgment of what God's intentions for us are ! In that private judgment he is, of course, sincere and disinterested—and " Sincerity " covereth a multitude of sins, where the activities of the elect are in consideration ; to the conclusions bred by his study of the Word he is unswervingly loyal.[3] That it is really to himself that he is attached wholly escapes him, as it escaped the later victims of these theological aberrations.[4] Like their master, the disciples identified the ideas of one man—a man understood to be no more than

---

Elizabethan Anglicans, Alexander Nowell, Dean of St. Paul's, preaching the official sermon at the opening of parliament in 1563, who in 1567 will be sitting in judgment on " fanatics ". Nowell's—anti-Catholic—thesis was that " Maintainers of false religion ought to die by the sword ". As for objectors, " Some will say, ' Oh bloody man ! that calleth this the house of right, and now would have it made a house of blood '. But the Scripture teacheth us that divers faults ought to be punished by death. And, therefore, following God's precepts, it cannot be accounted cruel." Quoted Neale, Elizabeth I and her Parliaments, I, 93. Had Cartwright's ideals prevailed, his reputation would have utterly eclipsed that of Bonner—the Bonner of Foxe's legend. For Thomas Cartwright, " God is a Presbyterian " (Pearson, State and Church, 37), the Presbyterian Church should be established, and " the evils of intolerance would continue, the victims and oppressors changing places " (Pearson, Cartwright, 106). " For this dissident majority . . . Cartwright recommended nothing short of imprisonment until they conformed, or else death ", McGinn, 123, quoting Cartwright, Second Replie, 68–69, 95, 115 and in Whitgift's Works, I, 201 ; see, too, McGinn, 118. As to Cartwright's personal severity to others who sinned, cf. the account, quoted in E. I. Fripp, Shakespeare, Man and Artist, I, 199, of his treatment of his " manservant who was whipped about the Market Place . . . for fornication with Mistress Cartwright's maid, the girl being set in the stocks, ' very great ' with child ". For Fripp, Cartwright is a " lovable man and popular, the ' Idol ' as well as the ' Champion ' of Warwick "—where these events took place.

[1] Quoted Pearson, 90 ; also in McGinn, pp. 119–120.

[2] Pearson, 92. McGinn says, more tersely, " this bloody-minded zealot ". Is it necessary to add that the party was as hostile as the bishops themselves, or the government, to any freedom of discussion ? " We do utterly mislike ", say the authors of the Admonition, in 1572, " that there is not in every country more straight looking to the printers in that respect [i.e. authors' and printers' names should be published], because our time is much corrupted with over much license therein." Puritan Manifestoes, 38.

[3] As to the source of Cartwright's certitude, he holds of course the view then so general, and which finds its place in the Homilies, that to those whom God has chosen, the meaning of Holy Scripture is transparently simple ; self-illuminating to the most illiterate—if these be God's children. Lack of such illumination is proof conclusive that the reader is one of those " strangers, infidels, men without God to whom God speaketh darkly ", as another of the band, Edward Dering, writes. Again it is part of Cartwright's teaching that while for any " lawful and profitable calling " all men need to be directly called by God, upon the man so called " God doth pour his gifts so plentifully, that he is as it were suddenly made a new man " ; cf. McGinn, 112–113, 111, quoting from Cartwright in Whitgift's Works, III, 189, 187 and I, 32.

[4] How far Cartwright could go in self-assertion—and he was not, in this, an eccentric among the Reformers—may be judged from his saying that, " The example of Christ [in forgiving the repentant sinner] is not always to be followed ". Quoted, McGinn, 131, with reference Whitgift's Works, I, 321–322, note (Parker Society ed.).

man, and for whom no divinely given charisma of infallibility was claimed—about the infinite God with God Himself; and their descendants did the same after them.   And for many of these last the inevitable reaction, when it comes, will be a reaction, not against Cartwright and his like, but against religion itself and the very idea that there is a God.

The only lawful officers in the Christian church, for Cartwright, are the ministers, the deacons, and the elders.   It is the minister who is presbyter, and there is no inequality of function or jurisdiction between one minister and another.[1]   The principal personal duty of all of them, even the highest, is to preach the word.   These ministers are called by the church, examined by the presbyterate of ministers, and ordained by these.   Although ministers are subject to the state in all those matters of conduct in which the layman is subject to it, the church is not subject to the state ; the ruler of the state is no more than a member of the church, and one of his duties as ruler is to protect the church and enforce the divine laws about religion.   But the whole government of the church and the regulation of the private lives of its members, lies with the church alone.   Geneva, Cartwright expressly holds out as the ideal commonwealth, the city of God realised on earth : " purified and exalted by the adoption of the discipline ".

The critics of the Settlement of 1559 are not, then, in 1572, merely protesting, and asking for freedom to follow their own consciences.   The official system set up by the parliament of 1559 the critics sternly condemn as contrary to Scripture, as damnably sinful therefore ; and they call for its abolition.   " . . . it hath been thought good ", say the authors of the *Admonition*,[2] " to proffer to your godly considerations a true platform of a church reformed to the end that, it being laid before your eyes to behold the great unlikeness between it and our English Church, you may learn, either with perfect hatred to detest the one and with singular love to embrace . . . the other, or to be without excuse before the majesty of our God . . . *who hath by us revealed unto you* [3] at this present the sincerity and simplicity of his gospel ".   And with the *Admonition* a new virulence of tone makes its appearance.   All the bad language used in Reform apologetic to describe the

[1] Bishop and priest are equals, and equally bound to the same principal function, to preach the word.   Cartwright's doctrine about the Christian bishop, and the passion which fired the whole anti-episcopal movement, can hardly be dissociated from the general reaction of religious-minded men everywhere against what, in the course of the later Middle Ages, the diocesan bishop had come to be.   Nothing could be more remote from the divine ideal as St. Thomas Aquinas expounds it, of the bishop as holding an office for the very performance of which holiness of life is a pre-requisite, a personage, from the radiation of whose holiness the people he rules become in their turn holy, than the typical bishop of the last centuries of the Middle Ages.   Now, in the first fervour of England's emancipation from " all that ", Cartwright saw perpetuated a conception of the episcopal office which reduced the bishop's direct and personal share in the evangelisation of his diocese to nothing at all ; cf. Hamilton Thompson, *English Clergy*, pp. 40–41, 43, 45, 46, and on p. 71, the following passage " . . . that completely stereotyped character which survived the ecclesiastical troubles of the next century, so that the post-Reformation Church continued its administrative course in the well-worn grooves marked out for it on these lines ".

[2] *Puritan Manifestoes*, 8.
[3] Italics mine.

" corruptions " of Rome, is now turned against the Elizabethan settlement. Its conception of the hierarchy is a thing " introduced into the church by Satan " ; [1] the Archbishop of Canterbury's court of Faculties, is " a place much worse than Sodom and Gomorrah " ; [2] the church is " governed by such canons and customs as by which Antichrist did rule his synagogue " ; [3] the Book of Common Prayer is " an unperfect book, culled and picked out of that popish dung-hill the breviary and the mass-book " ; [4] the archbishop's court is " the filthy quave-mire and poisoned plash of all the abominations that do infect the whole realm " ; [5] " this filthy court . . . this petty pope ".[6]

And the bishops, in their turn, denounced the party in the very phrases used, from the beginning, by the Catholics against themselves ; they denounced the party indeed on principles that were Catholic, and by implication took over from the Catholics, for the purpose of destroying their own domestic critics, something of that Catholic theory of the Church which, together with these critics, they had lately stigmatised as a human invention, a thing devised for the profit of the popes. Cartwright and his followers are, for the Bishop of Ely, guilty men simply because " innovators " ; [7] and Cox now traces their evolution as Fisher might once have traced his own ; " At first they attacked only things of little consequence ; but now they turn everything both great and small, up and down, and throw all things into confusion and are really a danger to the church ".[8] From Durham, Pilkington—of all men—states the danger very tersely in the statement : " These men are crying out that nothing is to be endured in the rites of the church, which is later than the Apostles ".[9] And that this is indeed the aim of these " factious and heady men, who in their writings and sermons and private conversation, condemn and pull to pieces the whole economy of our church, and bring all the bishops and other ministers into incredible disfavour with the people",[10] Cox also allows : " Their object ", he writes, " is to revive the ancient presbytery of the primitive church." However, the bishop goes on to say, " It cannot be otherwise but that tares must grow in the Lord's field, and that in no small quantity ".

As we read the exchanges that now take place between the Elizabethan bishop and his troublesome Protestant subjects we might be back in Mary's reign, Grindal saying to the accused pretty well what Grindal's predecessor would have been saying to Grindal, had Grindal ever been brought before Bonner.[11] Grindal, for example, examining the catch of the Plumbers' Hall

---

[1] William Chark, in a sermon at Cambridge, 1572, for preaching which he was deprived of his fellowship (Peterhouse) ; quoted Prothero, 197.
[2] Edward Dering to Cecil, Nov. 1, 1573 ; *ibid.*
[3] Sampson to the same, March 8, 1574 ; *ibid.*, 198.
[4] From the first *Admonition to the Parliament*, 1572 ; *Puritan Manifestoes*, 21.
[5] From the same ; *ibid.*, 32. [6] *Ibid.*, 33.
[7] Cox to Gualter, Feb. 4, 1573, *Z.L.*, 417.
[8] Same to same, Feb. 3, 1574, *ibid.*, 454. [9] To Gualter, July 20, 1573 ; *ibid.*, 426.
[10] " . . . and also with the magistrates and nobility ". June 12, 1573, to the same ; *ibid.*, 421.
[11] All this in June, 1567. Bonner, of course, is still very much alive, in the prison of the Marshalsea, and no doubt well aware of these incidents which were the talk of the capital.

incident in 1567, calls on one Smith to answer for all, but another enthusiast, Nixon, breaks in, whom the bishop silences, for the moment, with, " You are a busy fellow, I know your words, you are full of talk, I know from whence you came ".   And presently a great argument is in progress on the eternal question " What do the Scriptures quoted really mean ? "   Nixon says to Grindal, " Your garments are accursed as they are used " ;   and when the bishop asks, " Where do you find them forbidden in scripture ? " the other counters with, " Where is the mass forbidden in scripture ? "   Bishops, he says, never change ;   Grindal is just like the popish bishops—unable to find support in scripture for his acts he brings in the police.   The Lord Mayor is shocked by the comparison, and invites the bishop to share his emotion. But Grindal, keeping to the point, says to the prisoner, " All the learned are against you, will you be tried by them ? "   " We will be tried by the word of God ", another prisoner answers, " which shall judge us all at the last day." To which that staunchest of Protestants, Dr. Alexander Nowell, now dean of St. Paul's, rejoins, " But who will you have to judge of the word of God ? " only to be trenchantly served with, " Why that was the saying of the Popish bishops in Queen Mary's time . . . Then they would say, who shall judge of the word of God ?   The Catholic Church must be the judge." [1]

Twenty years after this, one of the most famous of all these heroes, Henry Barrow, brought before the Privy Council, had a tremendous altercation with Archbishop Whitgift.   It was not the first time that the two had met as accused and judge, and when the archbishop, worsted so far, said in his opening that Barrow was not a learned man he was told, " The Lord knoweth I am ignorant.   I have no learning to boast of : but this I know, that you are void of all true learning and godliness."   And when, in an unguarded moment, the Lord Chancellor,[2] pointing to Whitgift, asked rhetorically, " What is that man ? " the prisoner seized his opportunity with both hands.   " The Lord gave me the spirit of boldness ", he said later, " so that I answered : He is a monster, a miserable compound, I know not what to make him : he is neither ecclesiastical nor civil, even that second Beast spoken of in the Revelation ".   And then the court, uncomprehending but curious, asking him to be more explicit, Barrow opened his book at *Revelations* xiii. 12 : Whitgift was the one foretold who, speaking like a dragon, and deceiving men by false signs, would give life to the other beast that came out of the sea with names of blasphemy written on its head ; he was the one who would bring men to adore that beast, slaying all who refused to do so ; causing all to be marked with the mark of the beast, 666.   And turning to the second epistle to the Thessalonians Barrow showed the archbishop his portrait there too : " the man of sin, the son of perdition ", self-exalted above God, who " as God sitteth in the temple of God, shewing himself that he is God ".   This, for an archbishop who knew all about Antichrist—had he not begun his university career with an inaugural on the theme that Antichrist is the pope?— was too much.   " The Beast arose for anger ", Barrow tells us, " gnashing

---

[1] Usher, *High Commission*, pp. 57-58, quoting from *A Parte of a Register* (1593), 23-27.
[2] Sir Christopher Hatton.

his teeth, and said, ' Will you suffer him, my lords ? ' So I was plucked up by the warden's man from my knees and carried away." [1]

So might we surely be reading, in Foxe, some other prisoner's own account of his heroic defiance ; and the similarity of the psychology of these affairs is heightened when we read the comment which the modern historian of the court makes : " No doubt the account is exaggerated and was meant to prove the cruelty and tyranny of the commissioners." [2] Barrow, again, recalls the " meek lambs " who are Foxe's heroes when he tells the Bishop of London— John Aylmer—that he is " a wolf, a bloody persecutor and an apostate ".[3]

The upheaval which followed on the appearance, at last, in the inner circle, of a Reformer who was wholly religious—a leader who was competent, effective and in no way associated with the royal policies—did not, however, disturb the world of churchmen merely. It was, indeed, a clash between the queen and the parliament that occasioned the first *Admonition* from the clerics ; and for the next twenty years and more the movement to " presbyterianise " the church developed alongside a parliamentary movement to wrest from the crown some of its power over the church, a movement which necessarily, therefore, tended to achieve a greater degree of initiative for the House of Commons, wider scope and greater freedom of speech.[4]

The assault of the " primitive " section of the Reform party on the work of 1559 began, indeed, as an attempt to " complete " that particular parliamentary achievement through further parliamentary action. How these attempts, in 1566 and 1571, despite much zeal and very general support

---

[1] July 18, 1588. Barrow's own account, Arber, 40–48.

[2] Usher, *op. cit.*, 132, n. 3. How far are such " victims' " own stories about their judges reliable ? The question has already arisen in the affair of the Marian persecution of Protestants who are surely the closest of kin to these persecuted Elizabethans. " Much of the information regarding the intolerance of the bishops ", says McGinn, *op. cit.*, 123, " has been taken directly from the Puritan tracts, the ' bitterness and violence ' of which Pearson (*Cartwright*, 6) has noted. Since these tracts were instruments of propaganda, the Puritan complaint of ill treatment must be taken with some reservation ; for truthfulness, as Frere warns us (*History of the English Church*, 175), was never the strong point of Puritan writers ".

[3] Cf. p. 47 of Barrow's own account of his examination before Whitgift, Hatton, Burghley, Buckhurst and Aylmer, at Whitehall, on July 18, 1588, which is reprinted in Arber, *An Introductory Sketch to the Martin Marprelate Controversy* (1879), 40–48. John Penry, another Separatist whom Elizabeth and Whitgift were to send to the gallows, is no less explicit, in the same traditional way : " You shall find among this crew [i.e. the bishops] nothing else but a troop of bloody soul-murderers, sacrilegious church-robbers, and such as have made themselves fat with the blood of men's souls, and the utter ruin of the church." Strype, *Annals*, IV, p. 247.

[4] A movement to wrest also, from the queen, a declaration as to her lawful heir, and an engagement that she would marry. The relation of this threefold source of parliamentary discontent with the queen's policy (that really dates from the first parliament of the reign), to the growth of an independent spirit in the House of Commons is no new discovery. Cf. (for example), Lingard, in one of his rare reflective passages, " [The queen's] obstinacy, however, was productive of one advantage to the nation ; it put an end to that tame submission to the will of the sovereign, which had characterised and disgraced the parliaments under the dynasty of the Tudors. The discontent of the nation burst forth in defiance of every restraint imposed by the government : and the motives and obligations of the queen were discussed with a freedom of speech, which alarmed the court, and scandalised the advocates of arbitrary power." VI, 127.

in the parliaments, failed solely because of the queen's hostility, has been recorded. When, in 1572, Elizabeth summoned her fourth parliament,[1] the valiant men in the Commons began the struggle all over again with a Bill to restrict the operation of the basic Act of Uniformity to Catholics only. "This outrageous bill"[2] prospered as far as its third reading, when the queen met it (May 22) with a message that "from henceforth no bills concerning religion shall be preferred or received into this House, unless the same shall be first considered or liked by the clergy . . .",[3] that is, the bishops. And upon the heels of this, there followed that violent manifesto already noticed, *An Admonition to the Parliament*. This demanded a hearing for the case against the order established. If the queen refused the petitioners what they sought, the abolition of the episcopate as now understood, "We will by God's grace", said the authors, "address ourselves to defend his truth by suffering, and willingly lay our heads to the block . . .".[4]

In the next parliamentary session, in 1576,[5] the battle was renewed, and Peter Wentworth, in a historic speech, boldly protested against the royal direction of 1572. "Certain it is", he said,[6] "that none is without fault, no not our noble queen, since her Majesty hath committed great faults, yea dangerous faults to herself." It was the bishops, he declared, who were the real cause of the trouble, and to give them a free hand in matters of religion would be to make them popes—as he had himself said to the Archbishop of Canterbury. For this speech Wentworth was committed to the Tower— by order of the scandalised Commons, who "out of a reverend regard for her majesty's honour, stopped Mr. Wentworth before he had fully finished".[7] Nevertheless, in the very next session of parliament, five years later,[8] the attempt to wrest the control of religion from the crown was renewed.

---

[1] The first session ran from May 8 to June 30, 1572.

[2] Neale, *op. cit.*, 298. But why the passionate adjective in the historian of 1953 ? What has there ever been that is sacrosanct about the parliamentary arrangement we know as the Elizabethan Act of Uniformity ? And since when is it an outrage to plan the alteration, or even the repeal, of a statute ? The same writer, describing the events of 1572–1576, speaks (p. 371) of "the Puritan conspiracy". The term is surely inappropriate ?

[3] Prothero, 120, from the *Commons' Journals*.   [4] *Ibid.*, 199.

[5] Second session of the fourth parliament. It ran from Feb. 8 to March 15, 1576.

[6] Feb. 8, 1576 ; cf. Neale, *op. cit.*, 318–324, for extracts from the speech.

[7] Wentworth, who was born about 1530, was of an age with Sir Francis Walsingham (Secretary of State 1574–1590) whose sister, Elizabeth, was his present (second) wife. Wentworth sat for Barnstaple, for Tregony, and for Northampton in the various parliaments of the reign. He was again sent to the Tower in 1587, and a third time in 1593, for speaking his mind too freely in the House of Commons on the forbidden topic of the succession to the throne. The third time he was not released, and he died in the Tower, Nov. 10, 1596, " as much a martyr to parliamentary liberty as Sir John Eliot " ; Pollard, *H.E.*, VI, 463. Walsingham had died in 1590.

[8] Third session of the fourth parliament. It ran from Jan. 16 to March 18, 1581. Once again the queen blocked the attempt. Her " gracious answer " the Speaker, addressing Elizabeth, summarised as that the queen would herself give appropriate directions about " . . . those matters belonging to her as incident to that supreme authority which she hath over the clergy and state ecclesiastical " ; and the Lord Chancellor spoke of " her supreme authority granted to her by Parliament in those causes ". Quotations from Neale, *op. cit.* (i.e. *Elizabeth I and her Parliaments*, I), 414, 415.

The incident of 1576 drew from the queen, just one month after Wentworth's speech, a brisk reminder how real was her rule of the church. At the beginning of the session, said Elizabeth to Parliament, she had bidden the bishops reform church discipline, and she now declared to parliament that " if the said bishops should neglect or omit their duties therein, then her Majesty, by her supreme power and authority over the Church of England ", would so see to it as fully to content all her loving subjects.[1] And on March 29, 1585, the imperial voice spoke again to parliament about " the Church, whose over-ruler God hath made me ; . . . [as for faults and negligencies in the Church] All which if you my Lords of the Clergy do not mend, I mean to depose you . . . I see many over bold with God Almighty, making too many subtle scannings of His blessed will, as lawyers do with human testaments. The presumption is so great, as I may not suffer it . . . nor tolerate new-fangledness . . . I must pronounce them dangerous to a kingly rule, to have every man, according to his own censure, to make a doom of the validity and privity of his prince's government, with a common veil and cover of God's word, whose followers must not be judged but by private men's exposition. God defend you from such a ruler that so evil will guide you." [2]

At Heidelberg, meanwhile, Cartwright was soon well established. On January 25, 1574, he matriculated at the university, and straightway began to prepare for the press a book which contemporaries attributed to another exile, a younger man than himself, Walter Travers.[3] To this work Cartwright supplied a preface, and soon he was busy translating it into English.[4] The theme of Travers' *Explicatio* is the everlasting theme of this school—if the English church would be truly Christian it must fashion itself after the pattern of Geneva, for this church is faithful to the pattern set by God. Above all, the work upholds " the necessity of discipline ".[5]

Three years or so after the appearance of this treatise, the English merchants resident at Antwerp organised a church there, with the hearty assistance of Elizabeth's agent, William Davison, and of her Secretary of State, Sir Francis Walsingham ; " a church which although nominally

---

[1] Prothero, 209, from *Commons' Journals*, I, 112. For a very full account cf. Neale, *op. cit.*, 349–353.

[2] D'Ewes, *Journals*, p. 328.

[3] Born at Nottingham, the son of a goldsmith, about 1548—i.e. now a man of twenty-six or so ; educated at Cambridge (Christ's College, B.A. 1565 ; fellow of Trinity College, 1567). The book was entitled *Ecclesiasticae Disciplinae, et Anglicanae Ecclesiae ab illa aberrationis plena e verbo Dei et dilucida explicatio*. Pearson, *op. cit.*, refers to it as the *Explicatio*.

[4] *A full and plaine declaration of Ecclesiasticall Discipline owt off the word off God, and off the declininge off the Churche of Englande from the same.* The Latin original purports to be published at La Rochelle, 1574, the English is dated Middelburg, 1575. From the same press, about this very time (i.e. 1575), there came the story of those violent quarrels which had divided the exiled English twenty years before—the quarrels which foreshadowed the division revealed from the very morrow of the Settlement in 1559—*A Brieff Discours off the troubles begonne at Frankford anno domini 1554* : a history which is, of course, a highly controversial, party pamphlet. Pearson, 144.

[5] Cf. Pearson, 143 ff., for a summary of the contents of the *Explicatio*.

Anglican was virtually Presbyterian ".[1] Of this church Travers was the first minister, and on May 8, 1578, he was ordained at Antwerp by a group of other ministers, of whom Cartwright (contrary to what has been generally held) was not one.[2] This church was as like Geneva as a church could be which yet did not wholly abandon the Prayer Book of 1559.[3]

But these adventures, theological and liturgical, did not, ultimately hinder Travers' promotion. He returned to England to become chaplain to Cecil, and tutor to his son Robert ; and in 1581 Cecil's influence procured him a lectureship in the church of the Temple. But when, in 1583, the benchers wanted Travers for the vacant mastership, Whitgift, now Archbishop of Canterbury, successfully objected his lack of ordination. It was Richard Hooker who was appointed ; and for the next few years he expounded in the morning a doctrine which Travers contradicted in the afternoon— before audiences of absorbed lawyers.[4]

By this time there had been other events, all of which, to us 370 years later, may seem signs certain and sure that opposition to the Settlement of 1559, within the reformed ranks, was well on the way to become a permanent

[1] Cf. Pearson, 238. Walsingham's private secretary, Laurence Thomson, has also been thought to be the author of the *Explicatio*.   [2] *Ibid.*, 178.
[3] For the relation between this Antwerp church and Walsingham who, as Camden wrote, was a " most sharp maintainer of the purer religion ", cf. the interesting letters printed in Conyers Read, II, 262–266. When the merchants who supported the church informed him of " an intended alteration of the exercise of common prayer . . . contrary to, or at least no agreeable with the received order in the Church of this realm ", the Secretary of State warned Davison that " if it should come to her Majesty's ears it would greatly kindle offence " against him " for the furthering of the same ". Not that the Secretary misliked such a form of prayer, " only I would have all reformation done by public authority ". To allow " every private man's zeal " as warrant for reforming what was amiss would be dangerous. " Mr Travers, your minister there [not yet ordained, Walsingham is writing in March, 1578] knoweth my opinion in that matter ". And—surely with the queen in mind—the great personage goes on to say : " If you knew with what difficulty we retain that we have, and that the seeking of more might hazard (according to man's understanding) that which we already have, you would then, Mr. Davison, deal warily in this time when policy carrieth more sway than zeal. And yet we have great cause to thank God for that we presently enjoy, having God's word sincerely preached and the Sacraments truly administered. The rest we lack we are to beg by prayer and attend with patience." This passage is one among many reminders how far Elizabeth was from being any man's tool ; a reminder that, after twenty years, it could still seem uncertain to the queen's chief ministers how long she would continue to support a particular religious programme ; and a reminder that none of the councillors in whose lives religious belief played a real part were sympathetic to the policy which made what the Prayer Book and Ordinal of 1559 stood for, the final, true, and impossible to be improved, version of the religion revealed in Christ. What layman of note was there in these years who, if he were religious, was not " Puritan " in sympathy ? And cf. *infra*, p. 354, n., the evidence that Elizabeth, in these very months, was demanding that rebels in Flanders maintain the Catholic religion and refuse toleration to the Reformed.
[4] But, it would seem, to the scandal of some of the brethren. " I pray Mr. Hooker and I beseech Mr. Travers that they be of one accord in the Lord ", one of them wrote. " The time requireth it, the matter, your functions, the place, the scandal to the weak, the scoffs of the wicked, the despights of the godless, the desires of the godly." *Sir Hew Herbert's Treatise against Hooker*, in Peel, II, 48. In 1591 Travers left England for a chair of divinity at St. Andrews ; and then, from 1595 to 1598, he was provost of Trinity College, Dublin. Travers lived on until 1635. It was Cartwright who succeeded Travers at Antwerp, after some years spent at Middelburg as factor for the English merchants there. Prothero, 248–249, prints some extracts from the *Ecclesiastical Discipline*, i.e. the *Explicatio*.

feature of English life ; signs that already, and deriving from the criticism, there were new religious institutions in embryo. In 1572 there was organised at Wandsworth the first English presbytery.[1] In 1581 Robert Browne, who came of an ancient Rutland family,[2] set up, at Norwich, the first religious organisation deliberately conceived as something altogether independent of that which, in Elizabeth's eyes, was necessarily coterminous with the nation. In this Brownist version of the Christian religion, each local congregation was autonomous, owning no superior under God, in every way self-sufficing.

Judged "by the rules of God's word", say the Brownists, the organised body ruled by the bishops under the supreme authority of the queen has not " in this confusion and subjection Christ their prophet, Priest and King " ; its assemblies cannot be " esteemed the true, orderly, gathered, or constituted churches of Christ ", and the faithful should have no " spiritual communion with them in their public worship and administration ". All who have received " any of these false offices or any pretended function or ministry in . . . this false and antichristian constitution " ought, with the fear of God before them, to abandon it; and none should contribute, in any way, to the maintenance of this false worship, " under any colour whatever ". The faithful, having got themselves out of "this anti-christian estate unto the freedom and true profession of Christ ", will " unite themselves into peculiar congregations ; wherein, as members of one body whereof Christ is the only head, they are to worship and serve God according to his word . . .". And "if God withhold the magistrates' allowance " of their way of life, "they yet proceed together in Christian covenant and communion thus to walk in the obedience of Christ, even through the midst of all trials and afflictions . . .".[3]

Such were the beginnings of Independency. It is sad to turn from the idyllic language in which the aims are set out, to what the pioneers have to say, not only about the bishops and the clergy obedient to them, but about the clerics who stand with Cartwright. " As for the priests and preachers of the land ; they of all other men have bewrayed their notable hypocrisy,

[1] As to what exactly was set up at Wandsworth, in 1572, there is considerable doubt ; cf. Pearson, 74–81. For this writer, it " could not have been a Presbytery in the modern sense ", 76 ; it was " not the session of Wandsworth parish church ", 78 ; and it " did not occupy a position of conspicuous importance on the main line of Elizabethan Presbyterian history ", 79. Dr. Pearson hazards that it was " perhaps the court of a secret and independent body containing Congregational as well as Presbyterian elements ", 80.

[2] Born about 1550 (?), B.A. Cantab. 1572 (Corpus Christi College, whose master, Thomas Aldridge, was a leading member of the religious " left "). On leaving Cambridge Browne gave himself to open-air preaching, and although ordained began now to say that all ordinations were " an abomination ", and that the parochial system was anti-christian. His patron in the Norwich apostolate was Robert Harrison, another Cambridge man. Burghley more than once stood between Browne and the episcopal wrath he so persistently stirred : cf. A. G. Jessopp, in D.N.B., art. Browne, Robert. In 1586 Browne suddenly changed his whole way of life, and settled down as the peaceable resident parson of a village cure. The careers of these two scarcely support what Mr. Rowse's words might suggest, " Lower class elements . . . were liable in their clownish way to shade off into various sorts of separatist sects, Brownists, the Family of Love, Anabaptists ". Op. cit., 464–465.

[3] The quotations are from the Brownists' True Confession, 1596 ; or rather from the extracts from this printed in Hooker, II, 603, notes 1, 2, 3.

that standing erewhile against the English Romish hierarchy, and their popish abominations, have now so readily submitted themselves to the beast, and are not only content to yield their canonical obedience unto him, and receive his mark, but in most hostile manner oppose and set themselves against us. . . . These have long busied themselves in seeking out new shifts and cavils to turn away the truth, which presseth them so sore ; and have at last been driven to palpable and gross absurdities, seeking to daub up that ruinous anti-christian muddy wall which themselves did once craftily undermine. . . . With what equity now can these priests so blaspheme and persecute us for rejecting the heavy yoke of their tyrannous prelates, whom they themselves call antichristian and bishops of the Devil ? for forsaking their priesthood, which they have complained is not the right ministery ? " [1]

It was this movement which presently had the distinction to furnish the first Protestant martyrs put to death by Queen Elizabeth.[2] In 1581 Browne and a number of his congregation from Bury St. Edmunds (whither he had retired to escape the control of the Bishop of Norwich) migrated to Middelburg, in Holland. Here, as in the earlier Marian exile, books were written and printed denouncing the régime now in power in church and state at home. These were sent over to England and distributed by zealous supporters. Presently some connection with this propaganda brought before the judges of assize at Bury, in June 1583, John Coppin, a Brownist who had spent seven years in prison, and Elias Thacker whom he first met when both were prisoners. Coppin is alleged to have said, " The queen is sworn to keep God's law, and she is perjured ". Both are alleged to have refused to acknowledge the royal supremacy. They were found guilty and hanged at Bury, June 4, 1583.[3]

Here and there, meanwhile, all over the Midlands and East Anglia, there were parishes and groups of parishes where the clergy had not waited for any *Book of Discipline* to be authorised, or to be written even, but, by a kind of spontaneous religious instinct had, from the first years of the reign, organised for themselves a stricter and more methodical life ; much in the spirit (if not according to the very letter) of that discipline which had everywhere been the practice of the churches associated with Geneva, which Cranmer had provided for in the time of Edward VI, and for the establishment of which in England Sampson, for one, had shown himself so concerned while yet an exile. The clergy of these groups of parishes met every week for what came to be known as a " prophesying "—prayer in common, study and exposition of the Bible : " Which is done once in three weeks, when one interprets a piece of the Scriptures . . . for an hour, and the two others reply for half an hour, when we end with prayer ", so the account runs of the

---

[1] *Preface* to the *True Confession*, Hooker, II, 604, n. 2. It needs to be said that once the Brownists reached Middelburg, in 1581, they were soon fighting Cartwright, then sojourning in the same place of exile.

[2] Unless we count as such the Anabaptists burnt in 1575. For whom cf. Appendix, III

[3] See *D.N.B.*, art. *Coppin, John*.

earliest of these.[1] To these discussions the laity were often admitted, and parishes where these clergy officiated—and some of the best of the new clergy were to be found in such groups as these—were carefully governed by the minister and his elders, and the whole conduct of the parishioners was supervised, reported on weekly, and severely controlled.

At Northampton, for example, where the system had the approval and support of the diocesan bishop, Edmund Scambler, of the mayor also, " and other the Queen's Majesty's justices of the Peace within the county and town ", there was, in 1571, " a weekly assembly every Thursday . . . by the mayor and his brethren, assisted with the preacher, minister and other gentlemen appointed to them by the bishop, for the correction of discord made in the town : as for notorious blasphemy, whoredom, drunkenness, railing against religion, or preachers thereof, scolds, ribalds or such like ", in each parish there were " certain sworn men appointed for that service ", namely to present " in writing " the faults of their neighbours to this weekly meeting.[2]

The groups of parishes formed a *classis*, and the *classes*, in Travers' plan, were to be grouped together in provincial synods.[3] Here was a growing organisation, then, within the queen's church, that was living by a life unknown to the laws which established the church, a life independent of the royal injunctions, and the direction of the queen—an organisation whose ends were indeed spiritual, but which was made up of zealous men for whom ecclesiastical discipline was, in itself, a spiritual thing and a matter of faith.

To nothing in all her reign was Elizabeth more bitterly opposed than to this movement for spiritual autonomy.[4] That many bishops favoured the

---

[1] At Norwich. Letter of Edward Gaston to Haddon, Oct. 16, 1564 ; quoted Dixon, VI, 7, note, from P.R.O., *Eliz.*, *Addenda*, p. 562.

[2] Compare this with Cranmer's ideal, the provisions of the *Reformatio Legum Ecclesiasticarum* (de divinis officiis, c. 10). There are extracts from the regulations for the diocese of Peterborough 1571, in Prothero, 202–204, from Strype, *Annals*, III, 133–140 and 472. For the diocese of Norwich 1572, cf. Strype, *ibid.*, IV, 494, for Lincoln 1574, *ibid.*, III, 472, for Chester 1585, *ibid.*, IV, 546–549 (an extract in Prothero, 206–207 ; who also prints, pp. 204–205, extracts from Grindal's regulations, issued as Archbishop of Canterbury and metropolitan, in 1576). And cf., especially, the minute book of the *classis* of Dedham, 1582–1589, in Usher, *The Presbyterian Movement in the Reign of Queen Elizabeth*, pp. 25–74. For this exercise—the thing and the name—among the Protestant exiles of Mary's days, cf. par. 12 of the New Discipline, introduced into the church at Frankfort during the pastorate of Robert Horne, Queen Elizabeth's first Bishop of Winchester : " or else let Prophesy be used every fortnight in the English tongue, for the exercise of the said Students, and edifying of the Congregation. . . ." Arber, *Troubles*, 166.

[3] Cf. in Prothero, 247–249, extracts from Bancroft and Travers.

[4] This, I think, is generally agreed. Cf. Elizabeth, " who disliked all zeal ", Mandell Creighton, in *D.N.B.*, art., Grindal, Edmund. Also, ", . . . Elizabeth set her face against the designs of Cartwright, prevented her Parliament from advancing them, and against her opposition Cartwright and his co-religionists could make no headway ". Pearson, 413. This same historian, in *Church and State : A Study of the Political Ideas of Sixteenth Century Puritanism*, writes " The political danger-point in Presbyterianism . . . was the idea of sovereignty, so far as it related to ecclesiastical affairs. . . . Elizabeth saw that although the Puritans were conscientiously able and willing to take the oath of royal supremacy they did so with [a reservation] that would naturally mean a limited monarchy ", 61–62 ; also, " We are convinced that Elizabeth's fear that her sovereignty would be jeopardised by the legal establishment of Presbyterianism was justified. . . . Clericalism would have tended to rear its head ; ministers as God's interpreters would have tried to dictate in social and political affairs as

prophesyings, as an excellent means to encourage clerical learning and zeal—in a time when these were all too rare, and when everything conspired to hinder the improvement of schools and universities—in no way moved the queen from her opposition.   Nor had Parker been sympathetic to the movement.   But when, in 1576, Elizabeth bluntly ordered his successor in the primacy, Edmund Grindal, to suppress the prophesyings, her action provoked a crisis.

For the archbishop replied in a long letter,[1] the most extraordinary communication ever made to the queen by any of her subjects.   Grindal protests he is not unmindful that it is the queen who has made him what he is, " neither do I ever intend to offend your Majesty in anything, unless in the cause of God, or of his Church "—a phrase that recalls the words of Thomas More on the scaffold.   To " use dissembling or flattering silence" now, would be a poor return for all that the queen had done for him.   He then brings all the authorities he can cite to confute the queen's " strange opinion . . . that it should be good for the Church to have few preachers "—Elizabeth had told him that there were already too many of them, that four in a county were enough, and that no more was really needed than for the Homilies to be read.   Preaching of the Cross of Christ, he says, is highly unpopular with many people of influence—and so it is that they abuse the preachers.   " But God forbid, Madam, that you should open your ears to any of these wicked persuasions."   And the effect of the Homilies " is nothing comparable to the office of preaching ".

The archbishop admits the poor quality of the average parson's education, and reminds the queen how high a proportion of the parochial endowments is, since the monasteries were dissolved, in the hands of laymen.   In seven parishes out of eight there is not " sufficient living for a learned preacher ".[2]

Grindal then turns to the prophesyings, and begins by telling the queen that many of the bishops [3] " think the same as I do, viz. a thing profitable to the Church and therefore expedient to be continued ".   These exercises take place under the authority of the bishop of the diocese—an authority which bishops possess by the law of God as well as by the canons now in force. He explains in detail what takes place at these meetings, and goes to Scripture (the Old Testament and the New) to show the antiquity and the lawfulness of such exercises.   He speaks of the good results, to which other bishops, too, bear witness.   The system raises the morale of the whole clerical body, and removes " the opinions of laymen touching the idleness of the clergy ". Also, " Nothing by experience beateth down Popery more than that Ministers . . . grow to such a good knowledge by means of these exercises, that

---

well as in religious.   Intolerance would have been continued and a rigid uniformity enforced ". *Ibid.*, 63.   [1] Dec. 20, 1576 ; the text is in Strype, *Grindal*, 558–574.

[2] " And in many parishes of your realm, where there be seven or eight hundred souls (the more is the pity), there are not eight pounds a year reserved for a Minister." *Ibid.*, 565.

[3] He gives their names (p. 568), London [Aylmer] ; Bath [Berkeley] ; Lichfield [Bentham] ; Gloucester [Cheney] ; Lincoln [Cooper] ; Chichester [Curties] ; Exeter [Bradbridge] ; St. David's [Davies].

where afore were not three able preachers, now are thirty meet to preach at St. Paul's Cross ; and forty or fifty besides, able to instruct their own cures."

For all these reasons, Grindal says, " I am forced with all humility, and yet plainly, to profess that I cannot with safe conscience, and without the offence of the majesty of God, give my assent to the suppressing of the said exercises : much less can I send out an injunction for the utter and universal subversion of the same ", and he quotes St. Paul for the queen's meditation, *I have no power to destroy, but only to edify : I can do nothing against the truth, but for the truth.*[1]   2 Cor. x, 13.

If the queen, for this, wishes to remove him from his see, " I will, with all humility, yield thereunto, and render again to your Majesty that I received of the same . . . What should I sin, if *I gained* (I will not say a bishopric, but) *the whole world, and lose mine own soul* ? "

He then begs the queen to leave matters which touch " the doctrine and discipline of the Church " to the decision of the bishops and divines of the realm, as she leaves questions of the law to her judges—asking, with St. Ambrose, Is a bishop to be taught by a layman ?   And, secondly, he asks that " when [Your Majesty] deals in matters of faith and religion, or matters that touch the Church of Christ, which is his spouse, bought with so dear a price, you would not use to pronounce too resolutely and peremptorily, *quasi ex authoritate*, as ye may do in civil and external matters : but always remember that in God's causes, the will of God (and not the will of any earthly creature) is to take place."   To say " ' So I will have it ; so I command : let my will stand for a reason ' is the antichristian voice of the Pope."

Elizabeth, too, will one day die.   " Remember Madam that you are a mortal creature," one day to appear " before the fearful tribunal of the crucified, to receive there according as you have done in the body, whether it be good or evil.   And although ye are a mighty prince, yet remember that he which dwelleth in heaven is mightier, . . . *terrible above all the kings of the earth*." [2]   So, when these religious matters come before the queen, " set the majesty of God before your eyes, laying all earthly majesty aside ; . . . with all humility say unto him, *Not mine, but thy will be done* ".   After all, the prosperity of the reign is due to " the goodness of the cause which ye have set forth ; I mean Christ's true religion ; and, secondly, to the signs and groanings of the godly in their fervent prayer to God for you.   Which have hitherto, as it were, tied and bound the hands of God, that he could not pour out his plagues upon you and your people, most justly deserved."   Let the queen take heed, or there may come to pass what is written of Joash (2 Chron. xxiv), that *when he was strengthened, his heart was lifted up to his destruction, and he regarded not the Lord.*

Grindal's private judgment about the view Almighty God took of the queen's management of ecclesiastical affairs did not shake Elizabeth's private judgment about the right and wrong way of managing them.   The archbishop

---

[1] It is interesting that the archbishop always quotes the Vulgate, and (not very tactfully, perhaps) translates the Latin for the queen—as he translates even the tags he quotes.

[2] This sentence I have inverted, cf. *op. cit.*, p. 572.

was suspended from the exercise of his jurisdiction, and on May 8, 1577, the queen herself circularised the bishops, commanding them, " according to the authority we have ", to see to it that no services were held but those set out " directly according to the orders established by Our laws ". The prophesyings the bishops are to cause " forthwith to cease ", and those disobedient to their orders they are not only to commit to prison, but to report to the council, so that " their punishment may be made more sharp for their reformation ". Moreover, let the bishops themselves beware ! " We charge you to be careful and vigilant, as, by your negligence, if we should hear of any persons attempting to offend in the premises without your correction or information to us, we be not forced to make some examples in reforming of you according to your deserts." [1] And Grindal's heroic stand for conscience found not a single imitator among his brethren. As in 1534 the man of principle was exceptional in those places.[2]

When Grindal died in 1583, Elizabeth appointed in his place the man who had routed Cartwright in 1570 and driven him from Cambridge, John Whitgift, Bishop of Worcester since 1577. Here was a primate with no hesitations, an able controversial theologian and an unwavering ruler, determined to secure uniformity within the church, and conformity to the established order from all the clergy. And by the end of the reign, twenty years later, although the movement was far from dead, and although the theological views of what clergy of the Establishment possessed any theology were still, for the most part, identical with those of the " presbyterianisers " among them, these last had ceased to be a serious threat to the policy of organising the church under a hierarchy of diocesan bishops, and through what was retained of the ancient Catholic church law.

Zurich, it is interesting to note, began to be less happy about what in this book is called the " primitive " section of the Reform party, once the idea of the presbytery seemed to be taking hold of it. " I think that the greatest caution is necessary ", Bullinger wrote to the Bishop of London in 1574, " that the supreme power be not placed in the presbytery, much more that it be not an exclusive government " ; [3] and to Cox of Ely he wrote, only a few days later, that no church needed a government of its own which had such a sovereign as Queen Elizabeth, who could do more for " moral discipline " than " ten presbyteries in every church ". Presbytery, he declared, was very

---

[1] The letter is in Strype, *Grindal*, 574–576.

[2] For the interesting witness of a sympathetic clerical contemporary cf., once more, Harrison's *Elizabethan England* (1577), " In many of our archdeaconries, we have an exercise lately begun which for the most part is called a *prophecy* or *conference* erected only for the examination or trial of the diligence of the clergy in their study of Holy Scripture. Howbeit such is the thirsting desire of the people in these days to hear the Word of God that they also have as it were intruded themselves among them (but as hearers only). . . . But alas Satan hath stirred up adversaries of late unto this most profitable exercise, who . . . have procured the suppression of these conferences." Harrison says that the *prophecy* set ministers " to apply to their books, which otherwise (as in times past) would give themselves to hawking, hunting, tables, cards, dice, tippling at the alehouse, shooting-off matches, and other such like vanities " ; *op. cit.*, 66, 67, 68. A Presbyterian historian of our own day describes the " prophesyings " as " embryonic Presbyteries of the modern type " ; Pearson, *Cartwright*, 157.   [3] March 10 ; *Z.L.*, 458.

ike latent oligarchy. Was it not bound to degenerate into tyranny ? Look at Heidelberg, only recently ![1] How wise, was he not, *our* apostle Zwingli ! Of course, the queen's authority needs to be an effective thing, and it must correct licentious nobles and the corrupt plebs, as well as ill-living clergy. To which Cox, who had watched the whole affair for a good fifty years and more now, drily replied that the attempt " to compel our great men to submit their necks " to the discipline " would be like shaving a lion's beard ".[2]

4. THE BISHOPS OF 1583–1593 [3]

When Whitgift was named to Canterbury—a bare six weeks after the death of Edmund Grindal—three of the bishops appointed in 1559–1560 were still alive and active : Scory, at Hereford ; Scambler, at Peterborough ; and Sandys, who had passed from Worcester, via London, to York. Four sees were vacant : Oxford, since 1567 ; Ely, since 1580—to which Elizabeth would never again appoint a bishop, the revenues going at the moment, in large part, to Sir Christopher Hatton ; Bath and Wells, since 1581 ; and Chichester, since 1582. And Bristol was held, *in commendam*, by the Bishop of Gloucester. A passing mention, at least, is necessary about the bishops of the second generation, late Whitgift's colleagues, and now to be his lieutenants in the campaign against the dissidents for whom the queen's reforms were all too incomplete. There are twelve of them in all.[4]

The seniors by age were Edmund Freake of Norwich, 67, and Thomas Cooper, of Lincoln, 66, who had now been bishops eleven and twelve years respectively. How Freake came to the many high promotions showered on him from the early years of Elizabeth's reign does not appear. He had once been an Austin Canon, of Waltham Abbey, the last of all the monastic houses to surrender to Henry VIII. Freake, not yet a priest, signed the surrender, and was given an annual pension of £5. Bonner ordained him in 1545. Freake had married, and the lady, it was said, and with every appearance of truth, ruled the unfortunate bishop and, to the best of her power, the diocese too. The discontent had moved the queen to send down a special commission of enquiry, and Freake was now begging to be once more translated.[5] This same year saw him sent to

---

[1] Where Cartwright had lately been received, and where he was now hard at work, answering Whitgift and translating Travers. Cf. *supra.*, p. 179. " The Elector Frederick III (1559–76) . . . in July, 1570, formally established a Presbyterian system based on the Genevan model in Heidelberg. Soon the town was to become notorious for its church's despotic exercise of power. . . . As an [example] we may mention the case of the minister, Sylvan, who was beheaded for heresy, Arianism, in the Market Place of Heidelberg ". Frederick died in 1576. His successor was " a decided Lutheran ". Whereupon, " a reversal of policy was effected, and those divines who had ruled so long in the spirit of the Old Testament and the Roman Inquisition had to vacate their posts and depart from Heidelberg ". Pearson, 134–135.

[2] Bullinger to Cox in *Z.L.*, 466–467 ; Cox's reply, *ibid.*, 473.

[3] This section, I regret to say, is no more than what the articles (of very varied merit) in the *D.N.B.* disclose. [4] Not counting the bishops in the Welsh sees.

[5] He had begun as Bishop of Rochester, 1572.

Worcester, vacant by Whitgift's promotion. Cooper, too, had had to suffer from an unhappy marriage, a bad woman, it would seem. He was a poor man's son, a good student and an industrious writer. His Dictionary of classical learning was one of the household books of the day. Cooper joined in the Jewel-Harding controversy, produced a *Brief Exposition* of the Sunday lessons, which Parker desired to see in every parish church in the country, and in the last years of his life, translated now to Winchester, the bishop became the target of one of the Marprelate tracts, *Ha'ye any work for the Cooper*. At the time of his appointment to Lincoln Cooper was dean of Christ Church, Oxford. The prelate who was Bishop of Winchester in 1583 was another of the *seniores*, John Watson, now 63, but a bishop since three years only. He had been a Reformer in the days of King Edward VI, but in Mary's reign had so successfully converted himself that he kept his living and gained new benefices, the latest of them, the chancellorship of St. Paul's, only nine months before Elizabeth came in. A year later he had changed sides again, and was already archdeacon of Surrey. He voted on the official side in the famous convocation of 1562 and in 1570 began his connection with Winchester, where, as the dean, he became the great friend of the bishop, the Robert Horne who had been the pastor at Frankfort. In Whitgift's story Watson plays no part at all, for he had now only a few months to live, dying in the first weeks of 1584. Thomas Cooper was his successor.

John Aylmer, the Bishop of London since 1577, was about the same age as Watson. His first patron had been that Marquis of Dorset who was the father of Lady Jane Grey, and Aylmer was one of the girl's tutors. In Edward VI's reign he had climbed as high as the archdeaconry of Stow, in Lincolnshire. Mary's reign he spent abroad, at Strasburg and Zurich. He came back, in 1559, in time to take a part in the Westminster Abbey disputation with the Catholic bishops which the government arranged. And then, as archdeacon of Lincoln, he went back to Lincoln, and for fifteen years was an active diocesan administrator, under the two bishops Nicholas Bullingham and Thomas Cooper—a good apprenticeship for the sixteen years to come in London. As bishop he showed himself a ruler of exceptional severity. He harried the Catholics, and the Puritans, and his own clergy, ceaselessly, ruthlessly—with the fullness of the ill-temper to which his portrait testifies no less than the records ; all to the continual embarrassment and annoyance of the government. And who shall wonder that, with ten young children to provide for, the elderly man used all his wits to make his tenure of the see as profitable as might be ?

A fifth bishop in his sixties was John Piers, first of Rochester (1576) but now of Salisbury, and destined, on Sandys' death, in 1588, to be advanced to York. Piers was a scholarly bishop, once of Magdalen College, Oxford, ordained according to the Catholic rite and beneficed in Queen Mary's reign. After Elizabeth's accession he climbed steadily the *cursus honorum*, dean of Chester, dean of Salisbury, dean of Christ Church. Parker and Whitgift joined to recommend him for Norwich in 1575.

Leicester was to urge his promotion to Durham in 1587. He was one of the rare bishops of this time who did not marry.

Whitgift had been six years a bishop when the queen translated him to Canterbury. Of the seven bishops who remain to be considered, one alone was his senior by appointment, Richard Barnes, who had been at Durham since 1577 and who before that was Bishop of Carlisle (1570–1577) and earlier still (from 1567) suffragan Bishop of Nottingham. It is hard to say what qualifications Barnes had, save promise, for his promotions began almost as soon as the new régime itself, when he was no more than 25 or 26. Within two years of the queen's accession, he was canon and chancellor of York. He had, however, Burghley for his patron, which is part explanation of the appointment to Carlisle (at 38) and to Durham. On both occasions " a string of manors " was surrendered to the crown. His successor was John May, brother of the famous canonist and civilian Dr. William May who had advised the crown in the matter of the consecration of Matthew Parker, and who had been appointed to York in 1560. John May was a Catholic in Mary's reign, or passed for one, for it was then (1557) that he was ordained. In the early years of the new reign he had the Earl of Shrewsbury for a patron—the sixth earl who was for so long the unwilling gaoler of the Queen of Scots, and who passed, with many, for being a Catholic at heart. May's life, between his ordination and the appointment to Carlisle, in 1577, at the age of 47, was spent in university administration, master, like Whitgift, of a Cambridge college, and a teacher of theology. Another one-time master of a college in the same university, was John Young, appointed to Rochester, at 42, in the year that followed May's appointment to Carlisle. Young, a Londoner by birth, had always been a Reformer, it would seem, and was at one time closely connected with Grindal, who ordained him, in 1561. He has the rare distinction that he remained at Rochester for the whole of his episcopal life, twenty-seven years no less.

Of the three bishops appointed in 1579, four years before Whitgift's translation, William Overton, then 54, was a one-time fellow of Magdalen, Oxford, and in Mary's reign had been sufficiently Catholic to be given the living of Swynnerton in Staffordshire. The university, however, was his real life, down to his appointment as treasurer of Chichester in 1567. He was famed as a preacher, and something has already been said of his judgment about religion in Sussex as he found it. John Woolton, ten years younger than Overton, who now became Bishop of Exeter, was a Lancashire man and a nephew of the famous Dr. Alexander Nowell, author of catechisms and, in the pulpit, the victim of one of Queen Elizabeth's more celebrated interruptions. As a mere youth Woolton had gone abroad with the other Marian exiles, and he was ordained in the first year of the new dispensation, June 4, 1560. The " Puritan " Earl of Bedford, Francis Russell, was his powerful patron, and through this influence Woolton began to acquire an ecclesiastical interest in Devonshire. By 1565 he was a canon of Exeter, and thence onward very active as a writer and as a preacher in the west country. When the queen re-founded the collegiate church of Manchester, Woolton was named its first warden, and then, ten months later, he was given the see of Exeter. The third of these bishops of 1579, William Chaderton, was the youngest of all the bench. He too was a Lancashire man, of the ancient family Chaderton of Chaderton, some five miles to the north-east of Manchester. The Manchester Grammar School and Cambridge had educated him—the Cambridge of Mary's reign, where in 1558 he became a fellow of Christ's College. Leicester was one of his patrons, Cecil another. At 27 he was Lady Margaret professor of divinity, and the next year president of Queen's College—this last through the influence of Cecil and the court, as his servile acknowledgment survives to show. In that same year he became also archdeacon of York. Next, after leave asked of Leicester, Chaderton married, and in 1569 he followed Whitgift as the regius professor of divinity. In the theological controversies Chaderton was a very active member of the Whitgift party. In 1570 he begged for the vacant deanery of Winchester, but was refused it. Nine years later, however, Leicester's influence obtained for him, at the age of 39, the see of Chester, and he was also given, *in commendam*, the wardenship of the collegiate church of Manchester—thus securing a residence in the town meant to be the headquarters of the campaign he was planning against the Catholics of Lancashire. Chaderton now showed himself as one of the main forces in the queen's ecclesiastical commission for the northern province. One feature of his activities was that the children of the recusants were handed over to him " with the view of guarding them from the seductions of the papists ". Chaderton was to govern Chester for the next sixteen years, and to be in all that time the most active of Whitgift's colleagues in the pursuit of the enemies of the Settlement of 1559.

John Bullingham, Bishop of Gloucester, the twelfth of these bishops, had been a bishop not quite two years, when Whitgift arrived at Canterbury. He was then about 53—the same age as the new primate. He came from Gloucestershire, was educated at Magdalen, Oxford, and he had then gone abroad to avoid the revolutionary changes of Edward VI's reign. He returned, upon Mary's accession, to complete his university studies, to be ordained, and to be taken by Gardiner as one of his chaplains. At the first royal visitation under the Act of Supremacy of 1559 he refused to conform and was deprived. It is unfortunate that we have no knowledge at all of what happened next. But by 1565 Bullingham had conformed, taken his bachelor's degree in the new theology and received from Grindal a prebend in St. Paul's. From then on he is well beneficed, and in 1581 he was given Cheney's two sees, Gloucester and Bristol.

During the all-important first ten years of Whitgift's primacy, 1583–1593, five of the sees that were vacant at the time of his promotion were filled,[1] and since four of the bishops of 1583 died in those ten years,[2] there are nine

---

[1] Worcester, Bath and Wells, Chichester, Oxford, Bristol.
[2] Watson 1584, Scory 1585, Barnes 1587, Sandys 1588.

new prelates to be noticed, if any record is to be made of episcopal appointments as a pointer to state policy in religious affairs.

For Bath and Wells, and for Chichester, the government chose two
venerable survivals from the generation of Sandys and Grindal, contemporaries of the now ageing Burghley, Thomas Godwin, Dean of Canterbury these eighteen years, and Thomas Bickley. Of Bickley's life in the
quarter of a century since the queen's restoration of the reformed religion
we know no more than the list of his promotions, but in Edward VI's reign,
as a fellow of Magdalen, Oxford, his fiery zeal had shown itself in a spectacular sacrilege when he publicly trampled on the Blessed Sacrament in
the chapel of his college. It is not surprising that, on Mary's succeeding,
Bickley fled to the Continent, but to France and not to Germany. Now,
in 1585, at 67, he took Curtis' place at Chichester. Godwin had been a
fellow of the same Oxford college in those same years, and then master of
the Grammar School at Brackley. He married, turned to medicine in Mary's
reign, and was not ordained until the Elizabethan restoration, when he became one of Bishop Nicholas Bullingham's chaplains (1560). Godwin had
a gift for popular preaching, and for as long as eighteen years he was Lenten
preacher to the queen. When Sampson was deprived of his great position
at Oxford, Dean of Christ Church, it was to Godwin that it was given.
But within a year he had surrendered this and was Dean of Canterbury.
Here he had troubles with his chapter, and also with the archbishop, Parker.
And when, shortly after his appointment to Bath and Wells in 1584, he re-
married a second time, at the age of 67, he was immediately in trouble with
the queen.

It was very rare for Elizabeth to give a see to a man so old as 60, but the
fourth of these whom she appointed, Matthew Hutton, Bishop of Durham
in 1589, was a man of real distinction. Like the bishop he replaced, Richard
Barnes, he came from Lancashire, and after a successful career at Cambridge
(master of Pembroke Hall and regius professor of divinity, at 33) the queen
gave him the deanery of York, in 1567. And here, for twenty-two years,
progress halted. In 1570 he was, indeed, spoken of as Grindal's successor
in London, but Parker objected, the suspicion that he favoured the Puritans.
In the last ten years of his life, as Archbishop of York and Lord President
of the Council of the North, Hutton was a power indeed, and he is found
at the end urging the younger Cecil to deal leniently with the Puritans.[1]

William Wickham who followed Cooper, first at Lincoln (1584) and then
at Winchester (1595), was 45 at his first nomination, a product of Eton and
King's College, Cambridge; and then vice-provost of Eton, canon of St.
George's, Windsor, a royal chaplain, Master of the Savoy Hospital, and
at 38 Dean of Lincoln. It was his lot to be appointed to preach at the
state funeral of Mary, Queen of Scots in Peterborough Cathedral, an awkward
" assignment " indeed, in which Wickham showed himself a man of charity.
Burghley is spoken of as his patron.

[1] As, when Bishop of Durham, he had begged Burghley to deal mercifully with a Catholic,
Lady Margaret Neville.

What brought Richard Howland, also at the early age of 45, to the see
of Peterborough in 1585 was the upheaval caused by Archbishop Grindal's
death in 1583 and the need to translate the unfortunate Edmund Freake.
Whitgift was moved from Worcester to Canterbury, and Freake from
Norwich to Worcester. Then Scambler, after twenty-four years at Peterborough, was moved to Norwich. And Peterborough was given to this
very notable Cambridge dignitary. Howland was a theologian, educated
at Christ's College and at Peterhouse. He had sided with Cartwright in
the famous events of 1569–1570, and had been one of those who petitioned
Burghley in 1571 for the restoration of this great figure to the life of the
university. But after the year of the *Admonitions* to the Parliament, he had
gone over to the official party, without, however, making enemies of his old
associates. Howland's moderation made Burghley his friend, and when in
1577 he went, through Burghley's influence, to the mastership of St. John's
the appointment was very popular. Howland's rule gradually calmed that
long-distracted college. This "man of gravity and moderation, and of
neither party nor faction", was not married, which was an additional inducement to the queen to favour him, as she did when, personally, she
chose him to look after the turbulent county of Northampton.

Howland, when he met his fellows in the House of Lords, would find a
good half dozen who, like himself, had come to their episcopal promotion
after the test of ruling a college in one of the universities. Among the group
promoted during Whitgift's primacy there was a second such, John Underhill,
rector of Lincoln College, Oxford, for twelve years when Elizabeth, in 1589,
provided in him a bishop for the incredibly neglected see of Oxford ; it
had been vacant for twenty-two years. Underhill was an Oxford man by
birth, educated at Winchester (in Queen Mary's time) and at New College
(1561). He was teaching moral philosophy by the time he was 25, and
next was involved in some conflict with the visitor of the college, Robert
Horne, Bishop of Winchester (1576). Then, at 32, he was made the rector
of Lincoln. It was Leicester who saved him from Horne, and Walsingham's
influence that secured him Oxford. On his death, after a short three years
as bishop, the see was once more left vacant.

Herbert Westphaling, given Scory's see of Hereford in 1585, at 54, was
also an academic type and an Oxford theologian, but from Christ Church.
He, too, had been in early years associated with those who, later on, were
to urge the completion of the work done in 1559. He was, for example,
one of those who petitioned Leicester for Sampson's appointment to Christ
Church. It was Grindal who ordained him, and Cecil who gave him his
canonry at 29. Westphaling was a preacher, and had a name for success
in converting recusants, and so won a place on the council's list of those
" fit and able to cope with Jesuits ".

Deans of cathedral churches were a more usual type of ecclesiastic to
promote to the episcopate. Five of the nine bishops we have been considering were already deans when the *congé d'élire* brought them to the notice
of the electing canons. One of these was John Coldwell, who, after ten

HENRICVS BVLLINGERES.

Sic candor, pietas, sic et doctrina relucent ,
Bullingere, tuo semper in ore simul .
Quam doctus fueris, pius, et candoris amicus,
Sat tua scripta probant.candida,docta,pia .

Cum priuilegio.

HENRY BULLINGER, 1504-1575

JOHN WHITGIFT, ARCHBISHOP OF CANTERBURY 1583-1604

THOMAS CARTWRIGHT, 1535-1603

HENRY HASTINGS, EARL OF HUNTINGDON, 1535-1595

years as Dean of Rochester, became Bishop of Salisbury in 1591, at the age of 56. He was a Cambridge master of arts, once a fellow of St. John's College, a physician also, married, and domestic chaplain (and physician) to Archbishop Parker. As a writer on medicine he has some place in history. Raleigh accused him of impoverishing his see; certainly he died deep in debt. We know much more about another promoted dean, Richard Fletcher. Of all the bishops Fletcher was the one personally most pleasing to the queen, and a rare specimen of a type remarkably uncommon in the Church of England, an ambitious man of the world with only his wits to live by. His father had taken orders, some years after Fletcher's birth, according to the rite of Edward VI. The son, born in the year of Henry VIII's decease—fourteen years younger, then, than the elderly queen whom he was to please—was educated at Trinity, Cambridge, became a fellow of Corpus Christi and, at 26, married. He was handsome, distinguished in manner, a preacher; and he won Elizabeth's good graces at first sight. The queen made him her chaplain-in-ordinary in 1581, and Dean of Peterborough two years later; he was then 36. Nor was it his only good benefice. Fletcher's atrocious bullying of Mary, Queen of Scots in the last moments of her life is his only claim on the attention of the general historian. He wrote Elizabeth a revoltingly pious account of the horror. When, two years later, she gave him the see of Bristol, her " well-spoiled " chaplain only received it on terms which, it has been said, amounted to a secularisation of the see. The new bishop spent far more time at the court than in Bristol or Dorsetshire, living mainly at Chelsea. Then, in January 1593, Edmund Freake having at last departed this life, Fletcher was translated to Worcester, whence piteous letters soon came to Burghley—London being now vacant—begging a second translation for, the bishop explained, he " delighted in London ", and longed for the court " where his presence had become habitual and looked for ". And so it was arranged. And now the poor man made the mistake which undid all. He not only married a second time, but chose badly; a young beauty whose name was a byword. Whereupon the queen drove him out, forbade him ever to come to court, and ordered Whitgift to suspend him from the exercise of his functions— which the primate did, a bare month after he had confirmed his election to London. The letters may be read in Strype in which the bishop grovels to Burghley, and then when the queen, after six months, relaxes the suspension, grovels still more piteously for leave to come to court. It was never granted, and the bishop's spirit was utterly broken. And one day, suddenly, as he smoked his pipe, death took him—at 49. He died insolvent, with eight children unprovided for.

5. ARCHBISHOP WHITGIFT

With Whitgift's promotion to Canterbury, the man had arrived who was to make all the difference.[1] Within two months of his appointment he

---

[1] Contemporaries, well informed, could say this; e.g. Hooker's close friend and associate, George Cranmer, writing in 1598, by which time the archbishop had triumphed, thus lauds

made his first move. What he proposed, after consultation with the other bishops, is set out in the so-called Articles of 1583 :[1] resolutions for common episcopal action on the main practical questions about which there was now controversy, together with a new test for all officiating clergy as well as for those licensed to preach.

In the first place comes a decision to put the new laws against the recusants[2] into stricter execution. There are also articles that touch the layman, ordering, for example, strictness in the matter of substituting money fines for the public penances imposed by ecclesiastical courts, and tightening the rules about the publication of banns of marriage.

The bulk of the resolutions, however, regard the clergy only. The rules about dress, laid down in the *Advertisements* of 1566, are renewed. Religious services " in private places "—this does not mean family prayers—are " utterly inhibited " ; they are " a manifest sign of schism and a cause of contention in the Church ". The long standing complaints about the quality of *ordinandi*, and of the indifference of the bishops to this, are met by renewing the ancient rules: no man is to be ordained who is not in possession of an appointment to a benefice or ecclesiastical salaried post ; candidates must be twenty-four years of age, and if not university graduates " at the least able in the Latin tongue to yield an account of their faith, according to the Article of religion agreed upon in Convocation " in 1563—by which is meant an ability to say on what Scripture texts the truth of these articles is based they must also bring to the bishop about to ordain them some testimonial as to character, from their college (if they are university men), " or from some justice of the peace, with other honest men of that parish, where he hath made his abode for three years before ". Bishops who ordain men not thus qualified are to be suspended from ordaining for two years. If the Court of Arches is invoked, to compel them to institute men " not of the ability before prescribed ", the archbishop will find means to halt the court.

Clergy of that school which considers that the sermon is the all-important thing, and the liturgical services of morning and evening prayer and the Holy Communion very secondary by comparison, are corrected by a rule that no one is to " preach, read or catechize " who does not, " four times in the year at the least ", say service and minister the sacraments, according to the Book of Common Prayer.[3] And it is also laid down, that no one is to

---

his hero : " It may be remembered that at first, the greatest part of the learned in the land were either eagerly affected, or favourably inclined that way. The books then written for the most part savoured of the disciplinary style : it sounded every where in pulpits, and in the common phrase of men's speech : the contrary part began to fear that they had taken wrong course ; many which impugned the discipline, yet so impugned it, not as not being the better form of government, but as not so convenient for our state, in regard of dangerous innovations thereby likely to grow. One man alone there was, to speak of, . . . who . . . stood in the gap, and gave others respite to prepare themselves to their defence ; " letter to Hooker, in *Hooker*, II, 598.

[1] G. & H., 481–484 for the text. Peel, I, no. 119, pp. 172–174, gives another version. Whitgift was elected to Canterbury Aug. 24, 1583, and the Articles were sent to the bishops Oct. 19, following.   [2] 23 Eliz., c. 1, for which cf. *infra*, pp. 343–344.

[3] The examination of John Wilson by the Bishop of London's chancellor, Dr. Stanhope, in November, 1587, shows the difficulty which this rule, it was hoped, would correct

preach who has not been admitted priest or deacon " according to the laws of this realm ".

Then there is the new test : no one is to preach, minister sacraments, or execute any ecclesiastical office, who does not make an explicit, signed acceptance of the royal supremacy ; of the Book of Common Prayer also, and of the ordination service, as in nothing contrary to the word of God, lawfully to be used therefore, with a promise always to use " the said book " and to use no other ; and an acceptance of the Articles agreed by Convocation in 1563 and set forth by the queen's authority, all of which articles, he must declare, are " agreeable to the word of God ".   The minister is not to be free to choose what version of the Bible he will use in the public services : the " one kind of translation " which alone may be used henceforward is the version of 1568, the so-called Bishops' Bible.

Whitgift's " test " was the fourth of its kind since 1559, and the most searching of them all.   In the test which accompanied the *Advertisements* of 1566, the Articles of 1563 had not been mentioned.[1]   Convocation, in 1571,[2] had only preachers in mind when it ordered that each should " by subscription " accept the Articles of 1563.   And the written acknowledgment of the Articles imposed by the Act of Parliament of that same year 1571, although obligatory on all future ordinandi and on all future nominees to benefices with cure, could be understood to refer to those Articles only which " concern the confession of the true faith and the doctrine of the sacrament ".[3]

" After he [i.e. Wilson] had read the articles, and promised to give a true answer, Stanhope said :

   S. Well, I can tell you, Mr. Wilson, if you mean to preach here, you must minister the
         communion every year thrice at the least.
   W. There is one to do that already in the place.
   S. That is no matter, you must at the least join with him in that action to shew that
         you divide not your ministry.   Would you divide your ministry ?
   W. My ministry shall be only to minister the Word.
   S. But the laws of the realm neither know nor allow any such ministry.
   W. But the laws of God do both.
   S. Yea, but I am set to maintain the laws of the realm.
   W. And I am set to maintain the laws of God, and declare the truth thereof.
   S. Well, it must be as I tell you, and further, you must subscribe to certain articles."
Peel, II, 227.   Wilson, who sought a licence to preach, was only in deacon's orders.

[1] G. & H., 475.

[2] Canon VI, for which cf. *supra*, 158–159, G. & H., 476–477 (translated) and Prothero, 201.

[3] The point of the controversy about the precise obligation imposed by the Act of 1571, is admirably illustrated by the different ways G. & H. (p. 478) and Prothero (p. 64) print the crucial clause of the Act.   In G. & H. it reads, " every person . . . shall . . . declare his assent, and subscribe to all the articles of religion, which only concern the confession of the true Christian faith and the doctrine of the sacraments, comprised in a book imprinted, intituled : Articles, etc., etc." Prothero does not print a comma after " religion " ; and, in his account of the Act, *Introduction*, p. xxxviii, he interprets the passage thus : " subscription to such of the articles as ' concern the confession etc.' ".

Which is the correct reading ?   " The question is very difficult to answer ", Hardwick wrote, a hundred years ago now (*op. cit.*, 225).   From the beginning a fight was made for the position that the obligation should be understood in the more restricted, " Prothero ", sense ; and in the end it became a kind of convention that " the articles relating to faith and doctrine (so far as these may be separated from the rest) are [nos.] 1, 2, 3, 4, 5, 9–18, 22 " [of the series as printed today in the Book of Common Prayer], Hardwick, 225, referring to Gibson's *Codex*, p. 321.

Moreover, of the clergy already in possession of benefices, the Act of 1571 only obliged those to subscribe who had been ordained otherwise than by the rite in the Ordinal of Edward VI that Elizabeth had now re-established—the numerous one-time Catholic priests, that is to say, and such odd figures as William Whittingham, ordained by the presbyteries of Reformed churches beyond the seas.[1] But now, in 1583, all must sign who wished to exercise any clerical function, and they must pledge themselves as accepting all the Articles of 1563.

The new test, which was presented to the whole body of the clergy in the next few weeks—the most vigorous episcopal action in their regard for nearly twenty years—caused an immediate swarming of the men it was meant to bring to order.   The critics fell upon the test immediately, as contrary to the statute of 1571, and they seized the opportunity to attack the Book of Common Prayer, the Ordinal, and the Thirty-nine Articles too.   The war of earlier years was vigorously renewed.

Three sets of systematic, critical analyses of the bishops' policy have been preserved.[2] As to the Catholics, these " primitives " are as worried as the bishops, " seeing the multitude of Recusants after so long a time of the gospel so greatly abounding ".[3] They think the bishops are largely to blame, through their slackness at visitations, and—it is alleged—a willingness to connive where Catholics are wealthy and there is a chance of good bargaining with them about properties.   On the other hand, " throughout the land, where preaching is, Papistry is not ".[4]

It is worth noting that this list of sixteen articles held as certainly imposed by the Act of 1571 does not include either of the articles about whose " authenticity " there was also much controversy.   These were (1) The opening sentence of the present article 20, that first appears in 1563, " The Church hath power to decree Rites or Ceremonies, and authority in Controversies of Faith : And yet " [then follow the unchanged words of the article of 1553]. (2) The whole of the present article 29.

As to the addition to article 20, the Latin printed text of 1563 (the first authoritative text of the Elizabethan revision of Cranmer's Forty-two articles) contains it, and so does the English printed text of 1571, but not the Latin text of this same year.   Article 29 (although in Parker's Latin MS. of 1563 which all the bishops signed) does not appear in print until 1571 when it is in both the English and the Latin versions of the articles.

For the convenience of the reader here is the English text of these two articles as 1571 left them : Article 20, " The Church hath power to decree Rites and Ceremonies, and authority in Controversies of Faith : And yet it is not lawful for the Church to ordain any thing that is contrary to God's Word written, neither may it so expound one place of Scripture that it be repugnant to another.   Wherefore, although the Church be a witness and a keeper of holy Writ, yet, as it ought not to decree anything against the same, so besides the same ought it not to enforce anything to be believed for necessity of salvation."   Article 29 : " The Wicked, and such as be void of a lively faith, although they do carnally and visibly press with their teeth (as St. Augustine saith) the Sacrament of the Body and Blood of Christ, yet in no wise are they partakers of Christ : but rather to their condemnation do eat and drink the sign or Sacrament of so great a thing."

[1] The bishops are exempted from the obligation to subscribe.

For which cf. Peel, I, nos. 120–122, pp. 174–195, a summary by the editor with many verbatim extracts.   Such documents as those published in this great collection often serve the purpose of speeches from the front bench of the opposition—criticism of government policy, and of the way this is executed.   Like such speeches, the criticism also is at times ill-informed and prejudiced.   But, on the other hand, it also gives at times a clue to the actual effect in the country of the laws enacted at Westminster and the decisions arrived at in the queen's council.   [3] Peel I, 174.   [4] Ibid., I, 175.

For this party, what was all-important in the appointment of clergy was that each parish should itself " call " its own particular minister. The bishops' remedy—the renewal of ancient ordination regulations—at a time when, so the critics insist, " such a swarm of unworthy ministers have been daily made *de faece populi*, which range in every country like to greedy flies for some 20 nobles by the year and meat and drink . . .",[1] in no way satisfies their passionate desire for reform, and they mock at the futile repetition.[2] " In the present great lack of preachers ", they also say, " it is not well that laymen of good life and learning should be prevented from reading in the churches " ;[3] and why " are those made ministers in foreign churches to be excluded from preaching " ?[4] " For seeing we maintain one profession of religion and live in one Communion, what cause is there why we should refuse their ministers, or by refusal disgrace the ministry of foreign churches ? "[5]

What stirs the opposition most of all, of course, is the new test. Even the demand made in it of assent to the royal supremacy is criticised. " Some ministers fear to subscribe to the statement that the Queen's authority is according to the Word of God, because it is not clear how far that authority extends."[6] Another critic objects that this particular demand is superfluous: " Without doubt the Queen possesses all authority ; long may she continue to do so without ' contradiction and to[o] curious sifting and enquiry of the manner or limitation of the same ' ; indeed the only people who object to this supremacy are the Papists."[7]

There is strong criticism of the new demand to approve the Prayer Book as in all things agreeing with God's word. Is it meant, by this, that the book is perfect ?[8] There are many ministers who use it loyally, but who would conscientiously hesitate to say about it what is now required of them. Why not tolerate their scruples ? What the points were, " whereat their conscience stumbleth ", is no mystery. One objectionable feature is that the lessons from Scripture are " appointed barely to be read, without interpretation and application ". The service, again, is so long as to " hinder preaching " ; and because it is an unescapable duty that the minister shall read all that is in the book, this may lead people to think that the service itself " meriteth, and is good service to God " ; and also that to read the service is the whole reason for there being a minister. There should be no chancels, " as in the popish churches . . . making a division between the priest and the people ".

Is it not " uncircumspect to pray God to have mercy upon all men without limitation ? " or for " the unity and concord of all nations, be they friends or enemies ? " and for prayer to be made " for all infidels and heretics ? " The idea of a special place [the font] for the administration of baptism is displeasing, and the " wicked opinion " that baptism is absolutely necessary ; and the signing of the child with the sign of the cross during the ceremony. Confirmation is a dangerous practice, it is declared, leading men to think

[1] Peel I, 180. [2] *Ibid.*, I, 180–182. [3] *Ibid.*, I, 177.
[4] *Ibid.*, I, 193. [5] *Ibid.*, I, 188. [6] *Ibid.*, I, 188 ; this the editor's summary.
[7] *Ibid.*, I, 183 ; this the editor's summary, with a quotation from the text.
[8] *Ibid.*, I, 199.

" baptism is not sufficient ", and, since only bishops may confirm, that con
firmation is more important than baptism. The use of the ring in the mar
riage service is another practice that is disliked ; also the service called th
" churching " of women after childbirth, and the allowance that children i
danger of death at their birth may be baptised by the midwife ; and finall
at funerals, is it not " absurd, whensoever the minister burieth Protestant
Papist, or Atheist, Heretic, Usurer, or Whoremonger, good or bad, to tha
he is his brother, as the book appointeth, and that he committeth him to th
ground . . . in sure and certain hope of resurrection to eternal life ? " [1]

The bishops' demand about the Thirty-nine Articles—this is a basi
criticism—goes beyond what is required by the Act of Parliament imposin
subscription to them,[2] namely, acceptance of the " doctrinal " articles only
This is the only objection raised on this point, in the three analyses. Othe
critics, however, now took the opportunity to criticise the Articles themselve
in some detail. What is it that exactly happens to a man through hi
" consecration " as a bishop ? Is Article VII correct—that the civil law o
Moses is not received—seeing many of its precepts " stand in force " ? Doe
not Article XVI suggest the " popish distinction of sin, deadly and venial ? '
Is it not dangerous to say that a man may fall from grace ? The article tha
speaks of election (XVII) says nothing of reprobation. Can it be said truly
that the doctrine of predestination " of itself is dangerous ? " or that there
can be any man to whom it " may cause a dangerous downfall " ? The nineteenth article, describing " a visible Church ", leaves out one of its necessary
marks, Discipline. Is the article about the calling of ministers (XXIII)
complete ? Does not Scripture itself " set down who they be that should call,
what they are to be called, and in what order ? " and should not this be
mentioned in the article ? Is it right to give " the name of priest . . . to
the ministers of God's word " ? And can the commanded approval be
given to the Books of Homilies that are a permanent obstacle to the formation
of a preaching (and therefore) instructed clergy ? [3]

What the primitives had not yet realised was that the queen, personally
most interested in these controversies, was also wholeheartedly against the
ideals of their party. Their efforts to paint Whitgift as a friend of the papists,
and to suggest that this new vigorous policy was a menace to the royal
supremacy, and an offence against the praemunire code, were so much
waste time.[4] In December 1583 the archbishop received from the queen a
new commission, under the Act of Supremacy. The Court of High Commission was henceforth the principal engine of his power, and a sign that all
could read of the identity of purpose and of views that united the sovereign
and her chosen primate.

---

[1] All these objections to the Prayer Book itself are taken, not from the three sources last
mentioned, but from *Questions to be answered concerning the archbishop's urging of subscription.*
Ibid., no. 124, pp. 196–201.
[2] 13 Elizabeth, c. 12. *An Act to reform certain disorders touching Ministers of the Church.*
G. & H., 477–480. The Act of 1571 already mentioned.
[3] All this from the source cited *supra*, in last note but one, pp. 197–199.
[4] For examples of these efforts, cf. Peel, I, 196.

To secure that the clergy, everywhere, signed the newly devised articles, and that the signatories were loyal to their bond, Whitgift acted systematically through this court and in it developed a procedure so rigorous that it moved Burghley to protest openly.[1]

The archbishop was not, of course, the inventor of the procedure. This court, not inaptly described by its own historian as a " Star Chamber for ecclesiastical cases ",[2] was no more than a development, the final development indeed, of the commission first appointed by the queen in 1559, according to the terms of the Act of Supremacy.

The commissioners, nineteen in number in 1559,[3] are to punish offences against the Acts of Supremacy and Uniformity. A quorum of six suffices, and they are " to enquire by oaths of twelve good and lawful men, as also by witnesses and all other ways and means ye can devise ".[4] The queen wills and commands them " to use and devise all politic ways and means for the trial and searching out . . . as by you . . . shall be thought most expedient and necessary ; . . . and to award such punishment to every offender by fine, imprisonment or otherwise . . . as [shall be thought meet and convenient] ".[5] And they are given power, " to call before you . . . suspect persons . . . and witnesses as you . . . shall think meet . . . and

[1] The archbishop's proceedings, Burghley wrote to him, July 1, 1584, were " so vehement and so general against ministers and preachers, as the Papists are thereby generally encouraged ". The Articles of 1583 had, in fact, now passed into a questionnaire, to be answered on oath by all ministers ; and the statesman found it " so curiously penned, so full of branches and circumstances, as I think the inquisitors of Spain use not so many questions to comprehend and to trap their preys . . . this kind of proceeding is too much savouring of the Roman inquisition ". The archbishop's canonists could, perhaps, justify it ; " but though *omnia licent* yet *omnia non expediunt*." The shudders of the old fox did not take in Whitgift for a moment. At this very time, in order to wring answers to the ' Bloody Question ", so " curiously penned " at Burghley's directions, the rack and the " scavenger's daughter ", the gauntlets, the rope and pulley, and the " needles under the nails ", were in continuous employment in the Tower, " to comprehend and to trap " the unfortunate Catholics; upon whom, indeed, Burghley would willingly have seen the archbishop operating. " In charity ", Burghley had written, " I think they ought not to answer to all these nice points, except they were very notorious offenders in papistry or heresy ". And it was only a matter of months since Burghley had publicly defended the torturing of Catholics. Whitgift's *tu quoque* is dated July 3, " I cannot but greatly marvel at your Lordship's vehement speeches . . . seeing it is the ordinary course in other courts likewise. . . . And I think these articles to be more tolerable, and better agreeing with the rule of justice and charity, and less captious, than those in other courts. . . ." Strype, *Whitgift*, III, 104–112 ; for extracts, cf. Prothero, 213–214. Also, the High Commission never used torture—nor, of course, could it pass sentences of death or mutilation.

[2] Usher, *High Commission*, 96.

[3] In 1583 the commissioners are forty-four in all, viz., the Archbishop of Canterbury ; the bishops (for the time being) of London, Winchester, Ely, Lincoln, Salisbury, Peterborough, Worcester, Norwich, Chichester, and Rochester ; the suffragan bishop of Dover ; the (present) deans of Canterbury, St. Paul's, Westminster, Windsor, Salisbury, and Rochester ; the (present) archdeacons of Canterbury, London, and Essex ; the archbishop's chancellor ; the Dean of the Arches ; three doctors of divinity ; four members of the government (Knollys, Walsingham, Mildmay and Sadler) ; the Master of the Rolls, the Lord Chief Baron, and two Masters of Requests ; the Recorder of London ; the Attorney-General and the Solicitor-General ; three Masters of the Court of Chancery ; three doctors of the Civil Law ; the lieutenant of the Tower. A quorum of three of these suffices, provided one of the three is one of twenty-two specially named. Cf. Prothero, 417b.

[4] Prothero, *op. cit.*, 228.   [5] *Ibid.*, 230.

to examine [them] upon their corporal oath . . . " ; [1] and " to commit . . to ward " those in any way obstinate or disobedient, " there to remain until . . . by you . . . delivered ".[2] The commission is thus, from the beginning, a court ; and as a court it follows the pattern increasingly fashionable since the accession of Henry VII, and is yet another instance of the natural affinity between the " totalitarian " tendency of the Tudors as administrators and the affection of most of their time for Roman Law procedure as the instrument adapted, *par excellence*, for governments that propose really to control the lives of their subjects. And the warrant that appoints these commissioners who are to see to it that the Acts of 1559 really go into operation, is very similar, of course, to that by which Mary, two years earlier, had provided a means for the discovery and arrest of suspected heretics.[3]

The powers of these commissions were granted *ad bene placitum*, and new commissions were issued in 1562, 1572, and 1576.[4] At first these commissioners were no more than a body chosen to carry out the directions of the council in some particular matter concerning religion : they did not really form a body with a life of its own ; all initiative, all policy, lay with the council and the commissioners were simply the council's agents, acting according to defined instructions. Then gradually, and more by a " change in emphasis ' in the form that named these personages than by a change in the form itself " certain of the ecclesiastical commissioners for the province of Canterbury " were transformed into the judges of a permanent ecclesiastical court—a transformation that was already complete by the time Whitgift was named archbishop (1583). Litigants with grievances in any matter of church jurisdiction were now finding that to petition the ecclesiastical commissioners to look into their affairs and to judge them was the speediest way to obtain justice.

And if the court developed as rapidly as it did because the practical possibilities of the new institution made a strong appeal to the small man everywhere, the tendency of the commission to become a court was greatly helped, also, because the bishops realised that by means of it they could give a new reality to the ancient sanctions of church discipline. Fifty years after the collapse of Wolsey's legatine authority, a super-episcopal organ of church administration, equipped with coercive jurisdiction that was a reality, was functioning once again—but this time it was functioning with the greatest good will on the part of the bishops. Now, for the first time since the inauguration of the new religion, ecclesiastics *as such* found themselves furnished with sanctions really adequate to enforce the various details of the new order. Excommunication as a sanction had, in the long run, failed too often : nothing less than the concrete punishments of fine and imprisonment would ensure obedience, from the Reformed as well as the Catholics,[6] to the fundamental Acts of Supremacy and Uniformity. Without these punishments,

---

[1] Prothero, *op. cit.*, 230.   [2] *Ibid.*
[3] Cf. Vol. II, 271–272 ; and Usher, *High Commission*, 337–339.
[4] Prothero prints the relevant passages of the Commission for 1559, 1562, 1572, 1576, and 1601 ; and the full text of that for 1583.
[5] Usher, *High Commission*, 64–65.   [6] Cf. Appendix VI, pp. 422–440.

without a court that could decree them, that had officers of its own to collect the fines, and prisons of its own to house the convicts, the bishops' jurisdiction would, by the end of Elizabeth's reign, have been a dead letter.[1] It was Whitgift himself who said this, in so many words, to Elizabeth in 1593, " It is the only means we have to punish and restrain sectaries and contentious persons which refuse to observe laws and to keep order." [2]

What really brought this development to all its fullness was the personality of the two remarkable men who dominated the High Commission in the last fifteen years of Elizabeth's reign, Whitgift and Richard Bancroft : the last named a great figure indeed, whose appearance in the high places of the Elizabethan *Anglicana*—so it has recently been declared—came " only just in time to save the English Church from complete disintegration by decay ".[3] It is thanks to Richard Bancroft, above all, that the statesman-appointed churchmen of the statesman-constructed church ultimately find a way to run the church independently of the statesman ; the Royal Supremacy, it is discovered, can be made to serve the cleric's turn too, and to become a means whereby there is restored the reality of the cleric's hegemony in the church. And alongside this reaction, that steadily develops once Bancroft becomes one of the High Commission in 1587, there is beginning a second reaction, whose historical consequences are not less of the highest importance, a reaction against Calvin's doctrines about election and reprobation. In this reaction, too, Bancroft will play his part ; and we may perhaps see the young divine as a symbol of that new age, now preparing, when the view that government through bishops is a thing good in itself (good always therefore) and not a matter of church politics merely, will come to be thought of, in the queen's religion, as another part of that theology which renounces Calvin, all his works and pomps.

Whitgift's articles of 1583 met with some resistance. In November, 1583, there were suspensions of clergy who refused to sign ; and there were further suspensions in 1584 ; [4] and appeals and petitions to the council, to parliament and to the queen.[5] The year 1585 opened with a great campaign of prayer

---

[1] Usher, *High Commission*, 99 ; whose thesis is here summarised. " When laymen cheerfully remained excommunicated for years, as was not uncommon in Elizabeth's reign, it became clear to all that the validity (*sic* !) of the old ecclesiastical process had disappeared. The Church no longer possessed a method of coercing the disobedient suitor at law " ; *ibid.*

[2] Quoted *ibid.*, from Brit. Mus. Add. MSS. 28, 571, fo. 172.

[3] Gregory Dix, *The Shape of the Liturgy* (1945), 703 ; this judgment is made not of Bancroft alone, but of Bancroft and the other " neo-Anglicans " of the time, and it is not made with reference to the work, now about to be described, of the High Commission, but to their " elaboration of a properly Anglican doctrinal position ".

[4] " Over two hundred ministers in Lincoln, Norfolk, Suffolk, Essex and Kent ", Black, 162 ; for details of these cf. Peel, I, pp. 209–245. Pearson, 241–242, speaks of " many " suspensions.

[5] Cf., in Peel, I, nos. 134 and 164, petitions to the queen ; no. 163, *A Supplication to Parliament*, i.e. to bring the queen to reform the church ; nos. 141–145, 168, " supplications " to the council from Norfolk, Essex, Lincolnshire, and from Walter Travers. Also the extremely interesting contemporary accounts of the discussions between these ministers who have refused to subscribe and the officials of the High Commission, in which we can see most vividly the conflicting mentalities of Whitgift and his critics ; e.g., *ibid.*, I, 209–220,

and fasting in the camp of the true believers, while in London a General Meeting drew up plans for a renewal of the fight through parliament.[1] Here they failed, time and again. A petition to the House of Commons (February 25) was rejected.[2] A petition asking Convocation to remodel the settlement of 1559 after the pattern of Geneva was not even read.[3] And in the House of Commons the same fate befell the Bill, and the prayer-book annexed, " digested and framed by certain Godly and Learned Ministers ".[4]

A petition was now sent off to the long-exiled Cartwright begging him to come home. He returned in April, 1585.[5] Parliament was now dissolved; it had been hostile to the ideals of the party, although a parliament so bitter against the Catholics as to enact the Statute which made it death for a priest to be found in the country, and death for all who gave him any assistance.[6] The conferences of ministers, however, continued to function, and within a few months Travers had ready for them the most important of his books, the *Disciplina Ecclesiae sacra Dei verbo descripta*, " the Puritan Book of Discipline *par excellence*, . . . a complete outline of the system of ecclesiastical government desired by the Puritans "—a vade-mecum for whoever wished to reorganise religious life after the pattern of Geneva.[7]

In the autumn of 1586, a new parliament having been summoned (Sept. 15), a second campaign by petition began—petitions to the queen, to the council, to parliament,[8] and to all the great men about the court. The language of the petitions was temperate : they were the work of

---

the case of the ministers and preachers of the diocese of Chichester ; pp. 248–252, the Bishop of Winchester (Thomas Cooper) and the Vicar of Wandsworth ; pp. 275–283, the same bishop and Whitgift with Spark and Walter Travers, *coram* Leicester, Walsingham and Lord Gray, " apparently written by Travers " ; pp. 286–291, the case of Eusebius Paget, minister of Kilkhampton, in Devon, the charges against whom illustrate the rule that no one is to preach who refuses to celebrate the communion service. Paget is charged with saying that the sacraments are " dumb elements ", of no avail without preaching ; and of a minister associated with him it is said that he " has several times refused to administer the communion, and has said, " Do they make so much a do for chewing a piece of bread and drinking a cup of wine ' ". In *ibid.*, II, 39–48, there is an account of the troubles of one of the most famous of all these ministers, John Udall, the vicar of Kingston-on-Thames, that includes a most detailed list of his alleged offences and wrong theological notions, thirty-six points in all.

[1] The fifth parliament of the reign, opened Nov. 23, 1584, dissolved March 29, 1585.

[2] Pearson, 251.

[3] *Ibid.*, 252. There is also a petition to Convocation in Peel, I, no. 180 (pp. 296–303). This petition is " in the name of the ministers that had refused to subscribe the articles lately enforced upon them ", and is a detailed exposition of the thesis that many things in the Book of Common Prayer are directly contrary to the Word of God.

[4] Pearson, 251.   [5] *Ibid.*, 229.   [6] 27 Elizabeth, c. 2.

[7] The quotations are from Pearson, 252 and 141. The book was ready by 1586 and it circulated in manuscript. In 1644, when the " presbyterianisers " were at last in control, and able to carry out the destruction of the episcopal system and institute the Discipline, the book was translated into English as *A Directory of Church Government*. The Latin original was printed in 1907 in Paget's edition of Hooker's *Ecclesiastical Polity, Book V*. Pearson's warning (p. 141) should be borne in mind, that because Travers' book of 1574 (the *Explicatio*, cf. *supra*, p. 179) " was frequently called *The Book of Discipline* even by contemporaries ", it is frequently confused with the book of 1586, as Cartwright's translation of the earlier book is confused with the translation published in 1644.

[8] The sixth parliament of the reign, which was opened Oct. 29, 1586, and dissolved March 23, 1587.

loyal subjects, harassed in conscience by the new unprecedented demands of the bishops. The petitions came in from all over the midlands, from the east and the south-east; they bore the signatures of clergy and laity, of the local gentry, of justices of the peace; and, taken to be what they declared themselves, the appeal of " many thousands of the most trusty, most loving subjects that her Majesty hath ", they made a great impression.[1]

Nevertheless, when on February 27, 1587, Antony Cope actually introduced the Bill to " make void . . . all laws now in force touching Ecclesiastical Government ", and to replace the Prayer Book of 1559 by the Form of Prayer devised at Geneva by the exiles of Mary's reign, he struck the rock of rocks. The queen intervened, and forbade all further consideration of the matter, while Cope was sent to the Tower and other members too were imprisoned. This was the end of the presbyterian party's hope to complete through parliament the achievement of 1559.[2]

Seven drafts have survived of Bills for the reform of the church, prepared by this party, to show in detail what it was they planned.[3] One of these [4] proposed to reform the ministry by enacting (i) that all one-time mass priests ordained " to sacrifice for the quick and the dead ", should within six months openly, and in plain words, abjure, with true repentance, the heinous sin of their ordination, and " be admitted ministers by a new vocation and election to the preaching of the gospel "—or else utterly cease to be employed in the ministry; (ii) that all clergymen convicted of evil-living [5] since their calling to the ministry are to lose their clerical employment, and never again to be so employed; (iii) that all who were admitted to the ministry while they yet lacked " God's gifts of true interpretation and utterance of God's holy word ", are, upon proof of this before the statutory examiners, to be " published no ministers " ; the local civil authority is to arrange for their future maintenance ; (iv) that no man is to be " called " unless " to some certain congregation or parish then vacant " ; and before he is " called ", there is to be a public examination to test " whether he be of sound judgment in the interpretation of the holy scriptures . . . and has the gift of utterance to preach unto the people " : all this being found in order, and the man's good character certified, he is then to be presented to the congregation by some neighbouring minister, and they " by holding up their hands " shall declare their will to have him " to be their pastor ". Whereupon the minister sent from the

---

[1] For evidence of the pressure to which Whitgift was subjected by the Presbyterian-minded among the lords of the council, cf. the insolent letter from Robert Beale, once a Marian exile, and now clerk to the council (July 7, 1584), Whitgift's correspondence with Burghley about this (these in *Bath MSS.* II, 26–30), and also Sir Francis Walsingham's letter to the archbishop (with more than a hint of threats of the law and disgrace) in *Hatfield MSS*, III, 109–112.   [2] Pearson, 255–256.

[3] All calendared in Peel, *op. cit.*, some of them printed in full.

[4] *An Acte for the reformation of the Ministerie in the Churche of England and for the supplyinge of the same with convenient and sufficient ministers.* Peel, I, pp. 304–311.

[5] A detailed list of enormities is given, at the head of which is " revolting from the gospel to idolatry ".

conference [i.e. of ministers], and the elders with him, " shall lay their hands upon the said new chosen pastor ", and the minister pronounce him " lawfully admitted to be pastor in that place " ; (v) that there shall be, monthly, a meeting of the conferences of ministers " in sundry parts of the shire ", thirty to forty ministers to each conference.   The prophesyings forbidden in 1576 are to be made obligatory, by Act of Parliament, in 1586 ; and it is the justices of the peace who are to fix the assembly places for each conference.

To bring home to the members of parliament the urgency of this question of clerical ignorance, and clerical ill-living, the party presented a survey, carefully detailed, of the clerical establishments in the places complained of—the value of the living, the name of the incumbent, his professional competence and his manner of life.   The " sum total " of parishes thus surveyed is 2537 (between a third and fourth of the total of parishes in the country).[1] Of the incumbents, 1773 are set down as "no preachers", 472 only as " preachers ".   Only in the surveys of Cornwall, Lincoln, Norfolk, Essex and Warwickshire are there comments on the moral character of the incumbents.   The account given of Cornwall reads like an appendix to the reports on the monasteries prepared by Dr. Layton for Cromwell, in the unenlightened days of fifty years before :   141 of the clergy are named ; of the character of 54 we are told nothing, 22 are described as good, and 65 as really wicked men. In the 416 parishes of Norfolk which have a non-preaching minister conditions are better than in Cornwall ; on 91, out of the 361 clergy named, no comment is made ; of the remaining 270, only 71 are bad men.   In Essex 55 out of the 199 named are set down as men of bad life, and in Warwickshire 26 out of 159.[2]   In London—i.e. within the walls of the city—there are 97 parishes, it is stated, and " if diligent search by authority might be made, there would not be found within the walls of this city . . . above 4 godly, learned, sufficient, resident and diligent ordinary pastors, attending only upon their flocks, not failing them in teaching and catechising every Sabbath ".[3]

---

[1] For the documents of this " Survey of the Ministry ", cf. Peel, II, 88–174.   The detailed survey covers the following counties : Cornwall (98–110), Lincoln Lindsey (111–129), Oxford and Oxfordshire (130–142), Berkshire (142–146), Norfolk (146–156), Essex (156–165), Warwickshire (165–174) ; there are summary accounts of Rutland (92), Bucks (94), Surrey (94), Middlesex (95), London, city and archdeaconry (95–96).

[2] How far can we rely on these surveys ?   On the truth of their information about the evil life of some of the new clergy, for example ?   Whether there is any means or not to evaluate this critically, what is certain is that it cannot be disregarded simply because " Bancroft, Whitgift's right-hand man at Lambeth and ultimate successor there, called them ' libels ' rather " (Rowse, *England of Elizabeth*, 474) ; nor on Frere's general principle that " Truthfulness was never one of the Puritans' strong points ".   Rowse, *ibid.*, 476, sets aside the Cornish survey, " the most spicy and vindictive ", and arbitrarily prefers to it, as " more moderate and representative ", the survey of Warwickshire.   Along with these " surveys ", we may also consider the testimony *de statu ecclesiae* of the Lancashire rectors in 1590 (Chetham Soc., Old Series, no. 96, *Chetham Miscellany*, *V*), that " the churches are almost empty and drunkenness and illegitimacy are on the increase ", so Leatherbarrow, 120, for whom also, 136, " It is clear that the Lancashire Rectors . . . were members of what may be called the left wing of the Lancashire clergy ", but " no doubt their picture was a faithful one ".   [3] *Ibid.*, II, 95.

This lamentable state of things a second Bill [1] proposes to remedy by carrying to the fullness of destruction Henry VIII's projected reformation of the Canon Law. An entirely new machine is to take its place. There shall be elected in every parish, so the Bill enacts, a committee of six laymen, who "together with the minister" constitute "the presbytery of the parish", and act as censors and judges of the whole lives of the parishioners, hearing all those cases concerning private lives which were the business of the church courts. The presbytery is to punish offenders by admonitions, and excommunications, calling in the civil power to imprison those who ignore their sentences, and do not abandon the sin in which they were taken. Presbyteries which neglect their duty are to be "constrained" by the Justices of the Peace at their sessions. But such matters as probate, tithes, and marriage suits— all of which are " cases mere civil "—are, for the future, to be dealt with by the Justices of the Peace for the shire. The canon law and the whole system of church courts, with their fees and ecclesiastical censures, is effectively abolished.

If there were not preachers enough, nor trustworthy clergy, to man even a third of the parishes in England, it was attempting the impossible to enact the establishment of these thousands of presbyteries that called for instructed godliness everywhere, lay and clerical.

Next, however, came the *Bill exhibited to Parliament for reformation of the ministry*.[2] There is no hope of a learned clergy, it is here announced as an axiom, unless the posts are sufficiently paid. The Bill therefore proposes, first of all, a means to improve the revenues of the benefices, and then a scheme to secure that the best of them are reserved for the learned [i.e. university taught] clergy. All the legal developments of past centuries by which tithes have been diverted from their true purpose, the support of the clergy who actually serve the parish, are abolished. Unlearned incumbents, in places where this reform has increased the value of the living by £20 or more, are to provide for their parish a resident learned preacher, under pain of deprivation. In those many cities where livings are insufficient "to maintain learned ministers ", and where the full tithes are also insufficient, the householders are to pay their minister " being a learned preacher ", a tax equal to 10 per cent. of the annual value of their houses. The Act of 1571, it is recalled, already reserved livings above £30 yearly to bachelors of divinity, or those licensed by a bishop to preach. Bishops have, however, as is notorious (says the Bill), taken too easy a view of what makes a preacher. For the future, then, no preacher shall be given so valuable a benefice who is not either a bachelor of divinity or an M.A. of five years standing.[3]

---

[1] *An acte for the restitution of christian discipline in the Churche of England, and for the abolishing of the Canon Lawe in that behalfe.* Peel, II, 1–4. The patronage of Henry VIII is claimed in the opening sentences of the Bill.

[2] *Ibid.*, II, 196–198.

[3] " Of almost 10,000 parishes there are not much above 500 that are above £30 in the Queen's books ", a disputant on the other side wrote : Matthew Sutcliffe, *False Semblant, etc.* (1587), p. 69, quoted in Hooker, II, 516 note 1. Hooker himself writes (in 1597) that " not a fourth part of the livings . . . [are] able to yield sufficient maintenance for learned men." *Ibid.*, II, 516.

Furthermore, none shall be admitted to a benefice of £20 a year who is not a master of arts and a preacher ; and none to a benefice of over 20 marks (£13 6s. 8d.) who is not either a bachelor of arts or a preacher lawfully appointed by a bishop.

These three Bills were meant for the session of 1586. For that of 1587 two more were prepared, that dealt with the forbidden subject of the Prayer Book. *A Bill for the further reformation of the Church offered with the booke in the Parliament A°. 1587,*[1] is a lengthy manifesto that sets out the party's view of what that church should be, in which the queen, Whitgift and Cartwright (to say nothing of Cecil and Leicester, Hatton and Walsingham) found themselves. Running through it all, is the evident and bitter disappointment that the policy since 1559 has halted what (according to the party) all good men had really had in view from the first days of change in the time of Henry VIII. It was only " the necessity of sudden change to be made ", that compelled the queen, in 1559, to leave the work incomplete. " Your highness established a certain form of church government and common prayer, and caused certain penal statutes to be made for the strict observation of the same "—but, also [alas], did this by reviving and restoring laws and statutes of Henry VIII and Edward VI, which were, necessarily, imperfect instruments for the godly work. For in King Henry's time, when the heavenly light was still dim, the knowledge needed for the task was slender ; and although King Edward, indeed, attained " unto a clear knowledge of the true worship of God by the further increase of that heavenly light ", there were too many " deformities and corruptions " to be purged, and so he, too, " was enforced for a time still to permit " the operation of the great system of the canon law.

The Bill goes on to instruct the queen, in detail, that " whereas our Saviour Christ hath set up in his Church for the building up of his saints " a ministry of Pastors and Teachers, and of Elders " whose office is in having a special eye upon the life and manners of every one within their charge ", who are to rule and guide the church and to choose and ordain those called to any office of service [2]—whereas all this is what God has willed, " for Teachers, Elders and Deacons our Church lacketh altogether, retaining only some shadow of the two latter in Churchwardens, Sidesmen and Collectors, mere civil offices ". On the other hand, the church " doth embrace a calling of Lord Bishops not agreeable to the word of God ", a corrupt following of the Apostles, in fact ; who now usurp all the functions of the Presbytery, and are responsible for the present lamentable professional insufficiency and ill-living of the clergy. As the Prayer Book of 1559, and the Ordinal, are the warrant for all this departure from God's law, be it then enacted that, for the future, " the book hereunto annexed, entitled ' *A booke of the form of Common Prayers etc.*' . . . be authorised, put in use and

---

[1] *Peel*, II, 212–215. This is, apparently, one of the Bills introduced by Antony Cope.
[2] And, " for clearing of doubts and questions that may arise, the Lord hath ordained conferences, and assemblies of the governors of many Churches in Synods and Councils, both provincial and national ". *Ibid.*, 213.

practiced ", and all other laws that set forth religious services, rites, orders, or government of the Church be " utterly void and of none effect ".

There is a second Bill on the same subject, and of the same date.[1] This time the preamble is short. The Prayer Book of 1559 is declared to " join too much with the conformity of the popish churches ". The framers of the Prayer Book of 1549 were deservedly praised for the reformed version of it which they produced in 1552. Even in this, however, there are still many things that " do evidently dissent from God's word ", things that offend " the consciences of many good subjects that profess the gospel ", and so bring them in danger of " great penalties ". The Bill then enacts that, in place of the book of 1559 there shall be used the book called *A Forme of Common Prayer*.[2] No other is to be used in public services, and no prayer not in accord with its spirit is to be asked in private services of prayers. " De-pravers " of this book, or of the confession of faith it contains, are to go to prison until they give security for future good behaviour. In public services the psalms may be sung " in meter ", and the minister may offer *ex tempore* prayers, so long as these accord with the confession of faith.

Next, since the authority " now committed to the bishops and arch-bishops " of governing the Church of England rightly belongs " to an assembly of lawful ministers and elders ", the Bill commits that authority to such assemblies—one for every county—and proceeds to say how these shall be appointed. It is worthy of note that this omnicompetent body, the Assembly, sovereign in all matters spiritual, is limited by the proposed statute, when it inflicts penalties, to spiritual punishment ; it is specially enacted that, " they deal not with any penalty of body or goods ". Above these county assemblies there is set the " general assembly " of the province, York or Canterbury, whose members are chosen by the county assemblies, as a court of appeal. And, if the need should arise, the queen may be peti-tioned " for a general synod of the whole realm ". This, it is, and not the queen, that is to be the ultimate authority, " from which no man shall further appeal ".

[1] *An Acte for the establishing of a Booke intituled A forme of Common Prayer and Adminis-tration of the Sacraments to be used in the Churche of England, with a Confession of Faith annexed in the beginning thereof.*

[2] This is the prayer book used in the services of the church of the Marian Exiles at Geneva, the work of Knox, Whittingham, Gilby, Foxe, and Cole. It was printed by John Crespin, and issued on Feb. 10, 1556. After the return of the exiles, in 1559, " many editions were printed for the use of the Puritan Congregations in England ". The first known of these " bears no date, but was probably printed in 1584 or 1585 ". Schilders, of Middelburg, printed at least three further editions of the same book, in 1585, 1587, 1602, " for the use of the English Puritans. . . . Many other editions must have appeared for the use of the Puritans, but of them all trace has since been lost." The quotations are from Dr. W. D. Maxwell's work, *The Liturgical Portions of the Genevan Service Book used by John Knox while a minister of the English Congregation of Marian Exiles at Geneva, 1556-1559*, Edinburgh and London, 1931, pp. 8, 75. This learned work does not reprint " the long Confession of Faith, nor the Preface Letter," but it includes the text of the Sunday Morning Service, Baptism, the Lord's Supper, Marriage, Visitation of the Sick, Burial of the Dead, Election and Ordination of Ministers. The book used at Geneva was reprinted in *The Phoenix* (1709), Vol. I.

It was at the moment when the manoeuvres of the presbyterianising section of the establishment seemed likely to check—and perhaps to destroy— what the newly appointed Whitgift was working for, that there appeared in the controversy the man who was to be the archbishop's principal support, his second self indeed. This was Richard Bancroft, an Oxford theologian, now in the early forties,[1] who for some years had been chaplain to one of the queen's principal favourites, Sir Christopher Hatton, soon to be named Lord Chancellor.[2] Bancroft, who was a hard and rapid worker, had great organising gifts ; he could write a telling pamphlet, and preach a sermon that would change public opinion—and he revealed himself, too, as a born police-man. Such was the scholar who now replied to the party of Travers and Cartwright, answering the pamphlets of the party in a masterly way, and showing how, despite the carefully moderate language of the petitions, the real aim was to remake the whole administration of the church after the Cal-vinist model. More usefully still, Bancroft was able to show that the pres-bytery-men were indeed but a party—they were not the mass of the church-men, nor did their numbers run to thousands and thousands. Bancroft knew enough to be able to convince the council that this flood of seemingly spontaneous petitions was, in reality, the fruit of careful organisation on the part of a really small group of ministers.[3] Here was his great service to the government, to make it clear that it did not need to take seriously the seeming menace of the petitions ; the policy of 1559 need not be changed ; this

[1] Richard Bancroft was born in Lancashire, 1544. His mother was a niece of Hugh Curwen, at this time Archbishop of Dublin and later (1567) Bishop of Oxford. Bancroft was educated at Cambridge (Christ's College, B.A. 1567) and there is some ground for believing that in the first clash of the Puritans and the ecclesiastical authorities, the young man's sympathies were with the Puritans. But he soon came within the orbit of one of their strong opponents, Richard Cox, Bishop of Ely, whose chaplain he became in 1576. It was seven years later, during the assizes at Bury St. Edmunds, that an accident set Bancroft on the track of Brownist " sedition " ; and he thereby became a means to the trial of the two Brownists then convicted and hanged.

[2] Sir Christopher Hatton, Bancroft's first important lay patron, was his senior by some four years only. He had been at Oxford (but left without a degree) and at the Inns of Court (but was never called to the Bar). At the queen's court he soon attracted Elizabeth's atten-tion, became one of the Gentlemen Pensioners (1564, aetat. 24) and captain of her body-guard (1572). The two now treated each other with the most affectionate familiarity, in speech and in writing, and " malignant gossip " (J. M. Rigg, in D.N.B., Hatton) said he was the queen's paramour. He had entered parliament in 1571, where he ultimately came to be looked on as spokesman for the queen's wishes. Elizabeth, who showered gifts upon him, of money and of lands, knighted him in 1578 and made him a Privy Coun-cillor ; and in 1587, to the no small indignation of the lawyers, she made him Lord Chan-cellor—some compensation for the agonies he had endured as Raleigh, twelve years his junior, replaced him in the elderly queen's affections.

[3] How Bancroft came by this knowledge, Usher explains. He kept up " an untiring correspondence with the local officials of the suspected districts. When an answer came that led him to believe a man was in league with the classis, some of the Privy Council spies, placed at his service by Walsingham, very quickly uncovered the truth. His best information was derived from the interception of hundreds of letters exchanged by the Puritan clergy and gentry." Reconstruction, I, 50. How far Bancroft's eagerness could carry him this same writer illustrates (ibid., 57) from his letter of Dec. 23, 1589, to Naunton. Bancroft needs evidence, and in order that Naunton may get a sight of papers that are in Scotland the queen's commissioner suggests that he should pretend a willingness to be converted to Presbyterianism.

handful of critics could be safely disregarded ; whenever the government chose to suppress them, the nation would look on unmoved. The layman —this Bancroft did *not* say, of course—could breathe easily once more ; the peculiar institution he had planned and planted on the country in 1559 was not in any real danger from these zealots—the layman's absolute control of the clergy, that is to say, and the consequent security that his own life would remain absolutely independent of clerical control ; the lion could grow his beard as long as his taste preferred.

The great movement was, then, not at all what it pretended to be, and those who had organised it had deliberately given it this false appearance— the holy men had descended to the political arts, it is suggested ; and the notion is now first mooted that will always hereafter cling in some measure to the " Puritan ", that " godliness " and trickery can dwell together with mutual satisfaction.

Bancroft's literary duels date from 1585 and 1586. It was in 1587 that he was named to the High Commission, and in 1589 that he preached the sermon at Paul's Cross which, in the history of this affair, played the part of a modern prime minister's broadcast at a national crisis. This sermon, preached as parliament assembled,[1] was " the turning point in the history of Elizabethan non-conformity ",[2] in the history, that is to say, of the fortunes, within the Elizabethan *Anglicana*, of those who stood by the traditions of Sampson and Humphrey and Lever and Coverdale—and of Tyndale too. " The incomparable sermon " [3] is a lengthy affair, sixty-eight pages in the reprint of 1709. It exposed the far-reaching aims of the anti-episcopal party ; it said something of their methods, as ecclesiastical politicians ; and, in order to discredit, once and for all, the popular (and seemingly most reasonable) demand of the party for a return to the system of primitive Christianity, the sermon invoked the testimony of all the centuries since, in proof that the system attacked—the episcopal system—was no novelty, that the thing now in possession had been in possession from the very beginning. Bancroft does not, however, say that the episcopal system is a divinely commanded part of the Christian religion. He goes no further than to point out that wherever we read of the Christian Church, we find that it is a body ruled by bishops.[4]

As the preacher's text might foretell, the " presbyterianisers " are de- nounced as false prophets.[5] And to make it clear that they are such, Bancroft

---

[1] Sunday, Feb. 9. Cf. the Abbot of Winchcombe's sermon, under similar circum- stances, in 1515 ; Vol. I of this work, pp. 151–152.   [2] Usher, *Reconstruction*, I, 50.

[3] So George Hickes, the editor of 1709 (the last reprint), whose scholarship has pre- served this important document in the *Bibliotheca Scriptorum Ecclesiae Anglicanae*, 247–315. Bancroft's text, 1 John iv. 1, gave the preacher all the scope he could desire : Believe not every spirit, but prove the spirits if they be of God ; because many false prophets are gone out into the world.   [4] Hickes, 291.

[5] False, because they apply signs of true prophecy to a false end, says the preacher, who now (without feeling any need to apologise to the coming more humane time for what he is about to relate) illustrates his theme by an example : " Of this number I may very well account the late obstinate heretic, Francis Ket, who was within these two months burnt at Norwich." *Ibid.*, 251.

14

revives a conception of the Church the repudiation of which, as a lie found out, had been the very basis and justification of the whole revolt against the authority of the popes. Alas for Tyndale,[1] and for Jewel too—in flat contradiction to Jewel whose works Bancroft is, none the less, presently to command, as Bishop of London, shall be in every church of his diocese. In order to cut the ground from under the feet of his opponents Bancroft now turns to that famous line of argumentation which would rule the heretic out without any examination of what he has to say in explanation or defence of his beliefs—the argument that proves the heretic wrong because what he teaches is something wholly new, that goes back to Tertullian,[2] whom the preacher of 1589 quotes extensively.

The interest of this polemic is great indeed! The advocate of a perfect reformation is now told that the church he would reform is "that Church which maintaineth without error the faith of Christ . . . which holdeth up the true doctrine of the Gospel in matters necessary to Salvation and preacheth the same".[3] And a sixteenth-century Reformer is quoted to support the ancient father, and to warrant the truth of the (surely popish!) saying, "Out of this church, *Nulla est salus*, there is no salvation".[4]

This doctrine, that the church is an infallible guide, is all very new— as good Reformed religion, that is to say—in the England of 1589, less than twenty years after the imposition of articles of belief that seemingly say the contrary. Administrative necessity is driving Bancroft—as the need for unity had, forty years before, driven Calvin—to attempt to reconstruct the Reform in the image and likeness of the *Catholica*, and so to reconstruct it for the sake of these very attributes for claiming which the *Catholica* had been most reviled by the innovators.

The beginning of heresies, says Bancroft, quoting from St. Cyprian, is when men begin to please themselves ;[5] and he recalls St. Jerome's pithy words : "The covetous man worshippeth his money, and the heretic his own opinion ".[6] While Rome has adopted the evil policy of locking up the

---

[1] Whose burning words we may profitably recall, as Dr. J. F. Mozley quotes them : " And hereby ye see that it is a plain and evident conclusion, as bright as the sun's shining, that the truth of God's word dependeth not of the truth of the congregation. And therefore when thou art asked, why thou believest that thou shalt be saved through Christ, and of such like principles of our faith ; answer, Thou wottest and feelest that it is true. And when he asketh how thou knowest that it is true ; answer, Because it is written in thine heart. And if he ask how thou camest first by it ; tell him whether by reading in books, or hearing it preached, as by an outward instrument, but that inwardly thou wast taught by the Spirit of God. And if he ask, whether thou believest it not because it is written in books, or because the priests so preach ; answer, No, not now ; but only because it is written in thine heart ; and because the Spirit of God so preacheth, and so testifieth unto thy soul : and say, though at the beginning thou wast moved by reading or preaching, yet now thou believest it not therefore any longer ; but only because thou hast heard of it of the Spirit of God, and read it written in thine heart " ; Mozley, *Tyndale*, 222, quoting *An Answer unto Sir Thomas More's Dialogue*, published July, 1531 (no other reference given).

[2] In the *De Prescriptione adversus Haereses*.   [3] *Hickes*, 254.   [4] *Ibid.*, 255.

[5] *Ibid.*, 261.

[6] *Ibid.* Nowadays, he says, the chief cause of heresy is the hope of a share in the loot of church property ; *ibid.*, 262.

Scriptures and forbidding them to be translated into the modern languages, these other false prophets, his English adversaries, " would have the people to be always seeking and searching [the Scriptures] " [1] which habit is one of the marks of heresy—and Tertullian is again quoted, " always to be beating this into their followers' heads : Search, examine, try, and seek." [2] Whereas, as St. Augustine says, " Faithful ignorance is better than rank knowledge ", and St. Gregory Nazianzen—still more to the point— " It falleth not within the compass of every man's understanding to determine and judge in matters of religion, but of those who are well experienced and exercised in them." [3] Nowadays all are experts in " this art of the Scriptures ". Whereas—on Tertullian's authority—once " constantly built by a lively faith upon the notable foundation " which is Christ, " you then content yourselves, seek no further . . . do not desire to seek any further ".[4]

In order to illustrate how the " dutiful children " of the church " ought to submit themselves without any curious or wilful contradiction ", Bancroft reminds his listeners of the accepted irrevocability of the decision come to at Nicea about the divinity of the Logos. And, " now that popery is banished ", why should we not attribute as much " to the decrees of our learned fathers in their lawful assemblies " as, in days gone by, was attributed to Nicea and Chalcedon ? If men may find fault now with official commands and regulations imposed by the church, they will soon be attacking the Articles set out in 1563 ; whereupon Bancroft develops another point of his " counter-reformation ", and indicts the critics for exercising their private judgment against the decision of the church. Here he makes great play with the fact that Calvin, also, was opposed to such individualism as they profess, quoting that apostle on the rôle of the *examen doctrinae privatum et publicum*, and how it is the second of these that is the more important.[5] " For ", says Calvin, " if authority and liberty of judging shall be left to private men, there will never be any certainty set down, but rather all religion will become doubtful." [6]

One last point about the great sermon. It was always an important part of the bishops' case against these troublesome clerics, that their speculations were as harmful to the state as to the church. And Bancroft professes to be shocked that they make so little of the supremacy of the queen in religious affairs. " Can there be in a Christian Commonwealth ", he asks, " such an absolute order of ecclesiastical government, as they brag of, set down for the only form, which is necessary to be observed, without any mention of the civil magistrate ? " [7] In the revised version of their book, it is true that " they have remembered the Civil Magistrates, but that in so cold and sparing a sort, as in my opinion, there is not a priest in Wisbeach who will refuse

---

[1] *Hickes*, 271.   [2] *Ibid.*, 272.   [3] *Ibid.*, 272.

[4] *Ibid.*, 273. *Nobis curiositate opus non est post Christum Jesum : nec inquisitione post Evangelium* : Bancroft quotes the actual phrase.

[5] *Hickes*, 275–276.

[6] Quoted, *ibid.*, 276, as part of Calvin's commentary on the text with which Bancroft's sermon began.   [7] *Ibid.*, 287.

. . . to subscribe unto it ".[1]   And about the Royal Supremacy as a fact in the life of the church, about the rôle of the queen in the religious life of her people, Bancroft is singularly explicit.   Elizabeth is now, rightly, in England, all that the pope used to be thought to be.   And the whole controversy about authority, with the Catholics, has simply been as to which of these two potentates has the right to this authority.   " The issue between them [i.e. the scholars opposed in the controversy] was ever this, Whether the King within his Dominions, or the Bishop of Rome might, by the word of God, rightly challenge the aforesaid authority." [2]   And as for the arguments of the " presbyterianisers " against the Royal Supremacy, they are the same as the arguments of the papists, Harding and Stapleton.[3]

In this sermon of 1589, there is much more for the future to develop than the exposure of a shrewdly organised attempt to "presbyterianise" the church of Queen Elizabeth's Settlement.   For the future to develop—for Bancroft's views are ultimately, long after his death, very successful; the Catholic Church's teaching about what the Church of Christ by His foundation is, now slowly begins to take root in the minds of some of the clergy of the new *Anglicana* ; and in a century when their battle is fierce against the assault of the spiritual children of the pioneers of the native Reformation, the Catholic idea receives from them much attention, much sincere homage indeed and acceptance, and it does their cause no little service.

The Richard Bancroft who preached the famous sermon was an ecclesiastic high in the confidence of the government, since it was he who had given the High Commission the finality of its usefulness.   This was now to be displayed in the grand manner, in the tracking down and punishment of the recalcitrant.   All through 1587, after the collapse of the attempt on parliament, the *Book of Discipline*, still in manuscript, circulated from conference to conference, and the ministers and their supporters seemed well on the way to become organised as a Presbyterian church within the queen's *Anglicana*.[4] A General Assembly was held at Cambridge in September, 1587, and at Warwick in April, 1588,[5] and for a third time at Stourbridge in September, 1589.[6]   In a sense all this was strictly constitutional—the party was no more rebellious in its intentions than were the followers of Robert Aske fifty years before.   All this work of conference and assembly was purely preparatory, a means of holding the brethren together until the great day arrived—a day to be brought on by strictly lawful means alone.   Since the beginning of the new controversies in 1584, however, there had been divided counsels in the party, the inevitable divisions between temperaments keen on action, and the more cautious, politically-minded leaders.[7]   And just four months or so before Bancroft's celebrated sermon, there came from the younger section the first of the *Martin Marprelate* tracts : bitter attacks on prelacy and on

---

[1] *Hickes*, 287.   The castle of Wisbeach, in the Isle of Ely, was at this time a prison for the more learned of the Catholic priests, in durance for refusing the Oath of Supremacy. Cf. *infra*, p. 364.   [2] *Hickes*, 292.   [3] *Ibid.*, 307.
[4] *Pearson*, 259.   [5] *Ibid.*, 260.   [6] *Ibid.*, 263.   [7] *Ibid.*, 247.

prelates, lively, scurrilous and extremely damaging, printed on a secret press, that moved all over England as the pursuivants began to get busy, until finally, in August 1589, it was discovered and taken at a hamlet in the environs of Manchester.[1] And with the Marprelate tracts, about whose authorship there is still much mystery, there were replies to the great sermon, letters about it to Bancroft from Cartwright, pamphlets by other scholarly theologians like John Reynolds, the president of Corpus Christi college Oxford,[2] and by evangelists with Marprelate affiliations such as John Penry.

In the late autumn of 1589 the arrests began, leading ministers of the various *classes* in Northamptonshire and Suffolk, and then Cartwright himself. Next, an associate of the Marprelate organisers was captured, John Udall, the vicar of Kingston-on-Thames. He was tried at Croydon assizes, July, 1590, for publishing seditious literature in contravention of the Act of 1581, and found guilty.[3] In 1591 there was a " plot " to dethrone the queen and one of the three men concerned in it was hanged.[4] Then, in 1593, Henry Barrow and John Greenwood, " Separatists " whose views were akin to those of Robert Brown, and who had spent the best part of the previous seven years in prison, on a warrant from the High Commission, were put on trial for circulating seditious literature, condemned and executed (April 6) ;[5] and on May 29, the man who may have been Martin Marprelate

[1] *Pearson*, 278, considers that these tracts " hurt the cause of Puritanism and hastened the fast ebbing tide ". For Dover Wilson, Martin is " the great prose satirist of the Elizabethan period ", who " may rightly be considered a forerunner of Swift ". (*Cambridge History of English Literature*, III, 374–398, a literary account which should be read.)

[2] Whose brother, William Reynolds, had by this become a Catholic, and, ordained priest, had lately been busy as a reviser, and defender, of the new translation of the Scripture known as the Douay Bible. For William Reynolds cf. *D.N.B.*, and Southern, 51–52, 258–262.

[3] He was not sentenced to death until February, 1591. In the interval he was offered his life on condition that he recanted the opinion put forth in the book for publishing which he had been tried, *A Demonstration of the trueth of that Discipline which Christ hath prescribed in his worde*. The main obstacle to the efforts made to save him (for he refused to recant) was Whitgift. When the archbishop withdrew his opposition the queen signed his pardon, January 1592. But Udall died a few days later, before the formalities of his release were completed.

[4] " Bancroft unearthed a conspiracy to kill the queen as a necessary prelude to the introduction of the Discipline " ; so Usher, I, 65. " Three men ", he continues, " Coppinger, Arthington and Hackett . . . expiated their fault on the scaffold." The facts are as follows : William Hackett, the *fons et origo*, was a one-time serving man whom a lucky marriage had turned into a maltster. Once " converted ", he seems to have lost his reason, a violent, half-crazy fellow, whipped through more than one town for his extravagancies. He came to London about Easter 1591, and there met Henry Arthington, a Yorkshire gentleman, and Edmund Coppinger, also of good family, who had a post in the royal household. Hackett persuaded these two that he was lately come from heaven, personally commissioned by the Holy Ghost to inaugurate a new age on this earth, and, as a beginning, to dethrone Elizabeth and set himself in her place—another detail was the abolition of bishops, and the rule of the holy men. On July 19 of that same year the three set out in a cart to preach this revelation in the principal street of the capital—with the natural result that a week later they were standing their trial charged with treason. Coppinger starved himself to death in prison (!), Hackett was executed at Charing Cross on July 28, and Arthington, after a recantation, was released in 1592 ; so *D.N.B.*, s. vv. *Hackett* and *Coppinger*.

[5] Of these two, John Greenwood, according to Whitgift, was a poor simple fellow—Barrow, said the archbishop, " is the man ". He was the senior by ten years and now a man in the forties (B.A. Cambridge, 1570). From Cambridge he had gone to Gray's Inn, and then, caught in the fringes of the gay life of the court, had given himself to " atheism " and its

himself followed them to the gallows, the Welshman, John Penry, charged with plotting, in Scotland, a rebellion against the queen.

Penry," one of the finest spirits of an age exceptionally rich in spiritual and intellectual achievement ",[1] was an Elizabethan in the full sense, for he was born five years after the queen's accession, in 1563. He was bred, like his friend Udall, in the Whitgift-purified Cambridge of 1579–86. He had refused to be ordained, in protest against clerical worldliness, and gave himself, at first, to preaching in his native country. In the hunt of 1589 he was so lucky as to escape into Scotland. But on his return journey to Wales, three years later, he delayed over long in London, and was arrested, March 22, 1593, the vicar of Stepney calling in the police. Penry, unlike Udall (and others), had no highly-placed patrons [2] to ward off the doom before him. When the High Commission had finished with him he was handed over to the Queen's Bench, and the documents supplied by the Commission sufficed to condemn him.[3]

Penry was, moreover, associated, not with the party who believed that to leave the Elizabethan establishment (whatever its defects) was to leave the Church of Christ, but with the men who held that, as an organisation, it was but a human thing which it was the duty of a follower of Christ to leave.[4] Upon his return to London from Scotland, in September, 1592, Penry attached himself to the very congregation with which Barrow and Greenwood had been associated.[5]

In Penry's *Note Book* [6] are drafts of letters to Burghley, written in prison, and of petitions for the Brownists imprisoned with him. The memory of the bad days of Mary Tudor is much in the writer's mind. These days have

---

practical sequelae. A sermon, to which he went in mocking curiosity, converted him ; he gave up law for theology, and about this time first made Greenwood's acquaintance. By 1585 (so Usher, I, 59) both men had split away from the main body of the " presbyterian-izers ", and were organising private services of their own. It was while holding such a " conventicle " that Greenwood was arrested, in the autumn of 1586. Barrow was detained (Nov. 19) while visiting his associate. After their condemnation (March 21, 1593) there was, apparently, much division of opinion in the council whether the sentence should be executed. Burghley was on the side of mercy, but (so Pollard, *H.E.*, VI, 465) he was powerless against the combination of Whitgift and the queen. For Barrow's earlier encounter with Whitgift, cf. *supra*, p. 176.

[1] Dover Wilson, in *The Library*, Oct. 1907, quoted in Peel, *Penry*, vii. Peel's *Introduction* to this book (pp. vii–xxv) is the best portrait that has yet appeared of Penry and his aims. " Puritan fanatic " is the summary description of Rowse, 543 (in the index to the book).

[2] In 1586 Udall had Lord Howard of Effingham to intercede for him and the Earl of Warwick, Leicester's elder brother ; later he had Francis Hastings, Earl of Huntingdon, and at the end Sir Walter Raleigh and Alexander Nowell, Dean of St. Paul's.

[3] For Rowse, 475, the sole interest of Penry's surely moving story is what it reveals of Bancroft's " brilliant detective work ", who " surpassed himself in getting hold of the private papers, written in Scotland, of John Penry, upon which he was condemned for treason ". Penry, says the more measured Dover Wilson, was " hanged on a trumped-up charge of treason, thus paying with his life for the part he had taken in the Marprelate controversy ". Quoted Peel, *Penry*, xxi.

[4] " That by God's commandment all that will be saved must with speed come forth of this antichristian estate . . .". The Brownist's *True Confession* (1596), article 32, printed in *Hooker*, II, 603, n. 2.

[5] Peel, *Penry*, xviii.

[6] The book referred to in these notes as Peel, *Penry*.

now returned, he is bold enough to say explicitly. The directness of his speech, after the endless " tact " and insincerity, is most refreshing. " We profess the same faith and truth of the gospel this day ", the Supplication of the Brownists declares, " which her majesty, this state, and all the reformed churches this day under heaven do profess. We go further than they go in the detestation of all popery, that most fearful Antichristian religion, and draw nearer in some things unto Christ's holy order and institution.

" This is our cause. For the profession whereof there are of us almost fourscore persons, men and women, young and old, lying in cold, hunger, dungeons, and irons, only in the prisons about London, not to speak any thing of other prisons of the land. Thereof towards the number of some 56 taken the last Lord's day . . . hearing the word of God truly taught, and praying and praising our God for his favours shewed unto us, her Majesty, your honours, and this whole land, and desiring our God to be merciful unto us, unto our prince, and to our country. Being employed in these actions we were taken in the holy place where the holy martyrs were enforced to use the like holy exercises in the days of Queen Mary."

Now they have been committed to prison by the Bishop of London, and " This bloody man and his assistance will neither allow them meat, drink, fire, bedding, nor suffer others that will do the same, to have any access. . . . These godless men have put the blood of war about them in the day of that peace and truce which the whole land hath professed to make with Jesus Christ. Bishop Bonner, Story, Weston, etc. dealt not after this sort. Those whom they committed close they would also feed, or permit to be fed by others." [1]

" Are we a free people under our natural prince ", he asks Burghley, " or are we held for slaves and bondservants under some cruel and unjust tyrant ? " [2] What is life worth for Protestants of this school under the queen's rule ? " Were it not for the hope of a better life it were better for us to be Queen Elizabeth's beasts than her subjects : yea, her Christian subjects. For were we her beasts, going under her mark, the proudest prelate in the land durst not attempt to take us into their own hands." [3]

For Penry, his way of being a Protestant is the true Reformation : " Mr. Cranmer, master Tyndale built it, these present destroyed the same. King

---

[1] Peel, *Penry*, 45–47.   [2] *Ibid.*, 68.

[3] *Ibid.*, 59. The victims had to revive the legend of the worst man ever, in order to do Whitgift justice : " No bishop that ever had such an aspiring and ambitious mind as he ; no not Cardinal Wolsey ; none so proud as he, no not Stephen Gardiner of Winchester ; none so tyrannical as he, no not Bonner." Peel, *Penry*, xxii, from *Dialogue wherein is plain laid open, etc.* When one of these Separatists, a member of the congregation of Barrow and Greenwood, died in prison (Feb. 16, 1593) his coffin was laid at the door of the judge who had committed him, suitably inscribed : " This is the corpse of Roger Rippon, a servant of Christ, and her majesty's faithful subject, who is the last of 16 or 17 which that great enemy of God the Archbishop of Canterbury, with the high Commissioners have murdered in Newgate within these five years for the testimony of Jesus Christ. His soul is now with the Lord, and his blood crieth for speedy vengeance against that great enemy of the saints, and against Mr. Richard Young who in this and many the like points hath abused his power for the upholding of the Romish Antichrist, prelacy and priesthood." *Ibid.*, xx.

Henry the 8 permitted it and the Lord Cromwell helped it. Queen Elizabeth and the Lord Treasurer suffer it to be pulled down." [1] What Queen Elizabeth and the Lord Treasurer had actually achieved he describes in the passionate apostrophe that was later quoted as evidence against him. " Surely with an impudent forehead [England] hath said, I will not come near the Holy One ; and as for the building of his house, I will not so much as lift up a finger towards that work. As for the gospel and the ministers of it, I have already received the gospels and all the ministers that I mean to receive, . . . a gospel and a ministry that will stoop unto me, and be at my beck, either to speak or to be mute, when I shall think good. Briefly I have received a gospel and a ministry that will never trouble my conscience with the sight of my sins. Which is all the gospel and all the ministry which I mean to receive." [2] And to Burghley, the pious Catholic squire of Wimbledon in Queen Mary's reign, he gives the charitable warning of what was most noxious in the régime of 1559 : " It is dangerous, my lord, to be ambiguous in religion, either truth or falsehood would be embraced, indifferency, neutrality can take no place. . . ." [3]

While Barrow and Greenwood and Penry lay in the queen's prisons awaiting their fate, with such thoughts about the régime in their minds as these papers reveal, the government was busy in parliament with a new kind of Bill—a penal law directed against Protestants such as these ; directed against them not as heretics (as Cranmer would have liked to legislate against Lutherans), but as subjects disobedient to the foundation laws of the revolution of 1559, the Acts of Supremacy and Uniformity. This is a statute against Barrow and Greenwood and Penry, but it will not touch Cartwright ; and once again the country is sharply reminded of the close connection between the crown and the practice of religion. The criminal whom the new statute [4] has in view is the man already guilty of refusing to attend the public services of the church. Should such a man, now, whether in print, or by writing or by speech, persuade another against the Royal Supremacy ; or, with a view to encouraging him against the Supremacy, persuade another either not to attend church, or to go to a " conventicle " ; or should this Protestant recusant merely join with, or be present at, a " conventicle " ; if upon conviction for any of these offences he does not make submission within a month, he is " to abjure the realm for ever " : that is to say, pledge himself on oath to leave England and never return. Those convicted who refuse to abjure, or who, after abjuring, contrive to remain in the country, and those who return from exile without the queen's permission, are to be hanged. All who give such evaders shelter are to be fined £10 for every month they have harboured the fugitive. Moreover, upon abjuring the realm the criminal forfeits all his moveable properties to the queen, and with these all the profits, for life, from his landed

---

[1] Peel, *Penry*, 75.   [2] Strype, *Annals*, IV, 246.   [3] Peel, *Penry*, 76.
[4] 35 Elizabeth c. 1. *An act to retain the queen's subjects in obedience.* Text in G. & H., 492–498 ; see also Prothero, 89–92.

possessions. The Act was proposed as a piece of special legislation, to cover an emergency : it was to continue in force only until the end of the next session of parliament.[1]

6. HOOKER

The grim conventicle Act of 1593 crowned the activities of the first, well-filled ten years of Whitgift's rule at Canterbury. And from the pen of his indefatigable lieutenant, whose triumph, also, the statute assuredly marks, there came in the following summer the two classic accounts of the long crisis that Bancroft's name always recalls, the *Survey of the Holy Discipline* and *Dangerous Positions*.[2] These two books, for all their importance to students, have not, however, been reprinted for three hundred years. Like their author's own great effect, as a divine, as Bishop of London and as Archbishop of Canterbury, upon the religious life of his time,[3] they are nowadays all but forgotten. But in this same year there was another book published, no less closely connected with the crisis, and indeed the product of the crisis, which, since the author's mind was touched with genius, rose high above the particularities of the occasion,[4] and, once it was really studied, won enduring recognition as a masterpiece of original thinking. This was Richard Hooker's eight books *Of the Laws of Ecclesiastical Polity*.

To the ultimately widespread effect of Hooker upon the formation of minds loyal to the religion whose heart is the Book of Common Prayer, the whole theological work of the centuries since doubtless bears witness. Like all great thinkers who face the task of re-interpreting the old in the light of the new, and of showing the unity of old and new, Hooker's importance, for the ages that follow, is twofold : he advances thought by his own personal contribution, and, a wider service, he becomes a classical expositor of ideas generally held.[5] *Mutatis mutandis* this is to claim for Hooker, among his

---

[1] But in 1597 a new Act (39 Elizabeth c. 18) extended it for another four years, and in 1601 a further Act (43 Elizabeth c. 9) gave it three more years of life. It was again renewed in 1604 (1 Jac. I, c. 25) and in 1624 (21 Jac. I, c. 28).

[2] *A Survey of the pretended Holy Discipline* : and *Daungerous Positions and Proceedings, published and practised within the Iland of Brytaine under pretence of Reformation.*

[3] Bancroft and the other ". . . neo-Anglicans . . . knew . . . that the elaboration of a properly Anglican doctrinal position was accomplished only just in time to save the English Church from complete disintegration by decay. One has only to study the unemotional, purely factual, reports on the growing disorganisation of church life, and the general emptiness of the churches, and the increasing neglect of all worship, which reached the Privy Council in a steady stream from the judges of Assize and the emissaries of the Ecclesiastical Commission from all over the country in the 80s and 90s of the sixteenth century. . . " ; Gregory Dix, *The Shape of the Liturgy* (1945), 703.

[4] ". . . it was Hooker's greatness to realise that secondary problems could be solved only by raising fundamental issues ". E. T. Davies, *Episcopacy and the Royal Supremacy in the Church of England in the XVI century.* Oxford (1950), 43.

[5] One interesting example of his general influence—where much indeed might be quoted—which is, at the same time testimony to the existence of a presumption, among his co-religionists, that Hooker is everywhere accepted, is the way in which, in the year Victoria came to the throne, Newman, defending Pusey's orthodoxy against bitter criticism from within, can be satisfied to throw out the challenge that nowhere has Pusey gone counter to " that religious system which has been received among us since the date of the Ecclesiastical Polity ". *Tract 82*, reprinted in *The Via Media* (1877), II, 147.

own, the kind of prestige which, let us say, St. Thomas Aquinas enjoys with Catholics. Hooker is no more than a private individual, and more than this must not be claimed for him ; but from the early years of the seventeenth century there begins to be active in the Church of England a " Hookerism " —ideas derived from him, and through him, begin to be as powerful as was Calvinism of the years that are the subject of this book. Hooker matters indeed, and he matters from the beginning, from the very publication of his books—for the historian's purpose at least.

For what concerns his own time, Hooker is doing over again the work of Whitgift against Cartwright and Travers, both of which writers he continually quotes at length ; and he is doing again the work of Jewel, setting out in a systematic way the belief of the Church of England. He is more advantage-ously placed than the bishop who was the patron of his promising boyhood, for it was in the press of fierce criticism that the original, slender *Apology* was developed ; and his method, too, makes him so easily Jewel's superior that it seems odd to compare the two, as controversial writers. What first strikes the reader, as a difference between Hooker's work and all else that he has so far read, on either side of the " Puritan " controversy, is its utter calm, the great charity of the language, the peace in which it is all thought out—and it was thought out, we know it now,[1] not in some remote parsonage on the Wiltshire downs, but in the heart of the city of London, in the society of some of the most active contenders of the events of 1585–93. Hooker has the impersonality of the man wholly devoted—and, in the first place, not to victory or success but to the exposition of truth as a means to win over the other side.[2]

The work is addressed " To them that seek (as they term it) The Reforma-tion of Laws and Orders Ecclesiastical in the Church of England ",[3] and the first necessity, he declares, is for all to consider anew " what law is, how different kinds of law there are, and what force they are of according to each kind ".[4] So it is that, in Book I of the treatise,[5] Hooker must needs be the philosopher and invoke all the ancient masters, and such fathers of the church as St. Augustine, whose thought the medieval schoolmen had preserved and developed : and with them he will invoke these schoolmen too. This is somewhat startling. It is sixty years, almost, since Layton announced from Oxford to Cromwell that Dunce was set in Bocardo, and

---

[1] Thanks to Professor Sisson whose *The Judicious Marriage of Mr. Hooker* (1940), has, for the first time, set out the facts of Hooker's life, during and after the inception of his great work.

[2] Not that Hooker labours under the defect of natural impassivity. There are hints enough that he too had a temper, and a real antipathy to what he could call " the purified crew " ; but even in these " hints " he remains free from scurrility. " If Aristotle and the schoolmen be such perilous creatures ", he retorts on the critic of his first four books, " you must needs think yourself an happy man, whom God hath so fairly blest from too much knowledge in them ". Quoted, I, 373, with the relevant passage from *Christian Letter*, 43, referring to the matter of Bk. III, ch. viii, 10.

[3] *Preface, Hooker*, I, 171.   [4] *Ibid.*, 172.

[5] Pp. 189–285 of vol. I of Keble's edition, as revised by R. W. Church and F. Paget, Oxford, 1888 : the edition used here, and quoted as *Hooker*. Book II is pp. 286–337 of this same volume, Book III is pp. 338–416, Book IV is pp. 417–488.

now, in defence of what had then begun, Dunce is cited as an honoured authority.[1]

It is again the philosopher, interested first of all in ideas as such, who next proceeds, in the second and third books, to examine critically two postulates of the other party, fundamental to their case : these are (shades of the primitive reformers !) " That Scripture ought to be the only rule of all our actions ",[2] and, " That in Scripture there must of necessity be found some particular form of Polity Ecclesiastical, the Laws whereof admit not any kind of alteration ".[3] In Book IV the general charge of the party against the settlement of 1559 is considered, namely the corruption of " the right form of church polity with manifold popish rites and ceremonies ".[4] These four books made up the first volume, published in 1593. The fifth book of the work, which did not appear until 1597, is twice the length of all the first four books combined,[5] and with it Hooker begins his examination of " the specialities . . . in controversy " :[6] the " specialities " considered in the fifth book being, " the cause alleged . . .wherefore the public duties of the Christian religion, as our prayers, our Sacraments, and the rest, should not be ordered in such sort as with us they are " : and also the ritual " whereby the persons of men are consecrated unto the ministry ".[7] Book VI opens the analysis of the controversies about jurisdiction in the church, with a consideration whether " laymen, such as your governing Elders are, ought in all congregations for ever to be invested with that power ".[8] In Book VII the question is " Whether Bishops may have that power over other Pastors, and therewithal that honour, which they have with us ".[9] The last book deals with " this power, a power of Ecclesiastical Dominion, communicable, as we think, unto persons not ecclesiastical, and most fit to be restrained unto the Prince or Sovereign's commands over the whole body politic " :[10] the Royal Supremacy, in fact.

As is well known, the sixth and eighth books did not appear until 1648 —nearly fifty years after Hooker's death ; and the seventh not until 1661. Except as evidence of what one particular supporter of the changes of 1559, one of the very greatest, was thinking about these matters (somewhat to

---

[1] " Wherein I confess, notwithstanding, with the wittiest of the school-divines ", he writes, introducing a passage from Scotus' commentary on Peter Lombard, *Preface, Hooker*, I, 260. St. Thomas, too, he quotes easily, " the greatest amongst the school-divines ", *ibid.*, I, 381, and can borrow from him a pregnant summary.
Hooker cites Cajetan's great Commentary on St. Thomas, Bellarmine too, and even the *De Sacramentis in Genere* of Cardinal Allen (lately indicted for treason with Campion and his companions), *ibid.*, II, 555. The story of Pope Clement VIII's comment on Hooker's erudition, as Stapleton translated to this great canonist the first book, which is a treatise on Law, is well known.
[2] *Ibid.*, I, 172 ; " this point, which standeth with you for the first and chiefest principle whereon ye build ". [3] *Ibid.*, I, 172. [4] *Ibid.*, I, 172.
[5] *Hooker*, II, the whole volume, pp. 598 of text.
[6] *Ibid.*, I, 173. [7] *Ibid.*, I, 173.
[8] *Ibid.*, I, 173. Book VI is *Hooker*, III, 1–139. For a discussion of the extraordinary circumstance that the introductory chapters of this book disappeared between Hooker's death in 1600 and the publication in 1648, cf. Sisson, 96–108.
[9] *Ibid.*, I, 173. Book VII is *Hooker*, III, 140–325.
[10] *Ibid.*, I, 173. Book VIII is *Hooker*, III, 326–468.

the embarrassment of his associates)[1] these books hardly concern this history.

Few great writers could more easily be misinterpreted than Hooker through the quotations of a commentator anxious to prove a thesis. And even in the comparatively simple matter of illustrating, by quotations, his acknowledged positions in the great controversy, the danger of uncon- sciously misleading remains very real.[2] For the scholar who has re- constructed the truth about Hooker's own life, demolishing a legend all but contemporaneous with its hero, and who modestly reminds us that he is himself no divine, Hooker is, by reason of the *Ecclesiastical Polity*, a pioneer of " that development of the Reformation in England which in some ways became a counter-Reformation . . ." ;[3] of the movement of reaction, it might be allowed, against the spirit that had produced the Reformation itself, and had prevailed down to Hooker's own day, if what he began did indeed find " its logical outcome in the High Church of Laud ".[4] Hooker, it would seem, is in the full flood of general reaction when he insists on the place of the human reason in the right use of the Scriptures : " For whatsoever we believe concerning salvation by Christ, although the Scripture be therein the ground of our belief ; yet the authority of man is, if we mark it, the key which openeth the door of entrance into the knowledge of the Scripture. The Scripture could not teach us the things that are of God, unless we did credit men who have taught us that the words of Scripture do signify those things." [5]

Here is the beginning of the end, so far as Hooker prevails, in one of the territories which the Reformed have made their own, of the system which was a main feature of the popular propaganda of all the first reformers. No longer, then, is each man to feel confident that what his mind conceives, as he prayerfully cons the sacred text, is the message thereby divinely sent to him. And one of the first lessons which reflection, the use of his natural reason, will teach a man is the rôle, and the right, of the church as witness to what the Scripture is. " Scripture ", indeed, " teacheth all supernatural revealed truth, without the knowledge whereof salvation cannot be attained." And, " The main principle whereupon our belief of all things therein contained dependeth, is, that the Scriptures are the oracles of God himself ".

---

[1] " When the whole story is told it may be questioned whether Hooker was in all respects in harmony with his allies on the controversial ground which it was his function to defend on behalf of the Church. The most significant divergences, however, did not appear until a later date. It was, indeed, difficult to ensure a statement of the position of the Church which would meet with the approval of the varying shades of orthodox opinion in a rapidly develop- ing institution " ; Sisson, 6 ; cf. also *ibid.*, ch. iii, *The Posthumous Books of " The Laws of Ecclesiastical Polity* ".

[2] Cf. Davies, E. T., 41, *op. cit.* " It is this ' quotable ' character of Hooker's admirable writing which probably accounts for the very diverse views held of his teaching ; and High Churchmen, Liberals, Modernists, and Evangelicals have all in turn appealed to *The Laws of Ecclesiastical Polity*, and never in vain." And G. R. Cragg, quotes Brian Sanderson, Regius professor of divinity at Oxford down to 1648, and Bishop of Lincoln in 1661, to the effect that those who agreed " with Hooker in matters of doctrine " could be called Puritans ! *From Puritanism to the Age of Reason* (1950), 25.

[3] Sisson, 100–101.   [4] *Ibid.*   [5] *Hooker*, I, 321.

But, " This in itself we cannot say is evident " ; and " Scripture . . . presumeth us taught otherwise [i.e. than by Scripture] that itself is divine and sacred ". So the question arises, " by what means we are taught this ". And thus we are brought to the rôle of the church. " That which all men's experience teacheth them may not in any wise be denied. And by experience we all know, that the first outward motive leading men so to esteem of the Scripture [i.e. that it is the oracle of God] is the authority of God's church. For when we know the whole Church of God hath that opinion of the Scripture we judge it even at the first an impudent thing for any man bred and brought up in the Church to be of a contrary mind without cause." [1]

It is a first count against the likelihood of any individual's new theory about the meaning of Scripture being true, that it goes counter to the opinion held by " the whole Church of God ". Hooker stands amazed at the spectacle of individuals, full of zeal, of course, who read their bibles and thence conclude that, they too being prophets and apostles, to them also are given the rights and powers recorded in Sacred Scripture as divinely granted to Isaias and St. Paul : such individuals, " . . . when they oppose their *methinketh* unto the orders of the Church of England . . . their sentences will not be greatly regarded ".[2]

What Hooker has in mind, of course, above all else, is the demand that the Discipline of the Genevan system shall replace the episcopate as being the true intention of God and set forth, as such, in holy writ. As to this Genevan system, " Our persuasion is, that no age ever had knowledge of it but only ours ; that they which defend it devised it ; that neither Christ nor his Apostles at any time taught it, but the contrary ".[3] He reviews thereupon, the career of Calvin, and recalls the facts—not yet fifty years old—of the first establishment of the system.[4] " It was the manner of those times ", he comments, " that every particular Church did that within itself, which some few of their own thought good, by whom the rest were all directed ".[5] But the system in possession from time immemorial is not to be given up at the bidding of individuals, learned and holy though they be. " The evidence " that the laws to be changed are what is alleged against them,[6] " must be great ". And, " If we have neither voice from heaven that so pronounceth of them, neither sentence of men grounded upon such manifest and clear proof, that they in whose hands it is to alter them may likewise infallibly even in heart and conscience judge them so : upon necessity to urge alteration is to trouble and disturb necessity ".[7]

St. Paul may have been, and was indeed, " resolute and peremptory ",

---

[1] *Hooker*, I, 376. This reference to " the authority of God's Church ", brought from the other side the immediate rejoinder, " Have we not here good cause to suspect the underpropping of a popish principle concerning the Church's authority above the Holy Scripture, to the disgrace of the English Church ? " For which, and Hooker's note on it, *ibid.*, n. 1.

[2] *Ibid.*, I, 430.   [3] *Ibid.*, I, 390.

[4] *Ibid.* (*Preface*, ch. ii), I, 127-129.   [5] *Ibid.*, 129.

[6] That is to say, " unnatural, or impious, or otherwise hurtful unto the public community of men, and against that good for which human societies were instituted ". *Ibid.*, I, 481.

[7] *Ibid.*, I, 482.

but this was because the truth was "made manifest unto him even by intuitive revelation ; . . . ye have it no otherwise than by your own probable collection ".[1] And what is it which, on this poor basis, is now called in question but " The Laws of the Church, whereby for so many ages together we have been guided in the exercise of Christian religion and the service of the true God, our rites, customs, and orders of ecclesiastical government ". And, " If they think that we ought to prove the ceremonies commodious which we have retained, they do in this point very greatly deceive themselves For in all right and equity, that which the Church hath received and held so long for good, that which public approbation hath ratified, must carry the benefit of presumption with it to be accounted meet and convenient." Hooker will not allow the argument that Scripture is a full and complete record of the practice of the Church in the time of the Apostles : ". . . is it necessary that all the orders of the Church which were then in use should be contained in their [i.e. the Apostles'] books ? Surely no," he says. And he is no less unmoved by another, kindred argument, which he sets out very takingly : " For it is out of doubt that the first state of things was best, that in the prime of Christian religion faith was soundest . . . all parts of godliness did then most abound, and therefore it must needs follow . . . the best way is to cut off later inventions, and to reduce things unto the ancient state wherein at the first they were."[5]

Hooker has brought reason to bear on the discussion of Scripture—philosophy, that is to say, the wisdom of the heathen Aristotle and the lore of the popish schoolmen ; he has invoked these against his opponents, and has refused to allow that the pious man, equipped with none of these, is the better interpreter of the sacred text.[6] Small wonder that they retorted on him the hideous, fatal charge, " Papist ".[7] He remained unmoved, and philosophically examining their invective he lights up for us, in an unexpected way, another dark corner of the history of the great change. It was, of course, much easier, he explains, for the zealots to rally the people to their cause by saying the ceremonies of the Prayer Book were popish, than by providing proof that they were, in themselves, hurtful to the Church. " The cause why this way seemed better to them was, for that the name of popery is more odious

---

[1] *Hooker*, I, 168. [2] *Ibid.*, I, 199. [3] *Ibid.*, I, 430. [4] *Ibid.*, I, 421.
[5] *Ibid.*, I, 421. [6] Which is the teaching of the official Book of Homilies, cf. *supra*, p. 112.
[7] About the enemies of reason, of trained minds and of universities who had been active in the war against the old religion from the beginning, he says, " But so it is, the name of the light of reason is made hateful with men : the ' star of reason and learning ' and all other such like helps, beginneth no other wise to be thought of than if it were an unlucky comet ; or as if God had so accursed it, that it should never shine or give light in things concerning our duty anyway towards him, but be esteemed as that star in the Revelation called *Wormwood*, which being fallen from heaven, maketh rivers and waters in which it falleth so bitter, that men tasting them die thereof. A number there are, who think they cannot admire as they ought the power and authority of the word of God, if in things divine they should attribute any force to man's reason. For which cause they never use reason so willingly as to disgrace reason." I, 365 (III, viii, 4). Hooker is careful to distinguish zealots of this type from the patron whom they invoke continually, Calvin, who was far indeed from their opinions in this matter, and whose letter to Bucer he quotes, " Philosophy is a noble gift of God . . ." *ibid.*, I, 373, n. 1 ; and with this " Beza's judgment of Aristotle "—all this in notes prepared for a reply Hooker did not live to write.

than very paganism amongst divers of the more simple sort, so as whatsoever they hear named popish, they presently conceive deep hatred against it, imagining there can be nothing contained in that name but needs it must be exceedingly detestable.   The ears of the people they have therefore filled with strong clamour : ' The Church of England is fraught with popish ceremonies : they that favour the cause of reformation maintain nothing but the sincerity of the Gospel of Jesus Christ : all such as withstand them fight for the laws of Antichrist, and are defenders of that which is popish.' These are the notes wherewith are drawn from the heart of the multitude so many sighs." [1]

Hooker is still bolder.   As though he had never experienced what risks came of speaking of Rome [2] without either the shudders appropriate to the thought of "the beast", or the protection of the famous texts in the Apocalypse, he now denied that customs were necessarily dangerous and to be forbidden simply because Rome, too, made use of them.   And he asserted that despite " the indisposition of the Church of Rome to reform herself . . . so far

---

[1] *Hooker*, I, 429. Whether the clamour is stronger than that of the official Homilies read, by the queen's orders, from three pulpits out of four, Sunday by Sunday, is a point interesting to debate.   Meanwhile, here is the judgment of one extremely intelligent contemporary on the worth (as honest reality) of that national hatred of popery, whipped up at every crisis, to menace, or to encourage, the policy of government—a phenomenon too often cited as proof how deeply love of the gospel had taken hold on the very simplest.   And how well Hooker understands the method of organising " reformations " !   " The method of winning the people's affection unto a general liking of ' the cause ' (for so ye term it) hath been this. First, In the hearing of the multitude, the faults especially of higher callings are ripped up with marvellous exceeding severity and sharpness of reproof. . . . The next thing hereunto is, to impute all faults and corruptions, wherewith the world aboundeth, unto the kind of ecclesiastical government established . . . [A] third step is to prepare their own form of church government, as the only sovereign remedy of all evils ; and to adorn it with all the glorious titles that may be . . . The fourth degree of inducement is by fashioning the very notions and conceits of men's minds in such sort, that when they read the scripture, they may think that everything soundeth towards the advancement of that discipline [i.e. of the programme of the revolutionary party] and to the utter disgrace of the contrary . . . From hence they proceed to an higher point, which is the persuading of men credulous and over-capable of such pleasing errors, that it is the special illumination of the Holy Ghost, whereby they discover those things in the words, which others reading yet discern them not ", and so on and so forth.   *Hooker*, I (*Preface*, ch. iii, 5 ff.), 146-150.

[2] On March 30, 1585, Travers had denounced Hooker to Burghley for such " unsound points of doctrine " as the statement that " the church of Rome is a true church of Christ ", and that its members could be saved, " yea, the pope himself ".   *Hooker*, I, 59.   Hooker's vindication has survived and so have some notes on the matter drawn up by Whitgift. Salvation is by Christ only—this is the foundation truth.   And, says Hooker, " this I think, if the Pope, or any of the Cardinals, should forsake all other their corruptions, and yield up their souls, holding the foundation again but by a slender thread, and did but as it were touch the hem of Christ's garment, believing that which the Church of Rome doth in this point of doctrine, they may obtain mercy.   For they have to deal with God, who is no captious sophister, and will not examine them in quiddities, but accept them if they plainly hold the foundation.   This error is my only comfort as touching the salvation of our fathers . . ." *ibid.*, I, 64, i.e. the " thousands of our fathers, which lived in popish superstition ".   *Ibid.*, I, 60.   Whitgift, however, noted that " Papists overthrow the foundation of faith, both by their doctrine of merit, and otherwise many ways.   So that if they have as their errors deserve, I do not see how they should be saved " ; and this, also, " General repentance will not serve any but the faithful man.   Nor him, for any sin, but for such sins only as he doth not mark, nor know to be sin ".   *Ibid.*, I, 64.   These citations are from Isaac Walton's *Life of Mr. Hooker* (1665), reprinted in *Hooker*, I, 1-99.

as lawfully we may, we have held and do hold fellowship with them. . . .
With Rome we dare not communicate concerning sundry her gross and
grievous abominations, yet touching those main parts of Christian truth
wherein they constantly still persist, we gladly acknowledge them to be of the
family of Jesus Christ ; . . . ." [1]

It is not, indeed, so much Hooker's views in detail that matter to this
chapter as the principles of the argument which he is offering against the
would-be " presbyterianisers " of his church.   In effect, reading all the pre-
Calvinian writers he has, inevitably, rediscovered for himself the corpus of
Catholic theology—as Newman was to rediscover it when, searching for
evidence as to the nature of the Church of Christ, he pushed his researches
back from the Caroline divines, his first masters, to the ancient writers whence
these had drawn.   In these older writers Hooker found much that he by no
means accepted.   But he found a wealth of good argument that must tell
against his opponents' case, and by the mere fact of using these arguments
about the kind of thing the Church is, he began to endow the Church of
1559 with a nature and with attributes, which, only thirty years before,
Jewel had rejoiced to be able to say that Church made no claim to possess,
because they were what no Church could possibly possess.   It is all done
in the calmest way conceivable, by a scholar into whose mind the thought
has never strayed that every popish reader of his treatise would immediately
say, as he met there so many familiar controversial ideas, this is but Satan
rebuking sin, one kind of heretic turning against another the kind of argument used by Catholics against all heretics, the argument from the very
nature of the act of heresy.[2]

Hooker, none the less, has nothing about him of the Catholic—of the
" Roman Catholic ", to use the term which friendly governments will
bring into use in the eighteenth century to replace in their laws the offensive
word " Papist ".   On every one of the points of belief at issue between

---

[1] *Hooker* I, 347.

[2] What else, indeed, than the kind of thing Hooker complained of, in Cartwright and
the rest, had been going on in England ever since the debates of 1536 which had produced
the Ten Articles of Henry VIII ? cf. the declaration then made, that, of the mass of common
Christian belief and practice certain items are essential—fixed, therefore, and impossible to
be changed—while other are accessories, to be changed as circumstances call for ; and the
implied declaration, moreover, that the question, What is essential, what accessory ? is one
to be decided simply by the learning of private individuals.   In 1536 these were the bishops,
abbots and other prelates of the ecclesiastical provinces of Canterbury and York, summoned
for the purpose, indeed, by the king in his capacity of Supreme Head of the Church.   In
1570–94 there had been no such assembly.   There had been a policy, which the queen
was determined should be executed ; an attack upon this by some learned theologians ;
a defence of it by others—and presently, the principal defender now promoted, vigorous
episcopal action to enforce the policy ; and a new polemic, out of which emerged the great
figure of Hooker.   Take away the action of the queen, and what is there, more than there was
at Geneva, of any activity but that of learned men insistent upon their own solutions ?
Hooker is insistent, against the English " Genevans ", that what is in possession cannot be
turned out on an *ipse dixit*, not even though this be of Calvin.   But in 1534–35, in 1547–53,
and in 1559, there had been some rare turning out, on precisely such grounds.   And if the
continuous, common use since Apostolic times is a decisive criterion, could such be claimed
for the doctrine about Grace which Hooker held, or for any of the conflicting doctrines about
the Eucharist put forward as the truth of Christ whether by himself or by other reformers ?

Rome and the Reformation he is stoutly, and as by a second nature, on the side of the Reformation. All that separates him from the Protestants he is opposing is the way in which these hold the beliefs which both parties have in common, and the *libido dominandi* which this generates, the spirit that would end with every minister more than a pope for his parish, assisted by daily and continuous divine inspiration. If he refuses to listen to such nonsense as the objection that, to call ministers of the gospel " priests " is a mark of the beast, it is not because ordination is, for him sacramental. Whitgift had already very sensibly replied to Cartwright, urging this point about the word " priest ", that in time the association between this word and what was once believed about the Eucharist would disappear.[1] Hooker, in his turn, now said, quite openly, that he had no liking himself for the word " priest ".[2] " Seeing then that sacrifice is now no part of the church ministry, how should the name of Priesthood be thereunto rightly applied ? . . . As for the people when they hear the name it draweth no more their minds to any cogitation of sacrifice than the name of Senator or of an Alderman causeth them to think upon old age or to imagine that every one so termed must needs be ancient because years were respected in the first nomination of both ". Although " in truth the word Presbyter doth seem more fit, and in propriety of speech more agreeable than *Priest* with the drift of the whole Gospel of Jesus Christ ".[3]

Holy Order is not, for Hooker, a sacrament. The system of government by bishops, though more consonant with Scripture, is not, so far as Scripture tells us, a matter ordained by God as an unchangeable rule.[4] The contention of Cartwright that " Ecclesiastical Polity "—the constitution of the Church of Christ—forms a part of Christian belief Hooker plainly denies : " . . . matters of faith, and in general matters necessary unto Salvation, are of a different nature from [such a matter as] the kind of church government " ;[5] and church government, which is " a form of ordering the public spiritual affairs of the Church of God ",[6] is not " matter of *mere* faith "[7] (as, to use Hooker's own term of comparison, " Articles about the Trinity "), but is " a plain matter of action ".[8] Hooker will not accept the starting-point of his adversaries, that church polity is a part of the doctrine revealed *de ecclesia Christi*. " There is no universally necessary polity." [9] The

---

[1] " As heretofore use hath made it to be taken for a sacrificer, so will use now alter the signification, and make it to be taken for a minister of the gospel." *Hooker*, II, 470, in the note. " But it is mere vanity ", he goes on to say, " to contend for the name, when we agree of the thing." To Cartwright speaking of " That ridiculous, and . . . blasphemous saying, ' Receive the Holy Ghost ' ", Whitgift answers : " The Bishop by speaking these words doth not take it upon him to give the Holy Ghost, no more than he doth to remit sins, when he pronounceth the remission of sins . . . He doth shew the principal duty of a minister, and assureth him of the assistance of God's Holy Spirit, if he labour in the same accordingly." Quoted, *ibid.*, II, 459, n. 1.

[2] *Ibid.*, II, 469. [3] *Ibid.*, II, 471–472, 472.

[4] " There is nothing in Hooker to serve as a foundation for an episcopacy by apostolic succession and divine institution " ; Sisson writes, 107, with his eye on the posthumous books of the Ecclesiastical Polity ; " indeed his reservations upon this matter might furnish ammunition for an opposition " (i.e. to the spirit prevailing in the reign of Charles II, when these books were first published). [5] *Hooker*, I, 353. [6] *Ibid.*, 352.

[7] *Ibid.*, 352. [8] *Ibid.*, 353. [9] *Ibid.*, 352.

fundamental difference evident since Cartwright's mission began in 1570 remains; and to say (what is so often said) that "the conflict with the Puritans was not at the outset an attack on their theology ", is to beg the question.[1]

Hooker is not explaining a doctrine when he deals with this main point of the controversy but deducing the rights of a system. And the whole business of the association of the episcopate with the State is thoroughly congenial to him. In this he is the true and legitimate heir to the Stephen Gardiner of the *De Vera Obedientia* : [2] " We hold, that . . . there is not any man of the Church of England but the same man is also a member of the commonwealth ; nor any man a member of the commonwealth, which is not also of the Church of England." [3] And this is why it is fitting that the head of the Commonwealth should be, and is, the head of the Church.

There is, in all this, no sign of incipient " Romanism " ; nor is there any in Hooker's loyalty to the new—to the Calvinian—beliefs about the way God has arranged that man shall come to his eternal salvation. Presently, between the publication of his first and second volumes, there was to be a new great controversy about this; an incipient rebellion, against the Calvinian teaching, that Whitgift would have liked to crush as he had crushed the opposition since 1583—only to find himself as peremptorily halted by the queen, for this unauthorised initiative, as his late opponents had been halted by her in their parliamentary manoeuvres. But something first needs to be said about the reception given to Hooker's book by his own time.

The great work, the ultimate outcome of his curious pulpit duel with Travers, had begun to take shape, there is reason to believe, round about 1588.[4] In " the general plan or trend of the work ",[5] it owed something to two of his one-time Oxford pupils, Edwin Sandys (son of the Edwin Sandys who had been Archbishop of York since Grindal's promotion to Canterbury in 1576) and George Cranmer, a great-nephew of the famous Archbishop of Canterbury. These brilliant young men [6] were lawyers ; Sandys was an influential member of parliament, and very much indeed " a coming man ". So that, although the work is indeed Hooker's and no other man's, it was planned and written in very close touch with high ecclesiastical personages, who looked for it to be what it actually showed itself—the very book the crisis called for. And once the first volume (Books I–IV) was finished, the printing was hurried so that it would be published while parliament was debating the government's Bill to put down the recusant Protestants. Curiously enough, it was on the very day that Sandys made his speech in the House of Commons, urging new severities in the Bill, March 13, 1593, that the printing was completed.[7]

Whatever the services of Sandys and Cranmer, encouraging Hooker to begin the tremendous undertaking and supplying friendly criticisms as the manuscript piled up, there seems no doubt that had it not been for the

---

[1] As the question is begged, so very often, in regard to a kindred matter, namely, the nature of the revolution accomplished in the Royal Supremacy of Henry VIII.

[2] As for Whitgift, cf. *supra*, p. 172, n. 2.   [3] *Hooker*, III—(i.e. Bk. VIII, ch. i, 2).

[4] Sisson, 90.   [5] *Ibid.*, 47.   [6] Sandys, in 1588, was 27.

[7] For all this, cf. Sisson, 12–13, 64, whose discovery all this history is.

keen interest of Sandys, and his business ability as well as his generosity, Hooker's book would never have found a publisher. The fact is undeniable that publishers shied at the sight of it : religious works, and especially works in support of the episcopal party, would not sell, they declared.[1] And it was only when Sandys offered to finance the affair—to provide the money for compositors, printers, paper and the rest : to stand the losses, if any—that publication was assured. The publishers' forebodings were well justified : it took eleven years to sell the 1200 or 1250 copies of the first edition of this book that the time was calling for—or the cause, at any rate, of the official view of English Christianity against the critical attack of the " presbyterianisers ".[2] And this at a time when the Genevan Bible was selling edition after edition.[3] The establishment of the work as a classic and a steady seller only began a generation later, about the time when Laud was appointed to Canterbury, with the edition of 1632.

The hopes of transforming the Church of England in the direction of Cartwright and Travers' version of Geneva seemed to be extinguished for ever. The court of High Commission was now unmistakably, not only " the most impartial ecclesiastical court in the realm ", not by any means just an engine to root out critics of the fundamentals of 1559, but a most important instrument of the government's policy, that had never wavered in thirty years, to make the English a people of one loyal mind.[4] " The whole ecclesiastical law is a carcase without a soul, if it be not in the wants supplied by the commission ", said Whitgift;[5] and it was by the ecclesiastical law that the layman was still ruled in some of the most important affairs of his ordinary life.

For the last ten years of Elizabeth's reign there was, if not peace, silence at least upon all these issues. And the Royal Supremacy continued to be a reality—with political considerations paramount in the conduct of ecclesiastical affairs at the highest levels. Bancroft's own elevation to the see of London supplies an example of this. No man had done the cause of the Supremacy greater service, none had simultaneously served so well what Whitgift stood for and the queen. When the Bishop of London, Richard Fletcher, died, in June 1596, Bancroft, now fifty-two years of age, was obviously the man who should succeed him ; and the primate immediately began to press on the government his great deserts and the promise, which all his career implied, of unique service in such a post for years yet to come.

[1] Sisson, 50. [2] Ibid., 52, 56, 67, 70.
[3] Thirty-four editions in the ten years 1593–1603 ; cf. Pollard and Redgrave, nos. 2093–2192. Mr. Rowse, then, would seem to be wrong (The England of Elizabeth, 476) : " In the fifteen-nineties the fact that the Church had won its battle is witnessed by the flood of apologetic literature on its side, culminating in a great work, Hooker's Laws of Ecclesiastical Polity."
[4] Usher, High Commission, 108. Bancroft " showed . . . that three civil lawyers, travelling round England under the Commission and with strict and minute orders from the Council had, at various crises, accomplished more in six months than the two Archbishops and twenty-four Bishops with all the Deans and Archdeacons in England could have consummated by their ordinary jurisdiction in as many years ". [5] Ibid., 110.

But, at first, all this went for naught. For the queen and the council saw, at the same time, how Bancroft's development of the High Commission was working for the exaltation of the cleric's part in the ultimate deciding of church policies ; if the control of the church was slipping into clerical hands, it was to Bancroft that this was due. And all Whitgift's efforts were vain, " until he and Bancroft practically surrendered themselves to the Cecils, father and son . . .".[1] If, as Bishop of London, Bancroft was to be a power—and to increase the authority of his position—this, in the government's intention, he was to do and to be, not by any means as a theologian, or as a masterful cleric, whether a Calvin or a Wolsey, but as a prelate whose " ecclesiastical functions were to be secondary . . . to onerous . . . duties of a quasi-political character ".[2] The Tudor bishop was still—and very much so—the servant of the Tudor state.

Nevertheless Bancroft, in the fourteen years of his episcopal service to that state, contrived to reverse the popular impression of church politics. By the time he died, in 1610, it was the " primitives ", the Puritans, as the nickname went that so annoyed them—who were hated and ridiculed in the capital ; it was the bishops who were now esteemed—as men of sense and religion.[3] Inevitably, in achieving so much, Bancroft had insensibly outmanoeuvred Cecil. With the terrifying Elizabeth gone, and her almost mythical prestige, and with the foreigner from Scotland ruling in her place, Bancroft, and not only Bancroft but the clerical element in that place where he now ruled as Archbishop of Canterbury, could not but profit immensely from all his early activities.

Whitgift, in his articles of 1583, had aimed another heavy blow at the party so hostile to the settlement, when he ruled that, henceforth, the only translation of the Bible to be used in the public services of the church was that made by the Elizabethan bishops, and first published in 1568, the so-called Bishops' Bible. For one of the main forces which, in all the years since 1559, had made for the survival and development of the primitive ideals among the Reformers, was the popularity of the translation of the Bible made at Geneva by a group of the Marian exiles, and first published there in 1560. The principal authors of this were William Whittingham, the historian of the Troubles at Frankfort, and Antony Gilby[4] and that Thomas Sampson,

---

[1] Usher, I, 113.   [2] Ibid.

[3] Ibid., 72. On becoming Bishop of London, Bancroft had to resign the preferment he then held—eight rectories and canonries ; and one of his first duties to the all but bankrupt see was to try and recover, from the estate of his last predecessor but one, something of what that prelate owed for dilapidations. This predecessor was the vigorously anti-Catholic, semi-Puritan, John Aylmer ; an enthusiastic gospeller whose activity went back to the days of Edward VI, who under Mary exiled himself to Strasburg, and then, as an Elizabethan bishop of London (1577–1594), was a perpetual embarrassment to the council by reason of his uncontrollable temper. He died at the age of seventy-five or six, leaving behind him a family of eight young children, to provide for whom he had successfully, " by severe economies and successful scheming ", bought land to the value of £16,000 (Elizabethan money) and had so arranged matters that this was not liable for claims.

[4] Born about 1514, and thus a man approaching 50 in the year the Geneva Bible was published. Educated at Cambridge (Christ's College) and described as one of the " most

with some of whose later activities we have already been occupied. A second edition was published in 1562 ; and a third edition in 1568—which was really the unsold copies of the first edition provided with a new title page, a device already found useful, years before, to sell off the surplus copies of Coverdale's translation.

Seven years later, Whittingham, now Dean of Durham, writes that this version is not in such demand that any more have been printed since 1568.[1] The popularity of bible-reading is a thing which really belongs to the second generation of Elizabethans. In this later generation that popularity is a fact, a great and important fact in many ways ; and it is above all the Geneva version which will then be the version in popular use. But we must abandon the notion—that underlies, for example, so much of Jewel's apologetic for the new establishment—of the generation contemporary with the changes of 1559 as a people thirsting for the chance to read those scriptures which the church of the popes has for centuries locked up from it, and falling eagerly upon the sacred text once the day of liberation has dawned. It is not with the generation that had reached manhood by the time that Mary's reign repressed the Protestant Experiment, that the Bible is popular— with those passing into middle age in 1575 when Whittingham wrote this letter—but with a generation that never knew that repression, nor had ever experienced any hindrance to reading the Bible as it chose. Bible-reading as a popular religious habit is, in fact, a mark not of a generation that has left the darkness for the light, or that has been brought out of darkness into light through its own study and love of Holy Writ, but of a generation bred in the light from birth, bred wholly, that is to say, in a religion where the Bible is exalted as the supreme and all-sufficient religious fact.[2]

---

acrimonious and illiberal writers " among the Reformers (art. *Gilby, Antony* in *D.N.B.*). On his return to England he found a patron as bitter as himself in the powerful Earl of Huntingdon. Gilby died in 1585, after twenty years as vicar of Ashby-de-la-Zouch.

[1] Dixon, V, 330, ref. Dore, *Old Bibles*, 347.

[2] The grounds for this statement are the dates of the editions of the various translations, 1535–1603, as given in Pollard & Redgrave, nos. 2063, foll. To go back nearly twenty years before the accession of Elizabeth, the last editions of an English bible which Henry VIII allowed appeared in 1541—the last 5 of 14 editions since 1535. Then, for eight years, no bible was printed. In the last four years of Edward VI (1549–1553) there were 14 editions (7 of the Matthews bible, 5 of the Great Bible, 2 of Coverdale's translation). In Mary's reign not only were there none bibles published, but there was a search for these translations in order to destroy them. What this search accomplished we do not know. The first bibles of Elizabeth's reign appeared in 1560, a reprint of the Great Bible and the new, Geneva, translation. The Bishops' Bible—the translation that Whitgift was to make obligatory, in 1583, for use in the public services—appeared in 1568. Between the queen's accession and this publication (1558–1568), there were published, in all, 5 editions of the bible : 2 of the Geneva version and 3 of the Great Bible. Between 1568 and Grindal's appointment to Canterbury in 1575 there were 12 editions : 1 of the Geneva book, 4 of the Great Bible (which now disappears) and 7 of the new Bishops' Bible. In the next eighteen years (between Grindal's appointment as archbishop and the Conventicle Act of 1593 that marks Whitgift's victory over the " Geneva " party) there were 42 editions of the bible, 33 of which are of the Geneva translation. And in the last ten years of Elizabeth's reign, the years when Whitgift is triumphant, there are 35 editions in all : another 33 of the Geneva book, and only 2 of the version officially imposed for public use. Of the 58 editions that appeared between the ruling of 1583, and the end of the reign, 51 were of the disapproved, Geneva book, and only 7 of the quasi-official Bishops' Bible.

Like every other translation of its time, the Geneva Bible was furnished with an abundance of explanatory and controversial notes ; [1] it was also the first English translation of the whole of Scripture to be printed in the modern, i.e. roman, type, and with the verses numbered ; it was illustrated, supplied with maps, and, after 1579, it contained also a catechism of doctrine, in which the Calvinism already evident through all the rich annotation of St. Paul's epistles, [2] was gathered into a convenient synthesis. If it was John Foxe's immensely popular *Book of Martyrs* that finally made the Englishman anti-Catholic almost by nature, it was this bible of Whittingham and Sampson that made the religious Englishman, also by nature, as it were, " anti-sacerdotal ", a Low Churchman if not a Free Churchman. It was then, " a book undertaken at the instance of a Calvinist congregation, by Calvinist scholars, for Calvinist readers ", [3] which, for the first sixty years and more after the settlement of 1559, shaped the spiritual outlook of the Bible-reading English. Beside the popularity of this private venture, the prestige of the " official " translation made by the new bishops was a very small force indeed. The preface to this, the Bishops' Bible, drew the queen's attention to another translation " not laboured in your realm, having inspersed diverse prejudicial notes which might have been well spared ". But the bishops were not encouraged to condemn or to suppress their rival ; [4] the queen ignored the hint and she did nothing at all to help their own version by any sign of authorisation. The Bishops' Bible was a very uneven piece of scholarship, [5] and it never displaced the Geneva Bible—from which, without acknowledgment, many of its own notes were taken. [6]

The theology of the popular bible of the day was unmistakably Calvinist ; and Calvin's own masterpiece [7] was popular also, in the translation

[1] " The insane principle that the Bible is best without an interpreter and can be used in education without explanation, was not invented before the age in which we live ". Dixon, VI, 249. The notes to Tyndale's translation had been, largely, Luther : the notes to this were Calvin. " Is it to be expected ", a critic of Whitgift's ban is quoted as saying, " that men will throw aside the Geneva version and the notes attached which have been so great a blessing ? " Peel, I, 176.

[2] " . . . the pithy, pungent, and voluminous notes which illuminated nearly every chapter were, as with its less tolerated predecessors, not the least among its attractions ". Dixon, V, 330.   [3] H. W. Hoare, *Our English Bible* (1911), 223.

[4] The official ban of the articles of 1583 is reflected in the acts of the bishops' visitations ; cf. (Peel, I, 220) the visitation of the diocese of Chichester, where one question àsked is " Whether the bible used in the parish church or chapel be of the same translation that is allowed by the bishops ".

[5] As Whitgift's clerical opponents were swift to point out in 1584. Few of the translators, it was said, were " exactly grounded in the sound and perfect knowledge of the Hebrew, Syrian and Greek tongues ". Peel, I, 176. Another point they urged was that " The restriction to one translation in public worship is unwise, for it will make the common people compare translations ". *Another awnser to the former articles contained in the petition of the ArchB. to her Majestie.* (1584), *ibid.*, I, 185–186. The quotation is the editor's summary. It may be noted that by now the Catholic (Douay-Rheims) translation, the notes in which criticised the accuracy of these other English bibles, was beginning to circulate.

[6] The illustrations provided for the pious and loyal student of the word of God are not without interest : portraits of the queen, of Cecil, and of—the Earl of Leicester.

[7] *Christianae religionis Institutio* . . . Basel, 1536 ; *Institution de la religion chrestienne en laquelle est comprinse une somme de piété et quasi tout ce qui est nécessoire à cognoistre en la doctrine du salut, composee par Iean Calvin et translatée en françoys par luy-mesme.* Geneva, 1541.

of Thomas Norton, first published in 1561 and five times reprinted in the next fifty years.[1]

This long examination of the new religious alternative thrust by law upon the Catholics of England in 1559, may, as it closes, recall that what was ultimately in dispute between the new and the old was the highly practical matter of the way appointed by God for man to save his soul. " Good master, what must I do to possess eternal life ? "

The answer given, in all these years, in all the official and quasi-official propaganda of Queen Elizabeth's *Anglicana*, was, substantially, the answer devised by Calvin ; and the last great religious stir of the reign was to show this yet once again. " As the only will and purpose of God is the chief cause of election and reprobation ", runs the annotation in the popular bible, " so His free mercy in Christ is an inferior cause of salvation, and the hardening of the heart an inferior cause of damnation ". Man's acts do not count for as much, in all this business, as the old religion had both taught explicitly and also implied in a hundred, sanctioned, devotional activities. And when, after nearly forty years, during which " the more *extreme* opinions of the school of Calvin, not excluding his theory of irrespective reprobation, were predominant in almost every town and parish ",[2] the first faint signs of reaction against this teaching began to show among the theologians, the nature of the Elizabethan establishment was revealed immediately : intuitively it showed itself as hostile to all but Calvin ; the first criticism of Calvin from within the Church of England provoked an uproar of condemnation that was unanimous. The last years of Elizabeth's long reign were indeed an age when, as one of the pioneers declared who led the reaction—a future Archbishop of York —Calvin's dictum, " which speaks little better of our gracious God than this, that God should design many thousands to hell before they were, not in eye to their faults, but to His absolute will and power ",[3] towered over every man's life.

The definitive edition is that of 1560, and it is this which was now popularised in England in translation.

[1] For Norton, a distinguished lawyer, as well as a zealot for the primitive purity of the Reformation, joint author of the first tragedy written in English, and in later years the self-confessed, enthusiastic torturer of Catholic prisoners in the Tower, cf. the account in *D.N.B.*

[2] Hardwick, 164 ; italics in the original.

[3] This was Samuel Harsnett, in a sermon preached at Paul's Cross, Oct. 27, 1584 ; quoted Hardwick, 164. The future archbishop, then but twenty-three, once a sizar of King's College, Cambridge, seemed, at the moment, to have ruined his promising career by this sermon. Forty years later he described in the House of Lords how, for this sermon, he " was checked by the Lord Archbishop Whitgift, and commanded to preach no more of it, and he never did, though now [i.e. 1624] Dr. Abbot, late bishop of Sarum, hath since declared in print that which he preached to be no Popery "—such was, in fact, the handy, noxious, epithet which the Elizabethan orthodoxy affixed to a critic of pure Calvinism. Harsnett was, in 1596, one of Baro's supporters (of whom in a moment) and soon after this became one of Bancroft's chaplains. In 1605 he was master of Pembroke Hall, in 1609 Bishop of Chichester ; promoted to Norwich in 1619, and to York in 1628, he died in 1631, seventy years of age, having lived to see his party so triumphant that the reaction of reactions was already evidently preparing.

The theological dispute of 1595, had for its protagonists, like that of 1570, the two leading divines of the university of Cambridge—the regius professor, William Whitaker, and his colleague in the Lady Margaret chair, Peter Baro.[1] It was, once again, the Lady Margaret professor whose views disturbed the peace. Baro, who was a Huguenot refugee, had, ever since the appointment which Cecil's influence secured for him in 1575, dealt critically with the theories which all around him professed. Gradually he was forming a school for whom Calvin and Bullinger were something less than infallible. The sales of their works began to decline ; and older authors, the Fathers, and even the schoolmen, began to creep back into favour.

There were complaints as early as 1581 that Baro was bringing in " new doctrines ", and a controversy, where his chief opponent was Laurence Chaderton. But the differences were settled amicably. Then, in May, 1595, a sermon by one of the fellows of Caius College, William Barrett, touched off the animosity that had smouldered for years. Calvin was here openly contradicted, and Beza too, with Bullinger and Peter Martyr : [2] Christ had died to save *all* mankind, it was asserted ; and God had not damned the reprobate to hell, before He created them, simply in order to demonstrate to man what an awful mystery infinite justice is. The controversy which now began raged for the next seven months, and not at Cambridge only, for Whitgift was soon appealed to. For Baro the archbishop had the harsh word that foreigners ought to mind their own business.[3] And with the aid of the regius professor, and the bishop-elect of London,[4] Whitgift drafted, and sent to Cambridge, November 24, nine articles that set forth what the *Anglicana* had hitherto believed on the matter, to be a standard of orthodoxy in university exercises.[5] These are the Lambeth Articles of November 20, 1595.

The Articles state :

1. God, from all eternity, has predestined certain people to life, and has reprobated certain people to death.

2. The motive or efficient cause of predestination is not a foresight of the faith, or the perseverance, or of the good deeds, or of any other thing in the persons predestined, but the will only of God's good pleasure (*sed sola voluntas beneplaciti Dei*).

3. The number of those predestined is defined and certain ; it cannot be increased nor diminished.

---

[1] For Baro cf. J. B. Mullinger, in *D.N.B.*, art. *Baro, Peter*. He was French by birth (born 1534), and, like Calvin, bred to the law (B. Civil Law, Bourges, 1556). Thence he turned to theology—at Geneva, where, by Calvin personally, Baro was admitted to the ministry.

[2] Cf. Barrett's retractation, made a few days later (Strype, *Whitgift*, III, 317–320) : *Temere haec verba effudi adversus Johannem Calvinum, virum de Ecclesia Christi, optime meritum . . . tum etiam nonnulla adversus Petrum Martyrem, Theodorum Bezam, Hieronymum Zanchium, Franciscum Junium et caeteros eiusdem religionis, Ecclesiae nostrae lumina et ornamenta acerbissime effuderim.* . . . The points alleged against Barrett, and his own comments, are printed *ibid.*, 320–321.

[3] *Non decet hominem peregrinum curiosum esse in aliena republica.*

[4] Richard Fletcher.

[5] Whitgift's letter to the university is in Strype, *Whitgift*, III, 279.

4. Those who are not predestined to salvation will necessarily because of their sins be damned.

5. The true, living, justifying Faith, and the holy-making Spirit of God is not extinguished, does not fail, does not pass away, in the elect, either finally or altogether.

6. The man who is truly a faithful man, i.e. possessed of justifying faith, is certain with the certainty that is the fulfilment of faith (*certus est Plerophoria Fidei*) that his own sins are forgiven and that through Christ he is eternally saved.

7. The grace that saves is not granted to, not communicated to, not conceded to the whole of mankind [as a means], by which they could be saved if they willed.

8. No man can come to Christ unless this be given to him, and unless the Father draw him. And all men are not drawn by the Father so that they may come to the Son.

9. To be saved is not [a matter] placed within the choice or the power of every man.[1]

These articles of 1595 were not, however, imposed for subscription. On December 5, the queen intervened, alarmed by the suggestion of Whitgift's letter that they were to be the theme of new debates.[2] They have, then, never had other force than, to use Whitgift's own words, " as the private judgments of those who drafted them, and who considered them to be true and correspondent to the doctrine professed in the Church of England, and established by the laws of the land. . . ." [3] At Cambridge, six weeks or so after the queen's command to the archbishop, Baro, preaching in the university church, set himself to explain how he could accept the articles and yet not abandon the theology he had been teaching.[4] He had failed to understand the menace in Whitgift's warning. The party of the articles were furious,[5] and Baro was called before the vice-chancellor, lectured, and forbidden to discuss the articles. All seemed set for a repetition of the events of 1570, and the expulsion of Baro from his chair, for attacking Calvin's teaching about grace, as Cartwright had then been expelled for urging Calvin's teaching about " ecclesiastical polity ". Again the university authorities wrote to beg the support of their chancellor—still Lord Burghley. They set out, in their letter, the whole story of " the late reviving of new opinions . . . among us " ; how Barrett, " about a year past . . . did preach popish [6] errors in St. Mary's . . . which he was enjoined to retract. But refused to do so in such sort as hath been prescribed him." His retractation, it was thought, added insult to injury. And so Dr. Tyndal and

---

[1] The translation is my own. The Latin text is printed in Hardwick, 361, and in *Hooker*, II, 596, n. 6, from Strype, *Whitgift*, Bk. IV, ch. 17.

[2] Cf. Robert Cecil's letter, of this date, to Whitgift, in Strype, *op. cit.*, II, 286.

[3] Letter to the university, as cited, p. 282. But Prothero understates the evidence of the document when he writes (p. xxix) that the Lambeth Articles are " interesting as showing the tendency to Calvinism which at that time prevailed even among the leading divines of the Church ".   [4] Jan. 12, 1596.

[5] " Flushed with their triumph ", Mullinger, art. *Baro, D.N.B.*

[6] For the contemporary use of this word, cf. *supra*, pp. 222–223.

Dr. Whitaker were sent to London " for conference with my Lord of Canterbury ". Whence " certain propositions (containing certain substantial points of religion taught and received in this university and church, during the time of her Majesty's reign, and consented unto and practiced by the best approved divines, both at home and abroad) "—the Lambeth Articles ; and so great peace at Cambridge until Baro's sermon. They complained, formally, that for the last fourteen or fifteen years Baro had been teaching the contrary of what was received since 1559, " and agreeable to the errors of popery ; which we know your lordship hath always disliked and hated ". And they beg him to arrest a movement whose end must be the return of the popish system.[1] But Burghley considered that the university had treated Baro over harshly,[2] and he gave the vice-chancellor no encouragement to imitate the Whitgift of twenty-five years earlier.

The Lady Margaret professor of 1596 foresaw, not only how slender were his chances of re-election to the chair, once his term was at end, but also the kind of life he would now be led at Cambridge. And choosing to leave before he was driven away,[3] Baro retired from the contest to London, where three years later, " in great poverty ", he died.

The Lambeth Articles of 1595, we may take it, are normal Anglicanism on this point and at this moment—and what they contain will continue to be the belief of the mass of the clergy for another generation at least, and to be popular for still longer with the pious layman.[4] None the less an age is now in sight when Calvin *De Gratia* will be fought and defeated no less effectually than Calvin *De Ecclesia*, although Calvin *De Eucharistia* will continue to be followed. The first—comparatively simple—stage is drawing to a close, of the development of what, in 1559, had displaced the Catholic Church at the will of the sovereign and the governing classes of England. Already a much more complex affair, the religion of modern England, is dimly showing in outline.

It is not the business of this particular history to embark whoever chances to read it upon the investigation which shall discover how the alternative

---

[1] This letter, March 8, 1596, is in Strype, *Annals*, IV, 319–322.

[2] This had been Whitgift's own first " reaction " to the university's censure on Barrett, ten months previously. But William Whitaker, the regius professor of divinity, deprecating the archbishop's lecture to the university doctors, reminded him that " Although these points [i.e. those attacked by Barrett] were not concluded and defined by public authority, yet for as much as they have been hitherto evermore in our Church held, etc., etc." The letter is in Strype, *Whitgift*, III, 338.   [3] *Fugio ne fugerer*, he is supposed to have said.

[4] On Feb. 24, 1629, a committee of religion of the House of Commons, appointed to consider religious grievances, set out its findings in four *Heads of Articles* (for which cf. G. & H., 521–527, and S. R. Gardiner, *Constitutional Documents of the Puritan Revolution*, 11). In the fourth of these, they say that the true reformed religion may be known by (amongst other matters here set out), " The Resolutions of the Archbishop of Canterbury and other reverend bishops and divines assembled at Lambeth for this very purpose, to declare their opinions concerning those points, anno 1595, unto which the Archbishop of York and all his province did likewise agree " (G. & H., 526), and by " The censures, recantations, punishments and submissions made, enjoined, and inflicted upon those that taught contrary thereunto, as Barrow and Barrett in Cambridge, and Bridge, in Oxford " ; where Barrow is, of course, Peter Baro.

set before the English Catholics of 1559 developed into that much more various thing. But it is a lawful speculation with which to leave the subject, one of great historical interest—and, very surely, of something more than that—whether what has here been called the Second Conversion of England was ever really accomplished. That the *massa* of 1559, the representative and descendant of the *massa* of 1529, ceased, ultimately, to be influenced, spiritually and morally, by the one set of beliefs—this is certain : did it ever really embrace and surrender itself to the influence of the other set ? Was England, at any time, ever more " Church of England ", or " Protestant ", than it was Catholic in 1529 ? or was it—ever—even as much so ? Was not more destroyed, after 1529—in the way of general, popular understanding and attachment to a system of Christian truth as a thing that really matters in practice—than was ever re-built ? Was the Englishman of 1603 more—or was he less—influenced by religion in his conduct than the Englishman of 1529 ? did he know more, or less, about Christ our Lord and His teaching ? The question whether the man of 1529 knew more, or less, about this than the man of 1954 we must leave for others to answer. But is it not from these generations that we must date the beginnings of what has troubled so many good men, of all kinds of belief, for a good century now, namely the unruffled " religionlessness " of so very many—indeed of whole sections, and of the very mass of the nation ?

In all the seventy-five years that followed Wolsey's fall [1] there never was, in fact, any great national movement of religious revival, a whole people clamorous for news of God and the truth about God and turning to the new teachers for what they had despaired of getting from the old. The clergy of these years who abandoned the old religion were no army of zealous apostles, fired with the one only aim, to bring men to Christ, and counting all else as dung. There were indeed such clerics, here and there.[2] But they were no more representative of their time than Fisher and the martyred Carthusians had been representative of the earlier time. There were not enough of such apostles, in the age of Parker and Grindal and Whitgift, to have manned even a single religious order. And with that thought, what a contrast this Elizabethan England presents to what was now afoot these forty years and more in Italy, and in Spain, where the great cities, and the country-sides too, were alive with the activities of a really national, religious revival, that was the work, in great part, of the countless members of the new religious orders, Theatines, Capuchins, Barnabites, Jesuits and the rest, whole-hearted servants of the divine ideal, who had literally given up all to follow this ; at once humanists, theologians and ascetics, the finest flower of them flung in world-wide missionary effort through all the newly discovered lands from Mexico and Peru to the Philippines and Japan. Here were men truly devoid of self, who, undisturbed by the personal failings and sins of

---

[1] 1529–1604.

[2] " Amongst all the works of the early Puritans there is not one on the character and life of Christ, nor one which gives any indication that they held even an imagination of the wholly spiritual nature of His kingdom." H. S. Skeats, in H. S. Skeats and C. S. Miall, *History of the Free Churches of England*, London, 1891.

authority, only demanded authority's permission to devote themselves ; men who, just as unconscious of their own personal superiority to authority, were to end, although they knew it not, by imposing on authority something of their own high standards.

With the appearance of the many contemporary saints of Spain and Italy, the daily following of the cross once more began to be a reality, even in the highest places of the Church and of the State. Philip II dies, after weeks of agony amid the stench of his own filth, whence none dare move him, either for the pain to the patient or the horror to themselves, and he dies reconciled to the manner of his death as reparation for his sins and as a means of union with Christ our Lord dying in agony to procure him the pardon of those sins, whose image the king has had fixed to the foot of his bed. Charles V's death, if less terrible, was no less a conscious act of Christian reparation. Is it mere accident that the pictures of Cranmer assisting Henry VIII's last moments, and of Whitgift beside the dying Elizabeth, are so different ? If brotherly love and active charity are the first signs, anywhere, of Christian revival, where are there any general signs of this in these generations when the doctrines of the Reformed religion are given their first opportunity to enrich the spiritual life of the English ?

In Mary's short reign no apostles had risen, from among the party in power, to revive that spiritual life. And in the nine times as long reign of her sister, none again had arisen from the party in power. Apostles there were indeed in Elizabethan England, the national counterpart of the Alcantarines of Spain, the Theatines of Italy, the Jesuits of Germany—it is to their spiritual adventure that we must now turn.

PART II

DELENDA

CHAPTER I

DRIFT

I

" TO the last, to the defeat of the Armada, manhood suffrage in England would have brought back the Pope "—the judgment is Froude's.[1] Whence no doubt, if he is right, the lasting consciousness in England of the debt owed to Elizabeth and to Burghley, rulers possessed of that transcendental greatness which understands the real needs of a people as that people never itself understands them.

Is Froude's judgment true, supposing, what is not at all certain, that it was a final and considered judgment ? The interesting thing about it, for what remains to be told of this history, is that the judgment accords, to the letter, with the judgment, made at the time, by the leaders of the militant, Catholic opposition to the Elizabethan Settlement ; a judgment that is, indeed, the starting point of their policy, to which, as to a matter where all men are agreed, they publicly appeal in justification of their long-continued endeavour to overthrow the queen's government. If Froude is right, then the opinions of Cardinal Allen and Fr. Robert Persons about the nature of what was going forward in their time [2] are worth more attention than is generally granted ; and there is something to be said for the claim that they,

---

[1] Froude's, unpublished, fragment of autobiography, quoted Algernon Cecil, *Six Oxford Thinkers* (1909), p. 169. Usher (*Reconstruction*, II, 266) would agree, seemingly, that the English were not yet won over to 1559 : " By tradition and habit the majority still inclined in 1583 to the old Mass." Froude is, notoriously, not exact in his sweeping statements ; and Usher, at times, is careless. Nor must I quote Professor Conyers Read as though I considered him habitually accurate in his generalisations, but on this matter it is interesting that he writes, " A large proportion of Englishmen, if not the actual majority, were Catholics, and it was never quite certain at what moment they might not rise in strength and demand the toleration for their faith which the laws refused. One of the gravest problems which faced Elizabeth's government was that of keeping the Catholics in check." *Mr. Secretary Walsingham*, II, 258. Would it distort what this scholar has written if, after " Catholics " one read " down " for " in check " ?

[2] Cf. Allen's " *A true, sincere and modest defence of English Catholics that suffer for their faith both at home and abroad, against a false, seditious and slanderous libel, entitled :* ' *The execution of justice in England* '. *Wherein is declared how unjustly the Protestants do charge Catholics with treason ; how untruly they deny their persecution for Religion ; and how deceitfully they seek to abuse strangers about the cause, greatness, and manner of their sufferings, with divers other matter pertaining to this purpose.*" 1584. The writer declares at the outset (Preface, p. 5 of the 1914 reprint, vol. i) that " the honour of our nation " is his real concern, "which otherwise, to her infinite shame and reproach, would be thought wholly and generally to have revolted from the Catholic faith ". The truth of the matter is that " the disorder " proceeds " but of the partiality of a few powerful persons abusing her Majesty's clemency and credulity ", and " that the whole state (excepting the authority of the Prince) may yet be rather counted Catholic than heretical ".

too, should be heard as though they were speaking, not from the dock, but from the more comfortable places beneath the royal arms—that they should so be heard, at least in this generation that is not so passionately interested in the question whether it is the Catholic or the Reformed view of the Christian religion that is true.

No one, it has been said by a present day authority, can really write impartially about these events.[1] As to this, the great personalities and their achievements do, indeed, still tend to influence our judgment through our sympathies, as well as through the reasoning intelligence. Any discussion will very soon reveal, this ; and will reveal, too, how close to us these events of three to four hundred years ago remain. The tradition of a great injustice that triumphed through fraud and force is still very much alive among the descendants of one part of the England of Elizabeth ; and the tradition of a great liberation, won in defiance of all the world leagued against us, survives among the descendants of other Elizabethans. The zest to pass moral judgments is very common ; and with it the belief that the ultimate question is one of right or wrong, and that it is capable of final solution. Such primitive notions, whatever the proportion of professional historians whom they consciously or unconsciously influence, still matter to that ordinary man for whom the historians write. And to this " idiot people ",[2] it will at times make all the difference whether the statement of the facts seems to form part of the plea in mitigation, or to be the summing up of the court.

A master-historian, writing of one particular problem of these times, has well described the difficulty that is present everywhere. " Few questions in history have been more keenly or more obstinately discussed, than whether [Mary, Queen of Scots] was or was not privy and consenting to the death of her husband ; but her advocates, as well as her accusers, occasionally leave the pursuit of truth for the pursuit of victory ; their ardour betrays both parties into errors and misrepresentations ; and the progress of the historian is retarded at every step by the conflicting opinions and insidious artifices of his

---

[1] " . . . it need hardly be said that a completely objective account of events in Elizabeth's reign, however desirable it may be in theory, cannot in actual fact be written." So Black, in the *Preface* (p. vi) to his masterly book, so often quoted in these pages, *The Reign of Elizabeth* (1936), where he sets out at length the reasons for this, surely pessimistic, estimate of the chances of the historian achieving what Lingard declared should be the common practice of the profession, to " view with the coolness of an unconcerned spectator the events which pass before his eyes " (*Preliminary Notice* to the last (1849) edition of the *History of England*, I, p. xxii). It is, of course, the fact that considerations other than the texts before their eyes have, at times, influenced many historians of this reign. Maitland is very much to the point, " The patient analysis of those love letters in the casket may yet be perturbed by thoughts about religion ", *C.M.H.*, II, 550. Since, in the pages that follow, Professor Black's presentation is, at times, questioned, the point of view from which he writes should be remembered : " . . . we have been compelled to observe events predominantly . . . through the eyes of the English government ", he says in his Preface (p. vi), carefully adding, " But the writer is aware, and the reader ought also to be aware, that there is another point of view . . .". This does not mean that the author means to write as an advocate for the government. Nevertheless, " the paramount necessity ", he finds, has been to place " the reader at the standpoint of the queen and her ministers ", and this [since no doubt, there cannot be room for everything in any book] " has prevented a rigorous following out of the principle " [of always taking other points of view into account].

[2] Rowse, *England of Elizabeth*, 265.

guides. In the conduct of Mary, previously to the murder of Darnley, I see nothing that can fairly impeach her character. There is no credible evidence that she was cognizant of the design, much less that she was the accomplice to the assassins. But in her behaviour subsequently to that event, there is much of more questionable tendency, which, in the supposition of her guilt, will be considered as the consequence of the crime ; in the supposition of her innocence, may be explained away by a reference to the difficulties of her situation. I shall narrate the facts with impartiality ; the reader must draw his own conclusions." [1]

" With impartiality " : Lingard's challenge to himself is made with the serene simplicity that marks all his work. And he will, indeed, systematically distinguish between fact and comment in every source he uses, and will let his readers see that he is doing this. And lest his own language accidentally colour the facts he is relating, and so turn his history into apologetic, Lingard will deliberately choose a cold, detached style, suspicious of brilliant imagery, and the happy epigrams that hit off the situation—as the writer conceives it—so perfectly.

As for presuppositions, " Supposition of guilt . . . supposition of innocence "—to the difficulty of discerning one's own presuppositions as one reads anew any particular history (to discard them once discerned is not so hard), there is in the history of the English Catholics under Elizabeth a further difficulty which is not a historical difficulty at all, namely, the question what is guilt and what is innocence, in the matter of organising to overthrow the government : can rebellion ever be anything but wrong ? is this particular rebellion one of the kind that is right ? As to the major question, we may cheerfully assert, against the unanimity of official theologians in the new *Anglicana* from Henry VIII to Elizabeth and beyond, that it can be lawful to rise against a tyrant. To answer the minor—whether it was lawful to rise against Elizabeth—would call for much leisure in which to study all those facts of the situation which such particular judgments must take into account.

Elizabeth might well, for example, have forfeited her *de iure* authority by her abuse of it, but what were the chances that a rising would succeed ? and what the assurance that the new régime would be wholly an improvement on the old ? Western Europe, in the second half of the sixteenth century, was not so clearly divided into a Catholic world (that was another Eden) and England—which was an Inferno. There is no reason to doubt that many an English Catholic would have echoed the words of the Jesuit, Henry Walpole, spoken after thirty years of the drive to exterminate the faith, " I heard Sir Francis Englefield say that the Catholics in England were much to be blamed for that though they desired the restoring of their religion, yet they would not allow of the means which were most or only probable, by admitting the Spaniards when they came, or when they should come, if ever they did again. Which speech I then much disliked, though professing then their religion, for that I ever thought their insolency and vice to be most

---

[1] Lingard, VI, 140–141.

odious to God, and that their coming hither by force would not only be the woeful ruin of the commonwealth and my dearest country, but also their example, especially of soldiers, make such as are of their religion to stagger, because for peace, moral virtue, and good government of the commonwealth, I in my poor judgment do not know any comparable unto England, not considering of religion at all." [1]

That the overthrow by a Catholic army, in 1569, of the government then functioning in England would have been a useful first step towards the revival of the Catholic faith is no doubt true. It would have meant freedom to live a Catholic life, e.g. to use the sacraments which, in the divine scheme, are " the chief means of our salvation ". But speculation about what the future would have been, had events so fallen out in 1569, and the Catholic success been maintained, will be wide of the mark, if it does not take into account the kind of Catholic the *padrone* was whom all these projects presuppose, King Philip II. The King of Spain's practice of the virtue called religion was, no doubt, exemplary. And he never wavered in his opposition to the new heresies of his time. But the history of his relations with the papacy shows the Catholic King as one of the great enemies of the freedom of religion. " Few rulers—except, perhaps, Henry VIII of England ", it has been possible to write of Philip II, " have ever maintained so consistently an anti-papal policy over a long period of years ".[2] In this history we see the pope of 1569, St. Pius V, in his primary rôle, as the strong man determined to free the Church from the stranglehold of the Habsburg state, and engaged, through all his reign, in a battle royal with Philip II, whom he even threatens with excommunication and with an interdict ; the king retorting with hints of an appeal to a general council. In Spain, so the nuncio reported, August 11, 1566, " I find the authority of the Holy See impugned on every point : all are opposed to it except the cathedral chapters, and even they are only actuated by self-interest ". In Philip's other kingdom of Naples, " the privileges claimed by the king [and they were acted upon] were such as to do away with the primatial power of the Pope " ; so the papal legate, Cardinal Bonelli, in 1571.[3] In this kingdom the pope was engaged in the herculean task of cleaning up after the neglect of generations, and at every turn his efforts were blocked by the king's *de facto* control of all the organs of ecclesiastical life. The pope's interference in the affairs of the king whom God was using as his instrument—so Philip II declared, November 26, 1566 —was ill-timed and ill-judged.[4] This is only one chapter in a story that

---

[1] The words quoted are from a statement made June 13, 1594, when a prisoner in the Tower of London, to the queen's commissioners (among whom Richard Topcliffe and Francis Bacon), *C.R.S.*, V, 256. Henry Walpole, of the famous Norfolk family, had been nine years a Jesuit when he came back to England, Dec. 4, 1593. He was arrested within twenty-four hours of his landing. After twelve months of imprisonment in the Tower and much torture, he was hanged, drawn and quartered at York, April 7, 1595. For his story, cf. Jessopp, *One Generation of a Norfolk House* (1878). There was, of course, in London at this very time a refugee from the Spanish Eden, whose own relations with the king might well have provoked this patriotic comparison. Cf., G. Marañón, *Antonio Pérez* (1954).

[2] Trevor Davies, 132.   [3] As summarised by Pastor, XVII, 68.

[4] For an outline of this contest during the reign of Pius V (1566–1572) see *ibid.*, 1–71.

continues for the whole period 1566–1598 ; the danger to religion latent in Spanish Caesaro-papism is a main element which all the popes of this time need to consider in all their policies. And it is an important part of the " background " of the history of the English Catholics under Queen Elizabeth.

" To narrate the facts ", then—the history of what befell those of the English who, in fidelity to the religious beliefs and practice traditional for the previous thousand years,[1] now rejected the arrangements made in 1559. It is the story of an attempt to destroy this fidelity by a penal code which, from the outset, threatens fines, imprisonment and even death ; of defiance of the new laws, at first sporadic, then gradually organised ; and of penal laws still more stringent provoked thereby. It is a story that has for its warp the foreign policies of England throughout the whole reign.

That Catholicism is a social whole, each part of which is necessarily affected by the fate of every other part, is taken for granted by the English statesmen who have planned to extirpate it, just as naturally as it is presumed by the Catholic apologists. Events in continental Europe will be used to justify new severities against the Catholics.[2] The kings of Spain and of France, and the pope too, will not at this critical moment see indifferently the next greatest power in Europe [3] pass from one side to the other in the religious conflict that has divided Western Europe for now forty years. And with the religious minority in England, who know how precarious is their own hold upon the government, the myth of the Catholic league against this country remains strong because all too likely : the myth is so strong as to withstand the contradiction of the most elementary facts about the international situation—for example, that France and Spain are so distrustful of each other that no peace between them can ever be more than a truce ; that both countries have been brought to the point of exhaustion by the war that ended in 1559 ; that France is the theatre of continuous civil wars for the thirty years that follow this peace of Cateau-Cambrésis ; that the revolt of the Netherlands is straining all Spain's resources through all those same thirty years ; that the papacy has, in fact, ceased to count in the counsels of the Catholic kings, who habitually ignore the recommendations of the

---

[1] In fidelity to the traditional *Heilslehre* and *Kirchenbegriff*.

[2] Cf. Sir Ralph Sadler's speech in parliament, Oct. 18, 1566 : " The late accidents in France [i.e. the first Civil War, that had turned out so disastrously for the Huguenots' English ally] the great tyranny and horrible and cruel murders and slaughters which have been committed and executed there upon those of the religion, the like whereof hath never been heard, nor read of, doth plainly show and declare the deadly hatred and malice of the Papists against the professors of God's gospel and true religion. . . ." Once the Catholic princes of the Continent have settled the religious problem of their own countries they will turn all their strength to restore the Catholic religion in England " where they may be sure to find a great aid of our nation of our English Papists ". Sadler Papers, II, 548–552 ; quoted Neale, *Elizabeth I and her Parliaments*, I, 138.

[3] The " pope and his confederates . . . hold this as a firm and settled opinion that England is the only sovereign monarchy that doth most maintain and countenance religion ". England is the " great obstacle that standeth between him and the overflowing of the world again with popery ". Sir Walter Mildmay, Chancellor of the Exchequer, speaking for the government, House of Commons, Jan. 25, 1581, quoted Neale, *op. cit.*, 382.

successive popes and defy their orders whenever national policies so demand.

The obvious facts of a political situation—it is notorious—have usually been more than religious enthusiasts are prepared to take into account, but it is hard to believe that the Elizabethan statesmen were really as unaware as the clerics they promoted—or as we tend to be—that " the main task which [Charles V] had left unaccomplished " to his successor was the defence of Spain against the Turks.[1] The overthrow of what Elizabeth had accomplished in 1559 was no more the principal concern of Philip II, in the years 1559–1572, than the progress of Lutheranism had been for his father. The permanent anxiety continued to be what it had been for forty years nearly : whether the Turks were to dominate Spain, and indeed Europe ; whether militant Mohammedanism, organised under a sultan, Soliman the Magnificent, who was " perhaps the ablest ruler in Europe during the century ",[2] was to triumph—a ruler whose domain reached from Buda, within a hundred miles of Vienna, to Basra on the Persian Gulf, who could put into the field a trained army of a quarter of a million, and who was, at the accession of Philip II, " undisputably " supreme in the Mediterranean.[3]

And it is these much-distracted, Continental potentates who will soon be seen by other Englishmen—leading English Catholics—as their only hope in this world ; these princes who, whatever the truth about the social unity of Christendom, can barely maintain their own power internationally, and who, whatever they do, must always act, first of all, to ensure their own interest. In these centuries, however—and for some time yet to come—there is only one way, even in England, for an opposition to triumph : by force of arms. And the classic way is for the opposition to become possessed of the nucleus of a powerful army outside the realm, and to conduct a successful invasion under the leadership of some kinsman of the sovereign, the means of triumph in 1485 and again in 1688. In the first years of Elizabeth's reign, however, the idea of salvation through this means is to be found only as the wishful thinking of individuals here and there, clerics all;[4] and such dreams are roundly condemned as mischievous and criminal folly by the very princes presumed to be willing to carry them out.[5]

---

[1] Chudoba, 84.　　　[2] Words I borrow from A. J. Grant, 214.　　　[3] Chudoba, 88.

[4] Maurice Clenock, for example, whom Mary had selected for the see of Bangor, writing from Louvain to Cardinal Morone, the cardinal-protector of England, Dec. 6, 1562 : " The bitter oppression grows daily, so that true believers trust to foreign aid for deliverance. . . . Better to strive for eternal salvation under a foreign lord than to be driven into the depths of hell by an enemy at home." Latin text in Meyer, 241, n. 1. Cf. also, in Bayne, 274, the proposals for depriving Elizabeth of the crown and recognising Mary Stuart as queen. This paper, in Pollen's opinion, was drawn up in ? 1561 by Dr. Nicholas Sander at Louvain (*op. cit.*, 77) ; by Morone according to Bayne, 121 ; for Meyer, 38, note 2, it is simply " anonymous and undated . . . apparently belonging to the year 1561."

[5] The Emperor Ferdinand I, for example ; Meyer, 52, and Bayne, 190–192, who prints (p. 298) the letter of the nuncio at the imperial court (June 17, 1563) describing the emperor's anger at the proposal to excommunicate Elizabeth : " *Io non so cosa la quale habbia mai commosso tanto l'Imperatore quanto il trattarsi hora di privar la Regina d'Inghilterra . . .*". Granvelle wrote to Rome, from Brussels, in the same strain (June 27) and Philip II also.

But whether with the Elizabethan Catholic, or with the Elizabethan government bent on exterminating his kind, the fortunes of Catholicism in this country are seen by all as intimately connected with that complex business the international situation. The story of the Catholic resistance to the revolution effected in 1559 cannot be told without continual reference to the history of foreign affairs. And among foreign affairs, as we need to remember, the relations of England with Scotland occupy the first place of all ; [1] and so there must enter into consideration the fact of the Queen of Scots, Mary Stewart. During all these years when, so it is said, the majority of Englishmen would have brought back the pope, and when severe, and ever severer, laws were making it harder and harder for that majority to remain what it wished to be—Catholic, that is to say—the next queen is there, before all men's eyes, and she is a Catholic. At any moment, so long as Mary was alive, a *coup d'état* was possible ; and down would come Cecil, government and all ; the whole pretence would be ended, and the minority be where minorities normally are. For Elizabeth to give the Queen of Scots that recognition as heir which she demanded as her right, would be as good as telling the Protestant party that its day of triumph was to be short. And then what ? And what if Mary were not only the heir, but, at this moment, the rightful queen ?

Whatever the proportion of the English who were Catholics in 1559, and the varying quality of the Catholicism of this great majority of the nation who had not been converted to the new beliefs, the most striking thing about their plight was their utter lack of leaders. Of the 16 bishops alive on May 8, 1559—the day on which the Acts of Supremacy and Uniformity received the royal assent—all but one had, by November, refused the new Oath of Supremacy and been deprived of their sees. And 12 of the bishops, the fact seems certain, had been immediately deprived of their liberty also.[2] Five of the 15 deprived bishops died within a few months.[3] By February, 1560, of the 9 in England, all but Poole were in custody of some kind or under surveillance ; and by the summer of this same year 6 of the 8 were in the

---

Meyer, 471–474, prints extracts from eight letters that passed between the Secretary of State (one day to be St. Charles Borromeo) and Morone, in which the effect of all this on the pope's judgment is clearly set out. They date from June 2 to July 17, 1563.

[1] Cf. Sir Francis Walsingham, when secretary of state, to Sir Christopher Hatton, " Scotland is the postern gate to any mischief or peril that may befall this realm ", July, 1578 ; Conyers Read II, 149–150. " . . . owing to a series of historical accidents the maintenance of England in the Protestant camp [i.e. between 1559 and 1573] depended to a very great extent on the course of events in the land of her northern neighbour ". Maurice Lee, Jr., *James Stewart, Earl of Moray* (1953), p. 5.

[2] Bayne, 54. Cf. the sworn testimony of Edmund Daniel, Dean of Hereford, and of Henry Henshaw, rector of Lincoln College, Oxford, given in 1570, at the enquiry that preceded the excommunication of Elizabeth. Phillips, 126, 127. The three not imprisoned were Morgan of St. David's, a sick man all this year, who died Dec. 23, Poole of Peterborough, also an invalid, and Goldwell of St. Asaph, who made his way to the Continent in June 1559. Bridgett, 232.

[3] Morgan of St. David's, Tunstall of Durham (Nov. 18, 1559), Bayne of Coventry and Lichfield (Nov. 1559), Oglethorpe of Carlisle (Dec. 31, 1559) and White of Winchester (Jan 12, 1560).

Tower,[1] Scot of Chester was in the Fleet and Bonner of London was in the Marshalsea. Scot escaped to the Continent in 1563.[2] The other 8, for as long as they lived, were the prisoners of the state, at times in prisons properly so called, sometimes in the custody of those who held their places since the consecrations of 1559–1562.

The reason for this careful segregation of the bishops, from the first weeks of the new régime, is obvious ; the pretext in law was, seemingly, that they were persons excommunicated for the offence of neglecting to assist at the new religious services. Their imprisonment was a matter about which the new government and its clerical allies were very sensitive, and the legend then carefully created, by Cecil himself,[3] that the deposed prelates—excepting Bonner—lived in a certain honourable retirement under formal restriction, has lasted until our own time, despite the detailed exposition of the facts made possible now that the state papers of the time are available for study.[4]

---

[1] Pate of Worcester, Bourne of Bath and Wells, Turberville of Exeter, Thirlby of Ely, Watson of Lincoln, Heath of York.

[2] In April or May. He died at Louvain, Oct. 9, 1564 ; Phillips, 197–198.

[3] See Bridgett's criticism of the legend, *op. cit.*, ch. I, and also Phillips, *op. cit.*, ch. III. The pedigree of the legend seems to be (1) the alteration made by Cox, Bishop of Ely, with the approval of Parker and Cecil (and without the knowledge of the author) in the treatise against the bull excommunicating Elizabeth, commissioned from the pen of Bullinger, 1570 ; (2) Cecil's pamphlet *The Execution of Justice*, etc. defending the death penalty as a sanction for the anti-Catholic laws, 1583 ; (3) Lancelot Andrews' *Tortura Torti*, 1609 ; (4) Camden's *Annales*, 1615.

The legend is admirably summarised in Pollard's account, *H.E.*, VI, 357. " The Marian bishops were, indeed, kept in a confinement which varied with their attitude to the government. Most of them were placed as guests in the homes of their successors ; [who, as Pollard's own note on this page shows, were doing their best to have these " guests " put to death] they were not required to attend Anglican services ; [whereas, actually, their imprisonment was, it seems, due precisely to their disobeying such a requirement] and some enjoyed facilities for hearing mass ; [i.e. from the report of a government spy we learn that Heath sometimes managed, by stealth, to have mass said in his house during a period when he was out of the Tower] Heath lived unmolested in his own house at Chobham, where he was occasionally visited by Elizabeth." For which last statement see Bridgett's account of Heath as " the pet specimen of Elizabethan clemency ", *op. cit.*, 108 ff., and Phillips, ch. XVIII. As for the life of the " guests " cf. the *Form to be observed by my Lords the Bishops in the ordering of such as were committed to their custody for Popery*, Brit. Mus., Lansdowne MSS, 155, fo. 198 f. printed *infra*, Appendix IV, p. 414. This *Form* was issued to the bishops by the council in 1577. There is nothing in the way the Elizabethan bishops spoke and wrote of their predecessors that will lead us to think that the severities prescribed in this little code were a revolutionary change for the worse, save Parker's references to Thirlby.

[4] It has been made a point in Elizabeth's favour that she did no more than imprison the deprived bishops ; e.g. " . . . they were but seldom sent to the Tower ", Pollard, *op. cit.*, 218 ; " . . . they were not subjected to the full rigour of the law ", Black, 16 ; " . . . despite a Protestant howl for vengeance not one was executed ", Bindoff, 193. The facts are against all three of these authors. All the bishops save one were imprisoned from within a few weeks of their deprivation ; the laws they had broken were the Acts that commanded them to take the Oath of Supremacy and to assist at the new services in their parish churches every Sunday and feast day, and they had suffered the penalties provided, i.e. deprivation (under the first of these Acts) and, under the second, excommunication followed by imprisonment at the behest of the Royal Commissioners appointed to administer the Act. And if " the Protestant howl " did not succeed, this was only because the government's legislation was faulty and because the bishop chosen for the experiment, Bonner, was too good a lawyer not to know this and how to make use of it. Cf. *supra*, pp. 42–43.

The bishops thus disposed of, and the clerical *universitaires* who remained Catholic,[1] to whom could the ordinary people look for any leadership worthy the name of organisation ? What non-Protestant nobles had appeared in parliament in the critical session of 1559, had voted with the government ; and in the elections to the House of Commons the government had had no difficulty—so far as we know—in securing the election of men likely to support it. We must not begin by supposing, what was not to come into existence for another good hundred years and more, the constituency with which we are familiar, nor the possibility of a national campaign in which issues are made clear, and opposing arguments countered by party propaganda ; and, supposing this, then ask why the Catholic case was not better managed. England was not yet ruled in this way. Parliaments were not yet that kind of thing.

Under the circumstances, all that the Catholic loyal to his faith could do was, as an individual, to disobey the law and risk the consequences. Since those consequences were serious always, and could be extremely serious, the question occurred to him, naturally enough, how far could he in conscience obey the law ? And the only law that affected everyone immediately was that obliging all to be present in the parish church at the religious service on all Sundays and feast days, under penalty of a shilling fine for every absence, to be levied by the churchwardens and applied as a poor rate— the prospect of a steady drain of several shillings weekly from the average householder, if, with himself, all his family followed a Catholic conscience, and if the churchwardens were keen and could not be managed.[2] And what was this service ? To sit in church and listen to psalms, said or sung, in his own language,[3] the words of which had nothing whatever to do with the doctrines now in dispute, and, as well as to psalms, to listen to prayers that were largely translations of the collects used in these parish churches for a thousand years. There was, of course, the homily—this would make little difference, unless the rector or vicar was educated and a zealot. The really insuperable difficulty, the new Communion Service, would come round

[1] Rishton (1585)—who matriculated at Brasenose College, Oxford in 1568 and took his bachelor's degree in Arts in 1572—says sweepingly, " The very flower of the two universities, Oxford and Cambridge, was carried away, as it were, by a storm, and scattered in foreign lands." More particularly he writes, " Some three hundred persons, of all conditions, went away at once into different parts of Europe, but especially, to the Belgian universities " [i.e. Louvain and Douay], Lewis, 261. " On the visitors going to the different colleges [in 1559] they did not obtain signature or oath from one in twenty ", Sander told the cardinal protector of England (Morone) in 1561, of Oxford. Sander was, at the time, fellow of New College. Dodd (1737) gave a list of 25 heads of colleges of both universities and of 35 fellows of Oxford Colleges, who left or were expelled by reason of the Acts of 1559. It is reprinted in T.-D., II, p. cccxvi.

[2] This Fine was " continually imposed and collected . . . consistently enforced throughout the period [1559-] " Kennedy, *E.E.A.*, I, p. cci.

[3] Meyer, 71–72, suggests that the novelty of a service in their own tongue would be a great attraction, arguing from what Harding and Sander wrote to the cardinal-protector, June 11, 1567 : " Experience has taught us, that even under Catholic jurisdiction people were so bitterly unwilling to surrender these very bibles [i.e. the heretical translation], that they rather clung to them all the more strongly the more the law forbade possession of them." Latin text, *ibid.*, 477.

very rarely, no more than once a quarter, with luck. Could it be so wrong to sit in one's own church on Sundays while the new services went on—as almost every Catholic did [1]—saying one's own Catholic prayers out of one's own Catholic primer meanwhile ? [2]

It is not surprising if such questions were eagerly debated. And when the more learned of the deprived clergy were consulted, the solutions differed. Dr. Alban Langdale, for example, deprived of his archdeaconry of Chichester for refusing the oath of Supremacy—and thereby, it might be thought, a kind of confessor for the faith—held that Catholics might do this with a safe conscience, provided they did so in order not to be disloyal to the queen and without any approval of the service and its implications.[3] William Allen, till lately the principal of a hall at Oxford, was, at the same time, preaching the contrary of this to his friends and kinsmen among the squires of Lancashire. The difficulties he would meet are very strikingly brought out in the letter of another Lancashire priest, who was, at this time, a much more notable personage than Allen. This was Laurence Vaux, a man now fifty years of age or so, who until the changes of 1559 drove him forth, had been at the head of the greatest ecclesiastical foundation in Lancashire, warden of the collegiate church of Manchester, and so responsible for the spiritualities of all the twenty townships of that great parish.[4]

[1] " . . . at the beginning of the reign of the queen, when the danger of this schism was not very well realised, for ten consecutive years practically all Catholics without distinction used to go to their churches . . .", Persons to Agazzari, Nov. 17, 1580. *Persons*, 58. Cf. also Edward Rishton, the continuator of Sander's *Rise and Growth of the Anglican Schism*, writing in 1585, " And thus by force or fraud it came to pass that the largest portion of the Catholics yielded by degrees to their enemies, and did not refuse from time to time publicly to enter the schismatical churches to hear sermons therein, and to receive communion in those conventicles ", English translation by Lewis (1877), 266–267.

[2] " There be many in the Diocese of Chichester, which bring to the church with them the popish Latin primers, and use to pray upon them all the time when the Lessons be a reading and in the time of the Litany. . . . Some old folks and women there used to have beads in the Church, and those I took away from them : but they have some yet at home in their houses." *Disorders in the Diocese of Chichester contrary ·to the Queen's Majesty's Injunctions*, P.R.O., S.P. 12, Vol. 60, no. 71. And cf. Birt, 427–430.

[3] The authorities for Dr. Langdale being of this opinion are Persons (C.R.S., II, 28, 180–181 ; IV, 2–7) and a MSS. treatise, now at Oscott College, Birmingham, for which cf. Bayne, 289, 290, 283. For the doubt whether Alban Langdale has been confused with his nephew, Thomas Langdale, the apostate Jesuit, cf. Gillow, IV, s.v. Langdale, Alban, 117–118. Alban Langdale, described in a report on recusants, 1561, as " learned and very earnest in papistry ", had been a fellow of St. John's, Cambridge. He had defended Transubstantiation against Edward VI's visitors of the university in 1549, and was one of the Catholic party in the Westminster disputation of 1559. From the time of his deprivation he lived in the household of Antony Browne, first Viscount Montague, the son of Henry VIII's old Master of the Horse, and the only lay lord to vote with the bishops against the Act of Supremacy in 1559.

[4] Laurence Vaux, born at Blackrod, in Lancashire, 1519, was educated (probably) at Manchester Grammar School, and at Oxford (Queen's and Corpus Christi). He was ordained 1542, at Manchester, and named to a fellowship in the collegiate church. In Mary's reign he was named warden. In 1559 he was deprived for his refusal to accept the new Acts of Supremacy and Uniformity and made his way to Louvain. In 1572 he became a canon-regular (Augustinian). He died in 1585 in the Clink prison, London, after five years of imprisonment. There is an excellent account of his career in T. G. Law's edition of his *Catechism*, Chetham Society, N.S. 4, 1885, pp. 96. Manchester parish had 6,000 " houseling people " in 1547.

This letter, dated November 2, 1566, is seemingly meant to be circulated. It opens abruptly : " I understand by your letter that ye be in doubt how to understand the letter sent from M. Doctor Sanders to me. . . . Concerning M. Doctor Sanders' letter, I am charged, to make a definitive sentence that all such as offer children to the baptism now used, or be present at the communion or service now used in churches in England, as well the laity as the clergy, do not walk in the state of salvation, neither we may not communicate or sociate ourselves in company with schismatics or heretics in divine things : there is no exception or dispensation can be had for any of the laity if they will stand in the state of salvation.   Ye must not think this be any severity or rigorousness of the Pope, Pius V, that now is God's Vicar in earth, to whom at this present God hath appointed the government of His Church in earth : . . . The Pope that now is hath no less zeal and good will to reduce England to the unity of Christ His Church than St. Gregory had, as he hath showed himself both in word and deed.   And partly I heard him myself express in words and deed, being with him in his own private chamber at Rome : by my special friends I was brought into his chamber to hear him speak himself what a benefit was granted in the Consistory for England, to the intent I might make more plain declaration to Mr. Doctor Sanders and Dr. Harding concerning the authority granted unto them in the Consistory by the Pope for the soul's health of them that dwell in England. . . . I must therefore without halting, colouring, or dissembling, let tell you that the Pope cannot dispense any of the laity to entangle themselves with the schism as is aforewritten concerning sacraments and service : that ye may not be present amongst them.   If ye associate yourselves at sacraments or service that is contrary to the unity of Christ His Church, ye fall in schism, that is to say, ye be separated from Christ His Church, and living in that state (as saith St. Augustine) although you lead never so good a life in the sight of the world, the wrath of God hangeth over you, and dying in that state shall lose the everlasting life in Heaven.   It is no small danger to continue in schism.   And ordinarily no priest in England hath authority to absolve from schism, except he have his authority from the Catholic See by Mr. Doctor Sanders and Mr. Doctor Harding, etc. . . . There is not one of the old bishops [1] nor godly priests of God that will be present at the schismatical service or damnable communion now used.   For the which cause all have lost their living, some be in corporal prison, some in exile, and like good pastors be ready to suffer death in that cause.   As it is the duty and office of the bishops to go before their flock as their leaders in matters of faith in religion, so the clergy and laity are bound to follow their examples, if they intend to be partakers with the bishops of the joys of heaven : and, thanks be to God, a number not only of the clergy, but, as well, of the temporality, both of them that be worshipful and inferior to them, do follow their bishops constantly, and will in no wise come at the schismatical service. Such as frequent the schismatical service now used in the church in England,

[1] Heath, Bonner, Bourne, Thirlby, Poole, Turberville and Watson are still alive, and all, at this moment, in custody.

must either contemn them as fond foolish men that refuse to be present at service, or else their own conscience will accuse them that they do nought in that they do contrary to the examples given them of the bishops. I beseech you to consider all the days that you have to live in this world, although ye might a thousand years, is but a moment in comparison of the life everlasting. What doth it profit a man to have solace, pleasure, and prosperity that can be wished in this world, when everlasting torments do follow the same, for by much trouble and adversity we must enter into the glory of God, saith the Scripture ; and as St. James saith, He that will flatter and dissemble with the world is enemy to God ? I pray you the comfortable promise of our Saviour Christ in His Gospel, Whosoever will confess Christ and the faith of His spouse of the Catholic Church before men, He will confess him before His Father in Heaven, and whosoever denieth Christ and His Catholic faith before men, Christ will deny him before His Father in Heaven : he that loseth his life for Christ or the Catholic faith shall find everlasting joys : ye that have followed Me, shall Christ say, shall sit upon the seats judging the tribes of Israel : and at the day of judgment Christ shall say, Ye be they which have tarried with Me in My tentations and adversities, therefore I dispose unto you a kingdom that you may eat and drink upon My table in the kingdom of heaven. Thus, to conclude, your good examples in the premises may not be salvation of only one soul, but upon your examples dependeth the salvation of a great number of the simple that know not the right hand from the left. Although this my rude letter appear hard, sharp, bitter, and sour, yet it is the truth, as I am persuaded in my conscience as I shall answer at the terrible day of judgment : and speaking in God's cause I may not halt or dissemble. What I write here to you I would wish Sir Richard Mollineux, Sir W. Norris, and other my friends to be partakers, not only to hear this my rude letter, but to follow this counsel. Although it be simple and rude, yet I doubt not but it is true, as knoweth the Lord, who ever keep you and yours in health and prosperity. November 2, Anno 1566. Yours ever, L. V.

" Whosoever will be saved, afore all things in heart, word, and deed, he must keep the Catholic faith firmly, wholly, and inviolate, or else without doubt he shall perish in everlasting pain. Thus saith our creed— Athanasius." [1]

One counsellor whom the Catholics consulted in the first years of the régime, was the Spanish ambassador, Alvarez de Quadra, who was a bishop as well as a diplomat. In a letter to his colleague the Spanish ambassador at Rome, August 7, 1562,[2] de Quadra explains how he has acted on such occasions. The prayer service about which the Catholics have consulted him, " does not contain any false doctrine ", he says, " nor anything wicked, for it is made up of scripture and of prayers taken from the Catholic Church,

---

[1] This letter (i.e. a copy) printed by Law, xxxii–ix, is in the P.R.O. SP/12, Vol. 41, no. 1.
[2] The Spanish original is printed in Bayne, 293–295, *q.v.*, also ch. viii, *Attendance at the English Church Service*, 159–181.

though from some they have cut out all that has reference to the merits and intercession of the saints ". Setting on one side, he says, the sin of dissimulation, and the harm that comes of the example given, the act of being present at such services is not, of its nature, an act that is evil. The bishop was torn between the fear of encouraging other Catholics to give way, and reluctance to condemn those who had gone to the service. To lay down a general rule, he remarks, was not easy, the Catholics being so differently situated and the question whether scandal was given so complex. What he had done was to console those who had gone to the services, by minimising the offence—lest they be driven to desperation ; and to encourage in their resistance those who, so far, had held firm. The matter called for authoritative decision, the bishop declared, and it was necessary that someone in England should be given the necessary powers for the absolution of those who, by unlawful acts of this kind, fell into sin. And he begged Vargas to lay all this before the pope.[1]

And when to such zealous priests as Laurence Vaux guidance was given, whether from the Council then in session at Trent,[2] or next, from the pope in

[1] The answer to the bishop's letter was given by the Roman tribunal called popularly the Inquisition, Oct. 2, 1562, printed in Bayne, 296–297. It is important to notice what this is, i.e. a reply given to what is explicitly set out in the opening words as the case put before them—*Casus est*, the document begins. This " case " is a correct summary of de Quadra's letter to Vargas—but how far is this letter a true picture of the dilemma of the English Catholics ? Bayne, 176, says " exaggeration which bordered on direct falsehood ". It is certainly not surprising that on the case presented the Inquisitors answered with a peremptory negative the question whether subjects who were faithful Catholics could be present at such services without danger of eternal damnation. Bayne also prints (297–298) the brief of Pius IV to the ambassador giving him powers to reconcile repentant heretics who wish to return to the Catholic Church. The pope also empowers the bishop to delegate these powers to suitable priests. This brief is dated Oct. 2, 1562. We know that the bishop received it, for he notified Philip II and asked his advice about how he should use these powers. What Philip replied is not known. But in less than a year the bishop was dead (Aug., 1563).

As to the reply of the Inquisition, it never came to the knowledge of the English Catholics. " None of the writers on the subject, neither Sanders, Allen, Martin, nor Persons, refer to it ; an almost certain proof that it was not known to them." Bayne, 180.

[2] For the appeal to Trent see Bayne, 162–173. A paper was drawn up, stating the case, and given to the Spanish and Portuguese ambassadors for despatch to the council. The Spaniard, as we have just seen, wrote directly to Rome. But his colleague, Mascareynas, did exactly as he was asked. Bayne prints (290–291) the Latin text of the petition. It is to be found in the Vatican archives among the papers relating to the Council of Trent. The only reference to the time is the statement that heads it, " given in to their Lordships the Legates, August 2, 1562 ". English conditions are more moderately described in this, the actual petition, than in the Spanish ambassador's letter to Vargas : it is evident, from a comparison of the petition dated Aug. 2 and the reply of the Inquisition, that the Inquisition had the actual text of the English petition before them, and not only the letter of Aug. 7 to Vargas in which de Quadra enclosed it. The last sentence of the petition is interesting, *Qui in Anglia nunc sunt Theologi partim metuunt partim varie respondent. Ibid.*, 291. This petition the legates sent on to Rome for the pope's own consideration. It would reach Pius IV about the time when he had before him the petition sent by Quadra with the bishop's letter to Vargas.

Did the Legates bring the matter before the council in any form ? No record of this has been found. But we have evidence that, within a few years of the petition, an alleged opinion of a committee appointed by the council was circulating in England ; and this opinion was quoted as a notorious fact by controversialists such as Gregory Martin (1578) and Persons (1580) and others. For all which, and for the question whether we have an authentic text of the opinion, cf. Bayne, 165–170.

person, who was to guarantee the news—the unwelcome news to many—as it spread around, that Catholics must choose between the two ways, and if they wished to be Catholics must never again even be present at the new rites ?

Percutiam pastores, it was Scripture and in the very record of the Passion of Christ, and had there been a first time verified, *et dispergentur oves gregis* The whole body of bishops swept out of existence at a blow, and all their officials ; their jurisdiction rendered a mere word ; and what was left but so many hundred thousand isolated individuals, and a world of rumours, and disputes that went on interminably ? what time ambiguity made its offers and slowly conquered. Isolated, indeed : " At no other period did Catholics see themselves so utterly forsaken by the Church, or so entirely cut off from communication with Rome, as at this period—especially in the seven years between the close of the Council of Trent and the Queen's excommunication. Neither pope nor council, neither emperor nor Spanish king, had done anything whatsoever for them ; not one priest had been sent to them. ' Who would ever have believed that until now [1570] the Roman court would have done so little to win back this island which has always been so faithful ? ' " [1]

And these isolated priests and squires, had they then known what forces were busy in Rome determining their fate! For it was with the two Habsburg sovereigns—with Philip II above all—that the last word lay ; they alone could be expected to act, to carry out, for example, a papal sentence of deposition ; and it was these two princes who, through all these first years of the reign, vetoed every suggestion of such papal action—Philip II, indeed, fearful lest actual contact between Elizabeth and the pope should occasion a crisis, successfully intervening to prevent all contact and holding up at Brussels the nuncios sent to Elizabeth by Pius IV, as Charles V had held up Pole at Dillingen a few years earlier.[2]

The full story of these diplomatic manoeuvres shows that, as so often, we must qualify the language which the most approved authors have used—in this instance about the pope's responsibility for the " isolation ". The efforts of the pope did not succeed ; and, since they were efforts " through

[1] Meyer, 67 ; whose quotation is from the *Discorso* of an anonymous English writer found by Meyer in the Vatican archives (*Misc.*, II, t. 84, fo. 32.) Cf. Kennedy for a like judgment (*E.E.A.*, I, p. cliv) : " In addition, the papal oracle remained silent and the thunders of a Roman pronouncement did not roar. Was the pope, too, at the mercy of policy ? Was the *vox Dei* smothered by the *vox clamantis* of the European wilderness ? Who could tell ? The Marian party could only wait in hushed anticipation as each day found its own sufficiency."

[2] " Fertile though the period was in strange contradictions between religion and worldly policy, one of the strangest is the circumstance that the Catholic King, who was afterwards to be the executor of the bull of excommunication, began, without intending it, by being the ally of the English reformers." Meyer, 35. Pollen, 64, describes Philip as keeping the ring " while Protestantism secured its final triumph throughout these islands " ; and also, " Philip certainly knew what would be the result of a complete victory by Elizabeth, yet, spellbound by fear of France, he looked on with but a few protests while the heretical Queen crushed the old order in England ", *ibid.*, 87. Neither writer, nor Kennedy (last note) has remembered the Turks—unlike Elizabeth, who ordered thanksgivings for Lepanto.

diplomatic channels ", the Catholics in England doubtless knew nothing about them. But what had happened was, in summary,[1] as follows.

Pius IV, the cool-headed jurist who took the place of Pole's enemy, the hasty-tempered Carafa pope, in 1559,[2] acted, one might say, with great speed. Only four months after his election, understanding well the impasse in which Elizabeth's intervention in Scotland had landed the queen,[3] he commissioned an envoy to her with " an olive branch " ; but he meant Elizabeth to realise that if she refused it he held a sword in reserve ".[4] This envoy was Pole's one-time agent for diplomatic business, Vincenzo Parpaglia. He left Rome on May 25, 1560, and by June 16 was at Brussels.

The pope, on May 3, had told Philip II's ambassador, Vargas, what he proposed to do ; and Vargas, the same who, from Venice, in 1553, had been so effectively hostile to Pole's mission,[5] protested effectively once again. When he wrote to his sovereign, Philip II, with quite unusual promptitude, replied on June 1, also protesting : the mission, he thought, could only irritate the queen and make the lot of the Catholics more harsh. The king also wrote to his government in Flanders to hold up Parpaglia, until further advised from Rome.

Elizabeth had heard, by now, what was afoot ; she was seriously alarmed, and showed this by increased severity towards the Catholics—it was now, for example, that the deprived bishops were transferred to the Tower and other public prisons. Philip's regent in the Low Countries, his half-sister Margaret, Duchess of Parma,[6] received the king's orders in time to halt the pope's envoy, and the Spanish ambassador in Rome worked so well that, on July 10, orders were sent to Parpaglia not to go further and to be guided by the advice of the Spanish king's government. Whereupon, between the regent and the king's ambassador in London a face-saving plan was devised, so that the pope (and the delicate situation) might be spared the shock of an English refusal to admit the envoy—a refusal which Elizabeth was now well-placed to give, the Queen-regent of Scotland dead (June 6) and the Treaty of Edinburgh signed (July 10). With de Quadra's letter to Parpaglia, of July 25, the first initiative of the Holy See, *vis-à-vis* Elizabeth, came to an end.[7]

Parpaglia left Brussels in November, 1560. Already Philip II was saying to the pope that the more opportune moment for intervention had now arrived, with the despatch to all Catholic princes—and even to the Protestant princes of Germany—of the formal invitation to be represented

---

[1] For an admirably documented account—a rare model, indeed—cf. Bayne, 40–61 and 73–116.

[2] The Cardinal Gian Angelo de Medici, a Milanese and no kin of the great Florentine family, born 1499, a courageous critic who withstood Paul IV to the face ; he was elected, unexpectedly, Dec. 25, in the last days of a conclave that had gone on since August.

[3] Bayne, 45.

[4] *Ibid.*, 46 ; and 250–251, i.e. Borromeo to nuncio in Spain, May 4, 1560 ; and, 254–256, Vargas to Philip II, May 6.   [5] Cf. Vol. II, 213–214.

[6] The real power in the Low Countries, at this time, was the chief minister, Antoine Perrenot de Granvelle (1517–1586), now a cardinal and Archbishop of Mechlin.

[7] Bayne (p. 61) thinks that Parpaglia's admission in June might have led to a rebellion ; no doubt against the Elizabeth-Cecil régime and the system of 1559.

at the General Council summoned to resume its work at Trent. In February, 1561, the Pope heard, through the Duke of Savoy, that according to Elizabeth's ambassador in Paris—the Earl of Bedford—the queen also wished to be invited.[1]

Pius IV now chose to bear the invitation a more dignified personage, Girolamo Martinengo, who had in his time served as nuncio at Vienna; and the envoy's commission was limited to the business of the council; there was no longer any note of menace. But the brief to Elizabeth, accrediting Martinengo and inviting her to be represented at Trent, had scarcely been drawn (March 4, 1561) when Vargas appeared, to say that his master, once more, must object. In a letter of February 9 Philip II had expressed his disapproval, for the same reasons that he had urged against the earlier mission [2]—Elizabeth, if irritated, might turn to France, and revenge herself on the Catholics in England. When Vargas put this to the pope there was a lively scene. But despite all the evidence that the pope put out in reply, and despite the arguments of cardinals called in as knowledgeable, Vargas steadily refused to believe that Elizabeth seriously desired to take part in the council.[3] He was in the right. All through this year, 1561— as we now know—from January to May, the queen's envoys in Germany and France were ceaselessly busy in an attempt to wreck the council, persuading the princes to take no part in it.[4] Why, then, this double-policy of the queen?[5] It was not, now, any desperate crisis of foreign affairs that invited her to make much of Spain. But the fleeting moment has arrived when it seems possible for the queen to make the only marriage she ever desired, and Elizabeth is caught by it.[6] Amy Robsart is but four months dead, and in January, 1561, Dudley is seeking through Henry Sidney the support of the King of Spain. On February 13 Dudley himself speaks of it to Philip's ambassador, and on February 15 the queen gives de Quadra audience to lay her mind before him. And all this de Quadra sends on to Spain. The king's reply is dated March 19. He welcomes the news, and since he is willing to make whatever profit he can out of the scheme he favours it. But he is utterly sceptical about the queen's good faith, and lays down a series of conditions. The queen must pledge herself to release the Catholic bishops, to grant toleration to the Catholics, to send ambassadors (and the Catholic bishops) to the Council of Trent, and to submit unconditionally to the decrees of the council.[7]

For a nuncio to appear in London now might, however, wreck the chances (whatever chances there are) of this delicate scheme. On the same day that

[1] Bayne, 77.   [2] *Ibid.*, App. 25 for the letter.

[3] Vargas to Philip II, March 15, 1561, *ibid.*, App. 27.

[4] Bayne, 79, quoting Elizabeth's instructions to her envoys in *Foreign Calendar*, 1560–1561, no. 826.

[5] " But at the same time as her ambassadors abroad were striving to unite England, France, and protestant Germany in opposition to Rome, she and her ministers at home were negotiating with Spain in a more friendly spirit, holding out hopes of reconciliation and professing readiness to send representatives to the assembly which was about to meet at Trent." Bayne, 84–85.   [6] For what follows, cf. Bayne, 85 ff.

[7] *Ibid.*, 87. The king's letter is in the *Spanish Calendar*, 1560–1568, 185.

he wrote to de Quadra the king wrote again to Rome, instructing Vargas to maintain the protest against the mission and telling him that Granvelle has been ordered to detain Martinengo, in anticipation that the pope, persuaded by Vargas, will send orders that the nuncio is not to proceed further.[1] Vargas was putting his last demand to the pope about the time that Martinengo reached Brussels (i.e. April 18) and Pius IV, as Vargas' letter of April 23 to the king [2] relates, was in fact won round to consent ; so that all the negotiations now going forward between the unconscious de Quadra and Elizabeth, and between de Quadra and Cecil—the question of the protocol, of the house to be hired for the nuncio at Greenwich and so forth—were sterilised ere they were yet concluded.   Cecil, who detested both the marriage scheme and the scheme to receive an envoy from Rome, was yet, by necessity, the patient official negotiator for both.   What next happened, and so profitably for his own position, can hardly have happened entirely by accident.

By the time Martinengo received his orders not to move from Flanders until Rome further instructed him, a miniature *révolution de palais* in London had brought down the whole house of cards.   De Quadra, to begin with, had deliberately disregarded his master's instructions of March 19, and had not even mentioned to the queen the pledges he was ordered to obtain from her.   He thought it a better way (and he persuaded Granvelle also of this) that Martinengo should be sent over without more ado.   His reception (or non-reception) would be a better test than signatures whether Elizabeth's offers were genuine.[3]   But on the very day of the favourable audience with the queen, April 13, which de Quadra reported to Brussels in his letter of April 14, a priest was arrested, as he was leaving England, in whose baggage a rosary was found and a breviary.   When examined the priest admitted the crime of having said Mass, and he gave away the names of some of his Catholic hosts, such great personages as Sir Thomas Wharton and Sir Edward Waldegrave, lords of the council under Queen Mary.[4]   Whereupon there was a general hunt for Catholic notables, a nephew of Cardinal Pole was sent to the Tower and a third one-time councillor of Mary Tudor was taken, Lord Hastings of Loughborough.   The imprisoned bishops were closely interrogated, and "the questions show the direction in which Cecil was walking.

[1] Philip II to Vargas, March 19, 1561, Bayne, App. 28.
[2] *Ibid.*, App. 29.   [3] *Ibid.*, 92.
[4] *Ibid.*, 99–103 for this incident and its consequences.   One detail is worth recording, in view of what the years were now to bring : the suggestion is made that the priest ought to be tortured, and it is made (with the jest appropriate for such a matter) by two ex-priests, the new Bishops of London and Ely.   " Some think that if this Priest, Haverd, might be put to some kind of Torment, and so driven to confess what he knoweth, he might gain the Queen's Majesty a good Mass of Money by the Masses he hath said : But this we lay to your Lordship's Wisdom, and so commit the same to Almighty God ", so the two prelates write to the Council.   They had been " to examine the Sayer and Hearers of the Mass at my Lady Carew's House . . .", they continue, " meaning thereby to find knowledge of more of that sort " ; But they achieved little, for " neither the Priest nor any of his auditors, not so much as the Kitchen Maid will receive any oath before us [and they] say also they will neither accuse themselves nor none other ".   Sept. 13, 1562, Haynes, 395.   The torture, be it noted, is to be used on the priest, as it will always be used, i.e. to wring from him an admission of sacramental ministry and the names of those to whom he ministered.

He desired to show that a project was afoot for restoring the old religion, and that Waldegrave, Wharton and Hastings, old councillors of Queen Mary, the imprisoned bishops and de Quadra were concerned in it. When the nuncio came over, the Protestant party would be forced to return to the Communion of Rome." [1]

While all this chase after the enemies of the state was in full cry came St. George's Day, and the annual meeting of the Knights of the Garter. At this eleven knights were present [2]—among whom Dudley : but when it was put to them, by Sussex, that they should petition the queen to marry Dudley, the knights preferred instead to make only a general petition, that the queen should marry : it was a defeat for the queen's desires that Elizabeth bitterly and openly resented, saying that when she did marry she would follow the taste of no one but herself. " These brave words veiled defeat." [3] And in reaction the queen swung over completely to Cecil who had defeated her. " Before the end of April he had persuaded her to refuse admission to Martinengo ".[4] He was able to tell de Quadra, on April 25, that it would not be possible to allow the nuncio to come : a conspiracy had been discovered, a papal legate was busy stirring up rebellion in Ireland ; and was not de Quadra, too, involved in all this, in a way ? [5] And at the ambassador's next audience Elizabeth accused him of spreading stories that Dudley was persuading her to become a Catholic.[6]

All was over, very evidently. It only remained to give this second invitation from Pius IV the *coup de grâce*. At the Privy Council, on May 1, when the question came up whether to admit Martinengo, the acting Lord Chancellor [7] silenced all possibility of support by an official explanation that, under the statute of 1559, anyone who voted for the admission of a nuncio was guilty of high treason.[8]

Spain, whatever the losses of the French in the recent war, had herself come out of it too badly damaged for the king not to be anxious, most of all, for the next few years, that France should not be the first to recover. Not only was Philip II, in these years, not in a position to carry out a papal

---

[1] Bayne, 102.

[2] Norfolk, Northampton (i.e. Parr), Arundel, Derby, Sussex, Pembroke, Montague, Howard of Effingham, Paget, Clinton, and Lord Robert Dudley ; *ibid.*, 108.

[3] *Ibid.*, 108.　　　　[4] *Ibid.*, 108.　　　　[5] *Ibid.*, 109.　　　　[6] *Ibid.*, 109.

[7] Which in effect is what the Lord Keeper of the Great Seal was, Sir Nicholas Bacon—after Cecil the most Protestant of the " technicians " in the council.

[8] The official minute of " the consultation had at Greenwich, May 1, 1561, by the queen's majesty's commandment ", is printed in T.-D., II, Appendix, no XLVIII. It should be compared with the account which Cecil sent, on May 8, to the third of the Protestant triumvirate, the ambassador at Paris, Sir Nicholas Throckmorton, for which see Pollen, *English Catholics*, 70–71. " When I saw this Romish influence towards about one month past, I thought necessary to dull the papists' expectation by discovering of certain massmongers and punishing of them as I do not doubt but you have heard of them. I take God to record I mean no evil to any of them but only for the rebating of the papists' humours, which by the Queen's Majesty's lenity grew too rank ". Fr. Pollen makes a good case (against Bayne's criticism) for describing Cecil's conduct as hypocritical ; but he is wrong in making Winchester one of Cecil's " best pillars ". The " my Lord Marquis " of Cecil's letter is Northampton, as the minute in T.-D. shows.

sentence against Elizabeth but, lest he drive Elizabeth into the arms of France, the king must tolerate whatever injuries and insults the queen's government chose to heap upon him. And in England his ambassador was commanded to damp down every show of Catholic enthusiasm for action, the which he did, repeating to those who approached him with plans the words of St. Paul, " Let every soul be subject to the higher powers ".[1] De Quadro's predecessor, the Count de Feria, had told Philip, in the first weeks after Philip had ceased to be King Consort, that " The Catholics in this country . . . place all their hope in your majesty ".[2] The bishop's successor, de Silva, was now to assure the king, " I have advised the Catholics to avoid all occasions for such accusations [as that they speak against the Queen] as it is not prudent to offend her. Rather let them treat matters which are not against their conscience with moderation and reserve, since respect for superiors is a duty they owe to God." [3]

2

The passive resistance of a large proportion of the parochial clergy to the zeal of the new bishops is a fact which has already been illustrated—the resistance, that is to say, of clergy who had not refused to accept what was put before them by the commissioners of the Royal Visitation of 1559. And from the Catholics who then did refuse, there was, from the beginning, a movement to dislodge the new thing ; even among the captive bishops there are signs of this. We can trace this reaction in such matters as the literary controversy of 1562–1568 ; in the work of Allen and Vaux in Lancashire ; in the attempts of, say, Sander and Clenock, to induce intervention from abroad ; in the endeavour to induce from Rome declarations about the questions of church attendance and the excommunication of the queen. It would not be right nowadays, with all that has come to be known since Simpson wrote, to accept as the whole story the indignant phrases written in his life of Campion. " They were all waiting ", he says of the Catholics of these years, " for something to turn up ; waiting like the drunken man for the door to come round to them, instead of shaking off their lethargy, and walking out through the door. They were waiting for Burghley to die, or for Elizabeth to die, or to marry a Catholic husband, or for the King of Spain to come and depose her ; waiting for fortune to change for them, instead of trying to change their own fortune ; and forgetting that fate unresisted overcomes us, but is conquered by resistance. It was this English dilatoriness, this provisional acquiescence in wrong, this stretching of the conscience in order that men might keep what they had, which made it possible that England should be lost to the Church, as it has since lost many a man who was quite convinced that he ought to be a Catholic, but waited till his conviction had

[1] Meyer, 70, quoting *Span. Cal.*, 389.
[2] Meyer, 34, quoting *Span. Cal.*, 1558–1567, p. 16.
[3] Pollen, 92, quoting the same, p. 389. De Quadra had scruples about such policies. " . . . if we are content to let God's cause go by the board ", he could write to de Feria, Feb. 12, 1560, " it will not take much to drag us down with it ". *Span. Cal., ibid.*, p. 127.

17

faded away. The Catholics waited for the times to mend ; and they waited till their children were brought up to curse the religion of their fathers, till they had been robbed piecemeal of their wealth and power, and found themselves a waning sect in the land they had once occupied from sea to sea." [1]

Nevertheless, it remains true that, among the Catholics in England, there is scarcely any sign of active opposition. In these first ten years of the reign the Catholics were, indeed, " patient, inoffensive, and law-abiding " When, however, historians proceed to say that there was no persecution in these years,[2] they can mean no more than that the government did not ever need to press its laws to their last extreme severity. But if persecution means a régime where, in a matter of religion, penalties are severe enough to deter the ordinary man from disobedience to the state, and then during the time when these laws endure the new obedience decreed becomes well-nigh universal, persecution there most certainly was—unless, what no one will assert, the quasi-universal obedience in these years (say, to the Act of Uniformity), derived from sincere conviction that the new beliefs were the true beliefs and the old belief in the Mass was idolatry. The priest who, after 1559, ceases to say Mass, the people who cease to go to Mass ; the priest who begins to use the new services, the people who begin to attend the new services— if their action is due, not to some such religious conviction but to fear of the law and its penalties, what else are all these but the victims of persecution ? The nature of the law is not altered because the law achieves its purpose silently and without bloodshed : a blockade is as truly, and as terribly, an act of war as a battle.[3] As well as those more obvious victims of persecuting laws whom all later history salutes as the punishment decreed is meted out, there is always the still more numerous array of those who have submitted in despite of conscience : victims of persecution, whose very obedience to the law is a contradiction of the statement that there has been no persecution ; victims who, by reason of these laws, have lost more, much more, than those who, unwaveringly, have gone to exile, to prison, to the stake, to the quartering block ; and in many cases have lost it irrecoverably.

A régime where there are people who obey a law about religion because they dread the penalties, is a régime of persecution. The Englishman who was a Catholic was indeed free, in these years : that is to say, the law would not interfere with his property, his liberty, or his life, so long as he was content never to hear Mass again [4] or to receive Holy Communion ; content that his children should be brought up without either ; willing to go Sunday by

---

[1] Simpson, 8–9.

[2] And most of our historians say this : cf., for example, " There was no persecution of Catholics ; the legislation of 1559 and even of 1563 did not amount to more than exclusion from office ", A. L. Rowse, *The England of Elizabeth* (1950), 440.

[3] *Preferisco io lo strangolamento*, said John Bull, in the Italian cartoon (apropos the economic sanctions of 1936) speaking to the Abyssinian holding up the bleeding head of his victim, *non lascia macchie*.

[4] Cf. the exultation with which Jewel (Bishop of Salisbury now) tells Peter Martyr, March 5, 1560, that the Mass will now cost " every individual spectator . . . 200 crowns." *Z.L.*, 90.

Sunday to his parish church to sit through a service he regarded as heretical and to listen to homilies which caricatured and ridiculed his own beliefs, and condemned them as idolatry, superstition, and treason ; so long as he carefully refrained from any expression of opinion on these extensive changes; so long as he had no ambition for a public career, no desire or need to be either lawyer or schoolmaster ; and so long as he did not have to sue a livery from the crown on coming into his property.[1] Otherwise he was speedily enmeshed. From the very first months of the reign, before the pope had even heard of England's apostasy, while Philip of Spain was still England's good ally, before any Catholic had so much as moved in thought against the victorious Protestants, means were ingeniously provided, in the very Acts that refounded their religious establishment, to make social life well-nigh impossible for all but the Protestant party and those Catholics who, by apostasy, real or feigned, would join them.[2]

What the religious observance was, during these first years of the restored religious supremacy of the crown, of all those who had not been won over to believe the new doctrines, seems fairly clear. The generality strove to combine with their Catholic belief, and their necessarily rare opportunities of Catholic practice, sufficient external observance of the Acts of Supremacy and Uniformity to escape the penalties ; we hear that many pushed their conformity so far that they received the communion of the new rite, priests even saying Mass and then, on the same day, celebrating the Communion Service.[3] The confusion within the party now victorious, that has been described already, assisted the development of this other confusion—among the Catholics : in such a situation Catholics could more easily pose as good " Queen's men " in matters of religion while, in their hearts, they " waited

---

[1] " These petty vexations, harassing enough to the sufferers, perhaps . . . " Black, 134 (a writer by no means unsympathetic to the Elizabethan Catholics).

[2] None would have been more astonished at the Liberal historians' picture of Elizabethan religious liberality (*vis-à-vis* the Catholics) than the first Elizabethan bishops—those who, in these " easy " years, were charged with the administration of these laws. Jewel, for example, commenting on the recent arrest of Bishops Bonner and Watson, of Abbot Feckenham and Dr. Scory, explains to Peter Martyr (May 22, 1560) : " For the queen . . . most manfully and courageously declared that she would not allow any of her subjects to dissent from this religion with impunity." *Z.L.*, 103. And Cox, ten years later, is even more explicit on the subject of what is just not going to be allowed. " Lastly ", he writes to Bullinger (July 10, 1570), " there are among us some papists, and those not of the lowest rank, who strain every nerve that they may be permitted to live according to their consciences, and that no account of his religion be demanded from anyone." *Ibid.*, 335. Which is an interesting contemporary reflection on the much-praised saying of the queen about her policy, that she made no windows to look into men's souls.

[3] Cf. Allen, years later, describing to Vendeville the situation at this time (letter of Sept. 16, 1578, Knox, *op. cit.*, 56). From fear of imprisonment and other penalties Catholics, in times past (*antea*), were so indulgent to themselves that not only did laymen who in their hearts remained unshaken in their Catholic belief, and who at home heard Mass whenever this was possible, go to the churches and services of the schismatics, and even sometimes receive the communion, " but also many priests would say Mass secretly, and publicly celebrate the heretical service and the Supper, often on the very same day (a frightful crime), sharing in the chalice of the Lord and in the chalice of the devils ". Cf. also Persons, quoted *supra*, 248, n. 1, and Rishton, 267.

for a day ", as the saying then went.   But immense harm was done, by these
years of drift, to what survived of the average Catholic's Catholicism,[1] and
a very thoughtful student, reflecting on what we know to have gone on,
suggests that the defining clarity of the queen's excommunication, when
it came, came too late:[2] England had, by 1570, ceased to be a country
where the mass of the people were anxious to be Catholics.   It must be
obvious that conditions had altered greatly for the worse in the seventeen
years since Mary's accession ; and how bad they already were in 1553,
after twenty-four years of the propaganda and the legislation of Henry
VIII and Edward VI, has been already—too often, perhaps—suggested
in these pages.

This situation may be chaotic, to the theologically-minded observer ;
to one not so interested in the question where is truth, and what will be the
fate of a people that loses it, the situation may offer in a high degree the interest which the transitional periods of all revolutions present ; to the leading
figure of English public life in these formative years of Elizabeth's reign, the
Secretary of State, Sir William Cecil, it is a situation that is unexpectedly
peaceful[3]—not perhaps the tranquillity that comes of order, but a state of
things where there are no disturbances, no demonstrations from leading
personalities, and where the opposition achieves nothing beyond talk in

---

[1] When the missionary priests from Douay began their work (from 1574 onwards), their
first task was to convince the Catholics to whom they were sent that it was sinful to attend
these non-Catholic services.   The success they achieved, in a very short time, seemed to
Allen remarkable.   " So it has come about ", he wrote, in 1578, " that not only has an immense number of our people right ideas about religion, but—what was for our priests a much
more laborious task, a matter where they faced keener opposition—it has come about that
they abstain altogether from the communion, from going to the churches, from the sermons
. . . and from all religious intercourse with the heretics : which in England, because of the
evil laws, is by far the most difficult thing of all, a matter where the sanctions are imprisonment and other penalties " ; to Vendeville, Sept. 16, 1578, Knox, *op. cit.* Persons, too, bears
witness that the Douay reminder was frequently resented, and the college criticised for its
action.   " Priests of the elder sort both at home and abroad . . . misliked their proceedings,
namely in that they prohibited Catholics in England utterly to go to the Protestant church,
which the other before in many points had tolerated, not having considered well the inconveniences thereof, nor the great obligation to the contrary in such a time of trial as this was ",
whence (so Persons) disagreement that went on for years. *History of Domesticall Differences*,
in C.R.S., II, 63.   Allen, in the eighth year of the Douay mission, is saying that he is grateful
to the pope (Gregory XIII) for this above all, that he has turned a deaf ear to the detractors of
the colleges and the missions, to those who " in order to excuse their own cowardice and
faintheartedness, are making out a case that all that is being attempted for our country is a
waste of time."   Letter (Latin) to Agazzari, of June 23, 1581, in Knox, *op. cit.*, 96.

[2] Cf. *The Elizabethan Apostasy*, by Mgr. George Andrew Beck, now Bishop of Brentwood,
Catholic Truth Society, p. 23 (1947).

[3] " Meanwhile the queen and her ministers considered themselves most fortunate in that
those who clung to the ancient faith, though so numerous, publicly accepted, or by their
presence outwardly sanctioned, in some way, the new rites which they had prescribed.   They
did not care so much about the inward belief of these men, or if they did, they thought it best
to dissemble for a time.   They were not a little pleased that even priests were found who did
not shrink from the new service ; for they were at first afraid that they would not be able to
persuade them to accept it, contrary to the example and commandment of their bishops and
the voice of their own conscience."   Rishton (1585), p. 268, in the English translation of
Sander by Lewis (1877).

corners, personal combinations, harmless alliances where the parties have in
common no more than the desire to be rid of a government and to be the
rulers in its place.

Cecil was, however, well aware, none more so, of the fires that burnt
below the treacherous ashes of his daily path : it was the busy, systematic,
bourgeois secretary, plain and unadorned, never happy unless at his desk,
who really influenced the queen's judgment and made the permanent impression—not the worthless and disreputable Leicester, still, it was rumoured,
her lover,[1] whatever his brilliance, nor Elizabeth's young kinsman Norfolk,
leader of the older aristocracy and England's solitary duke ; and throughout
these years the hates of these, and many others, seethed in consequence.

All this varied, jealous incompetence was fusing in a resolve to " free "
the queen from Cecil's influence, when, in 1568, the flight of the Queen of
Scots to England [2] brought the long malaise to a head. The one real crisis
of the reign was approaching. The situation was more critical than the year
of the Armada itself.[3] For Cecil was all-important to the Elizabethan reconstruction of England, and the foundations of this work were, even yet,
far from set.[4] Had Cecil now been driven out who was there, sympathetic
to his ideas, possessed of anything like his competence, whom the queen
could have put in his place ?

This anti-Cecil movement in the queen's council is not a religious reaction.
Its real spirit is exemplified by the bitter complaint of the Earl of Arundel,
that " a peer of his lineage should be overruled in council by an upstart ".[5]
There were Catholics, of a sort, among these lords and their associates and
they were soon to be allied with lords of ancient line who were Catholic
by conviction.

[1] The scandal that connected Leicester and the queen with the death of the earl's first
wife, Amy Robsart, in 1560, had died away. But there was still " talk " ; and Norfolk,
in 1568, put it to Leicester that if the queen and he did not propose to marry, he ought to
put an end to the familiarities that were so injurious to the queen's good name. Lingard, VI,
197, note (whose source is *Fénélon*, II, 120–122, i.e. the despatches of the French ambassador
at Elizabeth's court). These suggestions are not the invention of some contemporary
Elizabeth-hating papist. Norfolk was no more a Catholic than Leicester. Nor was Camden;
who wrote, apropos the Act passed in 1571 (13 Eliz. c. 1) to secure the rights to the crown
of the queen and her successors, " It is not to be believed with what jests shameless gossips
(*improbi verborum aucupes*) greeted this clause, ' except the same be the natural issue of
her Majesty's body ', for the lawyers call ' natural ' those children begotten outside marriage,
the children of nature alone and not of respectable marriage, while in the language of the
law of England, they call ' legitimate ' those children who are begotten of the body lawfully.
So far [did talk of this kind go] that, as a young man, I heard it repeatedly asserted that
that word had been put into the law by Leicester, with the design that at sometime or other,
he might, in the end, thrust upon the English some bastard of his own as the queen's natural
child." *Annales*, 211–212. It was not yet twenty years since Leicester's father had made
a bid to bring the crown into this family : no one was ignorant that Queen Elizabeth's reputed
lover and Lady Jane Grey's husband were brothers. Camden was a man of 20 when this
Act was passed. For the text of the Act cf. Prothero, 57–60.

[2] May 16.   [3] So Pollard, *H.E.*, VI, 277.

[4] " Cromwell's political heir, bred in the milder school of Somerset ", so Pollard, *ibid.*,
277 ; Cecil's " design remained the same as Cromwell's ", namely, the real supremacy of the
English sovereign, to be achieved through parliament, and he had to meet the same " threefold resistance ", i.e. of the Catholics, of local rights, of the nobles. It was this opposition
which, in 1568–1569, " all came to a head " ; *ibid.*   [5] *Ibid.*, 288.

Meanwhile in France, and for the third time, " the ambition of the French princes had marshalled, in hostile array, the professors of the old and the new doctrines against each other " [1] and at Jarnac, on March 13, 1569, the Protestant nobles had been heavily defeated. The queen began to think, once more, of Calais, and was " on the verge " of interfering in France.[2] But the discontented nobles of her council were resorting to the French king for counsel and aid. They suggested that Charles IX should place an embargo on trade with England : the general discontent that must thence ensue would surely shake Cecil's position. And the French king, they thought, might also " move the papal troops in the French service to the shores of the English Channel in order to encourage the Catholics and strike terror into the hearts of the protestants." [3]

The nobles made approaches to the Spaniards also. Cecil had lately (December, 1568) carried out a most extraordinary act of robbery. Spanish ships carrying £150,000 in gold to the Low Countries, the pay of Alva's army, were driven into Falmouth, and other ports, by fear of the pirates in the Channel.[4] Leave was now asked, and granted, for the conveyance of this treasure by land to Dover. Then the warrants were countermanded, the treasure was seized in the queen's name.[5] Whence some critical months with Spain : and whence, too, the Spanish ambassador's enthusiasm to entertain Cecil's opponents, " advising him as to the best means of defeating their own government ", leading him to think that " the golden opportunity had come " to drive out Elizabeth and set Mary Stewart in her place.[6] Through all these months, when foreign affairs were so critical, the treason is universal ; these nobles, who are all members of the council, and as Protestant as Cecil himself—certainly they are not Papists—regarded " every success of the English Government as a blow to their cause, and every rebuff as a victory ; and they took active steps to prevent the one and provoke the other ".[7]

It was in February 1569 [8] that Norfolk and Arundel made their approaches to the Spanish ambassador, the enthusiastic, over optimistic, Guerau de Spes, using as their intermediary a Florentine banker long resident in London,

---

[1] Lingard, VI, 278.

[2] Pollard, op. cit., 287. " Protestant pulpits resounded with exhortations to a war of vengeance for the slaughtered saints in France." Ibid. What does this sounding generality —" protestant pulpits "—amount to, given the religious state of England in 1569, as the evidence cited in earlier chapters makes this known to us ? How many clerics were there, by this date, licensed to preach in these pulpits ? If the words could be taken literally we seem to have here an early example of the idea, so familiar in the nineteenth and twentieth centuries, that England has a duty to interfere in order to punish, in the name of its own superior ideals, the sins of other countries.

[3] The summary is in Pollard's words (ibid., 286). When historians come to describe the very similar political activities of Allen and Persons, fifteen years later, their comment pillories these two personages as traitors uniquely monstrous. Much of this not very historical treatment is due to forgetting that Elizabeth reigned for nearly 45 years, and that 1583 is not 1603 any more than 1569 is : there is the unconscious assumption that the seemingly solid national unity against Catholicism of the last years of the reign is characteristic of the whole period. [4] Two into Falmouth, two into Plymouth, one into Southampton.

[5] Lingard, VI 231 : the only detailed account of the act and of the succession of lies with which the English government strove to excuse the robbery.

[6] Pollard, op. cit., 286. [7] Ibid., 286–287. [8] Black, 99.

Roberto Ridolfi. And in the first week of March the French ambassador presented his ultimatum to the government : did England want peace or war ? [1] It needed all the queen's " tact " to ease the strain. On the other hand, the cool judgment of Alva, governor in the Netherlands as well as commander-in-chief, was not overthrown by the prospect of such allies as Norfolk and Arundel. By May his master, too, was agreeing that threats of war were no way to recover the captured treasure ; [2] Spain was definitely out of the scheme, although the discontented nobles might not realise it yet, nor the Spanish ambassador (nor Cecil know it as a certainty). And in England the intrigues raged for the next three months. Cecil made a show of reconciliation with Norfolk (June 9),[3] and a show of admitting the lords to a say in the conduct of foreign affairs.

But it was not possible that the lords should win, in this contest with Cecil ; for they were secretly pledged to bring about first, the recognition of the Scottish queen as Elizabeth's heir and, secondly, Mary's marriage to Norfolk : here were the two matters—the succession and marriage—on which Elizabeth would not even hear of discussion, topics the mere mention of which invariably unloosed all the furies in her. It was Leicester who had now renewed in Norfolk the ambition to make Mary his wife,[4] and Leicester who had made himself the champion of the claim of Mary Stewart to be recognised as heir when, in May, he sent to her a pledge of support that Norfolk and Arundel and Pembroke had also signed. This letter offered the imprisoned queen restoration to the crown of Scotland and recognition as heir to Elizabeth, but on conditions: pardon for all her Scottish opponents, the English reformation to be accepted in Scotland, a league of perpetual friendship with England and a pledge never to impugn the right of Elizabeth to the English throne nor the right of any heir of her body, and, finally, marriage to Norfolk. On June 1 Mary wrote accepting the conditions, and on July 1 Norfolk contracted himself to Mary, and sent her in token the diamond ring which she would keep to the end of her days.

All that remained was for Mary's bitterest enemy, her half-brother the Earl of Moray, now ruling Scotland as regent for the baby king, to agree

---

[1] Black, 100.   [2] *Ibid.*, 101.   [3] Pollard, *op. cit.*, 288.

[4] Mary reached English territory, after her famous flight from Langside, May 16, 1568. Two days later she was taken to the castle of Carlisle ; she was, in fact, the prisoner of Elizabeth. Mary's demand for a meeting with Elizabeth was met by the counter-demand that she should submit to an enquiry into the charges against her of connivance in the murder of her second husband, Darnley, and of adultery with Bothwell, her subsequent (third) husband. On July 15 Mary was transferred from Carlisle to a more secure stronghold, Bolton Castle in upper Swaledale, and a new enquiry was proposed—into the conduct of those who had driven her from the throne, July 28. Mary, against the advice of her friends, agreed to this ; commissioners were named by all three parties, and the conference began, at York, on Oct. 3. Norfolk was one of Elizabeth's three commissioners and the Bishop-designate of Ross one of the Scottish queen's. It was during these conferences that the proposal of a marriage between Mary and Norfolk was first put out, by one of the queen's opponents, her one-time secretary, William Maitland of Lethington, to Norfolk himself, in the name of Mary's half-brother Moray, now the regent of Scotland, and here at York, as her prosecutor in effect. Upon Norfolk's return from York, Elizabeth made no secret of her displeasure at the mere idea, and Norfolk told her very plainly he had no intention of being a second Darnley. This will have been about Dec. 1568.

to this plan for his own supersession; and for the marriage scheme to be put to Elizabeth, as from Moray, by that Scottish Cecil, Maitland of Lethington. To us, so habituated, " conditioned ", to a knowledge of Elizabeth as the end of the long reign and its successes left her, all this sounds an incredibly naïve scheme to have come from lords of her council, men for so long in daily contact with the queen. But Elizabeth had, at this time, only been queen ten years ; and the long-enduring weaknesses of her situation, to us known only notionally, were as real to all the actors as the ultimate success of the queen is real to us.

The plan to restore Mary and to recognise her rights to the English throne was next raised in Elizabeth's council—all mention of the marriage most carefully suppressed ; it was approved, and sent to Edinburgh for the consideration of Moray (May) and of Mary's party also ; and Cecil, too, was so far won over (or pretended to be won over) that he promised not to oppose even the Norfolk marriage.[1]

Alva's scepticism remained unshaken. When new approaches were made he sent, in July, to the foolhardy ambassador in London a formal prohibition to meddle in the business—Mary's cause, he told de Spes, was being ruined by what was known of his intrigues with her servants and if he continued in this way her life would be in danger.[2] Then before the month was out, Moray, as so often already, had double-crossed his associates. The Scottish Estates, on July 25, declared that never would they consent to have Mary back as queen. And Maitland only saved himself from Moray's vengeance by a rapid flight. In August Elizabeth said openly to her council that she knew of their treasons, and how they were plotting in support of the Queen of Scots.[3] Then, while on a progress in Hampshire, she received from Moray

[1] Of Leicester, in this crisis, it has been written, " He obviously believed Elizabeth's fall to be at hand, and was arranging for the worst " (Lee, in *D.N.B.*, article *Dudley, Robert, Earl of Leicester*). Was Cecil, also, making long-distance preparations—is it even possible ? —to cross over to the cause of Mary and Norfolk, in case this should succeed ? to desert Elizabeth in 1569 as he had deserted Somerset in 1549 and Northumberland in 1553 ? And can the historians speak calmly of the mere possibility, who must soon be solemnly approving the sentence passed on Norfolk, and repeating, in simple sincerity, Cecil's shocked denunciation of the Catholics alleged to be, because Catholics, traitors to Elizabeth ?

[2] Alva to de Spes, July 14, 1569, *Span. Cal., 1568–1572*, p. 175.

[3] " Elizabeth . . .", says Pollard (*op. cit.*, 289) of this critical August, 1569, " seemed herself to be losing her hold over her government "—the very possibility will seem an outrageous supposition, if the whole reign has only been seen coloured by what the queen ultimately achieved. The first ten years of the reign are not, then, a time where Elizabeth's ideas necessarily bear all before them, when her will is absolute, and the ministers shake in their shoes at her frowns ? The queen can be deceived by her ministers and—for her own good, of course—is deceived by them ; she can know they are plotting against her and be uncertain of the result. Her own political gifts apart, how much better off is Elizabeth among her treacherous councillors, in this crisis, than her sister Mary was, fifteen years earlier? But even allowing—as I could not allow—that Elizabeth was, in fact, the stooge of her ministers, this by no means implies that England would to-day be a Catholic country but for accidents : Elizabeth and the ministers by whom (in the hypothesis) she was ruled, were as well agreed in the matter of the pope as Mary and her ministers had been divided. But the incident seems to show that the régime was, after ten years, more precarious than is generally allowed ; and it tends to make ridiculous the idea that the England of 1559–1570 was a country so solidly united that any effort of the Catholics to overthrow by foreign aid what was done in 1559 was, *a priori*, a shocking piece of anti-national wickedness.

an account of what the Estates had decided, and suddenly turned on Norfolk with a savage hint that she knew all.[1] Some weeks later Leicester, who was to have saved the situation by explaining to the queen the whole intent of the lords, and in particular the benefits of emancipation from Cecil's influence, and who had never been able either to find the courage to do this or the opportune moment, fell dangerously ill, and in quite another spirit he revealed the whole affair to the queen as she visited him (September 14).[2]

It was Elizabeth's own act that broke the nobles. Strong with the knowledge given through Leicester's treachery to his associates the queen suddenly rounded on Norfolk, and forbade him ever to think of marrying Mary. On September 15, in great wrath, he left the court, and so too did Arundel and Pembroke. When, six days later, he received in London the queen's order to return, he made his way instead to his stronghold of Kenninghall in Norfolk.[3] Was this to be the signal for others to join him, and for the revolt to begin? The guards around the Queen of Scots at Sheffield were strengthened, and orders were given that should Norfolk rise she was to be killed.[4] But after three days of tension Norfolk gave in. He wrote to the queen begging forgiveness (September 24) and " after many feints " [5] prepared to return. While he was on his way, Elizabeth received from Moray the letters which Norfolk had written to Mary.[6] Whereupon she ordered the duke's arrest. He was stopped at Uxbridge and on October 11 lodged in the Tower. Arundel and Pembroke, and Leicester also, were forbidden the queen's presence; Mary's ambassador, the Bishop of Ross, Ridolfi the Italian intermediary of the lords with the Spanish ambassador, Lord Lumley and Sir Nicholas Throckmorton were arrested (October 9).[7] When Leicester was " reconciled " he had to beg the queen's pardon on his knees; and, kneeling with him, Cecil also.

There was one part of England, at least, where the extraordinary intrigues, tearing this twelve months at the vitals of the Elizabethan régime, now passed rapidly into public life: that great region, namely, north of the Humber and east of the Pennines whence, thirty years before, had come the Pilgrimage of Grace that might so easily have shaken Henry VIII from his throne, the lands where the names of Percy and Neville were still so powerful as easily to warrant the only criticism of its acts which a Tudor government need notice, a general rising in arms. Here alone, we may presume, under the leadership of the earls of Northumberland and Westmorland, had there ever been a possibility that the contest between the lords and their new hated master would be put to the wager of battle—not, as will be seen, that either of these nobles were fire-eaters by nature. But the place, and the people, were apt for such demonstrations when governments went counter to the general desire. These countrysides were still all but wholly Catholic; and already, before the great intrigue had begun to crumble, before the duke's menacing departure from the court, Yorkshire and Durham

---

[1] Lingard, VI, 201.   [2] Pollard, *op. cit.*, 291.   [3] *Ibid.*   [4] Lingard, VI, 202.
[5] Pollard, *op. cit.*, 292.   [6] Lingard, VI, 203.   [7] *Ibid.*, 203–204.

were alive with meaningful talk, stirring with the hope that the ten years of Protestant triumph under Elizabeth were now to end as simply as the earlier triumph which the heretics had enjoyed under her brother.

In the early part of September, very early in the crisis indeed, " not much before the Duke of Norfolk's departure from the court there came into these parts a brute of a marriage betwixt the Scottish Queen and the said Duke " ; so Sir George Bowes, a notable of the North Riding, replied to Cecil seeking information about the causes of the general malaise. [1] Upon " the duke's departure in displeasure from the court to his house in London ", Northumberland was to explain, there " arose a great bruit in Yorkshire, the naming of a successor was in hand again ; and the Lords of the Privy Council wonderfully divided. The Duke home to his country, other noblemen to theirs, and so was it thought all the realm would be in hurly burly about the same ; which occasion moved me most especially, not only to send unto the duke, but also to assemble my friends, and to advise with them, and to know their inclinations." [2] And with this brute, or rumour, that gradually took hold of the whole population, there were, naturally, " doubts of troubles to come ".[3] This general anxiety lasted a good three weeks, " until it was certainly known abroad that the Duke was returned unto the court ".[4]

The people most anxious were the Protestants, who surmised that " such as not best liked the religion now used and set forth " were conferring " about an alteration of religion ". Whence, of course, " sundry warnings and messages " sent by zealous Protestants to warn one another to be ready, and " provide for their safety " in this land where, as another officer of state was shortly to report, there were not ten gentlemen who approved of the queen's alteration of religion.[5] Were there, in reality, any such secret meetings of Catholics ? Sir George Bowes, at any rate, had heard of none.

The most mischievous of the rumours was the " news " that the two earls of Northumberland and Westmorland were under suspicion. Both of these were notoriously Catholics, and Westmorland's countess was Norfolk's sister. But with the news of Norfolk's submission, and of the meeting of the earls with the Lord President at York (October 8), when they agreed to support the government in suppressing anything like a rising,[6] the rumours died down.[7]

Then, on Monday November 7, Bowes, five days only after his reassuring report to London, had to tell Sussex that Westmorland was, seemingly, assembling his retainers and tenantry at his castle of Brancepeth, four

---

[1] Nov. 2, 1569, Sharpe, 8.

[2] *Answers to interrogatories* put by Lord Hunsdon, at Berwick, June 1572 (sometimes called the earl's Confession) ; *ibid.*, 201.   [3] Bowes, as n. 1, *ibid.*, 8.

[4] *Ibid.*, 9, and for the next paragraph.

[5] This was Sir Ralph Sadler's opinion. When another high personage, Sir Francis Knollys, wrote, just a year before the Rising, to commend Bowes to Cecil, he said, " He is also a good Protestant, and his brother likewise, which is a rare matter in this country ". Oct. 24, 1568 ; *ibid.*, 380.

[6] The Lord President (the earl of Sussex) to Bowes, Oct. 9, *ibid.*, 5.

[7] A paper endorsed by Cecil, *Notes of uncertain brutes*, Nov. 2, printed, *ibid.*, 8.

miles south-east of Durham, and that with him at Brancepeth were North-umberland and the Sheriff of Yorkshire, Richard Norton. What had moved Westmorland to this action was fear, so Bowes thought, rather than " any evil pretended to be done ", fear lest " they should be surprised of the sudden ".[1]

The two earls had, in fact, just eight days before this letter, received a summons from the queen to betake themselves to the court. They had sent their excuses to the Lord President ; and Sussex, replying to these, on Friday, November 4, had repeated the summons. And now Westmor-land was gathering forces.

Many months later, when all was over and Westmorland a fugitive, Northumberland, the queen's prisoner, told at length what he could recall of the confused activity of the three weeks between the pledge of the earls to co-operate with the government and their refusal to obey the queen's summons to court.[2] " If his confession be true ", Lord Hunsdon wrote to Burghley, transmitting the document, " the rebellion was one of the strangest matters that hath been heard of . . .".[3] What emerges, in fact, from the earl's account, is that neither of the principals was ever a willing and whole-hearted rebel. The real driving force was a group of gentry, Nortons, Tempests, Markenfields, and others ; and the wavering earls were at last decided by the fear that they were destined to spend the rest of their days in the Tower, destined perhaps for what was ultimately Norfolk's fate, the scaffold on Tower Hill.[4]

What also emerges is the strength of Northumberland's own religious belief, the primacy of the spiritual in his action, and the purity of the re-ligious motives in his support of the Queen of Scots. When Burghley asked him " What was the intent and meaning of the rebellion ", the earl replied " The intent and meaning of us upon our first conferences and assemblies was only and specifically for the Reformation of Religion, and the preservation of the second person, the Queen of Scots whom we ac-counted by God's law and man's law to be right heir if want should be of issue of the Queen's Majesty's body, which two causes I made full account, was greatly favoured by the most part of Noblemen within this Realm, and especially for God's true religion." [5]

The earl's belief about this latent sympathy for Catholicism carried him very far. " Yea, I was in hope (although I had little for me), both the Earl of Leicester, and my Lord Burleigh had been blessed with some godly inspiration, by this time of the day to have discerned cheese from chalk, the matters being so evidently discoursed by the learned divines of this our time, and especially my Lord of Burleigh who is indued with so singular a judgment. I name them two the rather, for that they bear the sway about the Prince, able enough to bring her Majesty to the truth therein. And now finding myself deceived of that expectation, I can no more do but

---

[1] A paper endorsed by Cecil, *Notes of uncertain brutes*, Nov. 2, printed, 10–11.
[2] Northumberland, *Answers, etc., ibid.*, 195 ff.
[3] Hunsdon to Sir William Cecil, now Lord Burghley, June 12, 1572, *ibid.*, 207.
[4] Cf. Northumberland, *Answers, etc., ibid.*, 198 ff.   [5] The same, *ibid.*, 202–203.

shall pray faithfully to Almighty God to indue her highness and them with his grace that they may know him and fear him aright."[1] And these same considerations had guided Northumberland in the crisis that followed Norfolk's flight from the court. For the earl and his friends were only " aminded to join and to take part as the duke did if the quarrel should be for reformation of religion or for nominating of the heir apparent ".[2]

There was never any question of proclaiming Mary as Queen of England, supposing they had freed her ; " I do not remember I heard it opened, or moved at any man's hand to proclaim her Queen of England " ;[3] nor was she ever in touch with the rebels. Mary's only connection, if it may be so called, with the affair was her advice, when the earls consulted her, not to stir.[4] Northumberland's interest in Mary was twofold—" liberty of freedom of her whom we account the second person and right heir apparent ", and the hope " thereby to have some reformation in religion or at least some sufference for men to use their conscience as they were disposed ".[5] And Northumberland, at any rate, was extremely critical of the proposed marriage with Norfolk. He had sent a message to Mary " how much it was misliked, not only with me, but with sundry others, that she should bestow herself in marriage with the duke, for that he was counted to be a Protestant. And if she ever looked to recover her estates, it must be by the advancing and maintaining of the Catholic faith ; for there ought to be no halting in those matters."[6] Leonard Dacres was of Northumberland's opinion, but Westmorland, the duke's brother-in-law, and some of the Nortons, " liked well the match to be with the Duke ".

From the beginning the two earls, in these informal conferences with their friends, had been opposed to the idea of a demonstration in arms. And it is probable that the Rising of the North would never have taken place had the government in London[7] let well alone once Norfolk had submitted. The duke's warning to Westmorland—sent with the news

---

[1] The same, *Answers, etc.*, 203. This personal reference moved Burghley to ask, in the next questionnaire, " Who are the divines that you mean had so discoursed the matters, at this time, to cause the Earl of Leicester, and the Lord Burghley to discern cheese from chalk in religion ? " Whereupon the earl suddenly becomes alive. " Harding, Sanders, Stapleton, and others, hath, of late days, written so largely against the other divines, here within this realm ; not only showing how enormously they misconstrue the word of God, and abuse and falsify the ancient writers, as in D. Sanders vii book set out by the said D. S. called the Rock of the Church, which tends to the advancement of the supremacy. To be short, the unity which ever hath been, throughout Christendom, among those called papists ; the disagreement and great dissension continually growing, and that ever hath been among Protestants ; methink was, and is sufficient, to allure all godly and humble minds, from the dangerous sects now sparkled abroad among the said protestants." *Ibid.*, 212, no. 31.

[2] *Answers, etc.*, *ibid.*, 201.   [3] The same, *ibid.*, 193.   [4] The same, *ibid.*, 198.

[5] The same, *ibid.*, 193. This is, of course, about the time when the queen's Bishop of Ely is chafing at the Catholic's demand for freedom of conscience as a piece of unbelievable impudence, cf. *supra*, p. 259, n. 2.

[6] The same, *ibid.*, 192.

[7] Or Elizabeth ? Cf. Pollard, *op. cit.*, 292, who gives the queen the glory of provoking the rising she was to suppress so bloodily : " She was therefore well advised not to let matters rest. Delay would merely have postponed the rebellion to a less convenient season, and it would have been folly not to take advantage of the confusion into which the unmasking of Norfolk had thrown all sections of the opposition."

that he was about to make his submission [1]—not to rise, for this would certainly cost the duke's life, would alone have sufficed. But the duke had only been a fortnight in the Tower when the government decided to send for the earls. The gist of their replies, that while to come armed would be treason, to come unarmed would be to put themselves in the power of their enemies at the court—enemies proved, by the very summons, to be in possession of the royal ear—is the burden that recurs in the letters of every noble of the time : Sussex, the Lord President himself, for example, in his reports to the queen at this very time. And so, in the second week of November, the volatile young Earl of Westmorland, now readily agreeing with the fiery Nortons and Markenfield, began the muster ; and Northumberland, accidently stumbling into the nascent rising at Brancepeth as he sought in his own county a safer refuge than his Yorkshire house, was finally overborne and threw in his lot with the rest.[2]

As for the rank and file, it was a rising to free the faithful from the tyranny of the heretics, the Pilgrimage of Grace come again. Once more the banners displayed the five wounds of Christ crucified ; when the host occupied Durham the altars were restored, the Mass sung once again in the great cathedral crowded to the very doors. Sermons were preached that denounced the heresy of recent years and lashed the cowards who had pretended to conform, and the huge congregation knelt while the preacher absolved the contrite from the excommunication in which their surrender to heresy had involved them. There is record of similar scenes in other towns of the county, of an astonishing spontaneity, in all classes, towards the restoration of the old rites, and of priests openly confessing to their congregations that for ten years they had misled them. And in a bonfire on the bridge at Durham the heretic bible was ceremoniously burned, along with Jewel's *Apologia*, the *Homilies*, and the new Book of Common Prayer.[3]

The proclamation put out by the earls made no mention of the Queen of Scots, whose liberation was, however, one very real objective of the rising. What they published, in justification, was the case of the nobles against Cecil, with something of a case against Leicester ; their determination to free the queen from " divers new set-up nobles, who not only go about to overthrow and put down the ancient nobility of the realm, but also have misused the queen's majesty's own person " (Leicester, surely, presented as another Bothwell!), new men who, moreover, "also have by the space of twelve years now past, set up and maintained a new found religion and heresy contrary to God's word ".[4]

It was on November 14 that the earls occupied Durham. Four days later they were at Ripon, with 5,000 foot and 1,200 horse, while the queen's commander at York, the Earl of Sussex, was complaining, " Except it be a few

---

[1] Northumberland, *Answers, etc., ibid.*, 195–196.   [2] The same, *ibid.*, 198–199.
[3] For this varied detail (and more, of course), cf. in Sharpe, 252–263, *Proceedings of some of the Clergy and others in the County of Durham*, " from a manscript, *Depositions, 1565 to 1573*, in the Registrar's Office, Durham ".   [4] Lingard, VI, 210.

protestants and some well affected to me, every man seeks to bring as small a force as he can of horsemen, and the footmen find fault with the weather and besides speak very broadly." By November 20 the queen's lieutenant had still no more than 400 horse, and he reported that the justices of the peace and the gentlemen were keeping away. By this time the earls' host had come south of him. They had avoided York and from Ripon went by Knaresborough and Tadcaster to Selby ; at Bramham Moor, on November 24, like Charles Edward at Derby 200 years later, they halted and turned back. The castle of Tutbury, where Mary had been confined, was well over fifty miles still further to the south—too far for the rapid raid that might rescue her before her guardians could make the castle impregnable ; the possibility had been foreseen and the queen moved still further out of reach, to Coventry. And slowly the royal forces from the south were mustering.

The earls were no generals ; they seem to have had no plan, to have been half pushed into rising when they did by their keener followers ; there was no unity of command. The leaders give the appearance of never knowing what to do next, and all was really over the moment the cause halted in its march towards the south. In six days the host was back again in Durham, in the Neville country where it had all begun. The dissensions continued, and though Barnard Castle now fell to the rebels and the port of Hartlepool, the life had gone out of the movement. The royal armies were now moving up under Sussex and under Leicester's brother, the Earl of Warwick, one of the genuinely religious protestant lords. On December 16, at a council of war in Durham, there was a final wrangle between the earls—as to the real purpose of the rising ; and with this they dispersed their forces, and made for the safety of the Scottish frontier.

It only remained for the queen's provost-marshal to fix up the gallows and hang as many of the unresisting rank and file as he chose. All over Durham and Yorkshire the ghastly business went on. In the rising only five lives had been lost, but there was soon not a village from Leeds to Newcastle where one corpse at least did not swing from some tree in token of the power of the queen.

At its maximum, on Bramham Moor, the rebel host, so Bowes reported, amounted to 1,700 horse and 3,800 foot. Of these last, no more than 500 were " armed to any purpose . . . and these only with bows and arrows, jacks and bills ". It was a rising, he wrote to Cecil, " of artificers only and the meanest sort of husbandmen ". Bowes, as provost-marshal to Sussex, had personally chosen the victims to be put to death and had arranged the executions. These numbered 800 in all, " wholly of the meanest of the people, except the alderman of Durham, Plumtree their preacher, the constables [40 in number, according to the list] and a fifty serving men ".[1] The queen—as her letters show—was personally interested in the executions, pleased that so many of the poorer sort had been put to death, anxious not to spare too many of the better class, lest the distinction cause new troubles, anxious above all that the business be speeded up, so that

[1] Bowes to Burghley, Oct. 8, 1573, in Sharpe (from Harleian, 6991), 184, 185, 188.

the army could be disbanded and she be at an end of the huge expense of its maintenance. " I heartily pray you to use expedition ", Sussex wrote to Bowes, January 19, 1570, " for I fear this lingering will cause displeasure to us both. I would have you make the examples great in Ripon and Tadcaster ; and therefore, if you find not sufficient numbers within the towns that be in the doings of the late [rebellion], take of other towns, and bring them to their execution to those places ; . . . the like whereof shall be convenient to be done at Thirsk." [1]

Four days later than this Bowes was writing to his brother that he had now made an end of " six hundred and odd ; so that now the authors of this rebellion is cursed of every side ; and sure the people are in marvellous fear, so that I trust there shall never such thing happen in these parts again ". [2] Care had been taken to hang at least one man in every town or village whence any had left to join in the rising : where only one had left, the one was hanged.[3] Thus, from 109 villages and towns in Durham (excluding the county town) 845 had joined the earls : 201 were executed. In Durham itself another 80 were put to death :[4] one in ten of the adult male population.

The really well-to-do were attainted—only 9 were executed—and their lands and goods came to the queen. In addition, fines were levied, as a condition of being admitted to pardon when they submitted, on all who had in any way assisted the rising—a matter of another eleven or twelve thousand victims, according to Bowes.[5] Finally the north, from Doncaster to Newcastle, was harried and plundered by the soldiery of Warwick's army and brought to the verge of starvation, until the other commanders (responsible to the queen for the government of the north) protested violently. " I think a difference should be made between a rebellion in the Queen's own dominions and a foreign realm ", one of them wrote to Cecil, January 18, 1570 ; and another complained that " others beat the bush and the lusty southern armies have had the birds ". Cecil, as usual, had his practical advice to offer : in order to discover the rebels, take a few men in each township and imprison them and " as need should, being pinched with some lack of food " till this brings them to speak.

But none were pardoned except on condition they renounced their religion —they must take the oath of Supremacy.[6] And in the proclamation with which the queen announced the end of the period of martial law, and condemned those who had provoked the rebellion, the ambiguity of the Admonition of 1559 was repeated, to throw odium on the earls and to suggest to the Catholics that the assertion that religion had been changed in 1559 was a lie.[7]

---

[1] Bowes to Burghley, Oct 8, 1573, in Sharpe (from Harleian, 6991), 159–160. For Elizabeth, cf. Sussex, of Jan. 10, 1570, *ibid.*, 144, and her own letter of March 1, *ibid.*, 288.

[2] *Ibid.*, 163.

[3] " Besides the execution done in the great towns, there shall be no town where any men went out of the town to serve the earls . . . but one man or more as the bigness of the town is, shall be executed for example, in the principal place of that town." Sussex to Cecil, Jan. 4, 1570, *ibid.*, 134.

[4] Cf. Sharpe, 133–134, 140, 143, 151, 155, 250–252, for some lists.

[5] Bowes to Burghley, Oct. 8, 1573, *ibid.*, 187.

[6] Lingard, VI, 217, quoting the proclamation.   [7] *Ibid.*, 218.

3

The King of Spain was presently to quote the Rising of the North as an example of the mismanaged affair that can only do damage to the good cause, while it strengthens the enemy's hold.[1]

Meanwhile, as the last of the executions began to be a memory, the news leaked into England that away in Rome the pope had excommunicated the queen, had declared her to be no queen at all, or no longer queen, and had released all her people from their duty of allegiance. This bull of excommunication, signed by the pope [2] on February 25, 1570, or rather a copy of it, a Catholic was bold enough, on May 25, the feast of Corpus Christi, to fix on the door of the Bishop of London's residence, hard by St. Paul's Cathedral.

About this papal declaration there has never ceased to be discussion. But the specialist's warning of thirty years ago still holds good, that there is much we do not know of the circumstances in which the pope, St. Pius V, was induced so to reverse the policy of eleven years,[3] and, as old-fashioned writers would say, to " launch against Elizabeth the thunders of the Vatican ". But enough is now known to make nonsense of the view of the bull which language such as this implies. There appears, in fact, to be no doubt at all that what the pope had in view was not a resounding blow that should hurl

---

[1] In Aug. 1570, Philip II told the nuncio that he was opposed to schemes that forced him to show his hand where, yet, there was no substantial chance of success. And, as an example of what he would not approve, he spoke of the late rising in England. " In the beginning of these disturbances ", said the king, " these nobles who rose for the Catholic cause, were too hasty—perhaps because they could not do otherwise—in showing their hand ; for what they should first have done was to come to a better agreement among themselves, and then to send this for the consideration of the prince whose help they sought, who would then be ready at the time to give the help they needed. But throwing themselves into the affair without consideration (*intempestivamente*) they wrought only harm to themselves and made the enemy stronger still. . . ." Meyer, 479–480, who prints the nuncio's unpublished despatch of Aug. 4, 1570.

[2] This was Pius V, Michele Ghislieri, elected Jan. 7, 1566, in place of the pope who had hoped to aid the Catholic cause in England through Parpaglia and Martinengo (he died Dec. 9, 1565). Pius V was a Dominican, 62 years of age, a professional theologian whose service to the Inquisition had led to rapid promotion in late life once Carafa became pope in 1555. The new pope continued to lead the saintly life of all his earlier years, so as to fill with awe and reverence even the hardened diplomatists who thronged the Curia. " It has rarely happened in a pope that the sovereign has been so subordinated to the priest " (so Pastor, 66). And 140 years after his death he was canonised by Clement XI. As pope Pius V had a constant fear lest politics and law might obscure the first things ; and he ruled himself, ambassadors noted, by " theological principles ", and with no heed to the jurists (64, note 1). With reason he mistrusted, because of their relations with the various kings, the leading political experts among the cardinals, and thence came a tendency to decide everything for himself. For the greater part of the reign Pius V had no really first-class adviser on whose experience to draw for questions of temporal affairs. " Above all, the ambassadors [upon his election] lamented the pope's lack of experience in political affairs " (65). To this must be added the tendency of Pius V to expect the natural problem before him to be solved supernaturally ; he was a man to whom it was natural " to pay too little attention to the actual conditions with which he was faced " (66). The complex history of this great pontificate (1566–1572) can hardly begin to be understood without a study of Pastor's two volumes, 17 and 18 (1929)—nor the complexity of the whole action of this simple, single-minded man of God upon the life of his time. The quotations are from Pastor, vol. 17.

[3] " . . . the history of the Bull, about which we unfortunately still know very little " ; Pollen, *English Catholics*, 143, whose documented account, 142–159, should be studied.

Elizabeth from her throne, but relief for the *crise de conscience* reported to him to be torturing the English Catholics : [1] the majority of the nation, now oppressed by a heretical government, would like to rise against their oppressor, the queen ; felt that they ought to rise against her ; but were held back by the fear that to do so was sinful since, whatever her crimes, she remained their legitimate sovereign.[2] It was in order to resolve this difficulty [3] that the pope sent the case of Elizabeth's wrongdoing into the court called the Rota, on February 5, 1570, for judgment. Witnesses were examined to prove the charges against the queen and on February 12 the sentence was delivered that Elizabeth was indeed a heretic, and had forfeited her pretended right to rule. Thirteen days later the pope signed the bull which would communicate the decision to those for whom it was meant.

There is not a hint in the bull of the supposed opposition of the popes to Elizabeth as queen because of her illegitimate birth, nor of the rights of Mary Stewart ; nor is it anywhere said that Catholics *must* take up arms against Elizabeth.[4] No less unusual, in acts of this kind, the bull was never published by the pope in the ordinary way. And, just as none of the Catholic princes had been consulted about the wisdom of the action, so to none of

---

[1] This is not to suggest that Pius V was opposed, or indifferent, to the idea of overthrowing the English government by force : on the contrary, even before he can have had any plan to replace Elizabeth by Mary, the pope wrote to Alva, March 21, 1569, about the possibility of France and Spain combining to invade England. And when, eight months later or so, the first vague reports were coming in to Rome about the scheme of the anti-Cecil lords to marry Mary to Norfolk, the pope wrote both to Alva and the King of Spain (Nov. 3) asking them to help with money and troops the " noble English Catholics, who might perhaps marry Mary Stuart, and then receive England as a fief from the hands of the Pope ". For all which cf. Pastor, vol. 18, pp. 198–199.

[2] For Pollen (*Engl. Catholics*, 143), Dr. Nicholas Morton " certainly did much to give Pius V's policy towards England a new turn ". Morton, in exile for some ten years, served as the English penitentiary at St. Peter's. He had been active in Rome urging a militant policy both on the reigning pope and on his predecessor. In February, 1569, Pius V commissioned the penitentiary to return to England, to work perhaps as a penitentiary, and to gather information, but with a definite refusal to his request for a political mission ; and he was bidden first to consult Alva whether it was wise for him to cross into England. Morton met Northumberland and had perhaps an hour's talk with him, but solely on such matters as the want of priests. Another leader, Thomas Markenfield, said later that he had asked Morton whether the queen was excommunicated, and that the penitentiary had said she was excommunicated *in law*, i.e. by the fact of hindering a nuncio from entering the country. Northumberland denied this conversation. Morton was back in Rome before the great crisis of September 1569, and reported to the pope that the Catholics were ready to rise. Pollen's source is Morton's own account given in 1575 to Cardinal Alessandrino. Cf. Appendix V, no. 2, *infra*, pp. 420-421.

[3] The pope said this explicitly, more than once, to Philip II's ambassador, when the king's angry protestations began to come in to Rome. See extracts from the ambassador's despatches (April 10 and 28, June 10 and Aug. 11, 1570) in Pastor, vol. 18, p. 214, n. 2. There is other evidence in the letter of May 6 of the emperor's ambassador, Arco, *ibid.* Mr. Rowse, *The England of Elizabeth* (1950), 442, writes, somewhat after his own fashion, " St. Pius V was not the less a fool of a friar for being a saint. He should have thought first of means of executing his Bull before publishing it." This is the comment of one unaware of the real purpose of the pope's act.

[4] The Latin text of the bull is printed in full in T.-D., III, App. no. II ; for an English translation, cf. Appendix V, *infra*, p. 418. In Pollen, *op. cit.*, 150, there is a photograph of the original.

18

them was any notice sent of what was done.   Here is a sentence of deprivation, then, launched, as it were, upon the air ; with not even a general demand that Catholic princes rally to the cause of the Church and expel the sovereign deprived.   So far as such a thing could be done, the excommunication of Elizabeth was shrouded in absolute secrecy.[1]   The only action which Rome took in the way of making it public, was that, for the sake of notifying the Catholics in England, copies of the bull were sent to the Governor-General of the Netherlands, with a request that they should be displayed at various seaports, where English people might see them and the news thereby percolate into England.   And a copy in cipher was sent to Ridolfi in London. No attempt was made to serve a copy on the queen.   It was from Alva that Ridolfi received the half dozen printed copies one of which Felton pasted on the Bishop of London's gate.

This is all in very singular contrast to the usual story of Pius V's de-claration.[2]   It is, apparently, the true story ; and it will, no doubt, stir the mirth of the profane as the older version once stirred their indignation. What a cumbrous way to settle a difficulty of conscience !   And yet, whatever the way chosen, the act would need to be public, the only kind of act the news of which could be trusted gradually to leak through and to make its way behind what, nowadays, we might call the Iron Curtain, into the land where only now and then did a messenger from Rome penetrate, by

[1] While, as will be said, means were taken that the bull should come to the knowledge of the Catholics in England, the proceedings of the Roman trial of Feb. 5–25 were not known, in Rome itself, until some months later.   In April the imperial ambassador there could only report them as hearsay, and the pope spoke to Philip II's ambassador of what had been done as something he proposed to do.   It was not until May that any copies of the bull appeared in Rome, and even then it was immediately withdrawn from sale.   Even so late as July 17 the nuncio in Madrid only knew of the excommunication by hearsay, and that a copy of the bull had reached Spain from England.   For this, cf. Pastor, vol. 18, pp. 216, 218, quoting : for Spain, the letter of the Spanish ambassador to Philip II of April 10, printed *Correspondencia diplomatica entre España y la Santa Sede durante el pontificado de S. Pio V* (ed. D. L. Serrano, 4 vols, Rome, 1914), III, 291 ; for the nuncio, a despatch of July 17, *ibid.*, 456 ; and for the imperial ambassador, an unpublished letter of April 15.   It was through England that Philip II, too, received his first news of the event—at the end of June, i.e. four months after the bull was published ; and this from copies sent by his ambassador in London, de Spes.   See the king's letter to de Spes, June 30, in *Corresp. de Felipe II*, III, 369, quoted Pastor, *op. cit*, 218, n. 3.   For the " reaction " of the Catholic powers, cf. Pastor, *op. cit.*, 217, 218 ; Alva, May 18 ; Charles IX of France, Aug. 11 ; Philip II, July 15.

[2] For example, Pollard, *op. cit.*, 368, saying that the bull " erected rebellion into a religious duty ".   Black, *op. cit.*, 135, writes of it as " cutting the gordian knot of the English question in a manner that would have commended itself to Innocent III-"—of all the popes the one, surely, whose professional mentality was most distant from the views that governed the conduct of Pius V.   It is, however, to Ranke, and not to the better informed Pastor, that this historian goes for his portrait of the pope, " grim bigotry, rancorous hatred, and sanguin-ary zeal for persecution ", and while, for a full discussion, he recommends Meyer, 78–83, he ignores Pollen.   His interpretation of the bull is that it " aimed at destroying the allegi-ance of [the queen's] subjects, [and] by coupling all who continued to obey her laws and mandates in the same anathema, it not only legalised rebellion but, by implication, positively commanded it " (136).   " Thus to every man who in his heart respected the authority of the Holy See, the bull must have come as an ultimatum, ordering him to choose between his conscience and his political obligation ", *ibid.*   Neale is more exact, " theoretically [the bull] had converted every Catholic into a potential rebel and made his faith tantamount to treason ", *Elizabeth I and her Parliaments*, I, 191.

stealth and in disguise, at the risk of his life, and with the minimum of credentials to guarantee, even to the Catholics, what he was and what he came
for. How, next, to devise the necessary public act, that would yet—despite
its public character—avoid the fatal error of putting the Catholic princes
in the difficulty that, at the command of the pope, they must either attempt
the obviously impossible or give the scandal that they appeared to flout the
papal will ?

And how was it possible, without stirring up fresh miseries for the Catholics
in England, to produce such an act which, while it could make no immediate
difference whatever to the status and power of the queen whom it declared
no queen, was *ipso facto* a declaration of war upon her claims ?

Elizabeth's legists might take pleasure in the technical neatness of what
the Roman lawyers had devised ; but even had they known enough to have
been able to make clear to the queen all that, for example, Fr. Pollen shows
the bull to have been intended to be, it always remained possible to cite it as
a declaration of ill-will against her, a message to the Catholics that whenever
the opportune moment came they could rise against her without sin, and
could even (this deduction would some years later be made) arrange to take
away her life. The bull put into the hands of the hostile government the
handiest instrument of all for completing the propaganda inaugurated by
Henry VIII, thirty years earlier, that identified the profession of the Catholic
faith with disloyalty and treason ; and it gave the queen's ministers the easiest
of all themes to develop in justification of penal laws. " You belong to the
Church whose head has forbidden you to acknowledge me as queen."
What was the English Catholic to say to this ? " You have gone back to the
Church whose head has forbidden those who acknowledge him to acknowledge me as queen." How was the convert, the man " reconciled ", to
counter this ? [1]

On the other hand Allen was able, in later years, to claim credit in open
controversy with Cecil, for " the notable discreet and sincere dealing of
Catholics all this while, about fifteen years, that this sentence hath been
extant and published ; and their manifold endeavours to mitigate and ease
the burthen thereof, in all such as might thereby have remorse to obey and
acknowledge the Queen's regality. Never writing of the matter, nor dealing
in it, but to the end of pacification, public rest, and security of the state,
brought into brandle and doubt by this unhappy alteration in religion." [2]

---

[1] Again, this is not imaginative reconstruction : these points were at the time clearly
put to the pope by Alva and the Spanish ambassador, urging upon him a revocation of the
bull or a mitigation, at least, that would make the lot of the Catholics in England less bitter.
The pope, in June, 1570, approved Alva's delay in publishing the bull, and " seemed to be
not altogether sorry if the Papal sentence did not come to the knowledge of Elizabeth ",
Pastor, *op. cit.*, 219. But he refused to withdraw the bull—once issued, how could he do
this ? And he could only suggest (in August) that Alva might make it known to the Catholics
in England that the pope would not consider them excommunicated (for their acknowledgment of Elizabeth as queen, despite the bull) while they continued to live in England. To
this Alva made the natural comment that he had no means of contact with the mass of the
English people, " and that no one in England would be bound to believe " him even if
he could find means to publish this statement. For all this, cf. Pastor, *op. cit.*, 219.

[2] *Defence of English Catholics* (1584), I, 85.

Whatever the " paper logic " of the matter, the bull never, in fact, made any difference to the loyalty towards Elizabeth of the generality of her Catholic subjects, priests or laymen ; and none, in all that time, stirred them, in the name of the bull, to hostile acts against her. But, from the beginning, the bull played into Cecil's hands. He would ignore the patent fact that Catholics were loyal, and insist that they could not, since 1570, be sincerely loyal any longer : he could know better than the Catholics themselves what their religion commanded them. He might, said Allen, " have had all the learned of our nation either silent in the question of the excommunication, or miti-gators of it still ".[1] But the opportunity was one not to be lost, of forcing the dilemma, of exhibiting Catholics as straining principles until they snapped, of showing them as manifestly untrustworthy once they began to explain themselves in logical distinctions.

The Catholics in England might, indeed, have hoped that the sentence would be " suffered after a sort to die " [2] and " by moderation and sweetness to temporise betwixt both their Superiors ",[3] leaving the matter " to God's judgment, that he might, either in this world or in the next (where both Pope and princess must come to their accounts), discern of the controversy betwixt our two superiors . . .".[4] It could hardly be expected that a government whose whole aim was the destruction of their religion would fall in with the Catholics' desires. And in the session of parliament which followed the act of Pius V, new statutes, with savage penalties, would be enacted to give the dilemma force of law, and to make it a practical, con-crete difficulty in the ordinary Catholic's life, an ever-present menace to his peace.[5]

One seemingly immediate effect in England of the bull was a great invasion scare—due, in reality, to the coincidence that this summer of 1570 saw the fourth marriage of Philip II, and a great fleet sent to Antwerp to escort his bride. Apparently every beacon along the southern coast was ready for lighting, and what troops the country possessed guarded the danger spots while the great fleet made its double journey through the Channel. Preachers, of course, denounced meanwhile the latest manifestation of Anti-christ's ill-will, pamphleteers mocked the ineffective gesture, and the talents of Bullinger were pressed into service to refute the argumentation which the sentence implied. Elizabeth affected to despise what had been done, but strove, through the emperor Maximilian II, to have the sentence reversed ; [6] and she immediately reversed her own policy in Scotland, where, since the renewal, upon the murder of Moray (January 23, 1570), of the war between " King's lords " and " Queen's lords ", English troops had been burning and wasting in the interests of the anti-Marian party. At the end of May, 1570, the English army was recalled to Berwick ; the queen's lieutenant, the Earl of Sussex, managed to bring about a truce ; and in October Cecil

---

[1] *Defence of English Catholics* (1584), I, 85–86.   [2] *Ibid.*, 86.
[3] *Ibid.*, 85.   [4] *Ibid.*, 82.   [5] Cf. *infra.*, p. 342.
[6] Maximilian II to Pius V, Sept., 28, 1570, quoted Pastor, *ibid.*, 221 and the pope's reply of Jan. 5, 1571.

(much against his will) [1] was sent to Chatsworth to lay before Mary Elizabeth's plan to replace her on the Scottish throne.

Were Elizabeth's intentions serious ? It was certainly a gesture away from that support of Calvinism for which, amongst other things, the pope had explicitly condemned her. It was a gesture, also, towards the court of France ; and the proposals for a marriage between Elizabeth and the French king's eldest brother, about which Cecil, in December, 1570, began to sound the French Court, was a still stronger move in the same, more orthodox, direction.

Parliament was to meet in the new year, 1571, and Cecil was also, no doubt, turning over in his mind the details of the new laws with which it would now be well to fetter still further the life of the Catholics. And while the commissioners from Scotland debated and wrangled with the queen's ministers in London about Mary's attitude to the plan put to her at Chatsworth, her own representative, the Bishop-designate of Ross, was conferring with the Spanish ambassador—the same de Spes whose hair-brained enthusiasm Alva was for ever rebuking—and the Italian banker Ridolfi. " The first-fruit of the Bull of 1570 ", says the latest historian of the reign, " was the Ridolfi Plot." [2] The plot, if that is the right name for these conversations, was the outcome rather (if of any one specific cause) of the realisation that the proposals of Chatsworth were disingenuous ; and it is Lingard who, with his usual startling simplicity, seems to describe essentially what happened, " . . . these three foreigners arranged among themselves the plan of another insurrection in favour of the Scottish queen ".[3]

By the end of March, 1571, Ridolfi, self-appointed to this great task, had " contacted " the two for whom he had designed the principal rôles, the imprisoned Mary and the no less effectively imprisoned Duke of Norfolk ; and then, after a farewell audience with Elizabeth, he had made his way out of the country (March 25, 1571) to Brussels first and Alva, then to Rome and St. Pius V, and finally to the court of King Philip. It was June before he came to Madrid, and long before that Cecil knew the main part of all he had talked over with Ross and de Spes.[4]

---

[1] Lingard, VI, 239, note 1, quoting a letter from Cecil, " I am thrown into a maze, that I know not how to walk from dangers. Sir Walter Mildmay and I are sent to the Scottish queen. God be our guide ; for neither of us like the message."

[2] Bindoff, 212.   [3] Lingard, VI, 253.

[4] Neither Black nor Pollard has sufficient space to do justice to himself in the account each gives of the Ridolfi conspiracy—" this grotesque conspiracy ", Black truly describes it (p. 118). But Pollard is widely astray when (p. 298) he numbers among the plotters Alva, who ridiculed the scheme from the first and did all in his power to warn Philip II against it, and against Ridolfi, a talkative ass if ever there was one ; *muy liberal en el hablar*, Alva wrote (see Pollen, 174, n. 1, for the correction of the phrase usually attributed to Alva, *un gran parlachin*). The most detailed, critical and documented account of Ridolfi and his schemes is in Pollen, *op. cit*, 160–184, who is, however, not always clear. " How far the conspiracy which Ridolfi left behind him was an objective reality, how far a creature (*sic !*) of his own imperious imagination, we shall never know ", is his very moderate conclusion 173. See also Lingard, VI, 253–273, and, for a documented and dated account of Ridolfi's Continental adventures, Pastor, vol. 18, 226–240.

We need to distinguish between what we know today of Ridolfi's schemes, as the papers in the archives of Rome and Spain have revealed them, and the more meagre (though still important) information which Cecil gathered from what papers of Ridolfi now fell into his hands and from the avowals made under torture, and the threat of torture, by those he now arrested—the Bishop of Ross, and the secretaries and agents of Ridolfi and the Duke of Norfolk. And this testimony needs to be critically examined before judgment can be based on it. One thing is very clear—the Ridolfi conspiracy involved no one of the English Catholics : Ridolfi's hopes and beliefs that they would do wonders once the scheme was announced to them, obviously commit none but Ridolfi. And, so far as Cecil knew, all that Ridolfi had done was to make proposals to Mary and Norfolk, to win their assent to these, and to pledge the pope and the king of Spain for aid in carrying out the scheme—to convince Mary and Norfolk, that is to say, that once he, Ridolfi, properly introduced, had laid the scheme before these Continental potentates they would give all the help needed. And this would be great !

What exactly was it that Ridolfi persuaded Mary and Norfolk could now be done ? the scheme, which, says Pollen, captivated the pope, which Alva ridiculed, and which the Council at Madrid was debating in the summer while in England, unknown to them, Cecil was slowly rounding up the agents of the plotters and extracting his evidence from them ? Certain lords in England, Ridolfi wrote to the pope, September 1, 1570—before ever he had held a consultation with Ross, or discussed the matter, even indirectly, with Mary or with Norfolk—will, once Alva sends arms, with the aid of all the Catholics, set Mary free and restore the Catholic religion. Mary's party in Scotland will pour over the border in support. Eight peers are named [1] and four knights,[2] and the forces each will bring into the field : 45,000 men in all, one of the greatest armies the sixteenth century ever saw ! [3] Details added later were the marriage of Mary and Norfolk, and the deposition of Elizabeth in favour of Mary.

What exactly the pope did for Ridolfi, when the banker reached Rome, April, 1571, beyond giving him a warm recommendation to the king of Spain, we do not know.[4] Letters were also prepared, under date of May 8, for Mary, Norfolk, Ross, Arundel, Derby, Montague, and Lumley.[5] Not

---

[1] ? Guglie, Derby, Southampton, Montague, Arundel, Lumley, Windsor, Worcester.

[2] Sir Thomas Stanley, Sir Thomas Gerard, Sir Thomas ? Fitzherbert, Sir John Arundell.

[3] For this letter cf. the Calendar of Roman Papers, 1558–1572, pp. 346–350.

[4] The pope's letter, May 5, 1571, is printed by Laderchi, *Annales*, 1571, no. 6. Pastor, *op. cit.*, 230, n. 2, prints a passage from a letter of Ridolfi to Mary to the effect that the pope approves all that has been arranged between Norfolk and herself and " the other nobles of the kingdom ", and that he has approved the plan. Through all the business of estimating the realities of the Ridolfi conspiracy, one leading consideration is Ridolfi's own character. Pastor has discovered, and prints in part (*op. cit.*, 215, n. 4), a memorial of Ridolfi to the pope who succeeded Pius V, which seems to bear out Alva's ruthless condemnation of his incapacity and Lingard's judgment of him as dishonest and a bragging charlatan. Whatever Pius V may have thought of the schemes, I would not take Ridolfi's unsupported word as evidence of the pope's mind. The fact that the Holy See made use of his services as banker and man of affairs proves nothing beyond the man's technical capacity in his own profession.

[5] Pollen found minutes of these in the Vatican archives, *op. cit.*, 177, n. 1. Were any

until June 28 did Ridolfi reach Madrid, and on July 7 the Council discussed his proposals—now somewhat more detailed, it would seem, and involving the chance that Elizabeth might meet her death in the business.[1] The outcome of it all was that the king was willing to take part in the scheme and sent orders to Alva to make ready, but, characteristically, left the final decision to Alva's judgment. And Alva, as may be imagined, decided to do nothing at all.[2] By the time the orders reached him the news was out in London, and the last chance of the Italian banker's dream destroyed. Norfolk was sent to the Tower on September 7. In January 1572 he was tried for high treason, on the evidence furnished by the letters of Ridolfi, the avowals

of them ever sent, ever written ? As to the action of Pius V in general, towards Elizabeth, Meyer, op. cit., 90–91, in order to show that, in " the battle with poisoned weapons " that began, as he considers, with the excommunication, " There was not much to choose between the contending parties ", quotes two " pious biographers " of St. Pius V, one writing in 1605, the other in 1647 (vere, 1595). One says, " the pope laboured with all zeal to excite the English to rise and destroy Elizabeth " (which is certainly not the case), and that the means through which he did this, Ridolfi, was " a Florentine gentleman residing in England in the guise of a merchant ", which is also not the case. The illustrations are offered by Meyer in order to show " the temper of the time ", and that " The plan of seizing Elizabeth living or dead, either by insurrection, revolution, or assassination, was considered in those days quite as pious a work as the naval league which Pius V formed about the same time ", and through which the great victory of Lepanto was won. Meyer has not a word to say about the historical value of these two biographies. But Pastor (op. cit., vol. 17, 420–424), writing some years later, has taken the trouble to evaluate them critically—a worth-while service, for they are the foundation of all the subsequent accounts of Pius V. Of Gabuzio, from whom the " Meyer " quotations in this note derive, Pastor says he " shows a tendency to embellish and exaggerate his account ", and that his work " reads like a translation " of the earlier of the two lives (by Catena) which, in turn, is marred by " the error of over-estimating the achievements of his hero ", and a tendency " to exaggerate the successes of Pius V and to keep silent about his failures ". Pastor also wrote of " the directly false statements into which Catena, in his wish to exalt the fame of his hero, allowed himself to be drawn ". How can the unsupported assertions of such writers be regarded as proof ? Meyer does not reproach the pope for what he considers his action in all this—to do so " would be an anachronism in morals " ; for the same reason, " Lord Burghley's actions also lose the revolting character which has been attributed to them by Catholics until the present day ", 92. Through Camden, who quotes Catena at length (Annales, 227–229) as the secretary of Pius V's Secretary of State, for the express purpose of showing e qua officina prodierit, et a quibus haec coniuratio fuerit conflata (i.e. the Ridolfi schemes), this bragging and inaccurate panegyrist has set the tone for much of the later English writing about Pius V and English affairs.

[1] For the much discussed question whether these Spaniards and Italians—I do not, of course, mean the pope—were now planning to murder Elizabeth, see Pollen, op. cit., 177 ff.

[2] One of the tasks left to Alva was " to come to an arrangement with Norfolk and de Spes for simultaneously obtaining possession of the Queen, the Tower of London and the English fleet at Rochester ", Pastor, op. cit., 233—a " very easy " matter, thought de Spes, who had already (12 June), outlined this plan for Philip II : " If on the landing of 12,000 to 15,000 soldiers with a corresponding force of cavalry, the English should obtain possession of the Queen, the enterprise would have half succeeded. It would also be well to capture Cecil, Leicester and Bedford, as well as the fleet at Rochester." Ibid., 233, n. 1. Comment would spoil this. But what of the king who used such a man for the work of the embassy in London ? It is upon the action of minds of this quality that the fortunes of Catholicism in England are going to turn, very largely, in the next critical twenty-five years. For the Madrid phase of the Ridolfi affair Pastor, op. cit., 231–236, should be studied. Alva's comments (letters of Aug. 3, 27, Sept. 5) show the realities : Norfolk, neither resolution nor courage ; de Spes, blinded by his hatred of Elizabeth ; Ridolfi, a hare-brained fellow who can't keep a secret ; and " the national pride of the English " will never endure to be helped by the foreigner.

of Ross and of his secretary. He was found guilty, and, after four months of hesitating Elizabeth, under great pressure, signed the warrant,[1] and he was executed June 2.[2] And just one year later the surrender of Edinburgh Castle to English forces " terminated the long warfare, open and covert, which Elizabeth had waged against Mary Stewart in Scotland since 1560 ".[3]

[1] How determined the queen's ministers were that the Queen of Scots and Norfolk should now be put to death, and what extraordinarily ferocious aids they found in the preachers and the bishops, is part of the general history of the time. What, until Mr. Neale's new book, has never been anything like so clear, is that nothing but the opposition of Elizabeth stood between them and the full attainment of their purpose ; cf. *Elizabeth I and her Parliaments*, 247–281. To what lengths Burghley and the rest can be thought still able to go, in the fourteenth year of the queen's reign, some sentences of this cool Elizabethan scholar are witness : " Time and again, to the despair of her advisers, the Queen wavered over the Duke's execution. . . . Greater pressure was required than the Privy Council could exert ; and Parliament alone was capable of that. There was also the problem of Mary, Queen of Scots. . . . How much pressure was needed to extract Elizabeth's consent to summon a Parliament, we can only surmise. Probably a great deal . . .", *op. cit.*, 241. The queen, at this critical moment, fell seriously ill (March, 1572), and it was thought she might die. And what then ? The Queen of Scots sought out in her Derbyshire prison by the lords of the Council, as Elizabeth at Hatfield House thirteen years earlier, and saluted as queen ? Graver words than any of mine, and a weightier judgment, assure us that such were the chances : " . . . had the illness turned out to be fatal, the odds are that the cause of Mary, Queen of Scots would have triumphed : her complicity in the Ridolfi Plot, along with her manifold offences, would have proved little hindrance to the throne." *Ibid.*, 242. Norfolk was condemned in January, 1572 ; the writs for a new parliament went out, March 28 ; the parliament, called (said the government's declaration) " to devise laws for the safety of the Queen's majesty " (*ibid.*, 244) was opened, May 8.

[2] Norfolk died in the reformed faith he had always professed, attended at the scaffold by Alexander Nowell, Dean of St. Paul's, and by his old tutor John Foxe, the martyrologist. " Norfolk blundered to his fate more from sheer stupidity than from conscious treason ", Pollard, *op. cit.*, 298. He perished " a victim to his own inordinate ambition and crooked ways ", Black, 120. " The Duke of Norfolk was convicted in 1572, contrary to all law and justice, of a treason resting on presumptions and inferences only ", Taswell-Langmead, *English Constitutional History*, edited Plucknett (1946), 575, in a section on *The Law of Treason*.

[3] Conyers Read, II, 130.

Chapter II

LEADERSHIP

I

THE long drawn out crisis was over : the doubtful were now fully instructed about the strength of the bond between the queen and her chief minister.[1] Moreover, a pact of mutual defence had been signed with France, in April 1572,[2] whose chief importance was that the French government thereby abandoned the cause of Mary Stewart ; and the breach with Spain was healed by an arrangement of April 1573 ; Elizabeth, as the sixteenth year of her reign begins, is strong indeed. There will be no interference with her policies from without : events have proved there is no likelihood of successful reaction from within. It is these same years that have seen the first flare of serious trouble from the Protestant primitives, the alliance between their theologians and a determined group in the House of Commons—and over this also her government has been victorious. And death has even removed the Protestant heir to Elizabeth's place.[3] More than ever is the queen indispensable to the men of 1559, and her life precious. Should anything now happen to her, what descendant of Henry VII could take her place ? Elizabeth, however, was barely forty ; although she might not marry the French king's brother—would not marry him, in all likelihood—she had probably many years of life before her to rule in peace the new England that we can safely describe as, by this time, coming into existence under her auspices.

For her Catholic subjects it promised to be a harsh and hopeless age : new laws to restrict the exercise of their religion ; new suspicions to dog them in ordinary life ; a new depressing certitude—bred of the recent, catastrophic failure of the Catholic earls—that things can now never be different. While, for those who knew all about it and were scrupulous, there were new perplexities stirred by the papal bull.[4] But now, for their

---

[1] Now, since February 1571, Lord High Treasurer and a peer, Lord Burghley.

[2] Which not all the horror at the crime of St. Bartholomew, four months later, disturbed.

[3] The Lady Catherine Grey. Mary had executed her sister, the Lady Jane, in 1554. Elizabeth, in 1561, had the younger woman arrested, upon the news that she had married ; and in prison, or under house-arrest, she kept the lady until her death, 1568. There was a third sister, Mary Grey, a dwarf, it is said, who in 1565 made a ridiculous marriage with the queen's gigantic serjeant-porter, Thomas Keys ; whereupon they too were arrested and kept in separate confinement until Keys' death. No doubt the Turk also, who could bear " no brother near the throne ", could have explained how natural his conduct was.

[4] How was the ordinary Catholic to know about the bull ? by what means, in the England of 1570, could it have been brought to his knowledge ? and who was to interpret for him and

consolation, a force wholly new in kind would begin to act upon their lives ;
and, within ten years, so renew a right spirit within them that their situation
would truly be transformed.   This force was the college founded in 1568,
in the university town of Douay, in the Low Countries : from which, for
the remainder of Elizabeth's reign, there came to serve the Catholics of
England a steady succession of trained missionary priests.[1]

The more carefully the nature of this invention, so to call it, is studied
and the detail of its organisation, the more one is inclined to see in it one of the
primary achievements of what is commonly called the Counter Reformation.
Here is a work to be ranked, for its quality, with the Council of Trent, and
the Society of Jesus, and the Roman Oratory, and the Carmelite renaissance
that we associate with St. Teresa and St. John of the Cross, the greatest
religious achievement of Elizabethan England.   And like all our classic
achievements it did not come into being through any fiat of high authority,
but, poorly born, through the zeal and determination of private individuals
whose very existence was unknown to the magnates.[2]   Like all the other
phenomena of the Catholic revival the English movement too had its saints—
in the technical sense of the term : 120 martyrs, officially recognised as
such by the Church in our time, put to death in the thirty years between
the arrival of the first Douay missionaries in 1574 and the death of the
queen.

The soul of the movement was William Allen.   He came from Rossall,
in the Fylde of Lancashire—then a bleak and sparsely populated county,
somewhat isolated from the general life of England by its frontiers of moors
and mosses, and its unusually wretched means of communication ; a
county where the largest town was the great village of Manchester ; where
there was but one great lord, the Earl of Derby, and where the land was held
by a multitude of small squires.   Lancashire, by its geographical character, its
social organisation, and the peculiarly stubborn intelligence of its people,
was a natural stronghold for any minority determined to fight back.[3]   And
when the great defeats of the seventeenth and eighteenth centuries came to the
Catholic cause, they found the priests and people of Lancashire still militant
and challenging, and in these darkest days the main strength of Douay
College and of the ecclesia of the martyrs.

---

make clear the implications of this sentence, given in a foreign tongue, and under a foreign
system of law ?   He might soon hear the Protestant interpretation : who was to give him the
pope's ?

[1] This college was the first foundation in a great work of English collegiate and monastic
restoration which, in the course of the next fifty years, produced a total of 44 houses in
various parts of the Continent—twenty-one of men and twenty-three of women.   Cf. the
table in Guilday, 40.

[2] " Had we only followed the fashion of present day colleges," Allen will write to Rome,
in a critical hour, Jan. 16, 1585, " this seminary would never have been founded.   It was the
work of men who were poor, who had no resources, and for a whole two years, in the latter
part of Pius V's time, the seminary kept going without any security that it would be helped."
Cf. the (Latin) letter in Knox, 246, *Si secuti fuissemus* etc., etc.

[3] For an interesting testimony to this aspect of the Lancashire *résistance*, cf. J. S. Leatherbarrow, *The Lancashire Elizabethan Recusants*, 12, 152-155.

Allen, who was a man of thirty-six when he first came to Douay, was born in the fatal year of the Submission of the Clergy, 1532. He was, then, the same age as the queen and Leicester, and a couple of years younger that Whitgift. About the time when Edward VI became king, Allen was beginning his studies at Oxford ; and it was from the vantage point of the university where Peter Martyr was the leading personage, with Jewel and Grindal and Harding prominent among the younger leaders, that the lad from Lancashire, growing into the man, observed, as student and fellow of Oriel, the Protestant experiment—what a heterodox minority, powerfully placed, were prepared to do, and what means they would use. He took his master's degree in 1553, served as proctor, became principal of St. Mary's Hall ; and he was in his twelfth year of residence at Oxford when the revolutionary changes of 1559 brought all to an end for him. Allen now gave himself to a vigorous apostolate, strengthening Catholics already prepared to disobey the new Acts of Supremacy and Uniformity, halting the waverers, bringing back those who had surrendered ; and presently, a marked man, he had no choice but flight. Like almost all these early refugees it was to Louvain that he went, and here, in 1562, he published the first of his many books, a treatise on Purgatory. Illness, and the fear of consumption, sent him back to Lancashire, somewhere about 1563–1564, and the apostolate was renewed, among the many Catholics who made an appearance of accepting the new services. This was in Lancashire, first of all, and then in the environs of Oxford, and finally in Norfolk. It was now that Allen showed his original quality, writing those tracts which spread so widely because short and to the point.[1] Once again there was a hunt for this active Catholic, and he soon became too dangerous a guest for friends to house. In 1565 he returned to the Low Countries, to study theology at Louvain and to be ordained priest at Mechlin in 1567.

It was in the following year that " hiring a suitably large house near to the theological schools ",[2] Allen launched his great enterprise, St. Michael's Day, September 29, 1568. Mary Stewart had been, for four months now, Elizabeth's " guest " : and it was while the complicated manoeuvres of Leicester and Norfolk and Cecil and the rest, just described, were occupying the attention of kings and princes, that over the seas in Flanders the new thing took root—*res quaedam pia hic ad Dei gloriam inchoata.*

The words are the earliest description we have of the scheme, written within a few weeks of the start, in a petition for aid, addressed to the Netherlands government by Jean Vendeville, professor of Canon Law in the university of Douay. Vendeville, one day to be a foremost figure in the public life of his country,[3] knew as well as Allen himself the aims of the

---

[1] *Mox late sparsae eo quod brevissimae.* Fitzherbert's *Life*, in Knox, 6.

[2] Vendeville to Viglius, Nov. or Dec., 1568 ; cf. note that follows.

[3] Vendeville was to end his life as Bishop of Tournai (1587–1592) and President of the Council of Justice (one of the three councils through which the King of Spain ruled the Low Countries). His letter of Nov. or Dec., 1568 to the then president (Viglius) is in Knox, *op. cit.*, 22–23, and also in T.-D., II, p. cccxxx. Along with Allen's later letter to Vendeville (Sept. 16, 1578, Knox, 52–67) and his letter to Maurice Chauncey (Aug. 10, 1577),

new foundation, for it was in Vendeville's company, on the long journey homeward from Rome some months earlier, that Allen's first plans had been talked out; and it was Vendeville, seemingly, who had suggested Douay as a suitable place to begin. It was Vendeville, also, whose influence smoothed over all the first difficulties and who interested in the scheme the charity of three neighbouring Benedictine abbeys. And it was possibly through Vendeville that Allen came to make his first, all-important contact with the Jesuits: the new religious society, scarcely thirty years old as yet, its founder dead but a dozen years or so, is about to make its first appeal to the English, and to begin its great career in this new field. Vendeville, too, it was who steadily encouraged Allen through the stage when all his own, hypnotised by the lowliness of the beginnings, prophesied failure, and spoke of futility.[1] And with Vendeville we must, on Allen's authority, name as a main stay in these earliest years, Allen's Welsh contemporary, Owen Lewis.[2]

But Allen, as English contemporaries also realised, was born a great man.[3] Vendeville had lauded him to the Council of King Philip's government as a scholar who spoke and wrote with distinction, and as a most experienced controversial writer. This was true enough. But the peculiar merit of the future cardinal was to see differently from others—and to see exactly—the shape of the events passing before the eyes of all.

He understood well, and from the beginning, the full power for ill of Cecil's encouragement of "ambiguity"; he saw how, as a German Lutheran

---

one of the London Carthusians whom Cromwell had imprisoned, forty years ago now, and at this moment prior of the English Carthusians at Bruges (*ibid.*, 31–37), it is a main source of our knowledge of Allen's first intentions and plans.

[1] *toti enim opere pene praefueras, et prima vivendi subsidia comparaveras, cum nostri adhuc contulissent parum, nec magnum operae pretium ad regni conversionem tam minutum collegium futurum putassent.* Allen to Vendeville, Sept. 16, 1578, Knox, 53. Other evidence of the isolation in which Allen began the great work and of the steady, hostile criticism it had to face from English Catholics, is to be found in the *Letters and Memorials of Cardinal Allen*, cited here as Knox, and elsewhere in the correspondence of those times. One piece of evidence, from Allen himself, has already been quoted, *supra*, p. 282 n. William Holt, S.J., provides another in his account of the way the Catholic religion was preserved through 38 years of persecution (*Douay Diary*, 376): "There were not lacking critics who found fault with this wise and religious plan. Some of them were of the kind who condemn scholastic theology without knowing anything about it; others were afraid that it would not be possible for any length of time to house and feed such a crowd of students." This was written in 1596.

[2] ". . . *in hoc seminario inchoando summus et suasor et adjutor extitit*", Allen wrote of Lewis to the Cardinal Secretary of State, June 13, 1575, Knox, 26. Lewis, Anglesey born 1532, educated Winchester and New College, Oxford (fellow, 1554), B.C.L. 1559, left England for Louvain in 1561. In the new university of Douay he held the chair of Canon Law 1566–1572. Thence he passed to the practice of the law—*officialis* of Cambray and archdeacon of Hainault. A lawsuit took him to Rome (and to still higher preferment) in 1575. Gregory XIII made him a referendary of the two *Segnaturae*. He became vicar-general to St. Charles Borromeo at Milan. Through Philip II he was made Bishop of Cassano, 1588. And, had his own death not followed Allen's by a few months, Clement VIII—it is not impossible—would have given him the red hat.

[3] *Ad res magnas et natus et aptus :* Nicholas Sander to the Cardinal Secretary of State, March 31, 1576 (Knox, *op. cit.*, 28). It will be a great error, he adds, if the Holy See does not first consult him, in all questions concerning the Catholics of England.

historian of our own time has described, the great apostasy of Elizabeth's reign " did not take place suddenly and of set purpose, but was the result of silent compromises with conscience " ;[1] he realised that, " what began as outward compliance with the law would . . . gradually result in actual membership in the national Church ".[2] Allen's great achievement was that he discovered a means to break up the silence in which those surrenders were taking place. Allen is the personification of plain, truthful speech, that means the thing said, that says exactly what is meant—the characteristic sometimes supposed to be so peculiarly English as to be almost a national monopoly ; and where it exists a characteristic fatal to the success of such manoeuvres as the religious policy of Elizabeth and her ministers. Their chosen ambiguity Allen tears off pitilessly, and thereby reveals in himself the very antithesis of the lying spirit of 1559 ; Allen is anti-1559 incarnate, and his lifework the most direct challenge conceivable to the queen's plan for religious unity. " Our aim ", he could say, " is and has always been, to train Catholics to be plainly and openly Catholics ; to be men who will always refuse every kind of spiritual commerce with heretics." [3] Beneath his cultivated, courteous manner, alongside his simple, universal friendliness,[4] there burns a spirit as fiercely hostile to that of the *politique* as was ever the spirit of Cartwright or Barrow. After the long years of hypocrisy— of judicious compromise—the plain " yea " and " nay " of the priests whom Allen formed comes through the horrible atmosphere of the state's arrangement with a truly bracing sweetness. Here, too, are Englishmen uncorrupted by the profitable, organised insincerity of their age ; safe against the poisons that flow down from that court whose very life is the preposterous adulation of Elizabeth as the virgin goddess.[5] Here, too, is virile protest against

---

[1] Meyer, 70 ; the word omitted here is " only ". Cf. also, Black, 19, for the same idea succinctly expressed, " Time and the slow moral attrition of repeated church attendance might be relied upon to convert unwilling obedience into a real conformity ".

[2] *Ibid.*

[3] Allen to Vendeville, Sept. 16, 1578. Knox, 59. There is more than one glimpse in Allen's letters of the kind of Catholic too often produced by the régime of the years following 1559—the pattern Catholic desiderated by the Cecilian policy, into whose conscience the queen " made no windows ". In this very letter, for example (*ibid.*, 55) : " Their wise elders, recalling former days, compared the imprisoned Catholic bishops and other ecclesiastics with these new superintendents, the pseudo-bishops . . . and with their own domestic clergy ; and sometimes, when at home and among their own, they would, in secret, complain that their unfortunate children must have men of this sort to educate them, and that with such tutors they could not be bred to a good life, but must be wholly corrupted and perish. This was the way in which, amongst themselves, these Catholics lamented ; but in public, through fear of the laws, they attended the sermons of the heretics and the schismatical services, loving rather the world than the glory of God."

[4] Allen's own advice to Owen Lewis, describes his own innermost self, ". . . wisdom and . . . great patience and . . . condonation of each other for God's sake and our country's and common church's sake " ; May 12, 1579, Knox, 83.

[5] The court where, said one who knew it well, " There was no love but that of the lusty god of gallantry, Asmodeus ". Harrington, *Nugae Antiquae* (1779), II, 209–210. And cf. Topcliffe's letter to Elizabeth (now *aetat.* 60) asking her " pleasure " in the matter of torturing Fr. Robert Southwell, and describing the contortions his cruelty will produce in the victim (cf. *supra*, Illustrations, no. 31) and, with this, cf. the same dirty ruffian's brag of the familiarities permitted him by Diana's affection. This last in C.R.S., V, 210–211. " Unfortunately, however, Elizabeth did not live a life of faith . . . and the queen's personal

official acts and against official ideals, and against an almost national enslavement.

The need, the duty, of resistance to the government in spiritual matters was the theme of all Allen's apostolate from the very beginning, from those first years after 1559 spent in Lancashire, in Oxford and in Norfolk.   To be present, from time to time, at the sermons and services of the heretics, far from being a venial matter and of no consequence to a man's membership of the Catholic Church, was, in fact, a crime so fearful that those guilty of it could not, by any manner of means, be regarded as Catholics.[1]   And as Allen saw this more clearly than most,[2] so in his practical way he also saw, as the years went by, the plight in which the hoped-for restoration would find itself, the actual plight of the returned Marian exiles in 1559 : too few trained men for an immensity of evangelical work that needed to be begun straight-way.   Hence the plan for a college to house the learned clerics now scattered all over the Netherlands, and to train other young preachers and writers ; [3] and then, about the time when the first of the new generation were ready for ordination, came the second thought : that these new priests should go back to England now, and keep the faith of the Catholics in being, instructing and exhorting them, hearing their confessions, saying Mass for them, marrying them, baptising their children, giving them the last sacraments.[4]   In the

---

popularity in the early part of her reign was itself an evil, when it made fashionable the oaths she swore, and the dissipation and sacrilege she indulged in ".   Haweis, 146.

[1] *Nicolai Fitzerberti de Alani Cardinalis vita libellus*, Rome, 1608, printed Knox, *op. cit.*, 3–21.   Fitzherbert was a confidential secretary of Allen's last years : *Tantam esse criminis huius atrocitatem ut qui se eo contaminaverit, nulla ratione manere in catholica communione possit ;* the crime being, *perniciosa quaedam opinio . . . licere sibi ad haereticorum conciones atque conventus sine graviori piaculo et ab ecclesia catholica dissidio accedere aliquoties ;* which opinion, says the biographer, *persuasum erat illis, in principio hoc suo metu tantoque rerum et vitae proposito periculo* . . . . p. 5.   Cf. also Rishton, as cited, Lewis, 80.

[2] There is a second ambiguity about the religion established by the queen's majesty—as a religion practised—which the Douay movement did not fail to expose : the Royal Supremacy.   Rishton, for example, explaining this, " in order that foreigners unversed in our affairs may understand the present condition of the state ", and detailing the new depend-ence of the clergy on the crown for all that affects their spiritual authority, goes on to say, very bluntly, " . . . the very Protestants have been long ago ashamed of these most foolish laws ; they have attempted to hide the baseness of them from people unacquainted with English affairs, by saying that nothing is meant by them beyond a declaration that the king or queen is supreme over ecclesiastics as well as over lay men . . . it is plain that by this law the king or queen is supreme not only in civil affairs . . . but in the things of God also. . . . This is not all their folly ; they say that this spiritual jurisdiction is a part of the kingly authority, not granted now for the first time, but restored and given back to the crown as its ancient rights. . . . But we must pass on ", he concludes, " and leave these matters in the hands of God, who will judge the cause of His Church, and make their princes like Oreb and Zeb, Zebee and Salmana, who said ' Let us possess the sanctuary of God for an inheritance ' ".   Rishton, in Lewis, 249–251.

[3] Putavimus enim egregium esse habere semper extra regnum homines doctos paratos ad restituendam religionem cum opportunum esset, *licet haereticis regnantibus nihil tentandum speraretur.*   Allen's view of the prospects, about 1568–1570 (the words here in—my—italics) is very interesting.   The quotation is from the letter of Sept. 16, 1578 to Vendeville, Knox, *op. cit.*, 54.

[4] The new idea came from one of the newly ordained, Lewis Barlow, " . . . one of them named Mr. Barlow, if I remember not amiss (and sure it ought to be remembered to his perpetual praise) offered to go into England . . . and he was the first missioner of that happy

fifteen years since 1559 many of the priests who then remained faithful had died ; now, at last, others were provided to take up their work. The great note of this mission would be the incompatibility of religion and heresy, and if the venture prospered it would halt what otherwise must happen, in the ordinary course of human events—the drift, into ultimately real membership of the queen's establishment, of the remnant wholly faithful, as yet, to the belief of their fathers ; it would also provide a means for the return to a conscientious life of those Catholics who, in good faith or in bad faith, followed the ministrations of Elizabeth's *Anglicana* ; and it would be the only way to convert the real, genuinely Protestant, English and so save their souls.[1]

It was the boast of Douay College, from very early days, that it was the first realisation of that new Tridentine idea, the seminary—a college where aspirants for Holy Orders should be trained and taught.[2] Whether this be so or not, Allen's college was undoubtedly a new kind of thing, in the spirit that gave it life and in the routine of its studies and religious exercises. One need only compare, for example, the organisation of the last colleges founded at Oxford and Cambridge, on the eve of the great change, by such bishops as Foxe and Wolsey and Fisher.

That there was a new earnestness in the Elizabethan foundation is not surprising—a very real sense of crisis, of the hour having at last arrived when indeed it behoved all to arise from sleep ; the feeling that, although not too late, it is late indeed. And the first requirement in all, spoken of as something pre-supposed in all and always found, is a grave, understanding, whole-hearted dedication to God for the work of the mission. Scholarship there is to be, there needs to be—this is explicitly stated ; good teaching, good methods, an incredible amount of hard work in class rooms and in studies.[3] But the first things are never, for a moment, out of sight ; and

---

mission." Persons, *Certain notes of memory concerning the first entrance [of the Jesuits] into England* . . . [1605]. MS now printed in C.R.S., II (1906), p. 190. And Allen, *Sed postquam coitum feliciter est . . . cœpimus tum cogitare hoc collegium non solum utile esse posse ad servandos istos qui in eo, hoc exilii nostri tempore, educarentur, aut ad futurum catholicismi semen ; sed ad praesentem religionis propagationem, aut restitutionem clerique antiquioris iam deficientis supplementum, si recte in eum finem instituerentur et domum ad suos remitterentur, futurum salutare :* Allen to Vendeville, Sept. 16, 1578. Knox, *op. cit.*, 54.

[1] It being axiomatic, with these Catholics, that the chances of a Protestant saving his soul were slender—as, to the Calvinist, the chances were slender that a Papist would be saved. Cf. *supra*, p. 223, n. 2, for Whitgift on this.

[2] Pius V gave to the college *approbationem et confirmationem Apostolicam.* So that, *Collegium istud primum putatur in orbe Christiano erectum ad normam Seminariorum, qualia in singulis provinciis seu Dyocesibus institui voluit Sacrum Concilium Tridentinum. Douay Diaries*, 4.

[3] Cf. Allen, explaining to Rome why the college is, financially, *in extremis*, Jan. 16, 1585 : " Many, and most experienced, teachers we must have, to train our men for the sacred war against the heretics, to write books in various languages explaining and defending the Catholic Faith, to instruct with learning and with skill, those who come to us from England, those whose faith is weak, the doubtful, those devoid of all religion, the openly heretical ". The Latin text is in Knox, *op. cit.*, 245, *Necessarii sunt nobis.* . . . Persons is not less insistent. " Send us only men who are well-prepared and especially men who are well trained in Controversy ", he writes to the rector of the English College at Rome, Nov. 17, 1581, " for

they are present as the first things—and what they effect, as the source of all the rest, is a college where the common life is one continuous act of mutual charity. Never was there an institution more free from the professional, conventional charity of the Christian Pharisee that has rotted so much good will in its time. Here was the reality, the friendliness which is the flower, and first evidence, of charity, *quae pares aut invenit aut facit*. And when the president describes the life he seems to write as one of the community, very grateful to the rest for what he enjoys : " . . . the things that we do be so agreeable to every man's mind ", he tells Richard Hopkins, invitingly, " that we could not hold them from them if we would. And many surmise strange things of our order that never saw them ; but never none that saw them, that I know of, was desirous to leave them. A little government there is and order, but no bondage nor straightness in the world. There is neither oath nor statute nor other bridle nor chastisement ; but reason and every man's conscience in honest superiority and subalternation each one towards others. Confession, communion, exhortation hath kept us these nine or ten years, I thank God, in good estimation abroad and in peace amongst ourselves with sufficient livelihood from God and in good course of service towards the church and our country ".[1]

When Allen, at Vendeville's request for guidance—Philip II had charged him with the foundation of two seminaries—set down his lengthy account of Douay College, he was speaking after ten years experience of the new task.[2] It will be noticed that, in the letter to Richard Hopkins, he makes no claim that the harmony of the life was the outcome of the accident that a number of fine characters happened to be living in the same community. The president of the college was under no illusions about human nature. This very

---

one learned man is worth more here than a hundred unlettered ", Persons, 62. Cf. also his protest to his own superior general about a Jesuit proposed for England, " not very suitable as regards talents, though extremely suitable in the matter of spiritual zeal, humility and other virtues ". *Ibid.*, 262 ; also, 241, 245, 252, 257. Aquaviva cancelled this appointment. Persons' *Punti per la missione d'Inghilterra*, now printed, C.R.S., IV, 94, has preserved a similar protest from Fr. William Holt to Agazzari, April 25, 1583, demanding maturity, practical sense, learning and zeal as much more important than getting through the course speedily. There are frequent references in the letters of the missionaries to the need that priests be well trained. Fr. Robert Southwell, S.J., for example, writes to the rector of the seminary at Rome, Dec. 22, 1586, " Certainly any priest here can be of great use, but most of all priests who are really skilled in dealing with cases of conscience and the controversial questions ", C.R.S., V (Latin text), 316.

[1] Allen to " Mr. Richard Hopkins, residing at Louvain ", April 5, 1579, Knox, *op. cit.*, 76, from Dodd, II (1737), printing an original that has since disappeared. " Nine or ten " has been substituted for " nineteen " of Knox and Dodd. " Nineteen " is not possibly right, and Dodd " was not a careful copyist ", says Knox. Hopkins, a one time barrister, occupied himself, among other good works, in translating the *Libro de la Oracion y Meditacion* of Lewis of Granada (1505–1588), a masterpiece of the new Catholic spirituality and intended, like the *Introduction à la vie dévote*, for those with no technical training in theology. This translation Hopkins dedicated " To the Right Honorable, and Worshipfull, of the fower principell howses of Cowrte in London, professing the studie of the Common Lawes of our Realme ". It was published in 1582 and it is on record that Hopkins sent a copy to the godly man who was now the queen's principal secretary, Sir Francis Walsingham. Cf. also Southern, 197–206.

[2] There is a doubt whether the date of this letter is 1578 or 1580 ; we do not possess the original letter, but only a draft (with corrections in Allen's hand) and a later copy.

letter is written with the plight of the English exiles at Louvain in mind, worn out now with the tedium of twenty years of disappointed hopes, lack of regular occupation, and, in the end, of petty, personal animosities. And presently there were to be " broils ", of extraordinary heat, in Rome between students and rector in the newly established college. If Allen knew well that the parish clergy of bygone days had failed from lack of adequate instruction [1]—*scientia competens*—he was also aware how the effort of the learned clergy of the exile had been handicapped by their lack of a systematic religious training, how self-sacrifice and subordination were, with them, according to every man's taste ; Allen has said this explicitly.[2] The priests now sent to England must be so formed—Allen had this most clearly in his mind as a primary objective—that, in their inevitable isolation, without any superior to guide or admonish, these young men would continue to lead prayerful, ascetic, devoted lives.[3]

It was in a spirit that recalls the hard, practical sense of St. Ignatius Loyola, analysing the elements of the being called Man before drafting practical instructions to assist men to pray and practise virtue, that Allen, reflecting on the actual situation in England, developed a system through which the facts of that situation were themselves to become a means to produce the kind of priest the situation needed.

He has himself described the Douay training. " . . . We make it our first and foremost study, both in the seminary and by means of our labourers in England also, to stir up, so far as God permits, in the minds of Catholics, especially of those who are preparing here for the Lord's work, zeal and a just indignation against the heretics. This we do by setting before the eyes of the students the exceeding majesty of the ceremonial of the Catholic Church in the place where we live, the great dignity and practical work of the sacrifice and sacraments, and the devotion and diligence with which the people come to church, confess their sins, and listen to sermons. At the same time we recall the mournful contrast that obtains at home : the utter desolation of all things sacred which there exists ; our country, once so famed for its religion and holy before God, now void of all religion ; our friends and kinsfolk, all our dear ones and countless souls besides, perishing in schism and godlessness ; every jail and dungeon filled to overflowing, not with thieves and villains, but with Christ's priests and servants, nay, with our parents and kinsmen. Then, turning to ourselves, we must needs confess that all these things have come upon our country through our sins. We ought therefore to do penance, and to confess our sins, not in the perfunctory way we used in days gone by when, for custom's sake, we confessed once a year ;

---

[1] Cf. Allen to Chauncey, Knox, 32–33.

[2] Letter to [?] the Jesuit General [? 1576] in C.R.S., IX, 64, 66. The Douay priests *specialibus regulis et institutis informati, cum caeteri, licet docti et alias idonei sint, suo more propriisque studiis et impensis viventes, se libenter et ultro fere non dent.* . . . The college, because *huic operi specialiter comparatum, dabit semper homines obedientissimos.*

[3] *Ibid.*, 66. The Douay régime is *valde necessarium*, if the dissensions are to be warded off that arise so easily *inter eos qui clanculum, libere, et sine necessitate reddendae rationis suae vitae et doctrinae, ibi opus domini facient ubi nullum habent superiorem cui pareant.*

19

but we should go into our whole past life and, in order to the perfect examination of our consciences, perform the spiritual exercises under the fathers of the society; we must choose a holier kind of life and one better fitted to secure our own salvation and that of others. We should likewise enter into a holy union with these fathers, or others, of unceasing prayer for our church and country, in union with the many afflicted catholics who live there; and we should excite ourselves to pity and tears for them; but above all for those who are perishing so wretchedly at home, thinking over in what way we, even we, may be able to snatch some of them from ruin, remembering that this would work off a multitude of our own sins. Lastly, we ought to resolve to confess more frequently, communicate more devoutly and study more diligently, so as to prepare ourselves for the priesthood, which Christ has given us the opportunity of receiving even in exile,[1] beyond all our hopes and deservings; seeing that we have found so much favour with foreigners that they assist us, nay more, that Christ's own Vicar does not disdain us, miserable and unworthy though we be, but entertains us at his own expense for that end which God has predetermined. Therefore we should desire to correspond in some measure with God's providence which has brought us forth unharmed from Sodom, and we should long to serve Him in the sacred priesthood; not because that order, as was formerly the case and always should be, brings with it profit or honour among men, but because we wish at this present time, when it is an office contemptible in the world's eyes and even perilous, to labour for Christ and the church and the salvation of our people in tears and penance.

" We remind ourselves, too, that the days of this life and of pleasure are few, uncertain, evil; that they are happy to whom it is given to suffer something for their country, kinsfolk, religion and Christ; that the time of this world is most brief, during which the impious persecutors lord it over these holy sufferers; and while the memory of the one becomes forthwith glorious in the sight of God and men, the infamy of the others is infinite and everlasting;[2] as may be easily seen not only in the ancient martyrs, but in those also whom, almost within our own remembrance, public acknowledgment of the faith has rendered glorious in this world and happy—it is certain—in heaven. There is nothing then which we ought not readily to suffer, rather than look on at the ills which afflict our nation." [3]

[1] Allen himself was ordained at Mechlin, in 1567.

[2] In the *Defence of Catholics* (I, 47), Allen, six years later, boldly makes an explicit, challenging comparison between the *gloria postuma* that will be Elizabeth's and what will be recalled of the victims, " What worldly honour the two King Henrys of England had (I mean the second and eighth), which in the days of their reign, no doubt, was great : or what esteem soever the Princess present and her greatest ministers have now, by the height of their room and fortune in this life ; it is but a very dream, shadow or phantasy, to the glory of Thomas of Canterbury, John of Rochester, Chancellor More, Father Campion, and the rest ".

[3] Allen to Vendeville, Sept. 16, 1578, Latin text, Knox, *op. cit.*, 62–63, English translation by Knox, in *Douay Diaries*, xxxviii–xxxix, used here with a few changes. This same letter is the source for all that follows about the studies and college exercises.

The daily round at Douay begins with Mass at 5, at which all are present, and litanies for the conversion of England. All the priests say Mass every day; and on all Sundays and the greater feasts the rest receive Holy Communion. All say, every day, the Divine Office. Twice a week all fast, for the conversion of England, the peace of the Church, " and of that country where, by God's providence, we live in exile ". The feasts of St. Gregory the Great, of St. Augustine the apostle of England, and of St. Thomas of Canterbury are kept with especial solemnity.

Such piety even is not, however, enough. *Domine, bonum est nos hic esse ;* but the appointed theatre of the priests' lives was the hostile world of England. And if for the priest's own sake—that the supernatural virtue of Faith may be fruitful, and the gifts of Understanding, and Knowledge in operation—he needs theological instruction, how much more these missionaries to a country where truth has been dumb for half a century, and where heresy alone has had a hearing ?

Once again Allen is an original. What first impresses one about the scheme of studies he devised—organised in a three-year course—is the immense importance given to the study of the text of Scripture. " Our adversaries have at their fingers' ends, in a heretical translation, all those passages of Scripture which seem to make for them . . . and they produce the effect of appearing to say nothing but what comes from the Bible." Also, says Allen, they have the great advantage of an English version of the Bible ; and of power and grace in the use of their mother tongue, " a thing on which the heretics plume themselves exceedingly ". So at Douay there is to be much practice in preaching in English. As to Scripture, there is a daily set lecture on the New Testament, twice a day a running commentary on the Old and New Testaments, chapter by chapter. There are dictations of the texts around which the new controversies rage, with a note of the wrong interpretations, and of the argument against these ; there are weekly disputations on these texts, students set to defend the heretical position and, in turn, to criticise it ; and twice every week a student gives an address on one or other of these texts, as though speaking to persuade an audience of heretics.[1]

" We now teach scholastic theology chiefly from St. Thomas ", Allen writes, thereby again declaring himself one of the new men, for Peter Lombard's reign, as the inevitable introduction to the science, was not yet ended. There were two lectures daily, then, on the *Summa*, and once a week a disputation.

The main task of the missionary is to help the ordinary man. Whence the greatest possible attention to make the missionary a good catechist and a sound practical confessor. So he is formed on the catechism of Canisius,

---

[1] Allen, of course, held the chair of controversial divinity in the new university—a university whose very ratio was the study of theology with this practical end in view. His priests worked through the Old Testament in public twelve times during the three years' course, and the New Testament sixteen times. Both Greek and Hebrew were taught with the practical end that the texts could be read in the original tongue, and the captious, philological objections of the heretics guarded against ; *ibid.*, 65.

says Allen, and study of the so-called *Catechism of the Council of Trent* is urged upon him ; and as he is taught how to say Mass, so that he may the better teach others he is taught how to say the Rosary. Moral theology is taught in the informal way we now associate with study circles, and the classic text of the day is used, the *Manuale* of Martin Azpilcueta, commonly called Navarrus.[1]

One last point : the history of the Church in England is thought to matter greatly, and St. Bede is carefully studied, " in order that [the priests] may be able to show our countrymen from [his history] that our nation did not receive in the beginning any other faith but the Catholic faith which we profess and was converted to no other form of Christianity except that which we preach to them, and that their forefathers bore the name of Christians and were such only as members of this Catholic Christendom ". Which, adds Allen, " is a very telling argument with the more sober sort ".[2] Another English writer, who is recommended as the best of all for an understanding of the errors of the English heretics, is the Carmelite, Thomas of Walden.

All this is a far cry from the bishops organising colleges in England on the eve of the change, and from that re-organisation of them as Catholic institutions under Queen Mary in which Allen had himself taken some part, as the principal of a small Oxford house—to say nothing of what the new Elizabethan episcopate was able to achieve.

It is not surprising that Rome rejoiced at the appearance among the English of such a leader as Allen. " It is impossible to imagine what conceit they have of D. Allen and those of his school ", an English Jesuit wrote from Rome in 1579 to another English Jesuit then in Poland, " as of their rare spirit and courage in matters of adversity and conscience, which they have seen in scholars of the seminary here ".[3] Pope Gregory XIII, who had succeeded Pius V in May, 1572, had by this time come to Allen's assistance with an allowance of 100 gold crowns a month, to be increased, in 1580, by another 50 a month.[4] And in the crisis of 1578 that drove the college to Rheims the pope acknowledged and protected it as his own work, *seminarium quod Duaci constitueramus*.[5] To Allen personally the old pope was markedly, movingly grateful. At an audience in November, 1579, when the president spoke of " the pope's students " Gregory corrected him : " Not mine, Allen, yours." [6]

---

[1] *Suo tempore notissimus*, says a modern practitioner, Dominicus Prümmer, O.P. ; his time was 1493–1586, and a complete edition of his works appeared in five folio volumes at Lyons, 1594.

[2] The *Historia Ecclesiastica* of St. Bede had been translated some years before this (in 1565) by Allen's colleague, Thomas Stapleton, the greatest mind among all these exiled scholars. This remarkable piece of English prose (cf. Southern, 89–94) was reprinted in 1930, ed. Philip Hereford.

[3] Robert Persons to William Good, March, 1579, *Persons*, 7–8.

[4] The King of Spain, in 1578, granted the college a pension of 1,600 florins a year, and this (through the efforts of Persons when in Spain, 1582) was later increased to 2,000 florins a year.

[5] Brief to the cardinal Louis de Guise, Archbishop of Rheims, May 18, 1578, Knox, *op cit.*, 40.   [6] *Tui sunt, inquit, Alane, non mei. Douay Diaries*, 158.

The first four priests trained in the new college were ordained in 1573,[1] the first four were sent to England in 1574.[2] In the four years before a temporary success of the Calvinists at Douay brought about the removal of the college to Rheims, 75 priests, in all, were ordained and 52 had been sent into England. The next seven years (1579–1585) saw a most remarkable expansion of the work : 200 ordained and 216 sent to England. It was now, 1585, that Allen, called to Rome by Gregory XIII and destined to remain there for the rest of his life, gave up the direct control of the college. The extraordinary prosperity of those seven years was not maintained. But in the next seventeen years before the death of the queen another 167 priests were ordained and another 170 went back to England. Of these 438 priests sent to the work of the English mission by Douay College,[3] 98 were put to death, 67 of them in the years 1582–1591.

No single part of England had the monopoly of these vocations to the heroic life. The college diary gives no nearer clue to their origins than the diocese in which the students were born. Of the 436 priests whose origins are thus recorded, the north of England claims [4] 183, the diocese of Lichfield and Coventry [5] 37, the west of England [6] 45, London 30, south of the Thames [7] 25, eastern England [8] 28, the diocese of Oxford [9] 21, of Lincoln [10] 19, Wales and the Welsh border [11] 48.

Where the majority of these priests worked in England, and how they fared individually, is all but unknown to us. Of the life which, from the beginning of the venture, they had to lead, let Allen give us a picture. " . . . This is certain that priests there had need to pray instantly, and fast much, and watch and ward themselves well, lest the needful use of sundry enticements to sin and necessary dissimulation in things of themselves indifferent, to be fit for every company, bring them to offend God, and so, whiles they labour to save others, themselves become reprobate ; wherein they must also be more careful of their ways, for that every man's eyes be cast upon them as on such as take upon them to be guides of other men's lives and belief, whose faults many a man spieth that prayeth not for them ; as most men mark their misses, and few consider in what fears and dangers they be in and what unspeakable pains they take to serve good men's turns

---

[1] They were Richard Bristowe (diocese of Worcester), Gregory Martin (diocese of Chichester), Thomas Ford (diocese of Exeter) and Thomas Robinson (diocese of Lincoln). *Douay Diaries*, 6.

[2] They were Lewis Barlow (diocese of Gloucester), Henry Shaw (diocese of Chester), Thomas Metham (diocese of York), Martin Nelson (diocese of York) ; *ibid.*, 24.

[3] Also, from 1579, the English College at Rome had begun to send missionaries, and from 1589 the English College at Valladolid.

[4] Dioceses of York 75, Chester 75, Durham 20, Carlisle 13. Lancashire is in the diocese of Chester, and so is the N.W. part of the West Riding of Yorkshire.

[5] The counties of Stafford and Derby, part of Shropshire, part of Warwickshire.

[6] Dioceses of Exeter 16, Bath and Wells 15, Salisbury 12, Bristol 2.

[7] Dioceses of Canterbury 10, Rochester 0, Chichester 3, Winchester 12.

[8] Dioceses of Norwich 12, Peterborough 8, Ely 8.   [9] The county of Oxford.

[10] The counties of Lincoln, Leicester, Bedford, Huntingdon, Buckingham, and (part of) Hertford.

[11] Dioceses of Llandaff 10, St. Asaph 10, Bangor 3, St. David's 3, Worcester 11, Gloucester 6, Hereford 5.

to their least peril.   I could reckon unto you the miseries they suffer in night journeys, in the worst weather that can be picked ; peril of thieves, of waters, of watches, of false brethren ; their close abode in chambers as in prison or dungeon without fire and candle lest they give token to the enemy where they be ; their often and sudden rising from their beds at midnight to avoid the diligent searches of heretics ; all which is great penance for their feathers, and all to win the souls of their dearest countrymen ; which pains few men pity as they should do, and not many reward them as they ought to do." [1]

This letter to Prior Maurice Chauncy was written in August, 1577. As yet nothing has transpired to give a semblance of likelihood to the government's charge (which later it will develop so well) that the new priests are, in fact, simply spies and traitors.[2]   Dr. Sander, it seems, has yet to convince the foreign potentate that an invasion of the queen's realm is feasible, even if desirable ; England has not yet been " invaded "—inevitable, and blessedly useful word !—by the two famous Jesuits, one of whom is not yet a priest, while the other is a classical master in a college in Bohemia ; we are still in the fullness of the régime of " no persecution ".   But the new episcopate is uneasy at the effect of the foundation of 1568.

Douay College, one of its priests declared in 1576, was by now famous throughout England.   And it was so not only because it had sent out some thirty or forty priests, but because it had already become the active centre of a new movement of resistance.   Apart altogether from the work of training priests, the college was influencing the English layman directly, in a most remarkable way ; this was a work thrust upon Allen and his community by the laymen themselves who, once the news of the foundation spread, flocked to the college in great numbers.[3]   These young visitors from the English universities, deeply impressed by the learning and way of life of their exiled fellow countrymen, by the spectacle of the Catholic revival in these provinces,[4] and by this new English college, returned home to infect others with a like enthusiasm.   They roused the curiosity of many more to enquire about the faith of the Catholic Church, and to go to Douay to see for themselves. So it came about that a good many of the younger generation began to make their way to the college ; and so the first falling away from the heresy, it was

---

[1] Letter to Maurice Chauncy, Aug. 10, 1577, Knox, 36.

[2] *Nos . . . quos vocabant patriae et Reginae inimicos et proditores*, Allen will write, a year or so later ; to Vendeville, Sept. 16, 1578, Knox, 59 ; this, again, before any political moves by Rome, or stimulation of such from Spain.

[3] Multique mox ex Angliae scholis et academiis, vel recens instituti suorum Collegii fama vel catholicae institutionis desiderio, iuvenes confluxissent, ac nobiles etiam adolescentes vel curiositate (ut fit) vel etiam parentum voluntate non pauci venissent.   Allen to Vendeville, Sept. 16, 1578, Knox, 54.

[4] *Ibid.*, 58.   The religious revival in the Catholic Low Countries was a fact that greatly impressed these refugees bred in the England of 1540–1570.   " If you but made trial of our banishment ", Edmund Campion wrote, in 1572, to his erstwhile patron Richard Cheney, Elizabeth's bishop of Gloucester, " if you but cleared your conscience, and came to behold and consider the living examples of piety which are shown here by bishops, priests, friars, masters of colleges, rulers of provinces, lay people of every age, rank, and sex, I believe you would give up six hundred Englands for the opportunity of redeeming the residue of your time by tears and sorrow ".   From the translation of the letter in Simpson, 513.

noted, was among the nobler types of the younger men, of all classes but especially of the students of arts in the universities, and of the Common Law in London and also of young men of the court circle.[1]

Allen and his associates soon struck out a systematic procedure for the religious instruction of these earnest visitors.   Those who had not come with a view to being priests were lodged at the college until, fully instructed according to their age and capacity, they were reconciled to the Church, with repentance for their former life and for their schism.   And, in a kind of offensive, the Douay men wrote to Oxford and Cambridge to call away to the new life the friends and associates of past years.[2]

There also came to the college not a few visitors who were genuine heretics, some of them ministers and preachers.   All of these were, in the end, reconciled.   After a year or two in the college they wished to be priests, and were ordained and sent to England, where one of them had since been martyred.

But all the English whom business of any kind brought to Douay, or who passed through that town *en route* for France, Italy and the Low Countries, went to see the English students ; if not to see friends, then to look at the seminary of which they had heard so much.   Some of these visitors—a great part of them indeed—were wholly ignorant of all religion ; others were schismatics at least.   All were exhorted to stay at the college at least for a few days, and many did so ; those who were poor lived at the expense of the college for a month, and in that time they were taught the principal points of the Catholic religion, and how to make a good confession, and they were reconciled.   These *reconciliati* were, in their turn, apostles for the faith, once they had returned to England.[3]   Over 500 had been thus restored to the Church at the time when Allen was writing.[4]

[1] Prima ab haeresi defectio fuerit animadversa esse in nobilioribus iuvenibus omnium pene ordinum, maxime vero studiorum bonarum artium in academiis et juris Britannici Londini atque etiam aulicorum ; Knox, 55.

[2] Leading theologians among the heretics were also given a cordial invitation to visit the college. *Polliciti ipsis quamdiu hic manerent apud nos pro dignitate sustentationem et omnem humanitatem.* In all this there is no trace of that desire to light up Smithfield again, with which Allen has sometimes been credited.   And the letter is not written to one likely to have any objection to the " due punishment " of heretics as such. *Ibid.*, 58.

[3] Rursumque reconciliati ipsi non conquiescebant nisi idem etiam efficissent apud liberos, propinquos, famulos, amicos ; immo nonnunquam etiam liberi persuadent parentibus et uxores maritis ut fiant catholici et reconcilientur ; *ibid.*, 60.

[4] Sept. 16, 1578 ; *ibid.*, 54.   Allen also gives as a reason for many of the conversions, the goodness and competent learning of the Douay priests, contrasted by the converts-to-be with the ignorance and evil life of the clergy of the establishment of 1559.   This might be passed over as an unpleasing piece of self-satisfaction, but Walsingham is one day to say the same thing.   In December, 1586, he set down his thoughts on the great problem of arresting the new movement towards the Catholic faith—" the decay and falling away in religion ", in his words.   This evident fact is to be explained, he thinks, in two ways : the lack of learned and godly ministers, and the evil example of subtle persuasions of the seminary priests, " as well those that are restrained [i.e. in prison] as others dispersed throughout the realm ".   For which, cf. Conyers Read, II, 305, who prints a good part of this memorandum, and gives reasons for thinking Walsingham to be the author.   Cf. also, the petition of the House of Commons to the queen in March, 1576, only two years before Allen wrote this letter, complaining of the " great number of men admitted to occupy the place of ministers in the

When Persons came to describe for the Jesuits in Rome the fervent devotion of the Catholics in England, and their wonderful mutual charity, and to compare their brave resistance to the tyranny of Elizabeth with the all but universal treason to God in the time of Henry VIII,[1] he rounded it off by saying, " Truly, ' this is a change wrought by the hand of the most high ',[2] and to be counted among the greatest of God's mercies to this nation. Words cannot declare how greatly these colleges overseas have advanced the glory of God ; they are more fearful to the heretics than any armament of the Catholic princes ".[3]

The first condition of all this apostolic activity was a real change of mind among the Catholics in England—a new mental climate, as the jargon of today might say.   It is Allen who states the fact of the change, and who gives us the cause.   " Books opened the way ", he wrote,[4] explaining to a hostile world the aims of the new seminaries ; and, more explicitly, in the letter to Vendeville, " The books written in English by our people in Flanders (and printed there) on almost all the matters in controversy, did much to bring about this change in men's minds.   For in these books, written in a way adapted to the popular understanding, almost all the frauds of the heretics, the effects of heresy, the dissensions, blasphemies, contradictions, and absurdities, the heretics' falsification of Scripture and of learned authors, were made remarkably clear ; so that not only by the learned but by the popular voice we were judged to be superior to those whom we opposed ; and our adversaries, it was seen, only attained an equality with us through the power and arms of the state and what its laws enacted." [5]

The books to which Allen is referring in 1578 and 1581 are, principally, those which make up the Catholic side in the Harding-Jewel controversy of 1564–1567—forty-one works written by eighteen of the exiled scholars.[6] " Not less than 20,000 of these books ", Sander said later, " were imported into England and secretly sold." [7]   And he gave it as his opinion that they

---

Church of England who are not only altogether unfurnished of such gifts as are, by the word of God . . . [inseparable from] their calling, but also are infamous in their lives . . .".   Quoted Neale, *op. cit.*, 351.

[1] " In the reign of King Henry VIII, the father of this Elizabeth, almost the whole kingdom (bishops, prelates, and learned men innumerable), renounced the faith and the authority of the Pope at a single word from the tyrant.   But now, by the great mercy of God, in the persecution let loose by Henry's daughter, there are even boys and women who openly and before the judges not only profess their faith, but although threatened with death, refuse submissions that, to some people, might perhaps seem of little importance." *Persons*, 78 for Latin text.   [2] Ps. 76, 11.

[3] Written ? August 1581.   *Persons*, 78 for the Latin text here freely translated.

[4] *Apologie of Two English Seminaries* (1581), p. 26.

[5] Knox, 55–56 ; to Vendeville, Sept. 16, 1578.

[6] Pollen (*op. cit.*, 107, n. 1) gives the following names.   The Wykehamists are marked *. William Allen, George Bullock, Alan Cope, Thomas Dorman,* Lewis Evans, James Fenn,* Thomas Harding,* Nicholas Harpsfield,* Thomas Hoskins, Robert Johnson, John Martial,* Robert Poyntz,* John Rastell,* Nicholas Sanders,* Richard Shacklock, Thomas Stapleton,* Laurence Vaux ; and John Fowler, another Wykehamist, the printer.

[7] Quoted Pollen, 111, from the manuscript of Sander's *De Schismate* (English College, Rome), fo. 136.

did more for the Catholic cause than anything else in a good fifty years.[1]
With the foundation of Douay College this apostolate of letters, interrupted
when the Calvinists sacked Antwerp in 1566 and Louvain in 1568, started
up once more. To keep it in being became one of Allen's principal anxieties
—an anxiety appreciated and shared by one who was perhaps the most effective
writer of them all, Robert Persons. " Nothing has so helped, and is helping ",
the Jesuit wrote to Aquaviva,[2] " nothing will do so much to preserve our
cause in the future, and to make it known, as the printing of Catholic books,
works of controversy and works of devotion." More than once Allen tells
the Cardinal Secretary of State that the production of such books and their
distribution must be a leading activity of the mission to England. " We
need to write books of many kinds, if the nobles and people of England are
to be converted, and to provide for their conveyance over land and sea,
and for their distribution gratis in England—a most dangerous business,
the distribution of such books. By this means alone what we achieve is
hardly to be believed, at a cost (as is evident) that is more than we can bear." [3]

These books,[4] for importing, circulating, and possessing which the
Catholics were so heavily punished, which the Elizabethan bishops made such
efforts to search out, and which a special Act of Parliament proscribed in
1581, were wholly spiritual in their purpose and content—unlike those
productions of Knox and Goodman and Ponet and the rest banned under
Mary.   They are simple expositions of the Catholic teaching about the points
in controversy, critical accounts of the new theories, replies to the various
slanders and caricatures of Catholic belief ; and there is an especial insistence
that what was established in 1559, and is now being imposed under penalties,
is a different kind of religion, a heresy, and that no man can belong both to
this and to the Catholic Church. As to seditious writings, incitement to
rebellion, incitement to kill the queen—direct or indirect—Allen was able
to say to Burghley, before the face of all Europe, in a debate where the Lord
Treasurer was the challenger, that " our priests and Catholic brethren have
behaved themselves discreetly and nothing seditiously " with regard to the
papal sentence excommunicating the queen, " uttering in no preaching,
speech or book . . . any disloyal word against her Majesty ", a moderation
" kept in all places and persons of our nation, two only learned men of great
zeal and excellence indeed—Dr. Saunders and Dr. Bristow—excepted " ;
and that, upon Catholics objecting (who " wished the matter so offensive had
never been touched "), " not only Dr. Bristow omitted in his second edition
. . . that odious point, not fit at the time to be handled, but Dr. Saunders
also . . . suppressed to his life's end a very learned book made in defence of

---

[1] Quoted Pollen, 106, from *idem*, fo. 136.   [2] Oct. 21, 1581, *Persons*, 96.
[3] Jan. 16, 1585, in Knox, 245, here freely translated. See also, *ibid.*, 240–242 Allen's
letter of Sept. 27, 1584, and the passage, already noticed (cf. *supra*, p. 296) in the letter to
Vendeville of Sept. 16, 1578.
[4] Southern, p. 31, notes 206 titles known to have been published between 1559 and 1603 :
1559–1570, 58 ; 1570–1582, 47 ; 1582–1594, 21 ; 1594–1603 80 (which figure includes the
inter-Catholic controversial works of the Archpriest affair). Cf. *idem.*, 33–43 for an account
of the actual distribution of these books in England.

Pius V his sentence, and printed above fourteen years since ; [1] no copy thereof that is known being now extant." [2]

Of Allen's own books there should be mentioned his defence of the seminaries,[3] his account of the earliest martyrs,[4] and his reply to Lord Burghley's slanderous tract,[5] already quoted more than once. Laurence Vaux had produced a *Catechism of Christian Doctrine*,[6] Richard Bristowe *A brief treatise of diverse plaine and sure wayes to find out the truthe in this doubtful and dangerous time of Heresie* (1574),[7] and Persons, to omit for the moment

---

[1] Allen is writing in 1584.

[2] The quotations are from the 1914 reprint of Allen's *Defence of Catholics*, I, 76, 81, 82–83. About the content of all this literature, Black says nothing at all (*op. cit.*, 146–147) ; Pollard has just two, unforgivably misleading, references : (i) " Somerville's insane design to shoot the Queen, discovered in October 1583 . . . illustrates the effect of writings like Allen's on ill-balanced minds " (*op. cit.*, 384-385) ; (ii) " Parry was re-animated [in his design to murder Elizabeth, which both the priests he consulted—Watts and Creighton—had condemned as sinful] by a perusal of Allen's book ", *ibid.*, 388. The whole content of these Catholic books, in the period 1559–1582, is reviewed in great detail in Southern, *Elizabethan Recusant Prose*, 59–335.

[3] *An Apologie and True Declaration of the Institution and Endevors of the two English Colleges, the one in Rome, the other now resident in Rheims* (Mounts in Henault, 1581).

[4] *A brief History of the glorious Martyrdom of twelve reverend Priests executed within these twelve months, for confession and defence of the Catholic Faith, but under the false pretence of Treason ; with a note of sundry things that befel them in their life and imprisonment, and a preface concerning their innocency.* 1582 ; 1908 ed., *The Martyrdom of Fr. Campion and his Companions.*

[5] *The Execution of Justice in England for maintenance of public and Christian peace against certeine stirrers of sedition.* 1583. Reprinted, *Somers Tracts* (2nd edn.), I, and Harleian *Miscellany* (1809), II. For the full title of Allen's reply (*Defence of Catholics*) cf. *supra*, 239. It is surprising that neither of the standard histories of the reign make any mention of this extraordinary duel : the queen's chief minister publicly explaining a policy because he knows it is odious in the eyes of all Europe—" to justify before the world his war of extermination against priests ", says Meyer, *op. cit.*, 139—and the man replying who is responsible for the move that is now threatening the foundations of the minister's religious achievement. Not everything can be told, of course, in histories which have so narrow a space in which to manoeuvre. But whether the Elizabethan Catholics were traitors justly punished, or the unhappy victims of the malice and hypocrisy of Cecil's policies, is a leading question in the history of the time, and one to which both these writers have evidently given much thought. There is, however, not a reference to this Burghley-Allen " controversy " in Pollard, or Black ; nor is there any in Conyers Read ; and although Meyer, 139–140, disposes of Mandell Creighton's justification of the persecution by Elizabeth's government as a matter of politics (for which cf. *E.H.R.*, VII, 82, art., " The Excommunication of Queen Elizabeth "), he makes no use of Allen's *Defence*. He does not, as one would expect, confront Burghley's charges (the real source of so much of this apologetic in the modern historians) with Allen's replies. " Hypocrisy " is a word that comes very easily to historians who are Catholics when they write about the Elizabethan persecution of the Catholics. What they mean by it is that the government knew the victims were innocent of designs against the State, and put them to death in order to support a legend—the powerful, " friendly to the national enemy " legend—against them and against their religion. No sensible writer will attempt the proof of such a charge who has not an intimate knowledge of the detail of e.g. Cecil's correspondence and memoranda. One such, and a Catholic, was J. H. Pollen. He may be quoted, not as supplying an *ipse dixit* that settles the matter (in history there are no such things) but to illustrate what is said here about the use of the word " hypocrisy ". In *Plots and Sham Plots* (*The Month*, June, 1902, p. 614) he speaks of " the fate of the many victims who were slaughtered, in order to keep the Queen and the realm under the impression that they were threatened by a great religious conspiracy ". This is, of course, to class the Elizabethan statesmen (the architects of the Settlement of 1559) with the men who employed Titus Oates.

[6] In 1567. Reprinted, 1885, by T. G. Law, for the Chetham Society. Cf. *supra*, 248.

[7] This is the book often referred to as Bristowe's *Motives*. The author, a Worcestershire man, was somewhat younger than Allen (born 1538), master of arts (1562) and fellow of

other works, wrote the famous *Christian Directory*, upon which the spiritually bankrupt *ecclesia* of Cecil gladly seized and, making the work safe for Protestant use, published and republished it during these years.[1]

But the crowning glory of this scholarship was Gregory Martin's translation of the Bible, executed at the college between 1578 and 1582. The translator, a Sussex man,[2] was one of the original scholars of the new St. John's College founded at Oxford in 1557, and thereby the close friend of Edmund Campion ; a man who " went beyond all his time in humane literature, whether in poetry or prose ".[3] From Oxford he went to the household of the Duke of Norfolk, and at a critical moment in the duke's life (1570), Martin, faced with the choice between open profession of his faith and apostasy, left England for Douay, the college and the university. He took up his theological studies,[4] was ordained priest in March, 1573,[5] and spent the rest of his short life teaching theology and preparing his great translation. Unlike those classical translations of the English Reformers, Tyndale, the Geneva Bible, the Bishops' Bible, and the Authorised Version of 1611, the Douay Bible is not a translation from the original texts, but from the Latin version known as the Vulgate, which the Council of Trent had recently made the official version for public use. Like all the bibles of the time this Douay translation was generously annotated, all texts being explained which the enemy had misinterpreted.

This is not the place, very obviously, to discuss the merits of Gregory Martin's remarkable work.[6] But in the Preface, and in the Notes, the

---

Exeter College (1567), Oxford. He and Campion were then regarded as " the two brightest men of the university ". From the beginning of the foundation at Douay he was Allen's right hand man, acting as prefect of studies, and managing all in Allen's absences. He took his doctorate in theology at Douay in 1575. Bristowe died of consumption when barely 43 (Oct., 1581), at Harrow-on-the-Hill, sent back to England in the hope that his native air would halt the disease.

[1] *The first Booke of the Christian Exercise appertayning to Resolution*, 1582. The Protestant editions begin with that of Edmund Bunny, 1584. " Before Persons' death in 1610 his work had been reprinted four times by Catholics and at least fifteen Protestant editions had been published, in addition to seven Protestant editions of [the] second part.—Later, while a Protestant translated it into Welsh, Catholic versions appeared in French, Scotch, German, Latin and Italian, and of this Italian version there were some nine editions ", L. Hicks, S.J., *Introduction* to Persons, xlv. Cf. also, Herbert Thurston, S.J., *Catholic Writers and Elizabethan Readers*, in *The Month*, Dec., 1894.

[2] Born about 1540, at Maxfield, in the parish of Guestling, near Winchelsea.

[3] Antony à Wood, *Athenae Oxoniensis* (1813), I, col. 487. Seven of Gregory Martin's letters to Campion are printed in *Douay Diaries*, Appendix, 308–320.

[4] S.T.B., 1573 ; S.T.Lic., 1575.

[5] *Douay Diaries*, 6. Richard Bristowe was ordained at the same time, the first of the new priests, as Gregory Martin was the second.

[6] Cf. Southern, 231–262, for a good account, and a review of all the contemporary controversy about the translation, and of the later controversy about its literary merits. There is a very scholarly summary, by Dom Roger Hudleston, the *Introduction* (pp. v–xxviii) to the 1926 reprint of the Rheims Testament (*The Orchard Books*, Burns Oates and Washbourne, London). The college diary gives us the dates when Gregory Martin began his work and when he finished, Oct. 16, 1578 and March, 1582 (*Douay Diaries*, 145, 186). The translator tells us that it was lack of money alone that prevented the publication in 1582, at Rheims, of more than the New Testament. Not until 1609 was the Old Testament published—by which time the college was back at Douay ; whence the somewhat confusing references to

translator and his associates [1] have many things to say that are of interest to general history because reflections of—what we know so superficially—the views about the Settlement of 1559 of these Catholics upon whom it came.

"We do not publish" this translation, they say, "upon erroneous opinion of necessity, that the Holy Scriptures should always be in our mother tongue, or that they ought, or were ordained by God, to be read indifferently of all, or could easily be understood of everyone that readeth or heareth them in a known language". What has led to this translation is "special consideration of the present time, state, and condition of our country, unto which divers things are either necessary or profitable or medicinable now, that otherwise in the peace of the Church were neither much requisite, nor perchance wholly tolerable." [2] It is "compassion to see our beloved countrymen, with extreme danger of their souls, to use only such prepared translations and erroneous men's mere fancies for the pure and blessed word of truth", that has set these scholars to work. In a work whose avowed aim is to supplant translations already popular and asserted to be corrupt, it was natural to aim, above all, at a translation that should be literal ; and the Preface, defending this, says, "We . . . [keep] ourselves as near as is possible . . . to the very words and phrases which, by long use, are made venerable, though to some profane or delicate ears they may seem more hard or barbarous . . . acknowledging with St. Jerome, that in other writings it is enough to give in translation sense for sense, but that in Scripture, lest we miss the sense, we must keep the very words ".[3]

Fidelity to this ideal brought it about that, in more than one place, the gibe of Fuller has point, that this is "a translation needing to be translated ".[4]

"the Rheims Testament" and "the Douay Bible". This achievement of Gregory Martin and the rest must not be confused with the version commonly in use as "official" among English-speaking Catholics for the last 200 years, which last is a revision (by Bishop Richard Challoner) of Martin's work, that is so extensive as to be, in Newman's words, "little short of a new translation" (cf. his remarkable study of the various versions in *The Rheims and Douay Version of Holy Scripture*, reprinted in *Tracts, Theological and Ecclesiastical*, from *The Rambler*, July, 1859). Cf. also, Archdeacon Cotton's *Attempt to show what has been done by Roman Catholics for the Diffusion of the Holy Scriptures in English* (Oxford, 1855) and J. G. Carleton, *The Part of Rheims in the Making of the English Bible* (1902) ; "a total of nearly three thousand readings in the Authorised Version [are] due almost certainly to Gregory Martin ", Hudleston, *op. cit.*, p. xxviii.

[1] Allen and Bristowe (and William Rainolds) revised the translation, Bristowe wrote the notes.

[2] Cf. Allen to Vendeville, Sept. 16, 1578, explaining his hopes about a translation, Knox, *op. cit.*, 65.

[3] And the Preface kindly supplies two specimens of this careful, deliberate art : Against the spirituals of wickedness in the celestials (Eph. vi. 12) ; and, As infants even now born, reasonable milk without guile desire ye (1 Pet. ii. 2). And, in later centuries, with the vocabulary of our language long past its adolescence, there has been much merriment on such passages as : For consummating a word and abridging it in equity : because a word abridged shall our Lord make upon the earth (Rom. ix. 28), or, Beneficence and communication do not forget, for with such hosts God is promerited (Heb. xiii. 16).

[4] Quoted Hudleston, *ut cit.*, xviii. On the other hand, cf. A. W. Pollard, "the translation is much simpler than popular accounts of it make out " ; and "'hard places' do not occur on every page of the New Testament, and it is easy to find long passages in the Gospels without a difficult word in them, and which a good reader could make all the more dramatic because of the abruptness of some of the constructions and transitions " ; also G. P. Krapp, "the effect

The criticism would have embarrassed the translators far less than it has their later apologists. If, as Westcott declared, the vocabulary of this translation " is enriched by the bold reduction of innumerable Latin words to English service ",[1] there were also many Latin words not so patient of this reduction, words that were deliberately left in as irreducible, for the following remarkable reason, which, again, throws light on the religious mentalities actually in mortal combat at this time. The reason given is, " because we cannot possibly attain to express these words fully in English, and we think much better that the reader, staying at the difficulty of them, should take an occasion to look in the table following, or otherwise to ask the full meaning of them, than, by putting some usual English words that express them not, so to deceive the reader ".[2]

The Douay scholar is again countering " the erroneous opinion that the Holy Scriptures . . . could easily be understood of everyone that readeth or heareth them in a known language ". Translation is not enough. And the related idea, that faithful translation itself is not a matter of the philologist's skill in tongues, underlies the criticism, made in this Preface, of the heretical translations of the past half century : " We must not imagine . . . that our forefathers suffered every schoolmaster, scholar or grammarian that had a little Greek or Latin straight to take in hand the holy Testament." Translators of this kind, " frame and fine the phrases of the holy Scriptures after the form of profane writers, sticking not, for the same to supply, add, alter, or diminish as freely as if they translated Livy, Vergil, or Terence " : and, as More complained of Tyndale, " their intolerable liberty and licence " has changed " the accustomed callings of God, angels, men, places and things, used by the Apostles and all antiquity, in Greek, Latin, and other languages of Christian nations into new names, sometimes falsely, and always ridiculously, and for ostentation taken of the Hebrews ". And it is in deliberate protest against these practices that, in the Douay translation, such terms are exactly reproduced as " Penance, doing penance, chalice, priest, deacon, traditions, altar, host and the like " ; and " to signify to the people that these and such like names came out of the very Latin text of the Scripture ".

The work was rapturously received by the enemy. The Protestant scholars swarmed, and presently Cartwright,[3] Whitaker,[4] Fulke,[5] and Wither,

---

of the whole is not as grotesque as might be inferred from the more extreme examples of learned locutions . . ." ; both of these authors I quote from Southern, 241.

[1] *History of the English Bible* (1870), 258, n. 2.

[2] The quotations in this and the succeeding paragraph are from the Preface to the first edition of 1582—the pages of which are not numbered.

[3] Persuaded to the work by Leicester and Walsingham (J. B. Mullinger, in *D.N.B.*, s.v. *Cartwright, Thomas*) and rewarded by £100 a year from the queen (P.R.O., *Eliz.* (Domestic) Vol. CLIV, no. 48)—so L. Hicks, S.J., in *Persons*, 174, n. 3. Whitgift—the war between the two schools is now on once more—managed to prevent the publication of Cartwright's book : it might tell as much against 1559 as against Douay ; and not until 1618 did it appear.

[4] Now (since 1580) regius professor of divinity at Cambridge, and fresh from his exposition of the fundamental theme, *Pontifex Romanus est ille Antichristus, quem futurum Scriptura praedixit*. J. B. Mullinger, in *D.N.B.*, s.v. *Whitaker, William*.

[5] William Fulke (1538–1589) was a schoolfellow of Edmund Campion at St. Paul's. About the time when Campion's Oxford career was closing, Fulke was a principal figure in the

were busy replying to the annotations, and Fulke did Douay the great service of printing the whole of the translation in the book written to criticise it. And this folio was itself three times reprinted.

Three of Bristowe's many notes deserve quotation : they are valuable contemporary witness as to the way Catholics could regard the forces which, in a lifetime, had transformed their country.

On the *Apocalypse* of St. John (*The Book of Revelation*) ii. 5—Be mindful therefore from whence thou art fallen : and do penance, and do the first works. But if not, I come to thee, and will move thy candlestick out of his plaçe, unless thou do penance—the comment is made, " *Will move*. Note that the cause why God taketh the truth from certain countries, and removeth their Bishops or Churches into captivity or desolation, is the sin of the Prelates and people. And that is the cause (no doubt) that Christ hath taken away our golden candlestick, that is, our Church in England. God grant us to remember our fall, to do penance and the former works of charity which our first Bishops and Church were notable and renowned for."

On ix. 5 of the same book—It was commanded them that they should not hurt the grass of the earth, nor any green thing—this is said, " *Nor any green things*. The heretics never hurt or seduce the green tree, that is, such as have a living faith working by charity, but commonly they corrupt him in faith who should otherwise have perished for ill life, and him that is reprobate, that hath neither the sign of the Cross (which is God's mark) in the forehead of his body, nor the note of election in his soul."

And on the last verse of the New Testament—Come, Lord Jesus—is this prayer, " And now O Lord Christ, most just and merciful, we thy poor creatures that are so afflicted for confession and defence of the holy Catholic and Apostolic truth, contained in this thy sacred book, and in the infallible doctrine of thy dear spouse our mother the Church, we cry also unto thy Majesty with tenderness of our hearts unspeakable, COME LORD JESUS QUICKLY, and judge betwixt us and our adversaries, and in the mean time give patience, comfort, and constancy to all that suffer for thy name, and trust in thee.

<blockquote>
O Lord God our only helper and protector,
Tarry not long. AMEN.
LAUS DEO."
</blockquote>

" stirrs " at St. John's, Cambridge, described, *supra*, p. 160. He was a staunch leader on the Cartwright side in the later disputes, and for a time expelled from his college for his pains. Leicester was his patron and Fulke survived, to become master of Pembroke College, in 1578, and to be one of the bears set to bait the thrice-racked Campion in the Tower disputations of 1581. Fulke's first effort against the new translation is entitled, *A defense of the Sincere and True Translations of the Holie Scriptures into the English Tong, against the manifolde cavils, frivolous quarrels, and impudent slaunders of Gregorie Martin, one of the readers of Popish Divinitie in the trayterous Seminarie of Rhemes.* . . . Of Fulke, it has been written that his " language was unmeasured, and, even in that age, he was conspicuous for the virulence of his invective against his opponents ". E. Venables, in *D.N.B.*, s.v. *Fulke, William.*

2

Allen did not exaggerate when, to Vendeville, he wrote that four years of the Douay apostolate in England had made so great a difference. On June 21, 1577, John Aylmer, the third Bishop of London of the new line, writing to the Secretary of State, Sir Francis Walsingham, said at least as much about the evident revival, and about that feature of it to which Allen attached the most importance. " I have had conference with the Archbishop of Canterbury, and we have received from divers of our brethren, bishops of the realm, news that the Papists marvellously increase both in numbers and in obstinate withdrawal of themselves, from the church and services of God ".[1] And within a few weeks of this letter bishops and privy councillors were conferring, " How such as are backward and corrupt in religion may be induced to conformity and others stayed from like corruption ".[2]

It is at this time, in the summer of 1577, while the relations of England and Spain remain as amicable as the treacherous aggression of Elizabethan foreign policy will allow, and while there is yet no news of Anglo-Spanish-Papal plots (and not a Jesuit in the country, nor any of them even blessed with the idea of "invading" it), that the main lines of the policy, vis-à-vis the Catholics, are laid down which will henceforth be followed until the end of the reign. The plan and the determination—which will now never slacken—to activate the persecution, to inaugurate the terror, are the product of fear ; and the cause of the fear is one thing only, the evident fact that, under the influence of the new missionary priests, Catholicism is coming to life again, that Catholics are finding the courage to live as Catholics and to give up their hypocritical attendance at the new church services.

What this conference first recommends is a kind of census, to be taken by all the bishops, of all who refuse to come to church, " especially such as are of countenance and quality and do offend in example ". And these offenders should next, for two months, " be conferred with . . . by men sufficiently learned after a charitable sort ". If this has no effect pains should follow, and " by degrees ". First of all, " restraining of them of their liberties " with fines according to their ability to pay, providing that they are still willing to be conferred with ; then the offer of the Oath of Supremacy—the Acts of 1559 and 1563 are to come at last into general operation ; " lastly ", since the number of recusants " is so great " [3] that the " places of restraint " are not able to hold them, it might be well to apply the policy gradually, the " most corrupt " dioceses first of all, and in these " the principal persons ". There are further suggestions about schoolmasters, and about the servants of recusants, and also about the Catholic prelates of Queen Mary's time still in custody, the Bishop of

[1] Letter printed in C.R.S., xxii, no. 1. Cf. also Conyers Read, II, 280.
[2] This is the heading of the memorandum found by Conyers Read in one of Walsingham's letter books (P.R.O., S.P./12, Vol. 145, no. 10) and taken by him as embodying the conclusions of this conference of (?) July, 1577. Cf. his reasons, ibid., 282, n. 1. Extracts from it are printed infra, p. 415. [3] Not, " may be found to be so great ".

Lincoln (Thomas Watson), for example, the Abbot of Westminster (John Feckenham), the Archdeacon of Canterbury (Nicholas Harpsfield) and others.

On July 28 these, " who for a few months had enjoyed a certain amount of freedom ", were ordered back to the custody of the bishops.[1]   In October, 1577, the council sent out the orders for the " census " : every recusant, in every diocese, " with the value of their lands ".   And in return the bishops sent in 1,387 names ;[2] many fewer than if the test had been the communion.[3]

The bishops, in the conference about which Aylmer wrote to Walsingham, had wanted to introduce a new punishment, a really heavy fine for those who neglected to receive the communion of the new service. He thought it should bring in £1,000 a year to the queen. Nothing came of this suggestion : nor did the plan yet develop of locking up the wealthier Catholics. The queen was beginning to occupy herself, yet again! with the marriage proposals of the brother of the French king.[4] And orders were now sent out to magistrates and local notabilities " to forbear to persecute by way of indictment such as lately were presented, whose names you certified up ".[5]

This last letter was written in the winter of 1579–1580, it would seem, and meanwhile the government had not lost sight of the warning that prison accommodation would soon be overtaxed were the Catholic recusants really to be rounded up. A plan was drafted for the organisation of various castles as prisons for Catholics " of the better sort ". As to " the baser sort " there would be the punishment of a heavy fine.[6]

The government and its bishops had been, for three years, anxiously discussing what new severities would best meet the success of the Catholic mission—and the arrival of Nicholas Sander in Kerry, in the autumn of 1579, with his papal " army," eighty strong, had given them fine material for the cloak of deceit which their policy must wear—when, in June and July,

---

[1] The quotation is from the *Douay Diary*, Aug. 8, 1577 (pp. 127–128). For the government's decision, July 28, cf. Dasent, Vol. 10, p. 4.

[2] The lists of names are printed in C.R.S., Vol. 22.   [3] Cf. *supra*, p. 130.

[4] The suggestion of this as the reason why the drive against Catholics now slackened is Conyer Read's, II, 285. The heat was turned on or off, not according as Catholics were more or less dangerously traitors, but to suit the convenience of the government's policies.

[5] For the letter here quoted, almost certainly Walsingham's (and a private letter, not an official order), cf. Conyers Read, II, 283–284.

[6] Conyers Read, II, 282, n. 2 (q.v.) using " an undated paper " which was " certainly written before Feb. 20, 1579 ". It is partly in Walsingham's hand, and in places is corrected by Burghley. The paper is Brit. Mus. Harleian, 360, fo. 65. The castles proposed were : Banbury, for Warwick, Oxford, and Northampton ; Framlingham, for Norfolk and Suffolk ; Kimbolton, for Huntingdon, Buckingham, and Bedford ; Porchester, for Surrey, Hants, and Sussex ; Devizes, for Dorset, Wilts, and Somerset ; Melbourne, for Stafford, Derby, Leicester, Lincoln, and Nottingham ; Halton, for Lancashire, Cheshire, and North Wales ; Wigmore, for Hereford, Monmouth, Worcester, and South Wales. Those proposed for the north were Middleham, Knaresborough, Durham and Barnard Castle. Simpson, 234—so Conyers Read notes—has mistaken the date of this paper, making the plan a consequence of the success of Persons and Campion in 1580–1581, and he speaks of the plan as a thing realised. In my own book, *Rome and the Counter Reformation in England* (1942), p. 278, note, I have quoted Simpson without knowledge of his source and without seeing his erroneous use of it.

The Execution of

Iustice in England for maintenaunce
of publique and Christian peace,
againſt certeine ſtirrers of ſedition, and adherents to the traytors and enemies of the
Realme, without any perſecution of them
for queſtions of Religion, as is falſely
reported and publiſhed by the
fautors and foſterers of
their treaſons.
xvii. Decemb.
1583.

ꝭImprinted at
London. 1583.

THE LORD TREASURER AS APOLOGIST, 1583

SIR WILLIAM CECIL
LORD BURGHLEY

Si decem millia Pædagogorum habeatis in Christo. sed non multos Patres nam in Christo Iesu per Euangelium ego vos genui. 1 *Corm* 4

WILLIAM ALLEN
CARDINAL OF *S. MARTINO AI MONTI*

A · TRVE
SINCERE AND MO-
DEST DEFENCE OF ENGLISH
CATHOLIQVES THAT SVFFER FOR THEIR
Faith both at home and abrode: against a false, se-
ditious and flaunderous Libel intituled;

THE EXECVTION OF IVSTICE IN ENGLAND.

*VVher in is declared, hovv vniustlie the Protestants doe charge
Catholiques vvith treason; hovv vntrulie they deny their
persecution for Religion; and hovv deceitfullie they seeke
to abuse strangers about the cause, greatnes, and maner
of their sufferinges, vvith diuers other matters
perteining to this purpose.*

Psal. 62.

Vt obstruatur os loquentium iniqua.

That the mouth may be stopped of such as speake vniustlie.

Psal. 49.

Os tuum abundauit malitia, & lingua tua concinnabat dolos.

Thy mouth hath abounded in malice, and thy tongue hath
coninglie framed lies.

THE LORD TREASURER EXPOSED, 1584

1580, heralded by an immense amount of fuss,[1] the two Jesuits, Robert Persons and Edmund Campion, touched the Kentish shore.[2]

The co-operation of the Society of Jesus in the new mission to England was, in the nature of things, bound to come, sooner or later. In 1563 there were thirty or forty Englishmen in the Society, " a few of whom had completed their religious training ".[3] In 1578 Persons wrote to Campion, then at Prague, " We are here at Rome now twenty-four Englishmen of the Society whereof five hath entered within this month ".[4] And four months later this same English Jesuit was writing to Allen of his own wish to serve on the English mission.[5] Whether Persons knew it or not Allen had already, more than once, approached the father-general with a request for men. A paper has survived, written by him about 1576, that is a kind of report for the information of the general of the Jesuits on the needs of the mission, its resources and its prospects. This can hardly have been prepared except as part of a discussion to win the co-operation of the Society.[6] And in 1578, Allen made a direct appeal, in passionate language, to the general—" you who through yours gather in the sheep of Christ as far as the distant Indies " —to join in searching for the lost sheep that was in England.[7]

The father-general, at this time, was a Netherlander, Everard Mercurian. He had, in his time, been the provincial superior in the land where Allen had founded his college, and it is all but certain that the two men had then met. More than once, since then, he had been of service to the college, as Allen now gratefully reminds him.[8] And he must have

---

[1] " Our minds cannot but misgive us when we hear all men, I will not say whispering, but crying, the news of our coming ". Edmund Campion, from St. Omer, to Everard Mercurian, June 20, 1580, quoted Simpson, 175 ; q.v. for the whole letter, translated from More, *Hist. Provinciae Ang. S.J.*, 63. In the same letter we read " There is a certain English gentleman, very knowing in matters of state, who comes often to me ; he tells me that the coming of the Bishop of St. Asaph is canvassed in letters and in conversation. Great expectations are raised by it ; for most men think that such a man, at his age, would never undertake such a task, except there was some rising on foot."

[2] The most extraordinary language has been used about the event, even by historians ; e.g. Conyers Read : " In 1578 the Jesuits began to invade England in force " (II, 1) ; " In view of the fact that the Jesuits were invading England by force ", i.e. by the autumn of 1580–1581 (*ibid.*, 172) ; " In the autumn of 1581, the Jesuits, already in force in England, determined to invade Scotland " (*ibid.*, 177). This writer tends to see Jesuits everywhere, and Dr. Nicholas Sander becomes " one of the most famous of English Jesuits " (*ibid.*, 363). Persons noted at the time how, in order to blight the harvest of the Catholic revival, the move was devised to identify Catholicism with what was a much more fearsome bogy because quite unknown : " For from now on, in order to give rise to increased jealousy of us, they are beginning to wage war on the whole cause as identified solely with our names, and to call the Catholic religion the religion of the Jesuits " ; to Aquaviva, Oct. 21, 1581 ; Persons, 114 (Latin text, 105). " Jesuit " sounds more sinister even than " priest ", and so begins to be used, by scare-creators, of all priests, and then it comes to be accepted that all the priests, or a good proportion of the priests, for whom Elizabeth's government legislated were Jesuits. Cf. J. W. Willis-Bund, *Select Cases from the State Trials* (1879), with his section-heading, *The Jesuit Trials*. Cf., also, Meyer, 206, on the " lasting results " of the fact that these sinister personages did not go about England dressed as priests, " The ' Jesuit in disguise ' became a typical character in popular imagination ", to whom " political aims and schemes were attributed . . . without hesitation ".   [3] Pollen, *English Catholics*, 105.

[4] Nov. 28, 1578, *Persons*.   [5] March 30, 1579, *ibid*.

[6] Printed, C.R.S., IX (i.e. *Miscellanea*, VII).   [7] Oct. 26, 1578, Knox, 69.

[8] According to Persons, writing in 1605, it was Mercurian (whose agent was Possevino)

20

known how deep was Allen's sympathy with the spirit of the new Society, who can speak of himself in this letter as "Your servant and your son". Allen can only be reminding him of what he already knew when he now writes, that, from the beginning he has taken care to frame the spirit, the studies and the daily round of the college after the Jesuit pattern, than which (he goes on to say) nothing was better suited to the needs of the day, whether for the acquirement of learning, or deepening of piety, or—*quod maxime nunc requirimus*—the arousing of zeal for the salvation of souls.[1]

The Jesuit superiors thought the whole thing out very carefully. There was not a single chance or misfortune that came to pass as the years went by that they did not anticipate as possible. But the accident that in 1579 the Society was put in charge of the new seminary at Rome (an offshoot from Douay), and Allen's presence in Rome in the winter of 1579, carried the day. Mercurian gave in, and he commissioned for the work two really great priests, Edmund Campion and Robert Persons, with a lay brother to assist them, Ralph Emerson. With them, from Rome to the channel ports, there travelled another dozen ecclesiastics: elderly Marian priests who had been the last chaplains of the ancient English hospice in Rome (now become the new seminary), newly ordained priests of that seminary and Douay, Dr. Nicholas Morton, once a charter fellow of Trinity College, Cambridge, and canon of York (and Pius V's envoy to England in 1569), and the aged Bishop of St. Asaph, Thomas Goldwell.

Persons, easily disguised (to Campion's amusement) as a soldier,[2] crossed to Dover on June 11, and made such a friend of the searcher that the officer found him a horse and promised to look out for Campion (Mr. Edmonds), coming in a few days, and to help him also. It is a familiar story how the two great missionaries fared, and how after a rarely active thirteen months the one was taken and the other forced out by a chase so hot that he did not dare expose any Catholic home to the risk of giving him shelter. And what the two actually accomplished, still more what their brilliant offensive promised in the future, if it infuriated the more active of the new Elizabethan clergy, and alarmed the government as nothing had alarmed it in twenty years—this has also, for the co-religionists of the two missionaries, set their memory in a light that nearly four hundred years has not dimmed. What

---

who begged from Gregory XIII the monthly pension that was the first substantial help given to the college. C.R.S., II, 190.

[1] Knox, 69. We have also Allen's words to Maurice Chauncy, a year before this, " Consider the Jesuits' trade, who be men called of God to raise the necessary discipline of the Church and be the best ghostly fathers that the Church hath ", Aug. 10, 1577, Knox, 33. How close the relations were between Allen and the Society can best be seen from the warm, affectionate even, letters to him of the two generals, Mercurian and Aquaviva (1579–1585), published in C.R.S., IX (1911), 68–98. " Very noteworthy is the implicit trust which . . . Aquaviva places on Allen's judgment, even for the government of his own Jesuit subjects . . . [he] even empowers Allen to receive candidates into the Society for him ", Patrick Ryan, S.J. (the editor), *ibid.*, 13.

[2] " He was dressed up like a soldier—such a peacock, such a swaggerer . . ." Campion to Aquaviva, June 20, 1580, in Simpson, 174.

exactly was it that was special to their effort ?—the fact of their quite unusual gifts of intelligence and character conceded.

In the apostolate of Persons and Campion, we have, for once, the spectacle of the right idea brilliantly carried out : understanding of the first need, namely to know the position exactly ; the organised, rapid tour, next, to survey the whole country ; the " national mission " by two preachers of genius which this becomes ; a work of reconciliations and conversions over an area so extensive, and covered so speedily, that the two Jesuits seem simultaneously everywhere ; a work whose kind and whose effects cannot be kept secret—all the Catholics of England, it seems, knew of it, half expected (we feel) to meet the famous priests sooner or later ; and they knew, of course, as did all England, of the elaborate hunt to capture them.[1]

It is twelve months crowded with rumours and with adventures. Accident makes known the defence which Campion had prepared in advance against the slanders that would be circulated about his purpose; this paper [2] is attacked as " Campion's Brag and Challenge " ; [3] and then, a most unexpected happening, within a week or two a printed pamphlet appears that demolishes the assailants [4]—a pamphlet printed in England, at a press which Persons has had the wit to set up and which he has found men courageous enough to work. Then the government find an ex-student of the Roman Seminary who has abandoned Catholicism. He is made much of, indeed ; advertised as one who has preached before cardinals in Rome, and knows the innermost secrets behind the coming of the two Jesuits ; is set to preach in London, and to publish his findings in a book. And again Persons moves swiftly. Through Allen, from Rome, he secures an authentic copy from the Inquisition of the impostor's recantation, and in a second book printed at his secret press he blasts his spurious fame to shreds—and, incidentally, paints a remarkable picture of the organised charities of the papal capital for the edification of semi-pagan London.[5] Campion, intent on his theme that heresy is at the end of its hopes, writes his Latin tract in illustration,

---

[1] Cf. Persons, writing to Agazzari, Nov. 17, 1580, that he never dares stay more than two days in any of his many London refuges, and all day long is moving from place to place. *Persons*, 54, cf. also 85–86. Alphonso Agazzari, S.J., was rector of the English seminary at Rome.

[2] Printed in Simpson, 225–228.

[3] (i) William Charke, *An Answer to a Seditious Pamphlet lately cast abroad by a Jesuit, with a discovery of that blasphemous sect.* London, C. Barker, 1580, 8vo. (ii) Meredith Hanmer, *The great Bragge and Challenge of M. Campion a Jesuite, côfuted and answeared.* London, T. Marsch, 1581, 4to. Hanmer was vicar of Islington. " This doctor regardeth not an oath ", the recorder of London once wrote of him to Lord Burghley, " surely he is a bad man." Mr. Rowse records that he converted brasses in his church " into coin for his own use ; he then went into Ireland, and had a successful career as treasurer of Christ Church [cathedral] Dublin ". *England of Elizabeth*, 419.

[4] *A brief Censure upon two books in answer to M. Edmund Campion's offer of disputation.* Doway, by John Lyon, 1581, 16 mo. (a fictitious imprint, of course), pp. 86. For the full list of the books produced in this controversy cf. Simpson, 491–492, Gillow, V, 275 ff., and Southern, *op. cit.*

[5] *A Discoverie of I. Nichol, Minister misreported a Jesuite, latelye recanted in the Tower of London* . . . small 8vo., 194 pp. unpaged.

the brilliant, even amusing *Decem Rationes*. Persons, again, prints the work;[1] and the courage and ingenuity of William Hartley, a young Douay priest,[2] secures that there is a copy in every man's seat at the (Oxford) Commemoration of 1581, June 27. Add to this the first of Persons' English printed books, the *Brief Discourse . . . why Catholics do not go to Church*,[3] a simple, telling unveiling of the policy of craft; add what all this declared, the presence somewhere of a super-mind endlessly at work; add the failure of the close attempts to capture either of the priests; and we can understand the hatred for Persons, rightly guessed to be the organising brain of it all. In the debates of 1581 on the new anti-Catholic statutes where Campion is spoken of as " a wandering vagrant ", Persons is denounced as " a lurking wolf ". We do not need to read back into these months the political activities that will be his in the next few years [4] in order to understand why Persons was already so hated and so feared.

The letters of the two Jesuits make clear what an admirable organisation it was which they used so brilliantly; and, first of all, the miraculous amount of goodwill and generosity towards it, even among the wealthiest—indeed without this last, what they accomplished would have been impossible.[5] Persons arrived in London without, as we should say, a single Catholic address or a letter of introduction. To have carried such would have been folly indeed. " Arriving on foot, without a horse, [he] could get no lodging and was forced to go up and down, half a day, from place to place " [6] until a happy thought took him to the prison of the Marshalsea—the one place where

---

[1] *Rationes Decem : quibus fretus, certamen adversariis obtulit in causa fidei, Edmundus Campianus, Societate Nominis Iesu Presbyter : Allegatae Ad clarissimos viros, nostrates Academicos.* (So the title page of the original edition. Cf. Illustrations, no. 17.)

[2] Born in Derbyshire, 1557—at this time twenty-three. Educated at Oxford, St. John's College (the college of Campion), where he ended as chaplain. The president, Toby Mathew, later to be Archbishop of York, suspected him of Catholic sympathies and removed him from this post. Hartley left for Allen's seminary. He was entered there in August, 1579 and received minor orders a month later, the diaconate in December; and was ordained priest in Feb. 1580. He left Rheims for the English mission, June 16, 1580, and in October was sent to work among the scholars and students of Oxford—a bare year after his disappearance from St. John's. In Aug., 1581, he went to prison with the director of Persons' press, Stephen Brinkley, and the printers. He was tried, Feb. 1584, for conspiring to murder the queen, and condemned to death. The sentence was not carried out, and in Jan., 1585 he was deported to France. Later he returned to England and was hanged, in London, Oct. 5, 1588. William Hartley is one of the priests beatified by Pius XI in 1929. Cf. Challoner, 150, and Burton and Pollen, I, 522–531.

[3] *A Brief Discourse contayning certayne Reasons Why Catholiques refuse to goe to Church* . . . pp. 70.

[4] The worst offender, in this, is Simpson, *Life of Edmund Campion*, pp. 278–279, 342, whose case depends on writing as though what actually happened in 1582–1583, and was not really known to the government until 1584, had happened in 1580–1581 during Persons' stay in England as a missionary.

[5] Two other Jesuits, of later years, who met the like generosity from wealthy families, and were able thereby to make their own lives a real centre for the work of other priests too, were Fr. Henry Garnet (the friend of the Vaux of Harrowden) and Fr. John Gerard, whose autobiography, re-translated by Philip Caraman, everyone has recently been reading—far and away the best memorial of this heroic period. Fr. Garnet's twenty years of wide apostolate, from within the Vaux family group, has also been told with great skill in the book by Fr. Godfrey Anstruther, O.P., *Vaux of Harrowden* (1953).

[6] Persons' own account [of 1605], C.R.S., II, 200.

Catholics had not to fear identification ; and through the famous prisoner Thomas Pound (once a courtier of the queen) he made his first contacts with the Catholic nobles and gentry of the capital. From now on all was well. " We were abundantly provided (by the goodness of God) with all we needed ", he was to write ; " for each of us, without asking, was given clothes, money, and two riding horses with a groom. Besides this, a number of young men, of good birth and wealthy, offered to accompany us wherever we may go ; so do they intend thereby to share in all our dangers." [1] And so the great tour began, and the two Jesuits " passed through the most part of the shires of England,[2] preaching and administering the sacraments in almost every gentleman's and nobleman's house that we passed by, whether he was Catholic or not, provided he had any Catholics in his house to hear us." [3]

The chief of this band of laymen was George Gilbert, a gentleman of Suffolk, " who had been a great puritan in time past ". This disciple of Dering, Fr. William Good, S.J., had instructed and reconciled, and Persons had been his sponsor in Confirmation.[4] The story of the deeply spiritual lives of this group, of the way in which the Jesuits taught them to super-naturalise their gallant spirit, of all that was accomplished thereby, must be read elsewhere.[5] With the passing of the two great priests who captained them—and the coming of a terror still more exacting and, to men of property above all, most ruinous—the adventure ended, never to be renewed.[6] But in

---

[1] Persons to Agazzari, Aug. 5, 1580, in *Persons*, 41.

[2] In the late summer and the autumn of 1580 Persons worked through the counties of Derby, Worcester, Hereford and Gloucester, Campion through Berkshire, Oxfordshire and Northampton. In 1580–1581 Campion went to Lancashire, via the Catholic gentry of Nottinghamshire and the West Riding of Yorkshire.

[3] Persons, in Simpson, 233, no reference to source.

[4] Persons has described him well, " He put in execution so much as had been counselled him, drawing divers principal young gentlemen to the same purpose, who taking lodging together and sojourning in the chief pursuivant's house, who was of most credit with the bishop in those days, and dwelt in Chancery lane in London, were by his countenance and by the protection of one Dr. Adam Squire, son-in-law to the Bishop of London whom they fee'd, protected for divers years, and had access of priests unto them and sundry Masses daily said in their house until the Jesuits came in, when times grew to be much more exas-perated ". *The First Entry of the Jesuits into England* [1605], C.R.S., II, 201. When, in 1581, the hunt for Gilbert became so hot that his presence in England was dangerous to all his friends, Persons sent him to the Continent. At Rome he was received into the Society, and there died a most holy death, Oct. 6, 1583.

[5] For instance in Simpson (pp. 220–224), whose account is, however, wrong in one im-portant particular—these young men were not organised through membership in the famous Jesuit confraternity known as the Sodality, for which, cf. Pollen, in *The Month*, June, 1905, p. 592.

[6] . . . *eius opera conservari ac sustentari patres ipsi Societatis*, Allen wrote to Rome, introducing Gilbert to the Jesuit rector of the English College, June 21, 1581. Knox, *op. cit.*, 97. He also wrote—describing the admirable way in which this pious and munificent man had organised the " machine " which the fathers had worked—*Magnae res non possunt fieri sine magnis subsidiis. Ibid.*, 98. No doubt this was meant to be passed on. It is a topic that recurs in all this correspondence. High authority must be continually re-instructed about it. Lack of funds will be one main cause of future dereliction, for the expenses were immense and the Englishmen poorer and poorer as the persecution developed. None knew better than Allen the way in which the parsimonious suspicion of officials tends to sterilise the opportunities of apostles. The blight of Mr. G.'s Treasury-mindedness lies

these first months Persons' only thought was that, though he might not profit, he was certainly building for his successors ; "those who come after us will find things easier ; they will not be so hated as we are (who are the first) and they will find ready all the places I have prepared for them ".[1]

The general spirit of the Catholics, after four years of the new persecution, is no less impressive, as the two Jesuits describe it. "If I began to talk about the fervour of the Catholics I should never end", Persons wrote. "When a priest comes to them they greet him, at first, as though he were a stranger and unknown to them ; then they take him into a little room, well within the house, which is arranged as a chapel. There they kneel down, and very humbly beg a priest's blessing. They ask how long he is going to stay, and this they would like to be for as long as possible. If he says he will be leaving the next day (which is usual—there is risk in a longer stay) all, that same evening, prepare to confess their sins, and early the next morning they hear Mass and fortify themselves with the most holy Sacrament of the Eucharist ; afterwards there is a sermon, and the priest, giving them his blessing once more, leaves, escorted (as in almost all his travels) by some young men of birth." No one in England, he says, complains that the services last too long. All Catholics will hear as many Masses a day as are said, and if they can do so they will all go to confession every week. Best of all, "quarrelling between Catholics is a thing never heard of ".[2]

The priests were indeed busy men. "After mass has been said and sermons preached [this is Persons once more]—I am sometimes compelled to preach twice on the same day—I struggle with almost unending business. This consists mainly in solving cases of conscience,[3] in directing other priests

---

over ecclesiastical history too. And the apostle has to explain, to pour out in a heap and weigh on the government scale the good he is doing, lest the meagre supplies mysteriously cease, and the weary business of hands and knees to the influential begin all over again. Cf. the correspondence, in 1585, Allen-Cardinal Ptolomeo Galli, in Knox, pp. 240–246 : the college is in desperate straits, all resources have dried up in England, save good will, and the cardinal's prudent advice to Allen is to write off the good will as a liability. Cf. also, in the same strain, the letter of another notable who can keep his head while his fellow Catholics in England agonize for the faith, the nuncio to Philip II, reporting to Rome, Oct. 30, 1582, "The remainder of the memorial of the Jesuit father [i.e. Persons] contains a much exaggerated account of the great needs of the Catholics in that kingdom, and of the great ruin that will result in consequence ". *Ibid.*, 171.

[1] Persons to Agazzari, Aug. 5, 1580, *Persons*, 42–43.
[2] Persons to Agazzari, Aug. 1581. *Ibid.*, 77, 78. For a source—little studied—of the Catholic piety of the period cf. the many contemporary papers used in Challoner's *Lives of the Missionary Priests both Secular and Regular etc. . . . .*
[3] Confessors, preachers, schoolmasters—the three elements of the classical rôle of the Society, the means by which the spirit of St. Ignatius built such a barrier against the evils chronic through the centuries before. Allen, writing to the same correspondent, some months later, is impressive about the first need : "Problems of conscience are all the more numerous in England because there the Catholics are less well-instructed, on account of the heretics' control. And this business is especially urgent because the Catholics who live in the midst of persecution there have more delicate consciences (*magis timoratas* : the Public Record Office copy of this letter—which Simpson has translated, p. 296—has *minus* for *magis*) than in any other place I have heard of, and they are so taken with the [Jesuit] fathers that they do not easily accept the decisions of the ordinary priests unless it is confirmed by that of Fr. Robert." Letter to Agazzari, June 23, 1581, Knox, *op. cit.*, 97–98, here freely translated. The original is lost, and both copies are evidently imperfect.

to suitable places and occupations,[1] in reconciling schismatics to the Church, in writing letters to Catholics tempted at times by the course of this persecution, in trying to arrange temporal aid for the support of those who are in prison and in want. For every day they send to me, laying bare their needs." [2]

There were, too, the priests' own needs. When the news came that Alexander Briant, a young secular missionary and Persons' pupil at Oxford, had been taken and put to the torture, " for almost the whole of one night Campion and I sat up talking of what we should do were we taken . . .". This is a recollection preserved in Persons' *Life of Campion*, written in later years. At the time, however, he described the hazards, for Fr. Agazzari, with a simplicity that still moves us—all the more when we have lived (are still living) in an age when thousands, hundreds of thousands, have learned so to dread a knock on the door after nightfall : " Sometimes, when we are sitting merrily at table, talking familiarly about points of religion (for our talk is mostly of matters of this sort), there comes the insistent rapping at the door we associate with the police ; all start up and listen, hearts beating, like deer who hear the hunters halloo ; we leave our food, and commend ourselves to God in a brief movement of prayer ; not a word is spoken, not a sound is heard, till the servant comes in to say what it is. If it is nothing, we laugh—all the more merrily because of our fright." [3]

Persons, reflecting on the experiences of his three months tour, reveals himself as the first man to realise the problems that were inherent to the actual working of the mission to England. He is the pioneer discoverer, and he understands that unless a solution is found, a remedy applied, the problems will in the end prove fatal.

In his letter to Agazzari of November 17, 1580, he touches on some of these matters. He asks for more men—not fewer than five Jesuits are needed immediately, three Englishmen, an Italian and a Spaniard. This last should be a really distinguished man,[4] who would give himself to the special work of solving problems of conscience, *qui gravissimi hic occurrunt*, says Persons.

---

[1] Here is an example of what the Jesuit meant. The three priests you last sent over, he writes to Agazzari—Tyrell, Birkhead and Grately—arrived today, Nov. 17, 1580, to our great joy. " We have, without delay, found clothing for them, books, horses and all the rest of the business " (*Persons*, 47, for the Latin original). No man, if it lay with Persons, would arrive in London so destitute as he had come.

[2] Persons to the same, Nov. 17, 1580, *Persons*, 61.

[3] Persons to Agazzari, Aug. 1581, *ibid.*, 78.

[4] Persons is not shy about asking for the best men—the situation in England calls for such. See *Persons*, 105, for those he names in his letter to the father-general of the Society. Still there were limits, *P. Bellarminum non audeo postulare*, he writes. But whoever comes must be unusually good. " *Itaque iterum atque iterum vestram Paternitatem rogo ut non mittantur huc nisi homines valde idonei* " ; to Aquaviva, Oct. 21, 1581, *ibid.*, 105. And he wrote in the same strain, repeatedly, to the rector of the college at Rome. When, for example, he sent the news that three newly ordained priests had made London safely—very young, all three of them—and that others were daily hoped for, he added that it was better they should be mature, even though they came more slowly—*expectamus plures quotidie, sed quantum fieri potest maturos, licet tardius ad nos veniant. Ibid.*, 48, Nov. 17, 1580. The new problem is about to begin. Can foreign superiors train men suitably for English conditions?

And the newcomers must get from the pope the most ample powers.[1] Lack of sufficient powers means that the priests are often helpless in a situation entangled with all kinds of complications and doubts. It is just not possible to send these cases on to Rome for decision—to consult Rome, on any matter at all, is high treason, as it is to receive from Rome any document of any kind.[2] And so, for lack of authority on the spot, the missionary movement is greatly hindered.

And then the young Jesuit speaks the first word in a matter which all will discuss, henceforth, for the next hundred years and more : there is immense need here of a bishop of some kind, to bless the oils for baptism and extreme unction. For lack of a bishop we have been brought to the greatest straits, and unless the pope comes soon to our aid in this matter, we do not know where we shall presently be. The Bishop of St. Asaph's health and old age had held him up, but the refuges which Persons had prepared for him are still available for another. " Let us hope that his holiness will send us a strong man very soon ; it certainly matters to our common cause that we should have someone soon." [3]

The measures, the organisation and the leader envisaged by Persons— and, for all too brief a time, realised through him and in him—were obviously needed, were essential, by this time. As well as the president of the great college there was needed an organiser on the Douay side of the channel to arrange for the safe transit of the priests, the work Persons was to do in the winter of 1581–1582 and again in 1584 ; and there was need of a second organiser in England, with authority to co-ordinate and control the mission in general, an active man, who would move round continuously. The results of the failure to regulate, for example, the distribution of the missionaries would soon be all too evident : waste, loss, and in the end defeat, save for a sporadic apostolate here and there—which is what happened, in later years.[4]

---

[1] Powers to settle definitely such matters, no doubt, as involved excommunication, powers to dispense with the canonical impediments to marriage, and so forth.

[2] After all, the treasonable act for which Cuthbert Mayne was put to death was the possession of a Bull listing the conditions for gaining the Jubilee indulgence of 1575 ; and Roger Ashton, a gentleman of Lancashire, was hanged in 1593 for procuring a papal licence to marry his second cousin (*Challoner, op. cit.*, 186).

[3] The letter is printed in *Persons*, 47–56. All that has hitherto been available (it was Simpson's source) is the abbreviated copy published in Theiner, *Annales Ecclesiastici*, III, 216. The passages quoted are on p. 52 of *Persons*. Bishops resident in England would be required soon (and urgently) for other purposes than the consecration of holy oils—it was, for example, twenty years now since the sacrament of confirmation had been administered, the sacrament specially designed (one might think) for times of persecution ; and episcopal rule is the condition *sine qua non* of internal peace within the local *ecclesia*. If Persons seems not to see the greater needs, let us recall that he was only two years ordained at this time, and, if thirty-four years of age, only five years a Catholic.

[4] For which cf. my *Rome and the Counter Reformation in England* (1942), esp. 408–430. A very early warning about this problem was given by Bl. Robert Southwell, S.J., " It is certainly matter for regret, that there are many counties, each containing not a few Catholics, in which there is not a single priest, though earnestly begged for by many. Unless new supplies are soon sent the Catholic cause will suffer greatly. The evil is further increased by the fact that the priests actually at work in the harvest betake themselves in great numbers to one or two counties, leaving the others devoid of pastors." To Aquaviva, July 25, 1586, in C.R.S., V, 309.

For such a post of director-general in England Persons would have been ideal.[1]
He saw clearly the nature of the task, how to use well in England the fine
instrument Allen was producing through the college ; he had ideas that were
practical, and he had seen them work ; he knew how to enlist the sympathy
of the great, and to gather helpers as active and enthusiastic, and as dedicated,
as himself.   Rome had sent his fellow Jesuits to Abyssinia and to the Indies,
Nuñez and Francis Xavier, the one archbishop, nay patriarch, the other
legate *a latere*, clad only in their stuff gowns ; and so might Persons have been
sent to England as a bishop ; to direct was his metier, and, *nemo tam pater*,
he would have been acceptable, in 1581, to the Jesuit-minded missionaries
from the colleges.[2]   However, it was not to be—neither Persons nor any

---

[1] Cf. for example, this passage from his long letter of Oct. 21, 1581, to Aquaviva (*Persons*,
95–106), which is a kind of report on the whole mission : " When I first came into England,
I thought out as well as I could what part of the kingdom most stood in need of us, and what
part, as time went on, would be of most service to the cause.   I saw that there were three
districts into which, so far, the [seminary] priests had not penetrated.   First there was Wales
. . . not so much hostile to the Catholic religion as lapsed into dense ignorance about it due
to the lack of priests working there, and lapsed also into a kind of approbation of heresy
through being accustomed to it.   To Wales, then, I sent a certain number of priests, making
arrangements for their reception with a gentleman there.   A second district was Cambridgeshire, which the wholly heretical university of Cambridge had completely infected.   We
tried, in vain, many ways to improve this.   Finally, with the help of God, I slipped a priest
into the very university.   He went as a student, or a gentleman of studious disposition, and I
got certain assistance for him not far outside the town.   God blessed this enterprise, and
within a few months the priest had won over seven young men of promise, who are now
about to leave for the seminary of Rheims, as I hear from one of them who has just called
on me. . . .   The third district, the greatest of all in extent, comprises the four or five
counties near to the frontier of England and Scotland. . . .   Here almost no priest had
made his way."   *Ibid.*, 98. Persons then goes on to explain the importance of this district
and how he directed several missionaries to it.   This letter is unique, it seems to me, in
the way it reviews the general situation, thinks out the nature of its various problems, and
describes the means actually provided for their solution.   Here is all that we mean by a
sense of order.   The conditions of the English mission in 1577–1603 are all but fatal to
the survival of such.   But it will always characterise the Jesuit contribution to the
missionary work.
[2] The plan of sending to England just such a missionary bishop as Nuñez had evidently
been considered in Rome, but the pope did not like it.   Cf. the letter (July 13, 1580) of the
old Bishop of St. Asaph, who had left Rome for the English mission along with Persons, and
then fallen ill.   The bishop writes to the pope that he is astonished that after doing so much
for the Catholic revival in England the pope makes so many difficulties about creating three
or four titular bishops to preserve the faith there and propagate it.   Certainly the expenses
involved need be no difficulty.   " For God has so inclined the minds of the priests to spend
their lives in promoting the reduction of that kingdom to the Catholic faith, that, after being
made bishops, they would be contented to live as poorly as they do now, like the bishops
of the primitive Church."   The letter is in Simpson, 148–149, translated from Theiner,
Annales Ecclesiastici, III, 700.   Simpson's inference from it (stated as fact, " their request
had been refused because . . . ") is quite unwarranted, *viz.* that at Rome, " feudal power and
ecclesiastical authority had become so mixed up together in men's minds, that they feared
the scandal of a poor bishop, hiding from his pursuers, disguised like a soldier, mariner,
or serving-man, living in garrets, coves, or barns, wandering over the land, and at last dying
ignominiously on the gallows. . . .   Etiquette and routine prevailed."   This was the way,
of course, the bishops lived, whom Rome was now sending to Ireland.   According to one of
Persons' own contemporaries, William Holt, S.J., Allen himself proposed to Gregory XIII
that bishops should be sent into England, and the pope was still considering the matter when
he died—Holt notes that at the time when this was suggested there were still surviving in
Elizabeth's prisons the remnant of the bishops deprived in 1559, *ad quos pro quibusdam*

other was put in charge.   Allen, through whom the missionaries received their
spiritual authority, had the power to withdraw what he had granted ; and this
was the totality of local ecclesiastical authority which the mission to England
enjoyed.

Edmund Campion was taken on July 17, 1581, and with him (besides
various laymen) three of the Douay priests, Thomas Ford [1] and John
Collington and William Filby.[2]   With seventeen others [3] he was indicted
November 14, 15 ; and on November 20 tried at Westminster Hall, and
on December 1 put to death, along with Ralph Sherwin [4] and Alexander
Briant,[5] at Tyburn.   The way in which the Jesuit and his companions were
handled, their " judicial murder ",[6] the tortures, the Tower disputations,
the government publicity, made their prosecution a reaffirmation of the
original resolve of 1559, that no Englishman should profess the traditional
faith and live.   Campion's last words before he was sentenced, like those of
Thomas More, in that same place, forty-six years before, declare the
Catholics' understanding of the issue the government had raised, and the
spirit of their resolve to face it.

The Lord Chief Justice said to Campion and the rest, " What can you
say why you should not die ? "   And Campion replied, " It was not our death
that ever we feared.   But we knew that we were not lords of our own lives,
and therefore for want of answer would not be guilty of our own deaths.
The only thing that we have now to say is, that if our religion do make us
traitors, we are worthy to be condemned ; but otherwise are and have been
as true subjects as ever the Queen had.   In condemning us you condemn
all your own ancestors—all the ancient priests, bishops, and kings—all that

necessariis erat aliquando catholicorum accessus.   See Holt's (Latin) paper, *How the Catholic
religion was preserved in England during 38 years of persecution,* in *Douay Diaries,* 376–384 ;
the quotation is from p. 381.   The date of this paper is 1596.

[1] A Devonshire man, fellow of Trinity College, Oxford ; M.A. 1567, ordained from Douay
(one of the first three) 1573; B.D. (Douay), 1576, in which year he went to the English mission.
Beatified by Leo XIII in 1886.

[2] Born in Oxford, and there educated (Lincoln College).   Like Ford and Campion a
convert.   Ordained at Douay, March 25, 1581.   Beatified, 1886.

[3] Three of whom *in absentia,* viz. Allen (who headed the list), Nicholas Morton, and
Persons.

[4] Born in Derbyshire, fellow of Exeter College, Oxford ; " accounted an acute philosopher
and an excellent Grecian and Hebrician ", so Antony à Wood ; convert, ordained 1577 ;
one of the original students of the seminary at Rome ; returned to England, 1580, with
Campion and Persons ; captured November, 1580.   Beatified, 1886.

[5] Born in Somerset (like his tutor, Fr. Persons) 1553 ; educated Oxford (Hart Hall) ;
ordained at Douay, March 29, 1578, sent to England Aug. 3, 1579, arrested (in the raid on
Persons' London headquarters) April 28, 1581.   Beatified, 1886.   Of the others condemned
to death, Nov. 20, 21, 1581, 5 were spared ; 3 were put to death at Tyburn on May 28, 1582
(Thomas Ford, John Shert and Robert Johnson) and 4 two days later (William Filby, Luke
Kirby, Laurence Richardson, seminary priests like the last three, and Thomas Cottam, a
Jesuit).   Of these seven all were converts save Robert Johnson.   Shert, Richardson and
Cottam were of Brasenose College, Oxford ; Kirby a Cambridge graduate, of what college
is not known.

[6] J. M. Rigg, in *D.N.B.,* art. *Wray, Sir Christopher (1524–1592),* the Chief Justice of the
King's Bench, who presided at the trial.   Allen describes Wray as " a Catholic at heart, but
in outward act a Pilate ".   Cf. his letter of Feb. 9, 1582, to Agazzari, Knox, 112.

was once the glory of England, the island of saints, and the most devoted child of the See of Peter.   For what have we taught, however you may qualify it with the odious name of treason, that they did not uniformly teach ? To be condemned with these old lights—not of England only, but of the world—by their degenerate descendants, is both gladness and glory to us. God lives : posterity will live : their judgment is not so liable to corruption as that of those who are now going to sentence us to death." [1]

3

The capture of so many priests in the summer of 1581, the long drawn out spectacle of the killing of Edmund Campion especially, were evidence all too clear that the extermination of real Catholicism would be, from now on, a first consideration with the queen's government.   The event showed also that, as well as the will to destroy, the government certainly had the means. And the mind of Campion's colleague, once he was safe from the hunters, began to be occupied with schemes to change the government, to dislodge the tyrant—purely political schemes (albeit the ultimate goal was religious), schemes of foreign invasion.

Nowhere has Persons set down how this development began.   Allen had been introduced to the world of politics long before.   In the summer of 1575 the idea was mooted in the circle of English exiles at Rome of a raid on England that should set free the Queen of Scots, who, married to Don John of Austria, would be ruler in Elizabeth's place.   Philip II was won over to promise transport and maintenance for 2,000 men for six months (September 8, 1575), and towards the end of the year Sir Francis Englefield, a one time councillor of Mary Tudor, and an exile since 1560, was summoned to Rome to advise about the plan, and with him Allen also.[2]   They arrived by the following February, and although their reports (copies of which were sent to Philip II) are lost, we are in no doubt that the idea appealed to them.   A letter from Allen to Owen Lewis, of November 8, 1576, makes this very clear.[3] The plan is, *sancta erga gentem nostram consilia.*   Lewis is told, *omnia intus et exterius paramus.*   The preparations of which Allen here speaks were, no doubt, his efforts " to dispose men's minds for the coming enterprise, as the occasion might serve "—the rôle appointed him by Rome.[4]   But if this letter had ever fallen into the hands of Elizabeth's ministers, how effectively hostile counsel could have put it to the jury at the trials of the priests !   By the time Allen was writing to Lewis it was, however, all but all over.   The upheaval in Flanders which followed the deaths of the governor-general, de Requesens (March 5, 1576), and of the military commander, Chiappino Vitelli, had made all the difference.   When the new governor, Don John

---

[1] The best account of the trial is still Simpson, ch. XV, pp. 393–442.   Allen's, contemporary, comment is in the *Defence of Catholics*, ch. II (edition of 1914, I, 29–47).
[2] This summons was the occasion of Sander's commendation of Allen quoted *supra*, 284.
[3] For the full text of which cf. C.R.S., IX, 44–45.
[4] So Pollen, *English Catholics*, 201.   For a closely documented account of the affair— the only account, so far as I know—cf. Pollen, *op. cit.*, 196–220.

himself, arrived in November Flanders seemed all but lost to Spain, and had joined with Orange, in the Pacification of Ghent, to demand the withdrawal of the Spanish army. On December 17 Philip II wrote to Rome that the English scheme must be put off until Don John was master of Flanders ; and a month later, to the day, Don John wrote to Rome that there was no chance of his using the Spanish troops against England.[1]

The well-known letter of Sander to Allen of November 6, 1577, " O pityful change of things ",[2] reflects the bitterness of the disappointment when it was realised that this scheme had been abandoned.[3]

The pattern of these events of 1575-1577 is faithfully reproduced in the more talked-of negotiations of 1582-1584 : the initiative and the plan due to an ambitious foreign personage of all but the highest rank—who yet cannot act without his sovereign, and cannot commit his sovereign ; the goodwill of the King of Spain, not satisfied that the scheme has any chance of success, but anxious that the enthusiasm which prompts it shall not die out ; the English ecclesiastics, called in to give their opinion when the plan is ready. And even now, with the correspondence of Philip II and his ambassadors in London and Paris and Rome long open to all of us, with the correspondence of Allen and the letters and memoirs of Persons, how little we know of the actual rôle of the two Englishmen ! Half a dozen meetings in the course of some three years, of which nothing is known beyond what was then decided; as many memoranda detailing the hopes, enlarging on the prospects, and pleading for immediate action—but what was the share of Allen and Persons in all this ? What was their importance relative to those others, at whose invitation, or command, they gave their opinion, supplied information, wrote to princes, made tedious voyages to distant courts ? That they knew all that was agreed on, rejoiced at it, helped with all their heart, this very certainly we know. And I do not propose to embark on the absurd task of apologising for, or explaining away, what they undoubtedly regarded as a most dutiful and most Catholic activity—a most patriotic activity too : to make England safe for the Catholic mission, thereby to save England's soul. Were we to yield in the slightest degree to the threats of our enemy, Allen could write, in high indignation with the temporising Italian spirit, *actum esset de nobis et de republica*.[4]

---

[1] So Pollen, *English Catholics*, 211.

[2] The letter from which the often quoted phrases come, " The King of Spain is as fearful of war as a child of fire ", and " The State of Christendom dependeth upon the stout assailing of England ".

[3] Sander's letter is a reply to Allen's of June 7 and is printed in Knox, 38.

[4] To Agazzari, Aug. 5, 1584, Knox, *op. cit.*, 236–237. *Et de republica* : the old assumption, that Allen was driven by an exile's disappointment and resentment to connive at the enslavement of the land that would have none of him, no longer inspires the historians. But it is misleading to suggest that only after the Spanish defeat of 1588 did he begin to think kindly of his own (cf. Black, 375). " God's sake, and our country's and our common church's sake ; " these words, written to Owen Lewis in 1579 (Knox, 83), summarise fairly the whole spirit of the dual career, and when Fr. Robert Southwell called him " the father of his country " it was an understandable description. Letter to Agazzari, Dec. 22, 1586, in C.R.S., V, 316. Is Allen to be condemned as un-English for refusing to acknowledge that a minority was England simply because the minority controlled the government ?

Campion taken, the chase after Persons was so hot that he had now no choice but to leave England ; and sometime between August 13–21, 1581,[1] he made his way to France, to await there the instructions of his superiors in Rome. But before he left, he had made a contact with the new, pro-Catholic régime in Scotland.

In the thirteen months during which the two Jesuits had conducted their marvellous mission, a French cousin of James VI, Esmé Stuart d'Aubigny, sent to Scotland by the Duke of Guise,[2] had won the young king's favour ; Elizabeth's well-paid ally, the Earl of Morton, had been forced out of the council, and, June 17, 1581, had been put to death as one of the murderers of the king's father fourteen years before—despite frantic efforts on the part of Elizabeth to save him.[3] A historian of our own day will tell us that Elizabeth's hold on Scotland was, at this moment, weaker than at any time since those few months, in 1566, when Mary Stewart had driven out the cabal that had murdered Rizzio ;[4] and also—what is more evidently pertinent to the story about to be told—that Catholicism was still so strong in Scotland that " it would have required only a small expeditionary army, resolutely handled, from France and Spain, to turn the scales definitely against the protestants ".[5] Contemporary observers were of the same mind.[6] And as James VI was barely past his fifteenth birthday, and his new mentor— now created Duke of Lennox—was a Catholic, it is little wonder if Catholics began to hope; and the chief among them all, the imprisoned Queen of Scots. Mary now asked that some one should be sent quickly to Scotland who " could prudently work for the Catholic cause with the Duke of Lennox and her other friends ".[7] And so Persons, only a few days before he left England, sent to Edinburgh a seminary priest, an alumnus of Rheims, William Watts.[8]

Such is Persons' own account of his first introduction into the world of princes and men of state, as written many years later.[9] In the account

---

[1] See *Persons*, 95, n. 3 ; and, for the details of his leaving England, his own account, sent Oct. 21, 1581, to the Father-General of the Society, Claudio Aquaviva, *ibid.*, 95–97 ; also his *Autobiography* (1601) in C.R.S., II, 30, and his *Punti per la missione d'Inghilterra* (? 1608) in C.R.S., IV, 26–30.   [2] He arrived at Edinburgh, Sept. 8, 1579.

[3] Four months before the arrival of Esmé Stuart the French ambassador in London averred, " Estant ledict prince (i.e. James VI) entre les mains du dict comte de Morton, il est comme estant entre les mains de la Royne d'Angleterre " (May 14, 1579), quoted, from Teulet, III, 45, by Conyers Read, II, 156, whose judgment accords : ". . . by his death [Elizabeth] lost a strong useful friend. Never again was Scotland so completely at her beck and call as it had been during Morton's tenure of power."

[4] Black, 310.   It need hardly be said how Elizabeth's great intelligence now laboured in order to regain her position, her " ascendancy " (*ibid.*, 312), in Scotland. " The record of her intrigues, plots, and counter plots makes this one of the most baffling periods in the reign " ; *ibid.*   [5] *Ibid.*, 311.

[6] " The Duke of Guise ", Walsingham advised Burghley from Paris, Sept. 3, 1580, " is of late crept into very inward credit with the King [of Scotland] . . . there are daily consultations in the Duke's house, especially since advertisements are come hither out of Scotland that the King doth submit himself to any such direction as his mother shall give him " ; and Walsingham speaks of a " general hope " of " alteration of religion " in Scotland within twelve months, and of expectation of support from the pope and Philip II ; Conyers Read, II, 174, from Digges, p. 428.   [7] Persons, *Punti etc.*, C.R.S., IV., 20.

[8] *Ibid.*   [9] In ? 1608.

Persons sent at the time, October 21, 1581, to Aquaviva, there is no mention of the anxiety of the Queen of Scots as a starting point. Watts, Aquaviva is told, has been spending ten months, at Persons' suggestion, among the Catholics of the north and of the border counties. He returned, to report progress, " in the beginning of last summer ", and brought the information —in which Persons was especially interested—that there was no difficulty in crossing the border into Scotland. Persons thereupon put a plan before some leading Catholics whom he could trust ; they agreed to it ; and Persons next entrusted Watts with a mission to the court of Scotland. This plan had a purely religious aim—the conversion of the boy king.[1] But, from another source altogether, the correspondence of the Spanish ambassador in London, Mendoza,[2] we know that a priest, unnamed, took with him to Scotland, at this time, a message for the king from six leading Catholics, that was partly religious and partly political. Lennox was to be told that if the king would submit to the Catholic Church, many of the English nobles and a great part of the people, would at once side with him, and have him declared heir to the English crown, and would release his mother ; and the messenger was to say, also, that help would be forthcoming from the pope and the King of Spain and, it was to be supposed, from the King of France. Should James, however, not become a Catholic, he was warned that the Catholics in England would oppose his claim even more than the heretics.

It is to be regretted that we do not know the names of the six gentlemen who now put their credit behind this hare-brained [3] message to Edinburgh, and thereby began a new chapter in the history of wicked, mischief-pregnant futility. Mendoza is authority that " the end upon which they have their eyes fixed at present is the conversion of Scotland to the Catholic Church, without going into further particulars ". Hence, he tells Philip II, he has not " further opened out with them ". James VI once converted, this is in Mendoza's mind, England can be invaded from Scotland, with a rising of the Catholics in the north of England to assist. The ultimate good will be that these two countries will be permanently faithful allies to Spain.[4]

There seems little doubt that the unnamed priest of Mendoza's despatch was Watts.[5] Did Persons know nothing of this commission ? Seventeen years later, he categorically denied, to the Cardinal Protector of England, that he had ever engaged in affairs of state while in England in 1580–1581.[6]

---

[1] For this letter cf. *Persons*, 98–103.

[2] Mendoza to Philip II, Sept. 7, 1581, in *Span. Cal., Elizabeth*, III, 1580–1586, pp. 169–170.

[3] The word is harsh. What else is to be said of men who so lavishly promise the aid of foreign princes, and promise so lightly a general rebellion of their own people and who, at the same time, are saying to Mendoza that " oppressed as they are, they could not take up arms, or make any move, unless your Majesty send a great fleet with more than 15,000 men ", which ", the ambassador opines, " would be rather an army to conquer than to succour ".

[4] All this in the despatch of Sept. 7, just quoted.

[5] Cf. *Persons*, 125, n. 2, and xlvi, n. 75.

[6] *Ibid.*, lvi, n. 119. Such occupation was, indeed, expressly forbidden both Persons and Campion in the written instructions given them by their superiors at Rome. *Non se immisceant negotiis statuum neque huc scribant res novas ad status pertinentes, atque illic etiam neque ipsi sermonem injiciant aut ab aliis injectum admittant contra reginam nisi forte*

And we know that, while Watts was aware of the link between the six lords and Mendoza,[1] he did not pass on this knowledge to Holt.[2] As to the Queen of Scots, according to the letter to Aquaviva [3] it is not until Persons has received Watts' first report of his reception in Scotland (that is not until after September 15, and Persons is then in France) that he first attempts to make a contact with her.

Watts was not long in reporting progress. By September 15 Persons had heard from him. It was in October that he sent to Edinburgh William Holt ; [4] and in the winter of 1581-1582 these two priests employed themselves sounding the disposition, towards Catholicism, of the young king and the nobles. The prospects, they thought, were not unfavourable.[5]

Persons, meanwhile, was living at Rouen. The letter in which Watts described the situation in Scotland is wholly taken up with business that is purely religious, and it was, says Persons, " very satisfactory ".[6] Nothing can be more important than the conversion of Scotland, Persons will now begin to say : on this " depends every hope, humanly speaking, of the conversion of England ". So he wrote to Aquaviva, when he sent on Watts' letter, October 21 ; saying also, " In this business I am hanging entirely on your reply. In the first place, ought I to go forward with this business or not . . . . If it should seem [good] to you that I go on with it, then in addition to instructions which I beg you to send ", there will be need of money.[7]

---

apud eos quos insigniter fideles et longo tempore probatos habuerint, at quidem tunc etiam non sine magna causa (Meyer, Appendix), i.e. " They must not take part in affairs of state, nor write to us from there news concerning state affairs, and also, they themselves must not, over there, speak against the queen, nor allow to pass anything said against the queen by others, unless perhaps with those people whom they have reason to think are outstanding Catholics and tested through great length of time, and indeed even then not [to speak or allow such speaking] without some great cause." Conyers Read (op. cit., II, 279, n. 2) misrepresents the original somewhat when he summarises it, " not to take part in affairs of state ' except perhaps with those whose fidelity has been long and steadfast ' ". The prohibition about politics is, in the original, absolute.

[1] What the link was between the Spanish ambassador and the message sent to James VI by the six Catholic " lords ", Mendoza himself tells us, in the letter of Sept. 7, already quoted: " I have tried to spread the view in Scotland of how advantageous it would be to the king if he were to submit to the Catholic Church, although this is a difficult thing to do without it coming to the ears of this queen [i.e. Elizabeth] . . . I have therefore had to wait until I could discuss it with some of the principal Catholics here, by whose means alone was it possible to attempt it ". Mendoza goes on to say that he asked these Catholics to think it over, and to suggest a means by which he could communicate with the king. " They took solemn oaths to aid each other ", oaths of secrecy also, and " they decided to send an English clergyman, who is trusted by all six . . .".

[2] Persons, l.   William Holt was the Jesuit whom Persons had sent to Scotland to assist Watts.   [3] Ibid., 103.

[4] Ibid., 125, n. 2, for the date, soon after Oct. 20.

[5] Allen, in a letter of Feb. 18, 1582, to the Cardinal-Secretary of State, gives an account of the work of these two priests at Edinburgh in the winter of 1581-1582 (Knox, 114-115), enclosing for the personal consideration of the pope a brief report on the state of affairs in Scotland, written, it would seem, by Holt in this same month.

[6] It is printed Persons, 100-102. Watts only crossed the border on Aug. 26, as his letter says, and Persons, at Rouen, received this letter, sent via London, on Sept. 15, only nineteen days later.

[7] Persons to Aquaviva, Oct. 21, 1581, Persons, 95-106. The quotations are from p. 103.

It was very largely because of Persons' insistence that Jesuits ought to be sent as missionaries to Scotland—of which insistence this letter is but one example [1]—that, in January, 1582, Fr. William Crichton, a subject of James VI, and not of Elizabeth, was despatched from Rome by Aquaviva, instructed, naturally enough, to consult with Persons before sailing from France.[2] As Crichton made his way to Rouen, his confrère, William Holt, was riding from Edinburgh to London, with proposals from the Scottish, pro-Marian, lords, intended to bring about a religious revolution in Scotland. Holt reached London to find—to his evident surprise—that the personage whom he there " contacted " was the Spanish ambassador himself. And when Crichton arrived at Rouen, Persons took him to the château of Eu,[3] and the Duke of Guise, the leader of the militant party among the Catholics of France, and Mary Stewart's first cousin—and, of course, the personage responsible for Lennox' introduction to James VI ; and the three had a kind of conference " about the advancement of the Catholic cause in both realms of England and Scotland, and for the delivery of the Queen of Scots then prisoner in England ".[4]

Crichton reached Edinburgh in the first days of March, 1582, apparently. He presented himself to Lennox with credentials from Mary's ambassador in France, the Archbishop of Glasgow, and declared that he brought messages from the pope and the King of Spain. He was followed by William Holt, returned from his visit to London—and to the Spanish ambassador ; from whom came a request that Lennox would support a plan of the pope and the Spanish king for the release of Mary and the restoration of the Catholic religion. Lennox was willing to co-operate, but he made conditions about troops and about money which, later on, Guise (for one) thought excessive. And on March 17 Lennox sent Crichton back to France with his reply,[5] directing him to give Allen also full information about what was under discussion, " since the business concerned the welfare of England also ".[6]

All this the Scottish Jesuit did. He was back in France in April, had a meeting with Allen and the Archbishop of Glasgow at St. Denis, and then

---

[1] Cf. *Persons*, 96, n. 4.

[2] Persons had suggested this in his letter of Oct. 21, just quoted, cf. *Persons*, 115 : " If anyone is sent [to Scotland] let him come to the house of the aforesaid Archdeacon [i.e. at Rouen] where he will find everything in readiness and precise instructions from me."

[3] Forty miles from Rouen, 15 miles N.E. of Dieppe, roughly midway between Dieppe and the mouth of the Somme.

[4] The quotation is from Persons' *Autobiographical Notes* (1601), printed in C.R.S., II, 30. It should be noted that Guise, some eighteen months before the despatch of Esmé Stuart to Scotland, had been " in conference " with Philip II's ambassador in Paris about a scheme to liberate Mary by means of an armed descent on England, Franco-Spanish assistance, and himself and the Duke of Lorraine in command (Teulet, V, 144). What is the link between the English Jesuit and this high personage ? Persons' immediate superior (Hicks, in *Persons*, xi) was the French provincial of the Society, at this time Fr. Claude Mathieu. Mathieu was a confidential friend of the Guise (Knox, xxxiv) and he was also a leading spirit in that party among the French Jesuits who favoured the militant policies later to be associated with the famous *Ligue* that Guise called into being.

[5] All this is in Lennox' letter of March 7, 1582, to the Spanish ambassador in Paris, for which cf. Teulet, V, 235. It is translated in Knox, pp. xxxv–xxxvi, which is what is quoted here.　　　　　　[6] So Allen, April 24, 1582, to Gregory XIII ; *ibid.*, 130.

Top-left panel (title page)

Rationes Decem:
IBVS FRETVS, CERTA-
men aduersarijs obtulit in
causa FIDEI, Edmun-
dus Campianus,
ocietate Nominis IESV Presbyter:
ALLEGATÆ
larissimos viros, nostrates Academicos.

Ego dabo vobis os & sapientiam

qui non poterunt resistere

amno contradicere omnes
Psal.63.
e paruulorum factæ sunt plagæ eorum.

Top-right panel

Inst.li.1.ca.11.
nu.5.

ulni rabies negat in schola Sācti Spi-
ritus educatum, propterea quód sa-
cras imagines,illiteratorum libros,ap-
pellasset.

Dies me deficeret numerantem e-
pistolas, conciones, homilias, oratio-
nes,opuscula,disceptationes Patrum,
in quib⁹ ex apparato, grauiter & or-
naté nostra catholicorum dogmata
roborarunt. Quàm diu apud biblio-
polas ista venierint, tam diu frustra
nostrorum codices prohibentur: frustra seruantur aditus oræq maritimæ:
frustra domus, arcæ, scrinia, capsulæ
disquiruntur:frustra tot portis mira-
ces tabulæ suffiguntur. Nullus enim
Hardingus,nec Sanderus,nec Alanus,
nec Stapletonus, nec Bristolius hæc
noua somnia vehementiùs, quàm hi
quos recensui Patres,insectantur. Ta-
lia cogitanti accreuit animus & de-
siderium pugnæ, in qua, quoquo se
mouerit aduersarius,nisi gloriam Deo
cesserit, feret incommodū. Patres ad-
E.j.   miserit:

Bottom-left panel

Rationes Redditæ

me de tuis extermines, si tot luminib⁹
Ecclesiæ, tenebricosos homulos, pau-
cos, indoctos dissectos, improbos an-
tetulero?

Testes item Principes, Reges, Cæ-
sares, horumq respublicæ, quorum et
ipsorum pietas, et ditionum populi,
et pacis belliq disciplina,se penitus in
hac nostra doctrina catholica funda-
uerunt.Hic ego quos ab oriente The-
odosios, quos ab occidente Carolos,
quos Edouardos ex Anglia, Ludoui-
cos e Gallia, Hermingildos ex His-
pania,Henricos e Saxonia, Wences-
laos e Boëmia,Leopoldos ex Austri-
a,Stephanos ex Hungaria, Iosapha-
tos ex India, quos orbe toto dynastas
atq toparchas passim arcessere: qui
exemplo, qui armis, qui legibus, qui
solicitudine, qui sumptu, nostram ecclesiam nutrierunt? Sic enim præci-
nuit Isaias: *Erunt Reges nutricii tui,&*
Reginæ nutrices tua. Audi Elizabetha,
Regina potentissima: tibi tantus Pro-
pheta

Bottom-right panel

pheta canit, te tuas partes edocet.
Narro tibi: Caluinum & hos Principes vnum cœlum capere non potest.
His ergo te Principibus adiunge,dig-
nam maioribus, dignam ingenio, dignam literis, dignam laudibus, dignam
fortuna tua. Solum hoc de te molior
ego, & moliar, quicquid me fiet, cui
tanquàm hosti capitis tui, toties iam
isti patibulum ominantur.Salue bona
crux. Veniet, Elizabetha, dies,ille ille
dies, qui tibi liquidò commonstrabit,
vtri te dilexerint, Societas IESV, an
Lutheri progenies.Pergo.

Testes iam omnes oræ plagæq
mundi, quibus Euangelica tuba post
Christum natum insonuit. Parumne
hoc fuit, Idolis ora claudere,Dei regnum gentibus importare? Christum
Lutherus, Catholici Christum loquimur. Num diuisus est Christus? mini-
mé. Aut nos, aut ille falsum Christum loquimur. Quid ergo? Dicam,
Christus ille sit, & illorum sit, quo
K.j.   Da-

Nationes ad Christum traductæ.

1.Cor.1.

THE
NEVV TESTAMENT

OF IESVS CHRIST, TRANS-
LATED FAITHFVLLY INTO ENGLISH,

out of the authentical Latin, according to the best corrected copies of the same, diligently conferred vvith
the Greeke and other editions in diuers languages: Vvith
ARGVMENTS of bookes and chapters, ANNOTA-
TIONS, and other necessarie helpes, for the better vnderstanding of the text, and specially for the discouerie of the
CORRVPTIONS of diuers late translations, and for
cleering the CONTROVERSIES in religion, of these daies:

IN THE ENGLISH COLLEGE OF RHEMES.

Psal. 118.

*Da mihi intellectum, & scrutabor legem tuam, & custodiam
illam in toto corde meo.*

That is,

Giue me vnderstanding, and I vvil searche thy lavv, and
vvil keepe it vvith my vvhole hart.

S. Aug. tract. 2. in Epist. Ioan.

*Omnia quæ leguntur in Scripturis sanctis, ad instructionem & salutem nostram intentè oportet
audire: maximè tamen memoriæ commendanda sunt, quæ aduersùs Hæreticos valent plu-
rimùm: quorum insidiæ, infirmiores quosque & negligentiores circumuenire non cessant.*

That is,

Al things that are readde in holy Scriptures, vve must heare vvith great attention, to our
instruction and saluation: but those things specially must be commended to me-
morie, vvhich make most against Heretikes: vvhose deceites cease not to cir-
cumuent and beguile al the vveaker sort and the more negligent persons.

PRINTED AT RHEMES,
by Iohn Fogny

1582.

CVM PRIVILEGIO.

THE RHEMES TESTAMENT, 1582

GREGORY MARTIN, 1540-1582

ces of feare & horrour? it shalbe (sayeth the scripture) at midnight when commoulie men are a sleepe: it shalbe with hydeous noyse of trumpetts, sounde of waters, motion of all the elementes. VVhat a night vvill that bee trovvest thovv, to see the earthe shake, the hilles and dales moued from their places, the moone darckened, the starrs fall dovvne from heauen, the whole element shiuered in peeces, and all the vvorld in a flaminge fire?

Sainct Iohn sawe it in vision, and was maruailous a feard. I saw (saithe he) when the lambe had opened one of the seuen seales: & I harde one of the fower beastes saye (lyke the voyce of a thunder) come and see, and I sawe: and beholde a white horse, and one that satte vpon him had a bowe, and he went out to conquere. Then went there furthe a blacke horse, & he that sate vpon him had a payre of balãces in his hand: then went there forthe a pale horse, and he that satte vpon hym was named *death*: and hell folowed behynde hym: and he had authoritie geeuen hym to kyll by sworde, by death, and by beastes of the earth. The earth did shake, the sunne grew blacke lyke a sacke: the moone like bloode: the starres fell from heauen: the skye doubled it selfe like a folded booke: euerie hyll and Ilande was moued from his place: the kynges of the earth and princes and tribunes, and the riche & stoute, hid them selues in dennes, and in the rockes of hylles. Then appeared there seuen Angels with seuen trumpettes, and eche one prepa-

Apoc. 6.

D 5 red

THE FIRST BOOKE OF THE CHRISTIAN EXERcise, appertayning to resolution.

VVherein are layed downe the causes & reasons that should moue a man to resolue hym selfe to the seruice of God: And all the impedimentes remoued, which may lett the same.

Psal. 62. vers. 4.

Vnam petii a domino, hanc requiram: vt inhabitem in domo domini omnibus diebus vitæ meæ: vt videam voluntatem domini.

One thing haue I requested at gods hãdes, & that will I demaunde still: which is, to dwell in his house all the daies of my life: to the ende, I maye knovve and doe his vvill.

Anno. 1582.

VVITH PRIVYLEGE.

A

passed on to Rouen where he met Persons ; and with Persons in his company he reported progress to Guise at Eu. An illness of Persons now held things up ; his experience and his judgment were already so important to this group that, because of his illness, " nothing further can be done just now ".[1] But by the middle of May he had joined Crichton and the Duke of Guise in Paris. The two Jesuits were now received by the Spanish ambassador, and Persons told this personage how " the Catholics in England were extremely desirous this design should be carried out " [i.e. the plan to invade Scotland] for if all went well with it they could easily join in. England is so full of Catholics, Persons is reported as saying, that it can scarcely be believed. And as warrant for his certainty about their dispositions, he recalled his own experience, nearly twelve months ago now, of conversations in England with leading Catholics about such matters when he was " treating with them about their consciences ".[2]

Allen, and Mary's ambassador to the French court, and Guise had met, " within the last few days ", to discuss the plan, so Persons told the envoy of the King of Spain ; but the whole affair was being kept from the knowledge of the French king, for he could not be trusted not to betray it to Elizabeth. There was a further conference, a day or two later, at the residence of the nuncio, in which, as well as the nuncio and the three personages just mentioned, Persons also took part ; and just before May 24 there was a final conference, at which Fr. Claude Mathieu, the provincial superior of the Jesuits in France, also assisted ; the plan was now finally settled and Persons was commissioned to take the news (and a request for support) to Philip II, while Crichton was despatched on a like errand to the pope. The plan can be stated very simply : there was to be an attempt to stir up the embers of the Desmond war in Ireland, Guise was to land a small army on the coast of Sussex, and to Scotland a larger army was to be sent from Spain which, under the command of Lennox and James VI, would invade England ; meanwhile the English Catholics would rise and set Mary free.[3] On May 24, or 25, Crichton set out for Rome and on May 28 Persons left for Spain.

[1] The nuncio, to Cardinal-Secretary of State, May 8 ; Knox, xxxvi.

[2] Which, *pace* some innuendo, need not mean " hearing their confessions ". The ambassador's letter to Philip II of May 18, printed in Teulet, V, 246, is translated in Knox, *op. cit.*, pp. xxxvii–xxxviii, and this is quoted here. It has often been suggested that to spy out the land, with future political and military schemes in view, was the real purpose for which Persons came to England in 1580. Even Pearson (*Cartwright*, 236) can write, " The mission of Persons and Campion began in the summer of 1580 and took the form of a political campaign rather than a religious crusade ". Certainly the idea of the contrast between Persons and the (admittedly) saintly Campion appeals to historians who love a symmetrical arrangement of their material. Of evidence in proof of the charge there is hardly a sign —the words of the nuncio about to be quoted seem to me proof of no more than that exuberance about the unlikely only too characteristic of the establishment where Ptolemeo Galli presided. Writing in fact to this personage on May 8, 1582, the nuncio at Paris says, " Fr. Robert, the Jesuit, who came here from England, where he has been for two years busy with this affair " [i.e. plans for an invasion] (*padre Roperto, Giesuita chi e venuto d'Inghilterra, dove è stato dui anni trattando questo negotio*). Knox, *op. cit.*, 405, for the Italian original, and xxxvi for a translation, which I think is less exact than the one printed here.

[3] For this cf., in the Spanish ambassador's despatch of May 18, 1582 (Knox, xxxvii–xl translated from Teulet, V, 246 fol.), the account given him by Persons and Crichton. Also

Philip II, however, did not at all favour the project.[1] In this year, 1582, he had already far too many unsolved practical anxieties to welcome such another as this. As he told the new nuncio, Lodovico Taverna, who earlier in the year strove to interest him in English affairs, the war in Flanders was now calling for the whole of his attention. And the subjects of his newly acquired kingdom of Portugal were still very far from a peaceful acquiescence in his rule. The king's first move, on hearing that practical proposals and requests would be sent by the confederates at Paris, was to order his ambassador there to hold up the messenger. Persons, however, was well on his journey by the time this order reached Paris. When he reached Lisbon, June 15, it was several weeks before the king received him; and for long the Jesuit had to content himself with generalities of good will sent through the secretary, Idiaquez. When, finally, the king granted him audience, the main topic was the complaint that the pope had so little confidence in the good will of Spain. For Gregory XIII, despite his secretary's saying that the plan to attack England was as welcome as a crusade against the Turks—notoriously the desire nearest the old pope's heart—was very resolute not to give any aid until he saw the armies actually moving.[2]

And the plot of 1582 was still little more than the wishful thinking of half a dozen highly placed subordinates that no principal was really prepared to carry out[3] when, on August 23, a successful conspiracy in Scotland overthrew the Duke of Lennox.[4] It was the duke's influence with James VI that was the plotters' first essential—it was this alone that gave their talk any practical importance. Lennox out of the way, the whole affair must necessarily collapse. " Finally, when the news came of the capture of the King of Scots," Persons wrote to the pope, " His Majesty [i.e. Philip II] gave me leave to depart." [5]

This was not, however, the immediate end of the enterprise.[6] Elizabeth

---

the nuncio's despatch of May 22, enclosing a memorandum by Persons (Knox, 406–409, who translates it in great part, the memorandum fully, xl–xlii; in *Persons* also, the full text and a translation of the whole, 143–166).

[1] Cf. his chilling letter of June 11, Knox, xliii, translated from Teulet, V, 257 foll. " The two fathers of the Society of Jesus who spoke to you about Scotland, must have gone thither from motives of true zeal; but to advance so far as they did in the negotiation, and to communicate the plan to so many persons as they must have treated with, may be attended with much inconvenience as regards secrecy."

[2] And he offered only 50,000 crowns, when the total cost (so the Spaniards thought) would be 400,000. Persons' report in *Persons*, 169. For all this cf. Pastor, vol. 19, 431 and foll.

[3] Black's words, p. 296, about the rival plots of Don John and of Guise in 1578, apply also to these : " schemes that existed only in the brains of their promoters ".

[4] This is the conspiracy known as the Raid of Ruthven, in which James VI was captured while out hunting, by the anti-Catholic, pro-English, Earl of Gowrie, who held him a prisoner in Stirling Castle for the next ten months.

[5] *Persons*, 169.

[6] This last word is, in English, a common enough term for a common enough thing—in the next note Conyers Read can be seen using it of the Raid of Ruthven; and the word *impresa* is just as commonplace in Italian. But spell the word with a capital, and the sense of ordinary language is transformed. Mr. Neale, I think, conveys a wrong impression of the extent to which knowledge of such schemes as these—enterprises, if you like—was public property at the time, a leading feature of the day's international " news "; and a wrong impression also of the real importance of the conversations of these wishful thinkers,

had been privy to the Scottish conspiracy,[1] and it was Mary's anxiety, alarmed about the fate of her captive son, that now kept the varied group at Paris together. Was the tragedy of Lochleven to be repeated? And to whose profit?[2] In the months that followed the Raid of Ruthven Mary sent earnest appeals, to the pope, to Spain, and even to France, which had long ago seemed to wash its hands of the wrongs of the queen-dowager.[3] One result of this activity was that Guise now sent to Mary (October, 1582) a French Jesuit, Henri de Samerie—who passed as her physician—charged to find out what the queen could promise about the part her friends in England and Scotland would actually play in the enterprise, and also what arrangements exactly the Jesuits had made with the Catholic gentry in England about their rôle—and how far any actual preparations had been made.[4] The pope was still prepared to assist the scheme, even though—it was now declared— Spain held aloof. And in the first weeks of the new year, 1583, Henri III sent an envoy to Edinburgh, de Meyneville, whose real business was to organise, if possible, the rescue of the king and the re-establishment of the Lennox régime.

The papal secretary of state, however, was despondent. " The hope of doing anything better ", he wrote on February 28, 1583, to the nuncio at Paris, " seems to me to become fainter on all sides every day " ;[5] and a fortnight later, " So far as we understand, things are in a worse state in that kingdom [Scotland] than ever before ".[6] Lennox had now returned to France, but was lying dangerously ill, unable even to be consulted and soon to die. And Philip II's ambassador, sending this news, on February 14, was as despondent as the high personage in Rome. " In my poor judgment ", he wrote, " the affair is at an end for the present : for to all appearances this boyish prince will conform and adapt himself to necessity, and even, through his absence, forget Lennox, if requisite." [7]

Lennox died on May 26, but by then de Meyneville had returned to Paris bringing brighter news.[8] His report, and the " urgent sollicitations "

---

when he allows himself to write of the year 1580, " The Holy War of Catholicism against Protestant England—the Enterprise as contemporaries termed it—seemed imminent ; " *Elizabeth I and her Parliaments*, I, 370.

[1] Cf. Conyers Read, II, 179–180. " Walsingham himself seems to have given the signal for the enterprise " ; *ibid.*, 180.

[2] Mary's fears were not fanciful. Conyers Read (II, 182) says that Walsingham " remarked to one of his colleagues in the Council that the Ruthven raiders would either poison the young king or he would escape and bring them to the block ". And the Spanish ambassador in London thought that the only reason why Lennox made no fight was the fear that the Ruthven party would, in desperation, immediately kill the king ; *ibid.*

[3] And it was now that Mary wrote to Elizabeth the celebrated letter that set out in detail the long story of English ill-will towards her.

[4] The source of this is the report of the Nuncio at Paris, Nov. 6, 1582, to the Cardinal-Secretary of State, for which cf. Knox, *op. cit.*, 410–411.

[5] *Ibid.*, xlvi, 411.

[6] *Ibid.*, xlvi, 412.

[7] Teulet, V, 273, for the letter ; this translation is from Knox, xlvi.

[8] The Spanish ambassador thought him over optimistic : letter of June 24 to Philip II, Teulet, V, 281, quoted Knox, lv. For the English view that de Meyneville left for France broken and beaten, cf. Conyers Read, II, 191–192.

of the Queen of Scots and of Lord Seton,[1] the leader among her friends in Scotland, led directly to the next conference of the ambassadors with the English exiles. In the despatch of May 30, which gave the pope this information, the nuncio also wrote, in a general way, of what the Duke of Guise now proposed to do, and promised the details as soon as these were decided. The scheme to kill Elizabeth as a preliminary to the invasion would now, he believed, come to nothing.[2]

Twelve days later the conference had taken place. Besides the nuncio there were present Mary's ambassador, the Spanish ambassador in Paris, the late French ambassador to Scotland, de Meyneville, and the provincial of the Jesuits in France, Claude Mathieu.[3] All the nuncio could as yet say about the enterprise in its new form, when he reported this meeting, was that the death of Lennox had greatly increased the difficulties, and that much more would be required than the 80,000 scudi first asked. And he thought, as against Guise, that it was not possible to bring off the affair in September, nor indeed in this year 1583.[4]

On June 20 the nuncio sent to Rome the text of the *Disegno per l'impresa d'Inghilterra*.[5] This, on the face of it, is as crazy a scheme as ever passed through the mind of Ridolfi and his associates, postulating impossibilities as the condition of success and unaware of the impossibility of what is postulated.[6] There was to be a triple invasion : 2000 Spaniards to Ireland, an army of Frenchmen under Guise to land in Sussex, and—the principal attack—a much greater force, of 10,000 or 12,000, from Spain that was to land in the north of Lancashire. The Irish expedition, it is insisted, must land " a few days before " the other two—which seems to show that those who drafted the scheme were wholly innocent of the eternal uncertainties of oceans and tidal seas. " The principal lords of the kingdom ", Persons

---

[1] So the nuncio at Paris, despatch of May 30, Knox, *op. cit.*, 414, *stimolato molto da la Regina di Scotia et da Milort Seton.* Also, *ibid.*, *Dopo la venuta di Mons. di Menevil il Duca di Guisa si trovo molto riscaldato a questa impresa.*

[2] *Quel disegno sopra la persona de la Regina d'Inghilterra credo che andera in niente ; ibid.*, 414. For the probable character of *quel disegno*, cf. *infra*, p. 376, n. 3.

[3] Persons, who had lately arrived from Spain (he left Madrid April 30, 1583) after a year's absence from Paris, was not at this conference. He was now in residence at St. Cloud, and a day or two after the conference, the nuncio and the Spanish ambassador betook themselves thither, in order to put the discussion into better shape.

[4] One phrase in this despatch of June 11 (*ibid.*, 415) strikes a note familiar to whoever has read Walsingham's correspondence about Scottish affairs—money is needed, says the nuncio, to buy the support of Scottish nobles.

[5] For the text of which cf. *ibid.*, 416–419 (translated pages liii–lv). With this should be read the despatch of the Spanish ambassador of June 24 (in Teulet, V, 281 ; resumé, Knox, lv–lvi) which gives Philip II a much more realistic picture of the situation. There are still more details in the *Instructions* drawn up for Persons, who was now despatched to Rome by Guise, for which cf. Knox, lvi–lviii and (for the text) Teulet, V, 308.

[6] Cf. Black, 315, " The plot collapsed on the stocks before it was ready to be launched ". Did the plot ever get beyond the drawing-board ? And, *ibid.*, 313, " A more flimsy, fantastic, or immature plot for the subversion of a well-established kingdom could hardly have been devised." But this writer is surely substantially incorrect in his summary when he writes, " It was the jesuits, however, who took the initiative in laying the foundations for this wider and more pretentious plan ", and that " in May, 1582, a conference was held in France, *under jesuit auspices* ", 312 (italics mine).

was commissioned to explain to the pope, had sent assurances " that things are very well prepared especially towards the borders of Scotland ". The group in Paris, he was to declare, were " sure of having seaports where we can land in safety ", and the pope was told that " within a few days [of the landing in Lancashire] it will be possible to raise at least 20,000 horsemen " ; while arrangements had been made for ships to sail from the Lancashire port to meet the Spanish fleet and provide pilots for the awkward waters. In the *Disegno* itself it was said, very simply, that since the Catholics and the discontented subjects were in the majority " the conquest of that kingdom will be accomplished in a short time ".[1]

The group in Paris begged the pope to renew Pius V's excommunication of the queen, and to declare that the expedition was the pope's expedition, granting indulgences to all who aided or took part in it ; and they asked him also to appoint Allen Bishop of Durham so that, as papal nuncio, he could accompany the main force and so prove to this Catholic population that the expedition was an authentic, papal act and not " a foreign invasion ".

" Nothing but money is now wanting ", Persons was bidden to say to Gregory XIII. But, in truth, money was the least of the wants. No consideration, for example, would move the King of Spain to assist any kind of scheme, before his own mind had thought it all out anew. And again, the group's information was far from complete about the mind of the Catholics in England towards what was intended. It was to gather this vital information, and to organise the Catholic gentry of Sussex, if they proved favourable, that, at the end of August, Charles Paget crossed over to England. Another Catholic gentleman who began to busy himself with this work was Francis Throckmorton.[2]

Crichton's mission to Philip II was as sterile as the mission of twelve months earlier. But Persons achieved an astounding success at the court of Gregory XIII. The pope's enthusiasm went so far as to order the preparation in detail of all those juridical and diplomatic acts that must accompany such an expedition. A solemn declaration would announce once more the sentence of the bull of 1570, proclaim that the appointed time had now arrived, and that these armies were the armies of God, sent to carry out the sentence of the Church ; for all who aided, there were the spiritual favours granted to those who joined in crusades against the Turks ; and anathemas, likewise, for those who should stand by the excommunicated queen. A nuncio, or rather a legate *a latere*, accredited to the new queen should accompany the expedition, to publish the bulls, to proclaim the change of ruler, and to receive Mary's oath that she would restore the Catholic religion and bring up her son (now seventeen years of age, and no longer a child) as a Catholic. The

---

[1] And yet, on Aug. 28, two months later, it was necessary for Guise to send over Charles Paget to discover " what account is to be made of the strength of the English Catholics " ! Knox, lv, 418.

[2] It is " very evident that he was nothing more than an agent, acting according to the directions he received from overseas ". Conyers Read, II, 384. But in Neale, *Elizabeth*, 264, Throckmorton is presented as " one of the principal advisers concerned with the Enterprise '."

splendid array of the legate's faculties was set out, entrusted to Allen ; and for the last time the clerks in the papal chancery wrote the style and titles of the Bishop of Durham into a papal provision. All was complete, down to the very dates—September 24, 1583 : and there, in the archives, unpublished, never put into execution, these melancholy relics still repose.[1]

The promoters of the enterprise had been greatly heartened when, on the eve of the departure of their two envoys, the news had come from Scotland that the plan arranged by de Meyneville had succeeded and that James VI had escaped from the control of the Earl of Gowrie (June 27). The English government was correspondingly anxious. " The king's affection to her majesty is greatly abated ", the English envoy in Scotland reported, on July 31, and Sir Francis Walsingham, to whom he was writing, " would perceive this state to be in such case as it is very necessary to come to speedy resolution ".[2] So serious was the crisis that, to his disgust, it was Walsingham himself whom Elizabeth sent to Edinburgh. And so, while Crichton was striving against the unimpressionable inertia of Philip II at Madrid, and Persons rejoicing as the bulls and briefs and the rest of the paper work were drafted so liberally in Rome, the arch-enemy (unknown to them) was busy at the very heart of all their hopes.

Walsingham, however, achieved little beyond the personal satisfaction of lecturing the youthful king, and soon after his return to England there was a real breach in the diplomatic relations of the two kingdoms. But now, most unexpectedly, and by a kind of accident, there came to Elizabeth's secretary of state a revelation of what had been planned at Paris in the summer. It was not a complete exposure, but it was enough suddenly to frost the hopes of which Allen's bulls were the symbol, and to render unavailing any new chance there might be in Scotland where the English party was now " pretty well broken, and Elizabeth in no mood to reconstruct it ".[3]

Walsingham had for some months been watching very closely the movements of the French ambassador at Elizabeth's court. The secretary, moved by that mingled hatred and fear of the Catholic religion as in truth idolatry that was characteristic of the primitive protestant, and of Mary Stewart as the wicked woman who might one day ride in triumphantly on the beast, was greatly preoccupied with the possibilities of danger from the Guise –Queen of Scots–French ambassador combination. And already, early in this same year, 1583, a fairly plain clue to the realities had escaped him.

---

[1] Cf. Meyer, 284–287, for details and sources. Fr. Leo Hicks, S.J., has done all of us the great service to print these documents in his edition of Persons' *Letters and Memorials*, 1942 (C.R.S., vol. 39), pp. 348–355.   [2] Conyers Read, II, 204.

[3] Conyers Read, II, 225. New chance there was none—as events very soon proved. If Walsingham's mission had done nothing else it had shown that the king—seventeen years of age in the previous July—was already the " youthful old man " he has been so often described. If he did not realise the weakness of his position (which is what Walsingham told him to his face) he knew the game he needed to play : deceit, already, had no secrets for him. And in no sense of the word was James sympathetic to the religion of the Catholic Church. The story should be read, in Conyers Read (II, 204–257), of the two years and a half that followed Walsingham's embassy of 1583, and of how James finally " sold out " to Elizabeth, on his own terms. And it is this young man whom his mother (at the bidding of the papal legate) is to swear she will bring up a Catholic !

For in March—while James VI was still a captive—the Jesuit, William Holt, who, disguised, had been in and out of the court during the Lennox ascendancy, was arrested at Leith on his way to a ship and to France, through the agency of Elizabeth's ambassadors, Sir Robert Bowes and William Davison. The Jesuit admitted that " a purpose " was in preparation for war against England " in the cause of religion " and the liberation of the Queen of Scots, and that the pope " and divers princes Catholic " were involved. More he would not say,[1] but he carried for the Father-General of the Jesuits a letter from Lord Seton which made it clear that expectations were principally based on the King of Spain. But the last point made little impression on Walsingham at the time. It was from France that he continued to expect the worst—and through Scotland.

Then, in April, the secretary found a Frenchman willing to spy on the French ambassador in London, and was able to place him in the ambassador's household. The spy speedily bought over the ambassador's secretary, and soon copies of papers were being passed systematically to Walsingham. They revealed nothing of importance ; not even Mary Stewart's letters gave any further information about " the purpose " to which Holt had admitted. The spy also sent in the names of Englishmen who frequented the embassy, who " never came to the house except by night ". One of these was Francis Throckmorton, and after receiving reports about him for a good six months, Walsingham had him arrested on November 4. And the third time he was tortured Throckmorton spoke.[2] He did not reveal the whole of what had been so hopefully planned at Paris : he did not know the whole. But what he had to tell was a complete surprise to the secretary—that the blow was to come not through Scotland but through the south of England, an invasion of Sussex by the Duke of Guise ; that forces were ready, and that the pope and Spain had undertaken to finance the scheme ; that what now remained was to rouse the Catholics in England and to decide at what point Guise should land his army—which explained the lists of ports and havens in Throckmorton's hand found in his possession, and the lists of names of Catholic nobles and gentry with an estimate of the forces they could bring.

[1] Elizabeth was very insistent that the Jesuit should be tortured to force him to tell more. " Her majesty doth look to hear of some further matter that may be discovered by Holt's confession, for that you have written he should be put to the boots by Colonel Stewart, which her pleasure is that you should urge to be accordingly put in execution. . . ." Walsingham to Bowes, March 28, 1583 ; and also April 16, in a second letter to the same, " Her majesty doth earnestly desire that Holt might be substantially examined and forced by torture to deliver what he knoweth ". Conyers Read, II, 378–379. But Holt still had good friends at court, and " with the connivance of James " (*ibid.*, 379) he contrived to escape.

[2] For Walsingham's personal care about the torturing, cf. his letter to Thomas Wilkes found in the P.R.O. by Conyers Read and quoted, *op. cit.*, II, 382. Wilkes is to join with Norton, the official torturer (Puritan champion in the House of Commons too, and translator of the edition of Calvin's *Institutes* that the more zealous bishops were now pressing on their clergy's attention). " I have seen as resolute men as Throckmorton stoop ", the secretary wrote, ordering further torture, " notwithstanding the great show he hath made of Roman resolution. I suppose the grief of the last torture will suffice without any extremity of racking to make him more conformable than he hath hitherto shown himself." And this in fact happened ; the rollers and cords had not yet " strained him to any purpose " before the accused (innocent until proved guilty) agreed to provide the crown with proofs of his guilt.

While Throckmorton lay in the Tower awaiting his ordeal at the hands of Norton, Persons returned to Paris with the news of the pope's enthusiasm for the scheme ; [1] and on the day after Throckmorton had agreed to talk, the briefs for Allen came in. He acknowledged them gratefully, to the cardinal-secretary and to the pope. [2]

Then, very tardily, the first news of the realities began to reach Paris. A letter of November 26 from the Spanish ambassador in London—Mendoza —told Guise of Throckmorton's arrest, of the papers found in his possession, and of the talk that he was to be tortured. Mendoza feared that all might come out, and his colleague at Paris shared his fears and repeated to the nuncio that there had been too much haste about the whole affair. [3] Even a month later than this, however, it was not known in Paris that Throckmorton had admitted " anything prejudicial to the cause ", when January 16, 1584, Allen and Persons, in a joint letter, once more urged upon the King of Spain the need to act immediately, while the Catholics in England were feeling the stimulus of the new severities that had followed Throckmorton's arrest, and before the government discovered—as soon it must—all that had been proposed in the conferences at Paris. [4]

Francis Throckmorton was tried for high treason, May 21, 1584, condemned and executed, after much delay, on July 10, 1584. And now all was indeed revealed, as the nuncio in Paris wrote to Rome. [5] The speech of the crown prosecutor at the trial, and the account published by the government made it common knowledge ; and then, just a day later than this letter of the nuncio from Paris, the Dutch admiral obligingly captured at sea, for Walsingham, Fr. William Crichton, and sent him prisoner to London : and Crichton had with him the dossier of the obsolete, abandoned plot of 1582— the still-born proposals of the Duke of Lennox. And Crichton, too, when interrogated in the Tower, admitted all ; [6] perhaps the deadliest part of his confession was his saying : " The enterprise failed by the death of the Duke of

[1] But without any promise from the pope that he would increase the subsidy to which he was pledged. The Spanish ambassador in Paris wrote very caustically to his master about Persons' diplomatic achievement (Nov. 15, 1583). Persons, he said, " was certainly in a hurry to obtain at Rome things which might have been deferred ; but as he was there, he must have thought it best to get it done apart from the rest ; the more so because the wish to see accomplished what he desires so ardently must have persuaded him (as often happens to the afflicted and necessitous) that the affair could be carried into effect in the way he imagined it ". Translated in Knox, *op. cit.*, lix, from Teulet, V, 317.

[2] Knox, 217, 218.

[3] The nuncio, Dec. 12, 1583, to the cardinal-secretary, in Knox, *ibid.*, 419.

[4] This letter—a copy, rather, in Italian sent to Rome for the pope's information—is in Knox, *ibid.*, 222–224 ; also in *Persons*, 193–195 (with a full translation). In both these works it is wrongly described as a memorial to Gregory XIII. It is obviously addressed to Philip II. Even in March, 1584, it is not understood how much Throckmorton has avowed, see a letter (? of Persons) in *Persons*, 199.

[5] Sept. 3, 1584. " A book has appeared in English in which is related the confession made under torture by the said Throckmorton, which contains (so Fr. Robert has told me) almost the whole story of the agreement about the enterprise, and involves chiefly the Duke of Guise . . . and he says that this Throckmorton had learnt all this from the above mentioned Don Bernadino " [i.e. Mendoza]. Knox, *ibid.*, 425.

[6] Cf. *ibid.*, 425–432, *An enterprise found about a Scottish Jesuit taken on the seas for the invasion of the realm ;* " A very dangerous plot set down about two years past, in the Italian

Lennox. He supposeth the intention remaineth ".[1] The Jesuit also admitted that it was from " his superior at Paris " that he had received these " discourses " in Latin and French and Italian, that were found upon him ; but there is no mention in his confession, nor in these papers, of either Allen or Persons.

This disastrous capture was the end. Already, June 24, the new nuncio at Paris had reported that " The English and Scotch who were acquainted with the enterprise have evidently given up hope ".[2]   The King of Spain had come to the conclusion that the plan would cost some 2,000,000 crowns— it was obviously not a present possibility. Persons was tiring heartily of his new occupation, and writing to Sir Francis Englefield, in Spain these many years, " If I could be rid of the whole, it would be a great ease and contentment to me, so all parties were satisfied ".[3] And towards the end of the year, with all possible explicitness, to the Queen of Scots he wrote, " Dr. Allen and I, having had a meeting together, had concluded—upon consideration of our thwarts and oppositions that we received daily in all our doings, and men of our side, and of the small success our former labours had brought forth— we had resolved, I say, to leave cogitation of such matters and to follow only our spiritual course, whereon all dependeth though in longer time, persuading ourselves that God would never permit such lets and hindrances from among ourselves except his divine providence did foresee that it was not yet time to relieve us temporally." [4]

With these admissions of disillusionment—and the half suggestion, surely, that they had been busy about business not properly their own— the tale comes to an end of the direct share of Dr. Allen and of Fr. Persons in schemes to overthrow the government of Queen Elizabeth. The next " enterprise " will be the Armada itself, and in the preparation for this neither of them was to be asked for advice or information—nor indeed, as Persons was to say very pointedly, were any of the exiles used : such was the Spanish opinion of their capacity or influence, and the Spanish mistrust also. And the next " privy conspiracy ", the so-called Babington Plot of 1586, would be hatched on English soil, without any engagements to foreign princes ; and with this affair only one ecclesiastic was connected, a priest who had long since ceased to function as such in any way, John Ballard.

In these great dreams, where Jesuits obediently moved from Paris to Edinburgh and from Paris to Rome and Paris to Madrid, as envoys, and as experts about the home front, the Catholics in England, writhing under the terror into which the repression of the statutes of 1559 had developed, had no share at all. The admirable articles of Fr. Pollen which first set out

tongue, for the invasion of this realm ", Sir Francis Walsingham wrote, Sept. 16, to the ambassador at Edinburgh, Sir Ralph Sadler, *ibid.*, 425, n. 3.   Cf. also 432–434, *William Creyton's confession what he had heard spoken.*
    [1] *Persons*, 433. Cf. also Walsingham to Sadler, as cited, " and as by the same Creighton is confessed there is an intent and meaning when the King of Spain shall be rid of his Low Countries' troubles to proceed to the execution thereof ".   [2] Knox, *op. cit.*, 424.
    [3] July 24, 1584, *Persons*, 226,   [4] *Ibid.*, 246.   Sept. 10 for Oct ? *ibid.*, n. 1.

critically the detail of the story might seem not so well named : it is not of *The Politics of the English Catholics* [1] that they treat, but of the politics of a very small group of exiles, and principally, of the two priests whose names recur at every turn. Were the president of the famous seminary and his extremely able Jesuit co-adjutor really the leaders of the English Catholics in any sense, save that they were leading influences at Rome for all that concerned the Catholics of England ? Is anything known of their political influence in England ? How far, in the first place, did any considerable number of the Catholics in England know anything at all, not of their activities around the council-table of the Duke of Guise, but even of their political views and their political hopes ? [2] This is a question that no man can yet answer. But there is the best of authority for believing that the Catholics in England would have learnt of these activities with real dread. The King of Spain's ambassador in London, analysing for his master the various elements in the situation, describes the English Catholics at this time as utterly cowed by the rigour of the persecution. From many passages these may be quoted, all from the spring of 1582, before the persecution had gone far beyond its tentative beginnings : to the King of Spain, " There are no signs of a disposition amongst Catholics here to rise unless they have foreign aid " ; [3] " I am replying to [the Queen of Scots] as regards [the English] Catholics that on no account should any declaration be made to them, and that they should not even be sounded, as they are quite paralysed with fear, and no good end would be gained by doing so . . ." ; [4] to Mary, Queen of Scots, " Many Catholic gentlemen are devoted to you but only to the extent of being sure unanimously to acclaim your Majesty in case of the death of the Queen, which the Catholics would do if they saw a strong fleet with foreign troops arrive on the coast, able to undertake the conquest of the country unaided. . . . I have been diligent in sounding their intention, and I must confess that I find no particularly strong spirit or effort to forward the matter themselves, nor do I perceive any close association, or league amongst them, each acting and thinking separately . . . [The efficiency of the government's spies has so terrified them] that they not only distrust one another, but avoid expressing their opinions ".[5]

In the activities of 1582–1584, in which Allen and the two or three Jesuits played the part described, it was, in reality, on the mind of the Duke of Guise that all had turned. His was the initiative, and it was his interest that

---

[1] These thoughtful papers (119 pages in all), informed, level-headed, well-documented, are still the best introduction to the story. See, *The Month*, 1902, Jan., Feb., Mar., April, June, July, Aug.

[2] Juridical authority over the Catholics in England they had none, of course. In all these twenty-five years since 1559 there had been no attempt to supply any kind of organisation through which ecclesiastical authority could be effective. Leaving out the three or four Jesuits now at work in England, there was not machinery even for the local government of the new priests : and the remnants of the Marian clergy faithful to their religion were, as they had been from the beginning, isolated units, each a law unto himself. On Feb. 17, 1582, Aquaviva wrote to Persons that the nuncio at Paris had been named *Ordinarius Angliae*, with power to grant dispensations to contract marriage. *Persons*, 106, n. 31.

[3] Feb. 9, *Span. Cal.*, *Eliz.*, III, 1580–1586, p. 293.

[4] March 28, *ibid.*, p. 457.   [5] May [? 6], *ibid.*, p. 467.

had inaugurated, and that sustained, the whole affair, from his first sending Lennox to the court of James VI in 1579. And the action of the Englishmen whom his choice brought into the affair was the action, of course, of private individuals, who can, in reality, speak only for themselves. It is a commentary on the lack of leaders among the Catholics—or on the poor quality that obtained among them—that it was to clerics alone that Guise turned for his counsellors and envoys. And it is illuminating, also, that in this age when, in England, the cleric had been finally pushed out of that control of temporal affairs which is the sphere proper to the layman, in the age of Cecil and Walsingham and the rest, the temporal affairs of the Catholics should continue to be the concern, in the main, of clerics, and the layman's subordination to these to be taken for granted—by the clerics.

That there were laymen who resented the share of clerics in these activities was inevitable. And from that resentment, in part, one element derived of the feuds that were presently to rend the fabric of Allen's great work.[1] In later years Persons recalled to Charles Paget how, when they first " dealt together in the city of Rouen ", in 1583, Paget complained " against priests in general and against Mr. Doctor Allen (after Cardinal) in particular and by name, about whom you and I had long dispute why he and other priests or religious men should meddle in public matters of our country and not you gentlemen . . .". Paget, so Persons writes to him, had against him the majority of " the gentlemen of worship then present in France " (whom Persons names) in " that very quarrel which you endeavoured to raise between gentlemen and priests, repeating often (as I well remember) why priests did not meddle with their breviaries only, and the like. And I answering you that if priests besides their breviaries, or with their breviaries, or by their credit in Catholic princes' courts, where breviary men were esteemed, could help and assist and serve you gentlemen also towards the reduction of our country, why should you not be content to use their labours to your and the public commodity without emulation ? "[2]

Paget and his associates were, however, very far from the perfection of political wisdom. They attempted the impossible when they thought to achieve their ends by double-crossing the Elizabethan government, and so they fell, time and again, into the hands of spies and *agents-provocateurs*.[3]

---

[1] " The fatal divisions, which so sadly weakened the Catholics in subsequent generations, were traced back by Persons to the offence taken by Morgan and Paget at being excluded from the conferences at Paris. Their irritation may not have been reasonable, they were doubtless a troublesome, unreliable pair. But this does not prove that their annoyance was altogether unreasonable and beyond expectation. Since then many have re-echoed their adverse censures." Pollen, *The Month*, 1902 (March), 303–304.

[2] Persons to Paget Dec. 20, 1597, extract printed in Knox, 391–394.

[3] Cf. also Allen (now a Cardinal) to Thomas Throgmorton, Jan. 4, 1591, *ibid.*, 320–324, for an insight into these complicated quarrels, whose importance is that they reflect rival policies. For Allen, in 1591, these lay opponents are " a few and very few discontented persons which are not . . . enough to give their names unto a faction, as though the English were divided among themselves, as some of folly may give out or of simplicity may believe ".

It is a commonplace that exiles who leave their country in the first crises of a long-enduring revolution know less and less of the realities of its life with every year that goes by, until in the end its national life becomes, in truth, most foreign to them, most unnatural even. By 1584 Allen had been away from England almost twenty years, Sir Francis Englefield longer still ; and in all the twenty-nine years of life that remained to Persons after his flight he would never see England again. Their judgment is no longer to be trusted, not about means of action merely, but about needs and their relative importance. The man who, in 1583, had been Philip II's ambassador in London for five years, had a very different impression of the feelings provoked by the persecution among the Catholics in England.[1]

" The schemes of Allen and Persons were so much criminal folly which, if carried out, could only have produced bloodshed and disorder ; and it is hard to say to what lengths a nation is not justified in going in order to protect itself." [2] In this commentary on the events of 1582–1584 the distinguished author is only saying about these two great figures, but in his own strong way, what most historians seem to hold. But how far is it the fact that these designs were " the schemes of Allen and Persons " ? Is there any evidence that the two priests were ever principals in these schemes, ever authors and origina-tors ? They are certainly called into consultation, as soon as Lennox and the Duke of Guise are of one mind ; and their opinion counts, apparently, whenever the question is discussed how far Catholics in England are likely to help the invaders. But for all the zeal of Allen and Persons in the matter, and the urgency with which they press the execution of these plans, is their rôle ever more than secondary ? [3]

It is another presupposition, in the traditional account, that Persons is the born conspirator, released at last in 1581 for the metier that suits his nature,

---

[1] And not only Mendoza. Charles Paget, so Persons was to write in later years (1601), returned from his mission of Aug.-Sept. 1583 with a " contrary answer to that which was expected by the Duke of Guise " [Knox, 391 n.]—the Catholic gentry were not enthusiastic. If it be true—what Persons goes on to give as told to him by William Watts—that this " contrary answer " was " procured of set purpose by Mr. Paget ", we are still left with a picture of partisans not so enthusiastic that they cannot be persuaded out of their enthusiasm by a story about " the facts " from one presumed in a position to know. Paget is alleged to have said to Watts, " walking upon the strand or seaside . . . at that time he expected his bark to pass into England ", that " he coming into England would in few days dissolve all that had been treated therein by Jesuits ". To which Persons adds " and so it ensued ". Cf. Persons' Autobiographical Notes, C.R.S., II, 32 ; where also we are told that Paget's task was " to draw the Earls of Northumberland and Arundel [Blessed Philip Howard] to join with the Duke of Guise for delivery of the Queen of Scots ".

[2] Pollard, *H.E.*, VI, 386. The last clause of the quotation introduces into the history of the event, once again, an apologia for the policy of the government—and its basis is not his-torical fact but a principle of ethics. This principle, invoked to clear Elizabeth, Burghley, and the rest, and to prepare the reader for the masterpiece of their anti-Catholic code, the Act of 27 Elizabeth, c. 1, is suggestively akin to " the end justifies the means ". Since, however, Allen and Persons considered it was they who championed the nation, and that what they were working to bring about was the delivery of the nation from a tyranny, on the reasoning hinted by Pollard their course of action would have been morally right and patriotic.

[3] Neale also writes as though he thought the schemes of 1581–1582 were primarily the work of the Catholic exiles. *Elizabeth*, 259.

and to which he now willingly gives the rest of his long life.[1]   This is curiously at odds with (what is certainly authentic) Persons' own, unconscious, description of himself as he tells how, upon his first coming to England, he strove to calm the London priests, dismayed by the fact that the Jesuits had actually arrived and, despite the ingenious slanders that were bound to ruin their work, were proposing to begin operations.   It would be an easy matter, Persons said to them, to answer whatever the prosecution might put before a jury about the political aims of the Jesuits.   Any jury would see immediately " that if foreign princes would have sent men hither to treat matters of State, they would have chosen other manner of men than we who all our lives have been mere scholars, neither would they have sent us so many together nor so openly as we have come ; neither would we ourselves have come on foot and so poorly apparelled from Rome, if we had come on princes' affairs ".[2]

The man so innocent as to think that to give such an answer settled the matter—answer to the London priests, answer to the crown prosecutors— is the last man, not to have made a good conspirator, but ever to have wanted to be such.   There is about his declaration a simplicity that would have delighted Cecil as much as it would have disgusted Mendoza, whose well known declaration indeed it might have provoked, that in matters of politics and diplomacy the priests had no capacity and were simply not to be trusted.[3]

[1] For example, Pollard, op. cit., 372, " a politician in a priest's disguise " (now, quoted by Bindoff (1950), circulating by the hundred thousand), and " that career of treason and intrigue ", ibid., 378 ; Black, op. cit., 146, " par excellence the politician and organiser of intrigue, plot and invasion against his native country . . . a kind of factotum, counsellor, and confidant " of all Elizabeth's enemies ; Rowse, The England of Elizabeth, " essentially a political spirit ", 461, " the cleverest intriguer, the most finished diplomat in Europe " 463, " the undescried heart of Robert Persons ", 462 (in which, nevertheless, this author proceeds to descry " a man with a complex ", needless to say an inferiority complex, with " resentment " as compensation for early frustration).

[2] Quoted Pollen, The Month, March, 1902, 295–296, from Persons' (MS.) Life of Campion. The Jesuit's final statement is good—and convincing as to sincerity : " If we have to deal with any men in these supposed matters of State it must be with Catholics, and what Catholic is there in England that would either believe us or look upon us hereafter if, after all these oaths and protestations to the contrary, he should see us begin with him to the contrary ". Ibid., 296, the whole page and a half should be read.   It must here be noted that, with this passage in mind, Pollard, op. cit., 376, accuses Persons of forswearing himself : " Both [Campion and Persons] had sworn to their fellow-Catholics that they came with no knowledge of, or concern with, affairs of state ; but though Campion confined himself to proselytising and literary controversy, Persons discussed political intrigues with Mendoza in London."   The only authority given by Pollard for this important statement is the article on Persons in the D.N.B., by T. G. Law ; but all that this writer says (without giving any authority at all) is that when Persons in November, 1580, was given shelter by Mendoza, he " received that bias towards political intrigue which marked every step of his subsequent career ".   As to " literary controversy ", Pollard is quite wrong : it was Persons who was the prominent figure, as even the bibliographies printed in the D.N.B. might show.

[3] Was Persons' whole life, after 1581, given to politics ?   For the editor of Persons' Letters and Memorials (1942), the only writer (surely) really familiar with his mind, really knowing his life and his books, " His mission to Rome [1583] may be said to have terminated his activity as a political negotiator.   With Allen he still continued to write on Catholic politics, offered advice to Catholic statesmen, and urged them at times to devote themselves to the interests of his English co-religionists, but he never again acted as an envoy " (Persons, lxi).   " Envoy " I take to mean not merely a messenger but an ambassador.   Cf. Persons, Aug. 26., 1582, from Spain, answering Watts of June 8, " I have laboured so vehemently in my particular business you know of that I am almost worn out both body and mind :

It is no purpose of this section of the book either to blame or to praise the political activities of Allen or of Persons. Historians who are Catholics have usually judged Persons very severely—much more severely than Allen. Fr. Pollen, a Jesuit himself, is perhaps the severest of all. The whole business of " making plans for the restoration of Catholicism by force of arms ", he considers, " an unfortunate development ", for which he blames principally not Persons but Fr. William Crichton. The whole thing was a tragic mistake ; and of Persons in particular, he writes, " he now adopted a course which was injurious to himself, to his Order, and to his country ". This is not, however, a condemnation of Persons (and Allen by implication) simply because they failed : " If Allen and the Jesuit were right in making so much of non-intervention in politics in 1580, they were certainly in error in not acting the same way in 1582." [1] Whether this was Fr. Pollen's last word about this particular matter I do not know, but it may also be said there was a world of difference between the situation in England in 1580 and in 1582— the difference made by the successful apostolate of Persons himself and of Campion ; and, also, that neither Allen nor Persons, was, in 1582, engaged in missionary work in England. Their real crime in the eyes of the government—their real importance—was not their share in the scheming of the Duke of Guise (of which the government knew all but nothing) but the success of the great invention, the mission to England.

---

infinite overthwarts of late have I had and many times I have almost despaired the success. And now again am I in hope and that very shortly to have good success " ; *ibid.*, 168. Also Persons' summary of the mission, i.e., to put before the King of Spain the matter " entrusted to me by the Duke of Lennox " ; the nuncio to Spain summarising Persons' report to him 20-30 Oct. 1582 ; *ibid.*, 179. And Persons' saying (*ibid.*, lvi, 119) that what was done in Paris in 1582–1583 was done by " common counsel ", meaning by others as well as by himself, proves he was no mere agent, as was, e.g. Watts, in 1581, when he took to Lennox the message of the six English notables.

[1] *The Month*, March, 1902, 301, 303, 303–304, 305.

CONFLICT

I

THE road which Campion and his companions had travelled, some scores of others were now to take. For the conflict, henceforth, is undisguised, between the architects of the system of 1559 and those who, in the name of all the thousand years before, refuse to make even the appearance of submission to it. The passionate zeal to destroy Catholicism [1] that glows beneath the formality of the Acts of Supremacy and Uniformity now begins to blaze—the passion of the ex-Catholic pioneers of the new beliefs to wipe out the idolaters ; the passion of the statesmen to wipe out whatever will not conform to their pattern of national uniformity. Catholicism has, at last, manifestly begun to make a stand. It has reacted, even ; and has declared war on the principle of ambiguity. To Burghley, and the rest, this is a challenge that is vital. They will not ignore it, cannot ignore it ; for the possibility seems real of a reaction strong enough to force a change of policy. This they cannot risk ; and to defeat the Catholic mission is, therefore, the most urgent problem before the government.[2] All the savagery threatened in the Acts of 1559 and 1563 will now be put into execution, and these laws be developed in order to simplify the process of extermination.

The government spokesman, Sir Walter Mildmay, preparing a more than sympathetic House of Commons for the introduction of " the notorious law which ushered in the period of severest persecution of the Catholics ", January 25, 1581, made it clear that the government realised that a turning point in the struggle had been reached ; and clear, also, what those Catholic activities were which now alarmed the queen's ministers.[3]

The offensiveness of the Catholics in England still lies in their disobedience to the religious laws of 1559, and in the false doctrine they profess—their fidelity, in mind and act, to the traditional religion now proscribed. The government is at this moment anxious because the number

---

[1] Conyers Read will say, of the Acts of Parliament of 1581 and 1585 (now about to be considered), " There can be no doubt that in these laws Parliament aimed at nothing less than the extermination of all Catholic preachers and of all Catholic sympathisers in England ". *Op. cit.*, II, 293. And Meyer, 92, " That [the complete destruction of Catholicism in England] was Burghley's object cannot seriously be denied ". Neither of these scholars is a Catholic. Neither is English. Neither is influenced by whatever it is that compels the native historian to shrink from statements so plain.

[2] " The Catholic menace " was " the chief business of the parliament of 1581 " ; Neale, *Elizabeth*, 252 ; whose authority I must not be taken to quote as though supporting Allen's view of what the " menace " is.

[3] For an account of the speech, cf. Neale, *Elizabeth I and her Parliaments*, I, 382–385.

is increasing of Catholics who refuse to act as though they were Protestants. Despite the long campaign since 1559, "the obstinate and stiff-necked papist is so far from being reformed as he hath gotten stomach to go backwards and to show his disobedience, not only in arrogant words but also in contemptuous deeds ". It has, then, been a general aim of the government's policy, in these twenty years, to bring about a change of mind in the Papist, to make Protestants out of Catholics ? So much for leaving a man's beliefs to himself if only he will, on Sundays, obey the queen and go to church. So much for " the queen's liberal-minded distinction between outward conformity and inward freedom ".[1]

The reaction, the scale of which is alarming the government, is declared to be the fruit of the papally-fostered activities of the priests trained in the seminaries abroad. The speech does not show any sign of that reluctance, on the part of the government, to be thought willing to punish for disobedience in matters of religion strictly so called, with which the modern apologists would seem to credit it. On the other hand, although the speaker is definite enough about " the implacable malice of the pope and his confederates against [the queen] ", the motive of which is that she has " loosened us from the yoke of Rome, and did restore unto this realm the most pure and holy religion of the gospel ", and although he cites, as examples of what the " malice " can effect, the rising of 1569 and the recent events in Ireland, he does not therefrom draw the general conclusion, " Catholics as such are traitors. Catholics are our enemies' fifth column " ; nor urge that the laws against Catholics must be stiffened because of this political danger. Nor are the new seminaries denounced as schools where Englishmen are trained to be traitors and assassins.

The pope has sent priests to England in order to encourage Catholics " to stand fast in their disobedience " to the queen's laws about religion, comforting them " with absolutions, dispensations, reconciliations and other such things of Rome ". The intent of these priests, " a sort of hypocrites, naming themselves Jesuits, a rabble of vagrant friars newly sprung up " is, first, " to corrupt the realm with false doctrine ",[2] and also " under that pretence to stir sedition "—the sedition, as the context makes clear, being the criminal refusal to attend church. Therefore it is that the government invites parliament to make severer laws against the Catholics, to teach them how little the blessings of reconciliation

---

[1] *Elizabeth I and her Parliaments*, I, 197.

[2] We have an example, from within a twelvemonth of Mildmay's speech, of a Protestant blaming the religion of his boyhood for what he considered the consequences of false doctrine—John Louth (1519–1590), archdeacon of Nottingham and a man of sixty when he wrote, " Now as to you pestilent papists . . . like devils You labour as much as any fiend in hell can do to bereave [Christians], by your doctrine, of everlasting life ". Nichols, *Narratives*, 17. And, in 1580, an indictment is laid against Edmund Campion that " being vested in alb and other vestments according to papistical rites and ceremonies, did say and celebrate one private and detestable Mass in the Latin tongue, derogating to the blood of Christ, and contrary to his due allegiance ". This last piece of information I owe to the kindness of Fr. Godfrey Anstruther, O.P., who has since published it in his *Vaux of Harrowden*, p. 115. The reference is King's Bench, 9/654, no. 58.

will avail " to save them from that punishment which we are able to lay upon them ".

Here is a state of things whose development, in a short seven years or so,[1] might well indeed have seemed impossible to the queen's chief minister, had it been predicted. Here was a revelation, indeed ; not that there were Catholics still in England, but that, after twenty years of general compromise and surrender and submission, the faith of so many was capable of such revival, of rebirth in strength of a new sort ; the rebirth, indeed, was more than possible, it was actually taking place, with all the nation looking on at it. Who could have foreseen that there would have been so much life to revive— in a body that was already so weak when the process of elimination began ?

It is not, then, the Catholics of 1559 that the government is now facing, but a people re-evangelised, toughened by new processes and instruments, a multitude whose religion is active, whose understanding has been enlightened, whose faith is instructed, and for whose leaders and guides Catholicism means combat and endurance until death. And for these Catholics, no less than for other Englishmen, with the religious conflict there is linked the future of their country. Allen, too, invokes the patriotic spirit.

These were Catholics of a kind Burghley had never known—quite unlike the kinsmen and friends and the clergy of his Catholic boyhood, in the years that preceded the divorce : here was resolution, fire, clear-mindedness, a habit of spiritual exercises, of prayer and acts of penance, and very frequent receiving of the sacraments ; a vocation, understood and accepted, of complete sacrifice of self ; and the core of it all was not a mere " cause ", and not just " the Church ", but Christ, the divine Saviour and the true universal King.[2]

It has often been noted, and very truly, as the leading weakness in Allen's later years that he had no personal contact with the new spirit that transformed so much of English life after 1570. And Burghley was similarly handicapped. By the time when he had come to the fullness of his importance in the government of England—by the date, let us say, of the papal jubilee year, 1575—the Catholic reform movement had brought about a real transformation of religious life in the Low Countries, in much of Germany and in Italy. Under the influence of the new saints and the new religious orders, and of the years of hard thinking in the universities whence came the theologians and the canonists and the trained administrators who made up the Council of Trent, all that state of things against

---

[1] 1573-1580.
[2] The readiest way to introduce one's self to the spirit of the Catholic *résistance*, to discover what it was that nerved the adventurers in the *maquis*, is to read the many contemporary letters which Challoner has incorporated in his *Missionary Priests*. In Southern's *Elizabethan Recusant Prose* there is a great deal about the content of the devotional literature of the movement. Janelle, *The Catholic Reformation*, has a good account of Persons' *Christian Directory*, and much may be learned from a study of the notes to the Rheims Testament. Best of all is the incidental testimony of such a work as Allen's *Defence of Catholics*.

which the Reformation was, self-confessedly, a resounding protest, had all but disappeared. It was now just forty years since Thomas More, a man as keenly aware as Luther himself of all that was amiss with Catholic life, had given his life as a testimony that the Church of the popes is, none the less, the one Church of Christ. Had he, *per impossibile*, lived on to see these times [1] how he must have rejoiced at the new spiritual rebirth, at so many changes for the better, in kind as in degree.

But how much of this was known to the " first men " who were the English contemporaries of these reforming saints? to Grindal say, and Whitgift, to Cartwright and Whitaker and Bancroft? and to Burghley? The most striking transformation of all, for example—the change of heart in the Roman Curia itself, wrought principally through the personal holiness of such a secretary of state as Charles Borromeo, of such a pope as Michele Ghislieri showed himself, and of the lowly priest who, moving ever in the background, did more than all the rest, Philip Neri?

It was from the heart of this new world, all aglow with the purifying fires of evangelical revival, that the men had come who were now bringing the word to the starved Catholics of England. And one important element of the new Catholic resistance was the men and women whom these heralds of the new renaissance won back from " religion as established by the queen's majesty": of the Elizabethan martyrs nearly one in three was a convert. That there were such converts, and many of them, was soon popular knowledge, so that it was taken for granted that any notably good Catholic was a convert.[2] And against no Catholics was the government more bitter, as witness the Statute of 1581, and the number put to death simply because they were converts.

Queen Elizabeth put to death, solely because of their religion, between the years 1577 and 1603, 183 of her Catholic subjects.[3] Of these, 123 were priests, 1 was a friar not yet ordained, and 59 were layfolk, 3 of them women. Three

---

[1] As his son-in-law William Roper, still alive and active in 1575.

[2] *Quia nunc sinceri Catholici dicebantur passim reconciliati.* Allen to Vendeville, Sept. 16, 1578; Knox, 59.

[3] A Catholic tradition that goes back to the reign of Elizabeth—and that the pope (Leo XIII), ratified in 1886—reckons also as martyrs five others, put to death before the beginning of the Douay mission : Thomas Plumtree, priest (1570), and Thomas Percy, ninth earl of Northumberland (1572), both executed for their share in the rising of 1569, but offered their lives on condition they changed their religion ; John Felton (1570), the layman who fastened the Bull of excommunication on the Bishop of London's gate ; John Story, kidnapped at Antwerp for personal reasons by Cecil, put to death for refusing to acknowledge the Royal Supremacy (1571) ; and Thomas Woodhouse, an old priest of Queen Mary's days, imprisoned since 1560 and put to death in 1573, also for refusing to acknowledge the queen's supremacy. "The government, as usual, was more merciful than the law, except in cases of treason. For this offence, and not for being a Jesuit, Thomas Woodhouse was hanged in 1573 "; Pollard, *H.E.*, VI, 371. But for a Jesuit to be in England was not a crime in 1573 ! " for this offence "—the treasonable act (who could guess it from the context ?)—was the denial that the queen is head of the Church. How can the government be truly said to be " more merciful than the law ", when a system obtains where the enactment of laws is as much the act of the government as the enforcement ? It is the merciful government which brought the cruel law into existence—in this case the very same officials.

of the priests were men ordained before the beginning of the queen's reign ; the rest were products of the new seminary movement. Four of them indeed, after beginning their studies in the seminaries of Douay and Rome, went to join the Society of Jesus ; another 6 were received into the Society after their ordination, while serving on the English mission or while they awaited their fate in the queen's prisons, as, in this way, another priest became a monk and yet another became a Dominican. Of the 123 priests put to death, all but 4 had passed through the seminaries, and 115 had been wholly trained there. Two of the 3 women martyrs were gentlewomen, the third came out of the upper class merchant society that ruled the northern metropolis, York. The occupation or social standing of 7 of the 56 men is not known ; 25 are listed as gentlemen, 1 was a student of Douay College, there are 5 schoolmasters and 4 men servants and 4 yeomen. And there is one of each of the following : printer, bookseller, glover, tailor, dyer, joiner, husbandman, ostler, waterman ; and one merchant, an Irishman from Waterford.

The historian of this persecution is not handicapped by such a circumstance as that the most of its victims can be no more to him than names on a list. Of very few, indeed, of those put to death can it be said that they are no more than silhouettes. But we do not know, as yet,[1] where all of them were born. There are, however, 8 Irishmen among the 183, 1 Scot, and 5 Welshmen. Then, from the west of England we know of 23, from the midlands 20 ; there are only 12 who are London born, 15 are from Lancashire, and 53 from Yorkshire. We are left with 46 of whose birthplace we are ignorant.

Where were these men and women put to death ? In London 76, of whom the priests were 55 ; in York 40, Durham 9, Lancashire and Dorchester 6 in each, Winchester 5, Oxford and Canterbury 4 in each, Gloucester and Derby 3 in each ; Chichester, Isle of Wight, Rochester, Isleworth, Lincoln and Newcastle-on-Tyne 2 in each ; and one in each of the following towns : Launceston, Exeter, Salisbury, Andover, Kingston-on-Thames, Chelmsford, Ipswich, Oakham, Warwick, Stafford, Wrexham, Beaumaris, Carlisle, Gateshead, Darlington. (See the map, p. 341.)

In these executions in the provincial towns the proportion of laymen put to death was somewhat higher than in London, 37 laymen to 70 priests. Ten of the 21 laymen killed in London are listed as gentlemen, as are 9 of the 13 in York, and 4 of the 6 in Winchester : at Dorchester only 1 of the 6 is a gentleman. The printer and the bookseller are both London martyrs, the ostler and the waterman also. Of the yeomen, 1 is a Lancashire man, the other 3 are from Yorkshire. The husbandman and the joiner are Hampshire men ; the glover hails from Gloucester, as does the dyer sent to his death in London for aiding a Gloucester priest to circulate

---

[1] In the last fifty years much more manuscript material has been printed than anyone has really studied, and much yet remains to be printed. Critical research (e.g. C.R.S., vol. V, among other works) has done much—in contrast is the failure to do anything more than repeat the *dicta* of Foxe. From the very time of the executions, the precise character of these deaths had an official importance for the Church ; for a summary account of the long official investigation of the fact of martyrdom, cf. Pollen's edition of Challoner (1924).

Allen's reply to Lord Burghley. None of the 5 reported as school-masters is among the London group; 2 came from Winchester (and are of New College, Oxford), the others are from Canterbury, Darlington and Wrexham.

It is interesting to note, not only that 49 of the " new " priests put to death were university men (40 Oxford, 9 Cambridge), but that the great majority of these belonged to the earlier period of the terror : of the 57 martyrs ordained in the great years of the seminary movement, 1577–1583, 35 were university men ; of the 42 ordained in the six years that followed, 1584–1589, no more than 12 were from the universities ; while of the 17 martyrs ordained in the last thirteen years, 1590–1603, only 2 were such. The stream of recruits from Oxford students and graduates [1] ran dry, then, long before the end of the reign. The transition period, when Oxford was filled with half-Catholics and with Catholics who compromised, had ended. By the last years of this period the seminary movement had drawn off the totality of sympathisers who were serious at heart. Again, from the time of the trials of Campion and his companions, the old propaganda had been singularly intensified—that Catholicism was neces-sarily anti-English : propaganda greatly assisted by the political events of 1584–1588.

Another detail that is interesting is the number of these martyrs of 1577–1603 who were converts—54 out of the 183.[2] Two of these convert-martyrs were women, and 9 of the men had been clergy ordained for the service of the new establishment.[3] Of the 52 men converts martyred, 31 had been educated at some time in the English universities, and 29 of these were later ordained. In all, this group of 52 produced 39 priests.

The 123 priests came from all classes of society, so far as we can judge from our scanty information about their families. Contemporary accounts of their lives [4] give 26 as of gentle birth. The vast majority, naturally enough, had never exercised any other profession than their ministry, but of a small group of 21 who came late to their priestly vocation, 8 had been schoolmasters, 5 fellows of Oxford colleges,[5] 2 had been students at the Inns

---

[1] From Cambridge there was never more than an occasional recruit.

[2] By converts is meant Catholics who were once, *bona fide*, of the queen's religion. This excludes from the list two Marian priests, James Bell, *d.* 1584, and Richard Williams, *d.* 1592, who had conformed and then, after a number of years' service in the establishment of 1559, had returned to the Church ; and a layman, John Rigby, *d.* 1600, who had also conformed (in appearance only) for a time. John Gerard has an interesting reference to conversions in his *Autobiography*, 79 : " . . . I reconciled many people to the Church ; some were heretics, but the greater number schismatics, for it was much easier to approach them than the others. . . . I cannot remember more than 8 or 10 converts from heresy. However, four of these entered religious Orders . . .". As an example of what he means by schismatics he cites this very John Rigby, whose story he tells at length, with moving simplicity, 80 and foll. What John Gerard means by " schismatic " he explains elsewhere, when he writes, " This young nobleman was a schismatic, that is a Catholic by conviction but conforming externally to the state religion ". Morris, *Condition of Catholics*, xxiii.

[3] Among them a successor of John Wyclif, the rector of Lutterworth, Robert Sutton, *d.* at Stafford, July 27, 1587 ; and a predecessor of Newman at St. Mary's, Oxford, Stephen Rowsham, *d.* at Gloucester, April, 1587.

[4] Incorporated in Challoner, *op. cit.*   [5] St. John's, 2 ; Exeter, 2 ; Trinity, 1.

THE
ELIZABETHAN
PERSECUTION

TOWNS WHERE THERE
WERE EXECUTIONS

NEWCASTLE
2 GATESHEAD
1 CARLISLE
9 DURHAM
1 DARLINGTON

6 LANCASTER   40 YORK

1 BEAUMARIS

2 LINCOLN

WREXHAM
1 DERBY
3
1 STAFFORD
OAKHAM 1

WARWICK
1

GLOUCESTER 4
3 OXFORD   1 CHELMSFORD
76 LONDON
ISLEWORTH 2 KINGSTON ROCHESTER
2   4 CANTERBURY

IPSWICH
1

1 ANDOVER
SALISBURY WINCHESTER
1   5
CHICHESTER
2

EXETER
1
DORCHESTER
6
LAUNCESTON
2 ISLE OF WIGHT

THE FIGURES SHOW THE NUMBER OF VICTIMS PUT TO DEATH
IN EACH PLACE

of Court,[1] 4 had been married, one had been a clothmonger, of Wakefield in Yorkshire, and one had been the college shoemaker at Rheims.

Sixteen of these priests were tried and condemned under the statute of 1352, which is still our law of treason. The rest owed their death to laws enacted under Elizabeth, the purpose of which was to wipe out the Catholic religion in this country—the Acts of 1559 [2] and 1563 [3] explicitly demanding, under an ultimate penalty of death, recognition of the supremacy of the crown in religious matters ; the Acts of 1571 [4] and 1581 [5] making reconciliation to the Church treason, and so punishing with death those who returned to the Catholic faith and all who had a hand in bringing this about ; the Act of 1585 [6] making treason, and so punishing with death, the very presence in the country of a seminary priest or Jesuit, and also whatever was done by others to shelter or assist the priests so proscribed.

And so five priests and seven laymen are hanged, drawn, and quartered for denying that with the queen lies the last word, for Englishmen, in all that belongs to the Church of Christ. One priest and two laymen suffer death for having said that the queen is a heretic. A priest suffers the penalties of treason for having in his possession a papal bull (that has no special reference to England, the matter of which is wholly spiritual ; a bull, moreover, that has expired),[7] and a layman for procuring a papal licence to marry his cousin.[8] A priest goes to the gallows for bringing into the country 500 copies of Allen's reply to Burghley, and with him a layman who helped to circulate the book ; [9] a printer also is executed for reprinting a tract by Gregory Martin exhorting Catholics to abandon the hypocrisy of attending services they considered to be heretical,[10] and a bookseller for having similar works among his stock.[11] Two priests suffer the penalties of treason because, having once conformed to the religion established by the queen's authority, they have since been reconciled,[12] and 3 other priests for bringing about reconciliations ; seven laymen were put to death for being reconciled, and another 5 for persuading others to be reconciled. And 94 out of the 123 priests were put to death simply because, being priests ordained abroad since June 24, 1559, they had returned to England : 34 laymen went to death with them, for giving them assistance in one way or another.

---

[1] Inner Temple, 1 ; Gray's Inn, 1. One of the lay martyrs was also of Gray's Inn.
[2] 1 Eliz., c. 1.   [3] 5 Eliz., c. 1.   [4] 13 Eliz., c. 1.
[5] 23 Eliz., c. 1.   [6] 27 Eliz., c. 2.
[7] This was Cuthbert Mayne, the proto-martyr of the seminary priests, executed at Launceston, Nov. 30, 1577 ; cf. *supra*, p. 312, n.   [8] Roger Ashton, June 23, 1592.
[9] Thomas Alfield and Thomas Webley, July 6, 1585.
[10] This was William Carter, once an apprentice of John Cawood, the elder : Tyburn, Jan. 11, 1584.
[11] James Duckett. The book which probably was used to sway the jury was Richard Bristowe's *Motives*. Tyburn, April 19, 1602.
[12] James Bell, Lancaster, April 20, 1584, and Richard Williams, Tyburn, Feb. 20, 1592.

The statute of 1581 that made reconciliation treason, whatever the means by which it was brought about,[1] spoke of this reconciliation as being a withdrawal of subjects " from their natural obedience to " the queen ; it was reconciliation " with that intent " which was the treason.[2]   But, in practice, this reservation was mere words—as the reservation " maliciously " had been a mere word in the Act of Henry VIII punishing as traitors those who denied maliciously the king's supreme headship of the Church.   All reconciliation was treated as, by the fact, a withdrawal of allegiance and an adherence to the queen's enemy.[3]

But what exactly was reconciliation?   A sinner is reconciled to God whenever, and as soon as, in repentance, he makes what theologians call an act of perfect contrition, or when he receives the sacrament of penance, i.e. goes to confession.   Reconciliation is also used to mean the return to the Catholic Church of one who had left it to join some other religious body. And, since there is but one baptism, reconciliation is used to mean not merely the coming back of such wanderers, but the conversion to the Catholic Church of men who, though baptised, have never been bred as Catholics, have never lived as Catholics.   To be reconciled could mean, in 1571 and in 1581, to go to confession (on the part of a good Catholic), or to give up the outward show of being of the queen's religion (on the part of a Catholic who had lapsed from Catholicism), or to be converted from belief in Protestantism to belief in the Catholic faith.   In practice the statutes were used to punish as treason all three acts.[4]

" My indictment was read ", one of those put to death for being reconciled tells us,[5] " and it was a sharp one.   Then my lord bid me speak, and I answered briefly in this manner : ' 1st, Whereas I am charged in my indictment that I was reconciled—it is very true ; to God Almighty I so was, and I think lawfully might be ; and, as I remember, it is also allowed in your Book of Common Prayer, in the Visitation of the Sick, that if any man find himself burthened in conscience he should make his confession to the minister,

---

[1] The statute of 1571 (13 Eliz. c. 2) had in mind reconciliation through " bulls and writings . . . procured from . . . the said Bishop of Rome and his said see ", Prothero, 61, 62.   The Act of 1581 (23 Eliz. c. 1.) touched reconciliation " by any ways or means put in practice " ; *ibid.*, 75.   [2] *Ibid.*, 75 : text of statute as there printed.

[3] The history of the Act as enforced, the way the courts took the statute in practice, might argue considerable simplicity in the historian of " the notorious law which ushered in the severest persecution of the Catholics ", when he invites us to acclaim " that inspired qualification ", and presents it as something which made " the approach political and secular "—as a sincere attempt, on the part of the government or the queen, made in all good faith, to distinguish between two kinds of converts.

[4] Cf. Allen (1584) recounting the charges against Richard Kirkman, James Thompson, William Hart and Richard Threlkeld, put to death at York, 1582–1583, " never charged nor suspected of any other treasons than of hearing confessions, absolving and reconciling sinners to the favour of God and to the unity of the Catholic Church again : which both in the priest that absolveth, and in the party that is absolved, they have made to be the crime of lése-Majesté under this false and most unjust pretence, that all parties so reconciled are assoiled of their obedience to the Queen and do adhere to her enemy, and admit foreign jurisdiction, power, and authority, which is exercised in Confession for remission of sins." *Defence of Catholics*, 14.

[5] The John Rigby already spoken of.   He was born *c.* 1570, at Harrock Hill in Lancashire, tried in London, March 4, 1600, put to death at St. Thomas Waterings, June 21, 1600.

which confession manifesteth a breach between God and his soul, and by this humble confession he craveth pardon of his sins and reconciliation to God again by the hands of his minister.

" ' 2dly, Whereas I am charged that I was reconciled from my obedience to her Majesty and to the Romish religion, I will depose the contrary ; for I was never reconciled from any obedience to my Princess, for I obey her still ; nor to any religion, for although I sometimes went to church against my will, yet was I never of any other religion than the Catholic, and therefore needed no reconciliation to religion.

" ' 3dly, Whereas in my former answers I said I went to church, it is true ; for fear of temporal punishment I so did, but never minded to fall from the old religion, and therefore needed no reconciliation to religion.

" ' 4thly and lastly, I humbly beseech your good lordships, as you will answer it before God, to explicate the meaning of the statute to the jury ; if the meaning thereof be to make it treason for a man fallen into the dis-pleasure of God through his sins, to be reconciled to God again ; by him to whom God hath committed the authority of reconciliation ; if this be treason, God's will be done.' Then said both the judges, It was by a Romish priest, and therefore treason. . . . Then said Justice Gaudy, Her Majesty and her laws are merciful ; if you will yet conform yourself, and say here, before the jury go forth, that you will go to church, we will proceed no further. ' My lord ', said I, ' if that be all the offence I have committed, as I know it is, and if there be no other way but going to church to help it, I would not wish your lordship to think I have (as I hope) risen thus many steps towards heaven, and now ill wilfully let my foot slip and fall into the bottomless pit of hell. I hope in Jesus He will strengthen me rather to suffer a thousand deaths, if I had so many lives to lose. Let your law proceed.' Then, said the judge to the jury, You must consider of it ; you see what is said ; you cannot but find it treason by the law." [1]

The Act of 1585 [2]—and the fact that it brought to their death men and women whose only " treason ", admittedly, was their resolution to persevere in the ancient faith, and to bring to others the spiritual means of a like

[1] The martyr's own account, printed in Dr. Thomas Worthington's *A Relation of Sixtene Martyrs* (1601), and quoted in Challoner, 240–241, whence it is now taken.

[2] By this Act, an " act . . . to destroy the Catholic mission in all its stages " (Neale, 267), 27 Eliz., c. 2, (i) all priests ordained, since June 24, 1559, by authority derived from the see of Rome, were ordered to leave the country within 40 days of the end of this session of parlia-ment ; (ii) those remaining after 40 days were to be punished with death as traitors ; (iii) all who harboured or assisted priests so remaining were to be hanged as felons ; (iv) all students in Jesuit colleges or in seminaries were given six months to return home and, within two days after their arrival, to change their religion—those returning and not presenting themselves within two days to take the oaths to be punished as traitors ; (v) for the future, i.e. after the appointed 40 days expire, it is not lawful for any Englishman ordained priest since June 24, 1559 . . . " to come into, be, or remain " in any part of the queen's dominions, under penalty of death as a traitor ; (vi) all who shelter or in any way aid such priests returning, are to be hanged as felons ; (vii) " Provided always ", i.e. if the priest thus proscribed will take the oath of supremacy within the 40 days, or within three days of coming into the country, acknowledging that not the pope but the queen is the supreme authority for Englishmen in matters of religion, nothing in this act will apply to him. The book quoted is *Elizabeth* (1933).

perseverance—has been the occasion of much apologetic on the part of the modern historians.[1] The statute is, in itself, so peculiarly ferocious [2] that they are " appaused " by it, as Foxe says of Stephen Gardiner. Its very ferocity has sometimes, indeed, been taken as the proof, and the measure, of the government's dilemma : the natural consequence of honest belief (caused by plots) that the new priests are traitors in the natural sense of the word, agents who throughout England will prepare and organise the Catholics for the great day of the invasion planned by Allen and Persons.[3] The missionary priests, however, were never so employed : nor were they given the training that would suit them for such a purpose. There was no link—this is certain—between the real business of Allen's life, the presidency of Douay College, and his occasional activities as an advocate, with princes, of schemes for the overthrow of Elizabeth's government by force of arms.

The contrary, of course, has often been suggested, and it used to be taken for granted.[4] The charge was openly made, at the time, by Burghley,

[1] Which no critic will allow such a book as this to ignore.

[2] Here, in translation, are two pattern indictments prepared by the government for trials, under this statute, of priests and their aids. The Latin text is in C.R.S., V, 164–165, from the originals, P.R.O., *Dom. Eliz.*, vol. ccxvi, n. 22.
i. " The jurors for our lady the queen present that William Gunter, late of London, clerk, born within this kingdom of England after the feast of the birth of St. John the Baptist in the first year [of the queen's reign, i.e. June 24, 1559] and ordained priest before the last day of June in the thirtieth year of the said reign, at Rheims, beyond the seas, by authority deriving from the see of Rome, thinking nothing of the laws and statutes of this realm of England, and in no wise fearing the penalty contained in them, was and remained on the said last day of June . . . in London, that is to say in the parish of St. Sepulchre, in the ward of Faringdon Without, in London, in a traitor's way and as a traitor, in contempt of our said lady the queen, her crown and dignity, and also against the form of the statute lately published and provided in this regard. . . ."
ii. " The jurors for our lady the queen present that while William Horner being a priest etc. [as in the preceding indictment, *verbatim*] was and remained etc. [as in the preceding] a certain Richard Lloyd, late of London, gentleman . . . knowing the said William Horner to be such a priest, on March 14 of the thirtieth year of the queen's reign, knowingly, willingly, and feloniously received, comforted, was a help to, and maintained the said William Horner being at large and not in prison, in the parish of St. Dunstan-in-the-West, in the ward of Faringdon Without, in London aforesaid, against the form of the statute published and provided in this regard and also against the peace of our said lady the queen, her crown and dignity."
These two indictments are sent with a covering letter of Sept. 12, 1588, signed by Hatton (as Lord Chancellor), Burghley, Walsingham and four others, to the sheriff of Staffordshire, with the instruction " the like indictments by you to be framed, *mutatis mutandis*, as the case shall require . . .".
The essence of the crime punished by this statute was thus explained by the judge at the trial of Blessed Henry Walpole, S.J., at York, April 3, 1595 : " Our laws appoint that a priest who returns from beyond the seas, and does not present himself before a justice within three days to make the usual submission to the Queen's Majesty in matters of religion, shall be deemed a traitor." Challoner, 226, from Yepez, 702.

[3] These priests " daily do come and are sent . . . to stir up . . . rebellion . . . within the realm ", says the very statute—repeating the assertion of the proclamation of April 1, 1582 (T.-D., III, pp. xxvi–xxvii) and the statute of 1571 (13 Eliz., c. 2), *ibid.*, pp. xviii–xix. And cf. a scholar of today, on the priests sent from Douay in the years 1577–1580, " whose object was to seduce the Queen's subjects from their allegiance . . . to foment rebellion . . .", Pearson, *Cartwright*, 235 ; a most surprising statement when made, unsupported, by a specialist writing since, e.g. Meyer.

[4] Simpson, because he was a Catholic writer, has been as mischievous here, through inaccuracy in dating, as was the hasty Acton about St. Pius V and the assassination plots.

that the seminaries were schools to train apostles of treason, and that to persuade men to turn traitor was one of the missionary priest's duties in England. The answer Allen then gave—in the *Defence*—ought to have stifled the slander as it was born ; it would have done so, had not the government very effectively prevented the circulation of the book.

The justification, to Allen's conscience, of all these political manoeuvres in which he had his part, was the papal sentence of 1570 excommunicating the queen. This was his authority for promoting activities that would otherwise have been, not merely treasonable in law and in fact, but mortally sinful : we shudder at assassination, the cowardliness of it appals us, but treason is more sinful still. And how could the priests have brought the Catholics to organise for such a notoriously sinful activity, unless by teaching them that, the queen being excommunicated, the acts were no longer sinful ? The meaning and effects of the papal excommunication of reigning princes must, by necessity—on this hypothesis—have been a major subject in the Douay curriculum. Whereas, " the governors of the students always of purpose [prohibited] . . . that in the course of our school questions and controversies concerning the Pope's pre-eminence, no matter of depriving or excommunicating princes should be disputed ; no, not so much as in generalities,[1] and much less the particularising of any point in our Queen's case ".

Here is a stock question of divinity, Allen says, a routine problem that all authorities discuss, the problem what is to be done about rulers who are apostates from the faith of Christ ; it is a problem, he notes, that Calvin considers and Zwingli too, and which both solve as the Catholic divines solve it. " Yet ", this problem, " because it is incident to matter of state (as now our country most unfortunately standeth), and consequently might be interpreted by the suspicious to be meant of her, whose case men liked best to deal in, it was thought best to pass over all with silence ."[2] So little, then, are the seminaries schools where treason is systematically taught, and professional traitors formed and apologists for assassination.

That Allen spoke truly is confirmed by the way the unfortunate priests answer their inquisitors when taxed about these matters. They do not reply in any uniform way, giving a stock answer to the subtly phrased questions that Burghley's civil law experts have drafted. They blunder about, with answers that are contradictory, and that land them in further difficulties, as a man not taught must always blunder about, when he is suddenly asked riddles that only the technically trained can solve.[3]

---

[1] In such tourneys, for example, as that when William Overton, canon of Chichester and one day to be a bishop, disputed, before Elizabeth, at Oxford in 1564. The question set was, " Whether it was lawful for a private individual to take up arms against a bad prince ". Overton defended the proposition that, " It is lawful for a private individual to consult the good of the republic, and that good was best consulted if the bad prince was killed ". *Ergo*, no doubt, all who belonged to Overton's church were conspirators ever on the look out for a chance to kill the prince thought bad, and the university a breeding place for political assassins. For Overton, cf. *D.N.B.* The quotation in the text is Allen, *Defence of Catholics*, I, 81–82.   [2] *Ibid.*, 82.

[2] Equally to the point, whether the priests really were trained political agents, is the Spanish ambassador's complaint to Philip II, " They [i.e. the priests] although ardently

The priests were innocent. And the government was as innocent as the priests—so the historians nowadays seem to suggest, who invite us to lament an inevitable tragedy of good Englishmen now locked in mortal conflict.[1]

Against the *a priori* view that the government really believed—and with reason—that the priests were *ipso facto* traitors in the proper sense of the word, it may however be urged that had they so believed they would have used their powers to the full, have rounded up and killed every priest in the country ; [2] that they would, at least, never have let any priest go free once they arrested him, let alone priests tried and found guilty, and sentenced to death as traitors. Yet Elizabeth banished priests by the dozen, among them priests sentenced to death for treason : and continually issued proclamations commanding priests to depart the realm—which is an odd policy towards subjects believed to be plotting the invasion of the country and the deposition and murder of the sovereign.[3]

It is a more likely view, one more in keeping with sixteenth-century methods, that sees the famous statute of 1585 as intended to strike terror : to cow the many converts, and the neo-Catholics of the rebirth evident to all as the fruit of the seminary movement.[4]

---

zealous as regards religion, cannot be trusted with matters of state unless they are taught word for word what they have to say ". April 26, 1582. *Span. Cal., Eliz.*, III, p. 350.

[1] Cf. in Black, 149, 150, who writes of all this with a rare generosity of mind : " the profound pathos of this terrible time. Up to a point both [i.e. Burghley and the missionary priest] were right ; . . . The fairest criticism that can be passed is to say that both parties to the conflict were the victims of a tragic dilemma, from which there seems to have been no escape but by the shedding of blood on the one side, and by self sacrifice on the other."

[2] Not an impossible task. By 1585, 229 priests had been sent from Douay, 33 from Rome : of whom 23 had been put to death, and another 70 were in various prisons.

[3] These deportations were not, however, the acts of mercy that Pollard, for example, suggests (*H.E.*, VI, 387). The prison system was such that it was not possible (so it would seem) for the government to ensure that the priests were not visited continuously by Catholics. In the Tower, John Gerard was indeed isolated, but of his stay in the Clink he says he would gladly have passed the rest of his life there, so convenient a centre was it for his apostolic work. The government could, without difficulty, have made away with all these priests, as they had made away with 23 others since 1577 ? Yes and no. Thanks to Burghley's astuteness in sending all over Europe the translations of his apologia for those executions, and thanks to Allen's exposure of what had really been going on in England (now circulating everywhere, except in England) Europe is now attending very closely. And to execute some 70 priests, and persuade the world that all are traitors ? or to execute them as reconcilers merely ? Mary Tudor had burnt 70 heretics annually for four years in succession. But there were no Protestant powers whose intervention she need fear. Nor was there, then, anything like such a proportion of the nation one in belief with the victims. Could the government have brazened out such a slaughter in 1585 ? That the thought of slaughter itself did not deter them may be argued from what they achieved in their first certainty of security, the weeks that followed the defeat of the Armada. It was a sample of what, according to the preachers (Haweis, 172–183), should have been done to the idolaters from the beginning— 8 executions in London on Aug. 28, and another 6 on Aug. 30 ; 7 in various places on Oct. 1, 3 more in London on Oct. 5. Nor did the government, in 1585, simply ship these priests out of the country. They first tried to make it a condition that each should swear never to return—thus breaking the missionary oath. They all refused ; and nevertheless were deported ; to discover, as they were about to be discharged on the foreign shore, that it was to be given out they had accepted the government's terms. The deportation was meant, in part, as a great act of propaganda : a demonstration that the missionary priests preferred their lives to their apostolic engagements.

[4] Walsingham left behind him a kind of memorandum, written about Dec. 1586,

In procuring the enactment of this statute of 1585 the government, however, has not suddenly—and inexplicably—become more cruel. The new law does not differ in spirit from those of 1581 and 1563 and 1559 ; it is but a means to make easier the extirpation intended already by these earlier Acts, a simplification that will bring to his death more expeditiously the priest guilty of refusing to acknowledge the crown as the lawful lord of all religious life. The death penalty has been there all along. In these twenty-six years, the government has been overcoming, step by step, the hindrances which the fact of strong opposition in the first parliament of the reign put in the way of its original purpose, namely to ensure the Elizabethan Settlement by means of statutes as bloody as the laws of Henry VIII. Public feeling, shocked by what is now about to happen, that priests will (for example) be captured as they land, even be taken from boats in the harbour, and then be hanged, drawn, and quartered for being found priests in England —should such feeling exist—can be silenced by bold propaganda. If Burghley's famous tract was a defence of the executions under the Statute of Treasons, was it not also a defence in advance, a preparation of the public mind for other executions to come ?

Nor are these cruelties simply a ripost, savage perhaps, but not incomprehensibly so if we remember that the country is fighting an aggression which imperils its life.[1] In all these twenty-seven years the real aggression— whether political or religious, whether the other party is Philip II or the pope —is wholly on the side of England.[2] And the great movement of which Elizabeth used to be held, in a popular way, the patron saint ; the movement, not to correct abuses in popular religion, but to bring about the acceptance

---

on how best to end the menace of recusancy. It is analysed in Conyers Read, II, 304–312. When he comes to consider " the mischief wrought by them [the seminary priests] abroad ", i.e. when at large in England, the secretary of state makes no mention at all of political activities, whether as agents or organisers or spies ; the nearest his charges come to this is when he speaks of these priests as comforting the Catholics with the hope that one day foreign help will restore Catholicism in England. The memorandum is printed, in part, in Strype's *Whitgift* (1822), III, 201.

[1] Cf. Conyers Read, II, 310 : " The persecution of priests during this decade ought to be regarded as essentially a war measure. The Queen and her government were fairly pushed to the wall, and they struck savagely at every one who bore the appearance of an enemy." Also, *ibid.*, where we are told that the great number of executions, 1581–1590 [102 in all, 76 of priests] was not due " to any special bloodthirstiness in those who controlled the government during this time. It was unquestionably due to the fact that between the years 1580 and 1590, England was exposed to greater danger from Roman Catholicism and its adherents than it had ever been or was ever to be ". This is apologetic in the spirit of Froude —assuming the truth of the government's contention (i.e. that it was only " political " Catholicism which it was fighting, and that its action was defensive), and justifying whatever the government did on the grounds of expediency. Whether the individuals put to death were, in fact, innocent or guilty is an irrelevancy that the historians need not examine. Here is another *a priori* surmise, set down with the same unawareness that such a way of writing history makes the historian an apologist for tyranny : " So too the neighbourhood where the priest was taken and tried had a direct bearing upon his fate. In districts where Roman Catholics were dangerously strong, priests sometimes had to suffer for the sake of example, who in more secure districts might have escaped " ; *ibid.*, 311.

[2] Cf. Neale, *op.cit.*, 247, " The question remained, how long could Elizabeth go on with impunity, fostering trouble for everyone else and escaping it herself ? "—which is written of the situation in 1580, when Anjou accepts the offer of the sovereignty of the Netherlands.

of a new theory of salvation, of a new set of religious habits deriving from this, a new idea of God, therefore—to say nothing of such a detail as a new theory of the place of the state in a man's religious life : all this great movement is in itself an aggression, surely, when introduced to the ordinary man's notice—as it is—not by sweet reason, or evangelical preaching, but by acts of state, commanding obedient acceptance under threats against liberty and against life itself.

It can hardly be repeated too often—for attention is hardly ever drawn to the fact—that, from the beginning of the reign, a man's mere failure to conform his conduct to the new arrangements about religion which the state has devised and sanctioned is, itself, a high crime : a crime which, if a man persevere in it, must mean his ruin and may mean his death. As to these priests who were now put to death in such numbers under the Acts of 1581 and 1585, and the laymen whom they converted or who helped them in their work, and who for this suffered with them, neither directly nor indirectly had any single one of them any share in the activity of those Catholics beyond the seas whose aim was the overthrow of Elizabeth, whether in the activities of foreign princes or of English exiles. Nothing of this sort was ever proved against them in the treason trials ; nothing of this was even charged against them in the rest. The great accomplishment of the Act of 1585 was that, henceforward, nothing of this needed even to be charged, in order to be rid for ever of the missionaries whose success in spirituals spelt ruin to the creation of 1559—nothing except the fact that being priests they were, and had remained, within the queen's dominions.

But granted that all these 183 men and women, claimed by the Catholic Church as martyrs for religion, were innocent in fact of any treasonable activity, what of the effect of the plots considered as maddening the mind of the ruler, reasonably causing panic and releasing his lower self, so that the innocent paid for the sins of others ? It is a long time since the comedy warned us all, " No scandal about Queen Elizabeth ". Native prejudice —tradition—is still alive ; and popular opinion, flushed with vague memories of the great victory over Spain, and of " spacious days " when the great queen reigned—wise, far-seeing, just, humane, the most English of all the English sovereigns—has a sharp reply when there is reference to the cruelties Elizabeth meted out to her Catholic subjects : " No plots, no persecution." And the historians, too, have often said this, each in his own tongue ; some, indeed, with real sympathy for the Catholics as unfortunate victims of ineluctable fate.[1]

---

[1] For example, in Pollard, op. cit., 378, " that career of treason and intrigue " on which Allen and Persons " now embarked [i.e. after the death of Campion] involved their more self-sacrificing brethren in great and needless suffering " ; or Meyer, 273–274, " Had there been no plots . . . the penal legislation of the last decades of the century, and all the terrible animosity to which it gave rise, would never have been heard of "—also, " the unfair judgment passed on the Catholic mission would have been impossible " ; which raises another question altogether, the ability of the historian to sort out the events chronologically, and also to distinguish between what was then known to the government and what is known to us ; or

Is it not the fact that the plots to depose, and to murder, the queen were the real, basic, cause of the anti-Catholic laws, and of the terror [1] that the Catholics endured, on and off, for nearly thirty years of the reign ?   The mere chronology of the events would seem to be enough to make the affirmative answer suspect.   And the plots (even as we know them, who know so much more about them than did the Elizabethan government) [2] were the affair of a bare score of individuals, while the persecution fell upon thousands whom no prosecution ever attempted to associate, in the slightest way, with even the knowledge of a plot.   When we turn from the picture presented by such official propaganda as Lord Burghley's famous tract, to the conduct of the trials in these years and the examinations of the Catholics under arrest, the contrast is remarkable.   In the examinations under torture of Fr. Campion and the rest there is question of only one thing—their religious activities.   Where did you say Mass ?   Whose confessions have you heard ? Whom have you reconciled ?   There is no question ever of matters of State—the excommunication, the invasion of Ireland, the plans of Spain. All the government wants to know is how far there has been disobedience to its laws about religious practice.   The theme of the government's action upon the Catholics never varies in all the forty-four years of the reign : You are disobedient subjects ; and for your disobedience to the laws of 1559 you are now about to be punished.   Once you agree to obey those laws your punishment will cease.   When one of those most frequently before the council for disobedience of this kind, Sir Thomas Tresham, ruined by the heavy fines of years, broken by continual imprisonment, protested to the Archbishop of Canterbury, " We [Catholics] ever have demeaned in all actions of civil duty, both before our imprisonments, and in the furnace of our many years adversity, as becometh faithfullest true English subjects ",[3] he was not answered that he was lying ; it was not said, " You are a Catholic, *ergo* a traitor ; you are one of the most prominent

---

again Neale, *ibid.*, 251, " The Government's answer was to destroy the priests as traitors.   The Spirit of Pity hovers over the victims, but Justice also has its place.   Some priests undoubtedly dabbled or even waded deep in treason . . . "—where " some priests " can only mean, " priests put to death ".   Who these priests were the author does not say.   The one priest put to death for political conspiracy and actually involved in this was John Ballard, the associate of Antony Babington.   He has never figured in any Catholic list of priests martyred for the faith.   In the only official Catholic paper I know where his death is mentioned, it stands out as the solitary occasion when a priest is noted as put to death and is not claimed as a martyr : *D. Joannes Ballardus, bis in Angliam reversus, una cum 12 nobilibus mortem subiit,* cf., in *Douay Diaries*, 292, a list of the priests sent to England from Douay, Rheims and Rome, 1574-1585.

[1] Cf. Pollen, *Religious Terrorism under Queen Elizabeth*, in *The Month*, March, 1905.

[2] " The question here is not of the facts as they were, but of the facts as Elizabeth and her Council saw them to be " ; Conyers Read, II, 279—a general truth that can be variously applied.   And Pollen's judgment—itself, at first sight, most surprising—is warranted, " . . . few aspects of the question are at first sight more surprising than the fewness and relative unimportance of the plots against Elizabeth, when they are regarded with any sort of calmness and criticism ".   *Plots and Sham Plots*, in *The Month*, June, 1902, 600.   Cf. also Meyer, 154, n. 1, " . . . the conspiracies against Elizabeth . . . to which an exaggerated importance has been attached . . .".

[3] March 25, 1590, quoted Anstruther, 177, from Rushton Papers, 51.

Catholics in the country, *ergo* a most important personage in the fifth column. It is for this you are punished " : the kind of answer we might expect had the government believed, with the good faith of its modern defenders, that the queen's Catholic subjects really were the famous fifth column.[1]

Politics were not the cause. It was a régime where, from the beginning, it sufficed that a man was a practising Catholic ; as it sufficed with Hitler to be a Jew, or with the queen's Catholic sister to be a heretic.[2] The effect of the plots, or rather of what general knowledge of them ever came out, was merely to serve the government with a pretext by which to justify its fiercer laws.[3] The first supplements to the original code, the Acts of 1571, did indeed precede all talk of the plots—they followed the excommunication immediately ; but it was not until the work of the Douay priests was seen to promise a revival of Catholic loyalty to Catholicism, with recognition that it was grave sin to pretend to be of the queen's religion ; with opportunity for reconciliation, and systematic religious instruction ; with a more virile spiritual guidance, and with the example of heroic devotion to the cause in the guides—it was not until all this was seen to be telling with remarkable effect, that the administration began to enforce the bloodier parts of these laws, and then to devise laws that were still more stringent.

This is not a theory " thought up " by the modern controversialist. It is what critics said at the time, openly : it is a main theme of Allen's reply to Burghley's justification of the executions of 1581–1583. The government, when in 1559–1560 they jailed the bishops and other prelates, little thought, Allen wrote, " that these old holy confessors, being worn out by years and imprisonment, a new generation would rise to defend their old bishops' and fathers' faith ".[4] And so, " When the politiques of our country, pretending to be Protestants, saw the Catholic religion, contrary to their worldly wise counsels and determinations and against their exquisite diligence and discipline and twenty years endeavour (in which time they thought verily to have extinguished the memory of our fathers' faith) to be revived in the hearts of the greatest number of the realm, and that neither their strange, violent and capital laws for the Queen's spiritual superiority against the Pope's pre-eminence . . . nor the execution of many by death and other penalties . . . according to the said laws, would serve, . . . they thought good . . . to alter the whole accusation from question of faith

---

[1] Cf. Anstruther, *Vaux of Harrowden*, for details from the examinations, and especially for the accounts of the various trials of Tresham and Lord Vaux before the council, 1581–1590 ; Tresham could protest to Elizabeth in 1584, " Let not us your Catholic native English and obedient subjects stand in more peril for frequenting the Blessed Sacrament and exercising the Catholic religion (and that most secretly) than do the Catholic subjects to the Turk publicly ", *op. cit.*, 155.

[2] Cf. the remark of A. L. Rowse, " the numerous trials [i.e. of Catholics] that make such sadly contemporary reading "—which was not, however, written with reference to the point of this paragraph. *England of Elizabeth*, 443.

[3] And the criminal act punished by the statute of 1585 (under which most of the priests were put to death) was still, in effect, the same act as that made criminal by the statute of 1559, viz., refusal of the Oath of Supremacy : on taking the oath the delinquent is immediately freed from all the liabilities incurred by his offences against the statute.

[4] *Defence of Catholics*, I, 58.

and conscience, to matter of treason " [1]—the trials of 1581, 1582 and 1584 under the statute of 1352.

Catholics are necessarily traitors ?　Already, in 1580, when Persons arrives in London, and before there have been any plots in which English Catholics have a share, he finds this everywhere taken for granted, or rather, insisted on.[2] It is the hold of this assumption—and not the news of plots—that renders possible the severity of the statute,[3] enacted a few months later, which makes it death to return, or be reconciled, to the Catholic Church, death to reconcile anyone, death to persuade anyone to be reconciled.　And it is with this same propaganda-bred idea already well started in the public mind that, in order to strengthen the idea against all possible criticism, the government next stages the first treason trials in 1581.[4]　And in order to strike down men who can by no other means be brought within the operation of the centuries-old Statute of Treasons, there is now devised, first, the bogus conspiracy charge, and then, the folly of this plan proved—for it shocks public opinion unpleasantly—the inquisition of the Six Questions.　We Catholics (once again this is Allen against Burghley), " having committed nothing by word or deed against our prince or laws, but doing all acts of honour and homage to her . . . are enforced to suffer death for our only cogitations and inward opinions, unduly sought out by force and fear ", opinions that are " yet not condemned by any Christian school in the world ", and which would not be " uttered by us but upon forcing interrogation ".[5]

Against the assumption of the propaganda, and the answers that may be given to the treacherous interrogatories, there is the notorious truth that Catholics are, in fact, loyal to their Protestant ruler.　In all these twenty-five years—Allen reminds the Lord Treasurer—when Protestants have " reacted " against their Catholic sovereign in Scotland, in France, and in the Low Countries after a fashion known to all, Catholics in England have been so loyal that the very bull of excommunication has been a dead letter.　Not so much as a disloyal word against the queen has come from any one of them :

---

[1] *Defence of Catholics*, I, 30–31.

[2] " . . . in the proclamation, in speeches, and in sermons they are made infamous in the eyes of the people, under the names of traitors and rebels."　Persons to Agazzari, Nov. 17, 1580, in *Persons*, 48.　Also, " There is an immense amount of talk here about the Jesuits . . . fables of every kind spread abroad . . . not only in private conversation but in speeches (*publicis concionibus*) and in books.　The main point of it all is that the Jesuits, and all the other priests too, are, it is declared, sent out by the pope as political spies, traitors and disturbers of the peace of the nation (*exploratores statuum, rerumque publicarum proditores ac eversores*) " ; Persons to Agazzari, August, 1581, *ibid.*, 73.　If *conciones* are sermons, this would appear as a contradiction of Haweis, 173, " The preachers do not seem to have gained any hold upon the truths on which the secretary and Lord Burghley, in his ' Execution of Justice ' founded their defence of the penal laws . . . Exhortations to the government not to spare the shaven and greased idolaters, and offensive pictures of the Roman missionary and schoolmaster, are sufficiently frequent in the sermons of the sixteenth century " ; and Haweis then quotes specimens (pp. 174–185) from a dozen preachers, beginning with the Archbishop of York, Edwin Sandys, demanding " Death, exile, confiscation, incarceration," as punishment for those who " join themselves unto the harlot inseparably ", but advising, " Touch them by the purse, it is the most ready way to take and tame these foxes ", i.e. the " little foxes " of the Canticle, ii, 15.　　　　　[3] 23 Elizabeth, c. 1.

[4] Trials, that is under 25 Edward III , stat. 5, c. 2.　　　[5] *Defence of Catholics*, I, 80.

" Not any one priest of the Society or seminaries can be proved by the adversary to have absolved in secret Confession any one man living from his allegiance ; or to have either in public or in private dissuaded any one person in the realm from his obedience in civil causes to the Queen." No priest was ever commissioned by the pope. or by any other authority, to discuss with Catholics in England " any such matters touching the queen ; neither is there any such thing implied in either the authority or act of reconcilement, howsoever the jealous enemy hath found knots in those rushes that of themselves are smooth ".[1]

None knew better than the government what Catholics really thought about these matters, none had done more to find this out. " Let the world see what one confession of treasonable matter you have wrested out by the so often tormenting of so many . . ." [2] You " have all sorts and sexes of Catholics in prison for their faith. . . . Hath any one of all the realm, in durance or at liberty, by fair means or foul, confessed that ever either priest or Jesuit persuaded them in Confession or otherwise, to forsake the Queen ? That ever they were absolved on that condition ? That ever they received Agnus Deis at their hands, or other spiritual token for earnest,[3] or [were] pressed to rebel or join with the enemy ? " [4] For this, Burghley insinuates, is what going to Confession now means.[5]

The brief apostolate of Campion and Persons (June, 1580–July, 1581) marks a turning point in the history of the English who were Catholics. What the government now attempted, in retaliation, became the settled policy of the next fifty years ; and the policy fixed, for much longer than that, the view of the ordinary man about the kind of Englishman one who was a Catholic must be. The winter of 1579–1580, when Mercurian and Allen came to their agreement that the Jesuits should take part in the mission to England, was a critical time for what, even after twenty years of power, it is not unhistorical to call, still, the Protestant party in England. Even after twenty years of continuous power, the success whose measure is security had not been attained. The old fear was active once again : how long are we going to have ? This sudden critical moment does not prove that England

---

[1] *Defence of Catholics*, I, 81. [2] *Ibid.*, 24.
[3] i.e. pledge. [4] *Defence of Catholics*, I, 42–43.
[5] The slander that the priests were using the confessional as a means to pervert the allegiance of the Catholics, and the point of Allen's challenge, is most clearly set out in Camden's account of what " wrested " from the parliament of 1581 the " new and severer laws against the Papists ".

" Nor did some of the priests conceal the fact that they had returned to England for no other reason than this, that just as that Bull [of Excommunication] had once and for all, in a general way, absolved everyone from all their oaths of fidelity and obedience to the queen, so they, by reconciliation in the confessional (*reconciliando inter confitendum*), would absolve individual Catholics from these obligations : and this it seemed easier to do at the same time when they were proferring absolution from every mortal sin, and the more safely done [then] because in a more hidden way, and under the seal of confession " (*Annales*, 348–349). Camden does not seem aware of the merciful intent of " the inspired qualification ". For this contemporary historian, as for the courts, it is all reconciliation, all going to confession, that falls under the law, and is meant to fall under it.

is still secretly Catholic in 1579, nor that Allen's view of the country was the right one : it does show that, for the Protestant leaders, the future was not yet so certain as, with the long centuries of unbroken success between ourselves and these events, we perhaps assume it to have been. The government, when the two Jesuit fathers returned, in 1580, to England, was not yet wholly delivered from very real, recent fears whether the Protestant venture—the Protestant control of policy—was going to last much longer.

The queen, it is certain, was never interested in the destruction of Catholics as such [1]—as idolaters, in the language of her bishops and her secretary of state.[2] And this her government must have known. No efforts along this line could ever have brought the queen to adopt a more severe policy towards the Catholics. But was Elizabeth, by the time the Douay mission began, convinced that Catholics were necessarily traitors ? that to indulge their consciences, to relieve them from the obligation to attend the new services, to allow them Mass and the ministrations of their own clergy, would be as much as to prepare her own dethronement ? [3] Or was the continued repression of the Catholics merely, in her eyes, a necessary, inescapable measure of policy ? religious feeling is so inflamed that real freedom of conscience, anywhere, must result in everlasting agitation, in broils and riots fatal to domestic peace and, ultimately, in chronic political intrigues that will make government impossible ? Whatever the truth about this, it is very interesting that, in the autumn and winter of 1579, the main anxieties of leading councillors have nothing to do with that recent papal expedition to Ireland which they will soon be exploiting against the Catholics as the danger of dangers. What is worrying the ministers is the fear that the queen is about to tolerate Catholicism, to halt the persecution at any rate.

What occasioned this alarm was the apparent seriousness with which the queen was now listening to the Duke of Anjou's proposals of marriage.[4]

[1] Elizabeth, early in 1577, had sent word to the States General in the Low Countries " that as a condition of her support the States must accept whatever religion the King of Spain might be pleased to impose on them. On this point she was limpidly clear. She was determined there should be no mistake about it. The creed in which the Hollanders had been brought up would do as well for them as it had done for their fathers." In the following October the queen repeated this advice saying there ought to be " no change of religion, no liberty of conscience, no separate chapels or conventicles to disturb the union ". Nothing, Orange wrote to the queen's agent, William Davison (Jan. 4/5, 1578) could have been more clumsy at the moment than this declaration. For all of which, cf. Froude, chapter 60, i.e. Vol. X, pp. 386, 420 of the 1893 edition.

[2] And of other councillors too, of course.

[3] As late as September, 1582, Leicester was writing to Walsingham, " Nothing in this world grieveth me more than to see her Majesty believes this increase of papists in her realm can be no danger to her. . . . If she suffer this increase but one year more, as she hath done these two or three years past, it will be too late to give or take counsel to help it ". Quoted, Neale, 252–253. What does Leicester mean, " too late " ? By this time twelve priests have been put to death, after a trial supposed to have proved them guilty of plotting to murder the queen. I do not forget that Elizabeth, to use this same scholar's word, p. 244, was " this superior deceiver ", nor that Leicester was no less tortuous than his sovereign.

[4] " But there was a new factor in this courtship. Alençon (i.e. Anjou) was conducting it himself, and with a dash that threatened to sweep Elizabeth off her feet." Neale, *Elizabeth*, 238 ; who, however, has not a word about the fears of the ministers that this may lead to some kind of toleration of Catholicism.

Elizabeth—just past her forty-sixth birthday—was, it seems, desperately in love with the idea of being married. Anjou, a Catholic *politique*, it is true, was yet the brother and heir apparent of the King of France : for the very name's sake he must, as Elizabeth's husband, win something for Catholicism from the Protestant queen. This is what Walsingham is afraid of, and Leicester and the president of the north, Huntingdon.[1] This is why Walsingham strives to " organise " opinion in London against the marriage.[2] And why Elizabeth begins to look for allies outside the council—to think, even, of bringing Catholics into the council.[3] The council is, at this time, more hostile to the marriage, more united in its hostility, says Burghley, than ever before. They are reluctant to express themselves formally to the queen—as always, and not surprisingly. Elizabeth, as always, has not the nerve to decide in the only way possible, that is to say, immediately.[4] There is a deadlock, and the uncertainty is complicated by such great changes in the international situation as the Spanish conquest of Portugal.

More than ever, from February 1580,[5] England must be the ally of France, and France will not have the alliance without the marriage, and the marriage must mean some concessions to the Catholics. Is there no connection between the wave of anti-Catholic propaganda now to be let loose, on the theme Catholic means traitor to England, and this menace to the hold of Burghley and his fellows on the government ?—no connection between their fear at this, and their alarm at the Jesuits' success in these same months, and the intensity of their own campaign to ruin the Catholic good name with all foreigner-hating Englishmen ?

There is certainly reason to believe that it was very largely in order to soothe the anxiety of the Protestant zealots—late so helpful in the contest with the queen about the Anjou marriage—that the government in 1581 sent Campion and his fellows to their doom.[6] John Stubbs [7] might openly

---

[1] Cf. in Pollen, *English Catholics*, 316, the quotations from the despatches of the French ambassador in London.

[2] For the view that Walsingham was, possibly, the inspiration of this cf. Conyers Read, II, 20, 22.   [3] And of making Edmund Plowden her Lord Chancellor ?

[4] Should the word be " courage " rather than " nerve " ? Is Elizabeth, queen for twenty years now, so safe that she can do as she likes ? Must she follow her ministers' policy ? It is no fantasy-ridden theorist whose words suggest the query. In the summer of 1578, writes Neale, *ibid.*, 237, " . . . councillors found Elizabeth quite unmanageable. . . . She consulted them as little as she dared." By " councillors ", Burghley, Leicester and Walsingham are meant ; and the business is policy towards the rebels in the Netherlands.

[5] The last king of an independent Portugal died Jan. 31, 1580, the military occupation by Philip II took place in July.

[6] " Their reason for pressing these matters [the trial of Campion and the rest] now is that they want them done whilst Alençon is here, in order to gratify the English and Scotch Protestants, and to discourage Catholics and make it appear that he cares nothing about religion, but that his only desire is to please the Queen." Mendoza to Philip II, Nov. 7, 1581, *Span. Cal.*, *Eliz.*, III, 1580–1586, pp. 210–211. So also Camden : " During his [i.e. Alençon's] stay here the Queen, to take away the fear which had possessed many men's minds that religion would be altered and Papists tolerated, overcome by unseemly petitions permitted that Campion of the Society of Jesus, Ralph Sherwin, Luke Kirkby, and Alexander Briant, priests, should be put on their trial ". *Annales*, 346–347.

[7] John Stubbs, a Norfolk gentleman, a radical in religion and cousin to Peter Wentworth, published, in Sept., 1579, a pamphlet entitled *Discovery of a Gaping Gulf*, *where*

express what the ministers secretly thought—and what Elizabeth knew they thought ; but what suited them better, before the country, was to magnify the danger of the expeditions of 1579 and 1580,[1] and to talk loudly of Dr. Sander, so that, as Persons wrote to Rome, " . . . it is now beginning to be called a war of the churches (*ecclesiasticum bellum*), and the boast is constantly made to the people that in a short time the event will make it clear whether the gospel or Popery is more powerful in force of arms ".[2]

The Irish expedition might indeed be welcome evidence of the pope's ill-will : it was also, no less strikingly, evidence that all that this could achieve against the queen was simply contemptible. Never was propaganda set to manufacture a national scare out of more paltry material. And this was the reality, as the government knew it.[3] In practice, however, it encouraged the fiction, " Catholics, because Catholics, are a danger to the state " ; and, propagated by proclamations—very powerful in a country where all else was rumour—the fiction, thus officially adopted, served to quiet the fears of the zealots and yet feed their hates, and to suggest the utter impossibility of the marriage of the queen to a Catholic prince. The execution, at this moment, as traitors, of priests tried for plotting rebellion and the very murder of the queen—of the popular, legendary Campion first of all—would reinforce this propaganda, and fix the fear as a reality in the public mind.[4]

England is like to be swallowed up by another French marriage, if the Lord forbid not the banns by letting her see the sin and punishment thereof. For this he was condemned to lose his right hand and, the barbarous sentence being carried out, lifted his hat in salute with his remaining hand calling out " Long live the queen ". He was then imprisoned in the Tower for eighteen months. The crowd was too much in sympathy with Stubbs' criticism of the marriage to rise to his heroic loyalty. They heard him in silence.

[1] The first expedition, with which Dr. Sander sailed, arrived in Dingle Bay, July 18, 1579, 80 strong. The second arrived in Sept., 1580, 600 men in all, and the news of it reached London by Dec. ; Pollen, 360. Walsingham had been able " to calculate pretty exactly the magnitude of [the] preparations " for the first expedition ; Conyers Read, II, 364. His real interest now was how strongly would this be reinforced. And he had news of this in time to send reinforcements himself, which reached Ireland two months before the 600 invaders ; *ibid.*, 365–366.

[2] Persons to Agazzari, Nov. 17, 1580, *Persons*, 48.

[3] Which is not to say that the propaganda was a failure. Persons speaks of " the Irish war " as one reason given in London, in 1580, for the increased bitterness of the persecution. Meyer's comment, 264, is justified, " Since Elizabeth's excommunication Rome had taken no more fatal step in English affairs . . . "—fatal in the opportunities it gave to the government to attack the Douay mission. And Persons and Campion realised this acutely. " Dr. Allen also told us that he had heard from Spain that Dr. Sanders was just gone into Ireland, by the nuncio Mgr. Sega's orders, to comfort and assist the Earl of Desmond, Viscount Baltinglas, and others that had taken arms in defence of their religion, and had asked the Pope's help, counsel, and comfort in that cause. Though it belonged not to us to mislike this journey of Dr. Sanders, because it was made by order of his superiors, yet were we heartily sorry, partly because we feared that which really happened, the destruction of so rare and worthy a man, and partly because we plainly foresaw that this would be laid against us and other priests, if we should be taken in England, as though we had been privy or partakers thereof, as in very truth we were not, nor ever heard or suspected the same until this day " —(i.e. the first week of June, 1580). Persons, *Life of Campion* (MS.), quoted Simpson, 146.

[4] The proclamations of July 15, 1580, Jan. 10, 1581, and April 1, 1582 (which is an elaborate justification of the execution of Campion, designed to counter the indignation evidently very general), are an extremely important instrument of this government propaganda of the notion that priests as such are traitors.

Were these trials, then, mere legal trickery on the part of the state ? It is certain that in any attempt to reach a conclusion about the good faith of Elizabeth, Burghley, and the rest in their policy during these years towards the English who were Catholics, study of the trials must be highly important. All the Catholics who were put to death were executed either as traitors, or as the accessories of traitors. Two questions arise : Were the treasons alleged treasons properly so called, or were they actions in themselves indifferent but lately " made treason " by Elizabethan statutes ? and, Were the prisoners, in fact, fairly tried ? The trials that are vital, for the question of good faith, are those where the priests were indicted for treason properly so-called ; and the history of these trials is a damning count in the case against the government.[1]

There were three sets of these trials, in November 1581, in March 1582, and in February 1584. " Campion ", says an acknowledged master of the history of these times, " was wisely put on his trial for treason by the Government, not under any recent act, but under the statute of 1352, made by a Catholic king and parliament ; and under it he was condemned . . .".[2] The historian's failure, here, to say precisely with what treason the prisoner was charged, the reference to the common religion of the accused and the medieval legislator, the invitation to share the writer's own implied approbation of the proceedings—approbation of what another authority [3] had roundly called " judicial murder "—bring this statement near to *suggestio falsi*. What the historian has refrained from telling his reader is, that Campion (and his fellows) were tried for conspiring, at places and dates mentioned, to murder Elizabeth—a charge, it is notorious, known to be false to the government that made it.[4]

It is unfortunate also (given the importance of this question of the good faith of Elizabeth and her ministers) that, in the great work whose subject is England and the Catholic Church under Queen Elizabeth, the account of the trials falls below the general high level of the book.[5] For here the trials are not classified according to the statutes under which the prisoners were indicted, i.e. according to the legal offences with which they were charged. But knowledge of this is a first preliminary to any enquiry about the moral guilt of the prisoners (as distinguished from their legal guilt), or about the good faith of the government. Instead, a distinction is attempted between

---

[1] As Meyer recognises, 153-154 : " The death sentences pronounced on these supposed conspirators constitute a heavy accusation against the administration of justice under Elizabeth ". Also, 179 : " The judicial murders systematically inflicted on those suspected of conspiracy."   [2] A. F. Pollard, *H.E.*, VI, 376.

[3] J. M. Rigg, art *Wray, Sir Christopher*, in *D.N.B.*

[4] See, in Simpson, 392-396, the story of the preparation of the indictment. And " wisdom " is a curious word by which to describe the careful concoction of a bogus plot which the decision to proceed under the Act of 1352 made necessary.

[5] By A. O. Meyer ; cool, critical, admirably documented, it is still, after forty years, the " last word " on its highly important subject. We are never told, however, in what proportion of these nearly 200 trials any authentic details have come down to us, there is no sign of a survey of the sources, and there is one notable error of fact—the statement that " nearly all the trials of Catholics took place in London ", whereas more than half of them were in various provincial towns.

trials where the treason alleged against the prisoner was an act, and trials where the treason consisted in an opinion. This mistake [1] is the cause of a curious account of the device of the " bloody question ", as a proceeding that is lawful, and, as a piece of political wisdom, natural and normal in sixteenth-century rulers. Law said that men were traitors for what they thought ; the executive had the right, then, to find out what they thought ; in a rough age, law, inevitably, used means for this purpose that were harsh.

But it never was legal doctrine in England that thoughts themselves could be criminal, and that a man suspected of treasonable thoughts could be interrogated about his ideas, and be punished for what his answers revealed of his mind.

The trials were (all of them) trials in the courts of common law ; and we need to distinguish the trials from the extra-judicial examinations which preceded—and even followed—them, and which were the usual occasion of the " bloody question ". All these prisoners were charged with definite offences, and these offences had nothing to do with those matters that were the subject of the famous interrogation : they were tried, for example, on the charge that at Rome and at Rheims on definite days they had plotted to murder the queen, or that they had denied the queen to be the supreme governor of all her subjects in all causes ecclesiastical, or that they had called the queen a heretic, or that they had a papal bull in their possession, or that they had reconciled to the Catholic Church someone who had previously conformed to the arrangement of 1559, or that being priests ordained since June 24, 1559, by authority derived from the see of Rome, they were and remained in England. These were the offences for which they were tried, brought in guilty, sentenced by the judge, and put to death. None was ever put on his trial charged that he had said, " In the event of the pope sending an army into England to restore the Catholic religion, I will take sides with that army ", or that he had persuaded others to take this view of their duty. There was no statute under which men could have been tried for such a declaration ; and the government never busied itself to enact such a law as would make criminal the expression (brought out under torture) of one's intended action in a future contingency. It would indeed have been a unique enactment.

But although opinions of this sort, never expressed until wrung from the prisoner by torture, could not be made the matter of a criminal prosecution—

---

[1] The mistake is that Meyer thinks this distinction is founded on English law : " Since the time of Henry VIII it was no longer unusual, in contrast to ancient and existing legal usage, to treat not merely *actions* but *opinions* as treasonable ". *Op. cit.*, 147 ; and also, *ibid.*, " this new legal doctrine ", and " While the modern sense of justice revolts against trials of this sort, we must remember, as we have already said (p. 147), that, according to English legal practice in the sixteenth century, *opinions* were chargeable with treason as well as *actions* " ; *ibid.*, 156. A general reference is given to J. W. Willis-Bund, *A Selection of Cases from the State Trials* (Cambridge, 1879), I, Introduction. Here (p. xl) the author writes, " With Elizabeth . . . the fact of holding certain opinions was again to be treason . . ." ; and what he seems to have in mind is what he has described earlier (p. xxxvi), " Nothing can be said in favour of making the question of belief in certain theological dogmas treason ". This is very far from warranting Meyer's statement.

nor silence about one's opinion when interrogated [1]—nevertheless, when the prisoner was condemned to die (as were most of the priests) simply for the offence that he, although a priest, had actually continued to live in his native country, and when he was hanged, drawn and quartered for this offence, it stilled nascent criticism for the government to be able to say that the victim (on his own confession) would, if the Spaniards had landed, have been on their side ; and that he would have had to be on their side, or else cease to be a good Catholic priest. This was the purpose of the so-called " bloody question ", of which something must be said ; and herein lay the malice, of which Catholics at the time complained : it was invented, they said, not to prove guilt and secure convictions but to cover the convicted with obloquy.[2]

It was after the execution of Campion, Sherwin and Briant, December 1, 1581, that interrogations designed to produce answers of this sort became part of the regular routine. Those executions caused a storm of disapproval in London.[3] The injustice of the trial was notorious, and the protestations, at the gallows, of loyalty to the queen were believed. Before putting to death the others condemned with them, the government bethought itself how to rob them of any like sympathy. Another six months was allowed to go by before they were executed, and as they lay in prison, under sentence of death, the Attorney-General [4] and the Solicitor-General [5] visited them with Six Articles, "most proper", said Lord Burghley in his apologia, "to try whether men are traitors or not ". And the answers given were published.[6]

[1] As to silence, it is set down against St. Thomas More, in his indictment, that when asked the dangerous question, *penitus silebat*. Now, in 1588, the Solicitor-General and the Recorder of London, sending to the council a draft of the test questions which they have been asked to frame " to discern those that carry traitorous and malicious minds against her Majesty and the state, from them whose simplicity is misled by ignorant and blind zeal ", have to say that silence, or the plea that they have not learning enough to answer, is not enough to bring the prisoners " within the compass of the law for any proceeding to be had against them in case of treason or felony ". If they are Jesuits or priests ordained since Midsummer, 1559, then, being in the realm, they can be tried under the Act of 1585. If they be lay persons, " some such other cause is to be holden with them . . . to discover their treasonable intention as your Honours . . . shall direct ". The Solicitor-General, Thomas Egerton, the future Lord Chancellor Ellesmere, had himself been in trouble as a recusant eleven years earlier. Thence, by 1581, he had proceeded so far as to conduct the prosecution of Edmund Campion. William Fleetwood, the Recorder, who had a well deserved name as a rigorous persecutor of Catholics, was an older man (born *c.* 1535). He was a protégé of Leicester and a parliamentarian as well as a lawyer and judge (M.P. for Lancaster, 1558, 1563, for London 1571, 1584, 1586, 1588). For the text of this letter cf. C.R.S., V, p. 151.

[2] Cf. Allen, *Defence*, 44–45 ; " Whereunto, because they did conjecture their answers would be odious in the sight of the simple, and specially of zealous Protestants (as it fell out indeed) they devised to publish and read them to the people at the martyrdom of the rest, that thereby they might at least conceive that they were worthy of death for other causes, though not for that whereof they were condemned, and so either less pity them, or less mark the former unjust pretenced matter of their condemnation."

[3] Cf. Simpson, 468 foll., for an account ; 493–499, for notes on the contemporary pamphlet literature—works in Latin, French, Italian, German and Spanish, as well as in English. The most striking testimony to the feeling in London is the work noticed in n. 6 following.

[4] Sir John Popham (1531–1607), later Chief Justice of the Queen's Bench.

[5] Sir Thomas Egerton (?1540–1617).

[6] Cf. *A particular Declaration or Testimony, of the undutifull and traiterous affection borne against her Majestie by Edmond Campion, jesuite, and other condemned priestes, witnessed by their*

The prisoners were asked : Whether the Bull of Pius V against the Queen's Majesty be a lawful sentence, and ought to be obeyed by the subjects of England ?

Whether the Queen's Majesty be a lawful Queen, and ought to be obeyed by the subjects of England, notwithstanding the Bull of Pius V or any other bull or sentence that the Pope hath pronounced or may pronounce against her Majesty ?

Whether the Pope have or had power to authorise her subjects to rebel or take arms against her, or to invade her dominions ; and whether such subjects so doing, do lawfully therein ?

Whether the Pope have power to discharge any of her Majesty's subjects, or the subjects of any Christian prince from their allegiance or oath of obedience to her Majesty, or to their Prince for any cause ?

Whether Dr. Saunders in his book of the Visible Monarchy of the Church, and Dr. Bristow in his book of Motives (writing in allowance, commendation, and confirmation of the said Bull of Pius V) have therein taught, testified, or maintained a truth or a falsehood ?

If the Pope do by his Bull or sentence pronounce her Majesty to be deprived, and no lawful Queen, and her subjects to be discharged of their allegiance and obedience unto her ; and after, the Pope or any other by his appointment and authority, do invade this realm ; which part would you take, or which part ought a good subject of England to take ? [1]

" They will know that we will do hereafter, if such and such a thing should chance ", Allen protested ; " they will sound all the Catholics' hearts in the realm, and (which is more than Antichristian violence) they will punish them as traitors by death most cruel, for their only thoughts. Yea (which God

---

owne confessions : in reproofe of those slanderous bookes and libels delivered out to the contrary by such as are malitiously affected towards her Majestie and the State.
Published by authoritie. Imprinted at London by Christopher Barker, printer to the Queen's most excellent Majestie, An. Do. 1582.

The opening words of this tract give the reason why it is published : " some disloyal and unnatural subjects . . . have published divers slanderous pamphlets . . . in excuse and justification of the said traitors . . . setting [them] out as . . . loyal . . . and obedient subjects . . . in no ways spotted with any stain of ill-disposed affection towards her majesty . . . not otherwise to be charged than with . . . matters of conscience, that were no way prejudiced to her majesty's state and government ". This is why the council, to counter these publications, now makes known " certain confessions taken of the said Campion and others before arraignment, as also certain answers lately made to certain articles propounded to those that were at the same time condemned of high treason, but yet spared from execution".

The tract gives the answers of ten prisoners to the six questions, and of Campion, Sherwin and Briant to questions about certain passages from Sander's *De Visibili Monarchia Ecclesiae*, and Bristowe's *Motives* and about the bull of 1570, all printed in the tract. T.-D., III, Appendix, no. III, prints the best part of the tract and the text of all the answers.

In C.R.S., V, there are to be found documents about the question in the *passio* of ten other martyrs, of various dates between 1584 and 1590 ; pp. 62, 76–77, 84–86, 169–173, 243, 325, 381. In four of these cases the questions were put at the gallows, in only one case— Christopher Bales, 1590, p. 331—at the trial.

[1] This is the text as printed in Allen's *Defence of Catholics*, I, 79. It differs, but never substantially, from that in his *Brief History of the Martyrdom of XII reverend priests*, which T.-D., III, reprints in App., no. III.

Himself doth not) for future faults never committed, nor perhaps ever like to come to pass." [1]

Put a man on the rack and ask him what he thinks about the pope's power to depose princes, and how he will act if ever the pope should send an army to carry out such a sentence ; keep the rack turning until you have got from the prisoner, not what he really thinks about the matter (which may be no thought at all), but what you want it to be thought that he thinks, so that you may use his " confession " as proof that this is what all Catholics think, and what all Catholics are hoping for, and are preparing to do.

" And this cunning course they have followed ever since in defence of that pretended justice ", said Allen.[2]   More than any knowledge of what half a dozen priests were plotting in France and in Flanders, it was this " cunning course " that began in the Englishman's mind that association of the ideas of priest and traitor that was, henceforth, to be one of the strongest bulwarks against a Catholic restoration.   Even today the " course " has its successes. The historian is rarely content to state the mere fact (though allowed to be such), that the priests put to death by Elizabeth were innocent of any real treason : at this point the historian begins to explain.   And the basis of his explanation is an interpretation of the answers which some priests gave to Lord Burghley's " bloody question ".   It is these answers that are still (in substance) offered as evidence that the Elizabethan government was right, when it suspected the loyalty of the Catholics, and as warranting the judgment that the harsh treatment meted out to Catholics as such—the Act of 1585, for example—was only natural : if not, indeed, inevitable.[3]

---

[1] *Defence of Catholics*, I, 89.   Cf., how four years later, the Jesuit poet, Robert Southwell, described the process.   They are asked, he says, " what it would be their mind to do, should this or that happen.   If they are not willing to answer, this, their questioner determines, is the clearest evidence of a mind that is rebellious and bent on treason.   If they reply that they will do nothing against the rights of queen and country, and the duty they owe to these, their answer is calumniously made out to be spoken insincerely and hypocritically. Indeed whatever may have been their reply, it in no way satisfies these judges unless they say something that can bring them within danger of the death penalty.   All answered the court mildly and, so far as might be, with no bitterness of speech, always giving testimony to their loyalty and obedience to their country and the rights of the queen ".   Letter to Aquaviva, Aug. 31, 1588, in C.R.S., V, 322.   " Wrong acts that are merely internal ", said John Gerard to Coke, in 1597, " are reserved to God's judgment ".   Gerard, *Autobiography*, 126.

[2] *Defence*, I, 45.   Cf. *infra*, 395, n. 3, S. R. Gardiner, on such " cunning courses ".

[3] Cf., e.g., Black, 148–149, where Burghley's thesis is stated and, without any criticism of this, the " other side " is next just as simply summarised, " loyalty to the Roman church involved acceptance of the papal bull " ; i.e. if missionary priests were put to death it was " *because they held opinions that were considered dangerous to the existence of the state*—opinions, moreover, from which they could not dissociate themselves without ceasing to be Catholics ". As to the last clause of this sentence, the fact is that, at this very time, and when he is sending on to Rome a copy of the government's tract just described, Allen can take it for granted that no Catholic confuses the theory about papal powers with his religious beliefs (cf. his letter of June 23, 1582, to Agazzari, in Knox, 146–147).   And Fr. Robert Southwell, S.J., writes in an equally matter of fact way to the general of the Society of Jesus, Aug. 31, 1588, describing how the imprisoned priests here answered these questions, " Since, therefore, this was not a matter that concerned the faith . . ." (*Cum igitur res ad fidem non spectaret* . . .), *Persons*, 322.   And Fr. Southwell had been trained in the Roman schools, under the very eye of Gregory XIII.   As to the first clause (here in italics), and the implication of the author's statement that " The majority of priests who suffered death, died not because they were proved guilty of conspiracy—that was the exception rather than the rule ", one can only feel

As to the part which the " bloody question " played in the trials of the priests put to death, it is certainly not the case that " . . . a considerable number of missionaries declared on trial that, in case of war, they would side with the invading army ".[1] And the same writer's conclusion is worth no more than the premise : " In the face of facts such as these it is impossible to speak of persecution from religious motives ".[2] Nor can the authoritative statement be allowed to pass, " While every priest was condemned to death who admitted he would side with his country's foes, mercy was shown to the small number who declared in favour of their country in its campaign against the Church. They were not set at liberty but their lives were spared." This vast and extremely pertinent generalisation has no foundation in the facts.[3]

2

Catholics are no longer troubled by rumours of what is in store, Fr. Robert Southwell wrote to his Roman superior, after their year's experience of the Act of 1585, " for the enemy has reduced us to such a state, that there is hardly any new cruelty that could be added ".[4] Moreover, the statute of 1581 which punished so savagely the convert, and the friend who persuaded him, and the priest who received him, had also made neglect of the new religious services an offence the penalty for which must presently ruin even the very rich.[5] For every month of absence from the Sunday service the fine was now increased to £20 ; if the offence continues as long as a year the recusant shall find two bondmen to the amount of £200, at the least, as surety for his good behaviour so long as his recusancy lasts. Moreover the huge fines are not to be levied, as was the fine enacted in 1559, at the

---

that the author is here the victim of Meyer's great error. The implication that there was a minority of priests, condemned and executed as such, who really were guilty of conspiracy, has no support in the facts. History knows no such priests. The charges on which, as a matter of fact, the missionary priests were condemned have been examined on p. 358, *supra.*

[1] Meyer, 295 and (giving his authority) 159–162. He has precisely one case to offer as the ground of this assertion—that of Francis Dickenson in 1589 ; but Francis Dickenson's words (quoted, 162) were not spoken at the trial, but when under examination. For the complete text of these examinations cf. C.R.S., V, 169–174. It is these documents which occasion Pollen's incisive comment, " We see here very plainly the two ideas of the persecutors : *First,* to make the Martyr confess that he is a priest coming into England. This ensures a sentence of death. *Secondly,* to ensure an unpopular answer to the ' Bloody question '. This, though it cannot be construed into a crime, will ensure execution." *Ibid.,* 169.

[2] Meyer, 295.

[3] The authority quoted for this generalisation is a " list of imprisoned and examined priests in July, 1588 ", published by J. H. Pollen, S.J., in C.R.S., V, 154–156. This paper is a very rough note in the hand of the queen's serjeant, John Puckering (with some additions by Burghley), of results of trials, i.e. pleas, verdicts, sentences, and proposed places of execution ; and also of answers to the fatal question, Would the prisoner take the queen's side if the pope should send an army into England ? In this list thirty priests are named, of whom eleven are classed (? by the editor) as willing to take the queen's part. The only priest on the list of whom it is definitely said, " take the Queen's part ", John Weldon, was however executed, Oct. 5. The only other hint of an answer given by a priest is (possibly) the words " ne resp." set against the name of Richard Leigh, also executed, Aug. 30.

[4] Southwell to Aquaviva, July 25, 1586. C.R.S., V, 308.

[5] 23 *Eliz.,* c. 1 ; Prothero, 75–76, T.-D., III, xxiv–vi, for the text.

discretion of the churchwardens, and to be applied as a parochial relief fund. One third is now to go to the crown, one third to be applied by the crown for the poor of the parish—and one third to the informer who has brought about the conviction. The recusant is to be at the mercy of his neighbours; and with such a premium on spying neighbourly good feeling is to suffer. If the recusant has a tutor for his children and the tutor absents himself from church, the master shall pay a fine for him also, of £10 monthly, and the tutor shall suffer a year's imprisonment. For saying Mass the penalty is now to be 200 marks[1] and one year's imprisonment; and for hearing Mass, 100 marks[2] and one year's imprisonment. Presently, when it is found not possible to extract such fines, because too few recusants are worth so much as to be able to pay a fine of £260 annually (Elizabethan money value), a new Act makes their destruction more easy. " If default shall be made in any part of any payment aforesaid " the queen may " seize and enjoy " all the moveable property of a recusant once convicted, and two-thirds of all his lands and tenements.[3]

The Elizabethan persecution, or campaign to destroy the Catholic faith among the English people, was thus by no means just a matter of some 183 capital executions. The bitter hostility aroused by the sight of the hated thing coming to life again, reached out to ruin hundreds, and thousands, for whom the gallows was perhaps only a distant menace. Spies, raids, arrests, fines, imprisonment, torture, the gallows—these, in the last half of the reign, were the common lot of the Catholic who refused to be, or to pretend to be, a Protestant; with the cruelty of the persecutor increasing with his success, and his own character sinking ever more closely into the brute.[4]

It is not possible to compute the numbers of the Catholics who were imprisoned for offences against this penal code. The Spanish ambassador, writing to Philip II, in 1582, that there are 11,000 Catholics in prison and that two-thirds of them are women is crazily over the mark—as is Persons,

---

[1] £133 6s. 8d.

[2] £66 13s. 4d. In a list of prisoners in the Counter, Wood St., London, dated June 14, 1586, we have " William Higham and Roger Lyne, gent, they were taken without Bishopsgate at Mass with Blackburn, alias Thompson, that was hanged : they are in execution for 100 marks apiece. They have been divers times examined before Mr. Justice Young ". C.R.S., II, 249–250.

[3] 28 & 29 Eliz., c. 6 ; Prothero, 88, and, more fully, T.-D., III, p. xxxvii–viii. The statute also makes void all conveyances of land made, since the accession of Elizabeth (now 28 years ago), not by a convicted recusant only, but by every Catholic who " forbears " to go to the service, if these are revocable at his pleasure or intended for the support of himself or his family.

[4] For an account of all this, in a work as far from sympathetic to the victims as it is to their principles, cf. Conyers Read, II, 293–300 ; and for a contemporary picture, The Autobiography of John Gerard, translated by Philip Caraman, S.J. Vaux of Harrowden, by Godfrey Anstruther, O.P. (1953), shows, in a most remarkable way, the actual effects of this régime upon a noble family and the world of its dependants. As for the brutality, cf. Meyer, 183, " No blot is more foul on the history of Elizabeth's latter years than the name of Richard Topcliffe. Every inhuman quality which the most heated imagination can picture is embodied in this example of unspeakable degradation . . . to invent fresh tortures became his business and his delight. . . . Had he not been sure of the queen's approval, the wretch could not have plied his trade."

reporting that a return made to the queen gives the names of 50,000 recusants. The most important official evidence we possess are certificates of the keepers of the London prisons, edited now nearly fifty years ago by Fr. Pollen.[1] From these forty-three documents and sets of documents we can learn much. There are four sets of particular importance—annual returns for the years 1583, 1584, 1586 and 1588.[2] For 1583 and 1586 there are certificates from 9 prisons, for 1584 from 8 ; the returns for 1588 are not classified according to prisons. In 1583 there is a total of 103 Catholics in these prisons, " committed for matters of religion ", of whom 33 are priests, 7 women. In 1584 the total is 100, 29 are priests, and there are 4 women. In 1586 there are 95 prisoners, 40 of them are priests, one a woman. In 1588 (September 30) there are 73 prisoners, 13 of them are priests ; there is one woman. All these are returns of prisoners " committed for religion ". There is also a list for the year 1595,[3] in which others also figure, a coiner for example, and forgers. But in this list there are, it would seem, 70 prisoners whose crime is their Catholic faith ; 10 of these are priests and 12 are women.

There are other lists in this dossier which show the executive meditating how best to deal with its prisoners. In December, 1586, for example, there are 42 priests in various London prisons.[4] The secretary of state, Sir Francis Walsingham, consults his spies, Nicholas Berden and Thomas Phellippes, about them and they report that one has " subscribed to the Queen's supreme authority in all causes " ; of another they know nothing, for a third favour is asked, 21 are recommended for banishment, 10 for imprisonment in the castle of Wisbeach and 8 for execution. None has yet been tried. Two of the 8 singled out for hanging are noted as having been banished already and having returned, and of one of these, Jonas Meredith, it is said, " he may do harm upon the other side ". The distinction between those to be banished and those to be sent to Wisbeach, " or such like place ", has nothing to do with degrees of guilt, but is simply one of means : " Such as are noted to be banished are therefor fittest because exceeding poor and contentious. Such as are noted for Wisbeach are well able to defray their expenses ;[5] of the graver sort and best accounted of for learning." The spy—or confidential agent—Nicholas Berden draws attention to other priests, still at large, " some of them more perilous than those in prison ", and among them one who " is a notable corrupter and "— after five years this is remembered—" conducted Campion and Persons and Edmondes through England ".

There is not a word, in these comments that are to influence the council's decision, that connects any one of these forty-two names with political action

---

[1] C.R.S., I (1905), 47–72 ; II (1906), 219–288.

[2] C.R.S., II, lists XVII, XVIII, XXII–L, XXXIX, pp. 228–231, 234–238, 251–253 and 282–284, respectively.   [3] *Ibid.*, list XLI, pp. 284–287.

[4] *A note of the prestes disposition and desert now in prison*, printed, *ibid.*, 272–276, as list XXXI.

[5] There is more than one statement as to this. And one list is headed *Preestes and others in the prisons about London fitte for Wisbech, able to bear the charges.* The date of this is c. 1587 ; cf. *ibid.*, list XXXIV, p. 272.

of any kind ; nor is it suggested that, by their answers to questioning, they have shown themselves " traitorously " minded. And, be it noted, this list is drawn up at a most dangerous moment for priests who are captives— it is December, 1586, the Queen of Scots has just been sentenced to death on the charge of being accessory to a plot to murder Elizabeth ; [1] the English queen is havering, longing to see Mary killed but not by any act traceable to herself ; she is suggesting to the Scots queen's keeper that he should himself make away with her. And Walsingham is anxiously pressing for the warrant that will solve all. Administrative expediency, rather than that spirit of Justice which, we have been sternly reminded, must temper our pity, is what, in fact, presided over the destiny of these captive priests who are Elizabeth's prisoners.

Few of those considerations that are so active in the minds of the historians who are the queen's instinctive apologists, make any appearance in the confidential notes that pass between the council and the keepers of the prisons. The prisoners—priests and laymen—figure, almost invariably, in these papers as " prisoners for religion ", as do the people we call Puritans and Separatists: Protestants and Catholics appearing, at times, in the same lists. " Against any of these ", it is written of a group of eight laymen, in a list signed by the Attorney General, " we find no matter, other than that they are obstinate Recusants, unless there be any matter known unto my Lords or Mr. Secretary which appeareth not to us ".[2] And again, " All these are in for Common Conversing with and entertaining and relieving of Seminary Priests " ; " All these " being three women and three men now in the Fleet and the Counters.[3]

The usual kind of note about a priest, when any information is given in these certificates is, for example, " Thomas Cotsmore, a Sussex man born, an old massing priest, taken at Arundel coming over from beyond the seas and sent in by your honours [i.e. the council] a two years since " ; [4] or, " Richard Ross, an old massing priest, a Yorkshire man born, sent in by the Lord Bishop of London and the High Commissioners a five years since ".[5] Of one, Richard Creagh, we are told, " a dangerous man to be among the Irish for the reverence that is by that nation borne unto him, and therefore fit to be continued in prison ". This is the captive Archbishop of Armagh.[6] Thomas Pound and Nicholas Roscarrock, men of great fortune both, who have lain in prison for years, are " for religion only committed and for intelligence with Jesuits and priests, two dangerous men and apt for any practise : fit they should be banished ".[7] Ralph and Richard Oldacres, " recusants, [are] . . . simple ignorant and poor men . . . the court examined them openly if they would come to the Church and they answered no it was against their

---

[1] October 27.   [2] C.R.S., II, 259, Sept. 25, 1586.
[3] Ibid., 258, *A Calendar of Seminarye Priests and others in divers prisons in London*, Sept. 25, 1586. Also signed, J. Popham, i.e. the Attorney-General.
[4] C.R.S., II, 224, March, 1583, in the Gatehouse.
[5] Ibid., 225, the same date and prison.
[6] Ibid., 238, May 27, 1585, the Tower of London.
[7] Ibid., 238, the same date and prison.

conscience and so they remain in charge . . ." [1] Again, " John Pinchin of
Clement Danes in the county of Middlesex gent., yielded himself a prisoner
[6 September 1582] to prevent the outlawry which was against him for certain
months which he refused to come to the church. Being inclined to the
Romish religion and doth yet refuse to go to the church ".[2] Trevennor
Rosecarrock of New Inn in the county of Middlesex had been " . . . found
guilty for hearing of a Mass and not coming to Church in one Whole year ".[3]
William Smyth, of the Middle Temple . . . and William Linger, of Thavies
Inn, both committed January 10, 1583, " for the Romish religion, and was
found guilty of not coming to Church in one whole year ".[4] " William
Warren of London, baker, Thomas Penkevel, of Penkevel in the county of
Devon gent, and Thomas Limerick, servingman . . . [committed] for not
conforming themselves in matters of religion, . . . being offered by me
. . . monthly to have their liberty to go with a keeper to the church to hear
the Divine Service, they utterly refusing to do the same, alleging that it is
against their conscience so to do." [5]

Of one priest, Christopher Bagshawe—once a fellow of Balliol College,
Oxford, in the days when Robert Persons was bursar—arrested in 1585,
we are told that he " was taken with letters from Charles Paget and the Bishop
of Ross to the Lord of Farnihurst and others in Scotland, and had a cipher
about him to Charles Paget ; " [6] and of another priest, Ralph Ithell, that he
was " accused directly by Ballard ",[7] of a share in the Babington conspiracy.
In 1588 Ithell appears as " a condemned priest in the Tower for Babington's
conspiracy ",[8] and Walsingham's agents had recommended that he should
be hanged.[9] Whatever the degree of his treason, it was readily forgiven
when he conformed to the queen's religion : in 1599 Ithell was given, by
the crown, the living of Aldham, Essex.[10]

In the seven years between Edmund Campion's arrest, July 1581, and
the last comprehensive list in this series, September 30, 1588, as many as
157 priests [11] passed through the London prisons, to judge from these papers
alone. Of them all, Bagshawe and Ithell and Ballard are the only ones of
whom treason, in the natural sense of the word, or political activity, is even
alleged. No one of the three has ever been claimed by Catholics as worthy of
respect or sympathy as a religious hero.[12]

---

[1] C.R.S., II, 244, June 13, 1586, the King's Bench.

[2] *Ibid.*, 226, March, 1583, in Newgate.　　　　[3] *Ibid.*, 237, April 8, 1584, in Newgate.

[4] *Ibid.*, 237, the same date and prison.　　　　[5] *Ibid.*, 238, the same date and prison.

[6] *The Lordes resolution upon the Prisonners*, Nov. 30, 1586, C.R.S., II, 265.

[7] *Prisoners in the towre and other persons apprehended lately*, Sept. 25, 1586. List XXVI,
signed J. Popham, the endorsement (here in italics) in Burghley's hand. *Ibid.*, 259.

[8] *Ibid.*, 280, list XXXVII.

[9] *A note of the prestes disposition and desert now in prison*, Dec., 1586, *ibid.*, 272, list XXXI.

[10] So *ibid.*, 210, note, quoting Newcourt, *Repertorium Ecclesiasticum Londinense*, II, 7.

[11] i.e., something more than 1 in 2 of the priests sent over from Douay-Rheims and from
Rome during these years. The chase was indeed hot. Not all these priests, by any means,
were arrested in London.

[12] This takes no account of the two foreigners, subjects of James VI of Scotland, William
Crichton, and Patrick Abdy his companion. One priest only is set down as having " subscribed to the Queen's supreme authority in all causes ", while in prison. This was Paul

The problem, how to find prison-room for the Catholics who refused " to conform to her majesty's laws in matter of religion " was very real, from the first beginnings of the war of retaliation waged on the mission from Douay.[1] After another sixteen years of the terror the problem was still acute, and the last of Elizabeth's statutes against these Catholic recusants, the Act of 1593, has been seen as meant to provide " the cheapest and most comprehensive method of detention . . . all the Catholics in England were kept in a sort of confinement ".[2]

However that may be, this statute [3] begins in good propaganda style, announcing, if not the facts, then what the government would like the country to believe are the facts. " Sundry wicked and seditious persons . . . terming themselves Catholics " (who, in reality, are " spies and intelligencers " for the queen's enemies and for some of her rebellious subjects abroad), hiding their " devilish purpose ", namely, conspiracy against the queen and the peace of the realm, " under a false pretext of religion and conscience ", are secretly wandering about the country on this business. Wherefore the Act provides that all Catholics over the age of sixteen who have been convicted of the offence of not going to the new religious services shall, within forty days of the end of this session of parliament, return to their homes and " shall not, at any time after, pass or remove above five miles from thence ".

Spence, committed to the Clink, Dec. 29, 1585, C.R.S., V, 272, 246. In these lists we meet also prisoners for religion from the Protestant party : Robert Lewes of Gloucester and William Druett in 1581, " of the precisian sort ", p. 220 ; John Nash of London, yeoman, in 1582, " for causes of religion as a precisian ", p. 226 ; Fra: Johnson, " Sectary ", in 1595 and George Johnson also, " Sectary in Conventicles to be indicted abjured ", p. 285 ; Christopher Cliff, March, 1585, a London cobbler, committed by Whitgift sitting in the High Commission: " the said Christopher Defyeth popery ", p. 249. And there are two prisoners, in 1581, who bring even the gaoler to the shudder still appropriate to their crime : " These two for horrible heresy—Richard Lewes of Ipswich, husbandman [and] Faith Arnold of Ipswich, spinster " ; p. 220.

[1] In July, 1577, for example : " Forasmuch as the number of recusants is so great as the places of restraint are not able to hold them, it may be thought expedient that the recusants of such dioceses as are most corrupt be first dealt withal, and in the said diocese the principal persons such as are by law to be reached unto " (Conyers Read, II, 281). Persons will hardly be exaggerating when, within a month or so of his arrival in London, he reports to Rome, " . . . in every county new prisons have been assigned ; for the old ones are already full of Recusants as they call the Catholics who will not go to their churches and sermons ". Letter to Agazzari, of Aug. 5, 1580, Persons, 46. Four years later, Allen's Defence (I, 10) appeals " to the conscience and knowledge of all the Catholics and Protestants within the realm, who of their equity will never deny, that most prisons in England be full at this day, and have been for divers years, of honourable and honest persons not to be touched with any treason, or other offence in the world, other than their profession and faith in Christian religion ". And at this very time, the Clerk of the Peace for Hampshire is complaining that " almost all other causes and grievances of the shire are omitted " because " the number of Recusants which at every sessions are to be indicted is so great ". The Trouble and Grievance growing to the Clerk of the Peace in Hampshire by the Recusants, P.R.O., Domestic, Eliz., Vol. 185, no. 83, quoted here from Conyers Read, II, 297. n. 4.

[2] It would be quite a mistake, of course, to assume that, because a law is enacted, it is necessarily put into full operation by the officers responsible for this. And Meyer's words (op. cit., 167), quoted here, would suggest some such argument on his part. In any case, the new Act, as will be seen, did not apply to " all the Catholics in England ", but only to those who had been convicted for the offence of recusancy.

[3] 35 Eliz., c. 2 ; for the text, cf. G. & H., 498–508.

Recusants in prison, or in foreign parts, are to do the same within twenty days of their release, or of their return to the country, and all convicted of recusancy in the future, within forty days of their conviction. For not attending the liturgies of the Book of Common Prayer, the Catholic is already liable to a fine of £20 a month, and to lose almost all his possessions at the first failure to pay ; now, whether he pays it or not, he is to endure, for life, confinement to a radius of an hour's walk from his home.

Recusants who had no home of their own were to return to the place where they were born, or to their parents' home ; and all, upon arrival, were to report themselves " to the minister or curate " of the parish and to the constable, and their names were to be entered in a register " to be kept in every parish for that purpose ".

The penalty—for not returning to one's home, for going beyond the five-mile limit—was severe : the loss of all property, goods and chattels, lands, rents, annuities.

The legislator is worried by the problem of huge numbers of recusants too poor to be worth fining—the kind who, at this moment, it seems, clutter up the prisons, costing the government mightily for their keep.[1] So the statute fixes a dividing line—an absolute estate, freehold, of £13 3s. 4d. annual value, all charges paid, *or* goods and chattels worth £40—and for convicted recusants worth less than this it enacts a special penalty for disobedience : if within three months of their arrest, whether for not repairing to their home, or for going beyond the five-mile limit, they have not conformed by making in church the submission provided in the Act, they are to abjure the realm ; that is to say, they are to take an oath before two justices of the peace that they renounce their country for ever, and to depart from such haven and on such a day as the justices determine. If such poor recusants refuse to make the abjuration, if they do not depart on the day fixed, if they ever return without the queen's permission, the penalty is death.[2]

The submission, by making which the convicted recusant, rich or poor, is freed from all the penalties imposed by this Act, is a public act of faith in the royal right to rule the church as what God Himself has arranged : " I, *A.B.*, do humbly confess and acknowledge, that I have grievously offended God in contemning her majesty's godly and lawful government and authority, by absenting myself from church, and from hearing divine service, contrary to the godly laws and statutes of this realm : and I am heartily sorry for the

---

[1] " To the end ", says the statute, " that the realm be not pestered and over charged with the multitude of such seditious and dangerous people as is aforesaid, who, having little or no ability to answer or satisfy any competent penalty for their contempt and disobedience of the said laws . . .". It is the complaint, repeated, made by the Hampshire Clerk of the Peace just quoted, that these convictions of recusants have so far brought no profit to the queen, for they " are not found to have lands or goods to answer their condemnations ". He also notes that condemnation makes no difference : there is, so far, no reformation of the recusants.

[2] Cf. Conyers Read, II, 304, for the interesting suggestion of a radical conflict of policy, the queen willing to legislate against recusants as a means of revenue, the council bent on destroying them—thence the fluctuations in the administration of the penal code. For examples of the difficulties which the Act caused, cf. Anstruther, 220–221.

AN ADMONITION
TO THE NOBILITY
AND PEOPLE OF ENG-
LAND AND IRELAND CON-
CERNINGE THE PRESENT VVARRES

made for the execution of his Ho-
lines Sentence, by the highe
and mightie Kinge Ca-
tholike of Spaine.

By the CARDINAL *of Englande.*

A°. M. D. LXXXVIII.

JEZABEL

Philippus II. Caroli V. filius, Hispaniarum, Indiarum, Neapolis, Siciliæ, Hierosolymæ, etc. rex catholicus. Mediolani, Brabantiæ, Geldriæ, etc. dux. Flandriæ, Hollandiæ, Hannoniæ, etc. comes. Aetatis suæ 59.
1586

THE SPANISH KING

POPE SIXTUS V, 1585-1590
FELICE PERETTI

THE
COPIE OF A LET-
TER SENT OVT OF

ENGLAND TO DON BERNARDIN

MENDOZA AMBASSADOVR IN FRANCE FOR
the King of Spaine, declaring the state of England, contrary to the opinion of *Don Bernardin*, and of all
his partizans Spaniardes and others.

This Letter, although it was sent to Don Bernardin Mendoza,
yet, by good hap, the Copies therof aswell in English as in French, were
found in the chamber of one Richard Leigh a Seminarie Priest,
who was lately executed for high treason committed in the
time that the Spanish Armada was on the seas.

Whereunto are adioyned certaine late Aduertisements, concerning the
losses and distresses happened to the Spanish Nauie, aswell in fight with the
English Nauie in the narrow seas of England, as also by tempests, and con-
trarie winds, vpon the West, and North coasts of Ireland, in their
returne from the Northerne Isles beyond
Scotland.

Imprinted at London by I. Vautrollier for
Richard Field, 1588.

same, and do acknowledge and testify in my conscience, that the bishop or see of Rome has not, nor ought to have, any power or authority over her majesty, or within any her majesty's realms or dominions : and I do promise and protest, without any dissimulation, or any colour or means of any dispensation, that from henceforth I will from time to time obey and perform her majesty's laws and statutes, in repairing to the church, and hearing divine service, and do my uttermost endeavour to maintain and defend the same." [1]

The great achievement of this policy of persecution was that it made the life of the ordinary Catholic a very nightmare of insecurity. At any moment, any one of a hundred chances might jeopardise his property, his liberty, his life. He was vulnerable through his servants, through his children, through his wife ; and his happiness was for ever at the mercy of a disappointed suitor, an envious competitor, the local zealot, the professional informer. How this code of laws and regulations wrought its deadly work can be read in a score of sombre contemporary memoirs that colour very horribly the black and white of the legal phraseology.

Sometime towards the end of 1594 a young Jesuit missionary in the north of England, Fr. Richard Holtby, sent in to his English superior, Fr. Henry Garnet, a long report [2] that is valuable to us, not only for the vivid picture of the sufferings which Catholics must now endure, even in that more favourable region, but for *obiter dicta* that go below the surface of the events and make us aware that, under the terrible pressure of the code, one age, with the Catholics, is giving place to another : there is beginning to be perceptible an understanding that the last chance of a Catholic England has gone, and the dawn of a new, less splendid, ideal—the happy future when what Catholics survive will be allowed to live. [3]

The writer speaks of " the weak and small number of God's servants ", and how more and more, after ten years of the persecution in full strength, all are lamenting that " the little sparkle of the catholic religion, as yet reserved amongst us, shall be quite extinguished ". [4] His own personal reason for this gloomy view—so very different from the enthusiastic picture of Catholic fervour which we find in the letters of Campion and Persons, only fourteen years earlier—is that he sees " in little storms what numbers are lost, yea, how many willingly cast themselves away, before they be greatly urged, and

---

[1] The submission leaves little doubt that, after 35 years, the real conception of the supremacy claimed by the crown in all causes ecclesiastical is, as Catholics always maintained, not a civil superintendence but a sovereignty truly and substantially religious : it is God's will that Englishmen attend the new services in obedience to the orders of the queen who has devised and imposed them, and the laws by which Elizabeth has brought this about are not merely " laws of this realm ", but " Godly laws ". If a view of the religion of Christ where this is fundamental is not substantially different from one in which the fundamental is a mysterious, infallible *magisterium* to which the whole church is subject and before which the whole church is equal, then words have no longer a meaning.

[2] For a printed text of which cf. T.-D., III, 75–148.

[3] I am well aware that it is also maintained—and not without very real evidence—that " the issue remained open, was recognised as remaining open, until well on in the 17th century "— but whatever the truth in this it must, I think, be understood of the issue within the governing classes.   [4] T.-D., III, 75–76.

how few there be that abide so long, until they come unto a just trial of their constancy ". Men who have endured like heroes for years, " in the end, tired with miseries and overcome with temptations, have yielded themselves unto the time " ; like " the famed gold of the alchymist's forge ", they are not " able to endure the seventh fire ", men and women of all degrees, " with some also of the clergy ". And the enemy, seemingly, never makes a mistake : " their policies take place, and their desires are accomplished ".[1]

The restriction of every Catholic to within five miles of his own dwelling has resulted in his life being brought still more closely under scrutiny. " To abide at home, if it be espied, we dare not ; and to fly far, we are forbidden by statute." [2] Catholics have now been disarmed, and except that " a guilty conscience suspecteth all it loveth not ",[3] what motive can the enemy now have for his suspicions, and for the raids and searches that continue everlastingly ? In every county the cohort of " officers, sergeants and pursuivants " is to be found, and the " secret spies, who, under cover of catholic religion do insinuate themselves into our company and friendship ". Catholics are far too much occupied with avoiding these present dangers, for them to have any interest in plots and policies of aggression. Travel is impossible for them : the search at the ports is so close, " of what profession, of what religion, from whence he cometh, whither he goeth, what he bringeth or carrieth with him, yea, and many times, attendance made for him and intelligence given of him, long before his arrival ".[4] At times the raids take in, not only " private houses, but also . . . common inns and whole towns, as Durham, and Yarm and many others, for all strangers and passengers . . . so that none . . . can light in any company, but that he shall be questioned, sifted, and examined of every peasant ".[5] It is such a serious liability to be known as the friend or relative of one who is a Catholic, that " even those who in their hearts, love our religion, hate our profession of the same ".[6] Family unity is broken up, parent and child, husband and wife, mutually suspecting the one the other.

The general air of the time is that Catholics should consider themselves lucky that they are allowed to live. All else is a favour, and favours are expensive, for " the chiefest favour must be procured, by their means that have spoiled us before ; and yet their lip-labour is so costly unto us, that it picks round sums out of our purses ".[7]

The leading spirit in all this is the Earl of Huntingdon, for twenty-two years now president of the council of the north, of " bloody and cruel mind against Catholic men and their religion ",[8] plentifully endowed with

---

[1] T.-D., III, 76.   [2] *Ibid.*, 77.   [3] *Ibid.*, 78.
[4] *Ibid.*, 79.   [5] *Ibid.*, 79–80.   [6] *Ibid.*, 80.   [7] *Ibid.*, 81.
[8] *Ibid.*, 85. This was Henry Hastings, the third earl of the line, born 1535 or 1536. He was the son of the second earl and his mother was Catherine Pole, daughter of Henry Pole, Lord Montague, whom Henry VIII was to put to death in 1538. Catherine Pole was, then, the cardinal's niece (and his executor). And as the only survivor of the grand-children of Margaret Pole, Countess of Salisbury, she was heiress to the claims of the House of York—a fact of which Elizabeth, though personally friendly to Lady Huntingdon, was always conscious. Catherine Pole's son, the third earl, had also married a Catherine, the daughter of John Dudley, Duke of Northumberland, and so the sister of Elizabeth's Leicester. He succeeded his father as Earl of Huntingdon in 1561, was a most enthusiastic

authority,[1] and grown marvellously ingenious with the years. " And although he be of a weak constitution of body, yet it is incredible what pains he taketh, both day and night, in watching, in writing, in travelling, without respect of frost, snow, and other importunate weather." [2]   The earl, " in religion . . . is taken for a prince of puritans " ; [3] and what the writer has to say of these faithful disciples of the primitive evangel of Tyndale and the rest is interesting. For example, that " their religion consisteth rather of a furious hatred, or presumptuous obstinacy to contradict others, than in any positive doctrine of their own, unless it be in singing of a psalm, or hearing of a sermon ".[4] To be " forward in the shew of puritanism " is the sure and certain road to the Lord President's favour.   Is Huntingdon sincerely a puritan ?   All that the writer will say is that " religion in magistrates is framed now, in England, commonly after Machiavelli's rule, to make a shew of a thing, where the substance wanteth, and any may serve well enough, if it agree with their policy ".[5] He recalls that Huntingdon is in the line of succession, " if any thing fall "—what a king, this Henry IX !—" and he supposeth, perhaps, that sort of people the fittest instruments to compass his purpose, as they accord best with his humour ",[6] an obstinate man, given to furious hates.

These puritans—real or pretended—who make up the mass of the earl's underlings, if only " zealous as they term [them] ",[7] are given a free hand in the business of harassing the Catholics of the north, " whereby they grow so malapert that . . . the best in the country dare not contrary them ".[8] And to these, all such promotions go as to be under-sheriffs—one result of which is that the superior officers of the administration, " of their own nature otherways modest and reasonable, are forced to use much cruelty, lest they be accused of slackness by their own substitutes, being factors of the president ".[9] This ultimate development—the rule in all régimes of despotic oppression— is familiar enough in this mid-twentieth century.   And so it is that, through fear, the better men " become more cruel than the rest, and, using themselves no otherwise than lions by kind, amongst whom they are nuzzled and trained, ' they learned to catch the prey, and to devour men : to make widows, and

---

adherent to the new doctrines, who in 1569 actually begged Elizabeth to allow him to sell his estates and raise an army to assist the Huguenots.   It was three years after this that he became Lord President of the North, and in 1579 the queen gave him the Garter.   He died in 1595, leaving no children.

[1] " The president in this north country hath had, and hath yet, as he taketh upon him, three several and principal authorities granted unto him, of president, of lieutenant, and also of a head commissioner, next after the supposed Archbishop of York, who is the foremost and first of that commission . . . neither can or dare the rest do anything, but strive only which way to please and feed his humour : yea, he useth these several offices in such sort, that he maketh one of them to countenance the other, and, confounding their distinct functions and places, applieth either of them to perform the office of the rest.   In this wise, sitting as a head commissioner upon religious matters, he terrifieth with the name of lieutenant, making no difference between peace and war, and threatening to execute martial law upon afflicted catholics, if they refuse to shew friendship and conformity to schism and heresy ; to which effect, provost-marshals were appointed in divers places, to put them in fear thereof " ; *ibid.*, 99–100.

[2] *Ibid.*, 86.   [3] *Ibid.*, 86.   [4] *Ibid.*, 87.   [5] *Ibid.*, 86.
[6] *Ibid.*, 86–87.   [7] *Ibid.*, 87.   [8] *Ibid.*, 87.   [9] *Ibid.*, 90.

to lay waste cities ' ".[1] And gradually—there have been the twenty-two years of a single administration to favour the development—" the whole country, framing themselves after these examples, and desirous to feed the humours of such heads, partly for fear, and partly to gain favour, are become ready and forward to execute whatsoever they are invited or called unto " ; [2] and so there came about the terrible affliction, at Candlemas 1593, that " the whole country over Yorkshire, Richmondshire, Bishoprick, Northumberland, were up, upon one night, to search and rifle catholic men's houses . . . such diligence used that . . . for divers days, and especially nights, going before, all fords, bridges and passages were laid, and the houses watched . . .".[3]

" Woe to those that are with child in those days ", it had been written in presage of another calamity ; and the latent savagery that " zeal " can call to its aid comes out rarely in the treatment of the womenfolk of the recusants. " Sometimes they are so uncivil, that they will search the very beds, where man and wife do lie, at their first breaking into the house, when they come in the night, as in London it is, most commonly; yea, sometimes into the beds, where women lie in childbed. Yea, they will not spare grave ancient matrons, and women of great place." [4] " When their wives are great, Catholics are forced to shift them from place to place, to conceal their lying in, lest their children should be christened heretically ; and sometimes want the sacrament wholly, through the malice and fault of the ministers, and want of due matter or form of baptism. Many women with child have been delivered before their time, to the danger of themselves and children, by the sudden and violent frights of pursuivants, who, like pitiless furies, rage every where alike, without compassion, or care of the diseased. Catholics have no less difficulty to avoid the danger of churching and purification, than of lying-in ; being watched in both respects, by malicious eyes." [5]

Richard Holtby has much to say about individual cases, about persecutors whom he names, and the particular acts of robbery for which they are known. He describes the effect of the commission of 1592 to question all Catholics upon oath whether they had been persuaded by any priest that if an invasion should be made by the pope or any other foreign power they should take part against their queen and country, and how this commission was extended by the president to other matters, and how the gentry who had Catholic wives were brought in.[6] These Protestant husbands were now forced to give recognisances that " morning and evening prayers, as is appointed and set down in the Book of Common Prayer, be publicly read in [their houses] three days in every week, at the least " and all the household—save the Catholic wife—" reverently [to] receive the holy communion, so often yearly, as is appointed in the said book of common prayer ". Furthermore, no Catholic other than the wife, they were to promise, would be allowed to visit the house,

---

[1] T.-D., III, 90 : the quotation is *Ezekiel* xix, 6, 7.   [2] *Ibid.*, 90.   [3] *Ibid.*, 90–91.
[4] Quoted from Fr. John Gerard's account of the Gunpowder Plot, in T.-D., III, 92, n. 1.
[5] This is a quotation (*ibid.*) from a letter to Richard Verstegan, 1592, the original of which is in the archives of Stonyhurst College.
[6] T.-D., III, 102–109. Holtby's narrative, once more.

and no member of the household have any contact with any Catholic, priest or layman. And the Catholic wife is to appear before the High Commission upon 14 days notice given.[1] Husbands who refused to accept these conditions were sent to prison. And the wives being thus brought in by their own husbands, " for saving the catchpoles some labour ",[2] are committed to prison, and " kept so strait and close . . . that no access of friends, unless they were such as sought to vex and pervert their constancy " [3] was allowed. There were cases, of course, where as time went by and the wife remained loyal to her conscience, marital affection was turned into hatred. " Others complained [of] their families misery at home, and accused the hard hearts of the wives : . . . others exclaimed against catholic priests, who, seeing both wives and husbands in misery . . . would not dispense with the one to commit now and then a sin, that both might live in earthly prosperity." [4] And no wife was released, unless upon bond " that no priest, or jesuit, or known Catholic should come in their . . . company, or at their house ; that they should have heretical ministers to come and confer with them ".[5] Little wonder that Catholics took to the woods and the moors, and hid in caves, carefully transformed into refuges " with enormous toil ", where they lay hidden, day and night, for weeks at a time.[6]

3

This harrying of the Catholics of the north, in the years 1592–1594, does not, of course, mark the end of the Catholic resistance. It is recalled here, at length, partly to bring home the degree of the strain to which the faith of the individual Catholic could now be subjected ; but also because the strain is taken in a spirit that is something different from what is described in the accounts of ten and twelve years before.

The intervening years had seen a succession of major reverses for the Catholic cause in the wider sense, i.e. in so far as the mission was a thing organised, and in need of patrons and protectors if it was to survive the pressure of the government's hostility. In the first place, the long eighteen years' campaign of the Protestant extremists against the life of the Queen of Scots

---

[1] T.-D., III, 106–107.   [2] Ibid., 121.
[3] Ibid., 122.   [4] Ibid., 123.
[5] Ibid., 125–126.

[6] For this, cf. the letter of Fr. Henry Garnet, the superior of the Jesuits in England, written seemingly in 1593, quoted, ibid., 103–105 (in the notes). A later letter from him (Sept., 1594), describing a night raid on the London Catholics, says, vividly, " The Friday night before Passion Sunday, was such a hurley-burley in London, as never was seen in man's memory ; no, not when Wyat was at the gates : a general search in all London, the justices and chief persons going in person : all unknown persons taken and put in churches, till the next day : no Catholics found but one poor tailor's house at Golden Lane End, which was esteemed such a booty as never was yet, since this queen's days. . . . Before that tumult of Golden Lane, about the latter end of February, they had laid a plot of these great stirs, and prepared the people's minds by a proclamation, wherein they commanded strait watches to be made, certain days in the week, every where, for priests and Irishmen, whose late attempts to kill the queen had been discovered ; and all Irishmen, not inhabitants in towns and citizens, banished England " ; which proclamation, Garnet goes on to say, was not " straitly executed and [is] now almost forgotten " ; ibid., 115–116, n. 1.

had at last succeeded.[1] Not only was she now put to death, February 8, 1587, but, so far as her enemies could manage this, she died as a criminal, justly punished for complicity in a plot to murder the English queen, her gaoler. And the events which led immediately to that dreadful morning at Fotheringay were coloured, for contemporaries, by three years of well-managed propaganda on the theme, " The Queen—our Protestant Queen—in danger from the Papists ". No better opportunity had arisen, so far, for a public display of that blind, anti-Catholic hatred which was a principal ingredient in the religion of those who brought about the settlement of 1559.

The first stage in that propaganda was the government's institution, in November, 1584, of the famous patriotic " Association ", which of itself suggested a nation clearly divided into Protestants—loyal to queen and country—and Papists, the would-be murderers of the queen. The bond which the council drew up for all the members of this brotherhood to sign opens with a declaration that to defend princes against those who menace their lives is a duty imposed on all subjects by God Himself. And so, " finding lately by divers depositions, confessions, and sundry advertisements out of foreign parts . . . [that there have been designs against the life of the queen] for the furtherance and advancement of some pretended title to the crown, [so that, if God had not intervened, the queen must have been dethroned or murdered] We acknowledge ourselves bound . . . to withstand all such intenders . . . of what degree soever . . . [and bound to make this declaration, viz], We . . . calling to witness the name of Almighty God . . . bind ourselves, everyone of us to the other, jointly and severally in the band of one firm and loyal society ; and do hereby vow and promise by the majesty of Almighty God, that . . . we will . . . pursue . . . all manner of persons, of whatsoever state they shall be . . . that shall attempt by any act . . . to the harm of [the queen]. And if any such wicked attempt . . . shall be taken in hand . . . whereby any that have [or pretend to have] title . . . to the crown [at the queen's death, may succeed] . . . we . . . bind ourselves never to accept any such pretended successor [in whose favour the deed is done.] And we also further vow . . . in the presence of the eternal and everlasting God, to prosecute such person or persons to death . . . and to act the utmost revenge upon them . . . [And] this our Loyal Band and Association we do also . . . confirm . . . by our oath corporally taken . . . with this express condition—[that if any associate fails, the rest will prosecute him as a perjurer and a public enemy].[2]

This Association, it is very obvious, " placed [the Queen of Scots] at the mercy of her enemies, who might, at any moment, plead a pretended plot

---

[1] As for " the long campaign ", does not Conyers Read (III, 1) open his chapter, *The Babington Plot*, with a reference to Walsingham being " finally enabled, after some eighteen years of ceaseless effort, to bring [the Queen of Scots] to the reckoning ? " And the crime of 1568, for which a reckoning was due ?   " Yet in pausing beside the grave of a very charming and a very unfortunate woman, one ought not to forget that she was perhaps, in herself, as great a menace as ever threatened the safety and welfare of England under Elizabeth " ; *ibid.*, 65.

[2] For the full text cf. Steuart, A. F., *The Trial of Mary, Queen of Scots*, 31–32.

in justification of her murder ".[1]   The bond was the act of the council, and was offered for signature as the newly-elected parliament assembled, November, 1584.   It was signed " by every man who had anything to fear from the displeasure, or anything to hope from the favour, of his sovereign ".[2] And this sacred engagement was sworn, in a kind of Protestant religious service, in the parish churches throughout the country.[3]

And then the government turned to give it sanction of law.   In the first statute of the new parliament it was enacted : [4] if any invasion or rebellion were made, " by *or for* any person that may pretend any title to the crown ", or if anything were " compassed or imagined " tending to the hurt of the queen by, or with the privity of, such a person,—a special commission could be set up to examine " the offences aforesaid " and give sentence ; and next, this sentence being published by proclamation under the Great Seal, the person sentenced would be excluded and disabled for ever from the Crown, and, also, all the queen's subjects " may lawfully kill every such wicked person, by whom or by whose means, assent or privity [either the invasion has been attempted, or the deed] against her Majesty's person compassed or imagined ".[5]

Should the queen actually be murdered, then, without further formality, the " person by *or for* whom " the deed was done shall be put to death, and all subjects are licensed to " pursue to death " those responsible for the crime.[6]

No subject, it is further enacted, is to be punished for anything he does in carrying out this law.   And as to the members of the Association, if they carry out the killing to which they are vowed their act will be taken as done by the authority given in this statute.

This Act and the companion law, already described, that made it death for the new priests even to come to England,[7] must be the bloodiest ever passed by a legislature whose members had any semblance of freedom in their actions, and who made any pretence of Christian ideals in their morality. Unless the killing of hostages can ever be justified, these are Acts prescribing what is bad in itself, and what cannot ever be made good.   And even if the explanations suggested by apologists for the Elizabethan tyranny really explained how such statutes came to be devised, and cleared the responsibility of those who made them, they would not change the moral character of the thing done.   But do the explanations offered really hold ?

The most obvious explanation is that the men responsible for these laws were men who would stick at nothing that would serve their purpose, provided they could, as we say, " get away with it ".   And, to confess my interest, I

---

[1] Lingard, VI, 371–372.   Or, as a later historian expresses it, " No clearer intimation could have been made to Mary that, if the plotting continued, her life would be in danger, if not actually forfeit ".   Black, 327 ; and Neale, very pithily, " a declaration of lynch law aimed at Mary, Queen of Scots ", *Elizabethan House of Commons*, 290.

[2] Lingard, *ibid.*   [3] Pollen, *The Month*, July, 1902, 71.

[4] 27 *Eliz.*, c. 1 ; Prothero, 80, 83.   Full text in Steuart, A. F., 33–35.

[5] The italics have been added, and the order of the last seven words reversed.

[6] Italics added.   [7] 27 *Eliz.*, c. 2.   Cf., *supra*, p. 344. n. 2.

will say plainly that I believe Burghley to have been such, Leicester of course and, in what relates to Catholics, Walsingham also.

Is it the case that what has been called " the Protestant Association ",[1] and that statute which legalised it, were the outcome of spontaneous national alarm, and of genuine anxiety, on the part of the government, that the queen was likely to be murdered ? It is customary to prove the existence of the alarm by a reference to the killing of the Prince of Orange, July 10, 1584, at the orders of Philip II, and to the schemes of 1582–1584 in which English Catholics had a part : " The news of these plots roused England to fury ; a voluntary Association was formed."[2] But none of these plots were directed to the killing of the queen.

An offer had indeed been made, to the Duke of Guise, in 1583, to see to this (by George Gifford) and rejected—but this incident played no part in generating the scare of 1584.[3]

Presently, within the parliamentary session now beginning (November, 1584), there would come the trial and execution of William Parry, with the sensational revelation (as one of his crimes), " That he directed letters to Gregory, the Bishop of Rome, certifying him of his intention and purpose aforesaid [i.e. to kill the queen], and desired absolution at his hands."[4] But the government already knew all that was ever to be known about the Parry plot long before the Association was launched, and even before Orange was killed. And never did it make any use of this marvellous material until difficulties arose in the debates on the Association Statute, and on the companion project that made it death for the new priests even to appear in England. Not until Parry, M.P. for Queenborough, attempting some super-feat of secret service ingenuity, spoke against the second statute as inhumanly cruel, did the government act. They then produced, in order to finish off Parry—the spy who knew so much and who could no longer be trusted— and to afford proof how necessary were these new bloody laws, the story Parry had told them months before. and which had then left them unmoved.[5]

From Throckmorton's admissions in December 1583, and from the papers (and admissions) of the Scots Jesuit, Father William Crichton, in September 1584, the government did indeed know that schemes for invading England and liberating Mary had again been in consideration between Guise and Philip II and the pope. But the only sign of any intention, or resolution or plot to murder the queen came from another quarter altogether, the talk of the half-witted John Somerville—that was a means to bring about the conviction of his wealthier father-in-law, Edward Arden, late high-sheriff of Warwickshire, and Leicester's enemy.[6]

---

[1] Pollard, *H.E.*, VI., 387. [2] *Ibid.*, 386.

[3] Not very surprisingly, if it be the fact that the offer was made " apparently with the approval of the English government " (A. Gordon Smith, *The Babington Plot*, 255). For " the very interesting conspiracy of George Gifford ", cf. Pollen, in *The Month*, June 1902 (607–614). It is to this offer that the letter of the nuncio in Paris refers (May 30, 1583), *supra*, p. 324, n. 2. [4] From Parry's indictment, quoted A. Gordon Smith, *William Cecil*, 218.

[5] For Parry, cf. the all but unnoticed study by Pollen, *The Month*, July, 1902.

[6] Very little has been printed about this affair, or plot, " if indeed it may be designated by the name plot ", Conyers Read, II, 381, n. 1. This note and a paragraph in Pollen (*The*

And although it was, indeed, " less than four months " after the murder of Orange that " the Council drew up the so-called Bond of Association ",[1] supposedly the product of a national movement of loyal anxiety caused by that event, it was all of four months : a long time for the horror of the murder to be in labour with the spontaneous reaction that figures in so many books—and not books (of course) by Protestant writers only.

That the killing of Orange, on July 10, 1584, caused an immensity of excitement no one will doubt. That this was excellent material for the government, arrived at a critical stage of its duel with the Catholic revival, is also true. And the way in which the killing was brought about—i.e. the victim outlawed by royal proclamation, for his alleged crimes, and all and sundry invited to kill him, with a promise of protection and of reward—is the pattern for what is now enacted in regard of the Queen of Scots, nowhere, so far, associated by any of her enemies with a desire to have Elizabeth murdered. Nor, of course (under the statute), need she have such a desire, nor anything more than the knowledge that such a murder is being considered, for her to be placed at the mercy of the daggers—swords, perhaps : daggers are hardly English—of the Association.

Although the Queen of Scots had never been a principal actor in the affairs of the English Catholics—or indeed an actor at all—her disappearance from the scene affected their immediate history very considerably. Whatever hope any of them may have had from the thought that Elizabeth's successor was certain to be a Catholic—or that Elizabeth might one day be displaced by her Catholic heir—was now gone, irrevocably. And when the pope, in the summer of 1587, gave the red hat to Dr. Allen, he could speak of his act as meant to console the English Catholics for the loss which they had suffered in Mary's death.[2] But more important than even this sense of loss, was the new problem, to whom should the Catholics now look as their hope, to Mary's son, the young King of Scots, or to the King of Spain, to whom Mary had made over her rights and her claims ? And upon this difference the handful of Catholics abroad, priests and laymen, who alone had the freedom to be politically active, were now to fall into a most bitter controversy that did not cease until the accession of James I, sixteen years later. Not even the catastrophic failure of the Spanish patron, in the year that followed Mary's death, could teach these politicians to see reality as it lay before them. The lesson was obvious. Henceforward any such controversy must indeed be " a meaningless anachronism ",[3] but less than ever does *phronēsis* rule their minds.

Month, 1902, 616) are the leading accounts. Black, 326, is in error saying Somerville was executed : he was found strangled in his cell. It was Edward Arden who was hanged, drawn and quartered. Somerville's wife and sisters were also sentenced to death and a priest, Hugh Hall, who, however, saved himself by becoming a spy in Walsingham's service (Conyers Read, as quoted). That Somerville was well known to be out of his mind seems certain.

[1] Black, 326–327. This account does not mention the general-permission-to-kill clauses of the statute, although the author does describe the government's act in setting up the Association as " this appeal to Texan [!] justice ", 327.

[2] Cf. the *Acta Consistoralia*, in Knox, 297.   [3] Meyer, 375.

For in the summer of 1588, that "enterprise" for which Allen and Persons, Morgan, Paget and the rest, had prayed, and worked, had at last been organised and set in motion—though not for the sake of the cause that was theirs. How the Spanish Armada sailed, on May 31, from a land which months of military preparations, and of endless religious exercises, had keyed up to a pitch of fearful anxiety rather than to expectation of triumph ; of all that happened, some weeks later, in the English Channel and in the narrow seas off Dunkirk, and then in the ocean to the north of Scotland and the west of Ireland ; of the extraordinary four months' silence which, in continental Europe, fell upon the fate of the fleet from the day it sailed—to be broken, in October, by the first, false rumours of triumph ; of the relief with which non-Spanish Europe learnt the truth ; all this is one of the best-known dramas of modern history.

Foremost among the doubters, before even the fleet sailed, was the pope, Sixtus V. He doubted whether the fleet would ever sail, and whether it would not be beaten once it met the English ; and, also, whether it would not be as well for the future of Catholicism if it were beaten. This pope had succeeded to the great patron of the seminaries and the missions, Gregory XIII, in 1585.[1] He was something like twenty years younger than his predecessor,[2] a professional theologian where the other had been a lawyer ; a Franciscan friar, successor to a pope who in thirteen years did not give the red hat to a single religious on the principle that monks should stay in their monasteries ; critical of the Jesuits, where Gregory had been to them all that was fatherly. And where Gregory had had but one real fault to find with the King of Spain —his everlasting delays—this successor set himself to correct, like another Hildebrand, the chronic mischief of Philip's conception of himself as a vice-pope for his own dominions.[3] Only twelve months before the Armada sailed Sixtus V was speaking of excommunicating the king,[4] and he spoke of it yet again in 1590.[5] Philip II was, of course, the ruler of a good half of the Italian peninsula ; and he was now master, once more, of the southern half of the Netherlands ; France seemed about to break up and the Spanish king to be about to impose upon the country a king of his own choice. " It is feared [in this court of Rome] ", Philip's ambassador informed him, "that if France were to succumb, Italy too would become the slave of your Majesty." [6] The pope's dilemma was great. He " could not deceive himself as to what would happen to the Holy See if there should be a complete victory on the part of the world-wide power of Spain [it is the Armada that is meant] for the usurpations of Philip II in ecclesiastical matters were still continuing and were giving rise to constant disputes ".[7]

---

[1] Felice Peretti, elected, after a three days' conclave, April 24, 1585.

[2] Gregory XIII, born Jan. 1, 1502 ; Sixtus V, born Dec. 13, 1521.

[3] Pastor describes it succinctly, " The aim of the King of Spain to assume the tutelage of the Church, and in a sense to share the office of the supreme apostolate with the occupant of the Apostolic See . . ." Vol. 21, p. 263.

[4] Aug., 1587. Pastor, Vol. 21, p. 269.   [5] *Ibid.*, Vol. 21, pp. 348, 350.

[6] Quoted Pastor, Vol. 21, p. 317 : no date given, but somewhere in 1589.

[7] Pastor's words, *ibid.*, p. 272.

The immediate importance to this particular history of this new, vigorous, strong-minded pope is not, however, his anxiety as to where Spanish Caesaro-papism would end, but the help which he gave the Caesaro-papist king towards the conquest of England. The convention of July 29, 1587, which the pope signed, has long been known.[1] On three conditions the pope pledged himself to give the King of Spain a million in gold (i.e. of *scudi*)—Philip had refused his offer of troops. Half the sum was to be paid once the Spaniards had landed, and the rest when they had won. The three conditions were : that the fleet sailed before the year 1587 was out ; that the future king was not to be chosen by Philip alone, but with the pope's consent, and he was to agree to receive England from the pope, as a fief ; that all church property confiscated during the Reformation century was to be restored.[2] The treaty was kept so secret that not until twelve months later did any of the cardinals know of it.

Sixtus V, for the five years and a little more that he reigned, endured all the torments of a capable man impossibly placed. For the English queen as a ruler he had, it seems, unbounded admiration. Had she only been a Catholic ! What an ally to counter the King of Spain, and to make up for the succession of *fainéants* in France ! And—the incredible thing is true— the pope actually endeavoured to convert her : [3] little can he have known of the reality of that personality, as little disposed, at fifty-five, to be the instrument of Sixtus V, had she been a Catholic, as she had been disposed, at twenty-five, to take lessons from Geneva or Zurich. Meanwhile, had Sixtus but known it, the pope had, in fact, as little influence upon her Catholic subjects, in politics, as ever he could have had upon the queen. And Burghley, in a manifesto broadcast in French as well as English,[4] was able to taunt the pope and the King of Spain, once the crisis was past, with the fact that not a Catholic anywhere in England had shown any sign of pro-Spanish feeling ; and to list some of the outstanding instances of their patriotic action. Which did not interfere with the government's plans to hearten the bitterest of its own supporters by a whole series of executions of Catholic " traitors " in the weeks that followed the victory.[5]

As part of the campaign of 1588 Allen had been induced to write—or to set his name to—an attack upon Elizabeth and her régime the language of which recalls, at times, the effusions of Knox and Ridley. This tract was written for distribution, once the Spaniards had landed, to be a means to rally any Catholics who still wavered. Printed off by the Netherlands government at Antwerp, it received no publicity at all, but it fell into the hands of

---

[1] It is printed in Meyer, 520–523, from a copy in the Vatican Archives.

[2] As though the pope had not, in the most solemn manner, condoned the possession of it thirty years before !　　　　　　　　　　　　　　　　[3] Cf. Pastor, Vol. 22, pp. 33–35.

[4] See notes on Illustrations, nos. 28, 29.

[5] Aug. 28, 5 priests, 1 friar, 2 laymen, in London ; Aug. 30, 1 priest, 1 woman, 4 laymen, at Tyburn ; Sept. 23, 1 priest, at Kingston-on-Thames ; Oct. 1, 3 priests and 1 layman at Canterbury, 2 priests at Chichester, 1 priest at Ipswich ; Oct. 5, 2 priests and 1 layman in London. For these events cf. Pollen's introductory notes to the documents in C.R.S., V, 150–165.

Elizabeth's ministers,[1] with what effect—as confirming the worst they had ever said, of Allen and his priests—may be guessed. Elizabeth is now spoken of as " an incestuous bastard, begotten and born in sin of an infamous courtesan ". There is a wealth of detailed abuse about her private morals no less than about her public policy, and the Catholics are invited to rise against this " infamous, depraved, accursed, excommunicate heretic ; the very shame of her sex, and princely name ; the chief spectacle of sin and abomination in this our age ; and the only poison, calamity and destruction of our noble Church and Country ". The mask has indeed slipped off, we may imagine the other side proclaiming, as it compared the language of this extraordinary manifesto with earlier works put out under the same signature.[2]

In the shorter *Declaration*,[3] also printed under Allen's name, it is related how the pope, seeing that without " the deprivation and deposition " of Elizabeth " there is no hope to reform those states " (which, oppressed by " pitiful calamities " are " become as infected members, contagious and troublesome to the whole body of Christendom ") has appealed to the " King Catholic of Spain " to use his armies to bring this about. And the pope, to make known how justly he is acting, and " to manifest God's judgments upon sin ", herewith sets out the case against the queen in detail— twelve points in all. And, so says the manifesto, the pope, now, " doth renew the sentence of his predecessors Pius V and Gregory XIII "[4] and excommunicates her anew and deprives and deposes her, and releases all her subjects from all oaths and obligations towards her, and commands that none yield her obedience of any kind, but, on the contrary, that all aid this work of her chastisement so that, the queen " which so many ways hath forsaken God and his church . . . may, abandoned of all, acknowledge her offence ".

These words are to bind from the moment " the inhabitants of the said country " have knowledge of them, upon which they are " to unite themselves to the Catholic army conducted by the most noble and victorious prince, Alexander Farnese, Duke of Parma, and Placentia, in the name of his Majesty . . .". Let there, however, be no mistake. It is not the intention of the King of Spain " to invade and conquer these kingdoms ", to " bereave of liberty or livelihood " any save " rebels and obstinate persons ", or to change the laws—except what " common accord ", between the pope, the king, and " the states of the land " shall decide is necessary for " the restitution and continuance of the Catholic religion, and punishment of the usurper and her adherents ".

There is to be punishment, also, for others, it seems. While care will be taken " to save from spoil the Catholics of these countries, which have so long

---

[1] Cf *supra*, notes to the Illustrations, nos. 25, 28.

[2] Cf. the comments of Conyers Read (II, 279, n. 2), " Of course . . . the charge against the priests on political grounds was greatly strengthened . . . particularly after Allen published his virulent pamphlet just before the coming of the Armada ". Allen, of course, never published it at all—the folly of the business did not go so far as to broadcast the fate of the bear before the bear was taken.

[3] A broadsheet printed in T.-D., III, xliv-xlviii.　　　　[4] In fact this was never done.

endured ", mercy will be shown " to such penitent persons as submit themselves to the Captain-General of this army "—even to some who pass for heretics. It was now all but forty years since the heretics established themselves in England as the government. A good half of the population had been born and had grown up to maturity under this rule ; and the children of many of these were now on the threshold of adult life. And whoever it was that drafted this extraordinary document is so remote from such an element of reality, that he now sets down this most amazing sentence of all, " Yea, for so much as information is given, that there be many, which only of ignorance or fear be fallen from the faith, and yet notwithstanding are taken for heretics ; Neither is it purposed, presently [i.e. immediately] to punish any such persons, but to support them with clemency, till by conference with learned men and better consideration, they may be informed of the truth, if they do not show themselves obstinate."

Finally, rewards are promised to whoever captures "the said usurper or any of her complices"—there is not, very notably, that invitation to all and sundry to murder the queen which we might have expected as inevitable from " plotters " such as the usual commentary on, say, the Sega correspondence, has in mind. Safe conduct is offered " to such as will resort to the Catholic camp, to bring victuals, munitions and other necessaries ", and a Plenary Indulgence to those, " being duly penitent, contrite and confessed ", who in any way assist " in the deposition and punishment of the above-named person, and . . . the reformation of these two countries ".

Burghley did not, however, publish the *Admonition* far and wide. England was not yet so whole-heartedly Elizabethan that such a hostile blast could have no other effect than to bind the nation still more closely to the queen. It could not yet be taken for granted that knowledge of such a work would bring harm to the Catholic cause, most of all.[1] And from the Catholic side there came, presently, a lengthy reasoned attack on the basic principle that underlay all this papal policy of recovering the lost provinces by force of arms.[2] On the facts, this writer denounced the motives of the papally chosen champion— the King of Spain's first, and real, interest was the extension of his own empire. He denounced, also, the quality of the king's Catholicism : what of the cruel exploitation of the natives in the Americas ? what of the king's usurpation of ecclesiastical jurisdiction, his ignoring the rights of the Church ? And Catholics must face the facts, "Wherefore, I think, we must yield to the time ; and for a time bear the yoke which Christ hath laid upon us with all humility ".

[1] Here is good Protestant comment on another event of this same year, September 5, five weeks after the defeat of the Armada. " Robert, Earl of Leicester dieth, who in his time became the man of greatest power (being but a subject) which in this land, or that ever had been exalted under any prince since the times of Piers Gaveston and Robert Vere, sometime Duke of Ireland . . . [so hated] that all men, so far as they durst, rejoiced no less outwardly at his death, than for the victory obtained of late against the Spanish navy " ; from Harrison's *Chronology*, still unpublished, quoted Harrison, 272.

[2] *An licitum sit Catholicis in Anglia arma sumere et aliis modis reginam et regnum defendere contra Hispanos?* Its author is given as a priest, Wright. An English version (? the original) is printed in Strype, *Annals*, III, ii, 583–597.

Here is an important sign of coming divisions among the Catholics. And, no doubt, the stories of the ill-treatment of the English volunteers who served with the Spanish forces would help to strengthen the case of such a writer.[1] Certainly the thousands of Catholics at home, for whom these publicists claimed to speak, would pay scant attention, after standing by the queen in the crisis of 1588, to leaders who still placed all their hopes on the national enemy.

In 1591 the queen issued a proclamation [2] which denounced the missionary priests more fiercely and contemptuously (and mendaciously) than ever before : " a multitude of dissolute young men who have, partly for lack of living, partly for crimes committed, become fugitives, rebels, and traitors." The seminaries were " certain receptacles ", where they were " instructed in school points of sedition ", and whence they were sent back to England to persuade the queen's subjects " to renounce their natural allegiance ", promising them, as the fruit of a Spanish invasion, the loot of " the possessions and dignities of our other good subjects ". Who will be astonished that it was in kindred style that Persons now wrote what " was at once an indictment and a justification " ? [3] The priests, he told the queen, " are not descended from the dregs of mankind like your ministers of the Word . . . there are more flowers of nobility in the three seminaries of Rome, Rheims and Valladolid than among all your clergy at home " ! And in words that Penry might have borrowed, he warned the queen, " Learn this, Elizabeth, that God is, and that He is the same who has chastised other kings, queens and monarchs and emperors before thee and far more powerful than thou art ".[4]

A new note is beginning to appear in the polemics of the mission. Not every one of the missionaries agrees that the novelty is to be encouraged. Presently the mission will experience internal divisions, and the same new note will sound loudly in the literature which both sides will put out— sounding a decline in charity it will testify that the golden age is coming to an end, that the " finest hour " (for the leaders) is running out.

Before the great controversy began, yet another Catholic book had appeared in which Persons had at least a share ; and it drew the attention of all England to him and roused the queen's animosity to the full. Elizabeth's fury, whenever the question of her successor was raised, had not abated after nearly forty years' rule ; and for a speech in the parliament of 1593, in which he asked the fatal question, the intrepid Peter Wentworth had, yet once again, been thrown into the Tower. And now, the very next year, it was Persons who took up the terrible topic.[5] Seven years before this, he had worked out,

---

[1] For this cf. Meyer, 245–246 and 357–358, using Persons' letter of April 4, 1597, to the secretary of Philip II, printed in Knox, 330 and foll.

[2] Oct. 18. Printed in Fr. Robert Southwell's reply, *An Humble Supplication*, etc. (1953).

[3] Meyers, 352. Persons' book was entitled : *Elizabethae Angliae Reginae . . . saevissimum in Catholicos sui regni edictum . . . Cum responsione ad singula capita . . . per D. Andriam Philopatrum presbyterum.* . . . Lyons, 1592, 1593. For other editions, cf. Gillow, V, 279.

[4] *Ibid.*

[5] *A Conference about the next Succession to the Crowne of England.* . . . Published by R. Doleman . . . 1594.

along with Allen, the rights of Philip II to the English throne, as the descendant of Edward III. What he now offered was a dispassionate legal and historical treatise, that concluded in favour of Philip II's daughter, another Elizabeth—Elizabeth II, had Persons had his way ! The two small volumes, coming at this precise moment, had the kind of success that filled all Catholics with dismay.[1] In the years to come Persons' Catholic opponents seized on his publication of the work as one of the major disservices done to the Catholic cause. In the history of the quarrels about to begin it has the importance that it gave to men who were already less than confident about Persons' wisdom as a leader, the best of pretexts for open revolt when next he moved in public affairs.

That next move was Persons' reputed share in the first stages of what has come to be known as the Archpriest Controversy. And between the crisis of the book on the succession and this later, really appalling dissension, there had come, in 1595, the quarrels that divided the thirty priests still imprisoned at Wisbeach. In these troubles a Jesuit, Fr. William Weston, was involved, not, by any means, as a fomenter or encourager of quarrels, but as a *casus belli*. The real quarrel was between these secular priests, the majority of whom would have liked to see this Jesuit act as a kind of informal superior of their common life. Inevitably, the Jesuit in charge of the fathers at work in England, Fr. Henry Garnet, was applied to, for advice and permissions, and so also drawn in. And, as various secular priests were invited to arbitrate, the news of the " stirrs " spread through the whole Catholic body. After nearly a year of dissensions, in which (it will readily be believed) more than one bitter thing had been said that would not soon be forgotten, a peace was patched up.[2] And this was barely done when, in the seminary at Rome, dissensions broke out between the students and the Italian Jesuits who, for sixteen years now, had administered the college. To deal with this crisis Persons was recalled from Spain,[3] and such was his personality that, by his mere presence and friendliness and willingness to listen, the crisis passed away without any permanent bad effect on the college life. " He whom we most feared, and whom we accounted for our greatest enemy, hath been our greatest friend ", one student wrote.[4]

These three crises, in three successive years, are the measure of what Allen had been to this extraordinary generation of English Catholics, their lot cast, as the great leader himself had noted, in " this exile, which of itself breeds murmurings, complainings, contradictions and discontents ".[5]

---

[1] The General of the Society of Jesus, realising " that Persons was exposing the whole Order to obvious peril for the sake of an impossible project " (Pastor, Vol. 24, p. 43) wrote, March 30, 1594, to prevent publication ; but he wrote too late. Pollen, *The Month* (1903), p. 524, prints the General's letter and Persons' answer to it.　　　　　　[2] Oct., 1595.

[3] Where he had lived continuously since Aquaviva sent him, in 1588, to gain the goodwill of Philip II at a serious internal crisis in the affairs of the Society. (For this, cf. Pastor, Vol. 21, p. 169.) It was during these years in Spain that the English Jesuit's influence with Philip II brought about the foundation of the seminaries of Valladolid, Madrid and Seville.

[4] Edward Bennett to Hugh Griffin, May 16, 1597, T.-D., III, lxxx.

[5] Letter to Agazzari, May 28, 1582, Knox, 136.

For in the year when Doleman's book on the succession was published Allen passed away,[1] sixty-two years of age, broken by constant overwork and the strain of a torturing and long-standing disease. Owen Lewis, who might perhaps have taken his place, died within the next twelve months. And the third great personality among the clergy, Stapleton, presently fell into the illness which was to carry him off three years later. Of the chiefs who had inspired the great days of the mission Persons alone survived.[2]

And from the ranks of the enemies of the mission, Leicester had fallen out in 1588, Walsingham in 1591. Burghley, well past seventy, was slowly falling into the state which some have thought was mocked at in Polonius ; and a new generation, his nephews Antony and Francis Bacon and their splendid patron the youthful Earl of Essex, was busy with endeavours to prevent the transfer of the Lord Treasurer's influence to his younger son, Robert, now in all but name the queen's secretary of state. Elizabeth, too, was ageing ; and then, in one very fateful year, 1598, she lost Burghley at last (August 4), and also saw her great foe the King of Spain pass into history (September 12).

It was not, however, the successor of Philip II whose personality was now to dominate the complicated diplomacy of the Curia Romana, but Henry of Navarre, now Henry IV of France. For, five years before the death of Philip II the Huguenot leader had made his submission to the Catholic Church,[3] and with this conversion the long thirty years of religious wars had ended for France. And in the last months of Philip's reign the new king had brought to an end the war with Spain also.[4] It was part of this settlement that Philip II now organised the Catholic provinces of the Low Countries in a quasi-autonomy, under the rule of his daughter Isabella and her husband the Archduke Albert.

A new Europe was already in sight, as the sixteenth century drew to its end ; and the new spirit abroad affected the fortunes of the English Catholics too, for it penetrated the Curia Romana, happy to feel that in the new France there was raised up a most powerful check upon the long Spanish domination of international affairs. It had been in the teeth of strong opposition from Spain that Pope Clement VIII—a creation of Sixtus V[5]—had ratified, in 1595,[6] the reconciliation of Henry IV, and had accepted him as a Catholic and the lawful King of France. In 1596 the pope had seen this new Catholic king make a treaty of mutual aid with Elizabeth, the old ally of his Protestant past ; and two years later, by the famous Edict of Nantes,[7] the king had

---

[1] Oct. 16, 1594.   [2] Fifty years of age in 1596.
[3] July 25, 1593.   [4] May 2, 1598, Treaty of Vervins.
[5] Clement VIII—Ippolito Aldobrandini—born Feb. 24, 1536, the fourth of seven sons of a Florentine jurist. Like three other brothers he made the papal service his career, as an ecclesiastical lawyer. The Farnese were his first patrons, then Pius V, after whose death his career halted a full thirteen years. Then Sixtus V, within a few months of his election, gave him the red hat, Dec. 18, 1585, and the post of Grand Penitentiary. In 1588–1589, as legate to Poland, Aldobrandini brought to an end a civil war between rival claimants to the throne. He was elected pope, Jan. 30, 1592. Clement VIII was a gentle, kindly man, of great personal piety, a disciple of St. Philip Neri.   [6] Sept. 17.   [7] April 15, 1598.

the *blessed* ~~intentio~~ of ~~his~~ our holly father, and y* ffervent desyre
of y* Cardinall, might w*out such promulticos of ~~false~~
y* *vtrue* ffrvasios and surprisd by y* Cath:kinge: y*
noble ffovers have take place. Ther was also to
~~vnder~~ add more affect to y* ~~people~~ ~~here~~ fores'th to
these terrible prognosticatios, such bodke proplns
in ffrace and in payg cottamg descriptios of
so mighty avemyes purposed for the ~~forsayd~~ conquest, as
though y* armys were *excepy* ~~very might~~ ~~and~~ great and
mighty, yet they war so compleyed in booke, as
in no age, any spavatio of all furcaio, ayeyst
the sarracyns and Turk, was coparable.

By these mreanes, this Quene thus forwarned, and terrifye
tooke occasio w* ~~heud~~ the ayd of hir people being not oly
firmly brodid, but thrughly invitated, for ther
own defece, as all hir whole realm and every corner
was fully furnishd w* armed people o hors & vabt cufo
tooke, and those contynually trayned and exerciseed in
warly manr. no ~~havyg~~ of moray to provide hors,
armer *po* weapo powder and all necessaryes, no ayt
of pvorars and vittells in every borge of y* realm
w*out exceptio. and which as it was most to be marveld
no ma copelled to serve, every ma voluntarly offred ~~he serve~~

Remembraunce for thes warrant to bee made
for theis pursuivant Topcliff gradated at the
counsell table   57

A warrant to the m[aste]r and keper of Bridewell to receive
and kepe as close prisoners Crystofer Bayliss alias Evers
a semynary preest John Bayliss his brother a taylor
Henry Garnuey Cuterdale Anthony kaye And John Coxed yoman
And no prisoner to resort to any of them But not Richard
Topcliff and not Richard Younge who is apoynted to
Examyn them and to provide powder w[i]th them according
to direction gyven to them by the L[ord]s.
                    directed To the m[aste]r and kepe of Bridewell

Another warrant from theis L[ord]s to Richard Topcliff
and Richard younge esquiers to Examyn these sayd
p[er]sons Crystofer Bayliss als Evers a semynary
preest John Bayliss taylor Henry Garnuey Anthony kaye and
John Coxed from tyme to tyme and yf they shall
fynde occasion to compell them or any of them
but onely torture upon the wadole as is shall for
the better understanding of the trewthe of matters
agaynst the m[aster] and the state etc.
                    directed To Richard Topcliff and Richard
                    younge esquiers

                                     112

                                                        (57)

Most gratious Soveraygne, Havinge Sr: Robert Sowthwell of my knowledge, & vn̄ ferrard in my stronge chamber in... I have made him assured for startinge, or hurtinge of him self, By puttinge vpon his armes a payr of hande cuffes: & him so can keepe him cast from... or confronne wt... any, But Nicolas yr vnderkeepe of the Ganthowse & my... Nicolas beinge the man yt... tooke him, by settinge of him into my handes, &...

...

TORTURE II

THE CARDINAL

arranged a *modus vivendi* with his own Huguenot subjects. And, next, the pope was to be brought, for a moment, to the point that the possibility of a *modus vivendi* between the Catholic Church and Elizabeth was actually suggested to him.

It is for this particular detail of a long and complicated story that, to the only historian who has made a special study of the relations of Clement VIII and England,[1] the Archpriest Controversy has any lasting significance. For, in the exchanges between the pope and the English priests sent to Rome in 1602, a matter of months only before Elizabeth died, that new age is foreshadowed when popes will recognise that heretical governments have come to stay, in lands that so recently were Catholic countries; and that the problem, henceforward, is not how best to overthrow a heretical government by force, but how to secure from the heretical ruler a measure of toleration for the Catholics, without appearing to bless—or even condone—the noxious principle that religious differences are unimportant.

Allen had been dead some two years and more when Persons, in 1597, put before the pope, as a means to arrest a disorganisation that must soon mean disintegration, a plan to appoint two bishops to rule the Catholics in England; one only of these would live in England, and his colleague in France or Flanders.[2] But the scheme did not seem feasible to authority. Instead, on March 7, 1598, there was appointed, as the superior not of the Catholic body but of the missionary priests who were seculars, an archpriest and twelve assistants: a novel and—speaking under correction—wholly unprecedented arrangement.[3]

What were things really like in England at this moment? Those who had brought about the disturbances at the college in Rome in 1596 had tried to make the pope believe that the priests and the Catholics in England were, like themselves, most estranged from the Society of Jesus, says a letter from the president of Douay College, January 4, 1597. It is, however, the contrary that is true, he continues, and much good work is being done in England, the faith advancing there as, perhaps, never before.[4] But, eight months later, another well-informed correspondent of the authorities in Rome, Fr. Oliver Manare, the superior of the Jesuits in Belgium, and a most level-headed administrator, is anxious about the " serious rumours that are spreading among the Catholics in England ": echoes, seemingly, of the late anti-Jesuit " stirrs " in the Rome seminary. His news is that priests there are being worked upon, and that trouble is preparing which, it may be, will prove as serious as what happened in Rome,

---

[1] Arnold Oscar Meyer, *Klemens VIII und Jakob I von Engeland*, in the *Quellen und Forschungen aus Römischen Archiven und Bibliotheken*, VII, 268–306 (1904).

[2] The Latin (original) text is in T.-D., III, pp. cxvii–cxix.

[3] *Ibid.*, pp. cxix–cxxiv, for the letters of the cardinal protector, Enrico Caetano, inaugurating this régime. There is some confusion as to whether the archpriest had any authority over the laity; cf. the three briefs of Clement VIII next mentioned.

[4] Richard Barrett to Agazzari, Douay, Jan. 4, 1597, *ibid.*, pp. xcii–xciii.

something worse than anything England has yet seen.[1] The divisions in the Low Countries have their effect on Catholic life in England too.[2] There would, then, be Catholics in England—priests at any rate—who would not receive in the joyous spirit of the sender such news from Rome as Edward Bennett's letter contains, written to the Welshman Dr. Hugh Griffin, now Provost of Cambray, " If you mean to do any good for our country, you must unite with the Jesuits . . ." ; and this too, " The pope hath determined to give all into their hands, and hath already given it ".[3] Already, in September, 1597, one trouble-maker in France, Dr. William Gifford, was writing to a kindred spirit in England, Dr. Christopher Bagshawe, that an appointment of some kind of superior was imminent and inviting Bagshawe to intervene.[4] The cardinal-protector of England had, in fact, been sounding priests in England about this problem, how best to end the state of "no subordination".[5]

The mere chronicle of the controversy that now began would fill a book. What needs to be said is that a small number [6] of the priests subjected to the new official resisted, from the moment the appointment was known to them, on the ground that this was not the pope's act ; and, also, that the most of those who so resisted were by no means scallawags nor trouble makers (*seditiosi*) either by nature or by habit, whether their views about certain Jesuit fathers as ecclesiastical politicians were warranted, or were mere clerical prejudice. The Jesuits cannot be left out of the story, because one reason for the resistance of these secular missionaries was their conviction that the new device of government by an archpriest was the invention of Persons, that it was he who was responsible for the choice of George Blackwell to fill the post, and also for the clause in the archpriest's instructions that bade him consult the Jesuit superior in England before deciding any matters of importance [7]—and that behind all this, alleged, manoeuvring lay the desire to swing the whole body of Catholic clergy in England to support Persons' policy in the crucial matter of the succession to the aged Elizabeth. With which last allegation these miserable quarrels attain the only importance which, in themselves, they ever possessed.[8]

In the fiercely critical years 1580–1588 the only articulate Catholics are the exiles—and about questions of politics they, too, are silent. So silent, indeed, that—this is all but certain—the priests at work in England knew at the

---

[1] Manare to George Duras, assistant to the Jesuit father-general, Sept. 18, 1597, *ibid.*, pp. xciv–xcviii.

[2] To the same, Oct. 12, 1597, *ibid.*, pp. xcviii–cii.

[3] Bennett was one of the " rebel " students, and now won over by the tact and kindness of Fr. Persons. His letter, May 16, 1597, is *ibid.*, pp. lxxx–lxxxii.

[4] Pollen, *Archpriest*, 23.   [5] *Ibid.*

[6] Nearly thirty priests supported the sending of William Bishop and Robert Charnock to Rome in 1598 with a protest ; so Pollen, *Archpriest*, 36.

[7] *Curabit archipresbyter in rebus maioribus iudicium quoque eius, consiliumque acquirere ;* quoted Pollen, *The Month*, Aug., 1902, 186, n. 1.

[8] " Behind the archpriest controversy, which at first sight exhibits nothing but a drama of personal animosities and quarrels to gain the upper hand, great differences on matters of principle lay concealed." Meyer, 420.

time just nothing about the share of their superiors in the various invasion schemes. From the time of the Armada, however, the knowledge surely began to spread among the missionaries that in these years their leaders had been busy tying the Catholic cause to the policies of the Spanish king. Allen's *Admonition* of 1588 and the broadsheet—if these were known— could leave no room for doubting that the leaders had pinned all their hopes for a Catholic future on a conquest by Spanish armies. Doleman's book of 1594 on the succession showed that their hopes were still based on Spain. And now priests in England, hitherto inarticulate, begin to speak, and to reveal that there is an opposition to all this—an opposition to the whole policy of working for the dethronement of the heretical sovereign as an essential condition of their success as missionaries. There is also active the opposition of those of the politically-minded who support the claim of the King of Scots.

The group of priests who doubted whether the appointment of an arch-priest was the pope's act sent two of their number to Rome to beg the revocation of the new system, and to ask, in place of the archpriest, a bishop whom the clergy should elect. They were not even heard but, by papal order, put under house arrest.[1] A papal letter [2] announced that the act of the cardinal protector, instituting the archpriest, had truly been the pope's act, and done by his orders ; but the letter made no reflection on the action of the priests who had hesitated to accept what was done and then appealed. The date of this letter is April 6, 1599.

There followed nine months of " peace ", during which the new dignitary showed, by his actions towards his late opponents, that he was one of that numerous class who should never be placed in authority over their fellows. A new appeal to Rome was soon in preparation among the priests who were prisoners at Wisbeach ; this time against Archpriest Blackwell's alleged misgovernment, and against certain Jesuits said to be his advisers and allies.[3]

Very soon the anti-Jesuit feeling took a very mischievous turn. One of the priests most active in organising the new appeal was Thomas Bluett, a veteran of the first days of Douay College, who was allowed by the government to leave his prison from time to time in order to beg alms whereby to pay the heavy bills for the keep of himself and his fellows there. Bluett, in the spring of 1601, came into the orbit of Richard Bancroft, Bishop of London now for some five years. And Bancroft had no difficulty, apparently, in drawing from the priest enough of anti-Jesuit discourse for the two to come to an understanding. The bishop could hope to repeat with the Catholics something of the success which his detective methods had attained, now ten years ago and more, with the presbyterian party in his own church.[4] And

---

[1] At the English College, with Persons made responsible for their custody. The envoys reached Rome Dec. 11, 1598. They were arrested Dec. 29.

[2] The brief, *Inter gravissimas*, printed T.-D., III, cxxviii–cxxix.

[3] The appeal, with 33 signatures, dated Nov. 17, 1600, is printed, *ibid.*, pp. cxxxiii–cxliv.

[4] Black's pithy summary is fair : " Here at last was the heaven-sent opportunity for which the government had been patiently waiting—the opportunity, namely, of destroying for good

Bagshawe, too, when brought before the council in October, 1598, had already been expounding a similar story. Not all the Catholics, not all the priests, by any means—according to these two secular missionaries—favoured the pro-Spanish policies for which the Catholics were denounced ; it was only the Jesuits who advocated these schemes : the secular missionaries stood aloof from them, were opposed to them, would like to see the end of them—and of the Jesuits, too, whose folly and pride were responsible for the mischief. And as though nothing could be dearer to the government than to see a host of loyal missionaries, free from penal laws, busy reclaiming the lapsed Catholics still nominally " Church of England "—provided only that there were no Jesuits among the missionaries—the priests who organised the new appeal to Rome inscribed on their task-sheet the papal withdrawal of the Jesuits from the English mission.

Here was a simplicity that Sir Robert Cecil and Bancroft knew how to use.[1] They allowed Bluett and four others out of prison, in order to collect the huge fund that the expedition to Rome would call for ; they arranged that, at the appropriate moment, the chosen envoys should be " banished " from England and provided with passports ;[2] and, meanwhile, they offered the group facilities for publishing their case against the other side, propaganda to convince England that Catholics were loyal Englishmen, and the Catholic priests, too—save only the Jesuits and their friends. Presently the attack turned on Persons himself, as the arch-enemy of peace, and Persons, of course, replied, and in kind.[3]

---

the unity of the Catholic party, and of discomfiting the jesuits by drawing the seculars to its side ", *op. cit.*, 377. The one source for the beginning of the Bluett-Bancroft meetings is Bluett's own account prepared for the two cardinals whom the pope appointed to examine the appeal in 1602, the (Latin) text of which is printed in Law, *Jesuits and Seculars*, 153–158 ; the document is summarised in the Calendar, *S.P. Dom.* 1601–1603, pp. 272–273. According to Bluett, he had reported himself to Bancroft, one of the High Commission, sometime in Feb., 1601, as a prisoner at large by permission of the gaoler, in order to forestall denunciation as a fugitive. The bishop showed him letters and books of Persons and other Jesuits which proved " most clearly " that they were doing their best to bring about a Spanish invasion, and to induce various individuals to murder the queen, and then asked him whether the secular priests were of the same mind as the fathers of the Society. The government, said Bancroft, thought all Catholics equally guilty, because all their seminaries were directed by Jesuits and all the priests were trained under Jesuit influences. Bluett assured him that none of the priests, nor any of the leading Catholics in England, had any knowledge of such schemes ; and as proof conclusive that the Jesuits did not enjoy the influence attributed to them, he revealed how the priests were about to appeal to Rome against what influence the Jesuits did in fact possess.

[1] Most of these priests had been prisoners for very many years. When Bluett came to London, in search mainly of advice—the archpriest had forbidden Catholics to give alms to any of these Appellants, he says—it was his first sight of the capital for twenty-four years. There is a touching simplicity about the concluding lines of his appeal to the cardinals, " What have wars and armaments profited us in all these twenty years ? the fleets and the plotted invasions ? all those most bitter treatises against the queen and against the council ? . . . Let us follow in the path where our fathers in God and our martyrs have walked before us, the Bishop of Rochester, for example, and More, and our holy bishops, who peaceably gave their all for the apostolic, Roman faith, and for the authority of the Holy See ".

[2] Cf. Bluett's letter to Mush, July 1, 1600, in T.-D., III, cxlvi.

[3] With " unbecoming warmth ", says Pollen, chastening the personage. But who will grudge such a trifle as this ?

The deputation [1] that went out to reinforce this second appeal [2] reached Rome February 14, 1602. They had their case well prepared, and drawn up (this time) according to the rules. Also, they were well introduced : they now had behind them all the influence, and experience, of the Roman ambassador of the French king. In a changed world the representative of Henri IV counted for much, and what might have been interpreted as a gross impertinence, now assumed the dignity of an affair of state ; we are, indeed, about to assist at the first battle in a campaign that will go on for fifty years nearly, between the kings of Spain and France, for control in the affairs of the Catholics of England. From the very arrival in Rome of the three envoys, February 14, 1602, the French ambassador there, de Béthune, was the " chief patron and promoter of their cause ".[3]

The detail of the running-fight between the two parties, before the commission of cardinals appointed to examine the matter and in the antechambers of various high personages, which filled the next eight months must be read elsewhere. The pope's decision was given in the brief *Venerunt Nuper*, October 5, 1602.[4] The archpriest was admonished very firmly indeed, and yet in kindly words ; the instruction to consult the Jesuit superior was revoked ; the appellant priests of 1598 were cleared of the charge of schism brought against them ; and the pope made a moving appeal for unity. The priests did not, however, obtain the recall of the Jesuits serving in England : their governmental patrons would be disappointed. And their plea to the pope that by removing the Jesuits he might induce Elizabeth to tolerate the practice of Catholic worship drew from him, in an audience, the comment that such hopes were a chimera, and, in the brief, a stern prohibition, under penalty of excommunication, of negotiating with heretics to the prejudice of Catholics *quovis praetextu vel causa ;* and it drew, also, a denunciation of the very idea that the pope could allow himself to be partner to an arrangement which suggested that truth and heresy had equal rights. For it was as such that the principle we call freedom of conscience first drew to itself the attention of the sixteenth-century cleric—whether orthodox or heretic. Whatever the ultimate *modus vivendi*, the principle that truth alone had rights was sacrosanct to almost all, on both sides. For Catholics to seem to propose that the pope should buy off the persecutor by surrendering such a principle was naturally scandalous.

Nevertheless, it was no longer to be unthinkable that the pope and the heretical government might, some day, come to the point of negotiating.

[1] Bluett, Mush, Anthony Champney and Dr. John Cecil, a priest whom the rest had taken into their company in Paris, a capable man, experienced in the ways of courts, possessing the confidence of the government of Henri IV—and, also (what was not then known), a one-time agent and spy of the English government on his fellows, in Spain and in Scotland. A sinister figure ; for all that " no serious loss of credit necessarily accrues to the Appellants for having taken Cecil into their counsels." Pollen, *Archpriest*, 70.

[2] The appeal, of Nov. 17, 1600, had been decided in the appellants' favour before they left England, by the brief, *Cum nobilissimum* of Aug. 17, 1601 (for which cf. T.-D., III, cxlix–cliv). But the defeated party, the superior of the Appellants, Archpriest Blackwell, held up the publication of it until Jan., 1602.

[3] Pollen, *op. cit.*, 70.   [4] For the text, cf. T.-D., III, pp. clxxxi–clxxxiii.

" If I who am a worm and no man could prevail so much with the queen ",
Clement VIII had allowed Bluett to say to him, " what might not your Holiness do, with the aid of the [King of France], towards obtaining consolation
for the English Catholics ? " [1]   And the nuncio at the court of the archduke
in Brussels, Ottavio Mirto Frangipani, so favoured this idea of negotiating
personally with the queen that he put to the pope a plan whereby he should
be kidnapped and carried a prisoner to England. [2]   Pius IV had been only too
anxious that Elizabeth should receive his nuncios.   The intervening forty
years of active hostility to the Catholic faith had put the queen outside the
pale—to say nothing of the sentence of excommunication.   In all that time
the only object for which a pope might decently allow his representative to
cross her threshold would be to receive the queen's submission.   Of that,
Rome knew it at last, there was no possibility at all.   And yet negotiations
could be spoken of !   No fact could proclaim more eloquently that a new
age had begun.

Thomas Bluett, of course, was quite wrong, if he thought that the prospect
of the papal good will had made any impression at all upon the old queen.
On October 2, 1602, just three days before the brief *Venerunt Nuper* was
signed, as it happened, Elizabeth opened her mind to the ambassador of
Henri IV.   The appellants, she acknowledged, were loyal subjects.   Religious
toleration was, however, a thing impossible even to consider.   The strain
of the allowed practice of two religions would be too much for the country
—it would be the end of peace, and the queen could only repeat the liberal
ideal of 1559 : if Catholics confined their Catholicism to their inward thoughts
they would be treated leniently. [3]   The failure of the appellants, then, to
bring about the withdrawal of the Jesuits—a failure proclaimed in the brief
of October 5, and underlined in the prohibition to negotiate with the heretical
government—was hardly the source of the ideas which now found expression
in the queen's proclamation of November 5 : [4]   her last word (as it happened)
on the duties of her subjects who were Catholics, for early in the new year
Elizabeth took ill, and on March 24, 1603, she died.

In its substance—an order to all priests to quit the kingdom within
a specified time—the proclamation of November 5, 1602, only repeats
proclamations of earlier years.   But, like the preambles to statutes, proclamations are a means for the government to explain its mind on questions
of the day ; and to make known, if not the truth about its own intentions,
then, at least, what it desires to be thought is the truth about them.   In
this last of the series directed against the missionary priests the queen is
evidently concerned with the impression made upon zealous Protestants by
the news that the government has been negotiating with the priests.   On the
other hand, while such faithful subjects need to be reassured that there is to

---

[1] Cf. Bluett's account in Law, *Jesuits and Seculars*, 158.

[2] Meyer, 530–531, prints the nuncio's letter, and notes the ironic comment of the pope's
secretary of state, written in the margin : *Il concetto è bellissimo.*

[3] Beaumont to Henri IV, Oct. 2, 1602, in Meyer, 453, from *Teulet*, IV, 264 and foll.

[4] For the text cf. T.-D., III, clxxxiv-clxxxviii.

be no change in policy, the proclamation is evidence that the government
wished to keep whatever new hold it might have obtained upon the priests.
There is no repetition, in 1602, of the slanderous language of the proclamation
of 1591, not even when, at great length, the queen sets out the alleged share
of the priests in the Spanish invasion schemes of the last ten years, or de-
nounces them for books that proclaim the duty of Catholics to fight on the
side of " any enemy the pope shall send, to subdue us and our dominions,
under pretence of restoring the Roman religion within our kingdoms ".

The distinction is noted between the secular missionaries and the Jesuits ;
the country is told of the recent conflict " between the Jesuits and seculars
combined with them . . . and certain of the secular priests dissenting from
them " ; and is made aware that the government is not ignorant of the danger
now that Jesuits and seculars have " very maliciously and wickedly combined
themselves together " for the destruction of the kingdom, namely through
this business of the appointment of an archpriest, by which " almost all
the secular priests . . . have in effect subjected themselves to be wholly
directed by the Jesuits " ; who, says the proclamation, are " men altogether
alienated from their true allegiance to us, and devoted with all their might to
the King of Spain ". So proud and presumptuous are all these priests that
they persecute mercilessly " any of their own sort, being of a milder temper "
who " do but seem to acknowledge the lenity of our proceedings ".

For this division among the missionary priests the government now carefully provides. The Jesuits and those secular priests who are "their adherents"
are to depart the realm immediately. The other secular priests, who protest
that the " continual plots and designs " of their brethren are " most wicked,
detestable, and damnable ", and who offer to be the first to denounce and to
resist by arms all such plots, are given until January 1, 1603, to depart.
Despite the obvious fact, acknowledged in the proclamation, that priests of
the second class are free of the anti-national malice alleged to distinguish
the Jesuits and the seculars whom they influence, and despite the queen's
desire to recognise this difference by a difference in the execution of the laws,
these priests too must suffer, the proclamation explains. The queen's
" natural disposition, ready at all times to apprehend the least cause to shew
mercy ", must be restrained. For even these anti-Jesuit priests, " labour
day and night to win and withdraw [subjects] from their sound and due
obedience ". Every convert they make is, by the fact, a recruit for " our
mortal enemy the pope, increasing his numbers and diminishing ours . . .
the same our enemy having had, as temporal prince, his banner in the field,
and still continuing his warlike stratagems against us ".

The loyal secular priests have, moreover, committed a new kind of crime.
Misunderstanding the queen's " sufferance and benignity ", as it would seem,
their insolence has reached the pitch " as they do almost insinuate . . . that
we have some purpose to grant a toleration of two religions within our realm ".
As for this idea, good men " grieve at it " ; it is " the bad that thirst after it " ;
and as for Elizabeth's own mind about the notion, she herself exposes the
chimera : " God (we thank him for it, who seeth into the secret corners of

all hearts) doth not only know our own innocency from such imaginations, but how far it hath been from any about us once to offer to our ears the persuasion of such a course, as would not only disturb the peace of the church, but bring this our state into confusion ". Yet once again we return to the principle of 1559: for the sake of the Settlement, no toleration of any other religion; and, therefore, the whole code of anti-Catholic laws, which the very opening words of this proclamation now describe as " ordinances, established by advice of our parliament, for the conservation of the true religion now professed in our kingdoms, and for the resisting of all disturbers and corrupters of the same (especially from foreign parts), and the receivers and harbourers of them ". It was in order " to seduce our people from their affection to religion and so, by consequence, from the constancy of their obedience to us " that " those Romish priests " were sent into this realm by foreign authority. And so it is that the subject who is also one of these priests, traitors by definition, is, in fact, less dangerous to England living abroad in the dominions of the queen's enemies, than when he lives at home, under the eye of the queen's government, but ministering *spiritualia* to the queen's other subjects—even the Jesuit, whose ill will and mischief-making capacity, the proclamation suggests, is well nigh infinite.

If these more loyal priests suffer, let them, then, blame for this the " intolerable presumption " with which they have repaid the queen's " notable clemency, never moved but by constraint to think upon any severity ". One concession the queen still makes to them, however. With those, who, before February 1, 1603, present themselves either to some lord of the council, or to the bishop of the diocese where they live " and before them acknowledging sincerely their duty and allegiance unto us, shall submit themselves to our mercy ", the queen " will then . . . take such further order ", as shall seem to her " most meet and convenient ".

The queen has a word for the Protestants who criticise her government's attempt to use the appellant priests. It has been a " further mischief " of her clemency, she declares, that " some other natures, apt to innovations and affected much to their own opinions . . . have broken forth . . . into factious invectives in print . . . as if no care were had by any but a few of themselves, to preserve religion ". The unknown authors of these pamphlets, " we would quickly make . . . to feel the weight of our indignation ", were they discovered.

Twelve weeks later, on the last day of grace allowed them, there came from thirteen of " the other sort of secular priests "[1] a most extraordinary protestation of allegiance, " a victory for the crown . . . although it did not lead to any consequences ".[2] This declaration[3] deserves to be called extraordinary, because what the signatories now promise the queen in proof that their allegiance is as genuine as that of their Protestant fellow-countrymen (the comparison is their own, explicitly stated) is nothing less than this, that

---

[1] The proclamation of Nov. 5, 1602 ; T.-D., III, clxxxviii.
[2] Meyer, 459.　　　　　　　　　　　[3] The text is in T.-D., III, clxxxviii–cxci.

they will not obey any commands from Rome to take the part of conspirators against her or of invaders, even though this be ordered under pain of excommunication ; for, they say, " we do think ourselves, and all the lay catholics born within her majesty's dominions, bound in conscience not to obey this or any such like censure ". This is the heart of the declaration. But it begins by carefully noting that the queen is now asking no more—" [of us who] by the laws of the realm [are subject] to death, by our return into the country after our taking the order of priesthood, since the first year of her majesty's reign "—than a pledge of allegiance. They " are most willing to give such assurance and satisfaction in this point as any catholic priests can or ought to give unto their sovereign ".

The thirteen priests set out their pledge in three parts—the third of which is the declaration already quoted that, in what concerns their allegiance, they will, if necessary, disobey the pope. In the first part they explicitly say that they acknowledge Elizabeth to have as much authority over all her subjects as any of her predecessors enjoyed. By God's law, and according to the teaching of the Christian religion about the duties of subjects, Catholics are bound to obey the queen " in all civil causes ". The word of God, they say, is their ground for now declaring that no authority, no cause, can warrant the Catholic, any more than the Protestant, in an act of disobedience to the queen " in any civil or temporal matter ".

The second part of the declaration is historical—a comment on the policy of the queen considered in relation to the acts of her Catholic subjects and of the Holy See ; and it is, its tone suggests, an acceptance of the English government's justification of the penal code, as set out (for example) in Burghley's tract of 1583. Alone of all the princes who have " departed from the religion and obedience of the see apostolic " Elizabeth, and her kingdom, have been the object, for years now, of conspiracies, and attempted invasions, under the pretence " of restoring Catholic religion by the sword " ; " a course most strange in the world", says the declaration. These "violent enterprises " it is which have brought the queen, " otherwise of singular clemency towards her subjects ", to enact " laws against Catholics " severer than, " perhaps " (say the signatories, tempering their panegyric with a sudden revival of critical judgment), would otherwise ever have been thought of ; Catholics as such, " by reason of their union with the see apostolic in faith and religion, were easily supposed to favour these conspiracies and invasions ". And so, acknowledging as fact one point after another of the official *apologia* for the persecution—including, it would seem, the charge that Catholics have plotted the queen's murder—the signatories seal their confession of their brethren's sins by a pledge, " to all the Christian world ", that whatever "any foreign prelate, prince or potentate" may direct under the plea " of restoring the Catholic religion " in the queen's dominions, they will defend the queen and the country against all attempts, and will denounce to the government whatever comes to their knowledge about plans of this sort.

There follows, next, the pledge that no threat of excommunication will move them from this resolve, and with it a bluntly phrased caveat. There will not be lacking critics to misconstrue the whole declaration, and to use it to discredit the signatories with the pope. To forestall all such, the priests beg the queen to allow them, while they are giving to Caesar what is Caesar's, " to make known by like public act "—nothing less than that they deny the jurisdiction recognised in her by the Act of Supremacy, and that they maintain, what it has been treason to maintain since the first months of her reign, viz. the spiritual authority of the pope. " And therefore we acknowledge and confess the bishop of Rome to be the successor of St. Peter in that see, and to have as ample, and no more, authority or jurisdiction over us and other christians, than had that apostle by the gift and commission of Christ, our Saviour ; and that we will obey him so far forth, as we are bound by the laws of God to do ; which, we doubt not but will stand well with the performance of our duty to our temporal prince, in such sort as we have before professed. For, as we are most ready to spend our blood in the defence of her majesty and our country, so we will rather lose our lives than infringe the lawful authority of Christ's catholic church." [1]

The full story of how this declaration came to be written and signed does not seem to be known. One of the copies of it that survive in the Public Record Office has an additional paragraph stating that, since it was not possible for all the priests to appear, four of them have presented the declaration in the name of the rest ; [2] and against this paragraph there is a note, " This was the explanation of the other, but it was refused ".[3] The text was, then, submitted to the government before they would allow it to be presented ; what was said in it the government had allowed to be said—the plain statement of the priests about their acceptance of the pope's authority as a thing divinely ordained, for example, and their resolve rather to die than deny this.

The list of signatories is interesting. In the first place, Bluett's name is not there—nor Bagshawe's, who had remained in Paris. But two of the recent delegates to Rome have signed, John Mush and Anthony Champney. And with them 7 others of the 33 who signed the appeal of November 17, 1600. One of these 7, Anthony Hepbourn, was presently to take the oath of Supremacy, and 2 others, Robert Drury and Roger Cadwallador, to give their lives rather than do so. Another of these 7 was John Colleton, who had stood in the dock with Campion and the rest in 1581. Francis Barneby had been one of the recent delegation to Rome, but, like Bagshawe, had not gone further than Paris. Finally, there were the original luckless envoys of 1598, William Bishop and Robert Charnock. Bishop was reputedly the author of the declaration,[4] and many years later he was to be the man in whom Rome revived episcopal government in England after an (actual) lapse of sixty years.[5]

---

[1] The text is in T.-D., III, cxc–cxci.
[2] The four were Bluett, Charnock, Hepbourn and Barneby. Pollen, *Archpriest*, 95.
[3] *Cal. Domestic State Papers*, 1601–1603, p. 286.
[4] T.-D., III, 56.
[5] The last two of the bishops deprived by Elizabeth, in 1559, Thomas Watson of Lincoln and Thomas Goldwell of St. Asaph, died in 1584 and 1585. Bishop was consecrated in 1623, Bishop of Chalcedon *in partibus infidelium*, and Ordinary for England and Scotland.

For Meyer, the act of the thirteen priests was a "show of disobeying the pope", put on, as the saying goes, in order to offset (in the eyes of the government) the failure to persuade the pope to withdraw the Jesuit missionaries. And the "path of resistance which the appellants made a show of taking" really led out of the Church and into Anglicanism.[1] It is truer to say that these priests were, in a certain sense, men before their time, when they denied so explicitly that the popes had the right to compel subjects, by threats of excommunication, to rise against an excommunicated sovereign. At a time when the complex problem of the papal authority over Catholic princes was being discussed anew, and when a solution was emerging that seemed unpleasantly revolutionary to such a pope, for example, as Sixtus V, these English priests, in circumstances very far from academic, took to the knot the sword of over-simplification. They stated the fact of their double loyalty so bluntly that it is the apparent incompatibility which now first strikes the reader. The priests do not draw attention to this difficulty ; they do nothing to resolve it. In a document drafted by permission of a government that desired nothing so little as such an explanation, how could they have done this ? whatever their understanding of the technical problem. Although they did not know it, these priests had the future with them. The age when this particular piece of church discipline had any rights had already passed away, and administrators would soon make the *de facto* surrender to this truth ; and moralists, registering this surrender, would invoke it in aid as they re-examined the old problem. What is not a matter of speculation is that the thirteen priests are witness, in 1603, to the continuity, through all the reign of Elizabeth, of that loyalty-despite-the-bull of which Allen had written twenty years earlier. Catholics in England were so loyal in practice, he had been able to say to Burghley, that the bull of 1570 had been a dead letter from the beginning [2]—and Allen had been able to say this without any scandal to his fellow Catholics, even in Rome. The declaration of 1603, indeed, did no more than put into words, on this point, what had been the mind of the Catholics in England for a whole generation.[3]

It is the association of the government and the appellant priests in 1601–1603 that is the novelty which puts it beyond doubt that a new age has begun—whatever the government's motives ; for we are hardly to suppose

[1] Meyer, 455.   [2] *Defence of Catholics*, I, 85–86.

[3] (Sir Thomas Tresham, e.g., had been as explicit in 1583, cf. Anstruther, 175.) In the face of this undoubted fact it was not reconcilable with good faith that the government should proclaim that, because a Catholic refused to abjure the theory of the pope's power to depose, it must therefore follow that he was making ready to act upon that theory, and so, very properly, be punished for his refusal, as one already plotting treason. S. R. Gardiner, writing about a later stage in the development of this government-invented dilemma—the oath of allegiance imposed under James I, in 1606—brings out well the wanton cruelty of such policies : " [the framers of the oath], however, forgot that there would be large numbers, even of loyal Catholics, who would refuse to take the oath. Men who would have been satisfied to allow the deposing power to be buried in the folios of theologians, and who would never have thought of allowing it to have any practical influence upon their actions, were put upon their mettle as soon as they were required to renounce a theory which they had been taught from their childhood to believe in almost as one of the articles of their faith ". *History of England*, I, 292–293.

that Cecil and Bancroft are now of the mind that a real toleration of the practice of Catholicism is the best policy. Events have brought it about, however, that persecutors and victims have met, elsewhere than in the courtroom or the torture chamber. In the inevitable way of humankindness there have even been interchanges that are friendly. The price of the advance is, on the side of the appellants, an admission not only that the past policies of the popes have been all that the state propaganda has described them, but also that there are other Catholics who are truly national enemies and whom the state rightly pursues. Had the willingness to pay such a price developed, had it spread until it affected a notable proportion of the missionary priests, the government would indeed, and within a short time, have gained its end—when the shepherds begin to fight the fate of the flock is certain. As it was, the action of the thirteen priests, out of some 300 and more, did little more, here, than offer to the state the surrender of a scarcely tenable bridgehead.

The possibilities can hardly have been noticed when, a matter of days only after the amended declaration was accepted, the mortal sickness of the queen drove all else from the minds of the government. The long-expected, greatly feared, moment was at hand : and there was still no decision, on the part of any authority, about the succession. But the great men had, long ago, decided for the King of Scots ; Cecil had made all the needed preparations —with the king, with the great personages in England, with the London authorities, with all the paraphernalia of officers of state, heralds, trumpeters and the like. Within a few hours of Elizabeth's death at Richmond, Sir Robert Cecil himself had proclaimed her successor, at Whitehall and Charing Cross and in the city, without a word of opposition, and with the usual ritual of cheering crowds, bonfires, and ringing bells.

CONCLUSION

AND what, now, of the Reformation in England ? Of the problem of the Catholics, for example ? And of that second religious problem, quiescent since the statute of 1593 : what of the antagonists of the Elizabethan Settlement within the Church of the Settlement ? History never finishes, and though to end a book tears the seamless web no less surely than to begin a book, even the longest book must sometime end. A moment in time when one kind of crisis is fading into another may seem appropriate for the artificiality of a close.

Within three years of the peaceful succession, in Elizabeth's place, of the son of Mary, Queen of Scots, come the events we know as the Hampton Court Conference and the Gunpowder Plot, critical for "Puritans", critical for Catholics—and, the second event, especially critical for the view of these last taken in the nation considered as devoted to the nation's religious settlement. And yet, in the aftermath of the plot, because the State, not knowing where to hold its hand, revealed only too clearly that its will to destroy Catholicism remained in all its strength, the gravest divisions among the Catholics which the State had so carefully fostered healed of themselves. The new test of the Oath of Allegiance was to prove the Catholics, as a body, to be unmistakably, unshakeably one.

Some of the Catholics had visited the new king in the closing months of Elizabeth's reign, to assure him of their support and to bespeak his favour. The English Presbyterians had not wasted their time in such futilities ; but when James left Edinburgh for his new realm they organised a statement of their grievances, and in the way traditional at the accession of new rulers, they begged for redress : " We to the number of a thousand ", so the petitioners presented themselves, " the ministers of the gospel in this land ".[1] The matter of the petition was that of all the petitions presented, fifteen to eighteen years before, in the time of Elizabeth. But the major demands—for the abolition of the bishops, and the adoption in their place of the system of elders and deacons, of kirk-sessions and synods—were no longer made. There were no longer any threats of the divine anger for opponents, and the language was most conciliatory. The ministers say explicitly that they are not " schismatics aiming at the dissolution of the state ecclesiastical ". What they long for is " the redress of divers abuses ", and relief from " a common burden . . . of rites and ceremonies " that are of human origin. The features of the Book of Common Prayer liturgy which they find objectionable are listed very simply. They ask for " a uniformity of doctrine [to be] prescribed ", and that " no popish opinion to be any more taught or

---

[1] The text of this, The Millenary Petition so-called, is in G. & H., 508–510.

397

defended ", but without any detail of what they have in mind. Then come the abuses complained of in clerical life and in the episcopal administration. It is now seventy-four years since the famous first session of the Reformation Parliament, and seventy-one since that Supplication of the Commons which was the prelude to the Submission of the Clergy. But all that was then complained of re-appears, substantially, as matter of complaint in this petition : commendams, pluralities, non-residence, excommunications for trifles, extortionate officials and unreasonable fees, overlong delays in ecclesiastical suits, the oath *ex officio*. The old Adam has survived the Reformation unharmed. And as there is yet no uniformity of belief, so there is not yet a ministry of " able and sufficient men ", who " preach diligently . . . especially upon the Lord's Day ". The petitioners ask that ignoramuses be no longer admitted to the ministry, that none be obliged to subscribe to the Articles beyond what the Act of 1571 commands, and to " the king's supremacy ". They also ask for an Act of Parliament to end the ambiguity that hangs around clerical marriage.

From this petition of April, 1603, came the Hampton Court Conference : three meetings in the wonderful country palace that once was Wolsey's, of bishops and divines, with the king presiding, January 14, 16 and 18, 1604. The king did more than preside. He was the principal opponent of the party of the petition, " talking much Latin ", said Sir John Harington, " upbraidings rather than argument " ; and if, as the bishops said, the king spoke by the power of inspiration, " the spirit was rather foul-mouthed ".[1] It was now that the liturgical radicals were told by the king, " I will have one doctrine, one discipline, one religion, both in substance and in ceremony " ; and that their aim, " a Scottish presbytery . . . agreeth as well with a monarchy as God with the devil." If this be all they have to say, was the king's final comment, after the discussions, " I shall make them conform themselves, or I will harry them out of the land, or else do worse ". All that came of the Conference was the great revision of the English Bible we know as the Authorised Version. The pleas of Dr. Reynolds for the imposition of the Lambeth Articles, and for the revival of the Prophesyings were rejected. But certain rubrics in the Prayer Book were made more definite, " that small things might rather be explained than changed ".[2]

This new edition of the Prayer Book is enjoined on all " as the only public form of serving God established and allowed to be in this realm ".[3] The bishops are ordered to see that offenders are punished according to the law that first authorised the book. And " those who mislike the state of religion here established " [4] are plainly told that the changes now allowed are to be taken as final.

Whitgift had been present at the Conference, but he was an old man, and now failing fast. Bancroft had been the effective leader of the bishops. On February 29, before the king's ruling was made public, the archbishop

---

[1] *Nugae*, I, 181, 182.
[2] So the royal proclamation of March 5, 1604, announcing the result of the conference ; printed G. & H., 512-518.   [3] *Ibid.*, 514.   [4] *Ibid.*, 513.

died, thanking God, it is said, that he would not be alive to see how the coming
parliament received the news of the bishops' victory. That first parliament
of James I met on March 19. Within a month the Commons were debating
" the re-establishing of the religion now established ",[1] asserting their right
to do this independently of convocation ; and making proposals that went
directly against the principles of the proclamation of March 5. And in the
long formal justification which they drew up of their general opposition to the
king throughout the session, they told him he had no power " to make any
laws concerning [religion], otherwise than in temporal causes by consent of
Parliament ", for all that they acknowledge the king to be " sovereign lord
and supreme governor in both [spiritual and temporal causes] ".[2]

The contrast is most striking between the seeming unanimity of all good
Englishmen, as Royal Proclamations state the case, and the attitude of the
majority of those good Englishmen who sit in the House of Commons ;
a contrast already evident in all the parliaments of Elizabeth's reign, which
is henceforward to be a permanent feature of political life for a good hundred
years. The life and death struggle between the " new monarchy " and the
parliament has begun. Nowhere will it be more fierce than around the will
of the monarchy with regard to the national religion. The ecclesiastical
system of 1559 has never been accepted without serious reservations—
outside the court that devised it. Now, through its laymen, the party
attached to the reservations will begin to matter more and more. Another
forty years and that party will, at last, have its way. And, to the end, this
party is remarkably consistent. What it will install in the day of its
triumph is what it has never ceased to demand since the very morrow
of the Elizabethan Acts of Supremacy and Uniformity: the perfection
towards which the régime of Cranmer in Edward VI's time seemed to
tend, and which, when there were no considerations of state to stand
in its way, was momentarily realised overseas in the tiny establishments
of the Marian exiles. What the king puts forward as the true religion
established, this party declares to be a novelty that approximates to
Popery. James I, for example, lays down that " preaching ministers " are
to take the Articles of 1563 and the two Books of Homilies " for a pattern and
a boundary, as it were " ;[3] Charles I, that the Articles taken " in their literal
and grammatical sense " contain " the true doctrine of the Church of England
agreeable to God's word ".[4] And to end " the curious and unhappy differences " that continue to " exercise the Church of Christ ", he orders,
in this same declaration of 1628, that " all further curious search be laid
aside "[5]—the curious search which six years earlier, with the same object
in view, his father had hoped to check when he forbade all but bishops,
or deans, " at the least ", to preach on such fundamental doctrines of the
Reformation as " the deep points of predestination, election, reprobation,

[1] Resolution moved April 16, 1604, by Sir Francis Hastings, S. R. Gardiner, I, 179.
[2] Ibid., 183. June 20.
[3] Directions concerning Preachers of James I, Aug. 4, 1622, G. & H., 516.
[4] Declaration, of Charles I, prefixed to the Thirty-nine Articles of Religion, Nov. 1628 ;
ibid., 520, 519.   [5] Ibid., 520.

or of the universality, efficacity, resistibility or irresistibility of God's grace ".[1]

The House of Commons, however, since they perceive " God's religion, in great peril now to be lost ", proceed immediately to propose very different remedies—despite Charles' announcement that he had so acted because " by God's ordinance . . . Supreme Governor of the Church within these [his] dominions ", and despite a complimentary acknowledgment that it was due, under God, to the king's " wisdom and goodness . . . that our holy religion hath yet any countenance at all among us ". There is a party in the church, they say [2]—" the Arminian faction "—" casting doubts upon the religion professed and established ". If this religion " is faulty or questionable in three or four articles ", unstable minds will presently be questioning the rest. And then, not only will there be divisions at home, and a division between the church and " the Reformed Churches abroad ", but these " unstable minds " will turn to Popery.[3] And the Commons propose to remedy the weak and sickly state of the national religion by a more rigorous execution of the anti-Catholic laws, as well as by purging the Church of England of the party that is working to undo the Reformation.

The king's declaration about the Articles has recently proclaimed that he " will not endure any varying or departing in the least degree " from " the doctrine and discipline of the Church of England now established." [4] The Commons, too, insist that the doctrine be not departed from ; they, too, are alive to the importance of the Articles, the " orthodox doctrine " contained in which, " according to the sense which hath been received publicly and taught as the doctrine of the Church of England ", is now being " suppressed and restrained " by the Arminians whom the king is favouring.[5] The Commons have their own touchstone of orthodoxy to propose : what the doctrine is that has been taught hitherto, may be known from the following, they say, namely, the Book of Common Prayer ; the Homilies ; the Catechism ; " Bishop Jewel's works, commanded to be kept in all churches, that every parish may have one of them " ; the public teaching of divinity professors and divines in both the universities ; the Lambeth Articles of 1595 ; the censures, punishments and submissions enjoined and inflicted " upon those that taught the contrary, as Barrow [Peter Baro] and Barrett in Cambridge and Bridges in Oxford ".[6]

For this majority of the House of Commons, then, there is, throughout these years, an orthodox doctrine which is not the same thing as that true doctrine now patronised by the king ; and the members ask, in 1629, for the severe punishment of those divines of the king's way of thinking who, on the controverted points, have been publishing works that are contrary to this orthodoxy. They demand explicitly that " the orthodox doctrine of our Church, in these now controverted points by the Arminian sect, may

---

[1] *Directions concerning Preachers*, G. & H., 517.

[2] Resolutions on Religion, presented by a committee of the House of Commons, Feb. 24, 1629 ; *ibid.*, 521–527. [3] *Ibid.*, 524. [4] *Ibid.*, 519.

[5] *Ibid.*, 525. [6] *Ibid.*, 526.

[be] established and freely taught, according as it hath been hitherto generally received " [1]—*nihil innovetur nisi quod traditum est*, in fact.

In what critical circumstances this parliament was dissolved,[2] just fifteen days after the passage of these resolutions, and how, upon this dissolution, there followed the eleven years " personal rule " of Charles I, are among the facts of English history that are known to all. When, in 1640, a parliament was once again summoned, the new House of Commons soon showed itself of the same mind as the old about the urgency of this question of " the orthodox doctrine ". It consented,[3] for example, to receive a petition which, setting forth a long list of reasons for the abolition, " root and branch ", of the system of bishops, noted how, as a novel defence against criticism, the bishops, "themselves having formerly held that they have their jurisdiction or authority of human authority, till of these later times, being further pressed about the unlawfulness, that they have claimed their calling immediately from the Lord Jesus Christ, which is against the laws of this kingdom, and derogatory to his majesty and his state royal ".[4] Also, one bad effect of the system, so the petitioners say, is " the faint heartedness of ministers to preach the truth of God, lest they should displease the prelates " —this " truth of God " being, it would seem from the passage that follows, those fundamental doctrines about Grace, forbidden, these twenty years, to all preachers but bishops or deans.[5] And when, six months later, in May 1641, the same House of Commons pledged themselves, by oath, to defend with their lives " the true reformed Protestant religion expressed in the doctrine of the Church of England against all popery and popish innovations ",[6] the act is witness, again, to the continuing general acceptance within that church of what was first systematised ninety years before, in the time of Edward VI.

What is the Englishman to believe as the truth revealed by Christ our Lord ? Or, rather, what is he to be made to accept as that truth ? One thing, certainly, is unanimously forbidden him—any return to the belief of his forefathers.

The Catholics, after the coming of the new line of kings, continued to be pursued—and explicitly, now—for the reasons that had produced the penal clauses of the Acts of 1559 : that their religion was not compatible with God's word ; that the Mass, in particular, was an act of idolatry ; and that to tolerate the practice of their religion must mean an increase in the number of Catholics and a continual recruitment from the Church of England. In the fifty years that follow the death of Elizabeth, these reasons will be stated over and over again, by all the parties hostile to the Catholics.

And there is to be a new " case " against these Catholics. While the peace with Spain, that was one of the new king's first acts, made the lie useless that

---

[1] Resolutions on Religion, presented by a committee of the House of Commons, Feb. 24, 1629; *ibid.*, 527.   [2] March 10, 1629.

[3] This is the first session of the Long Parliament—the second parliament summoned in 1640.

[4] The *Root and Branch Petition*, presented Dec. 11, 1640, is in G. & H., 537–545. This quotation is from p. 537.   [5] *Ibid.*, 538.   [6] Also in G. & H., 546.

every Catholic was a partisan vowed to the assistance of the enemy, a new legend was to be propagated of the Catholic as a secret assassin, an Englishman bred to bloodthirstiness by his very religion. The *Book of Martyrs* proved that his religion made the Catholic cruel ; the Gunpowder Plot that it made him treacherous. For whatever the true history of the plot, about one feature of the event there is no doubt at all—that the government seized with both hands the opportunity which it offered for propaganda against the very idea of Catholicism ; and one means that the government chose was the institution of a new holy day, with prayers in which thanksgiving, for the special act of Providence by which the plot was discovered, was made amid expressions of horror at the bloodthirstiness which Catholicism engendered.

Already, before the plot, announcing on February 22, 1604, a renewal of the persecution, the king had explained its religious character : " We hold ourselves obliged . . . to keep our subjects from being infected with superstitious opinions in matter of religion . . . the ministers and instruments of that infection are the priests . . . ordained in foreign parts, by authority prohibited by the laws of this land ".[1] When he addressed the Houses of Parliament, four days after the plot was discovered, the king, making a mock-plea for the Catholics who were innocent, was careful to say that their religion was not thereby acquitted.[2] The Catholics who are innocent of the plot are innocent because, presumably, they are ignorant of what their religion teaches, namely, " that it was lawful, or rather meritorious, as the Roman Catholics call it, to murder princes or people for quarrel of religion " ; a principle, the king notes, " that not even [the sects] of Calicut who adore the devil " maintain. Whereas, what alone led the plotters " to this desperate device ", was " the blind superstition of their error in religion ". As " Popery is, indeed, the ' mystery of iniquity ' " it is not to be wondered at that no Catholics who are really instructed in their religion " can ever prove either good christians, or faithful subjects ".

What few of those who heard the speech would know—and still fewer of the thousands who read it in the account of the plot published by the government—was that the king had been, for years now, in close correspondence with the head of this infamous religion. The pope had repeatedly written, to the archpriest and to the superiors of the Jesuits, commanding them to urge the Catholics to be patient, and to shun all political schemes and plots ; and the pope's nuncios in Paris and in Brussels had been continually active in the same way. And James had thanked the pope most warmly for his goodwill, expressing his sorrow that he could not do as much for the pope in return, in order to prove how deeply the pope's consideration moved him—all this through the English ambassador in Paris, Sir Thomas Parry.[3]

[1] The proclamation is in Wilkins, IV, 376 and T.-D., IV, lvii–lx.

[2] The speech is in the Lords' Journals, II, 358, and there is an extract from it in T.-D., IV, 62, n. 1.

[3] See the letter of Nov., 1603, in T.-D., IV, lxvi-lxxi, also the account in Pastor's *Life of Clement VIII* (Vol. 24 of his *History of the Popes*), pp. 45–60, 70–75. For the whole story of these relations the authority is A. O. Meyer, *Klemens VIII und Jakob I.* S. R. Gardiner describes the very reverse of what actually went on when he writes (I, 203),

And when, the plotters duly executed, parliament turned to enact laws still more cruel against this majority supposedly innocent of the crime, the legend was carefully written into the preamble of the statute.[1] It is " by the infection drawn from " their popish religion that Catholics become " ready to entertain and execute " such practices as the late plot. This was, indeed, " undertaken by the instigations of jesuits and seminaries ", for " the advancement of their religion ", and the plotters were " their scholars taught and instructed by them to that purpose ".[2] It was another statute of this same session [3] that provided that on every Fifth of November, in every parish church, the Act of Parliament establishing the observance of the new holy day should be read, and a special service used of thanksgiving " for the happy deliverance of King James I and the Three Estates of England, from the most traitorous and bloody-intended Massacre by Gunpowder ". In the special prayer which, this day, displaced the usual collect, God was thanked for delivering the King and Parliament, " by Popish treachery appointed as sheep to the slaughter, in a most barbarous and savage manner, beyond the examples of former ages ". And God is prayed, " O Lord, who didst this day discover the snares of death that were laid for us . . . be thou still our mighty Protector, and scatter our enemies that delight in blood : infatuate and defeat their counsels. . . . Strengthen the hands of our gracious sovereign . . . to cut off all such workers of iniquity, as turn Religion into Rebellion, and Faith into Faction ". Should the Holy Communion be administered, a special prayer is to be added wherein, again, God is declared to have " this day . . . miraculously preserved our Church and State from the secret contrivances and hellish malice of Popish conspirators ". And if there is no sermon preached, then one of six Homilies against Rebellion is to be read.[4]

Seventy years have passed since Thomas More went to the scaffold, and the new pattern of English religious life is now determined, in the main, as it will be for another two hundred and fifty years. More's own people are no longer the majority ; they are permanently proscribed, as idolaters and as enemies of their country ; upon them prejudice, no less than policy, continues to inflict penalties and disabilities for the best part of all that time ;[5] and their decline nothing does more to assist, it may be thought, than the

---

" Clement VIII would no doubt have had no objection to playing with James, as an angler plays with a salmon ". Meyer (*England and the Catholic Church under Queen Elizabeth*, 375), steering clear of metaphor, states the fact, " The king knew how to rouse and keep alive in Rome the hope that when once he was at the head of affairs a Catholic era would begin ". Cf. also, Pollen, *The Question of Elizabeth's Successor*, in *The Month* ; May, June, 1903.

[1] 3 Jac. I, c. 4: *An Act for the better discovering and repressing of Popish Recusants.* T.-D., IV, cxiii–cxxi.   [2] *Ibid.*, cxiv.

[3] 3 Jac. I, c. 1.

[4] The quotations are from the service appointed. This special service was laid aside by royal warrant in 1859.

[5] New penal statutes in every reign until George I inclusively, save in the three years of the Catholic, James II.

inability of Rome, during the critical seventeenth century, to establish among them any system of local control. Within the religion now established, these fifty years almost, the great division is rising to its climax, the inevitable convulsion is near, and the disappearance from the unity of the Royal Supremacy of a main element, to rate it no higher, of the primitive English Reformation. The ministers and congregations then expelled will maintain a corporate life outside the establishment, in that periphery where, meanwhile, small settlements of Baptists and Independents have been steadily increasing.

Nowhere, in all this variety of religious experience, does the humanity of the vast army cease to function : everywhere men think and question and compare. If doctrine does not develop, belief changes.

And in all this, where is the mind and heart of the ordinary man ?

APPENDIX I

Middlesex :
   London
   Westminster
Hertfordshire :
   St. Albans
Northumberland :
   Berwick
   Newcastle-on-Tyne
   Morpeth
Cumberland :
   Carlisle
Westmorland :
   Appleby
Lancashire :
   Lancaster
   Preston
   Liverpool
   Wigan
   Clitheroe
   Newton
Yorkshire :
   York
   Scarborough
   Hull
   Heydon
   Thirsk
   Aldbrough
   Boroughbridge
   Knaresborough
   Ripon
Lincolnshire :
   Lincoln
   Grimsby
   Stamford
   Grantham
   Boston

Derbyshire :
   Derby
Nottinghamshire :
   Nottingham
Leicestershire :
   Leicester
Cambridgeshire :
   Cambridge
Huntingdonshire :
   Huntingdon
Norfolk :
   Norwich
   Lynn
   Yarmouth
   Thetford
   Castle Rising
Suffolk :
   Ipswich
   Dunwich
   Orford
   Sudbury
Essex :
   Colchester
   Malden
Salop :
   Shrewsbury
   Bridgenorth
   Ludlow
   Wenlock
Staffordshire :
   Stafford
   Newcastle-u-Lyme
   Lichfield
Worcestershire :
   Worcester
   Droitwich

[1] Cf. the map, p. 19. The county of Durham is not represented. In Rutland and Merioneth there are only the county members.

Hereford :
  Hereford
  Leominster
Northants :
  Northampton
  Peterborough
  Brackley
  Higham Ferrers
Warwickshire :
  Warwick
  Coventry
Bedfordshire :
  Bedford
Buckinghamshire :
  Buckingham
  Wycombe
  Aylesbury
Oxfordshire :
  Oxford
  Banbury
  Woodstock
Gloucestershire :
  Gloucester
  Bristol
Kent :
  Canterbury
  Rochester
  Sandwich
  Deal
  Dover
  Romney
  Hythe
  Folkstone
Sussex :
  Lewes
  Winchelsea
  Chichester
  Arundel
  Midhurst
  Horsham
  East Grinstead
  Shoreham
  Steyning
  Bramber
Surrey :
  Guildford

Surrey (*cont.*) :
  Reigate
  Gatton
  Bletchingley
  Southwark
Berkshire :
  Reading
  Wallingford
  Windsor
  Abingdon
Hants :
  Southampton
  Portsmouth
  Winchester
  Petersfield
Wiltshire :
  Sarum New
  Sarum Old
  Wilton
  Ludgershall
  Malmesbury
  Marlborough
  Devizes
  Wotton Bassett
  Calne
  Chippenham
  Westbury
  Heytesbury
  Hindon
  Downton
  Bedwin
  Cricklade
Dorset :
  Dorchester
  Shaftesbury
  Wareham
  Poole
  Bridport
  Melcombe
  Lyme
  Weymouth
Somerset :
  Bath
  Wells
  Taunton
  Bridgewater

Devonshire :
   Exeter
   Dartmouth
   Plymouth
   Barnstaple
   Plympton
   Tavistock
   Totnes
Cornwall :
   Launceston
   Bodmin
   Liscard
   Truro
   Helston
   Lostwithiel
   Downeshed
   Newport
   Bosinney
   Camelford
   Grampound
   Michael
   Penryn
   Saltash
   West Looe
   St. Ives
Cheshire :
   Chester

Monmouthshire :
   Monmouth
Anglesey :
   Beaumaris
Carnarvon :
   Carnarvon
Denbigh :
   Denbigh
Flint :
   Flint
Montgomery :
   Montgomery
Cardigan :
   Cardigan
Radnor :
   Radnor
Brecknock :
   Brecon
Pembroke :
   Pembroke
Carmarthen :
   Carmarthen
Glamorgan :
   Cardiff

APPENDIX II

THE ELIZABETHAN ICONOCLASM

It would need an entire and lengthy chapter to describe at all adequately the Elizabethan destruction of the Catholic church furnishings, and the care now taken to desecrate and vilify objects which, for a thousand years, had been regarded as sacred, " so that no one popish ornament of all remaineth but is utterly defaced, broken in pieces and put to profane uses ".[1] It may be allowed, since for such a chapter there is not space, to refer to a remarkable account of what went on through the first six years of the régime inaugurated in 1559, set down by the very authorities responsible, and first made public now nearly ninety years ago. This is the *Inventarium Monumentorum Superstitionis*, preserved in the archives of the see of Lincoln, and edited by a Lincolnshire antiquarian, Edward Peacock, F.S.A., in 1866.[2] Here are accounts, given in 1566, by the churchwardens of 150 Lincolnshire parishes, to Elizabeth's commissioners, of the destruction so far accomplished. From this hard-to-come-by work two specimen reports are here reprinted —the spelling modernised and the contractions written out in full. " The greater portion of the returns are the original inventories, given in by the parish officers themselves." [3]

HABROUGH.[4]—Thomas Dagleise and John Webstar churchwardens, 30 April, 1566.

Imprimis one rood with Mary and John and the rest of the painted pictures—burnt Anno ii Elizabeth, Thomas Dagleise and John Hogg then churchwardens.

Item   our rood loft—pulled down, sold and defaced a year ago.

Item   our mass books with the rest of such feigned fables and peltering popish books—burnt Anno ii Regine Elizabeth by the aforesaid churchwardens.

Item   iii altar stones—broken in pieces and laid within the porch, one of them, and thother ii we have made stepping stones of at our churchyard stile.

Item   a vestment, albs, amices and such like linen belonging to the popish priest—the vestment we have cut in pieces and made a pulpit cloth of and of thalbs a surplice of.

Item   our handbells, cruet, crosses, candlesticks and censers, with a sacring bell, and the rest appertaining to the popish service—sold and de-

---

[1] The churchwardens of Little Bytham, in the document to be quoted, Peacock, 51.

[2] *English Church Furniture, Ornaments and Decorations, etc.*, cf. *infra*, Bibliographical Note, *s.v.*, Peacock.

[3] *Op. cit.*, 10.   [4] Peacock, 93.

faced four years ago, Robert Philipson and James Hall (as we think) then churchwardens.

Item banner cloths, banner staves, and a cross staff—broken in pieces the said four years ago.

Item a holy water vat—sold and defaced the said time.

Item a pax, a pix and a chrismatory—sold and defaced the said time by the said churchwardens in the said four year.

Item a sepulchre—sold and defaced this year.

HORBLINGE.[1]—The inventory of all such copes, vestments and other monuments of superstition as remained at any time within the parish church of Horblinge since the death of the late queen Mary, made by Thomas Buckminster and John Burgess churchwardens, the 18th day of March, Anno Domini 1565.

Imprimis the images of the rood, Mary and John and all other images of papistry—one Thomas Wright had and received in Anno primo Elizabeth, which he brake and burnt, John Brown and Robert Peiele being churchwardens.

Item all the mass books, portases, manuals, legends, grails, couchers and all other books of papistry—were sold to John Craile, mercer, by us Thomas Buckminster and John Burgess since the last visitation holden at Ancaster the 19th of February, 1565, who hath defaced the same in tearing and breaking of them to put spice in.

Item the rood loft—taken down by John Craile and John Brown who sold the same to Robert Gawthorne and John Craile who hath made a weaver's loom thereof and made windows and such like things.

Item iii altar stones—are broken, and troughs and bridges are made of them.[2]

Item two vestments—the one hath Thomas Wright of Horblinge, and hath cut it in pieces and made bed hangings thereof. And thother was given to Richard Colson, a scholar, and he hath made a player's coat thereof in Anno primo Elizabeth.

Item two albs—was cut in pieces and surplices made thereof to serve for our church.

Item the sepulchre—was sold to Robert Lond and he saith he hath made a press thereof.

Item the cross, censers, chrismatory, with two handbells, two candlesticks, with cruets and pax and all other things of brass, was broken in pieces and sold to John Skipper since Christmas last past.

Item a holy water vat of stone, broken.

Item three banner cloths—which were given away to children to make players' coats of, anno primo Elizabeth.

---

[1] Peacock, 107.

[2] Bridges—a detail in the inventory of Kelbie in the parish of Haydor will perhaps explain. " Item ii altar stones—which is defaced and laid in highways and serveth as bridges for sheep and cattle to go on so that there now remaineth no trash nor trumpery of popish peltry in our said church of Keilbie." *Op. cit.*, 110.

At Lincoln, in the house of Master John Aelmer [1] archdeacon of Lincoln, within the close of Lincoln, in the presence of the reverend father and lord, Nicholas [Bullingham], Bishop of Lincoln, of John Aelmer, archdeacon of Lincoln, and George Monson, esquire, the queen's commissioners, etc., the 19th day of March, 1565 [i.e. 1566] in the presence of Thomas Taylor, notary public. [2]

[1] Once tutor to Lady Jane Grey, and a future Bishop of London (1577–1594).
[2] The attestation is here translated from the original Latin.

APPENDIX III

Elizabeth and the Punishment of Heresy

That five men were burnt at the stake in this reign for heresy is a common-place of all the text-books. But since the documents are not so well known that reveal the mentality of the persecutors, here, from Rymer's *Foedera* (1713 edition, XV, 740–741) are the formulae for the executions of 1575.

Pro Nicholao Bacon Milite Custode Magni Sigilli Angliae, de Commissione speciali pro Haereticis Comburendis

Elizabeth, by the Grace of God, *Queen of England France and Ireland* Defender of the Faith *etc.* to our right trusty and right well-beloved Councillor, Sir *Nicholas Bacon* Knight Lord Keeper of our Great Seal of England, Greeting.

Where, the Reverend Father in God, Edwin [1] *Bishop of London*, Edmund [2] *Bishop of Rochester*, and our right trusty and well beloved, Sir *William Cordell* Knight Master of the Rolls, *Roger Manwood*, and Robert Mounson two of the Justices of our Common Pleas, with others our Commissioners sufficiently authorised by our Commission under our Great Seal of England, have travailed upon the Examination Hearing and Determination of *John Peeters* and *Henry Turwert* being Flemings born, and now lying in this our Realm, concerning their false Opinions and Sects of Anabaptists, holden and averred by them, wherein they have, before the said *Reverend Fathers* and others our said Commissioners, maintained their said most perilous and dangerous Opinions, for the which they are by definitive Sentence, declared by the said Reverend Father the *Bishop of London*, with the Consent of others our said Commissioners, justly adjudged and declared to be Heretics, and therefore as corrupt Members to be cut off from the rest of the Flock of Christ lest they should infect others professing the true Christian Faith, and are by them left under the Sentence of the great Excommunication to be by our Secular Power and Authority as Heretics punished, as by the Significavit of the said Reverend Father in God the *Bishop of London*, with the assent of others of our said Commissioners, remaining in our Court of Chancery, more at large appeareth, and although the said Anabaptists have since the said Sentence pronounced against them been often and very charitable travailed with, as well by the Ministers of the Dutch Church in the City of London, as by other Godly and Learned men, to dissuade revoke and remove them from their Anabaptistical and Heretical Opinions, yet they arrogantly and wilfully persist and continue in the same,

We therefore, according to our regal Function and Office, minding the execution of Justice in this behalf, and to give Example to others lest they

[1] Edwin Sandys—once a Marian exile.　　　　[2] Edmund Freake.

should attempt the like hereafter, have determined, by the assent of our Council, to will and require you the said Lord Keeper, immediately upon the receipt hereof, to award and make our Writ of Execution, according to the tenor in these Presents ensuing, and these our Letters signed with our hand shall be your sufficient Warrant for the same.

Per ipsam Reginam.

Et Warrantum remittitur praedicto Domino Custodi ut patet inferius.[1]

Brief for the Execution of Judgment against John Peeters and Henry Turwert heretics who are to be burnt.

Elizabeth, by the grace, etc., to the Sherriffs of London, Greeting.

Since it has been made known to us, by the Reverend Fathers in Christ Edwin, by Divine Providence Bishop of London, Edmund by the same grace Bishop of Rochester, and by our faithful and well beloved Sir William Cordell, Master of the Rolls, Roger Manwood [and] Robert Mounson, Justices of the Common Pleas, Alexander Nowell, dean of St. Paul's London, Gabriel Goodman, dean of Westminster, and by others, as Triers, Inquisitors, Judges and Commissioners, sufficiently and lawfully empowered by, among other things, our letters patent given under our great seal, bearing date of 11 May last, proceeding by the aforesaid authority against certain [men] John Peeters and Henry Turwert, Flemings by birth, resident in this our realm of England, defamed in the eyes of good and serious men by enormities like the wicked crime of heresy, and the detestable sect of the Anabaptists, the said John Peeters and Henry Turwert, appearing in person before the said Reverend Fathers and our other commissioners, did, contumaciously and out of a kind of pertinacity, uphold and defend the aforesaid wicked crime of heresy and the detestable sect of the Anabaptists, and each of them did uphold and defend.

By the definitive sentence of the same Reverend Father, the Bishop of London, with the consent of our other said Commissioners, justly, lawfully, and canonically passed against the same John and Henry in this matter, they are now heretics condemned and declared, and therefore to be thrown out and to be eliminated as rotten sheep from the Lord's flock, lest they infect our subjects with their contagion.

* Since, therefore, Holy Mother Church has not anything more that she ought to do and carry out on their behalf, the same Reverend Fathers and the other aforesaid Commissioners relinquished these condemned heretics, John and Henry, to our secular arm, to be punished with the punishment that is appropriate, as was certified to us in our chancery by the letters-

---

[1] What follows is a translation of the Latin original.

* From this point to the asterisk following the writ is almost word for word a repetition of that issued for the execution of Cranmer, for which, cf. this same volume of Rymer, p. 431.

patent set out above of the said Reverend Father the Bishop of London, with the consent of the others his colleagues in this matter.

We therefore, as being zealous for justice, and defender of the Catholic Faith, and determined to maintain and defend Holy Church and all its rights and liberties, and the Catholic Faith, and to root out and extirpate heresies and errors of this kind wherever found (so far as in us lies) and to punish with the appropriate punishment heretics so convicted, seeing that heretics of this sort convicted and condemned in the aforesaid manner, ought, according to the laws and customs of our realm of England in use about this matter, to be burned by fire.

We command that you cause the said John Peeters and Henry Turwert, now in your custody, to be taken to a public open place at West Smithfield, for the reason already mentioned, and this same John Peeters and Henry Turwert to be really burned in that same fire, in detestation of this crime of theirs, and for an example to other men lest they fall into the like crime; and this you shall by no means fail to do, at your peril.*

Witness the queen, at Gorhambury, July 15.

By the queen herself.

And the warrant is thence sent on to the said Lord Keeper of the Great Seal of England by her command.

APPENDIX IV

The Catholic Prelates as Prisoners for Religion

By the time the regulations were issued which are here printed, there were but few survivors of the ancient line of bishops. The first letter is the reply of the Secretary of State to the Bishop of London's warning of June 21, 1577, that the [queen's] bishops report in various places an alarming increase of Papists (cf. *supra*, pp. 132, 303).

Sir Francis Walsingham to John Aylmer, Bishop of London, July 28, 1577

"After my very hearty commendations unto your lordship, the inconvenience and mischief being daily found to increase, not only to the danger of her Majesty's person, but to the disturbance of the common quiet of this realm; and the lenity that hath been showed to such persons as obstinately refuse to come to the church in the time of sermons and common prayer: It is resolved, therefore, that for the redress thereof, there shall be some consultation, and thereupon some general order to be set down, which shall not be changed. And because it is intended that your lordship shall be present at the said consultation, I am for that purpose also appointed by my lords to require you to be there upon Thursday, and to bring with you Mr. Doctor Hamon, your Chancellor, and such as you shall think meet. And forasmuch as the special point of the said consultation will stand upon the order that may be taken generally with all them that refuse to come to the church, and in particular what is meetest to be done with Watson, Feckenham, Harpsfield, and others of that kind that are thought to be the leaders and the pillars of the consciences of great numbers of such as be carried with these errors, whether it be not fit they be disputed withal, in some private sort, and after disputation had with them, and they thereby not reduced to conformity, then whether it shall be better to banish them the realm, or to keep them here together in some strait sort, as they may be kept from all conference to the further maintenance of this corruption. . . . I have thought meet to give you of the same these short remembrances, that by thinking thereupon, and of some such other things as may further this good intention, your lordship may come the better prepared to the furtherance of so good a purpose. And so I bid your lordship most heartily farewell." [1]

The next paper is the plan devised at the consultation arranged by the Council.

---

[1] As printed in Bridgett's edition (1876) of Thomas Watson's *Holsome and Catholyck Doctrine* (1558), lviii–lix, from P.R.O., SP/12, vol. 145, no. 21.

How such as are backward and corrupt in Religion may be reduced to conformity, and others stayed from like corruption.

For the reducing to conformity of such as are corrupt in religion, and refuse to yield obedience to the laws of the realm, provided in that behalf, and the staying of others from falling into like corruption, three things principally are to be put in execution.

1. The first in taking orders generally with such as are recusants, as that they may be brought to obey the laws.

2. The second in providing, either by banishment or restraint, that Watson, Feckenham, and the rest upon whose advice and consciences the said recusants depend, may do no harm.

.   .   .   .

Touching the second point for the restraining or banishing of Watson and the rest : if banishment be not thought meet, then it is to be considered how they may be restrained in such sort as there may be no access had unto them, which may be performed by putting these things following in execution :—

First, in making choice of some apt place for the keeping of them.

Secondarily in appointing some man of trust to take charge of them.

Lastly, in taxing upon the bishops and clergy such as are non-residents, and have pluralities, some yearly contribution for the finding of them, and a convenient stipend to be given to their keeper.[1]

This third document is the circular to the bishops enclosing a copy of the regulations they are to follow.

After our right hearty commendations unto your lordship, whereas her Majesty heretofore, after the restraining of Feckenham, Watson, and others, very backward and obstinate in religion, upon persuasion and some opinion conceived that by granting them liberty they might be drawn in time to yield themselves conformable unto her Highness' laws, she was contented to have them enlarged, and bonds taken of them for their good behaviours, as that they should refrain all manner of conference, secret practices or persuasions, to seduce her said subjects by withdrawing of them from the religion presently received within this realm, and their dutiful obedience towards her Highness and her laws : forasmuch as it is informed that Feckenham, Watson and the rest, contrary to their bonds, promise, and hope conceived of their amendment, have and do daily and manifestly abuse the liberty granted unto them whereby many of her Highness' said subjects are by their secret persuasions lately fallen and withdrawn from their due obedience, refusing to come unto the church, and to perform that part of their duties which heretofore they have been dutifully contented to yield. Upon consideration whereof her Majesty foreseeing of what consequence the effects of these lewd persuasions and practices may be, if in

[1] Bridgett, as last note, lix–lx.

time they shall not conveniently be met withal, hath thought it convenient again to restrain them of their liberties, and to make choice of some of your calling, unto whom they might be committed, and carefully looked unto, and, namely, hath appointed the person of A. B. unto your lordship's custody, to be straitly kept and dealt withal, according to a form which we send your lordship herewith in writing, requiring you in her Majesty's name, at such time as the said A. B. shall be sent unto you to receive him, and in all points to do your endeavour strictly to follow the said form for the usage of him during the time he shall remain with you, unless upon some good report made by you of hope of his conformity, it shall be by her Majesty or us ordered, that he shall be more favourably dealt withal.

Wherein not doubting but you will thoroughly perform the expectation had of your care in this behalf, we bid your lordship right heartily [farewell].

A form to be observed by my Lords the Bishops in the ordering of such as were committed to their custody for Popery.

1. That his lodging be in such a convenient part of your house, as he may both be there in safe custody, and also have no easy access of your household people unto him, other than such as you shall appoint, and know to be settled in religion and honesty, as that they may not be perverted in religion or any otherwise corrupted by him.

2. That he be not admitted unto your own table except upon some good occasion to have ministered to him there, in the presence of some that shall happen to resort unto you, such talk whereby the hearers may be confirmed in the truth ; but to have his diet by himself alone in his chamber, and that in no superfluity, but after the spare manner of scholars' commons.

3. That you suffer none, unless some one to attend upon him, to have access unto him ; but such as you shall know to be persons well confirmed in true religion, and are [not] likely to be weakened in the profession of the said religion by any conference they shall have with him.

4. That you permit him not at any time and place while he is with you to enter into any disputation of matters of religion, or to reason thereof otherwise than upon such occasion as shall be by you, or in your presence with your good liking by some other, ministered unto him.

5. That he have ministered unto him such books of learned men and sound writers in divinity, as you are able to lend him and none other.

6. That he have no liberty to walk abroad to take the air, but when yourself is at best leisure to go with him, or accompanied with such as you shall appoint.

7. That you do your endeavour by all good persuasions to bring him to the hearing of sermons, and other exercise of religion in your house and the chapel or church which you most commonly frequent.[1]

---

[1] Bridgett, as last note, lx–lxi, from P.R.O., SP/12, vol. 114, no. 69.

There is no reference in these papers to any other cause in the prelates for these severities beyond what the papers themselves call " errors " of conscience, or a " corruption in religion " that is a hindrance to their being " reduced to conformity ".   And of Watson's own personal loyalty, so far as political questions went, the government had proof enough in the answer he had made to their interrogatories about the Bull of excommunication : " I reply that I do not know of this affair except by hearsay.   And that I have not ever, either read the said Bull, nor seen it.   I acknowledge (*confiteor*) our queen Elizabeth—despite any bull or declaration of the Roman Pontiff—to be our true and legitimate queen of England and Ireland, and that obedience ought to be paid her as queen by all her subjects.   I acknowledge—despite the said bull, or any other already made or that shall be made —that I owe obedience and fidelity to Queen Elizabeth as a subject to his legitimate prince." [1]

[1] Translation mine, from the Latin text in Bridgett, *op. cit.*, lvi, quoted from Goldast, *Monarchia Sancti Imperii Romani*, III, p. 66.

APPENDIX V

The Excommunication of the Queen

1. Text of the Bull *Regnans in Excelsis* [1]

Pius, Bishop, servant of the servants of God, in memorial of the matter.

The sovereign jurisdiction of the one holy Catholic and Apostolic Church, outside of which there is no salvation, has been given by Him, unto whom all power in heaven and on earth is given, the King who reigns on high, to but one person on the face of the earth, to Peter, prince of the Apostles, and to the successor of Peter, the Bishop of Rome. Him He has set up over all nations, and over all kingdoms, to root up and destroy, to waste and to scatter, to plant and to build, to the end that he may maintain in the unity of the spirit the faithful people bound together by the bond of charity, and present them unto Him their Saviour perfect and without loss.

In the discharge of this duty, We, whom God of His goodness has called to the government of His Church, shrink from no labour, striving with all Our might, to preserve in their integrity that very unity and the Catholic religion, which are now assailed by so many storms, by His permission from Whom they come, for our correction, and for the trial of the faith of His children. But the wicked are so many, and are growing so strong, that there is no part of the world which they have not attempted by their evil doctrines to corrupt ; among others labouring for this end is the servant of iniquity, Elizabeth, the pretended queen of England,[2] with whom, as in a safe refuge, the worst of these men have found a secure retreat.

This woman having taken possession of the kingdom, unnaturally claims for herself [3] the place, the great [4] authority and jurisdiction of the sovereign head of the Church [5] throughout all England, and has involved in miserable ruin that kingdom so lately recovered to the Catholic faith and piety.

She has forbidden by the strong hand of power the observance of the true religion, overturned by the apostate [6] Henry VIII, and by the help of the Holy See restored by Mary, the lawful queen, of illustrious memory. She has followed after and accepted the errors of heretics. She has driven the English nobles out of the royal council, and filled their places with obscure heretics. She has been the ruin of those who profess the Catholic faith,

---

[1] The translation is by David Lewis, from his translation of Nicholas Sander, *Rise and Growth of the Anglican Schism*, 301–304.

[2] *Praetensa Angliae regina* : perhaps more truly rendered as " Who claims to be the Queen of England ".　　　　　　　　　　　　　　[3] *Sibi usurpans.*

[4] *Praecipuam auctoritatem* etc. : better, " peculiar " or " especial ".

[5] " Of the sovereign head etc." is, in the original, *supremi ecclesiae capitis locum,* i.e. " the place of supreme head of the church etc."　　　　[6] *Desertore.*

and has brought back again the wicked preachers and ministers of impieties. She has done away with the sacrifice of the Mass, the Divine Office, fasting, the distinction of meats, celibacy, and the Catholic rites. She has ordered the use of books,[1] containing manifest heresy, throughout the realm, and the observance by her subjects of impious mysteries and ordinances, according to the rule of Calvin,[2] accepted and practised by herself.

She has dared to take away their churches and benefices from the bishops, the parish priests,[3] and other Catholic ecclesiastics, and has given them with other ecclesiastical goods to heretics. She has made herself a judge in ecclesiastical causes. She has forbidden the prelates, clergy, and people to acknowledge the Church of Rome, or to obey its mandates and the Catholic constitutions.[4] She has compelled many to take an oath to observe her wicked laws, to renounce the authority of the Roman Pontiff, to refuse to obey him, and to accept her as the sole ruler in temporal and spiritual matters. She has decreed pains and penalties against those who do not submit to her, and has inflicted them upon those who continue in the unity of the faith and obedience.

She has thrown Catholic prelates and parish priests[5] into prison, where many, worn out by sorrows and their protracted sufferings, have ended their days in misery.

All this being notorious and known unto all nations, and so confirmed by very many grave witnesses, as to leave no room for palliation, defence, or concealment, sin being added to sin, and iniquity to iniquity, the persecution of the faithful, and the ruin of religion daily growing more and more at the suggestion and under the direction of Elizabeth aforesaid, whose will is so obstinate and whose heart is so hardened [as we understand][6] that she has set at nought not only the charitable prayers and counsels of Catholic princes entreating her to return to a better mind and be converted, but also Our own by her refusal to allow the Nuncios of the Holy See to enter the realm, We, having recourse, by necessity compelled, to the weapons of justice, are unable to control Our grief that We must proceed against one whose predecessors[7] have rendered signal services to Christendom.

Relying then on His authority who has placed Us on this sovereign throne of justice, though unequal to the bearing of so great a burden, We declare, in the fulness of the apostolic power, the aforesaid Elizabeth a heretic, and an encourager of heretics, together with those who abet her, under the sentence of excommunication, cut off[8] from the unity of the Body of Christ.

[1] *Libros . . . proponi* : i.e. " books to be put forth ".
[2] *Mysteria et instituta ad Calvini praescriptum* : " rites and doctrines after the fashion of Calvin ". [3] *Ecclesiarum rectores* : this does not mean " parish priests ".
[4] " or to obey . . . constitutions ". The Latin reads, *Neve eius praeceptis sanctionibusque canonicis obtemperarent* : i.e. " or to pay attention to its canonical commands and their sanctions ". [5] *Ecclesiarum rectores.* [6] Omitted by Lewis.
[7] *Majores* : i.e. " ancestors ".
[8] " together with . . . cut off ". The original is *eique adhaerentes in praedictis anathematis sententiam incurrisse, esseque a Christi corpore praecisos*, i.e. " and that those who take part with her in the aforesaid matters have incurred the penalty of excommunication and are cut off etc."

Moreover We declare that she[1] has forfeited her pretended title to the aforesaid kingdom,[2] to all and every right, dignity, and privilege ; We also declare that the nobles, the subjects, and the people of the kingdom aforesaid, [and all others][3] who have taken any oath to her, are for ever released from that oath, and from every obligation of allegiance, fealty, and obedience, as We now by these letters release them, and [we][4] deprive the said Elizabeth of her pretended right to the throne,[5] and every other right whatsoever aforesaid : We command all and singular the nobles, the people subject to her, and others aforesaid, never to venture to obey her monitions, mandates, and laws.

If any shall contravene this Our decree,[6] We bind them with the same bond of anathema.

Seeing that it would be a work of too much difficulty to send these letters to every place where it is necessary to send them, Our will is that a copy thereof by a public notary, sealed with the seal of an ecclesiastical prelate, or with the seal of his court, shall have the same force in courts of law and everywhere throughout the world that these letters themselves have if they be produced and shown.

Given at St. Peter's in Rome, in the year of the Incarnation of our Lord one thousand five hundred and sixty nine, on the fifth of the calends of March,[7] in the fifth year of Our Pontificate.

CAE. GLORIERIUS
H. CUMYN

2. The Scruples of Conscience among English Catholics, 1569

The answers of the captive Earl of Northumberland, in 1572, to Lord Burghley's interrogatories reveal vividly how real these scruples could be.

19. Whom did first give you to understand of the bull, that came from Rome against the Queen's Majesty ; and by what means was that bull obtained ; and how many do you know that were privy and consenting to it ; and where, and how often, was Morton, an old priest, with you, to confer with you, upon that bull ?

I never perfectly understood of any bull that came from Rome, against the Queen's Majesty ; [being][8] then in Lochleven. I heard it reported, there should be one set upon the Court gates ; and afterwards set upon the Privy Chamber door, as was said. There was a scruple and division amongst us, after the Duke's first committing to the Tower,[9] whether we ought by

---

[1] *Ipsam* : i.e. " she herself ".
[2] *Praetenso regni praedicti iure* ; i.e. " the right she claims to the said kingdom ".
[3] Omitted in Lewis.   [4] This, in the original, is a separate clause.
[5] Cf. n. 2, *supra*.   [6] *Qui secus egerint* : i.e. " whoever shall act otherwise ".
[7] Feb. 25, 1570. Years reckoned according to the Incarnation of our Lord begin not on Jan. 1, but on March 25.
[8] Inserted by Sharpe, as, also, the stop after " Lochleven ".
[9] October 11, 1569.

God's laws to rise against our Prince, or no ; being our anointed Prince. We referred the judgment therof to learned men ; and the same being demanded of a couple, the one being singularly well learned (whose name I know not), the other being Master Copley, that reconciled me ; their judgments was (and shewed us the scriptures) we ought not to wager battle against our anointed Prince, unless they were lawfully excommunicated by the head of the church. Then said the other party, that was thought to be a lawful excommunication, when that the Pope did send to the Queen for sufferance to send his Ambassadors into her presence ; which being denied, they said that Doctor Morton's opinion was, for that cause, her highness was lawfully excommunicate ; and so, consequently, lawful to take arms against her. Thus much did Markenfield report, of the said Doctor Morton ; being at that time, beyond the seas. The most of us thought it not sufficient, unless the excommunication had been orderly published within the realm.

This scruple did not only persuade Sir John Neville and me to forbear the matter ; but also occasioned sundry other gentlemen to withdraw themselves from us. As for Doctor Morton, he was once at my house, and I spake with him about an hour ; and he opened unto me no such matter of any bull, or promise of aid from the Pope ; but lamented he saw so great want of sound and catholic priests, that he might give authority to them for reconciling such of the people as would seek. More than this dealt not I with him.[1]

[1] What is quoted here is the transcription printed in Sharpe, 204–205. It has been compared with the original in P.R.O., S.P./15, vol. 21, no. 56, I, fol. 168 at 6.

ELIZABETH AND THE CATHOLIC WHO WILL NOT PLAY THE PROTESTANT :
AN INQUISITION AND SOME OF ITS VICTIMS, 1561–1580

I

The first document [1] is, seemingly, a report made to the council (in 1561 ?)
by the commissioners appointed, under the Act of Supremacy, to exercise
certain parts of the queen's new jurisdiction in spiritual matters.   The
chief item in it—a list headed *Recusants which are abroad and bounde to
certayne places*, signed by Edmund Grindal, Bishop of London, Richard
Cox, Bishop of Ely, Dr. Walter Haddon and Sir Thomas Smith—is summarised, in some detail, in this note.   A second item in the report is a list
of *Certain evil disposed persons of whom complaint hath been made which lurk
so secretly that process cannot be served upon them*.   Twelve names are given,
all of priests, among whom are the late master of St. John's College, Oxford,
the late deans of Christ Church and of Durham, a one-time chaplain to
Bonner, and the chancellor to the late Archbishop of York, Nicholas Heath.
There is, thirdly, a list of seven reported to have " fled . . . over the seas ",
and, finally, a separately signed list of 16 personages committed to various
London prisons by the commissioners : the *Fleet*, Sir Thomas Fitzherbert ;
Dr. Scott, late Bishop of Chester ; Dr. Harpsfield, late archdeacon of London;
Thomas Wood, chaplain to the late queen ; [2] Dr. Cole, late dean of St.
Paul's ; Thomas Somerset, gentleman ; Dr. Draycot ; [3] Dr. Chedsey ; [4] the
Marshalsea, Dr. Bonner, late Bishop of London ; John Simes, a priest of
Somersetshire ; the *Counter* (Poultry), John Draycott, gentleman ; the
Counter (Wood St.), Dr. Young ; [5] John Sacheverell, esquire ; Thomas
Atkinson, late fellow of Lincoln, Oxford ; John Greete, a priest from
Hampshire ; the *King's Bench*, John Baker, a priest from Essex.   The
last list is signed by Grindal, Cox, William Downham, Bishop of Chester,
Gabriel Goodman (dean of Westminster Abbey) and T. Huycke.

As to the 61 personages named in the long list now to be summarised, all
but two are noted either as clerics or scholars.   Of the 46 clerics (reckoning
all fellows of colleges as such), 17 are noted as unlearned.   Parish clergy
are few.   There are 2 bishops in the list, and 2 deans—one of whom has
yielded to the queen's demands.   There are 2 archdeacons, and 6 doctors
of divinity.   The queen's commissioners, devising this plan to isolate the

----

[1] P.R.O., S.P./15, vol. 11, no. 45 (8 sheets in all).   For the loan of copies of the documents used in this Appendix, and for most generous offers of the fruits of much laborious
research, I am indebted to my friend Dr. William Trimble, of Harvard and the University
of Tennessee.   No. 45 is printed, in full, in Gee, *Elizabethan Clergy*, 179–185.

[2] And nominated by Mary for the vacant see of Salisbury.

[3] Late chancellor of Lichfield.   [4] President of Corpus Christi College, Oxford.

[5] President of Pembroke Hall, Cambridge.

more militant, or the better trained, of the clergy who have refused to turn their coats, are anticipating, by a good thirty years, the policy of the Elizabethan parliament towards all recusants ; and their action in 1561 is a corollary to the campaign against the bishops two years before.

RECUSANTS WHICH ARE ABROAD AND BOUNDE TO CERTAYNE PLACES

[Name]	[Status]	[Marginal Comments in the Original]	[Restrictions imposed by the Commissioners] [1]
Alexander Belsire [2]	clerk	wealthy and stubborn	Handborough in Oxfordshire, and 2 miles of this.
Doctor Poole	late Bishop of Peterborough	a man known and reported to live quietly, and therefore hitherto tolerated.	City of London and suburbs, and 3 miles of this.
Thomas Wyllanton	late chaplain to Dr. Bonner	stiff and not unlearned	Counties of Middlesex or Bucks or the city of London, and bound to appear once a term.
Robert Purseglove	late suffragan [bishop] of Hull, and before an abbot or a prior	Very wealthy and stiff in papistry and of estimation in that country	The town of Ugthorpe in Yorkshire and 12 miles of this.
Roger Marshall	once prior of Sempryngham	not unlearned and wealthy	Newmarket, and 6 miles of this.
Thomas Seagiswick	doctor of divinity	learned but not very wise	Richmond, and within 10 miles.
William Carter	doctor of divinity, late archdeacon of Northumberland	not unlearned but very stubborn and to be considered	Thirsk, and within 10 miles.
Thomas Harding	doctor of divinity	Learned. In King Edward's time preached the truth honestly and now stiff in papistry and thinketh very much good of himself	Monkton Farley in Wiltshire and within 16 miles, or Toller in Dorset, and 20 miles of this.
Richard Dominick [3]	clerk, late parson of Stratford, diocese of Salisbury	an unlearned priest but very stubborn	East Knoyle, in Wiltshire and 16 miles of this.
William Boyd	clerk, late parson of Guiseley[?] in Yorkshire	not unlearned but very wilful and stubborn	Southwell, in Nottinghamshire, and 24 miles of this.
David de la Hide	an Irishman, late scholar of Oxford [4]	very stubborn and worthy to be looked unto	Not to go within 20 miles of either university.

[1] The notes in this column summarise the original.
[2] The late-deprived president of St. John's College, Oxford.
[3] Prebendary of Salisbury Cathedral.
[4] ? Fellow of Merton.

RECUSANTS WHICH ARE ABROAD AND BOUNDE TO CERTAYNE PLACES

[Name]	[Status]	[Marginal Comments in the original]	[Restrictions imposed by the Commissioners] [1]
Edward Brombrough Robert Dawkes [2] George Simpson	} late scholars of Oxford	wilful scholars	as the last
Antony Atkins [2]	clerk, late of Oxford	an unlearned priest, very wilful	to remain in the counties of Gloucester or Salop.
William Thules	late scholar [?schoolmaster] of Durham, bound for his good behaviour in matter of religion		not to return to the diocese of Durham
Roger Thompson	clerk	late a superstitious monk of Mountgrace [3] and unlearned	not to return to the diocese of York and Durham.
John Rastall [4] Nicholas Fox Robert Davies William Giblett John Durham	} late scholars of Oxford	wilful scholars and not learned in divinity	restrained from the universities and bound for their quiet behaviour in matter of religion.
Richard Halse	late prebendary of Exeter	an unlearned priest	the counties of Devon or Cornwall, the city of Exeter, but not within 3 miles of either of his late benefices.
John Blaxton Walter Mugge	late prebendaries of Hereford	two stubborn persons . . .	the diocese of Hereford.
Robert Dalton	clerk, late prebendary of Durham	unlearned, wealthy and stiff	to remain with the Lord Dacres of the North.
Nicholas Marley	late prebendary of Durham	unlearned	the bishopric of Durham, but not to go within 8 miles of Durham [the city].
Thomas Redman	late chaplain to the late Bishop of Ely [5]	unlearned	the counties of York, Westmorland and Lancaster.
Henry Comberford	late of Lich[field]	learned but wilful and meet to be considered	Suffolk, with leave to go twice a year to Staffordshire, six weeks allowed for each of these journeys.

John Ramridge [6]   lately punished bound to be quiet and to go to the services and sureties found for his appearance when he shall be called.

[1] The notes in this column summarise the original.
[2] Fellow of Merton.
[3] A Carthusian. Mountgrace, near Northallerton in Yorkshire, was surrendered to King Henry VIII many years before this.
[4] Fellow of New College.   [5] Thomas Thirlby.   [6] Late Dean of Lichfield.

RECUSANTS WHICH ARE ABROAD AND BOUNDE TO CERTAYNE PLACES

[Name]	[Status]	[Marginal Comments in the Original]	[Restrictions imposed by the Commissioners] [1]
John Ceaton	doctor of divinity	learned, settled in papistry	the City of London and within 20 miles.
John Erle	clerk, late of Winton	an unlearned priest	Hampshire ; and to give notice at Hyde.
Laurence Vawse	late warden of Manchester	these two are thought to behave themselves very seditiously, and contrary to their recognisance secretly lurk in Lancashire. and are thought to be maintained there by [?] and gentlemen of that county	Worcestershire
Richard Hart	late one of the curates of Manchester		Kent or Sussex
Antony Salvin	late prebendary of Durham	meanly learned, but of estimation in his country	Kirkby Moorside in Yorkshire, or elsewhere in that county the city of York excepted, so that he does not go more than 5 miles north of Kirkby Moorside.
Robert Manners	late parson of Watton-at-Stane [2]	an unlearned priest	Baldock, in Hertfordshire and 20 miles of this.
Edmund Daniel	late Dean of Hereford	one that pretendeth a submission but yet stubborn	With the Lord Treasurer [3] or within 12 miles of the Lord Treasurer's house.
Thomas Hide	late schoolmaster of Winton	one very stiff and perverse	with the Lord Treasurer.
Robert Hill	late Commissary at Calais	very perverse in religion	Burton-on-Trent or elsewhere in Staffordshire.
Nicholas Banister		an unlearned priest	Lancashire, the town of Preston, always excepted where he had been a schoolmaster.
William Winck	late of Cambridge	not unlearned, subtle and stiff	Norfolk.
Clement Burdett	late of Bath	an unlearned priest	Crondall (Hampshire) or Sonning (Berkshire).
Doctor Tresham	late of Oxford [4]	a man whose qualities are well known	Northamptonshire.

[1] The notes in this column summarise the original.
[2] And prebendary of Lincoln Cathedral.
[3] William Paulett, Marquis of Winchester.   [4] Canon of Christ Church.

RECUSANTS WHICH ARE ABROAD AND BOUNDE TO CERTAYNE PLACES

[Name]	[Status]	[Marginal Comments in the Original]	[Restrictions imposed by the Commissioners] [1]
Alban Langdale	doctor of divinity [2]	learned and very stiff in papistry	to remain with Lord Montague or where his L[ordship] shall appoint and to appear within twelve days after monition given to the said L[ord] Montague or his officers before the Commissioners.
John Porter	late parson of Crondall in Kent	an unlearned priest	Maidstone or London or suburbs or elsewhere in Kent, Canterbury excepted, notifying the sheriff of his abode.
John Dale	late of Cambridge	not altogether unlearned but very perverse	Newmarket or within 10 miles of this, but not to go more than 4 miles in the direction of London or Cambridge.
Alan Cope [3] William Lowes	late scholars of Oxford		the said Cope is bound to appear within 14 days and Lowes restrained from the universities otherwise at liberty.

Stephen Hopkins   clerk, confessor (as he saith) to the Bishop of Aquila [4] and a daily resorter unto him. He was delivered out of the Fleet by the Queen's majesty's express commandment to the L[ord] of Canterbury.

Tristram Swaddel[?]	late Doctor Bonner's servant, and yet thought to be a practitioner for him	altogether unlearned but yet very subtle	
Thomas Dormer	late scholar of Oxford [5]		restrained from the universities.
Henry Johnson	clerk, late parson of Broadwas in Worcestershire	unlearned stubborn priests late of the diocese of Worcester	the county of Hereford.
Robert Shaw	late prebendary of Worcester		the county of Salop.
Robert Shelmerden	clerk		Northamptonshire.
William Burton	clerk		Oxfordshire.
Henry Saunders	clerk		Warwickshire.

[1] The notes in this column summarise the original.
[2] Archdeacon of Lewes.   [3] Fellow of Magdalen.
[4] Alvarez de Quadra, the King of Spain's ambassador in London.
[5] Fellow of All Souls ?

RECUSANTS WHICH ARE ABROAD AND BOUNDE TO CERTAYNE PLACES

[Name]	[Status]	[Marginal Comments in the Original]	[Restrictions imposed by the Commissioners] [1]
Edward Atislowe [2] Walter Russell Robert Young Robert Fenne [2] Ralph Keat	late scholars of Oxford	wilful scholars	restrained from the universities.

2.

The second document [3] whose date, according to the endorsement, is 1569, is headed, *An Abstract of the examination of such gentlemen of the Inns of Court which have been lately convented before the queen's majesty's commissioners appointed for causes ecclesiastical together with the interrogations whereupon every of them have been severally examined.* Three questions were put to these lawyers of the four Inns of Court:

1. Whether they and every of them have orderly upon Sundays and holydays gone to their parish church or other place of common prayer and there abiden the hearing of divine service, without some reasonable cause, and where they have so gone to service.

2. Whether they and every of them have yearly received the Communion according to the Law, viz. three times a year since midsummer the first year of the queen's majesty's reign.[4]

3. Whether they and every of them have not heard other forms of prayer or service than is appointed by the Laws, viz. mass, matins or evensong in Latin, or have been shriven or houseled after the popish manner.[5]

3.

The third of these documents, that also comes from the High Commission, is dated eleven years later than the last, and nineteen years later than the attempted round-up of likely leaders, in 1561, portrayed in the first of this set. The danger is still the same—Catholics influential in their own locality are still committing the crime of holding out against the Act of Uniformity, of refusing to conform to the new arrangements like those who believed the new doctrines. Here, in the commissioners' own report of their activities on circuit, we see the system of inquisition at work, its victories (and the victims), and its failures when it comes up against the spiritually heroic. It is now ten years since the Excommunication of the queen, and a matter of months only since the papal expedition to Ireland;

---

[1] The notes in this column summarise the original.
[2] Fellow of New College.
[3] P.R.O., S.P./12, vol. 60, no. 70.
[4] I.e. June 24, 1559, the date when the Act of Uniformity came into force.
[5] In all 22 barristers were called before the Commissioners and 14 appeared (Inner Temple 8 summoned, 5 appeared; Middle Temple 4 summoned, 1 appeared; Gray's Inn 5 summoned, 3 appeared; Lincoln's Inn 5 summoned and all appeared).

the time has arrived when all England is to be made to ring with the tale that the Catholics are harried for politics alone ; the organisers of the fifth column, some modern historians will say, are by now swarming from Douay and from Rome ; and at this crisis of national history the government makes a heroic effort, which only the queen's obstinate liberalism defeats, to turn the Eucharist into a test of loyalty. Thanks to the queen, it is urged, the Catholics are saved from the new affliction that, under penalties, they must regularly take the Communion. But what, in fact, already moves the queen's commissioners, and determines the fate of her Catholic subjects, is religion in the strictest sense of the word. As for the discipline of the Communion, *qui legit intelligat*.[1]

A Brief declaration of the proceedings of the most reverend Father in God Edwyn L. Archbishop of York, the right honourable Henry, Earl of Huntingdon, Lord President of her majesty's council established in the north parts, and other their associates her majesty's Commissioners for Causes ecclesiastical within the diocese and province of York in their several sessions holden in the city and county of York, beginning at York, the 18th day of July 1580 and from time to time and place to place adjourned and continued as hereafter followeth.

The First
Session.

AT YORK, on Monday the 18th of July, 1580

At which day the said Commissioners caused the keepers of the castle and other prisons in York, to bring into the cathedral church of York all such prisoners as were in their several custodies for matter of religion, at 8 of the clock in the forenoon, where was appointed and did preach, Mr. Thomas Cole, master of Arts, who earnestly exhorted the said prisoners being there present to forsake their vain and erroneous opinions of popery and conform themselves with all dutiful obedience to true religion now established as by the laws of God, and the Queen's Majesty grounded therein is required. But they were so far from yielding to any godly motion, that some of them by stopping their ears, some by coughing and unquiet behaviour never gave any attention to what was said neither would as much as say the Lord's prayer after the said preacher, being earnestly required by him to do so, that it might please God, all joining their petitions and praises together, the sooner to open their understanding to yield to his truth.

Afterwards the said commissioners sitting in the Common Hall in the City of York called before them the said prisoners whose names hereafter follow.

[1] What now follows is the full text of the document (P.R.O., S.P./12, vol. 141, no. 28) with the spelling modernised, and certain repetitions left out, as indicated in the footnotes. Some of the proper names I have not been able to make out. For the importance of this report, cf. the valuable study of A. G. Dickens, *The First Stages of Romanist Recusancy in Yorkshire, 1560–1590* (Yorkshire Archaeological Journal, vol. 35, pp. 157–181), to whom, however, this document was not known.

Out of the Castle of York

1. Thomas Field, priest.
2. William Fieldsend, priest.
3. Thomas   , priest.
4. John   , priest.
5. Stephen Hemsworth, priest.
6. John Staunton, gent.
7. Francis Hemsworth.
8. Brian Stapleton, esquire.
9. Robt. Bellasis.
10. Thomas Coupland.
11. William Smithson.
12. John Thackeray.
13. William Wryght.
14. John Gill.
15, 16. John Chamer and his wife.
17. William, his son.
18. Bridget, his daughter.
19. Katherine Norton, gent. [*sic*.].
20. Anne Cowper.
21. Katherine Wildon.

All these being severally persuaded with by the said Archbishop and other the Commissioners, would not yield to come to the church alleging none other reasons but that their consciences would not suffer them whereupon they were returned to prison whence they came.

All the priests named among these prisoners, as also one other following in the Kidcote, were after this sent to the Castle at Hull where they now remain.

Out of the Kidcote in York

1. Thomas Mudde, priest.
2. Thomas Harwood, gent.
3. Roger Geldard of York.
4. Thomas Lane of Haworth.
5. John Dilcocke of Pomfret.
6. Barnarde Stafford of Pomfret.
7. William Bowman of York.
8. Thomas Pereson of York.
9. Anne Cooke, wife of Ambrose Cooke of York.
10. Alice Pereson.
11. Margaret Watson.
12. Lucy Plowman.
13. Helen Williamson, wife of John Williamson.
14. Margaret Taylor, wife of Thomas Taylor.
15. Agnes Rawson of Micklefield, vid.
16. Agnes Johnson of York.
17. Alice Gibson of Huntingdon, vid.

These being likewise severally persuaded withal to yield to conformity refused so to do, and were returned to the prison whence they came.

Besides these, there were the same day committed by the said Commissioners for the like offences these persons following :

1. Alice Oldcorne wife of Thomas Oldcorne, now prisoner in Hull to the Kidcote.   to
2. Perceval Geldard of the city of York   to the Castle.
3. Margaret Thwaite, wife of John Thwaite, Esquire ⎫
   upon hope of conformity first to the custody of ⎬ to the Castle.
   Christopher Maltby, alderman. But at the next ⎭
   session at York
4. Agnes Clarke   to the Castle.
5. Elizabeth Wilkinson wife of William Wilkinson   to the Castle.

The same day these persons following yielded to come to the church and receive the Com[munio]n according to the laws of this realm.

1. Agnes Wigan, of York, Widow.
2. Phillida Bredon, servant to Thomas Oldcorne.

3. Henry Fairfax and Dorothy his wife, which Henry was bound in recognisance in £100 for himself, his wife and family so to continue.
4. Richard Eldon, bound in recognisance in £10 for himself, his wife and whole family to do the like.
5. Margaret Wryght, wife of John Wryght.
6. Anne Wilkinson, wife of Richard Wilkinson.
7. Alice Thorpe, of Huntingdon.
8. Ralph Lawson of Burghe esquire, entered into recognisance with William Lawson of Thorpe Bulmer gent., in £400 that he and his family shall frequent the church etc., and that the said Ralph shall be at the sermon at Ripon the 10th day of August next and there diligently hear the same etc. Also to apprehend popish priests and such like and to conform his wife etc. This said Ralph Lawson was first committed to the Castle of York where he remained prisoner 11 days before he yielded to conformity.

The Jury in the city of York. At the same time and place the Sheriffs of the City of York returned their precept with the names of a sufficient jury of good and lawful men as follows.[1]

All which being sworn on the behalf of our sovereign Lady the Queen (after an exhortation given them by the said Archbishop declaring the cause of their assembly and admonishing them of their duty which by virtue of their oath they were to perform) it was given them in charge to make diligent enquiry and true presentment of all such persons as did offend against her majesty's laws established for the good conformity of her subjects in matters of religion, and to bring in their verdict or presentment upon Wednesday the 27th of July following in the same place. At which day the court was adjourned till Friday the 29th of July then following and they required to bring in their verdict then, which they did as will appear.

The Second Session.

AT YORK on Friday the 29th of July, 1580

After a godly sermon made by Mr. George Slater, prebendary of the church of York, in the said cathedral church before the said L. Archbishop and L. President and their associates, with the Mayor and Aldermen of the City of York, and a great assembly of Justices of the Peace and others, the said Commissioners repaired to the Common Hall of the said city, before whom appeared the said jury, and by the hand of William Robinson, Alderman, being foreman, delivered in a presentment or verdict which with one consent they agreed upon. And then being commanded to make further inquisition as before, and deliver in their presentment the next day of Sessions to be holden by the said Commissioners at the said city for this purpose were dismissed.

Recusants Committed. At the same time and place were convented and appeared these persons following with whom order was taken as ensueth.

---

[1] The 20 names (4 aldermen, 2 gentlemen, the rest not specified) are omitted.

1. Jane Gascoyne, wife of Richard Gascoyne of Sedbergh, esquire, daughter of Richard Norton esquire, being earnestly persuaded withal by the said L. Archbishop and the rest of the Commissioners to repair to the church and receive the Communion would not yield so to do, and was committed close prisoner to the Castle of York.

2. William Calverley son of Walter Calverley of Calverley, esquire, confessed that of long time he hath not come to the church neither as yet could yield so to do. He confessed upon his oath that within the year past he hath heard a mass in a house of his own, he himself helping the priest to say it. But denieth upon his oath that he knoweth the priest's name that said it, or who were at it beside himself and his mother. After long reasoning and persuasion used by the said Archbishop, L. President and the rest he very obstinately persisted in his erroneous opinion and was committed close prisoner to the castle of York, and withall was enjoined *sub pena contemptus* to repair to the minster of York on Sunday and Sunday sennight following to hear Divine Service. And the keeper was commanded to attend upon him.

At the same Session

Recusants entering bond.

1. Robert Wryght of Huntingdon, esquire, entered into recognisances in £200 for all conformity of himself and his family in matter of religion. And to persuade his wife to the like or else to bring her in before the Commissioners the same day month then following.[1]

2. Elizabeth Barnarde wife of Henry Barnarde, of Haxby, yielded to come to the church and receive the Communion according to the laws of this realm. And a bond entered in £20 for performance of the same, and to certify the third of October next, and from time to time after as should be required.

3. Walter Wilson of Ashton, yeoman, entered into recognisance in £40 to repair to the church, receive the Communion, and certify the third of October next and after from time to time and that his wife and whole family shall do the like.

At BEVERLEY on Friday the 5th of August, 1580

The Third Session.

After a learned and godly sermon made in the church of Beverley by the aforenamed most reverend father, he with the said L. President and other their associates sitting in the Common Hall or Townhouse there, the Sheriff of the County of York returned his precept with the names of a sufficient jury as followeth.[2]

The Jury at Beverley.

To whom being sworn on behalf of our sovereign lady the Queen the said Archbishop declared the cause of their assembly putting them in mind of their duty and charge. And delivered to them (beside that which was given them in charge by speech) certain articles in writing to enquire upon,

---

[1] This demand, that the husband shall agree to arrest and hand over to the law, his conscientious wife, is one of the grievances mentioned in Richard Holtby's report, *supra*, 373.

[2] The 20 names omitted—3 are esquires, 16 gentlemen and 1 yeoman.

the Copy whereof hereafter followeth. And required them to give up their verdict or presentment in the same place the 22nd of this August to the hands of such Commissioners as should repair thither for the same.

Articles for the jury to enquire upon at this present

Statute A°
primo
Reginae
Elizabethae
Cap. 2°.

1. First whether any person whatsoever hath unreverently spoken any contemptuous words of the Communion of the body and blood of Christ, or Against the receiving thereof under both kinds.

2. Item, whether any parson, vicar or other minister, which ought to sing or say common prayers or to minister the Sacraments hath refused to use the common prayer and to minister the Sacraments in such wise and form as is set forth in the book of common prayer now by law and order established.

3. Item whether any parson vicar or any other minister hath or doth use any other order or form of common prayer or celebrating the Lord's Supper than is [?   ] in the said book of common prayer, or that have spoken in depraving of the said book or of any thing contained in the same.

4. Item whether any person or persons whatsoever hath or doth speak in depraving the said book, or procure any other common prayer or service to be said or maintain any person to say any other prayer, or administer the Sacraments in any other form than is in the said book. Or who interrupt any preacher or minister in time of preaching or divine service.

5. Item whether any person or persons whatsoever do absent themselves from their parish churches and divine service without just cause or do wilfully refuse to come to the church to hear divine service and receive the Sacrament according to the laws of this Realm.

Statute A°5°
Reginae
Elizabethae
Cap. 1°.

6. Item whether any person or persons do maintain the usurped authority of the Bishop of Rome by words or writings or do attribute a[ny] authority to the said Bishop within this Realm, or be procurers and counsellors of the same.

Statute
A° 13°
Reginae
Eliz.
Cap. 2°.

7. Item whether any person or persons whatsoever hath given or taken absolution by any Bulls from Rome or by cover of any Bulls, or put in use any bulls or other writings from thence and who they be.

8. Item whether any such person or persons whatsoever, have conceded any such absolutions, bulls or other like writings offered unto them or have given aid or assistance to any practising the same.

9. Item whether any person or persons whatsoever have brought into this realm any Agnus Dei, or any crosses, pictures, beads, or such like vain and superstitious things, or that deliver or offer to be delivered from any person authorised from Rome any such like thing with intent to be worn, or have received any such things and wear them.

10. Item whether any popish priests or other persons whatsoever, go from place to place, secretly to dissuade the people from true religion, and to reconcile them to popery, thereby to forsake their duty towards God and the Queen's majesty, and where and with whom you know or suspect any such to be recepted.

The same day appeared before the said Commissioners all these persons following with whom order was taken as ensueth.

1. Sir William Babthorp, of Osgoodby, knight, bound in recognisances to her majesty in £200 that he and his family shall dutifully repair to the church to hear divine service and receive the Communion according to the laws of this realm and to certify of their so doing from time to time, and to do his endeavour to conform his wife to do the like and to certify thereof. Lastly to apprehend all [royving] popish priests and other like evil popish subjects and bring their bodies before the Commissioners etc.
2. Ralph Hansbye of Bishop Burton, gent., £100
3. Robert Constable of Denton, gent., £100
4. George Fonberg of Newbold, gent., £100
5. Marmaduke Constable of Cliff, gent., £100
6. George St. Quintin, of Harpham, gent., £100
7. George Consett of Howden, gent., £100
8. Richard Langdale of Everingham, £100
9. William Constable of Constable Burton, gent., £100

These persons were bound in these several sums that they, their wives children and families, (except William Constable being unmarried and no householder) shall dutifully from henceforth repair to the church, receive the Communion and certify the third of October next and after from time to time of their so doing. Also to apprehend popish priests coming into their companies etc.

At BEVERLEY aforesaid, on Saturday the 6th of August, 1580

After a learned sermon made in the forenoon by Mr. William Palmer, chancellor of the Church of York, the said Commissioners repaired again to the Common Hall, before whom appeared the mayor of Hull with certain aldermen of the said town, and the keepers of the Castle and Blockhouses there, and brought with them out of the prisons at Hull, being requested by the said Commissioners so to do, these prisoners following, heretofore committed for matter of religion.

1. Roger Corkett, esquire.
2. Guy Jackson, gent.
3. William Lacy, gent.
4. John Mallett, gent.
5. Edward Cashe, gent.
6. William Justice, gent.
7. Henry Oglethorpe, gent.

And after the said L. Archbishop had made a brief repetition of the said sermon, applying the same to the present occasion, he with others the Commissioners reasoned with the said prisoners severally, and earnestly persuaded them to yield to conformity in true religion, and dutiful obedience to her majesty's laws established for the same. But they all being not able to bring any good reason for their defence to the contrary, persisted still in their papistical and erroneous opinion and would not yield to come to the church and embrace true religion now established. Whereupon they were returned again to their prisons at Hull. And were every one judicially enjoined by the said Commissioners that before the 27th day

28

of this August they should repair to some church in Hull to hear divine service and sermons *sub poena contemptus*. And their keepers were summoned to attend upon them from time to time for this purpose and put them in mind thereof. And the mayor of Hull was commanded to certify of their doing in the premises with convenient speed after the said 27th day.

And for so much as it was perceived that by the negligence of the keepers of the prisons at Hull, some disorders were committed among the prisoners there, the said L. Archbishop and L. President with the rest of their associates agreed upon certain orders to be observed as well by the Mayor and Aldermen of Hull as by the keepers of the prisoners there, copy whereof hereafter followeth.

Augusti 6, 1580.

Orders to be observed by the Mayor of Hull and the keepers of the Castle and Blockhouses there

1. First the Mayor of Hull for the time being, with three Aldermen, the Preacher and the Town Clerk, shall monthly survey all the prisons there and see that the keepers of the said prisoners do faithfully and truly observe such orders as hereafter following we shall give unto them.
2. Item if the said Mayor, aldermen, Preacher and town clerk shall find the keepers undutiful in their office, they shall forthwith signify the same unto us, and with all their opinions of a more fit keeper or keepers that we may remove the offenders and breakers of our orders, and place better in their stead.
3. Item that all prisoners which are popish priests shall be together in one prison and none others with them.
4. Item that all the gentlemen which be prisoners be together in another prison and none others with them.
5. Item that all the handicraft men, labourers and such others be placed in another prison and none others with them.
6. Item that all the women prisoners be together in another prison and none others with them.
7. Item that all children, servants, and others whatsoever not by order committed to be prisoners there, be utterly removed out of the prisons.
8. Item that the keepers shall suffer no man to have access or speech with any prisoner without special licence from the Commissioners or three of them, of whom the L. Archbishop or L. President to be one.
9. Item. If either money, apparel, bedding or such like shall be brought to any prisoner, it shall first be brought to the hands of the keeper of that prison, and he shall take a note in writing who brought the said money, apparel or bedding, to whom it was brought, from whom it was sent, and what it is, and keep a book thereof from time to time. And if any shall bring a bed of his own, yet the keeper shall have allowance of him and them for their chamber according to the order of the Fleet.
10. Item The keepers shall provide sufficient diet for the prisoners, good meat and drink and well dressed, and let every one have at their hands

only, according to his or her ability, paying and answering for the same according to the order and rate taken in the Fleet for prisoners there.

11. Item The keepers shall find maids and women servants to wash the linen of such prisoners as be sent there from time to time, receiving a competent price for the same.

12. Item The keepers shall suffer no [?] book or other like matters to be conveyed to or from the prisoners, except the same be first perused by the said Mayor, three Aldermen, Preacher and Town Clerk of the Town of Hull.

13. Item That whereas we have or shall enjoin any prisoner or prisoners within a certain time limit to repair to the Church to hear divine service, the keepers shall every day put the said prisoners in mind thereof with offer of their attendance to go with them for the performance of our injunction.

14. Item If any prisoner be committed who hath not paid fees unto the officers accordingly, the keepers shall suffer him or her to have no meat until they have answered the same officers such fees as are due unto them.

15. Item The keepers of the said prisons shall be bound with their sufficient sureties in £100 a year to deal faithfully with her majesty in this service and to observe such orders as we have or shall set down and prescribe unto them.

To these orders the said Commissioners subscribed their hands and delivered one copy thereof so subscribed to the said Mayor and Aldermen of Hull. And another copy likewise subscribed to John Alcock and John Beesby keepers of the said prisons. Which Alcock and Beesby at the same time entered into several recognisances with their sufficient sureties to her majesty's use in £100 a year faithfully to discharge the trust and service committed to them in that behalf.

THE NAMES of the prisoners at this present remaining at Hull for matter of religion, and how they were as well divided betwixt the keepers as also separated into companies as was thought convenient for doing least hurt by further infecting one another.

Prisoners at Hull, Augusti 6, 1580.

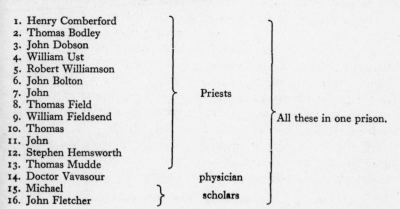

1. Henry Comberford
2. Thomas Bodley
3. John Dobson
4. William Ust
5. Robert Williamson
6. John Bolton
7. John
8. Thomas Field
9. William Fieldsend
10. Thomas
11. John
12. Stephen Hemsworth
13. Thomas Mudde
} Priests

14. Doctor Vavasour — physician
15. Michael
16. John Fletcher
} scholars

All these in one prison.

In the custody of John Beesby.

17. Roger Corkett, esquire
18. John Mallett, gent.
19. Henry Oglethorpe, gent.
20. William Lacy, gent.
} These in another prison.

21. William Justice, his wife
22. Edward Cash, his wife
23. Anne Launder
24. John Fletcher, his wife
} These women in another prison.

In the custody of John Alcocke.

1. Edward Cashe
2. William Stillington
3. William Justice
4. Guy Jackson
5. Thomas Leeds
6. Christopher Monkton
} gents. in one prison

7. Stephen Branton
8. Francis Perkinson
9. William Brimley
10. Oliver Walker
11. William Raynelds
12. Thomas Oldcorne
13. William Tesimonde

14. Robert Pooley
*15. Ralph Cowling
16. Ambrose Cooke
17. H. Wilburne
18. Christopher Hinton
} handicraft men in another prison.

Recusants Committed.

The same day were convented these prisoners following with whom order was taken as ensueth.

1. Christopher Monckton, esquire, who utterly refusing to come to the Church and receive the Communion, was by the said Commissioners committed to the prison at Hull into the keeping of John Alcock one of the keepers there.

Recusants entering bond.

1. Philip Constable of Everingham, esquire £100.
2. Edward Ellerker of Rysby, esquire £100.

They both entered into recognisances in these sums that they repair to the church and receive the Communion and to certify the 3rd of October next and after from time to time, to apprehend popish priests etc., To labour to conform their wives before Michaelmas and then to certify.

3. Ralph Ellerker of Northpark in Holderness entered into recognisances in £100 that he his wife and family . . . [as nos. 1 and 2].

4. George Creswell of N ? ekelinge gent. bound in £100 [as nos. 1 & 2]. And to endeavour to conform his wife before St. Stephen's day next and to certify thereof the first Session after Christmas.

5. John Lindley of the city of York, tailor, was at the same time and place bound in £100 that Ralph Cowling, at that present prisoner in Hull, should repair to the church, receive the Communion etc. as in former conditions, whereupon the said Cowling was by warrant enlarged, and set over to the next Sessions at Malton where he appeared and entered himself into like recognisance to the same effect and thereupon the former recognisance was released and he enlarged.

SUNDAY the 7th of August 1580 after morning prayers and a godly sermon made by Mr. Barnabas Shepherd, Bachelor of Divinity, the said Commissioners rode from Beverley to Old Malton to their next sessions.

* enlarged upon bond to be conformable, etc.

AT OLD MALTON on Monday the 8th of August, 1580 The Fourth Session. The Jury at Malton.

After a zealous and godly sermon made by the said L. Archbishop [—as at Beverley,[1] *supra*—the verdict or presentment of the jury to be delivered by August 22 next].

At the same time and place there were convented before the said Commissioners these persons following for not coming to the Church and receiving the Communion.

1. Edward Barton of Wetherby, esquire. He sufficiently proved his own conformity but confessed that his wife was faulty altogether, whereupon he entered into recognisances in £100 that he, his children and family should dutifully repair to the church receive the Communion etc., apprehend popish priests etc., and certify the 3rd of October next and so from time to time after. And to labour to conforme his wife before that time or to bring her in. Recusants entering bond.

2. Robert Ealande of Nonington, esquire, was bound in £100 for himself, his wife and whole family upon like condition.

3. Roger Mennell of Haunby, gent., bound in £100 upon the like condition.

4. Roger Gower of Applegarth, gent., bound in £100 upon the like condition, saving that he is to conform his wife before the third of October next or bring her in.

5. Roger Mennell of Kilvington, gent. After conference with him had for not receiving the Communion, he was by the said Commissioners enjoined sub pena contemptus, that he and his wife upon some one of the three Sundays then next coming should in the parish church of Thornton-in-the-Street receive the Holy Communion and upon Monday then next following bring in certificate under the minister and churchwardens' hands that he hath so done.

6. William Wright of Stangrave, gent., entered into recognisances in £100 himself and his family [as no. 1]. To conform his wife or bring her in.

7. Edward Thornton of St———, gent. Avouching his conformity in all respects, and no apparent proof to the contrary was enjoined by the said Commissioners to continue his conformity sub pena and so was dismissed.

8. Thomas Etherington of Whitwell in the parish of C——— entered into recognisance in £100 [as no. 1].

9. Sir Richard Cholmley of Rokesby, knight, entered into recognisances in £200 for himself and his family [as no. 1, save that there is no mention of bringing in the recusant wife].

1. Christopher Baynes of Norton, gent., being required to take an oath to answer as by law he was bound refused twice so to do, whereupon the said Commissioners for his manifest contempt imposed a fine upon Recusants Committed.

---

[1] To shorten the account the references to the Sheriff announcing the names of the Jury, the Archbishop charging the jurymen, and giving them the articles in writing, are left out in this and in the accounts that follow. At Malton the jury were 15 in all, 2 esquires, 13 gentlemen.

his head of £20, and for his disobedience and obstinacy in matters of religion he was committed to prison at Hull to the custody of John Alcock, with this injunction that before the 27th day of August then instant he should repair with his keeper to some church in Hull to hear divine service and receive the Communion, sub pena contemptus.

2. John Constable of Hatfield, gent., utterly blinded in popish error, after long reasoning and persuasion of the said L. Archbishop and L. President with the rest, he obstinately refused to come to the church and receive the Communion etc. Whereupon he was sent to the castle of York there to remain close prisoner.

The Fifth Session.

AT RIPON on Wednesday the 10th of August, 1580

After the learned sermon made by the said L. Archbishop [etc. as at Beverley, *supra*] [1]

At the same time and place were convented and appeared these persons following.

Recusants entering bond or otherwise conforming themselves.

1. Marmaduke Thurkeld of Easthorpe, gent., willingly entered into recognisance in £100 that he, his wife and whole family shall from henceforth dutifully repair to the church and receive the Communion etc., and certify the third of October next, and from time to time after as he shall be required, Also to apprehend priests etc.

2. Leonard Calverley of Kipling, gent., entered into recognisance in £100 upon the like condition.

3. John Wytham of Cliffe, esquire, entered into recognisances in £100 upon like conditions, saving that he is to conform his wife before the third of October next or to bring her in.

4. Thomas Proctor of Winterbourne, gent., entered the like recognisance for his wife, himself and whole family, saving that he is to certify of his receiving the Communion and his wife the first Session after Christmas next.

5. John Lindley of Otley, gent., for that it appeared not that he offended of any contempt or misliking of religion he was only enjoined to continue his conformity.

6. Antony Thackeray
7. John Smith
8. Antony Brathwate alias Casson
9. Richard Gilson
10. Isabel Atkinson
11. Christopher Scott
12. Henry Snawe
13. Antony Atkinson
14. Wilfrid Day

All of Ripon, bound in £20 a year for them self and their wives and families [as no. 1, but no pledge about priests].

15. Marmaduke Middleton
16. Richard Raymer
17.
18.   Backwith

Of Ripon parish [All these as no. 5].

Recusant Committed.

Christopher Marton of Ashton, esquire, being found a wilful offender in matter of religion, and a likely man to open more matter was committed to safe custody until further order should be taken with him.

[1] Jury of 16; 10 gentlemen, 6 yeomen.

Thursday the 11th of August, 1580, after a Sermon the said Commissioners departed to Skipton.

AT SKIPTON on Friday the 12th day of August, 1580

The Sixth Session.

After a learned and godly sermon made by the said L. Archbishop [etc. as at Beverley, *supra*] [1]

At the same time and place were convented

    1. John Proctor of Bordley, gent., 100 marks.

    2. Thomas Colthurst of Mytton, gent., 100 marks.

Recusants entering bond or otherwise conforming themselves.

They both entered into recognisances in these sums for themselves, their wives and families to come to Church and receive the Communion dutifully and to certify, the third of October next etc. Also to take roaming priests etc.

3. Ambrose Pudsey of Armfurthe, gent. [as nos. 1 & 2] saving that he is to conform his wife before St. Stephen's Day or bring her in.

4. Thomas Lyster of Gisburn, gent. [as no. 3].

5. Gamaliel Draper of Stubbin, gent. [as no. 3].

6. William Ingleby of Pudsey, esquire [as nos. 1 & 2].

7. John Nesfield, of [———], gent., willingly yielding to all conformity and it not appearing that he offended of any contempt or misliking, was only enjoined to continue his conformity, etc.

8. Beatrice Arthington, wife of Henry Arthington, gent., enjoined to repair to the Church according to the laws of this realm and to communicate before Christmas next and to certify of her so doing the first Session after Christmas next.

9. William Catterall of Newhall, esquire.

10. John Catterall his son.

They utterly denied themselves to be faulty and faithfully promised to continue dutiful in matter of religion now established and to apprehend popish priests etc. And no proof of offence appearing were dismissed.

AT WAKEFIELD the 15th of August, 1580

The Seventh Session.

On Sunday the 14th of August the said Commissioners being at Wakefield the said Archbishop preached in the forenoon. After the sermon there was a Communion ministered by Mr. Doctor Hutton, Dean of York, which did communicate the said L. Archbishop and L. President with the rest of the Commissioners, and sundry other Justices of the Peace and gentlemen. And at afternoon of the same day there preached before the said Commissioners and others Mr. Thomas Cole, master of arts.

On Monday, the said 15th of August, after a learned sermon made by the above named Mr. Doctor Hutton [the Sheriff presented the jury, and the Archbishop charged them, as on the other occasions, " making repetition of the sermon . . . and very aptly applying it "].[2]

---

[1] Jury of 18 sworn, 1 esquire, 6 gentlemen, 11 yeomen.

[2] Jury of 23 sworn, 5 esquires, 12 gentlemen, 6 yeomen

At the same time and place were convented before the said Commissioners these persons following.

> Martin Anne of Frickley, esquire, £200.
> William Hall of Swillington, yeoman, £100.
> Leonard Foster of Tadcaster, gent., £100.
> Thomas Leigh of Rothwell, esquire, £100.
> Gilbert Leigh of Skelton, in the parish of Leeds, gent., £100.

These persons entered into recognisances in these several sums [they themselves, wives and whole families to go to church, to receive the Communion and certify, to apprehend priests, and] Gilbert Leigh is to conform his wife and certify the same the first Session after Christmas next and if she refuse so to do then to bring her in.

Marmaduke Wentworth of Bretton, esquire, entered into recognisances in £100 that he and his family [etc. as in the other cases]. And to conform his wife and certify the same the first session after Christmas next or else then to bring her in. Further that the child his wife now goeth withal shall be baptised in the parish church where it shall be born according to the order in the Book of Common Prayer now by law set forth.

On Tuesday the 16th day of August, 1580, at Wakefield aforesaid the following appear before the Commissioners.

7. Thomas Waterton of Walton, esquire, entered into recognisances in £100 that he and his family abiding in the diocese of York shall dutifully repair to church and communicate etc. And that his wife after her return into the diocese of York shall do the like, And if she refuse to do so, then within one month after to present her body before the Commissioners at York.

8. William Leigh of Rothwell, gent., for that his offence in not coming to the church seemed not of contempt, and openly confessed his good liking to true religion now established, was only enjoined that he his wife and family shall orderly hereafter repair to the church and communicate according to the laws of this realm.

9. Andrew Young of Medley, his son John Young alleging that the said Andrew his father was impotent etc. was enjoined to signify unto his father that the Commissioners pleasure is that before Michaelmas next he shall procure the minister of the parish to come to his house that he may at home communicate and certify the same the third of October following.

10. Francis Hawdenby of Adlingfleet, esquire, confessed that he cometh to the church but [does] not communicate, whereupon he was enjoined to continue his conformity in [coming] to the church and before St. Stephen's Day to receive the Communion and certify of his so doing.

11. William Dyneley of Swillington, esquire, denieth himself to be faulty, and protesting his good liking to religion now established, and no sufficient proof appearing to the contrary was enjoined that himself, his wife and family should continue in dutiful conformity according to the laws of this realm and so was dismissed.

BIBLIOGRAPHICAL NOTE *

ALLEN, WILLIAM (later Cardinal), *An Apologie and True Declaration of the Institution and Endevors of the two English Colleges, the one in Rome, the other now resident in Rheims* (Mounts in Henault, 1581).

—— *A brief History of the glorious Martyrdom of twelve reverend Priests executed within these twelve months, for confession and defence of the Catholic Faith, but under the false pretence of Treason ; with a note of sundry things that befel them in their life and imprisonment, and a preface concerning their innocency* (8vo, 1582).

—— A TRUE, SINCERE AND MODEST DEFENCE OF ENGLISH CATHOLICS THAT SUFFER FOR THEIR FAITH BOTH AT HOME AND ABROAD, AGAINST A FALSE, SEDITIOUS AND SLANDEROUS LIBEL, ENTITLED : " THE EXECUTION OF JUSTICE IN ENGLAND ".

Wherein is declared how unjustly the Protestants do charge Catholics with treason ; how untruly they deny their persecution for Religion ; and how deceitfully they seek to abuse strangers about the cause, greatness, and manner of their sufferings, with divers other matters pertaining to this purpose, 1584.

ANSTRUTHER (O.P.), GODFREY, *Vaux of Harrowden*, 1953.

ARBER, E., *An Introductory Sketch to the Martin Marprelate Controversy*, 1879.

BATH MSS. = *Calendar of the Manuscripts of the Marquis of Bath, at Longleat, Wiltshire*, H.M.C., 1904–1907.

BAYNE, C. G., *Anglo–Roman Relations*, Oxford, 1913.

BAYNE, R., *Religion in Shakespeare's England* (1926), vol. I.

BINDOFF, S. T., *Tudor England*, 1950.

BIRT (O.S.B.), NORBERT, *The Elizabethan Religious Settlement*, 1907.

BLACK, J. B., *The Reign of Elizabeth*, 1936.

BOUVIER, ANDRÉ, *Henri Bullinger, successeur de Zwingli*, Neuchâtel and Paris, 1940.

BRIDGETT (C.SS.R.), T. E. and KNOX, T. F., *The True Story of the Catholic Hierarchy deposed by Queen Elizabeth*, 1889.

—— see also WATSON, THOMAS, *infra*.

BURGHLEY, WILLIAM CECIL, LORD, *The Execution of Justice in England for maintenance of public and Christian peace against certeine stirrers of sedition*, 1583.

BURTON, E. H., and POLLEN, J. H., *Lives of the English Martyrs*, Second Series, vol. I, 1583–1588. London, 1914.

C.R.S. 1. *Miscellanea, I*, 1905.

—— 2. *Miscellanea, II*, 1906.

—— 4. *Miscellanea, IV*, 1907.

—— 5. *Unpublished Documents relating to the English Martyrs*, Vol. I, 1584–1603, edited by John Hungerford Pollen, S.J., 1908.

CAMDEN, WILLIAM, *Annales Rerum Anglicarum et Hibernicarum regnante Elizabetha*, Leyden, 1625.

---

* This is no more than a list of the complete titles of books quoted in this third volume of *The Reformation in England*.

The following are the abbreviations used :—

      C.R.S. = Catholic Record Society, publications of.
      D.T.C. = *Dictionnaire de Théologie catholique*.
      E.H.R. = *English Historical Review*.
      H.M.C. = Historical Manuscripts Commission.
      L.R.S. = Lincoln Record Society, publications of,

CAMDEN MISCELLANY, IX = *A Collection of Original Letters from the Bishops to the Privy Council, 1564, with returns of the Justices of the Peace and others within their respective dioceses, classified according to their religious convictions,* ed. Mary Bateson, for the Camden Society, 1893.

CHALLONER, RICHARD, *Memoirs of Missionary Priests,* 1741, 1742. The edition used is that edited by J. H. Pollen, S.J., London, 1924.

CHUDOBA, BOHDAN, *Spain and the Empire, 1519–1643,* London, 1952.

CONYERS READ, E., *Mr. Secretary Walsingham and the policy of Queen Elizabeth,* 3 vols., Oxford, 1925.

CRAGG, G. R., *From Puritanism to the Age of Reason,* 1950.

CRANMER, Thomas, *Works on the Supper* = Vol. I of the Parker Society edition of Cranmer's works, 1844.

CREIGHTON, MANDELL, *Queen Elizabeth,* 1896.

DAVIES, R. TREVOR, *The Golden Age of Spain,* 1932.

DAVIES, E. T., *Episcopacy and the Royal Supremacy in the Church of England in the XVI Century,* 1950.

D'ENTREVES, A. P., *The Medieval Contribution to Political Thought,* 1939.

DENZINGER, H., *Enchiridion Symbolorum Definitionum et Declarationum de rebus Fidei et Morum.*

D'EWES, SIR SIMON, *Journals of all the Parliaments during the reign of Queen Elizabeth,* London, 1862, fol. 8.

DIGGES, SIR DUDLEY, *The Compleat Ambassador,* 1655.

DIX, GREGORY, *The Shape of the Liturgy,* 1945.

DIXON, R. W., *History of the Church of England,* Oxford, Vol. V, 1558–1563 (1902), Vol. VI, 1564–1570 (1902).

DORE, J. R., *Old Bibles,* London, 1888.

DOUAY DIARIES, i.e. *The First and Second Diaries of the English College, Douay,* edited T. F. Knox, D.D., London, 1878.

E.C.M., *The Reformation, The Mass and the Priesthood,* by E. C. Messenger, Ph.D., 2 vols., 1936, 1937.

ESTCOURT, EDGAR, E., *The Question of Anglican Ordinations discussed . . .,* London, 1873.

FITZHERBERT, NICHOLAS, *De Alani Cardinalis vita libellus,* 1608, in KNOX, *Letters and Memorials of Cardinal Allen.*

FOREIGN CALENDAR, 1560–1561 = *Calendar of State Papers* [in the P.R.O., and relating to Foreign Affairs], 1560–1561, ed. J. S. Stevenson.

FOXE, JOHN, *Acts and Monuments* (the " Book of Martyrs ") ed. Josiah Pratt, London, s.d. 8 vols.

FRERE, W. H., and KENNEDY, W. M. P., *Visitation Articles and Injunctions of the Period of the Reformation,* Vol. III (1558–1575), Alcuin Club Publications, London, 1910.

—— *History of the English Church under Elizabeth and James I, 1558–1625,* London, 1899.

—— and DOUGLAS, C. E., *Puritan Manifestoes,* 1907.

G. & H., *Documents illustrative of English Church History,* ed. H. Gee and W. J. Hardy, 4th ed., 1921.

GARDINER, S. R., *History of England from the Accession of James I to the Outbreak of the Civil War, 1603–1642,* vol. 1, 1863.

—— *The Constitutional Documents of the Puritan Revolution, 1625–1660,* Oxford, 1889 (many times reprinted).

—— STEPHEN, *A declaration of such true articles as George Ioye goeth about to confute,* 1546.

GEE, HENRY, *The Elizabethan Clergy and the Settlement of Religion, 1558–1564,* Oxford, 1898.

GERARD (S.J.), JOHN, *The Autobiography of John Gerard*, edited by Philip Caraman, 1952.

GILLOW, JOSEPH, *A Bibliographical Dictionary of the English Catholics.* 5 vols., 1885–.

GRINDAL, EDMUND, *The remains of Edmund Grindal, Archbishop of Canterbury*, Cambridge, *Parker Society*, 1843.

GUILDAY, PETER, *The English Catholic Refugees on the Continent, 1558–1793*, Vol. I : *The English Colleges and Convents in the Catholic Low Countries*, London, 1914.

HALL, HUBERT, *Society in the Elizabethan Age*, 1886.

HARDWICK, *A History of the Articles of Religion*, 3rd ed., London, 1884.

HARRINGTON, SIR JOHN, *Nugae Antiquae*, 3 vols., 1779.

HARRISON, WILLIAM, *Elizabethan England* (1576). The Scott Library edition : *s.d.* (?1888), ed. L. Withington.

HATFIELD CALENDAR = *Calendar of the Manuscripts of the Marquis of Salisbury, at Hatfield House, Hertfordshire*, H.M.C., 1883–1940.

HAWEIS (J. O. W.), *Sketches of the Reformation and Elizabethan Age, taken from the Contemporary Pulpit*, London, 1844.

HICKES, GEORGE, *Bibliotheca Scriptorum Ecclesiae Anglicanae*, 1709.

HILDEBRAND, FRANZ, *Melanchthon, Alien or Ally ?* Cambridge, 1946.

HOARE, H. W., *Our English Bible*, revised edition, 1911.

HOMILIES, *Certain Sermons or Homilies appointed to be read in Churches in the Time of the late Queen Elizabeth of famous Memory and now thought fit to be reprinted by Authority from the King's most excellent Majesty*, Oxford, 1832.

HOOKER, *The Works of Richard Hooker*, 3 vols., ed. R. W. Church and F. Paget, 1888.

HOPKINS, RICHARD (translator), *Libro de la Oración y Meditación*, by Luis of Granada, O.P. (1505–1588). Translation dated 1582.

HUDLESTON (O.S.B.), ROGER (editor), *The New Testament . . . printed at Rheims in 1582*, London, 1926.

HUGHES, PHILIP, *Rome and the Counter Reformation in England*, London, 1942.

IMBART DE LA TOUR, PIERRE, *Les Origines de la Réforme*, Vol. IV : *Calvin et l'Institution Chrétienne*, 1935.

JANELLE, PIERRE, *The Catholic Reformation*, Milwaukee, 1949.

JESSOPP, A., *One Generation of a Norfolk House*, 1878.

JEWEL, *The Works of Bishop Jewel*, 4 vols., Cambridge Parker Society, 1844–1845.

KENNEDY, W. P. M., *Elizabethan Episcopal Administration*, 3 vols., London, 1924.

—— The " Interpretations " of the Bishops and their influence on Elizabethan Episcopal Policy (Alcuin Club Tracts, VIII) London, 1908.

—— Parish Life in the Reign of Queen Elizabeth, 1914.

KIDD, B. J., *Documents of the Continental Reformation*, 1911.

KNOX (D.D.), T. F. (editor), *Letters and Memorials of Cardinal Allen*, 1882.

L.R.S., 23 = *The State of the Church in the reigns of Elizabeth and James I*, 1926 ed., for the Lincoln Record Society by C. W. Foster.

LADERCHI, J., *Annales Ecclesiastici ab anno 1566*, Rome, 1728–1737.

LAW, T. G., *A Historical Sketch of the Conflicts between Jesuits and Seculars in the reign of Queen Elizabeth*, London, 1889.

—— The Archpriest Controversy, Camden Society, 2 vols., 1896, 1898.

LEATHERBARROW, J. S., *The Lancashire Elizabethan Recusants*, Chetham Society, New Series, vol. 110, 1947.

LEE, Jr., MAURICE, *James Stewart, Earl of Moray*, 1953.

LEWIS, DAVID (translator), *Rise and Growth of the Anglican Schism*, by Nicholas Sander, London, 1877.

LINGARD, JOHN, *The History of England*, 5th edn., 1849. Vol. VI, 1558–1603.

McGINN, D. J., *The Admonition Controversy*, Rutgers University Press, New Brunswick, N.J., 1949.

MAGEE, BRIAN, *The English Recusants*, 1938.

MAITLAND, F. W., *The Anglican Settlement and the Scottish Reformation*, C.M.H., II.

—— *Collected Papers*, vol. III, Cambridge, 1911.

MAXWELL, W. D., *John Knox's Genevan Service Book*, 1556, London, 1931.

MEYER, A. O., *England and the Catholic Church under Queen Elizabeth* (1910), English translation, 1915, by J. R. McKie, of the Oratory.*

MÖHLER, JOHN ADAM, *Symbolism, or Exposition of the Doctrinal Differences between Catholics and Protestants as evidenced by their Symbolical Writings*, 1832. English translation by J. B. Robertson, 3rd edition, 1906.

MORISON, STANLEY, *English Prayer Books, An Introduction to the Literature of Christian Public Worship*, by Stanley Morison, Cambridge, 3rd edn., 1949.

MORRIS (S.J.), JOHN (ed.), *The Troubles of our Catholic Forefathers*, 3 vols., 1872–1877.

MOZLEY, J. F., *William Tyndale*, 1937.

NEALE, J. E., *Queen Elizabeth*, 1933.

—— *The Elizabethan House of Commons*, 1949.

—— *Elizabeth I and her Parliaments*, vol. I, 1558–1581, 1953.

NEWMAN, J. H., *Lectures on Justification*, 1837.

—— *Anglican Difficulties*, I, 1850.

—— *Apologia*, 1864.

—— *The Via Media*, 2 vols., 1877.

—— *Essays, Critical and Historical*, 2 vols., 1872.

—— *Tracts, Theological and Ecclesiastical*, 1874.†

NICHOLS, J. G. (ed.), *Narratives of the Days of the Reformation, chiefly from the manuscripts of John Foxe, the Martyrologist*, Camden Society (77), 1859.

O.L. = *Original Letters relative to the English Reformation, written during the reigns of King Henry VIII, King Edward VI, and Queen Mary : chiefly from the archives of Zurich.* Translated from authenticated copies of the autographs, ed. Rev. Hastings Robertson, M.A., Parker Society, 2 vols., 1846, 1847.

PARKER, *Correspondence of Matthew Parker, 1535–1575*, Cambridge, The Parker Society, 1853.

PASTOR, L. VON, *The History of the Popes*, English translation, vols. 15–24 (i.e., 1559–1605), London, 1928–1933.

PEACOCK, EDWARD (ed.), *English Church Furniture, Ornaments and Decorations at the Period of the Reformation. As exhibited in a List of the Goods destroyed in certain Lincolnshire Churches*, A.D. *1566*, London, 1866.

PEARSON, A. F. SCOTT, *Thomas Cartwright and Elizabethan Puritanism, 1535–1603*, 1925.

—— *Church and State : Political Aspects of Sixteenth Century Puritanism*, 1928.

PEEL, A. E. (ed.), *The Seconde Parte of a Register, Being a Calendar of Manuscripts under that title intended for publication by the Puritans about 1593, and now in Dr. Williams' Library, London.* 2 vols., Cambridge, 1915.

PEEL, *Penry. The Notebook of John Penry, 1593*, ed. A. E. Peel ; vol. 67 of the Camden Society, Third Series, London, 1944.

PERSONS = *Letters and Memorials of Father Robert Persons, S.J., Vol. I (to 1588)*, edited by L. Hicks, S.J., London, 1942. This is vol. 39 of the C.R.S. publications.

PERSONS (S.J.), ROBERT, Various memoirs and memoranda by, first published in C.R.S., II (1905), 12–218, and IV (1907), 1–161.

PESCH (S.J.), CHRISTIAN, *Praelectiones Theologicae* (edition of 1916).

PHILLIPS, GEORGE E., *The Extinction of the Ancient Hierarchy . . .*, London, 1905.

---

* Since the translator of this work by a Prussian Lutheran was a Catholic priest, the translation carries the *imprimatur* of the ordinary of the diocese where it was published. Such *imprimaturs* do not mean, as seems to be thought (cf. Black, *op. cit.*, 415), that the book is " official " Catholic history.

† In all cases what is quoted is the standard (Longman) edition.

POLLARD, A. F., *H.E.*, VI, = *The History of England from the Accession of Edward VI to the Death of Elizabeth 1547–1603*, 1910 (vol. VI of *The Political History of England*, ed. W. Hunt and R. Lane Poole).

POLLARD, A. W., and REDGRAVE, G. R., *A Short Title Catalogue of Works printed in England, Scotland and Ireland 1475–1640*, London, 1926.

POLLEN, J. H., *The Politics of the English Catholics during the Reign of Elizabeth*, articles in *The Month*, Jan.–April, June–August, 1902.

—— *The English Catholics in the Reign of Queen Elizabeth*, 1920.

—— *The Institution of the Archpriest Blackwell*, 1916.

—— *Religious Terrorism under Elizabeth*, in *The Month*, March, 1905.

PROTHERO, G. W., *Select Statutes and other Constitutional Documents illustrative of the reign of Elizabeth and James I* (1894, and many times reprinted).

PURITAN MANIFESTOES, cf. Frere and Douglas.

R.L.E. = CARDWELL, EDWARD (ed.), *The Reformation of the Ecclesiastical Laws . . . a new edition*, Oxford, 1850 : a translation of the *Reformatio [Legum Eclesiasticarum*, compiled 1552–1553.

RISHTON, EDWARD, cf. LEWIS, DAVID.

ROWSE, A. L., *Tudor Cornwall*, 1941.

—— *The England of Elizabeth*, 1950.

RIVIERE, J., *Mérite*, in *D.T.C.*, X (1928).

ROME CAL. = *Calendar of State Papers, relating to English Affairs, principally in the Vatican Archives and Library*, ed. J. M. Rigg, Vol. I, 1558–1571 (1916), Vol. II, 1572–1578 (1926).

RUPP, E. G., *The English Protestant Tradition*, 1947.

RYMER, THOMAS, *Foedera*, (1704–1735).

SANDER, DR. NICHOLAS, *see* LEWIS, DAVID.

SHARPE, CUTHBERT (ed.), *Memorials of the Rebellion of 1569*, London, 1841.

SIMPSON, R., *Edmund Campion, a Biography* (1866), the new, corrected edition of 1896.

SISSON, C. J., *The Judicious Marriage of Mr. Hooker and the Birth of The Laws of Ecclesiastical Polity*, 1940.

SMITH, A. GORDON, *William Cecil, the Power behind Elizabeth*, 1934.

SOUTHERN, A. C., *Elizabethan Recusant Prose, 1559–1582*, London, 1950.

SOUTHWELL (S.J.), ROBERT, *An Humble Supplication to Her Maiestie* [1595], edited R. C. Bald, Cambridge, 1953.

SPAN. CAL. = *Calendar of State Papers relating to English Affairs preserved at Simancas*, I, 1557–1567 ; II, 1568–1579 ; III, 1580–1586 ; ed. M. S. Hume, 1892–.

STEUART, A. F., *The Trial of Mary, Queen of Scots*, 1923.

STURGE, CHARLES, *Cuthbert Tunstall*, 1938.

STRYPE, *Annals* = *Annals of the Reformation . . . during Queen Elizabeth's happy reign* (4 vols. in 7 parts), 1824.

—— *Life of Grindal*, 1821.

—— *Life of Parker*, 3 vols., 1821.

—— *Life of Whitgift*, 3 vols., Oxford, 1822.

TAWNEY, R. H., *Religion and the Rise of Capitalism*, 1926.

TAYLOR, E. G. R., *Camden's England*, in Darby, H. C., *An Historical Geography of England*, 1936.

T.-D. = M. A. TIERNEY, *Dodd's Church History of England from the Commencement of the Sixteenth Century to the Revolution in 1688* (1737–1742, 3 vols.) with notes, additions and a continuation, 5 vols., 1839–1842.

TEULET, A., *Relations Politiques de la France et de L'Espagne avec l'Ecosse*, 5 vols., Paris, 1862.

THOMPSON, A. HAMILTON, *The English Clergy*, 1947.

TOMLINSON, J. T., *The Prayer Book, Articles, and Homilies*, London, 1897.

USHER, R. G., *The Reconstruction of the English Church*, 2 vols., 1910.

—— *The Rise and Fall of the High Commission*, 1913.

—— *The Presbyterian Movement in the Reign of Queen Elizabeth*, Camden Society, 1905.

VAUX, LAURENCE, *Catechism*, ed. LAW, T. G., Chetham Society, New Series, 4, 1885.

WATSON, THOMAS, *Sermons on the Sacraments*, 1876 (i.e. *The Holsome and Catholyke Doctrine*, of Bishop Thomas Watson, 1558, now edited by T. E. Bridgett, C.S.S.R.).

WESTCOTT, B. F., *History of the English Bible*, 1870.

WHITGIFT, JOHN, *Works*, edited J. Ayre, Parker Society, 3 vols., 1851–1853.

WILKINS, D., *Concilia Magnae Brittaniae et Hiberniae*, 1737, vols. III and IV.

WILLES–BUND, J. W., *Select Cases from the State Trials*, 1879.

Z.L. = *The Zurich Letters*. Second edition, Chronologically Arranged in one Series. Translated by Rev. H. Robinson, D.D., for the Parker Society, Cambridge, 1846.

INDEX

Abbreviations : *l.* = later ; n. = in the notes, where more than one note is shown by the figure in parenthesis ; *q.* = quoted.